IMAGES
of Rail

PORTLAND'S STREETCAR LINES

I0806376

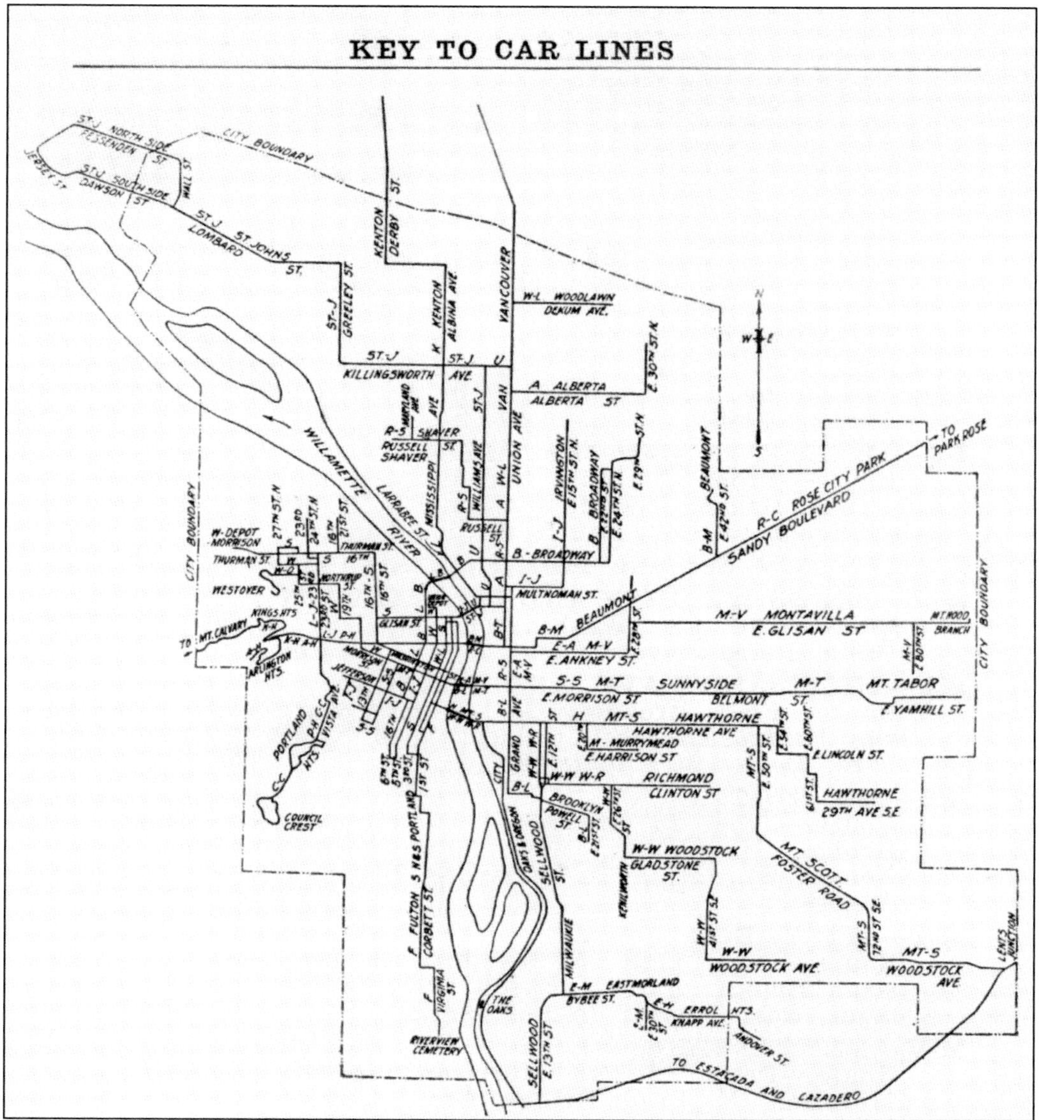

The 38 lines that constituted Portland's street railway system near its peak are shown in this map from *Pittmon's Portland Official Guide*. It appeared in the pocket guide from 1920–1937, a golden age for Portland streetcars. Route changes and line cutbacks were few, as the Portland Electric Power Company (PEPCO) took the helm from Portland Railway, Light and Power (PRL&P) in 1924. (Courtesy the author.)

On the Cover: Portland Railway, Light and Power Company's "Toronto" series streetcar No. 456 is westbound on Southwest Morrison Street at Fifth Avenue on the Depot and Morrison Street line. This picture was taken about 1909, when Portland's streetcar lines were growing rapidly. Another trolley is approaching in the background between the Portland Hotel, on the left, and the Marquam Grand Opera House. Both are long gone. (Courtesy the author.)

IMAGES
of Rail

PORTLAND'S STREETCAR LINES

Richard Thompson

ARCADIA
PUBLISHING

ISBN 978-0-7385-8126-2

Published by Arcadia Publishing
Charleston, South Carolina

Printed in the United States of America

Library of Congress Control Number: 2010926130

For all general information, please contact Arcadia Publishing:
Telephone 843-853-2070
Fax 843-853-0044
E-mail sales@arcadiapublishing.com
For customer service and orders:
Toll-Free 1-888-313-2665

Visit us on the Internet at www.arcadiapublishing.com

To my grandmother Marion Bissell Webb (1881–1970),
who took me on the trolley

Contents

Acknowledgments		6
Introduction		7
1.	To Goose Hollow, South Portland, and Council Crest	9
2.	To Nob Hill, Slabtown, and Willamette Heights	33
3.	To Albina, St. Johns, and Kenton	55
4.	To Vancouver, Irvington, and Rose City Park	71
5.	To Mount Tabor, Mount Scott, and Sellwood	99

ACKNOWLEDGMENTS

I am indebted to my late friends William K. "Bill" Hayes and G. Charles "Chuck" Bukowsky for their assistance during the nearly 40 years spent gathering the materials used in this book. Without their efforts, it would not have been possible.

Credit is due to Kenn Lantz for the loan of a large 1912 American Map and Reproducing Company Map of Portland and to Stanley Soho, whose hand-drawn streetcar line map appeared in the February 1969 issue of *Trolley Talk* magazine. These maps served as the basis for several maps created for this book.

I also wish to thank Mark Moore for graciously sharing images from his collection for yet another volume and Steve Morgan for once again taking photographs of modern streetcar operations to help bring this book up to date. The enthusiasm and dedication of individuals like these does much to preserve local history.

Finally I am very grateful to my partner, Jan Hofmann, for helping select photographs and proofread and to my good friend Tracy Brown for helping with maps and proofreading the manuscript through frequent changes.

Dates of operation for historic streetcar lines have been cross-checked using contemporary newspapers, guidebooks, and timetables wherever possible. I also have relied on two definitive secondary sources: *Portland Electric Power Company with its Predecessor and Subsidiary Companies 1860–1935* by Roy Robley and *Fares, Please!: Those Portland Trolley Years* by John Labbe.

Unless otherwise noted, all pictures in this book are from the author's collection. Original photographers are cited where possible.

INTRODUCTION

In Portland, as elsewhere, city neighborhoods predate the automobile. Our traditional neighborhoods owe their location, alignment, and growth almost entirely to a late 19th century innovation: the trolley car. The city's urban footprint still reflects the advent of the electric street railway and its impact upon neighborhood development.

The need for a public transportation system became apparent as Portland grew from a struggling village of 800 souls when incorporated in 1851 to a major West Coast city of 26,000 residents in 1885. In 1872, horses began pulling the first streetcars along Southwest First Avenue.

Because hills rising 1,000 feet to the west of the city slowed growth in that direction, street railway development spread elsewhere. By 1888, five competing companies were operating horsecar lines north and south from downtown, while another opened a line across the river connecting the cities of Albina, East Portland, and Portland.

Lines to more distant suburbs soon exceeded the speed, endurance, and reliability possible with horsecars. In 1887, the Willamette Bridge Railway Company turned to Industrial Age technology for a solution. Their Mount Tabor Motor line utilized former horsecars connected into trains drawn by steam "dummy" engines. These small locomotives disguised as streetcars were designed to have a less traumatic effect upon passing horses.

In 1890, as several more companies joined the effort to provide steam "motor" service on the less densely populated east side, the Portland Cable Railway Company brought another transportation innovation to Portland in the form of handsome cable cars built by the same company that provided them to San Francisco. Now residents could easily scale the heights to the west, where a posh neighborhood was sprouting.

With the advent of steam dummy and cable lines, people were able to live farther from the center of town. Even so, these much-feted technologies were eclipsed by a form of power that would further revolutionize the industry and extend lines beyond the dreams of early city planners.

The first electric railway in Oregon began running to Albina in November of 1889. That year proved a watershed in the development of Portland transportation; electrically powered streetcars were soon providing service on both sides of the Willamette River, and interurban routes were building toward Vancouver, Oregon City, and Estacada. By 1904, trolleys had replaced the last steam line, and cable cars had given way to electrics.

Unfortunately, the financial panic of the mid-1890s dried up needed capital, and a number of railway companies faltered. Three remained after a wave of consolidation: the City and Suburban Railway operated the largest street railway in the west, the Portland Railway embarked on an ambitious car-building scheme, and the Oregon Water Power and Railway took over the nation's first true interurban railroad.

In 1906, a final unification resulted in the Portland Railway, Light and Power Company (PRL&P) taking over operations of all local street railways. The construction of streetcar lines peaked during PRL&P's years in charge, when Portland had the third largest narrow-gauge street railway in the country. Car lines had spread throughout the metropolitan region, fostering homesteads, tracts, and additions.

In 1910, the public utility commissioner appraised company property at $18 million. By 1915, PRL&P was operating 43 lines over 171.57 miles of track with 583 streetcars. It was possible to ride the 18.7 miles from St. Johns to Lents on a single 5¢ fare (fare zones were not added until 1933). Automobiles were starting to be a threat, yet they were still expensive, unreliable, and subject to speed limits of 20 mph outside congested areas.

People were now using streetcars for more than basic transportation. Families did their downtown shopping by trolley or walked to nearby streetcar commercial districts. On warm evenings, they caught open "breezer" cars to cool off. On Sundays, they rode for fun—to explore unfamiliar sides of town or go out to the end of the line for an afternoon of picnicking, hiking, or fishing.

Portland's railway companies promoted ridership to a variety of attractions along their lines. Amusement parks opened at Council Crest, The Oaks, Jantzen Beach, and Lotus Isle. Sporting venues also appeared along car lines. The Portland Beavers played baseball at Vaughn Street Ballpark in northwest Portland. Automobiles raced at the Rose City Speedway, served by a spur line in northeast Portland. Similar racetracks were found in Irvington and at Sellwood's City View Park in the southeast. There was a golf course near present-day Benson High School in the northeast part of town, or golfers could ride to Golf Links Station in Sellwood to play at the Waverley course.

Even though streetcar ridership continued to climb until 1922, the trolley began to lose favor with a public that was becoming increasingly envious of the freedom and status afforded by automobiles. In 1927, three years after the Portland Electric Power Company succeeded PRL&P, the vital service provided by street railways started a long decline.

Fuel and rubber rationing, as well as an influx of shipyard workers, briefly sent people back to the trolleys during World War II. But ridership dropped again in the postwar era, establishing a new low for all forms of public transit. The last three city streetcar lines were converted to bus operation in 1950. Two generations would pass before Portland residents would rediscover the streetcar.

The author's previous Arcadia books, Images of Rail: *Portland's Streetcars* and Images of Rail: *Willamette Valley Railways*, told the story of Portland's street railway companies, the evolution of the streetcars that rolled out of their shops, and the saga of the interurbans that ran down the valley to Corvallis and Eugene. The focus in this volume is on the more than 40 historic car lines that served Portland and its suburbs from 1872–1950. Chapters are arranged according to Portland's geographic zones: southwest, northwest, north, northeast, and southeast. Lines in each region are listed beneath maps at the beginning of each chapter. All but a handful of lines for which the author could not locate photographs are included. Detailed car rosters and line maps can be found on the companion Web site http://vintagetrolleys.com.

One

To Goose Hollow, South Portland, and Council Crest

The story of Portland's streetcar lines begins in southwest Portland, where geography constrained early development to a shelf of land between the West Hills and the Willamette River. Rail magnate Ben Holladay answered a need when he opened the city's first streetcar line in 1872. His Portland Street Railway horsecars plodded along First Street, from northwest Glisan Street to southwest Porter Street, through the original shopping district.

During the next decade, competing lines expanded toward the West Hills. The Multnomah Street Railway opened two horsecar lines in 1882–1883, converting them to electric operation in 1890. The Washington Street line ran along what is now West Burnside Street. A branch line traveled down Southwest 13th Avenue to Montgomery Street in Goose Hollow. In 1890, the Portland Cable Railway inaugurated service to Portland Heights and Southwest Jefferson Street.

The optimistically named Transcontinental Street Railway opened the Montgomery Street line in 1886 and electrified it in 1891. It went to Southwest Fourteenth Avenue and Montgomery Street in the neighborhood named for the residents' habit of allowing their geese to roam freely through the wooded hollow.

New lines also extended southward through the immigrant neighborhoods known as Little Italy and Little Russia. In 1889, the Metropolitan Railway started a line on Southwest Second Avenue to the Fulton Park development a mile south of town. That same year, Transcontinental opened a long line serving both North and South Portland along Southwest Third Avenue.

Extensions to the elegant neighborhoods on Council Crest (1906) and Arlington Heights (1913) were the last two lines opened in Southwest Portland. The Council Crest line was the last to serve Southwest Portland neighborhoods until the introduction of modern streetcars in 2001.

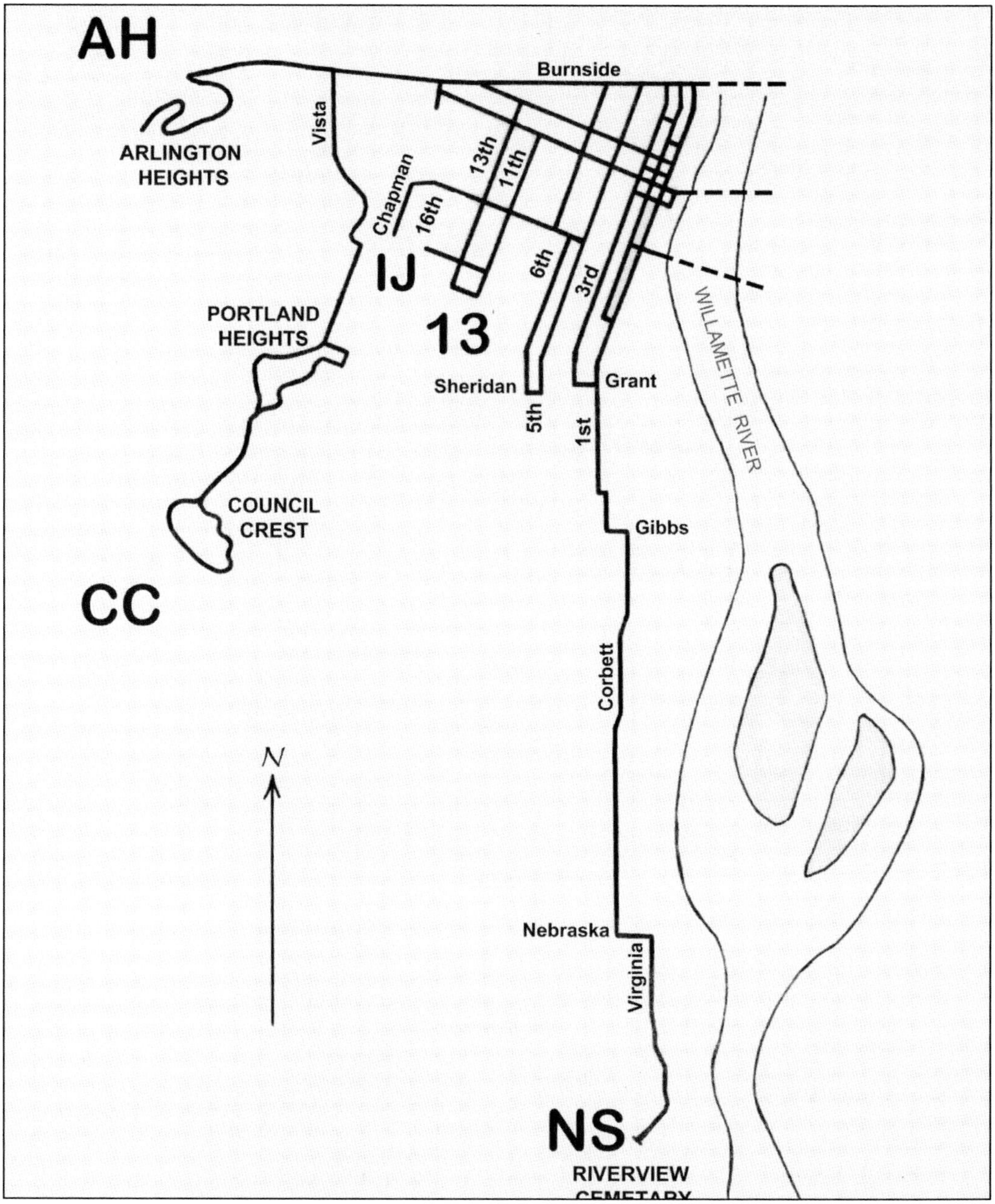

Lines in Southwest Portland included the following: Arlington Heights (AH), 1913–1941; Burnside Street, 1903–1915; Council Crest (CC), 1906–1950; Depot and Morrison (M) 1907–1923; Fulton (F), 1890–1923; Jefferson Street (J), 1892–1914; Irvington-Jefferson (IJ), 1914–1933; Montgomery Street (MG), 1886–1908; Morrison Street (M), 1886-1906; North and South Portland (NS), 1900–1937; Portland Heights cable, 1890–1904; Portland Heights (PH) trolley, 1904–1950; South Fifth (5), 1890–1909; Thirteenth Street (13), 1883–1937; and Washington Street (W), 1882–1904. Lines not appearing on this 1920s map had been discontinued or merged into other routes. For example, South Fifth became part of North and South Portland, and Jefferson Street merged with the Irvington line. In 1923 Depot and Morrison service was discontinued with the Willamette Heights line taking the northern end and Council Crest taking the southern portion. All but stub lines had terminals in downtown Portland.

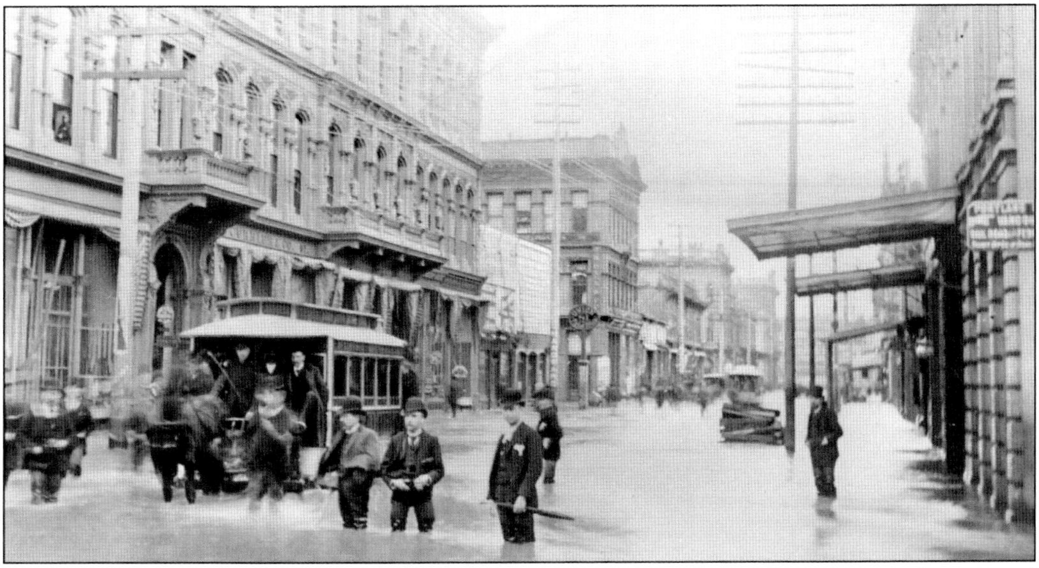

Portland's first streetcar line was Ben Holladay's 1872 horsecar operation serving the original business district along Northwest and Southwest First Street. Horsecars could plod through the periodic flooding seen here; however, this did little to slow down the adoption of newer electric streetcars, which supplanted horsecars on most other lines during 1889–1891. By the time the city's pioneer street railway ceased operation in 1896, it was the last horsecar line in town.

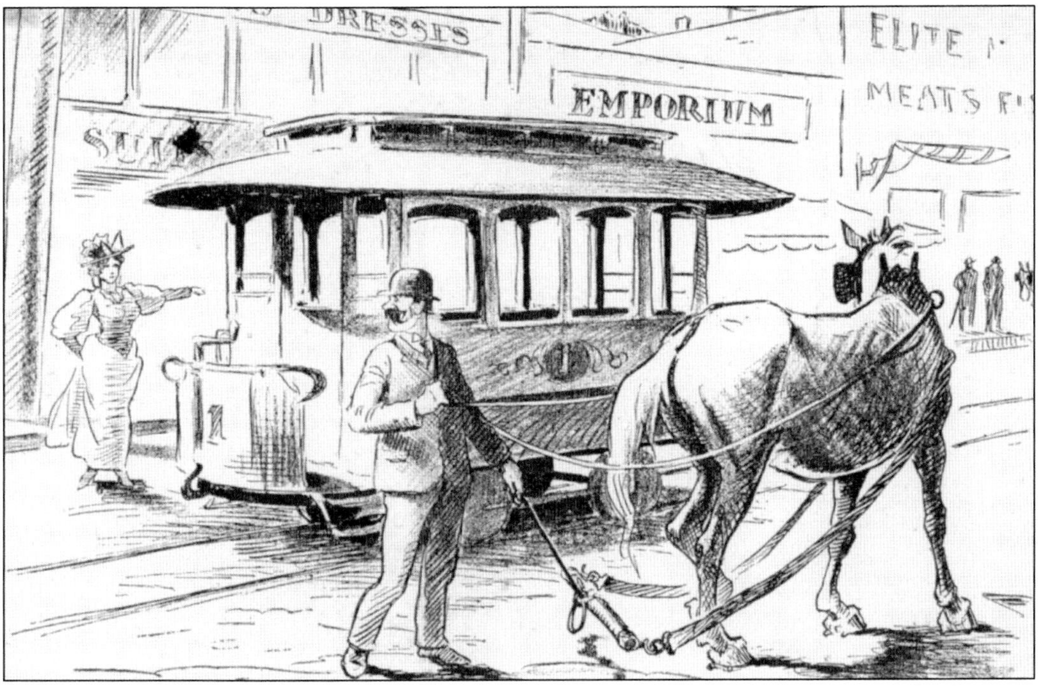

Portland's original "bobtailed" horsecars were replaced with double-ended cars. At the last stop on the line, the horse was moved to the opposite end of the car to reverse direction. According to this Quincy Scott cartoon from the March 15, 1934, *Oregonian*, ends might be reversed partway through a run if the driver wanted to impress a rider. Business practices must have been more relaxed in those times.

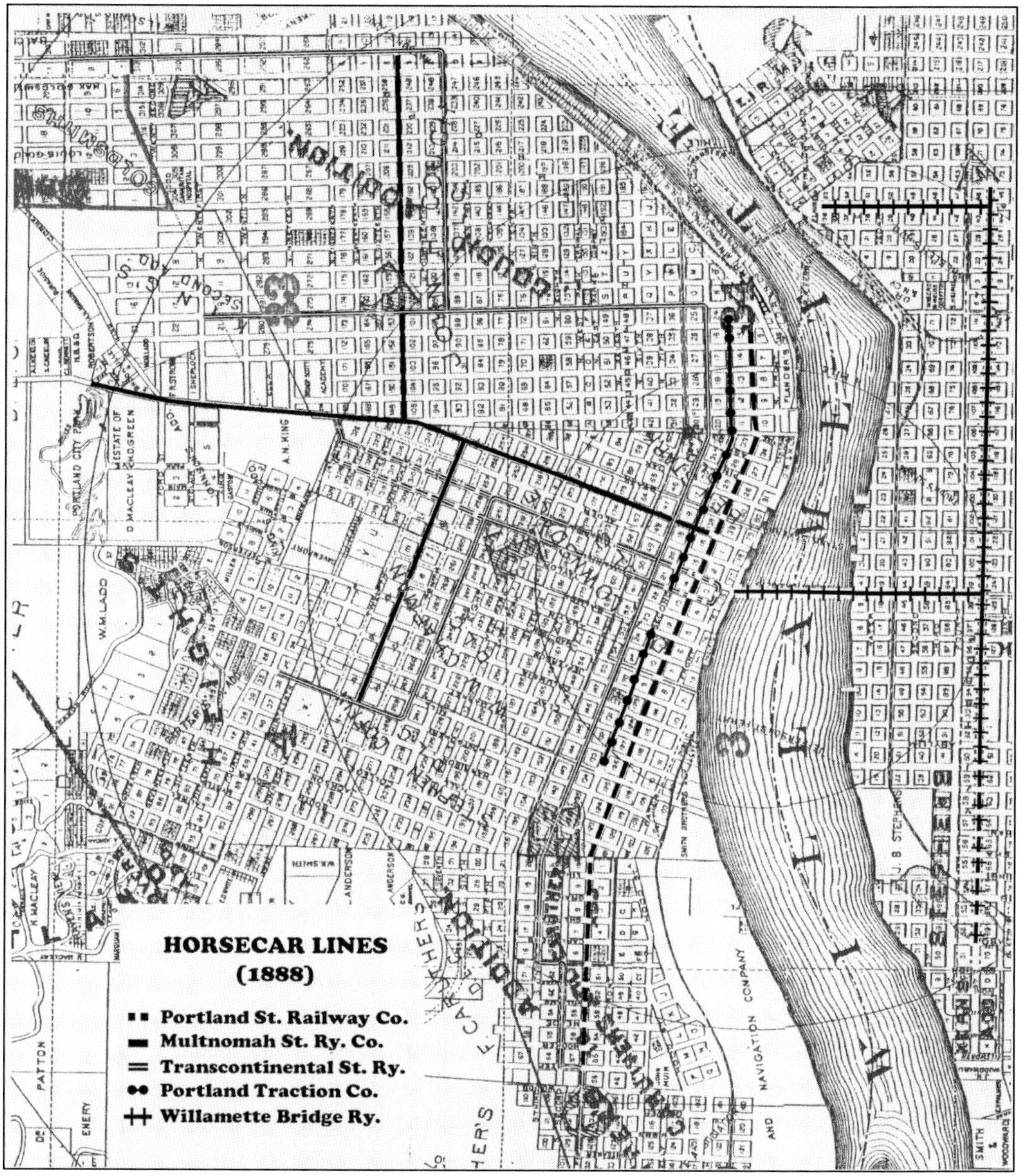

This 1888 map shows Portland's horsecar lines a few years before their conversion to electric operation. The horse-drawn railways begun by the Portland Street Railway (1872), Multnomah Street Railway (1882), Transcontinental Street Railway (1883), first Portland Traction Company (1888), and Willamette Bridge Railway (1888) formed the roots from which the nation's third largest narrow-gauge streetcar system developed.

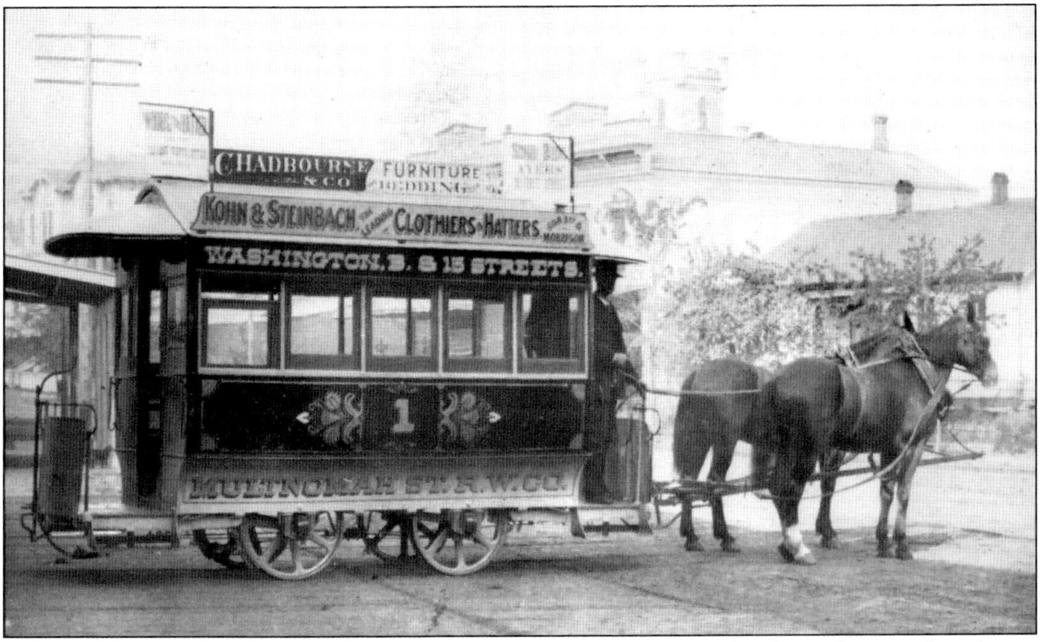

Multnomah Street Railway No. 1, festooned with advertising, waits by the carbarn on Southwest Washington and Sixteenth Streets in the mid-1880s. The Multnomah horsecars were doubled-ended, unlike cars first used on the Portland Street Railway and Willamette Bridge Railway. They had been intended for single-horse operation, but the hill on Southwest Washington Street (now West Burnside Street) proved too steep. (Courtesy Mark Moore.)

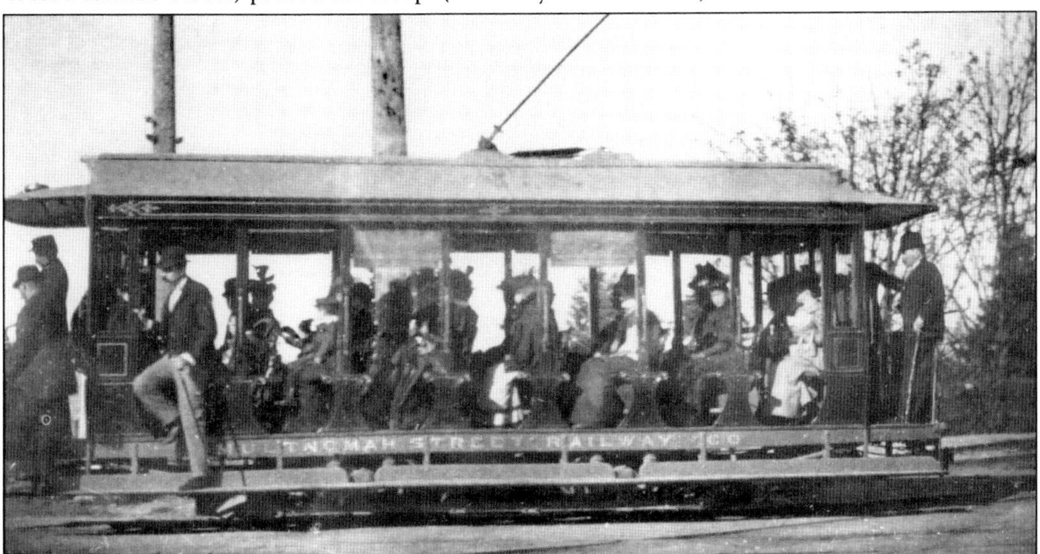

The Washington Street, Montgomery Street, and Thirteenth Street trolley lines were created from earlier horsecar routes. The Multnomah Street Railway used 10 open Brill cars like this to inaugurate electric service on their Washington Street line in March 1890. By the time it merged into the Portland Consolidated Railway Company in 1892, Multnomah was also operating electric streetcars on Southwest Thirteenth, Northwest Sixteenth, and Northwest Twenty-third Avenues. (Courtesy Mark Moore.)

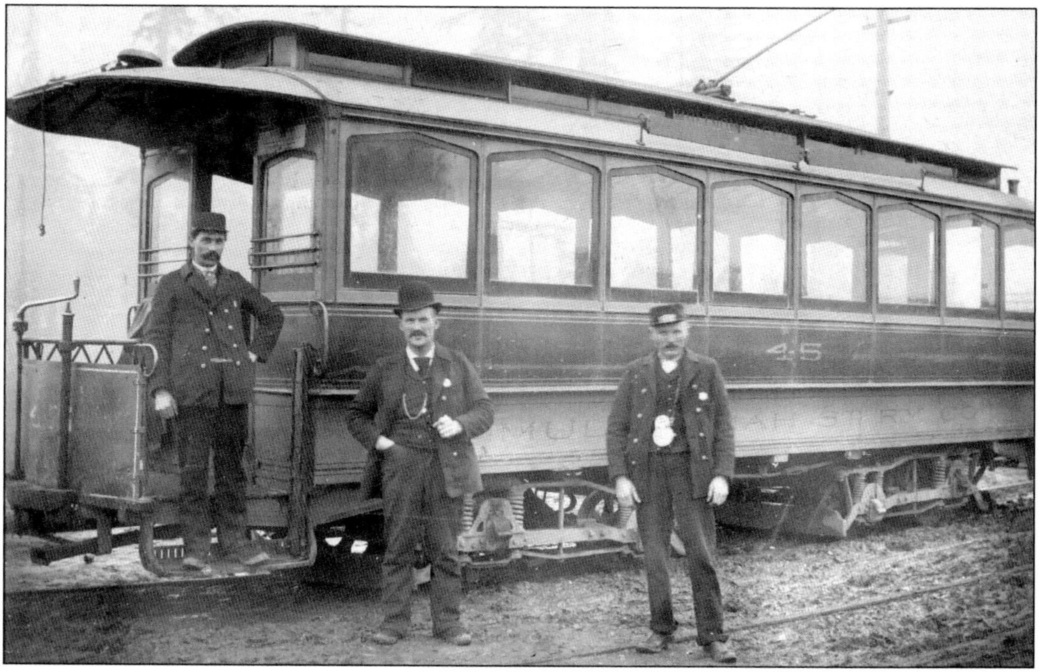

In 1891, the Multnomah Street Railway took delivery of six modern double-truck (eight-wheeled) Brill trolleys. They were nearly 34 feet long, carried more passengers, and negotiated the curving line better. Although the letter boards appear blank, the official and crew are likely posing with No. 45 at the forested terminus of the Washington Street line, what is now West Burnside Street near Northwest Twenty-third Avenue. (Courtesy Mark Moore.)

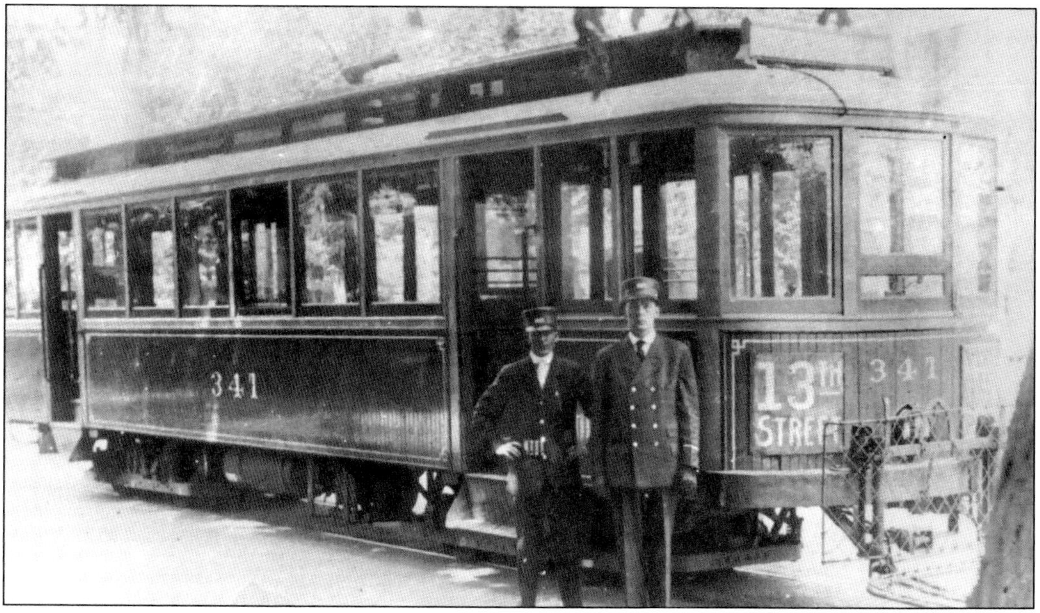

The Thirteenth Street line was a stub line running from Southwest Thirteenth and Washington Streets (via Thirteenth and Southwest Montgomery Streets) to Southwest Sixteenth Street in Goose Hollow. It began in 1883 as a Multnomah Street Railway horsecar line. PRL&P No. 341 is seen here at the leafy southern terminus of the line in 1913.

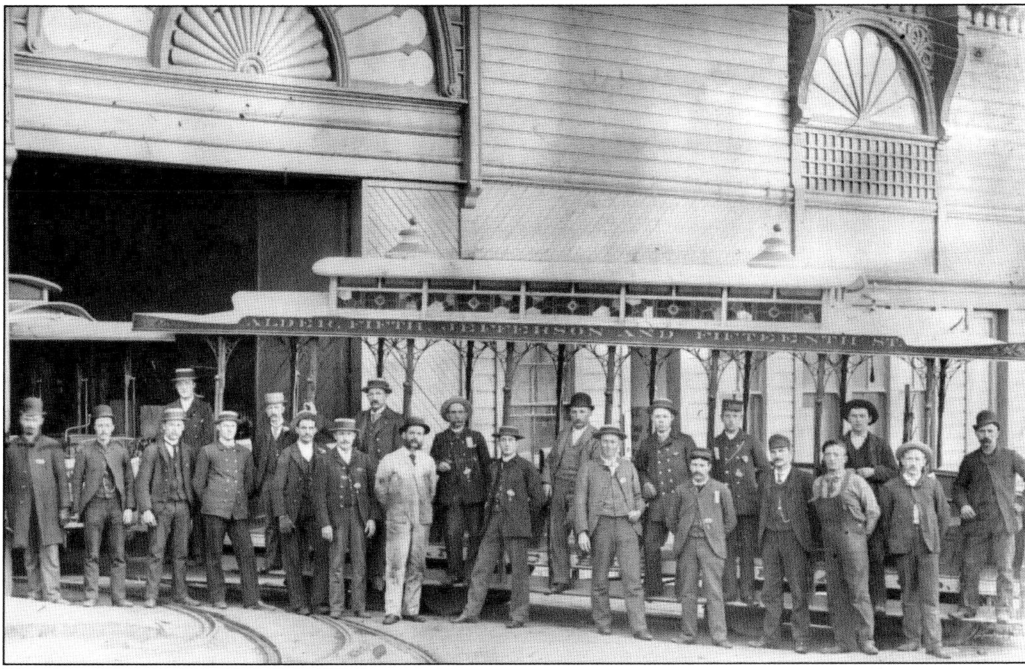

In February 1890, as the move to electric streetcars got under way, another technology joined the fray. The Portland Cable Railway commenced operation of lines running to Union Station on Southwest Fifth Street, out Southwest Jefferson to City Park, to the waterfront on Southwest Alder, and up Southwest Chapman Street to Portland Heights. Here conductors, gripmen, and mechanics pose in front of the ornate carbarn in Goose Hollow.

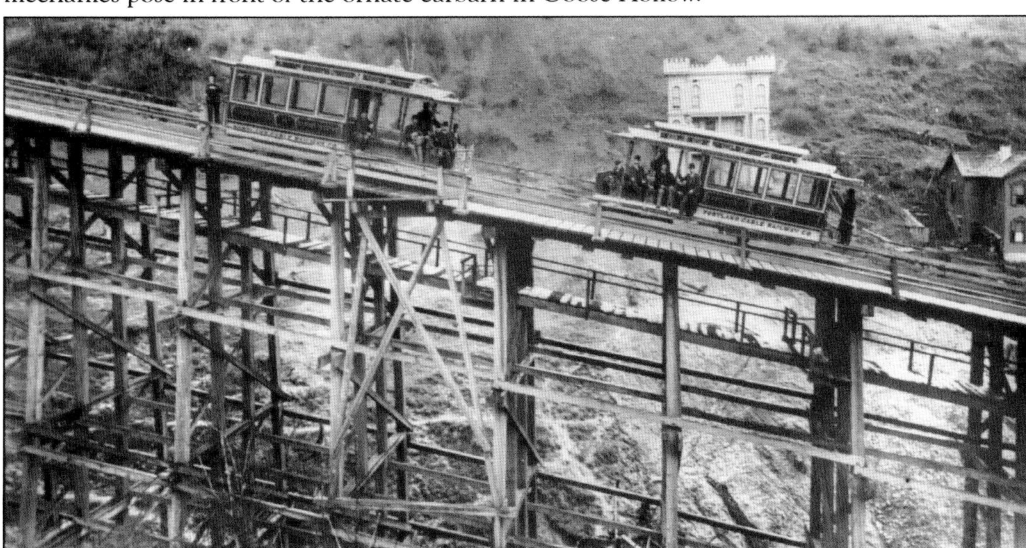

The 20.93 percent grade is apparent as two Portland Heights line cable cars meet on the Chapman Street trestle in April 1893. The press lauded this "superior car system," yet high operating costs resulted in portions of it being converted to trolley six years later. The last cable car ran in August 1904. The house in the background still exists. Note the pedestrian walkway beneath the tracks. (Courtesy Mark Moore.)

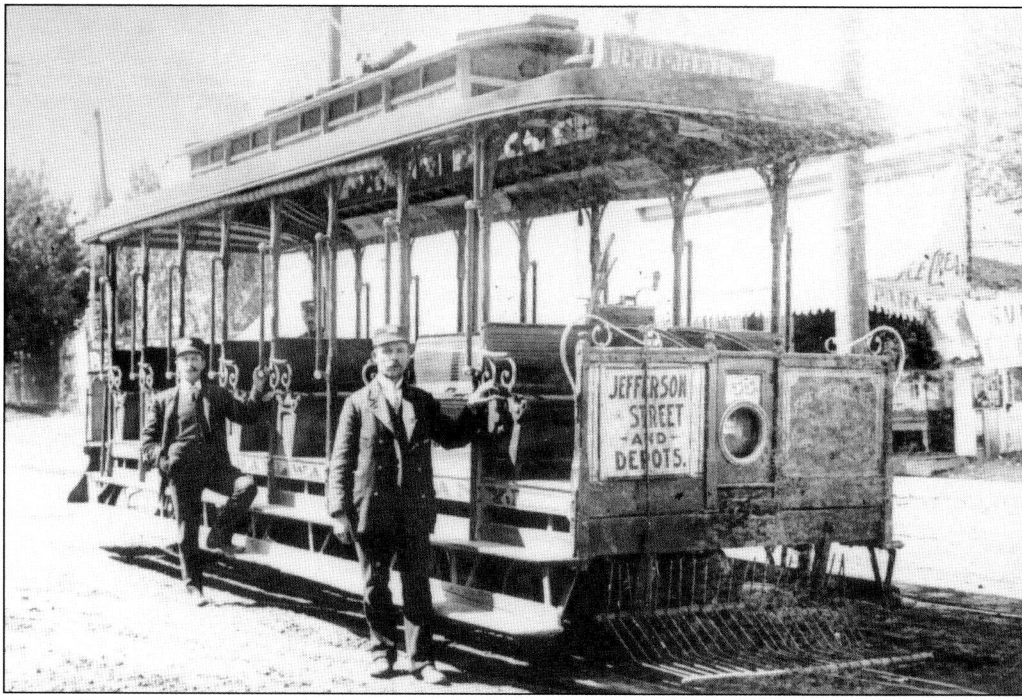

The Jefferson Street line and the South Fifth line started as cable routes. After May 1, 1896, only the steep line running up to Portland Heights from Southwest Eighteenth and Jefferson Streets was operated by cable. Some cars, like Portland Railway Jefferson Street line open No. 55, seen here, were converted into hybrids with both a cable grip and trolley pole so that they could be used either way.

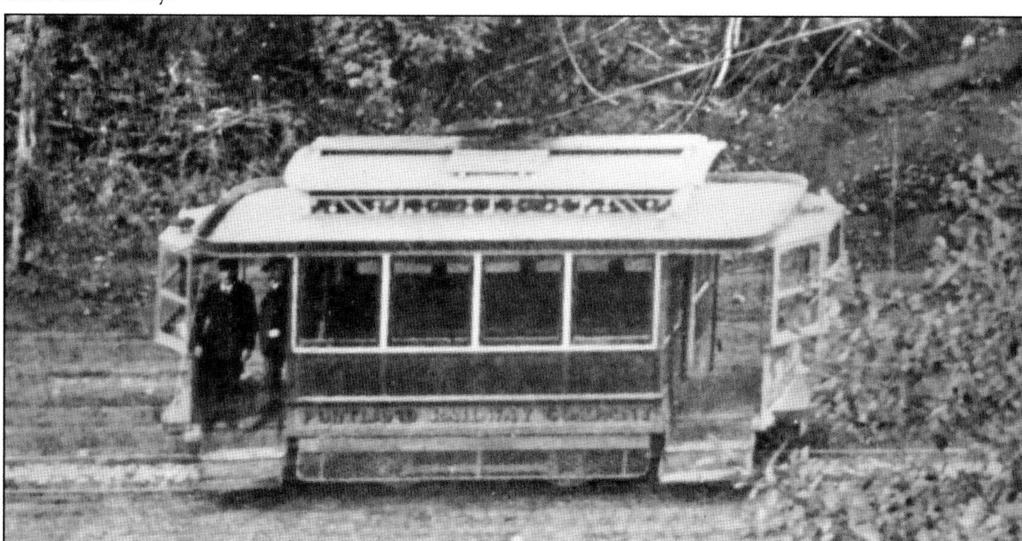

Portland Railway Company inherited a diverse collection of rolling stock in 1896, including this trolley built from the center section of cable car No. 17. No. 59 is seen sporting portable vestibules and passing under the new Ford Street viaduct on Southwest Jefferson Street around 1904. The little car was considered "junk" by 1910 and retired. Development on the Jefferson Street line was scaled back after construction of the Washington Park reservoir.

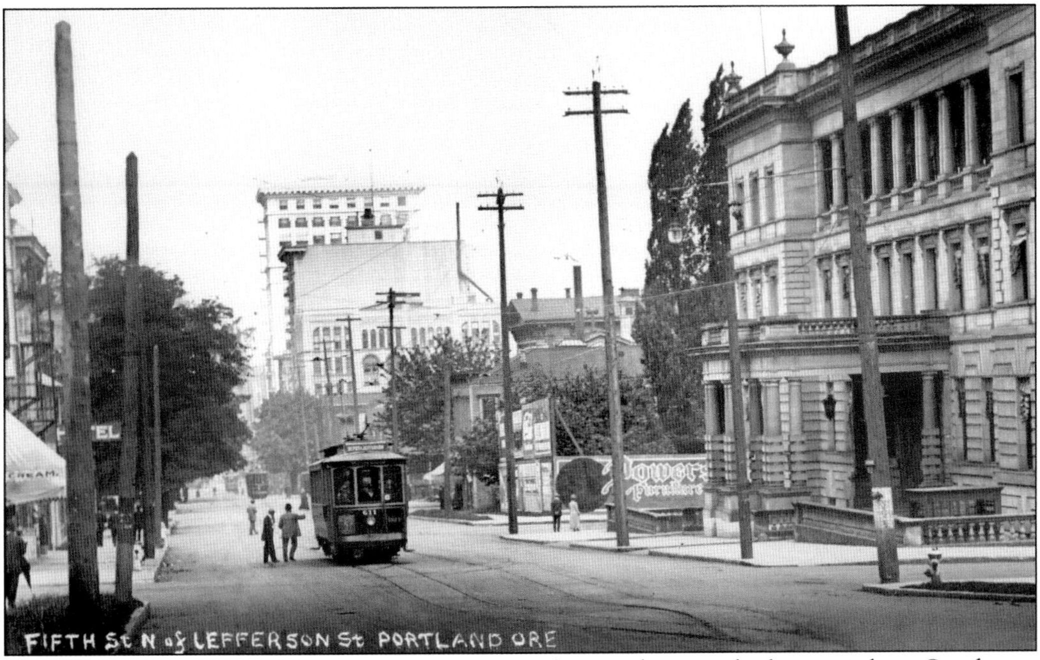

Streetcars are the only mode of transportation evident in this view looking north on Southwest Fifth and Jefferson Streets. PRL&P No. 611 is working the Depot and Jefferson line before 1910, when service to Union Depot was discontinued. In 1914, the Jefferson Street and Irvington lines were combined. A small hotel and ice cream parlor are on the left across the street from Portland's renaissance-style city hall.

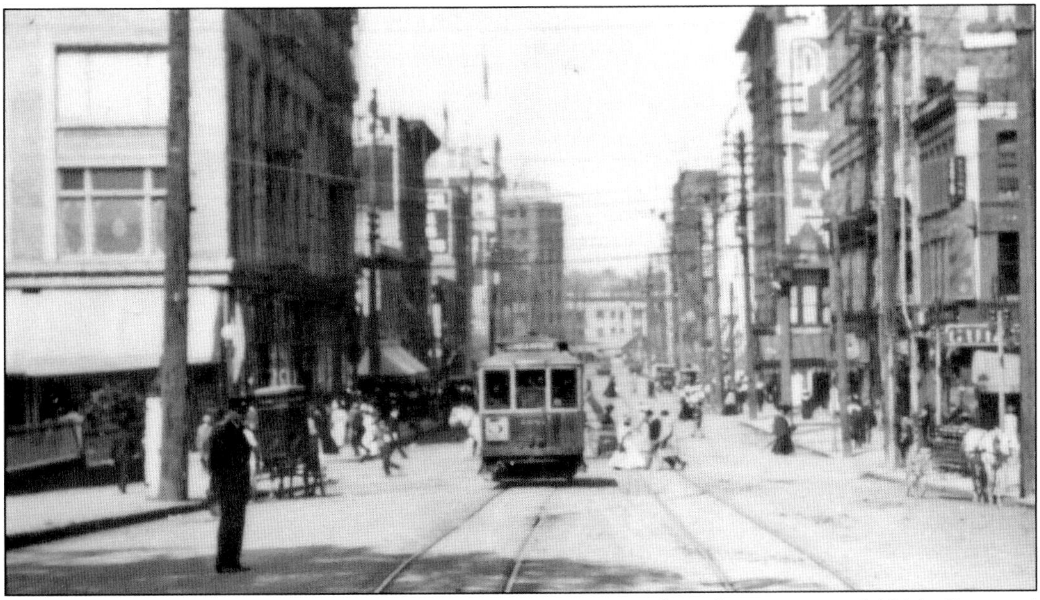

Not long after all traces of the cable conduit were removed in the autumn of 1904, City and Suburban *Standard* No. 100 drifts past the Meier and Frank Department Store on Southwest Fifth Avenue and Morrison Street. The South Fifth line operated from the Union Depot to Southwest First and Sheridan Streets until October 1909, when it became part of the Sixteenth Street line.

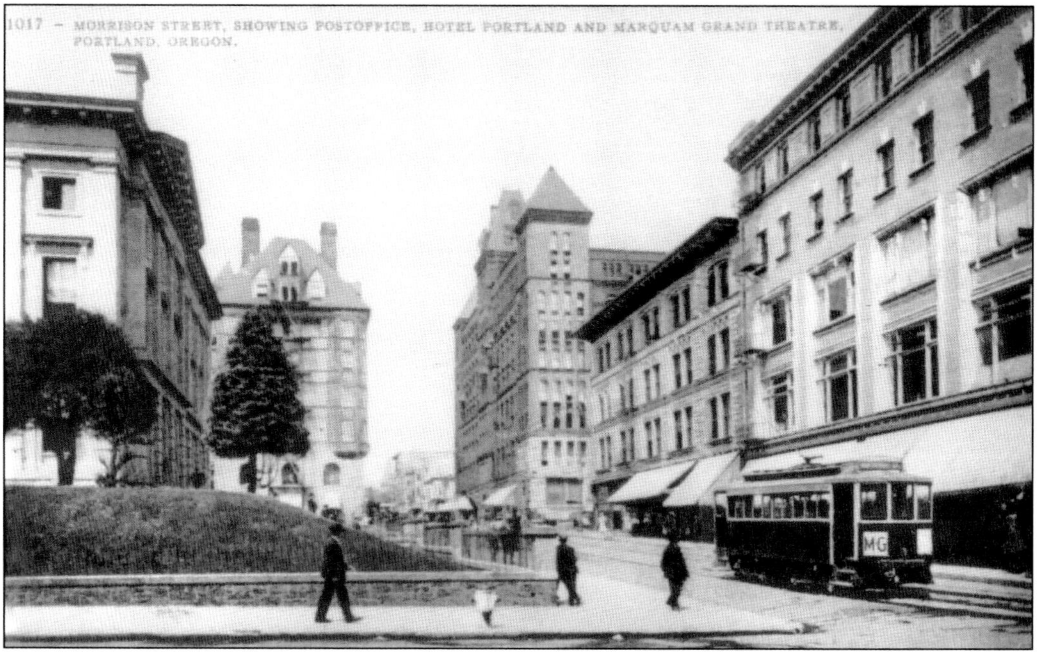

On this postcard, a City and Suburban Railway trolley built from spliced horsecars is seen heading east on Southwest Morrison Street at Fifth Avenue before the Montgomery line merged with the Mount Tabor Line in 1908. Buildings in the background include the Pioneer Post Office, the Portland Hotel, the Marquam Grand Theater, and the Meier and Frank Department Store, which was replaced by the current building in 1913.

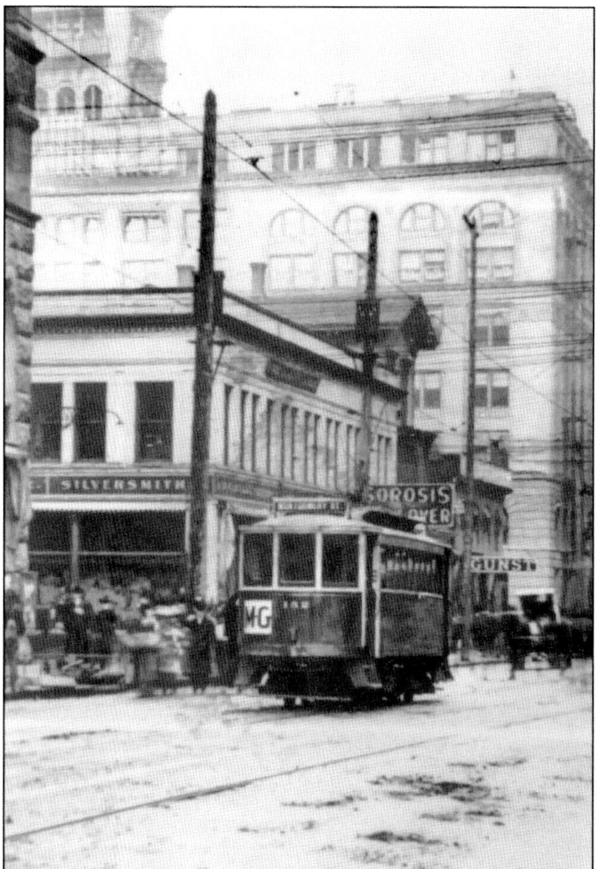

Southbound passengers are boarding the high-riding Montgomery line car No. 152 on the corner of Southwest Third and Washington Streets in 1908. Two years earlier, the chamber of commerce building, seen in the background, was damaged due to fire on an upper floor. Repairs were not completed until 1910, by which time two additional floors had been added. The 1892 building survived until 1933, although the chamber had lost ownership during the financial panic of 1893.

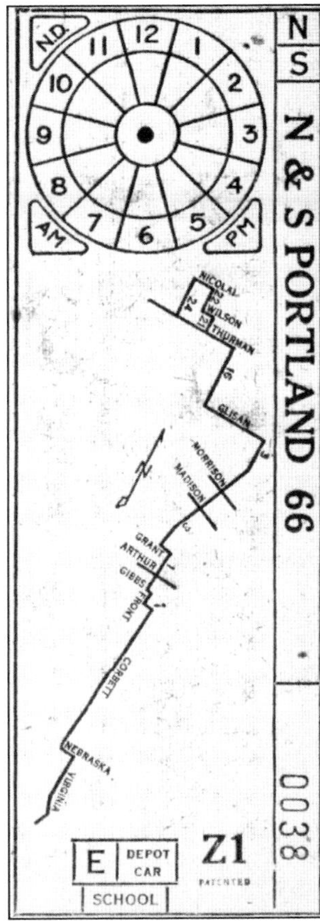

The North and South Portland line illustrated on this transfer was established around 1900 by the City and Suburban Railway using trackage begun by predecessors, including part of the Metropolitan Railway's line to Fulton. Initial service was from Northwest Twenty-seventh and Thurman Streets via Sixteenth, Glisan, and Third Streets to Southwest Corbett Avenue and Hamilton Street. The Fulton line merged with the North and South line in 1923. Conversion to trolley coach came on May 23, 1937.

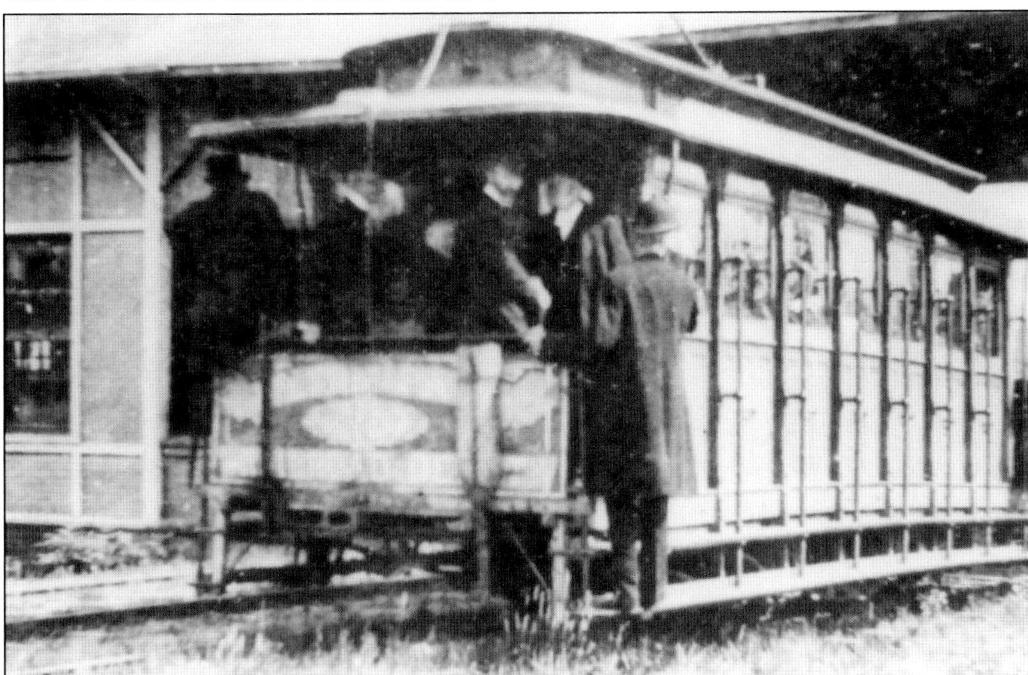

Metropolitan Railway launched the first electric streetcar line on the west side on January 1, 1890. This low convertible trolley has reached the southern end of the line, which ran from Northwest Second and Glisan Streets to Fulton Park and Riverview Cemetery in South Portland. In 1900, the re-gauged and relocated route was called the Riverview line, but it was Fulton when merged with the North and South Portland line in 1923.

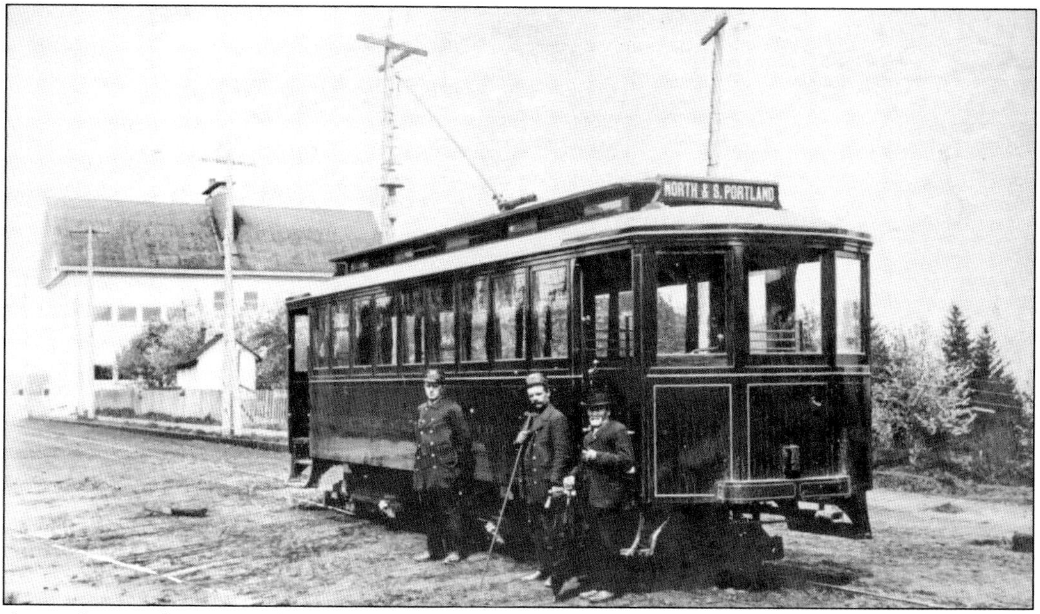

Around 1900, the City and Suburban Railway absorbed the Metropolitan Railway and inaugurated service on a lengthy line, serving both North and South Portland. The crew of No. 101, one of the first cars assigned to the new route, is seen here with an umbrella-toting gentleman at the original southern terminus on Southwest Corbett and Hamilton Streets. Holman School is in the background. (Photograph by Charles W. Love.)

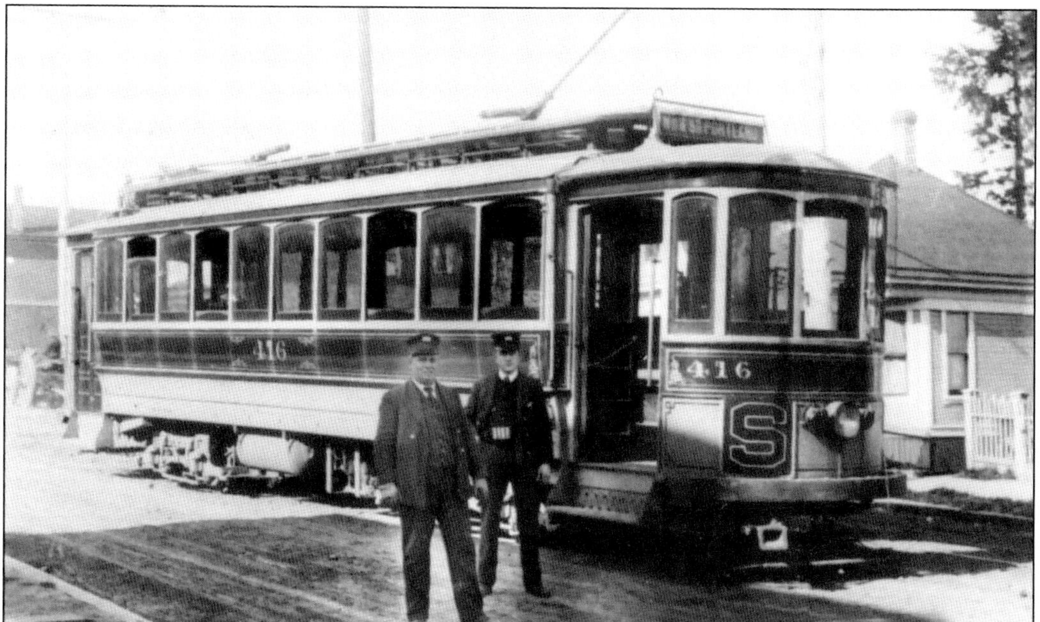

The hilly S line (North and South Portland) witnessed a number of runaway streetcars. On July 2, 1910, around the time this picture was taken, the brakes loosened while the crew was changing poles at the end of the line, and a passenger was injured when, upon the advice of others, she jumped from the rolling car. No. 416 was among the new trolleys replacing the 100 series on heavily traveled lines.

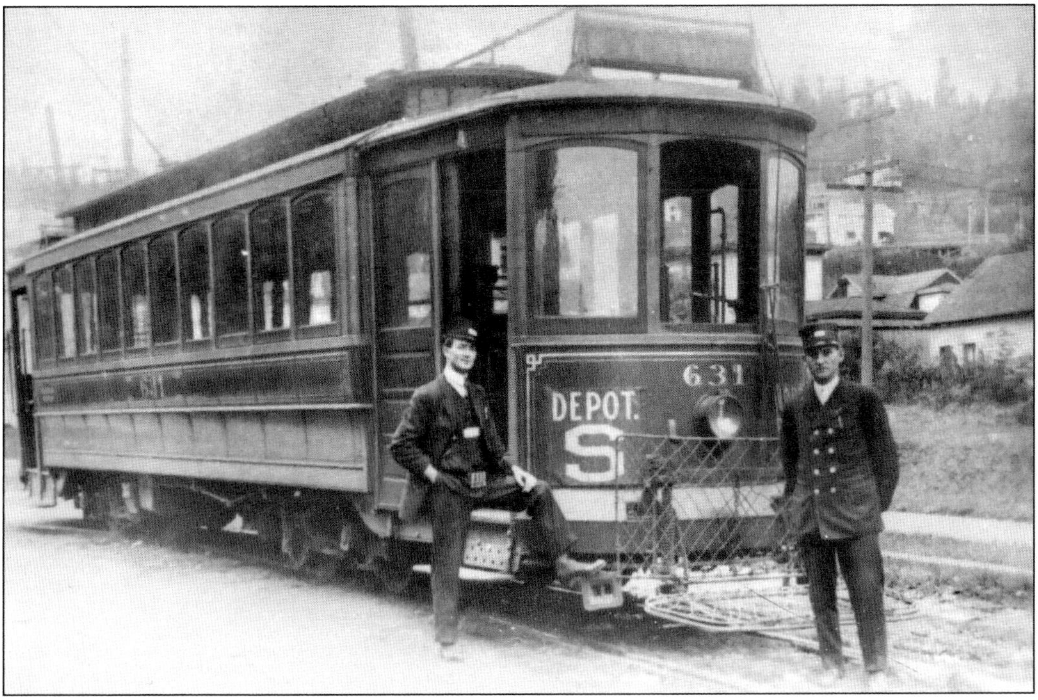

A car like No. 631, seen at the end of the North and South line around 1913, figured in a dramatic 1930s incident. The brakes let go while the motorman was taking a break at Southwest Corbett and Bancroft Streets one night. The empty car rolled down Corbett, crested the grade on Nebraska, and glided down to Virginia, where it derailed and crashed into Porcelli's grocery store. No one was injured.

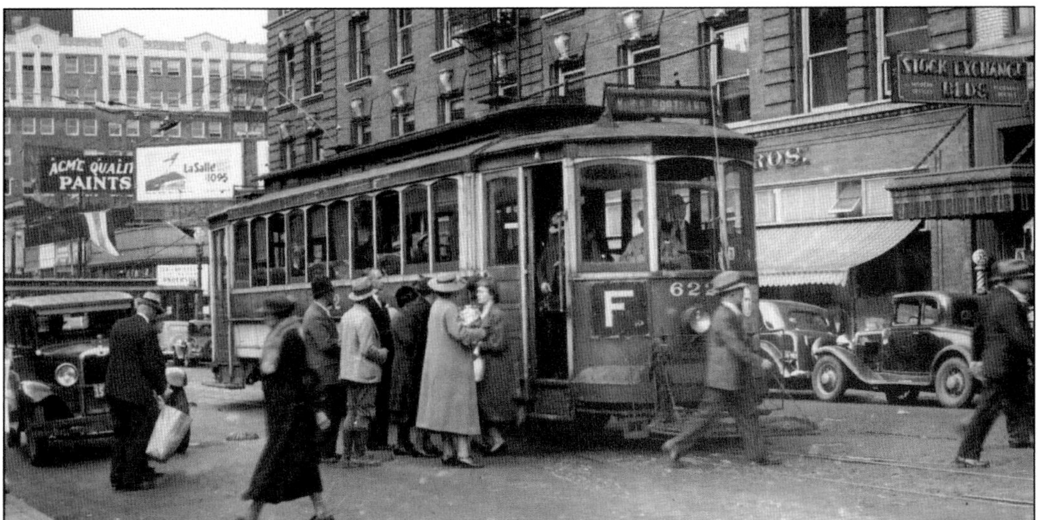

A worn-out looking No. 622 is taking on passengers on Southwest Third Avenue at Morrison Street during the last run for North and South Portland line streetcars on May 23, 1937. Double wires overhead are evidence of the trolley buses that would take over. After the Fulton line was discontinued on May 21, 1923, an F dash sign was used to signify North and South cars running to the former Fulton terminus.

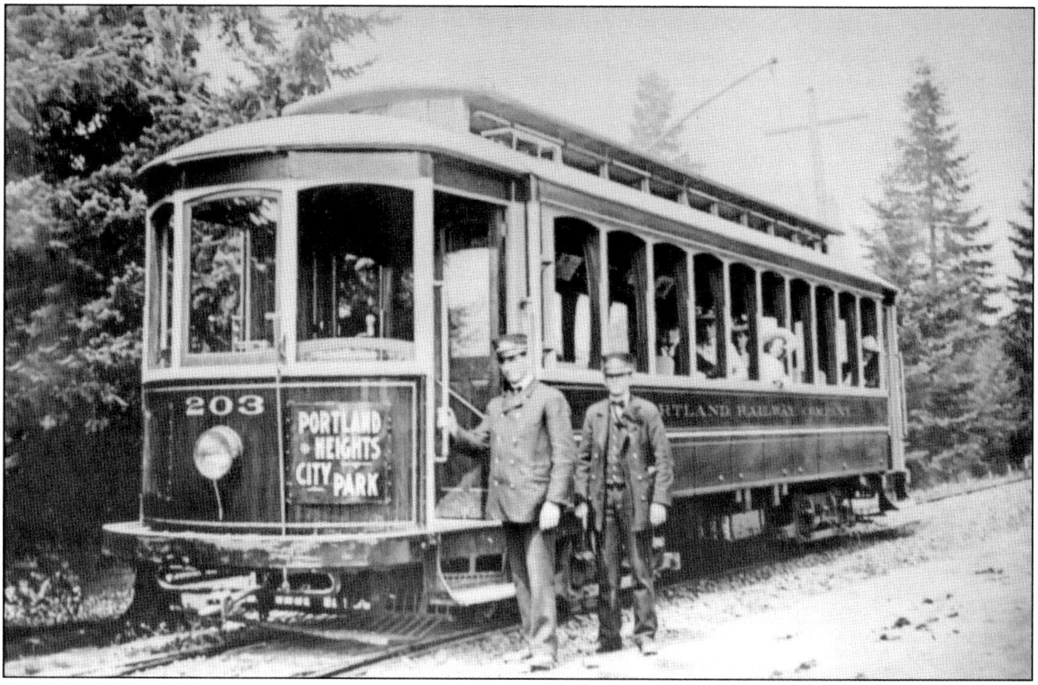

Portland's most illustrious trolley line began as a replacement for the cable car to Portland Heights in 1904. Following the abandonment of the steep Chapman Street trestle, the tracks were rerouted along Southwest Vista Street to Southwest Patton Road. In September 1906, a shuttle was added from here to Council Crest. Portland Railway No. 203 (later 503) is preserved at the Oregon Electric Railway Historical Society museum in Brooks.

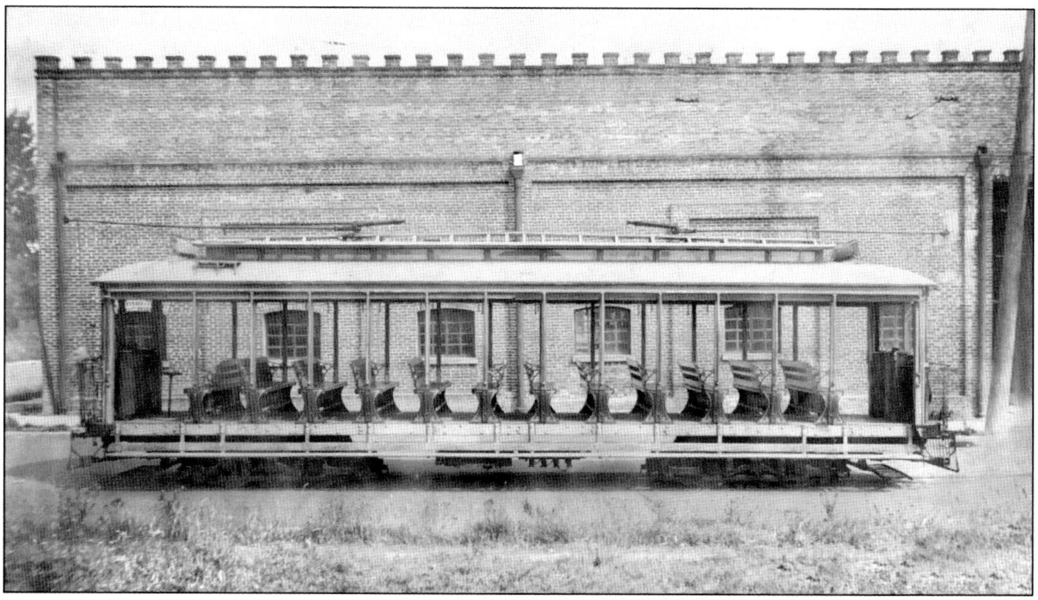

In 1907, PRL&P ordered 14 open cars from the American Car Company. Ironically, although they were equipped with four powerful motors and magnetic brakes that pressed directly on the rails, they were seldom used on the heights. Six years later, these Council Crest opens were rebuilt as closed cars. No. 260 is seen next to the Savier Carbarn prior to the 1918 rebuilding.

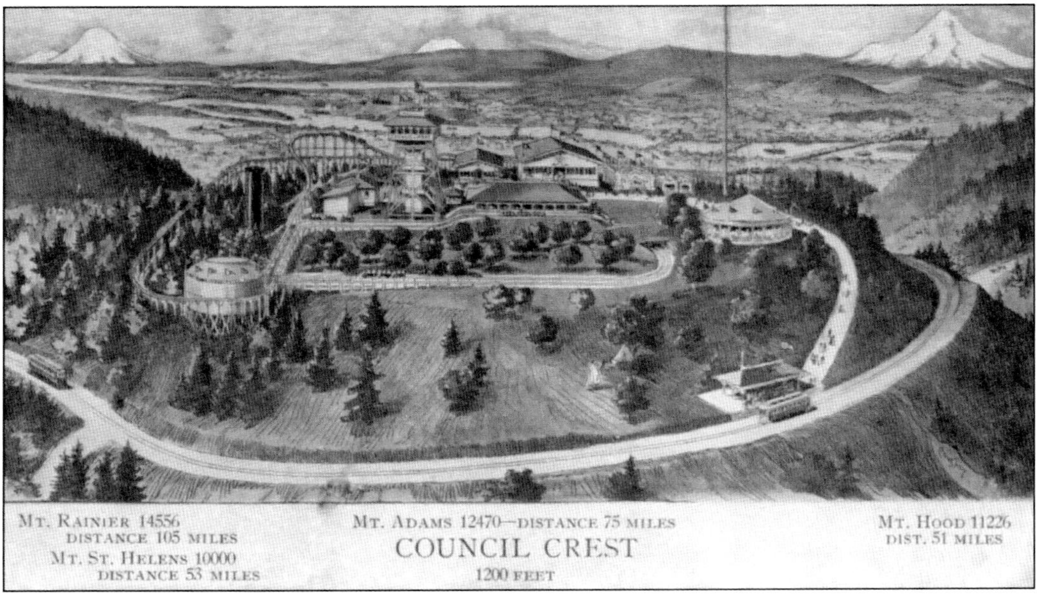

The 22-acre Council Crest Amusement Park opened on Memorial Day 1907. Financial problems led to its closure in 1929. Attractions included an observation tower (1,200 feet above the city), Ferris wheel, the largest open-air dance pavilion in the Northwest, a scenic miniature railway, canal boats, and a fun house—not to mention the 20-minute revenue-generating streetcar ride from town past mansions and forest. (Courtesy Mark Moore.)

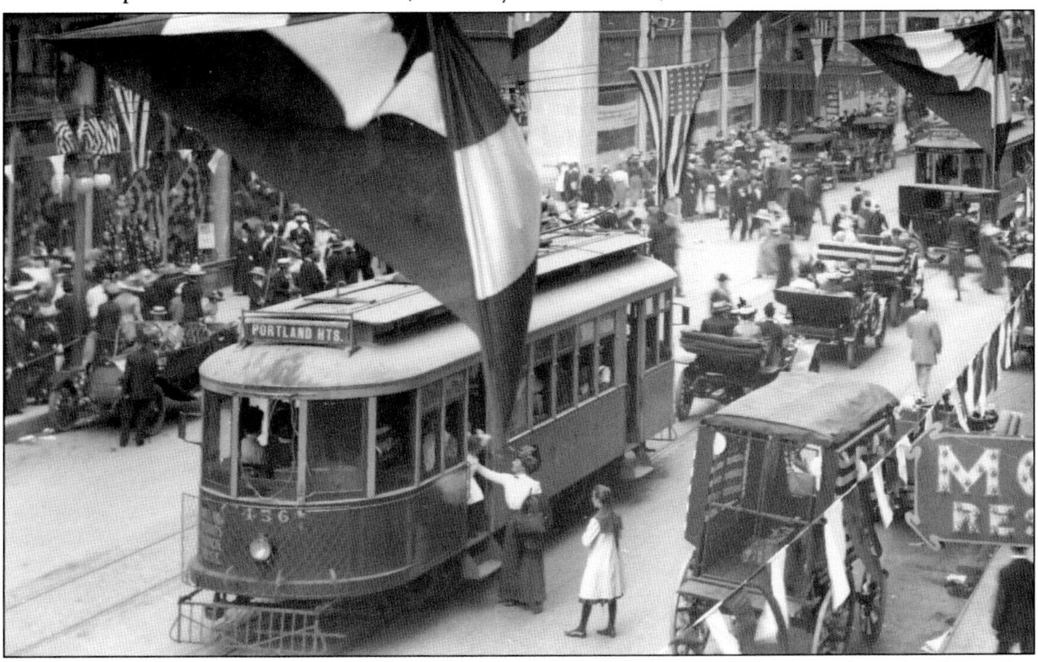

The trolleys that would come to be known as the *Council Crests* originally shared Portland Heights line duty with the *Torontos*. Round-nosed *Toronto* No. 456 is seen here following a Sixteenth Street line car on Southwest Fifth Avenue at Washington Street during a parade. It is around 1912, when the Meier and Frank Department Store on the left faced competition from the new Lipman Wolfe store on the right.

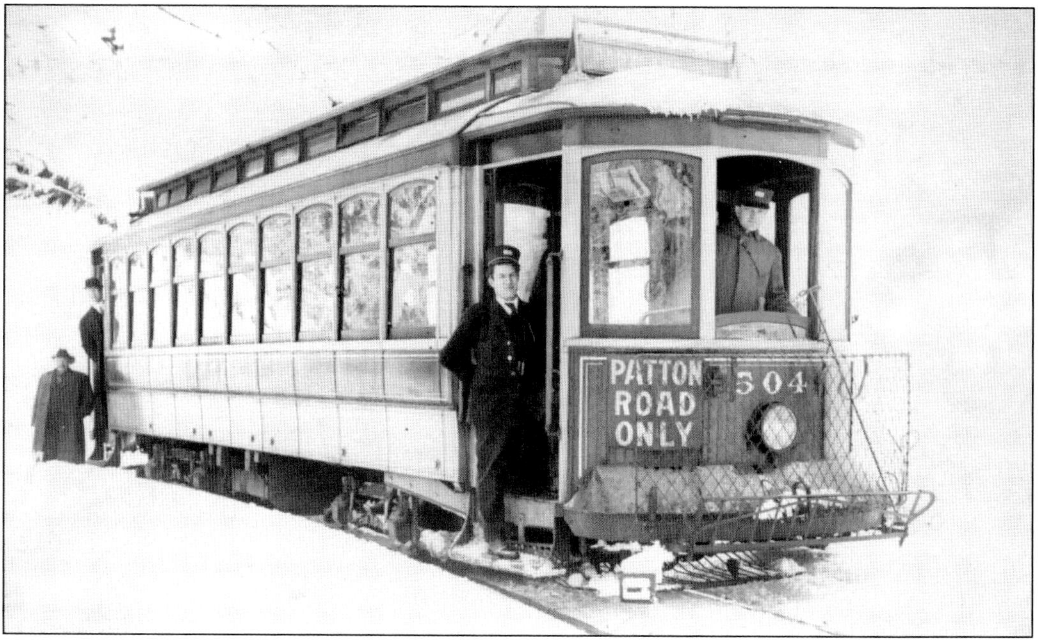

After Portland Heights cars began running to Council Crest, tripper service was established to the old terminus on Southwest Vista Avenue at Patton Road. Even though cars bearing the "Patton Road Only" dash sign turned back before reaching the 1,073-foot summit, they did often encounter winter snow, as seen in this frosty 1910s scene. (Courtesy Mark Moore.)

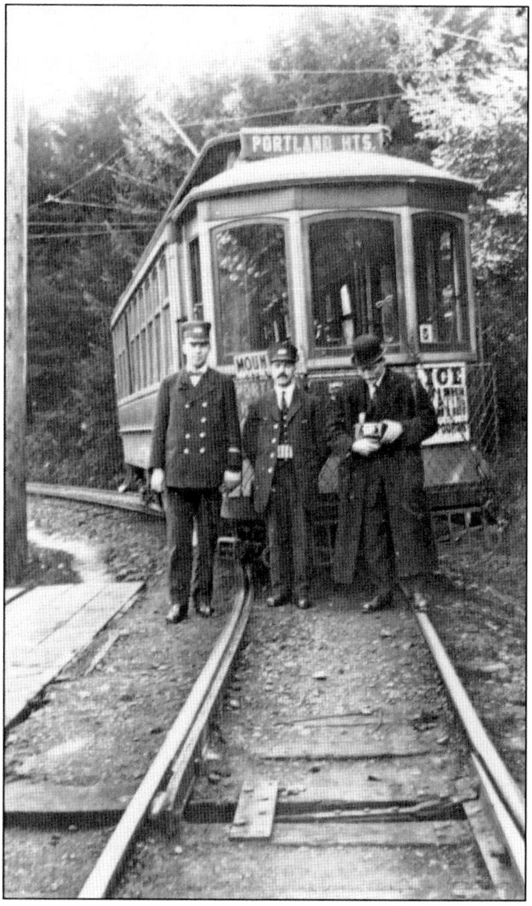

A passenger has disembarked to take a picture at Council Crest Park Station, which provided scenic vistas westward across the Tualatin Valley. Many considered the Council Crest line to be the most beautiful in America. The dash sign advertises skating at the Hippodrome, a 2,000-seat ice skating and hockey arena built in northwest Portland in 1914. It closed in the 1950s. (Courtesy Mark Moore.)

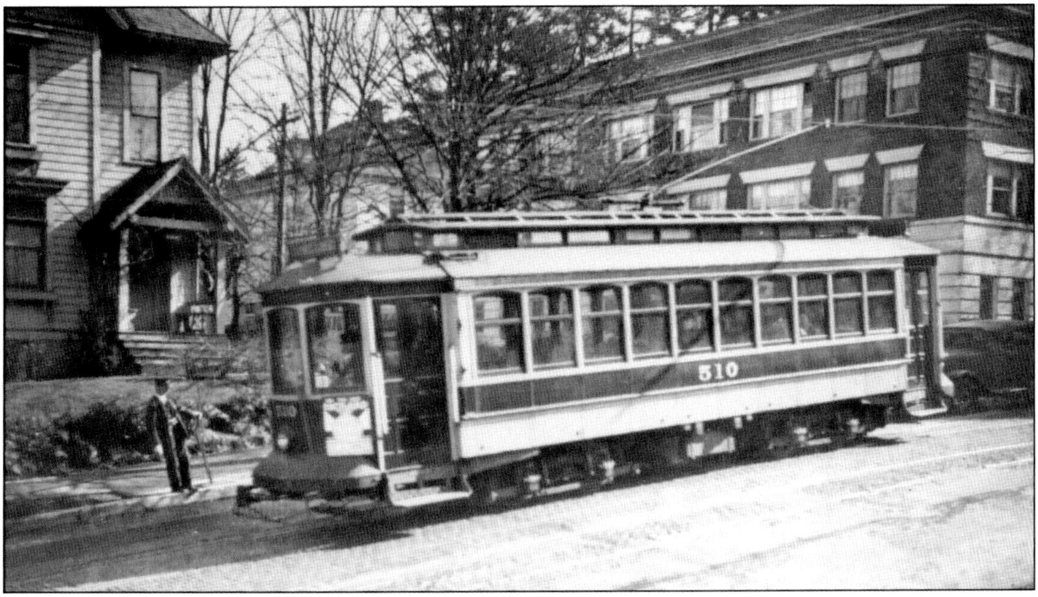

To prevent runaways, the Council Crest line incorporated switches that derailed trolleys if they did not make required safety stops. No. 510 is negotiating a derail on Southwest Vista Avenue while the conductor holds the switch closed. He will hop on the rear platform after the car passes and give the motorman two bells to proceed. When the line was converted to one-man operation in 1939, these derails were electrified.

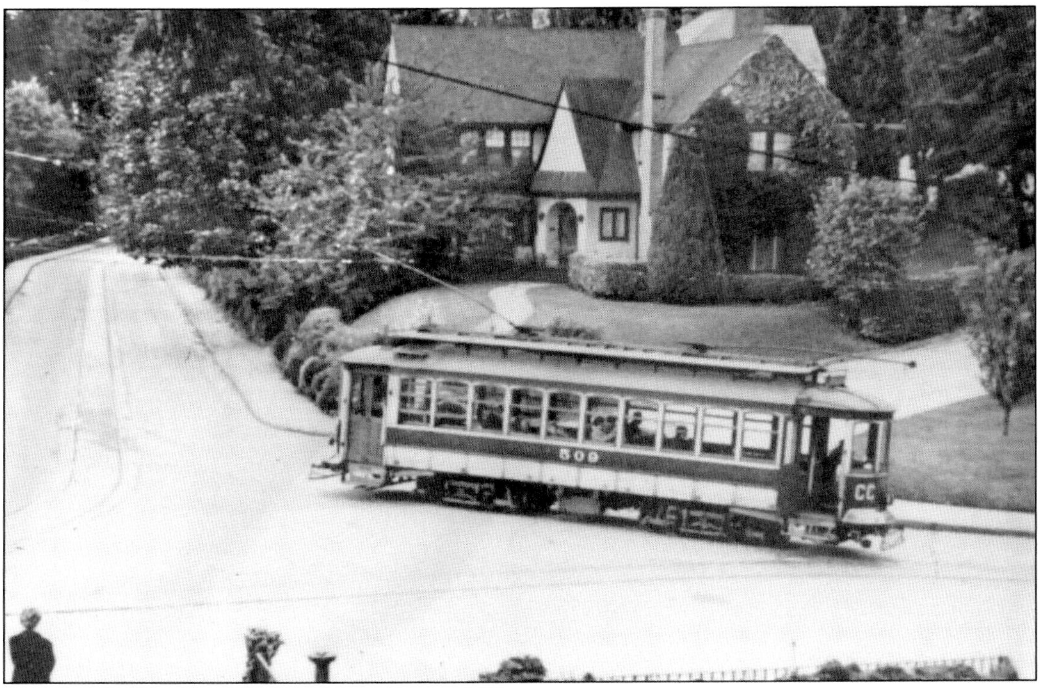

Council Crest line No. 509 swings eastward past a large Portland Heights home on Southwest Broadway Drive at Southwest Patton Road on a nice day in the 1940s. The Council Crest line got its start here September 20, 1906, running as a shuttle over the upper loop from the Portland Heights terminus to Council Crest Park.

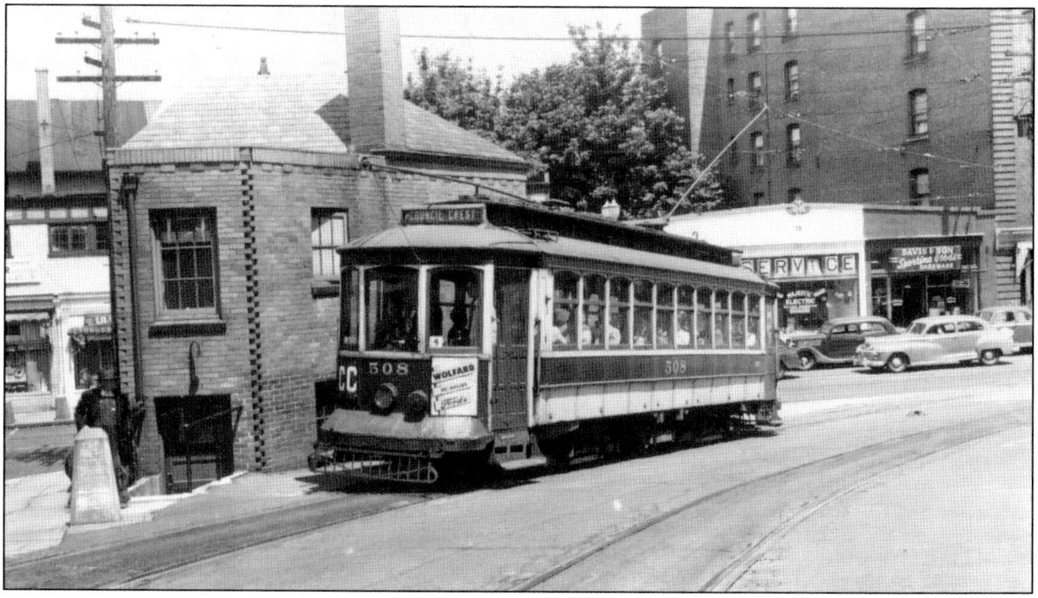

Council Crest No. 508 is traversing the short right-of-way connecting West Burnside Street to Southwest Vista Avenue in this 1940s snapshot. The concrete "dragons teeth" jutting out of the pavement at the left offered protection against derailed streetcars. Evidence of derailments on the line included gouged pavement on Southwest Vista Avenue and a chestnut tree filled with cement on Southwest Eighteenth Avenue. The building next to No. 508 houses an insurance office today.

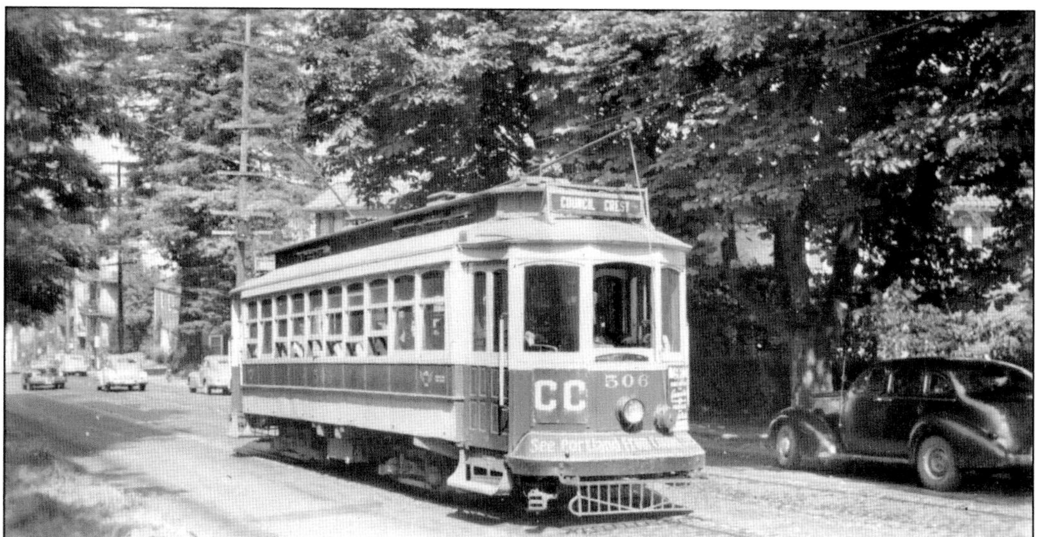

"See Portland from Council Crest" can be seen on the fender as No. 506 growls up hilly Southwest Vista Avenue, but crews have painted over the woodwork on doors and windows. That might have taken place after April 26, 1948, when the car derailed at the corner of Southwest Eighteenth Avenue and Spring Streets and slid into a power pole, slightly injuring two passengers. There were 68 curves on the line.

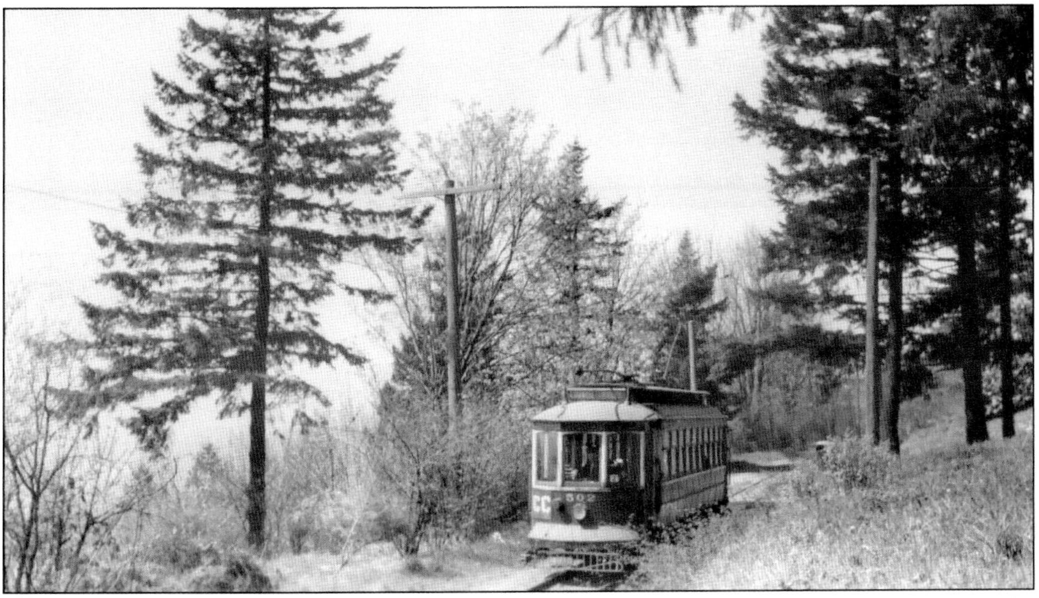

Car No. 502 has stopped at the highest point on the line overlooking the Tualatin Valley near the former Council Crest Park Station on an overcast 1940s morning. In 1909, a motorman on this same car became a hero when he jumped from the platform of his waiting streetcar and grabbed the reins of a runaway horse pulling a delivery wagon down Ford Street (now Southwest Vista Avenue). (Photograph by Al Haij.)

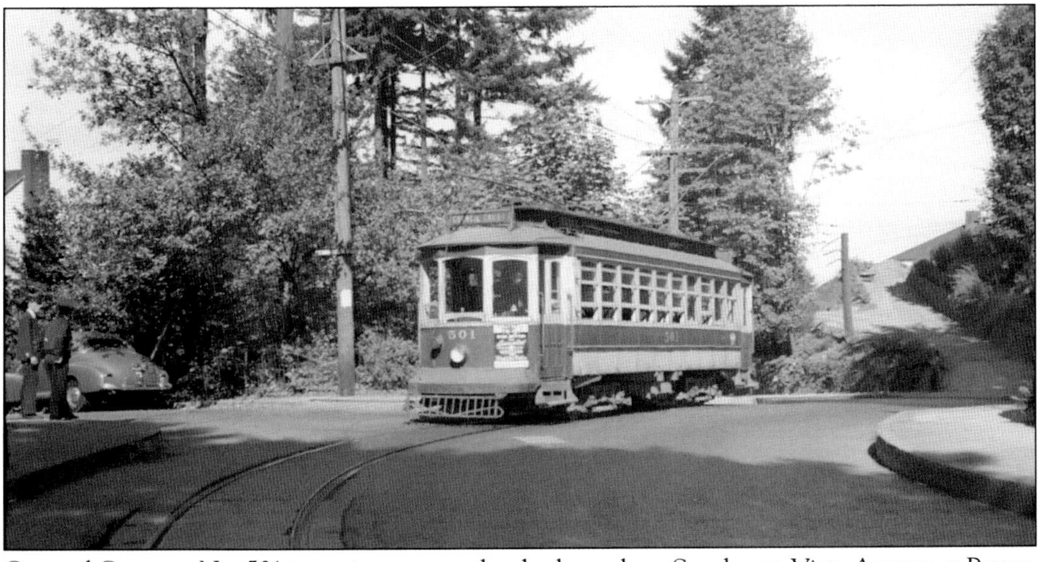

Council Crest car No. 501 is resting among the shadows along Southwest Vista Avenue at Patton Road during a late 1940s afternoon. A shift change may be taking place, as two crewmen appear to be conversing at left while another waits inside a parked automobile. (Photograph by John F. Bromley.)

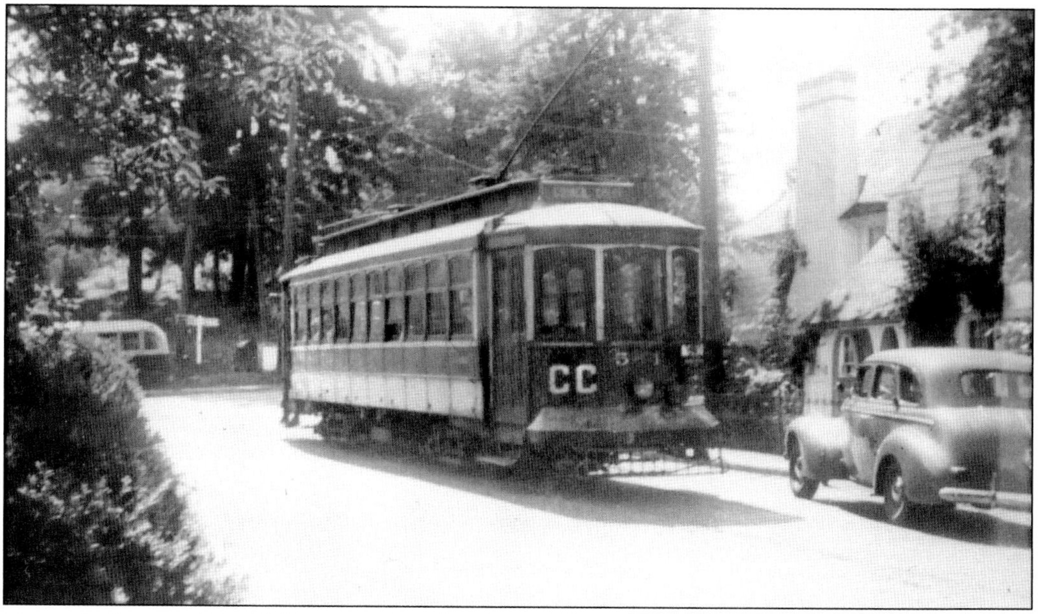

Council Crest car No. 504 has reached Southwest Vista Avenue and Patton Road in 1949. On August 10, shuttle buses had replaced trolleys on the upper loop to Council Crest Park. This location was once again the end of the line that ran past the picturesque houses of Portland Heights. One of the new buses is visible to the left. By this time, much of the private right-of-way was paved.

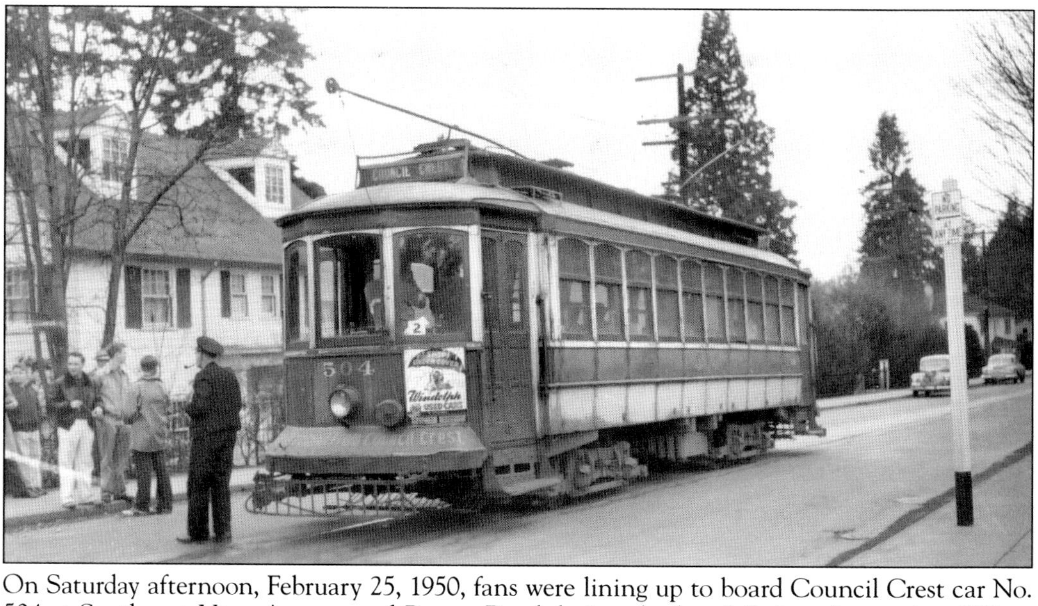

On Saturday afternoon, February 25, 1950, fans were lining up to board Council Crest car No. 504 at Southwest Vista Avenue and Patton Road during the last full day of operation. When the final car departed Southwest Vista and Patton at 12:50 a.m. the next morning, the Council Crest line was one of the last three local streetcar lines. Riders thought this had closed the book on Portland trolleys.

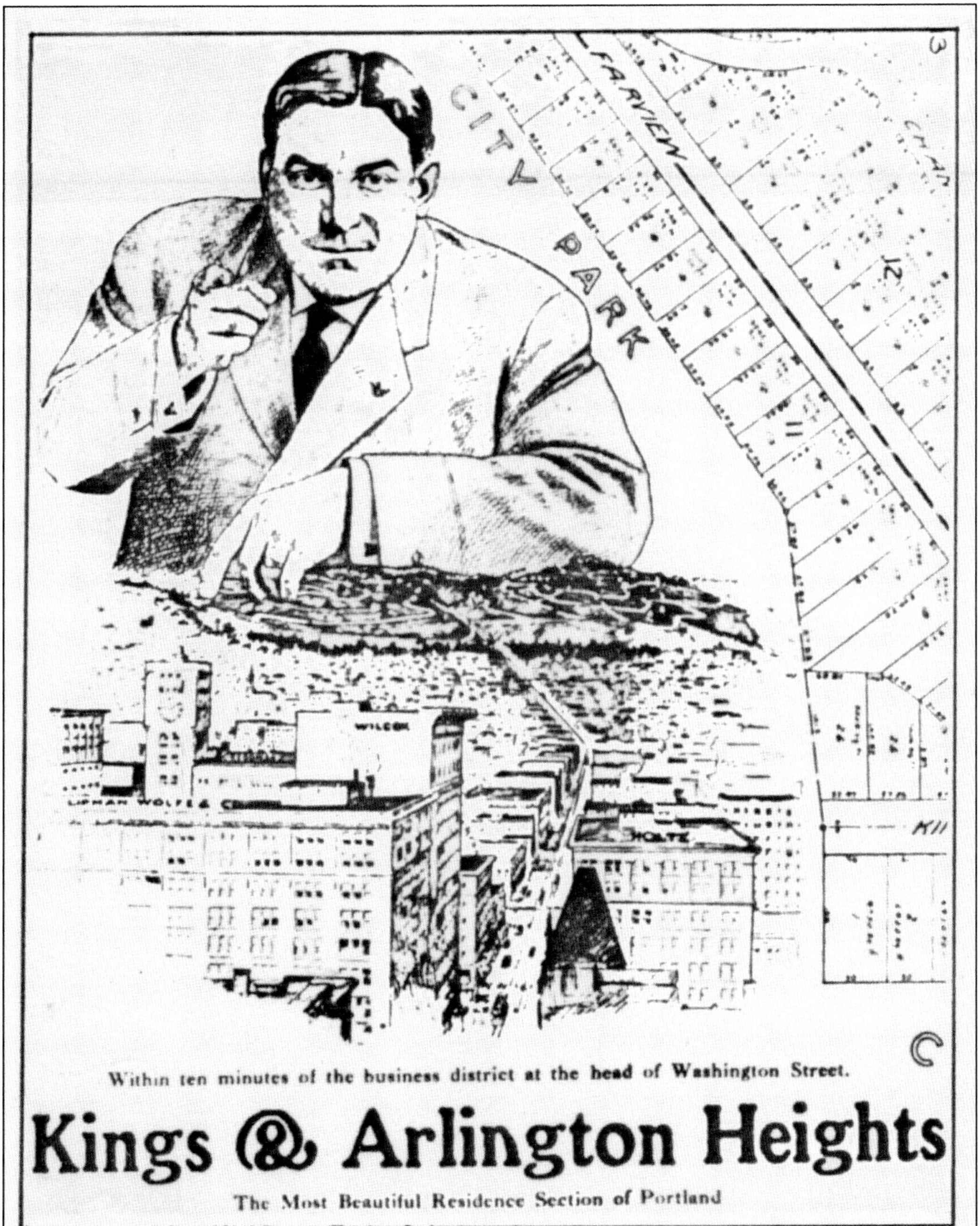

This 1912 advertisement for Arlington and Kings Heights, which flanked West Burnside above Twenty-third Avenue, shows available lots along Southwest Fairview Street in Arlington Heights. The largest developments in the city's history were "within ten minutes of the business district" because of stub lines built by the Dorr Keasey real estate interests. The King's Heights line opened in June 1911, and the Arlington Heights line followed in October 1913.

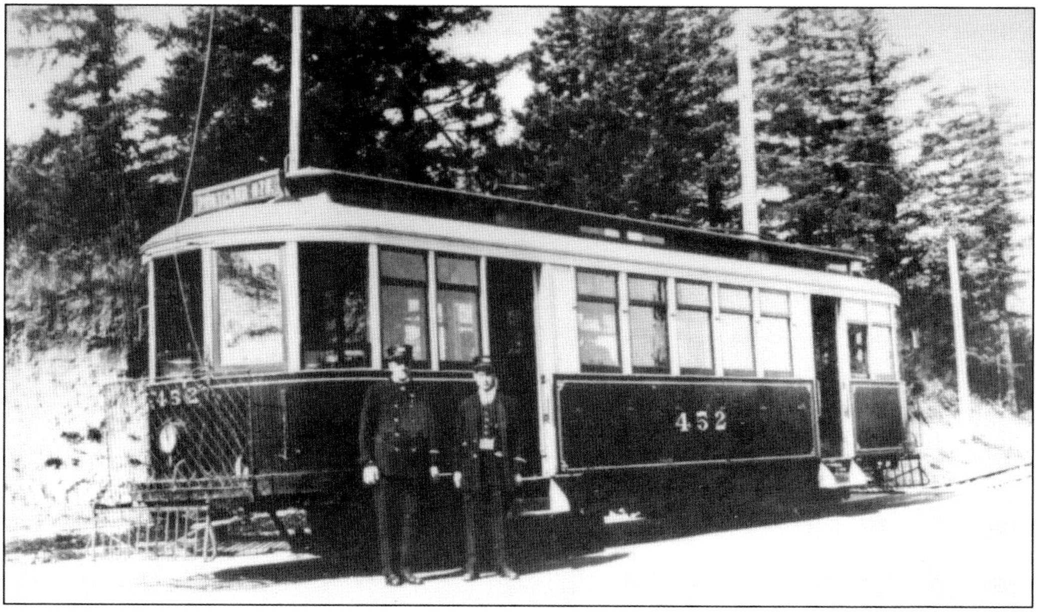

The stub line to Arlington Heights became the last new streetcar line in Southwest Portland when service was inaugurated from Northwest Twenty-third and West Burnside (then part of Southwest Washington Street) to Southwest Fairview and Champlain Streets on October 1, 1913. Both Arlington Heights and Kings Heights in Northwest Portland were served exclusively by *Toronto* cars like No. 452, seen here lying over at the southern end of the line.

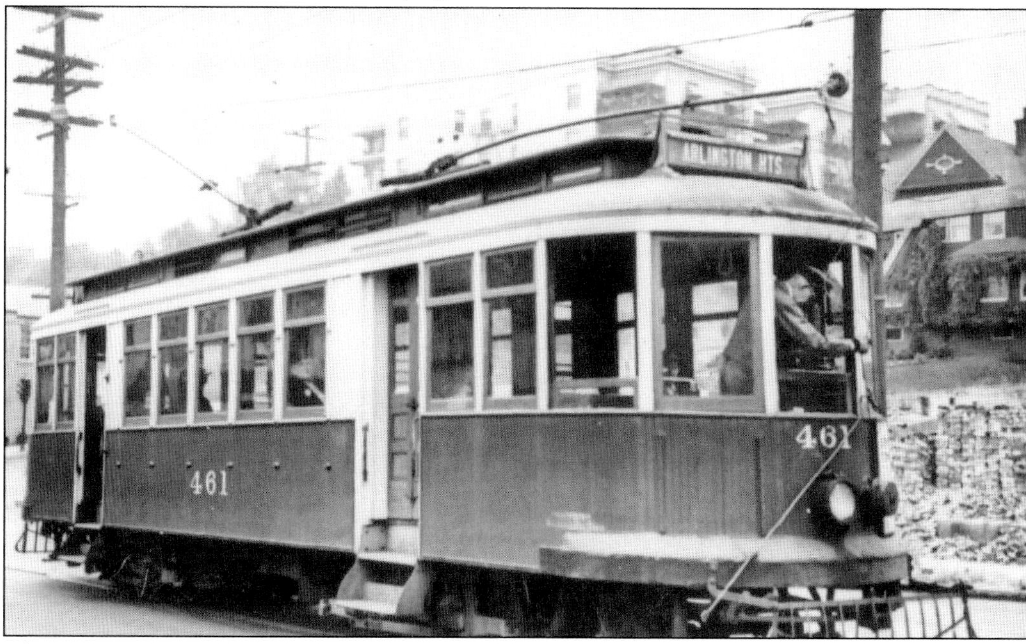

The motorman is reaching through the window to secure the pole on No. 461 at the end of the Arlington Heights (AH) line on West Burnside Street at Twenty-third Avenue. The car's fancy gold pinstripes have long since disappeared. The AH stub line was converted to bus May 9, 1941, not long after this picture was taken. The house and apartment building in the background are still there today.

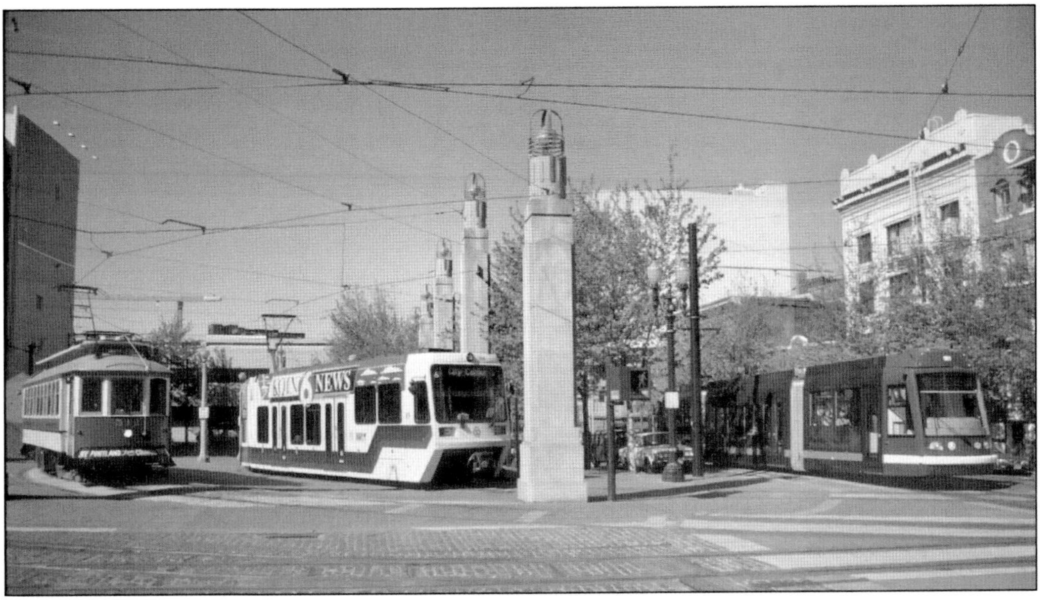

Streetcars returned in three waves: in 1986, the first Tri-County Metropolitan Transportation District (Tri-Met) MAX light rail line opened; in 1991, Vintage Trolley's reproduction Council Crest cars began running; and in 2001, the Portland Streetcar system began. All are represented in this scene on Southwest Eleventh Avenue and Yamhill Street on May 12, 2002: Vintage Trolley No. 512 (left), Red line MAX car No. 205 (center), and PS car No. 001. (Photograph by Steve Morgan.)

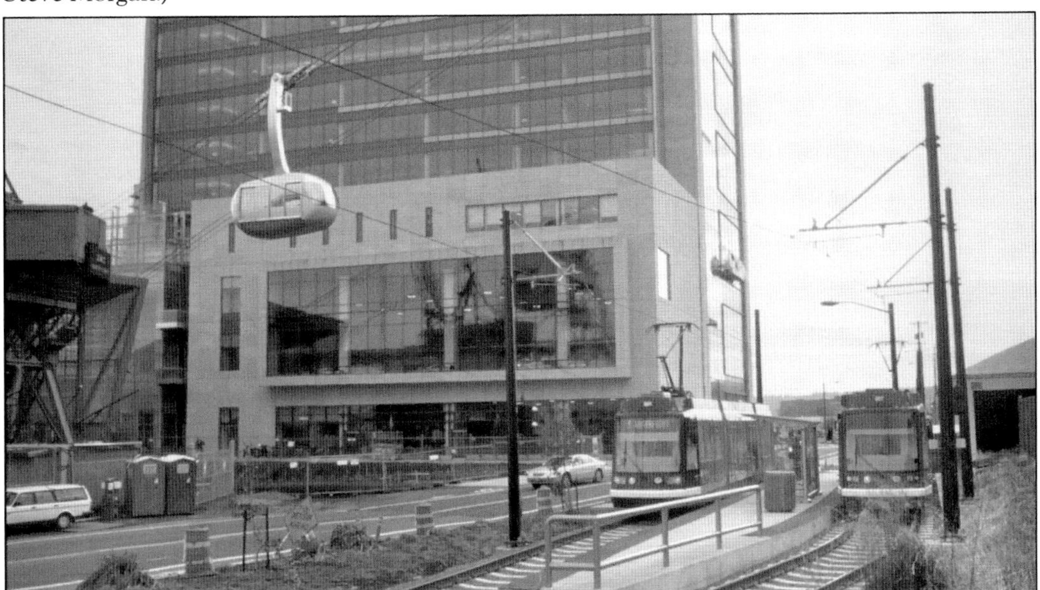

In the South Waterfront District, the Portland streetcar line helped foster development in the same way trolley line extensions had a century earlier. On January 22, 2007, two Skoda cars are lying over at the then southern terminal at Southwest Gibbs Street and Moody Avenue as a cabin of the new Portland Aerial Tram passes overhead, five days before the cableway to Marquam Hill opened. (Photograph by Steve Morgan.)

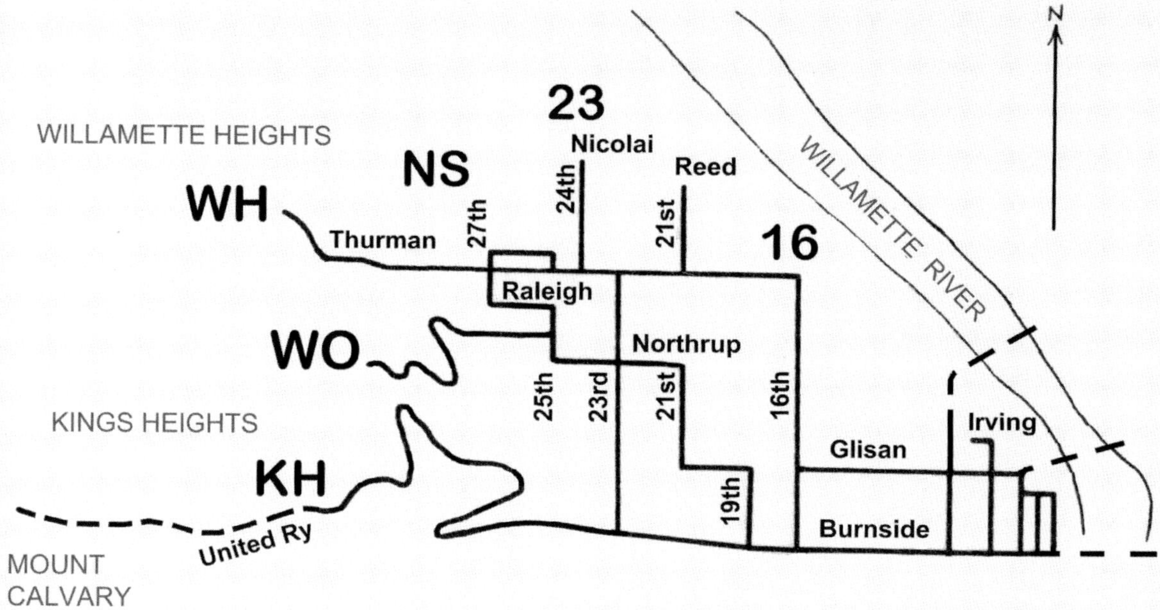

Lines in Northwest Portland included the following: Burnside Street, 1903–1915; Depot and Morrison (M), 1907–1923; Glisan Street (G), 1883-1900; Kings Heights (KH), 1911–1941; Lovejoy, 1910–1916; Mount Calvary, 1911–1927; North and South Portland (NS), 1900–1937; Savier Street (S), 1897–1900; Sixteenth Avenue (16), 1883–1937; Twenty-third Avenue (23), 1891–1950; Westover (WO), 1913–1941; and Willamette Heights (WH), 1923–1950. This 1920s map does not include lines that had been discontinued or merged into other routes. Savier Street became S, North and South Portland, after 1900, and Depot and Morrison was discontinued in 1923, with portions being blended into the Portland Heights and Willamette Heights lines. Lovejoy was a tripper on the Twenty-third Avenue line. Mount Calvary was a stub line operated by United Railways Company.

Two

To Nob Hill, Slabtown, and Willamette Heights

Contrasting neighborhoods appeared in Northwest Portland during the 1880s. A string of luxury homes on Northwest Nineteenth Avenue formed the core of Nob Hill, while a large working-class neighborhood called Slabtown (in reference to residents heating with wood from nearby sawmills) developed above Northwest Lovejoy Street.

In 1882, the Multnomah Street Railway extended its horsecar operations north of West Burnside Street along Northwest Sixteenth Avenue. The following year, rival Transcontinental Street Railway opened a line along Northwest Fourteenth Avenue.

By 1895, trolleys plying Northwest Nineteenth, Twenty-first, and Twenty-third Avenues had reached Willamette Heights. Syndicates headed by real estate king Dorr Keasey followed by building streetcar lines to large new developments in Kings Heights (1911), Arlington Heights (1913), and Westover Terraces (1913).

Closer to the river, a trolley line crossed the Willamette River from 1907 to 1911, connecting East and West Burnside Streets. It lasted an additional five years in truncated form, shuttling back and forth between Northwest Fifth and Sixteenth Avenues on West Burnside Street.

Portland's historic Chinatown and Japantown expanded north of West Burnside along Northwest Third and Fourth Avenues during the 1910s. Several trolley routes served this picturesque area, including the North and South Portland line.

Most routes were folded into others over the years or converted to bus. Yet, as the last trolley rolled into the barn in 1950, Northwest residents claimed two of the last lines as their own. Fifty-one years later, streetcars would return.

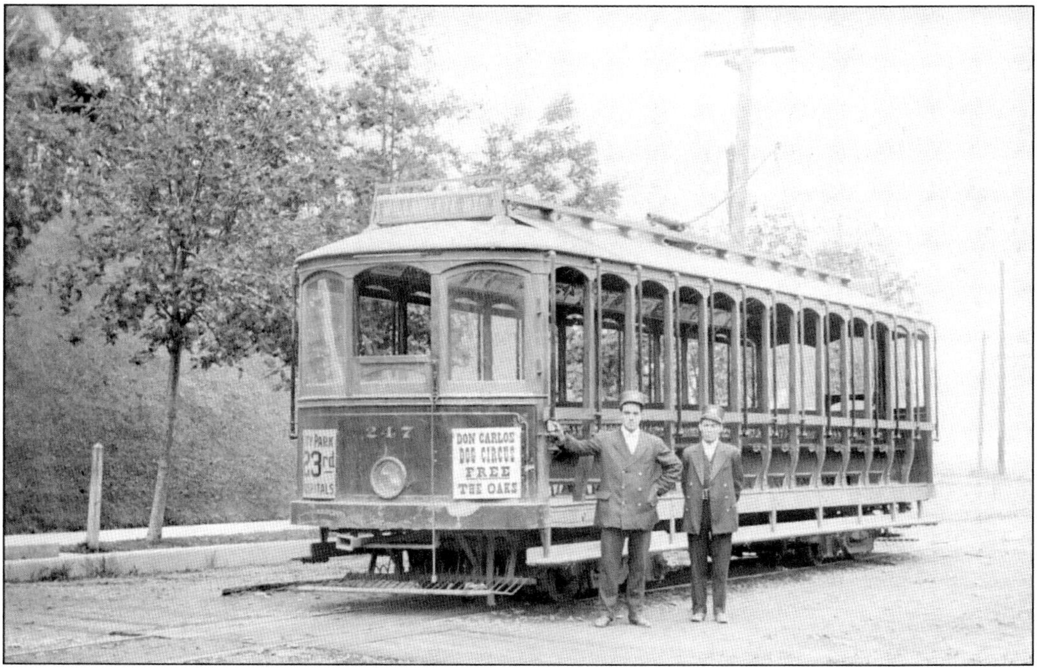

The oldest route in Northwest Portland began as part of the Multnomah Street Railway's Washington Street horsecar line, which added and extension on Twenty-third Avenue in 1891. Cars ran to Willamette Heights until the Twenty-third Avenue line terminus was changed to Northwest Twenty-fourth Avenue and Nicolai Street in September 1908. This photograph of open car No. 247 is at the earlier terminus on Northwest Thurman Street at Twenty-seventh Avenue. (Courtesy Mark Moore.)

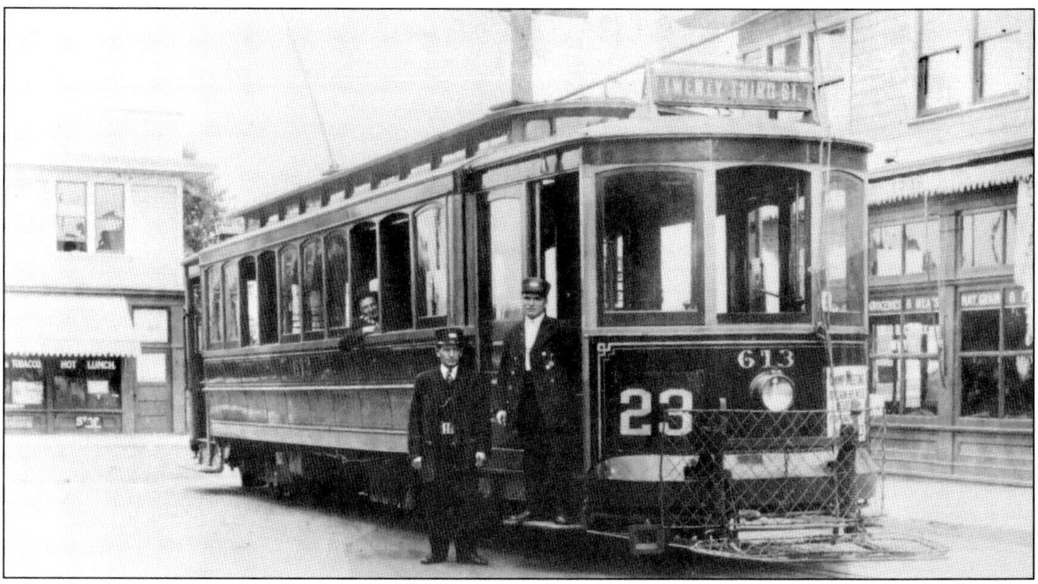

Car No. 613 is surrounded by stores at the Northwest Twenty-fourth and Nicolai Street terminus of the Twenty-third line during the 1910s. The lunch counter in the background offers hot lunches, cigars, and tobacco, while the market at right is selling groceries, meats, hay, and grain. The sign on the dashboard announces an upcoming camp meeting. (Courtesy Mark Moore.)

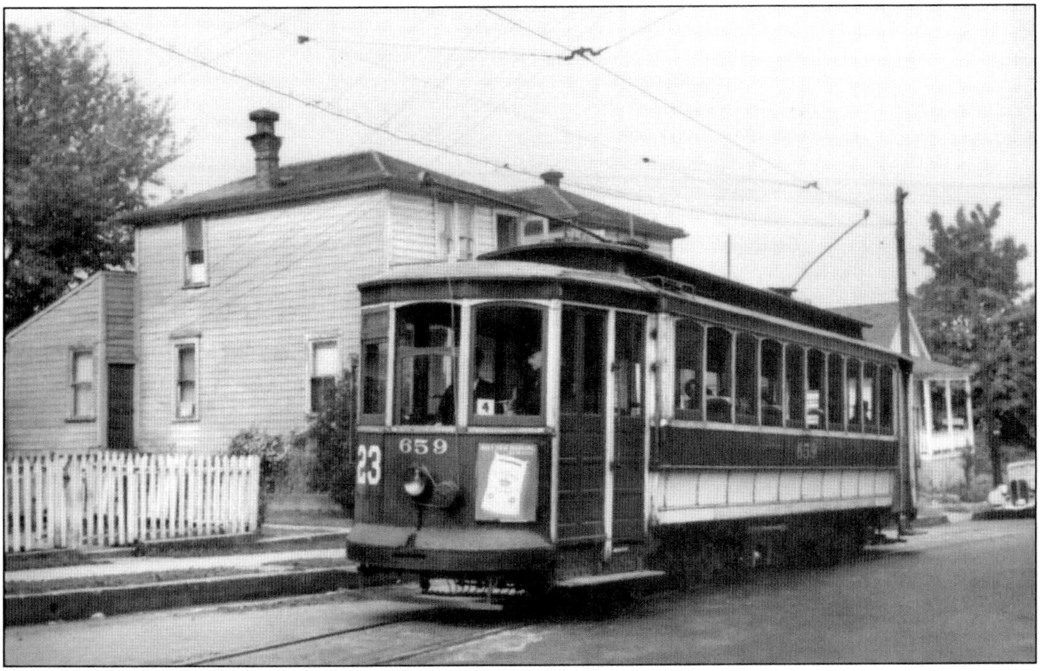

Twenty-third Avenue line car No. 659 rumbles through an early 19th-century neighborhood on Northwest Thurman Street at Twenty-fifth Avenue about 1942. The sign on the dash promotes better baking with flour manufactured by Northwest Portland's own Crown Mills (later Centennial Mills).

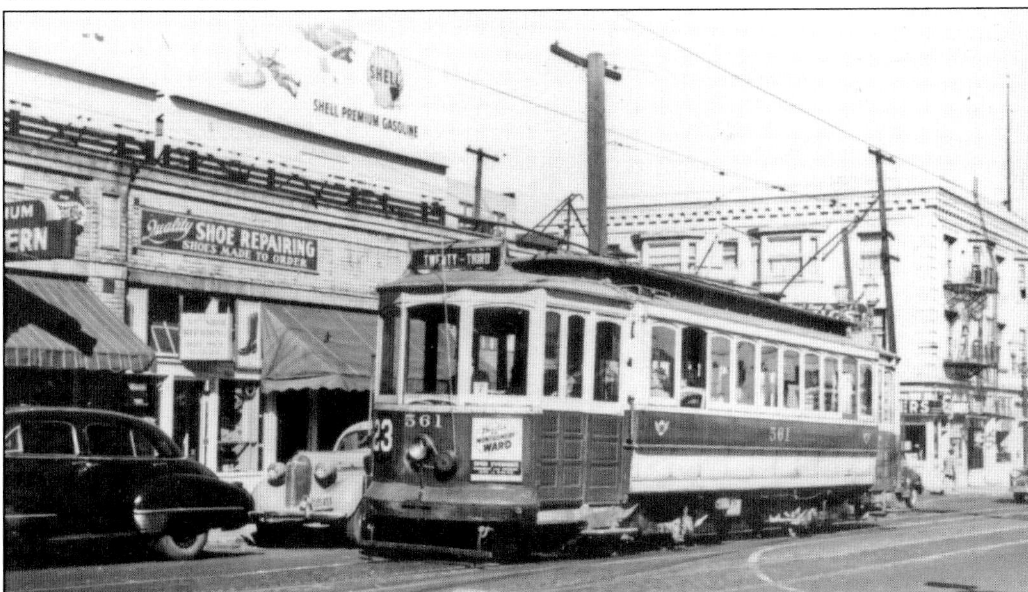

Twenty-third Avenue line car No. 561 is westbound on West Burnside Street between Northwest Eighteenth and Nineteenth Avenues. The building housing Quality Shoe Repair and the Stadium Tavern is now a parking lot, but the apartment building in the background is still in use. The granddaughter of the shoe repair proprietor remembers a long narrow store with a counter at the front and rows of shoes running the length of the building.

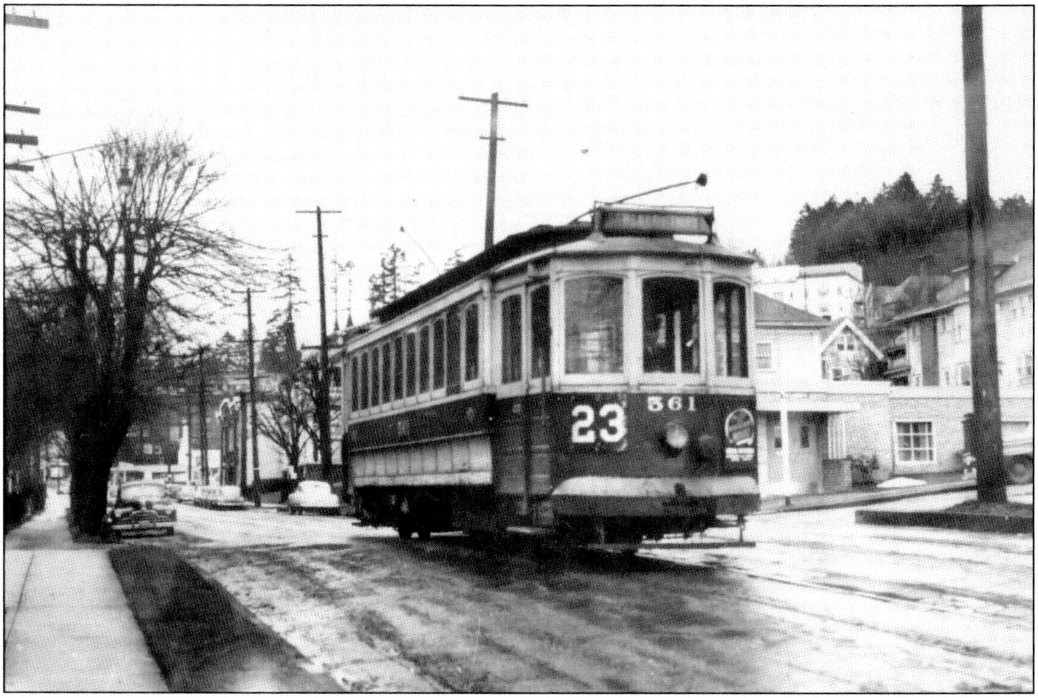

Time-weary Twenty-third Avenue veteran No. 561 is climbing the hill on Northwest Twenty-third Avenue at Northwest Flanders Street on a rainy day in January 1950. The fine woodwork on this 1910 American Car Company product has been painted over by the Portland Traction Company, final operators of Portland's city streetcar system. Today a lone car from this ubiquitous 145-car series survives in a California restaurant.

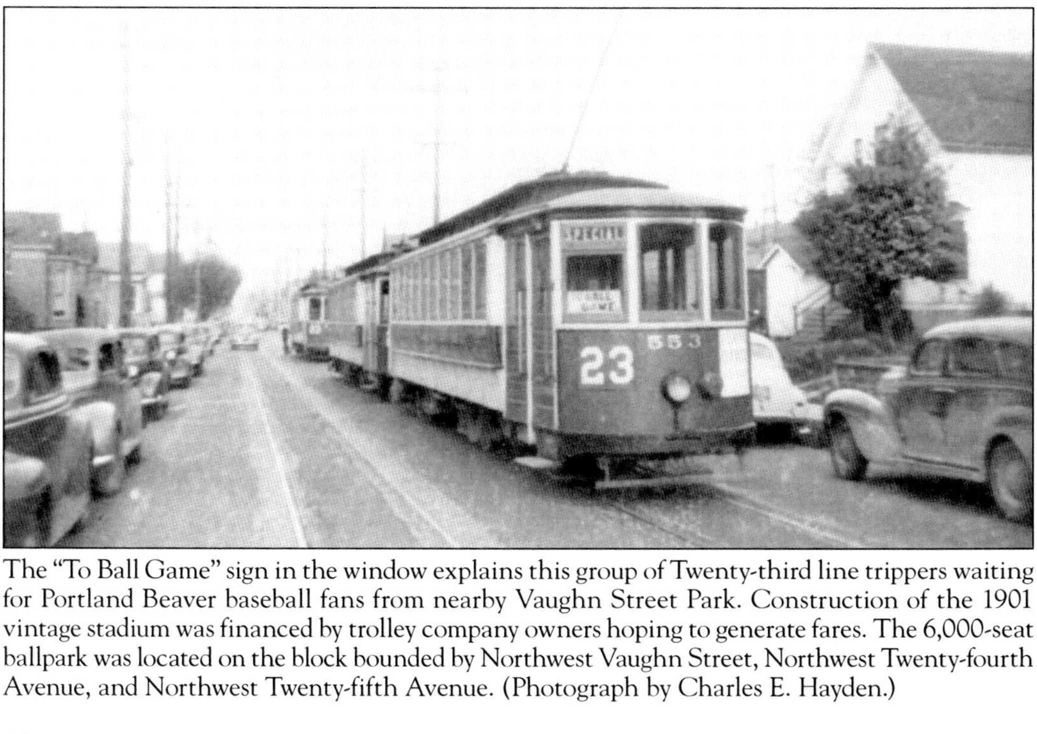

The "To Ball Game" sign in the window explains this group of Twenty-third line trippers waiting for Portland Beaver baseball fans from nearby Vaughn Street Park. Construction of the 1901 vintage stadium was financed by trolley company owners hoping to generate fares. The 6,000-seat ballpark was located on the block bounded by Northwest Vaughn Street, Northwest Twenty-fourth Avenue, and Northwest Twenty-fifth Avenue. (Photograph by Charles E. Hayden.)

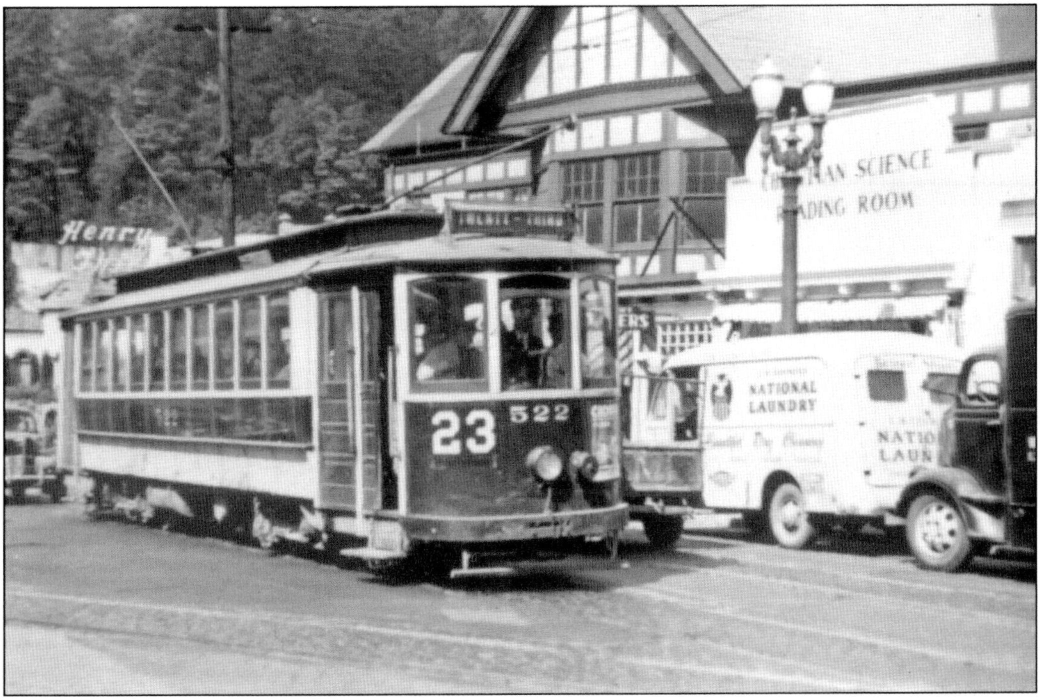

Two streetcars are rounding the busy corner of Northwest Twenty-third Avenue and West Burnside Street. The sign for Henry Thiele's popular restaurant can be seen in the background. The Tudor-style structure next to the Christian Science Reading Room is Murlark Hall, which housed a dance pavilion, theater company, golf academy, delicatessen, and soda fountain over the years. Both buildings are long gone. (Courtesy Mark Moore.)

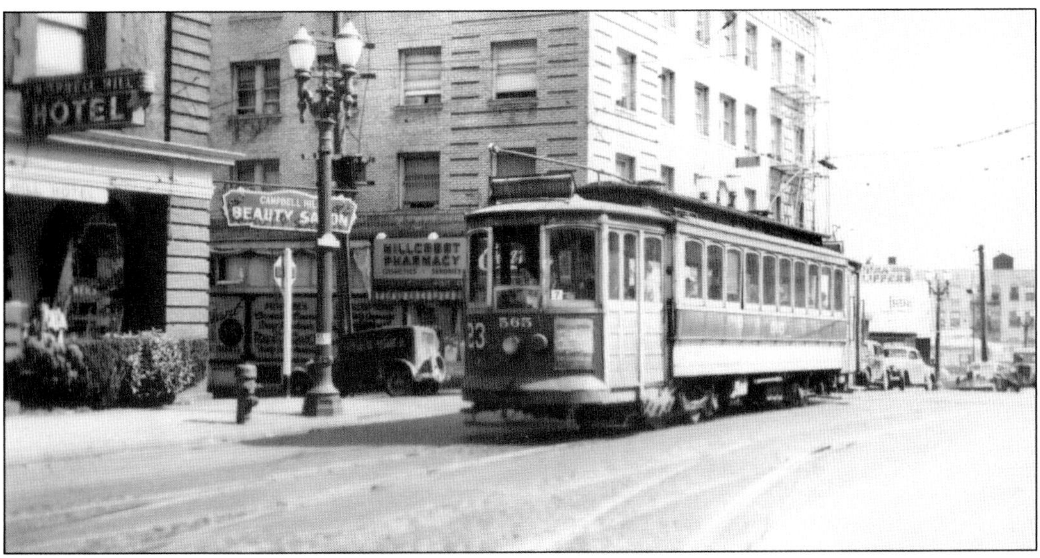

No. 565 wheels past the Campbell Hill Hotel on upper Burnside Street at Northwest Twenty-second Avenue. Although vacant in recent years, the 1904 hotel is on the National Register of Historic Places. The curved tracks in the foreground are for the Council Crest line.

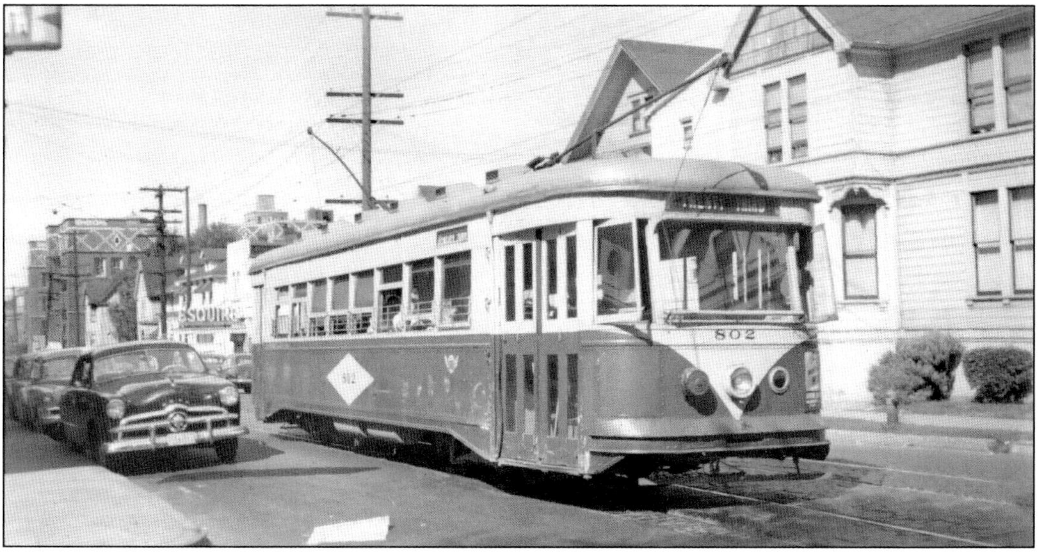

A streamlined *Broadway* car No. 802 hums past a brand-new 1949 Ford parked at the curb on Northwest Twenty-third Avenue and Johnson Street. The brick Good Samaritan Hospital and the Esquire Theater in the background are just memories today. It is interesting to note that the *Broadway* cars did not carry dash destination signs.

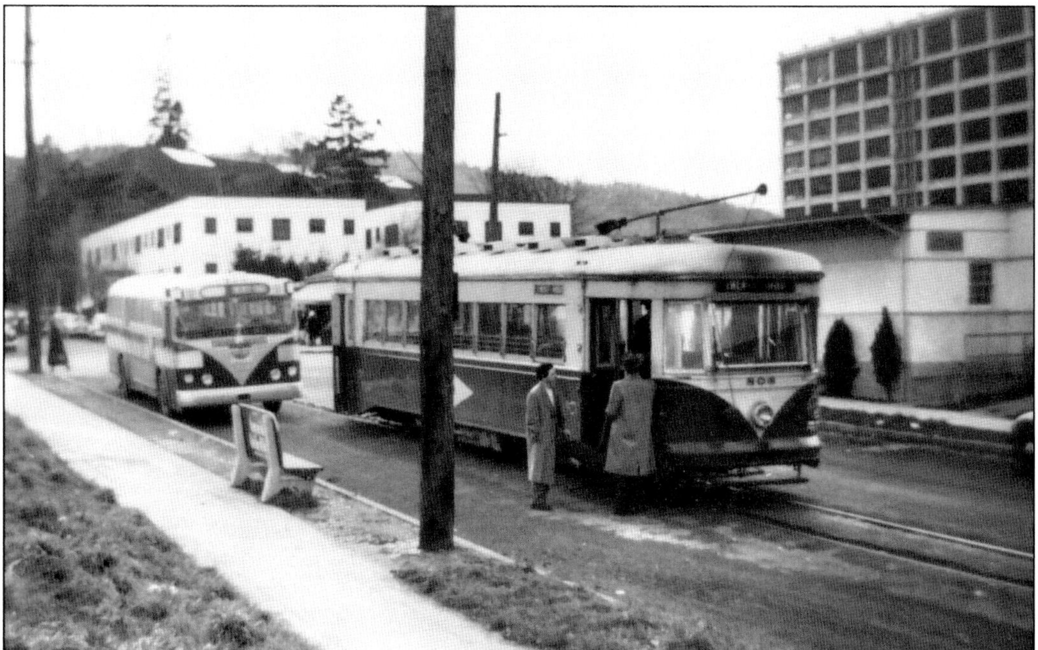

Montgomery Ward's looms behind the Monte Cristo Restaurant to the right of car No. 808 at the outer terminal of the Twenty-third Avenue line on Northwest Twenty-seventh Avenue and Upshur Streets. The roof of the Forestry Building from the 1905 Lewis and Clark Exposition, which burned in 1964, is in the background. The presence of the bus means it may be the last day for Twenty-third Avenue streetcars, February 26, 1950.

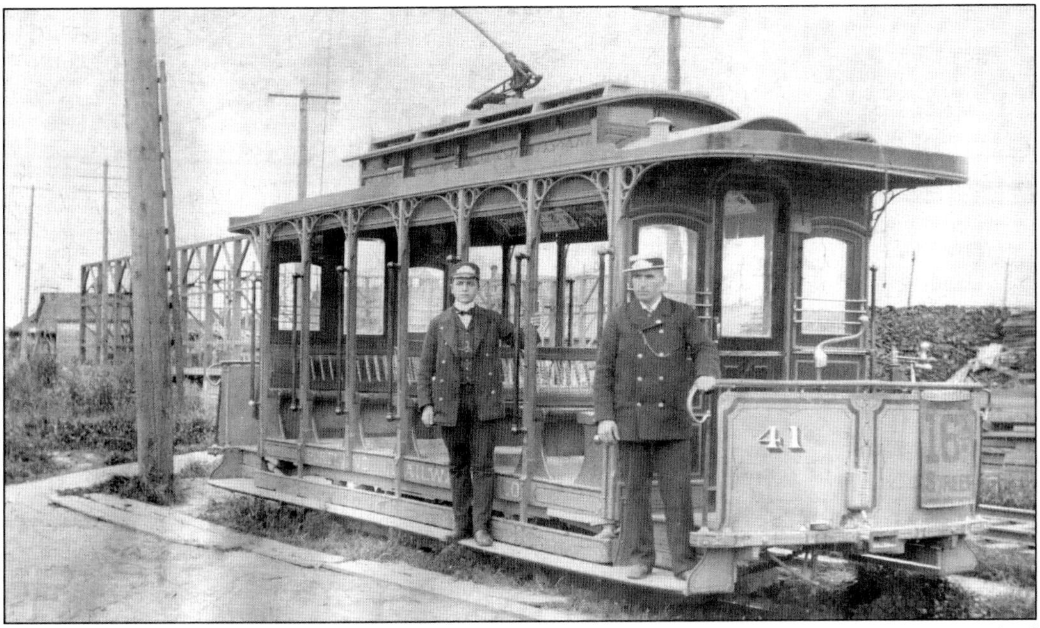

The Sixteenth Street line was originally a Multnomah Street Railway horsecar service. It had been electrified by the 1890s, when this picture was taken at the original northern terminus on Northwest Sixteenth Avenue and Thurman Street. Portland Railway No. 41's cable car–like appearance is natural since it was a Low Convertible built in Stockton, California, in 1890 by the same company that built Portland's cable cars. (Courtesy Mark Moore.)

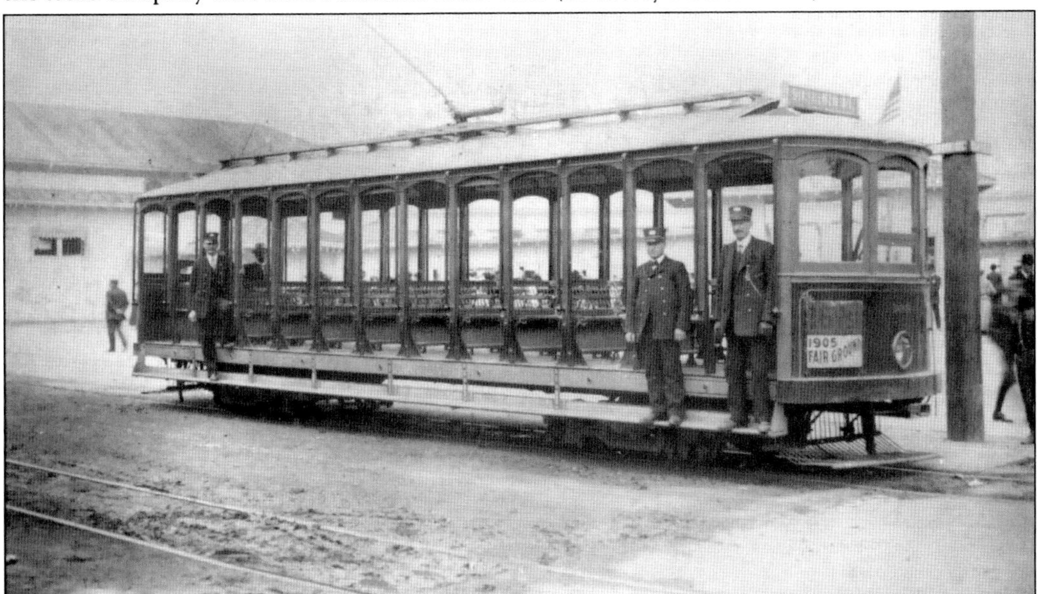

Sixteenth Street line car No. 109 awaits passengers by the peristyle gates to the Lewis and Clark Exposition on Northwest Twenty-sixth and Upshur Streets in 1905. These two-year-old Fuller open cars were more popular with fair-going crowds than the company since they could not be used in winter. The Portland Railway and City and Suburban Railway merged into the Portland Consolidated Railway in time to serve Oregon's only world's fair.

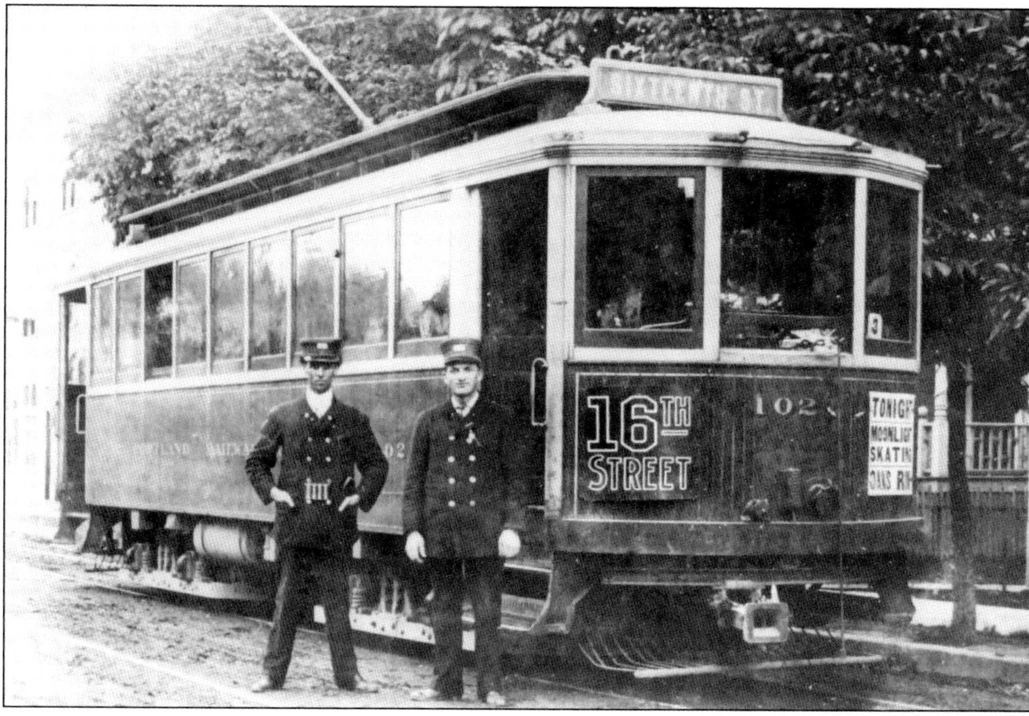

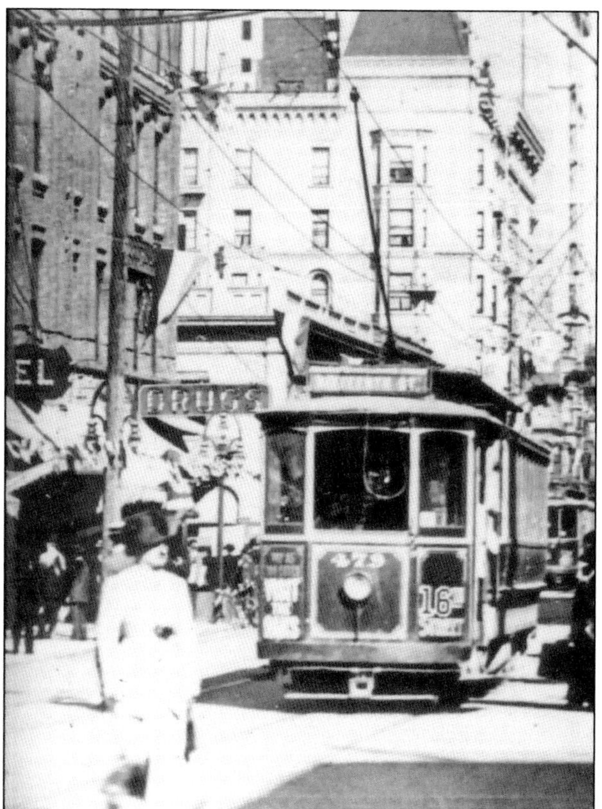

This view of No. 102 on the Sixteenth Street line was probably taken along Northwest Thurman Street not long before PRL&P took over operations in 1906. Horse-drawn streetcars of the Multnomah Street Railway first plied Sixteenth Street in 1883, with trolleys arriving in 1890. PRL&P added an extension from Thurman to Nicolai Streets around 1907. In 1910, the northern terminus changed again, to Northwest Twenty-first and Reed Streets.

A fashionably dressed woman steps across Southwest Washington Street as car No. 479 drifts by on its way to the new southern terminus at Southwest First Avenue and Sheridan Street. This longer route was a result of the South Fifth and Sixteenth Street lines being combined in October 1909. The tower of the Hotel Perkins in the background held a large golden steer that was placed there by builder and cattleman Richard Perkins.

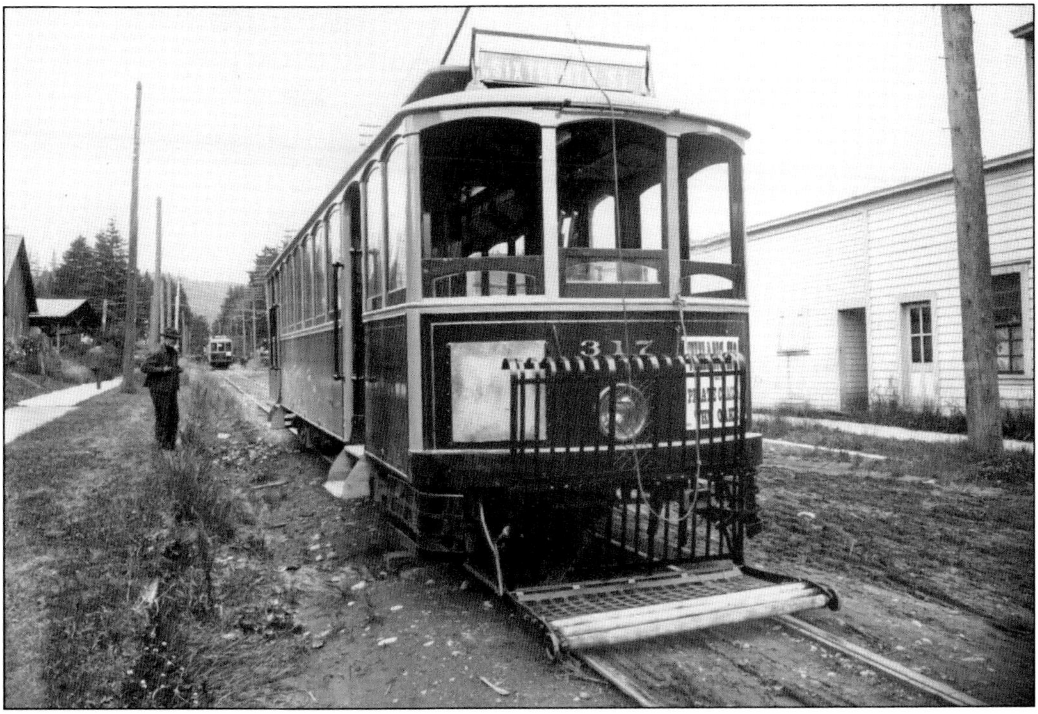

Two streetcars can be seen in a view that appears to have been taken on Northwest Thurman Street during the early PRL&P years. Outbound Sixteenth Street line car No. 317 has paused near several industrial-looking buildings. The three-compartment trolley is equipped with lever-type Fuller hand brakes and an experimental Eclipse safety fender, one of several types tried before Nelson fenders became standard in 1913.

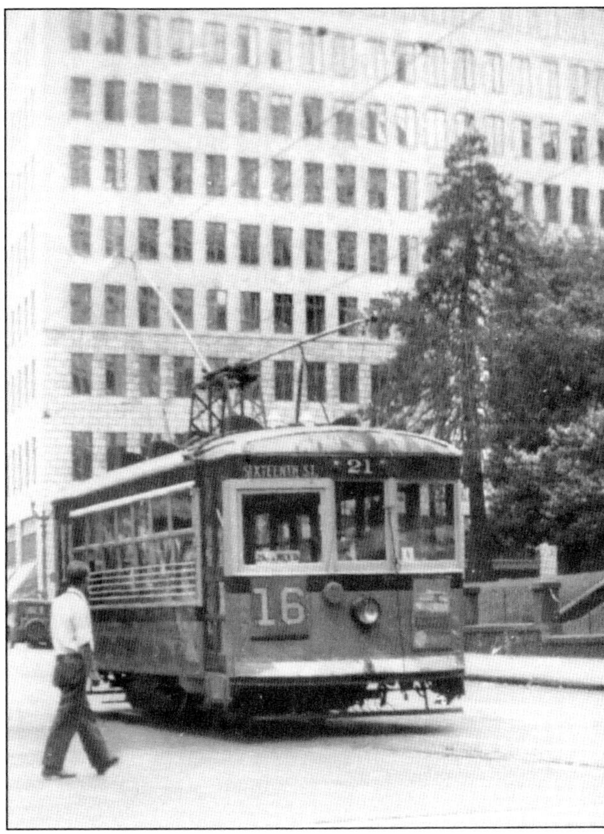

Northbound Portland Traction Birney No. 21 has stopped to pick up a passenger in front of the Pioneer Courthouse on Southwest Fifth Avenue and Morrison Street. It is 1935, and the little Sixteenth Street line car is sporting the grey, green, and cream color scheme first used by the *Broadway* cars. The Sixteenth Street line was converted to bus operation May 21, 1937.

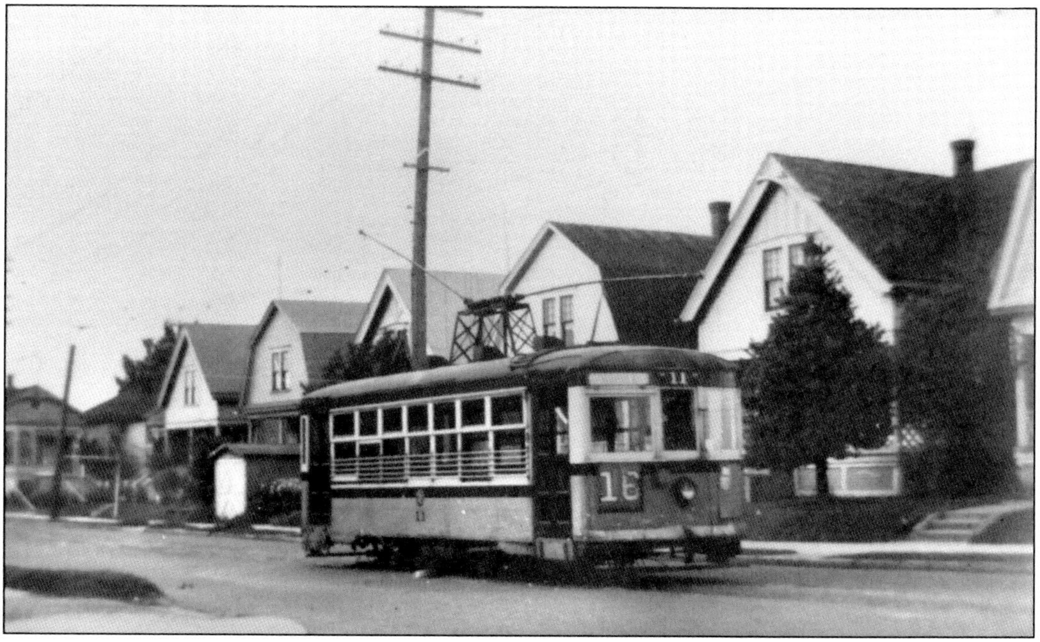

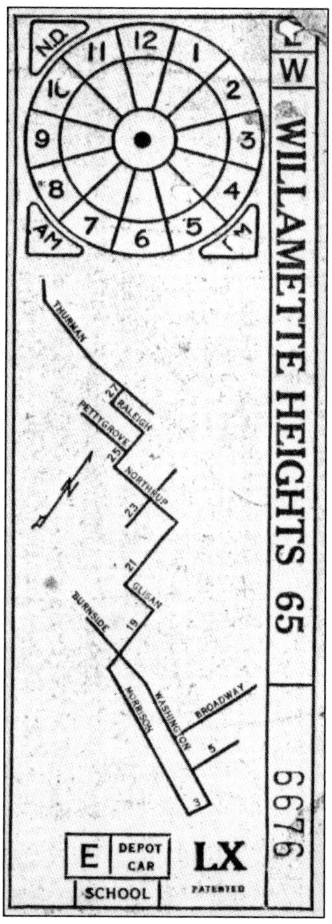

In 1926, the Sixteenth Street line was merged into the Williams Avenue line. But on February 26, 1933, Portland Traction Company established a new Sixteenth Street line running from Northwest Twenty-first Avenue and Reed Street to Southwest Jefferson and Chapman Streets. Birney cars, like this one, had been handling lightly traveled runs since their arrival in 1919.

Several lines served Willamette Heights over the years. The line that became Willamette Heights (WH) started in November 1907 when it shared tracks with the Depot and Morrison (DM) line. Cars ran from Union Depot to Southwest Morrison Street, then followed a stair-stepping route to Northwest Twenty-seventh and Thurman Streets. In 1923, the Depot and Morrison line became part of the Portland Heights line and Willamette Heights gained the route shown on this transfer.

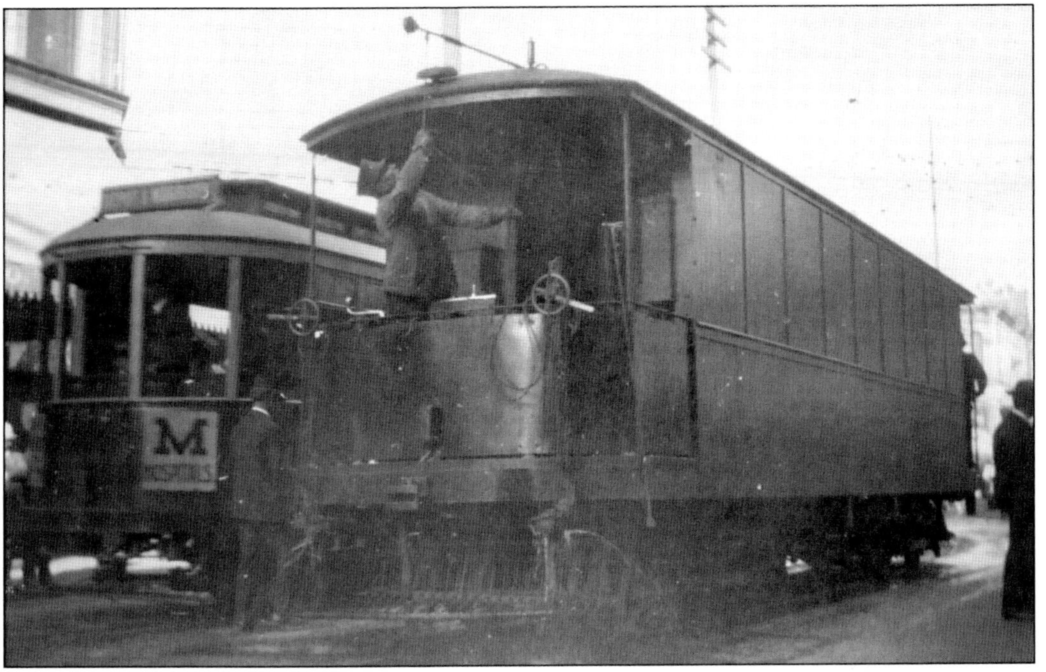

In this unusual picture, a sprinkler car is changing ends next to *Toronto* No. 452 on the Depot and Morrison line. Water still drips from the nozzles beneath the bumper, and there are puddles in the street. In the days before automobiles, street railway companies were responsible for such street maintenance chores. The two streetcars converted into street sprinklers in 1903–1905 had been retired by 1913. (Courtesy Mark Moore.)

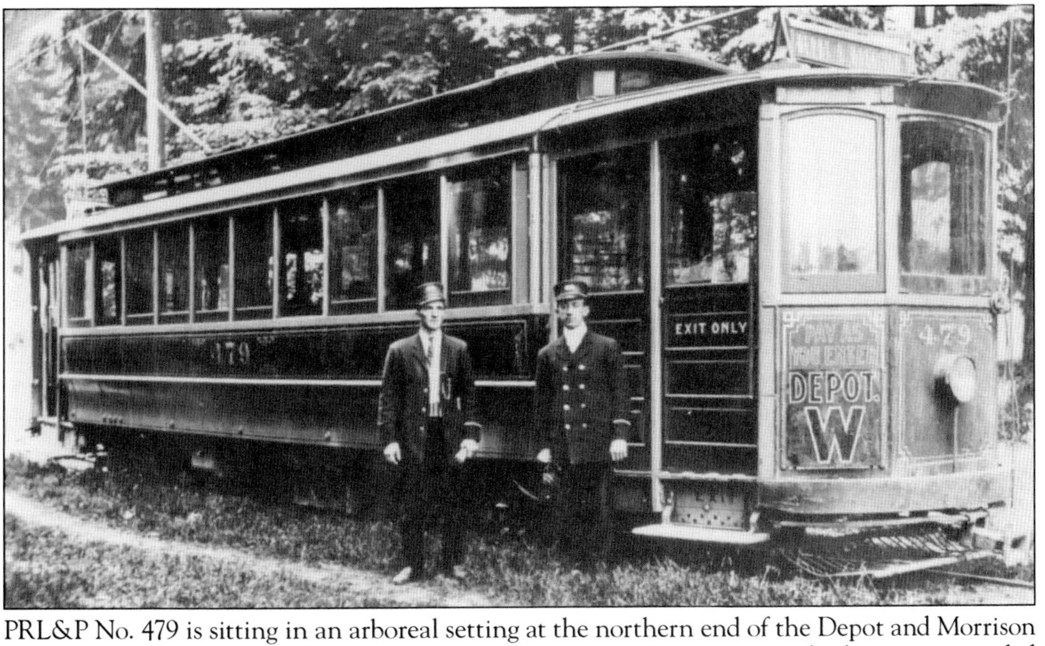

PRL&P No. 479 is sitting in an arboreal setting at the northern end of the Depot and Morrison line at Northwest Thurman and Gordon Streets. On October 28, 1909, the line was extended westward to this location from its previous terminus at Northwest Twenty-seventh Avenue and Thurman Street. A narrow footpath runs through the grass next to the car stop.

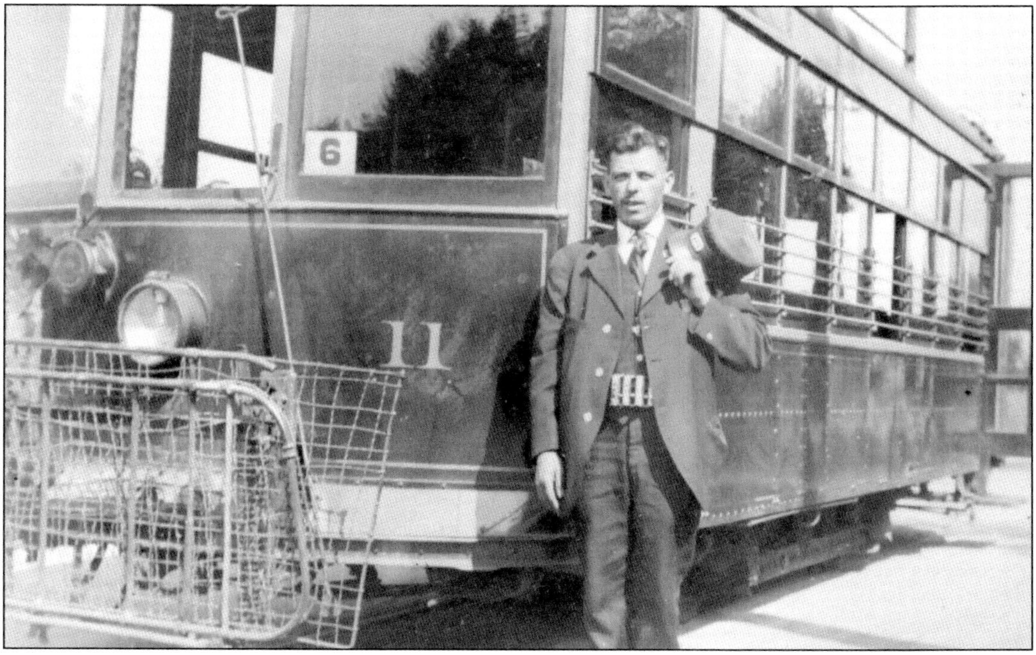

Motorman Alex Fediuk poses with Birney No. 11 on the Depot and Morrison line in the early 1920s. Mr. Fediuk was a Ukrainian immigrant who worked out of the Savier carbarn in Northwest Portland for most of his career. This lightweight four-wheeler first appeared in Portland in 1919. Birneys were employed mainly on the Sixteenth and Willamette Heights lines. Their original color was maroon with yellow trim and natural woodwork.

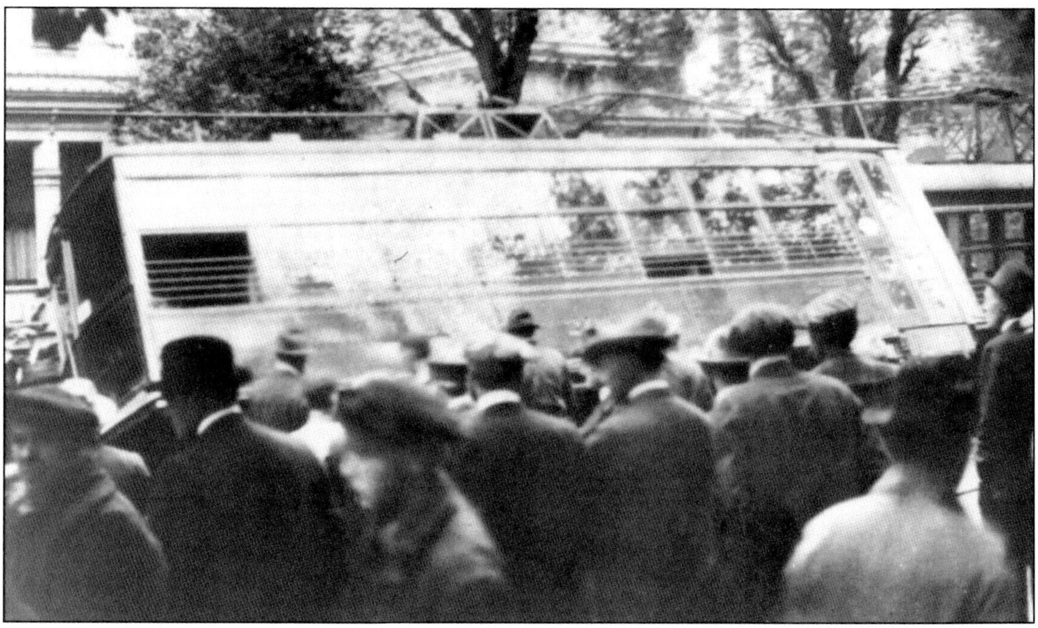

In spite of being safety cars, things did not always go smoothly for Portland's Birneys, as can be seen in this 1922 photograph showing a crowd of onlookers watching derailed No. 20 on the Depot and Morrison line. Birney cars were considered safer because they were equipped with features like "dead man" control that automatically applied the brakes if an operator let go of the handle.

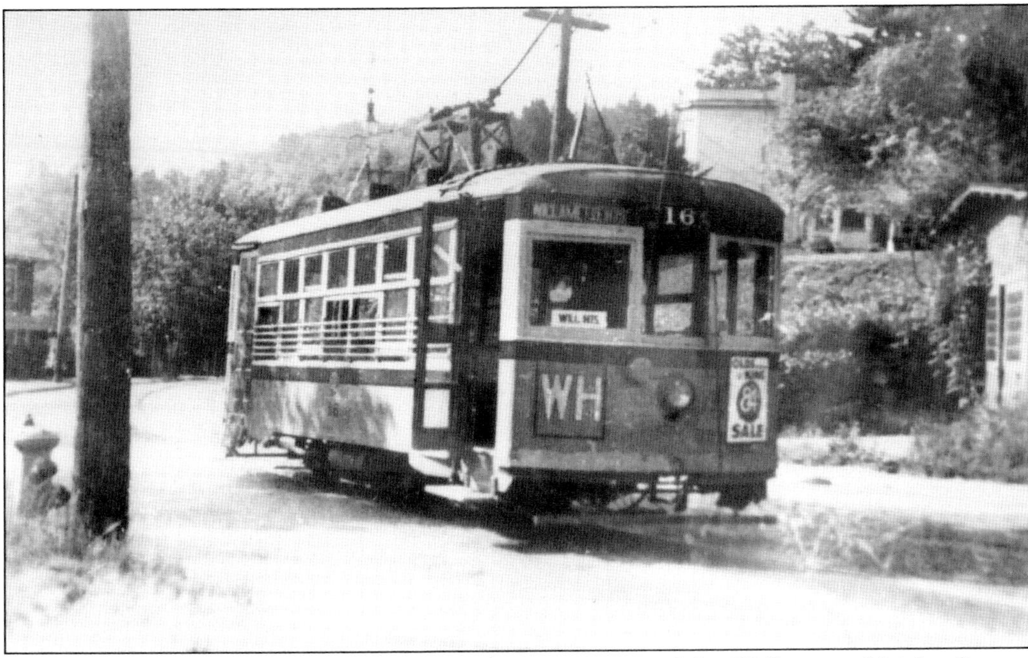

Birney No. 16 is changing ends at the northern terminus of the Willamette Heights line on Northwest Thurman and Gordon Streets in August 1935. In the 1930s, a permanent "WH" was painted on these diminutive cars. "Will Hts" or "Sherman St." signs were used in the window to indicate whether a car was inbound or outbound. Southwest Sherman Street became the southern terminus in June 1926.

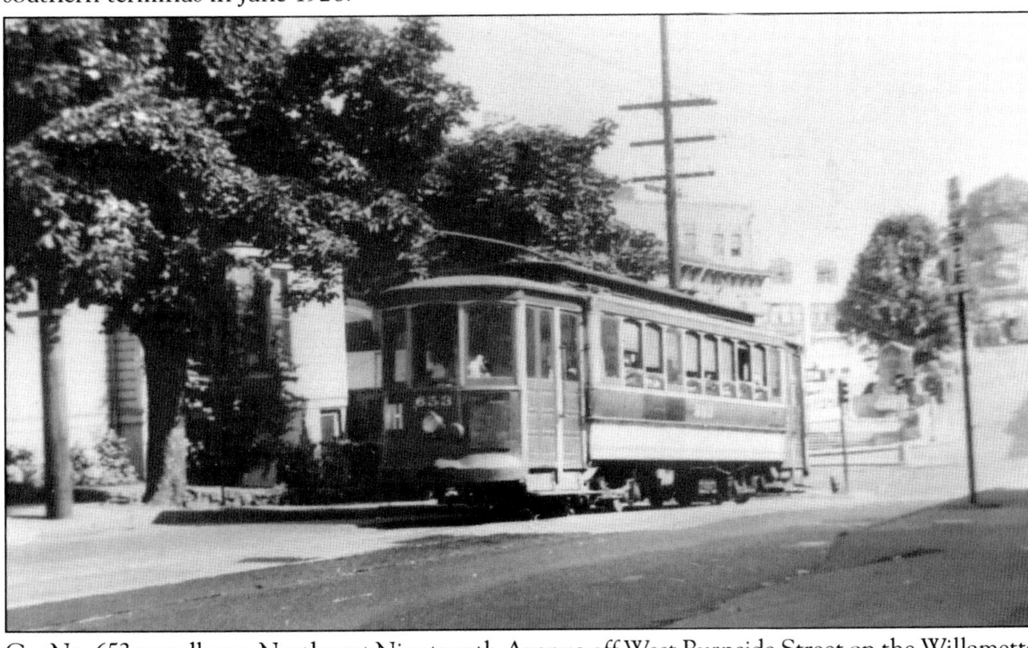

Car No. 653 trundles up Northwest Nineteenth Avenue off West Burnside Street on the Willamette Heights run in a once common scene. In the background is the memorial dedicated to Fire Chief David Campbell, who died in a fire on June 26, 1911, and to all Portland firemen killed in the line of duty. Note the touched up paint on the side of the hardworking trolley.

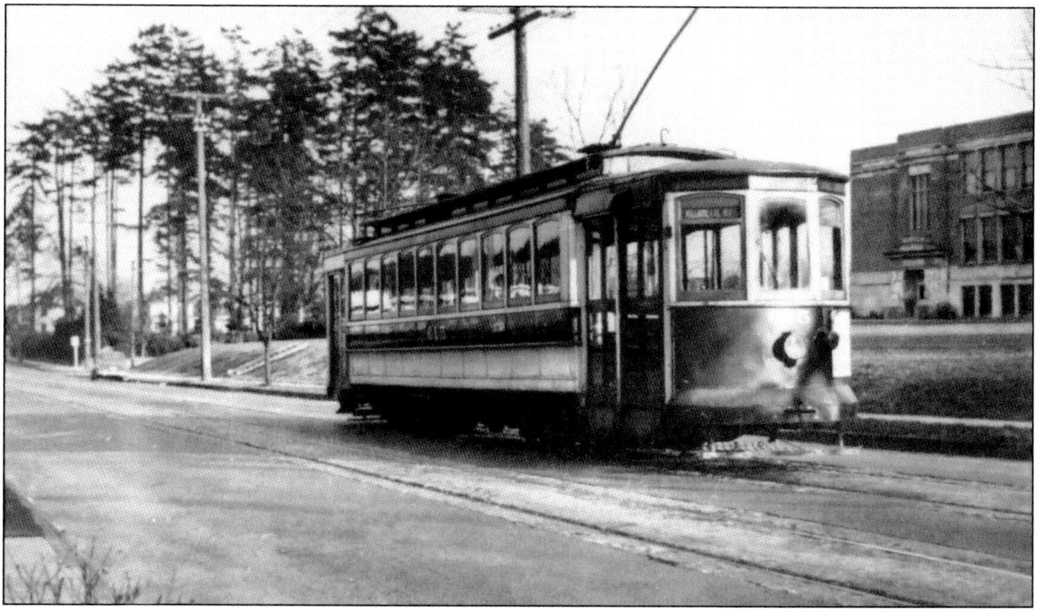

Willamette Heights car No. 615 rolls eastward past Chapman School on deserted Northwest Raleigh Street. The elementary school, named for early settler and prominent attorney William Chapman, replaced a Victorian wood frame school of the same name in 1923. It is best known today for its park and the birds (said to be the world's largest population of Vaux's Swifts) that return to nest in its chimney every summer.

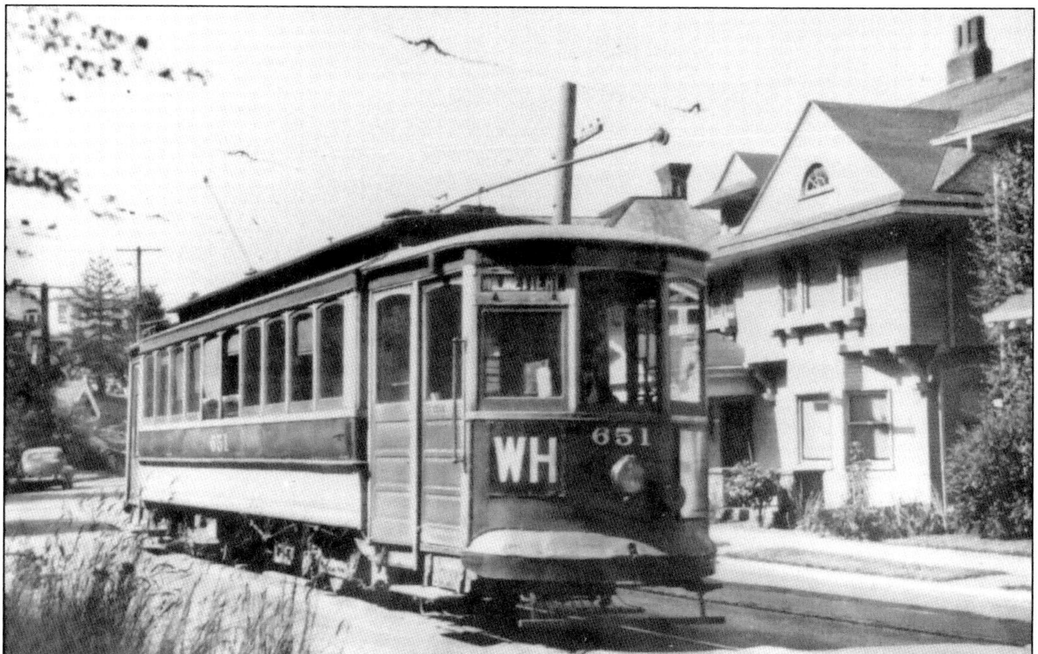

Car No. 651 is nestled among fine old Willamette Heights homes on Northwest Thurman Street near Northwest Thirty-second Avenue. The year is around 1948, and time is about to run out for this and all of Portland's historic trolleys. Classic wooden streetcars like No. 651 made up the bulk of Portland's street railway fleet for over 40 years, appearing on all but the hilliest lines.

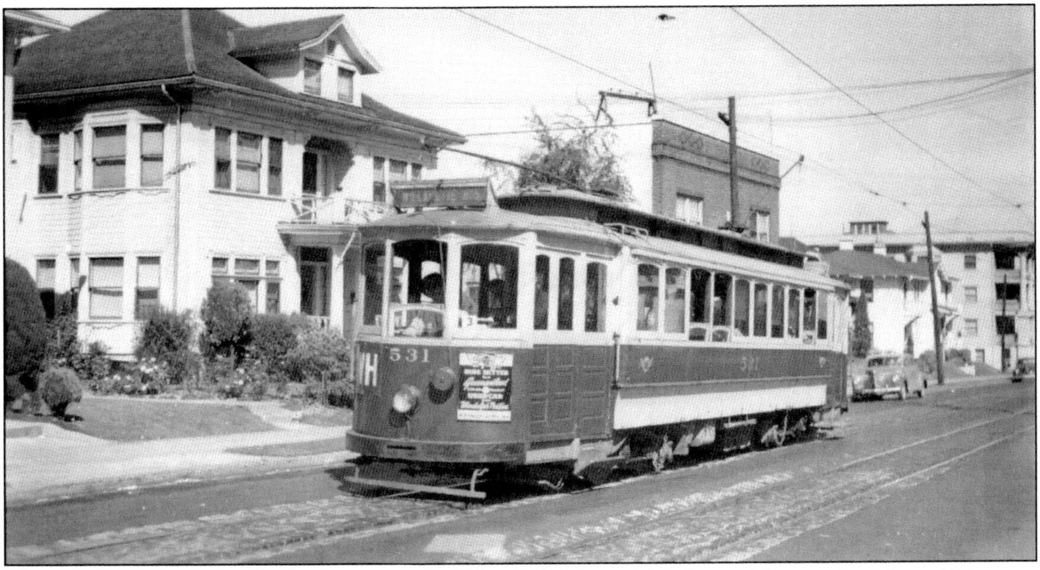

Willamette Heights line car No. 531 is headed west between Northwest Twenty-fourth and Twenty-fifth Avenues on Northwest Northrup Street during the final years. The apartment buildings in the background survive today. Note the brick paving between the rails. This was once a common feature throughout Portland.

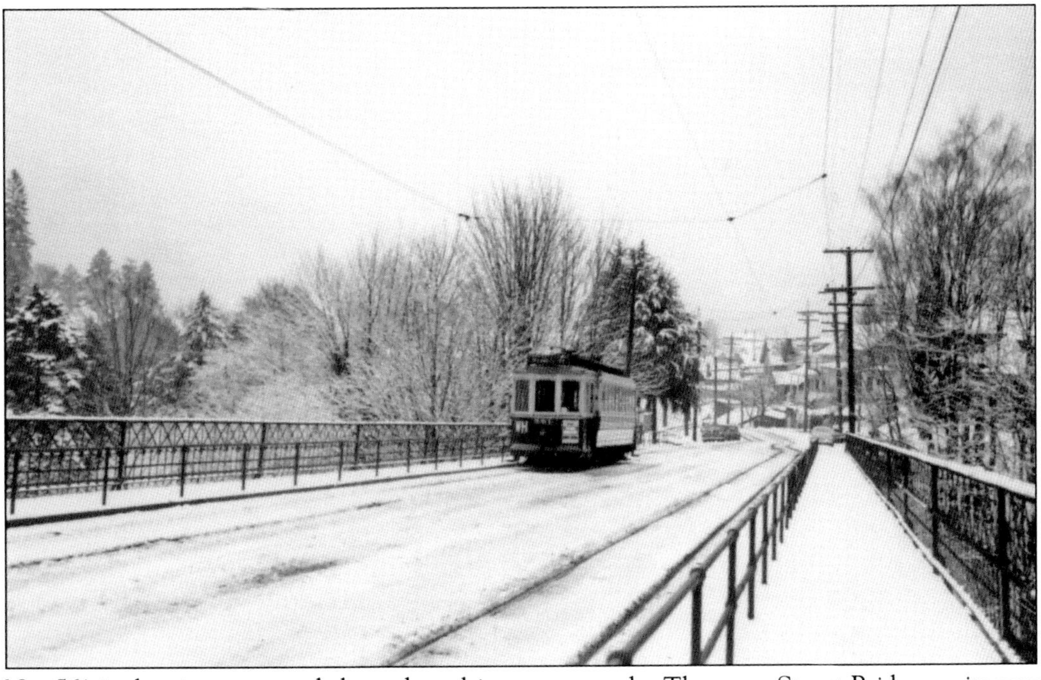

No. 561 is slogging westward through melting snow on the Thurman Street Bridge on its way to Willamette Heights. The 400-foot-wide deck truss bridge crosses Balch Creek Gulch. It was completed in 1905, in time for the nearby Lewis and Clark Exposition, which led to a rise in area population and home building. This is now the city's oldest bridge.

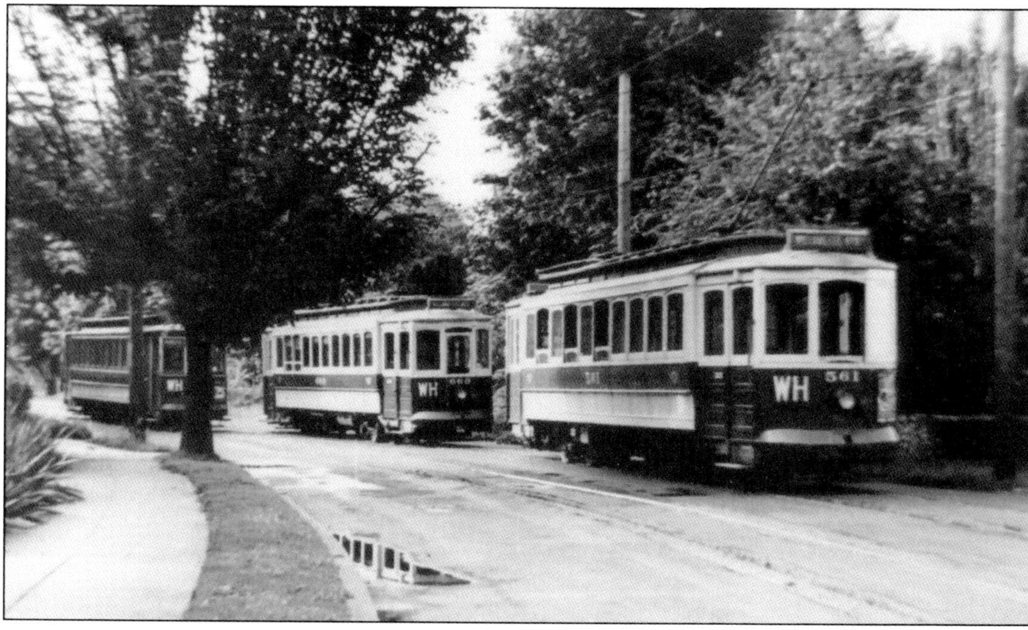

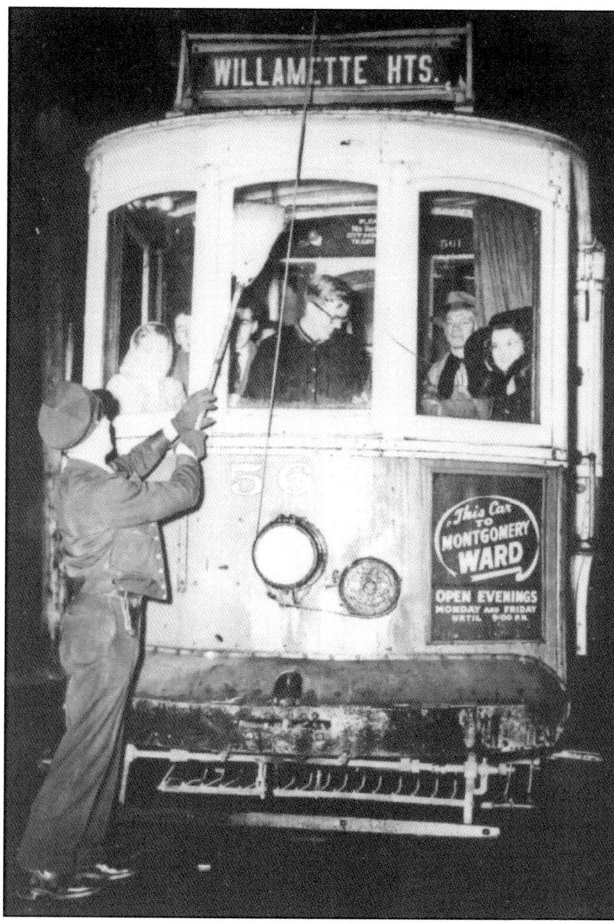

It looks as if someone was a little off schedule in this late 1940s picture of car Nos. 561, 660, and 657 lined up by the passing track at the end of the Willamette Heights line on puddle-strewn Northwest Thurman Street. No. 657 retired in 1948. The other two cars made it to the end of streetcar service in 1950.

Just before dawn on February 26, 1950, operator Jack Post uses a broom to clean the windshield (trolleys had no wipers) on veteran car No. 561 as he prepares to depart Southwest Fifth Avenue and Washington Street for the last run to Willamette Heights. When No. 561 got back to the carbarn, it was found that souvenir hunters had taken seat cushions, straps, handles, and other easily removed items from the historic streetcar.

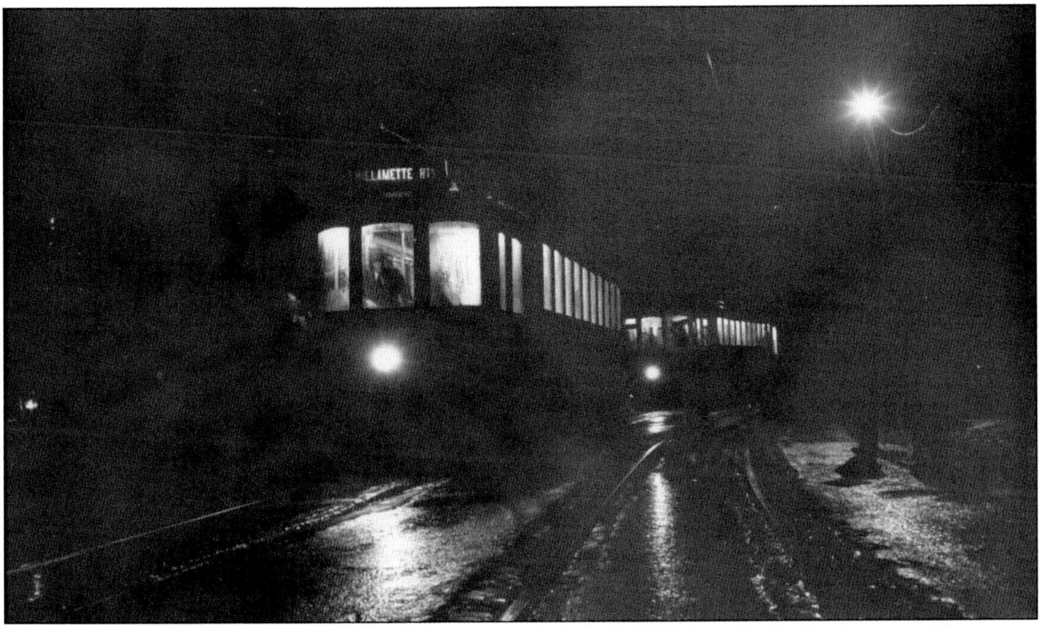

It is the end of the line in more ways than one. When these owl cars reached Northwest Thurman and Gordon Streets at 5:54 a.m. on February 26, 1950, they would be the last local streetcars to run for two generations. Two of the three cars needed to accommodate fans wanting to make the final trip are seen in this atmospheric shot at the end of the Willamette Heights line.

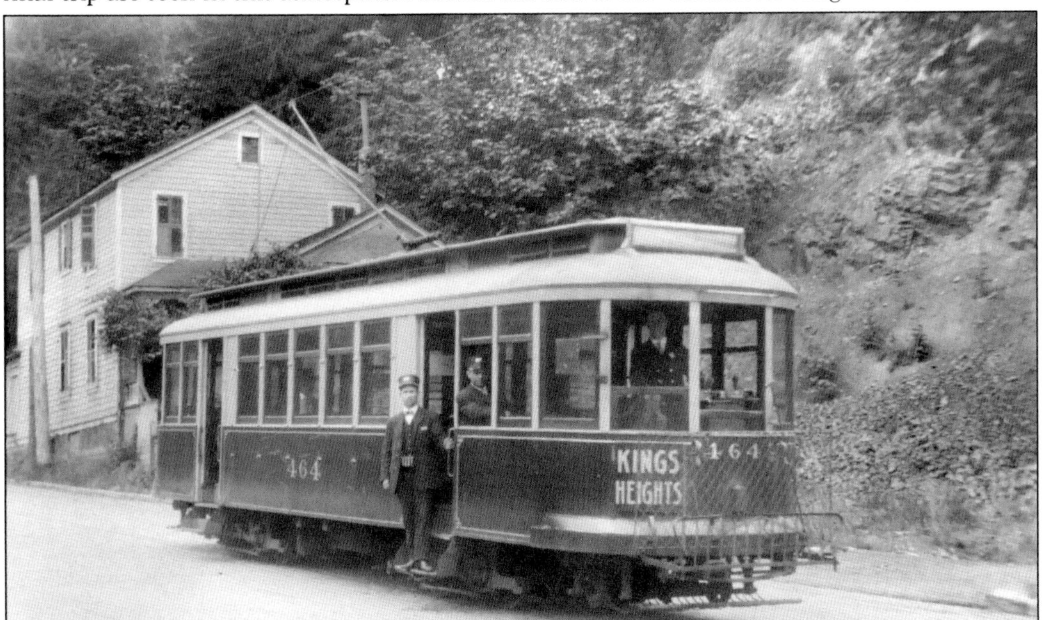

Car No. 464 is about to depart for Kings Heights from the foot of West Burnside Street near Northwest Twenty-third Avenue. It would shuttle over curving trestles and steep grades between here and the northern end of the line at Northwest Valle Vista Terrace and Hermosa Boulevard. The photographer who took this "instant postcard" had a studio on Council Crest. (Photograph by Cal Calvert; courtesy Mark Moore.)

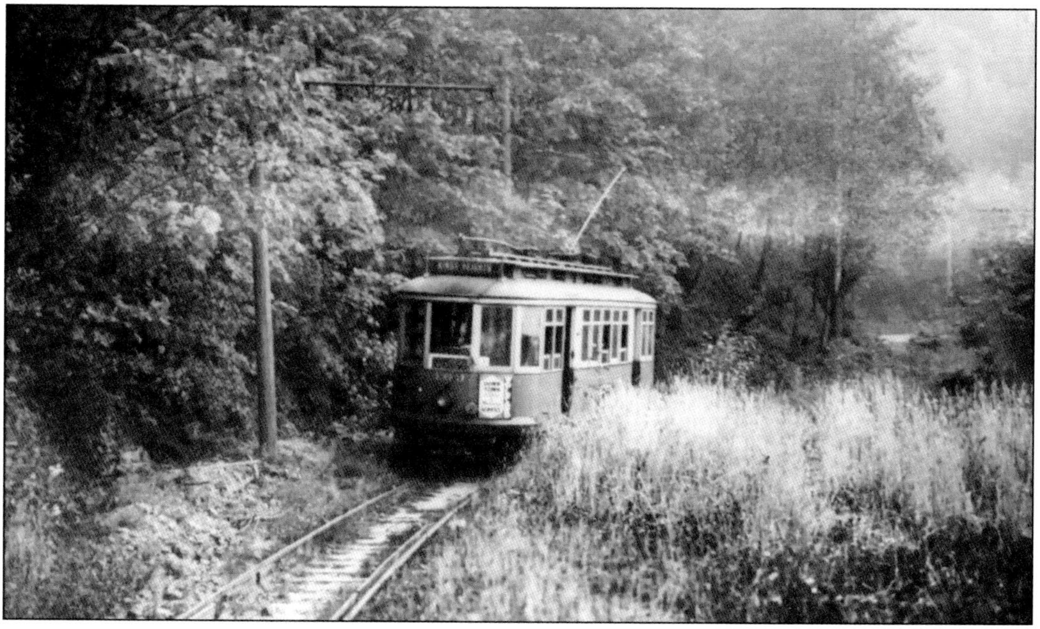

King's Heights line car No. 460 is travelling over a private right-of-way on present day Northwest Valle Vista Terrace wearing 1930s apple green and cream colors. The King's Heights line operated from 1911 until 1941, when it was converted to bus. A stub from the end of this line continued on to Mount Calvary Cemetery from 1911 to 1927.

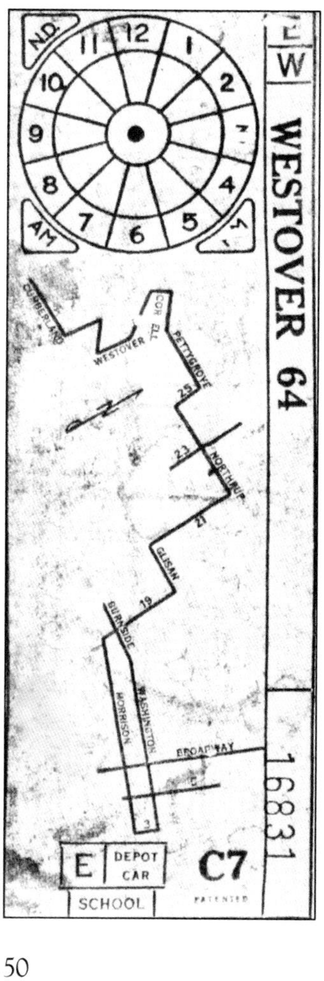

The Westover (WO) line began in July, 1913, as a stub from the Depot and Morrison line at Northwest Twenty-fifth and Pettygrove Streets to Northwest Ariel Terrace and Cumberland Street in Westover Terraces. Later the east terminal was changed to a connection with the Twenty-third line on Northwest Northrup Street. In 1927, the line was extended downtown. WO was converted to bus August 24, 1941.

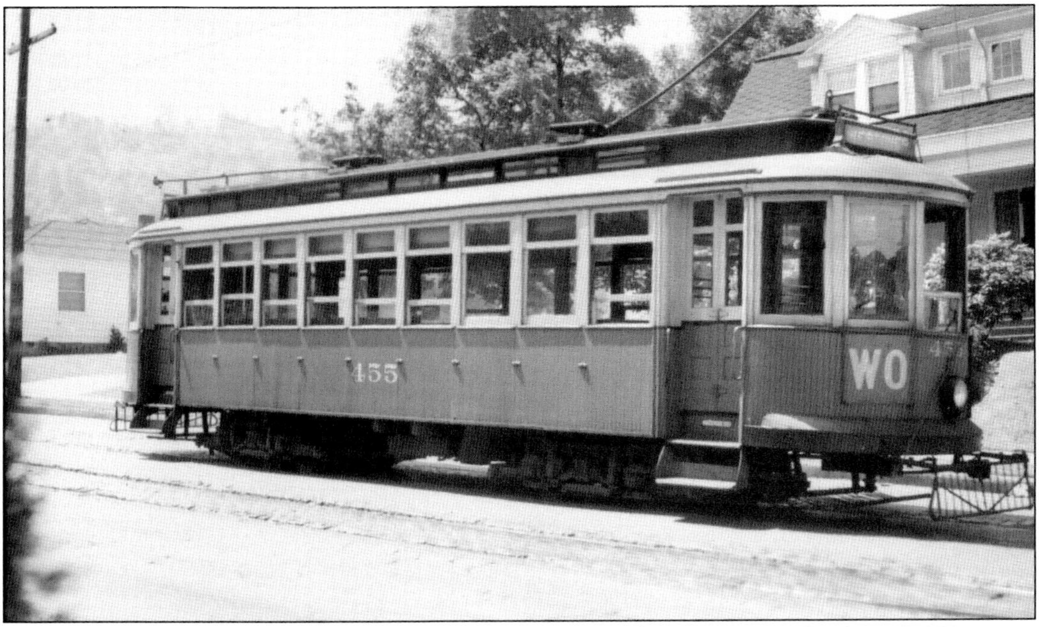

In the newspaper hyperbole of the time, Westover Terraces homes were said to have "1000 square miles in their front yards." For the home in the background, that view on this fine 1930s day included Westover line car No. 455 heading west on Northwest Northrup Street.

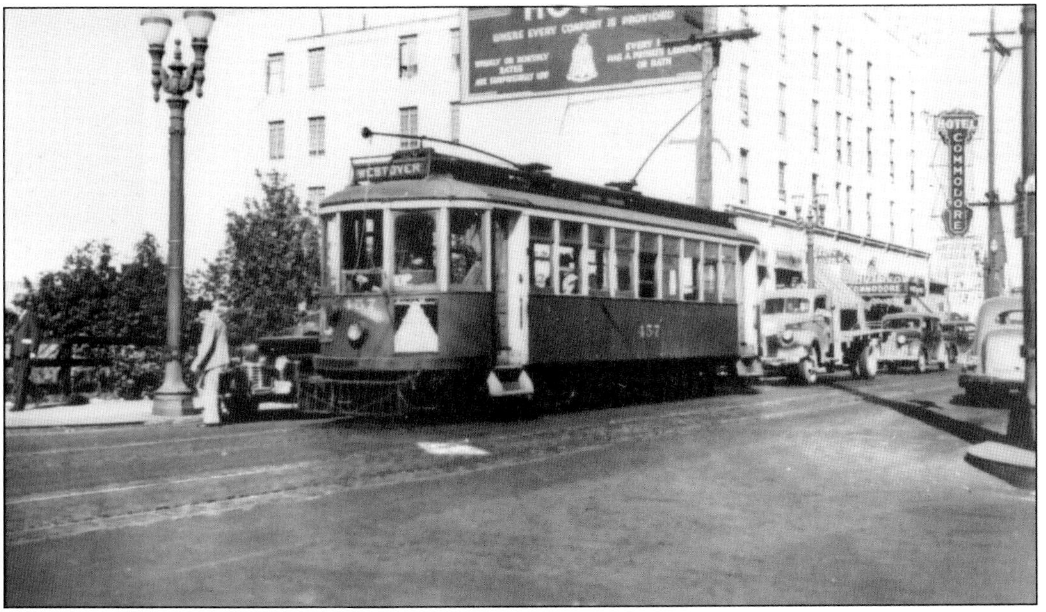

Westbound Westover (WO) line car No. 457, wearing the simple maroon and cream paint scheme seen during the last years, holds up traffic as it lets a passenger off on Southwest Morrison Street at Seventeenth Avenue. Service to downtown on the former WO stub began in 1927 but was cutback to rush hours only after 1938. The art deco Commodore Hotel in the background is on the National Register of Historic Places.

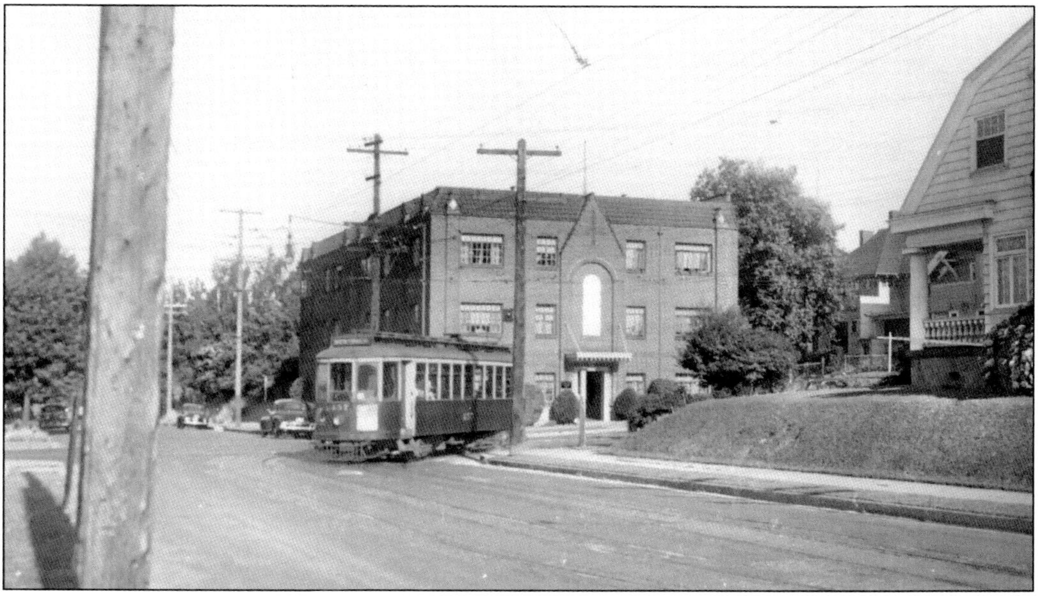

Westover line No. 457 rounds the corner of Northwest Twenty-fifth Avenue and Pettygrove Street on August 18, 1941, a week before the line was converted to bus operation. Since the 1920s, the Westover, Kings Heights, and Arlington lines have been described as unwanted orphans built by real estate interests rather than a streetcar company. The buildings in this photograph are still there today. (Courtesy Mark Moore.)

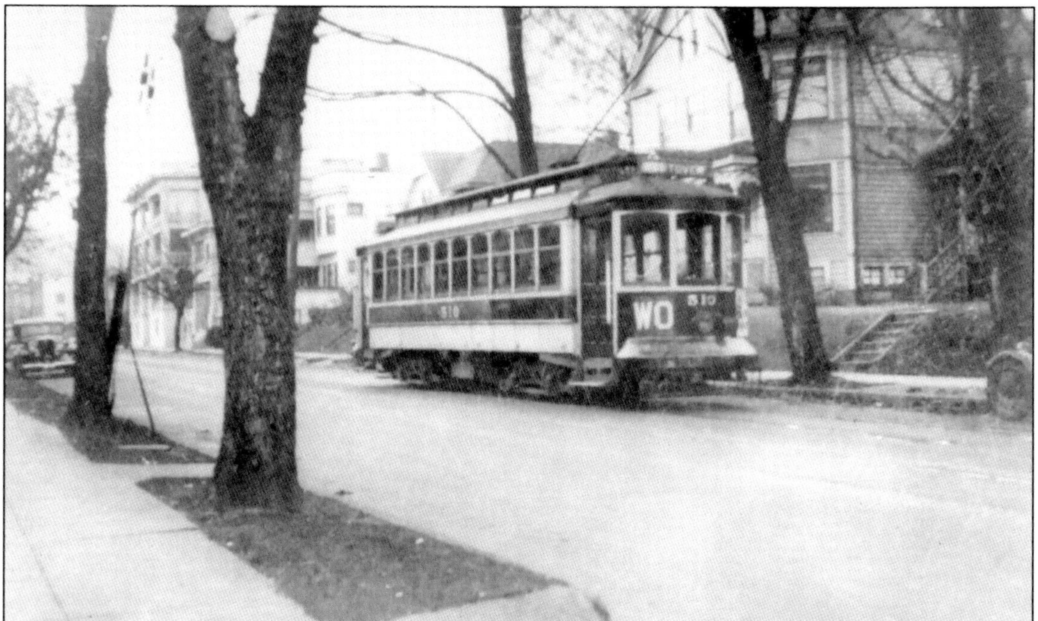

Council Crest car No. 510 presents an unusual sight as it heads west on Northwest Northrup Street between Twenty-third and Twenty-fourth Avenues on the Westover line. *Toronto* class trolleys 454–457 were normally used on this line. Like the Council Crest cars, they were equipped with four motors and magnetic brakes for hills. No. 510 retired in 1948 after being damaged by an electrical fire while on the Council Crest line.

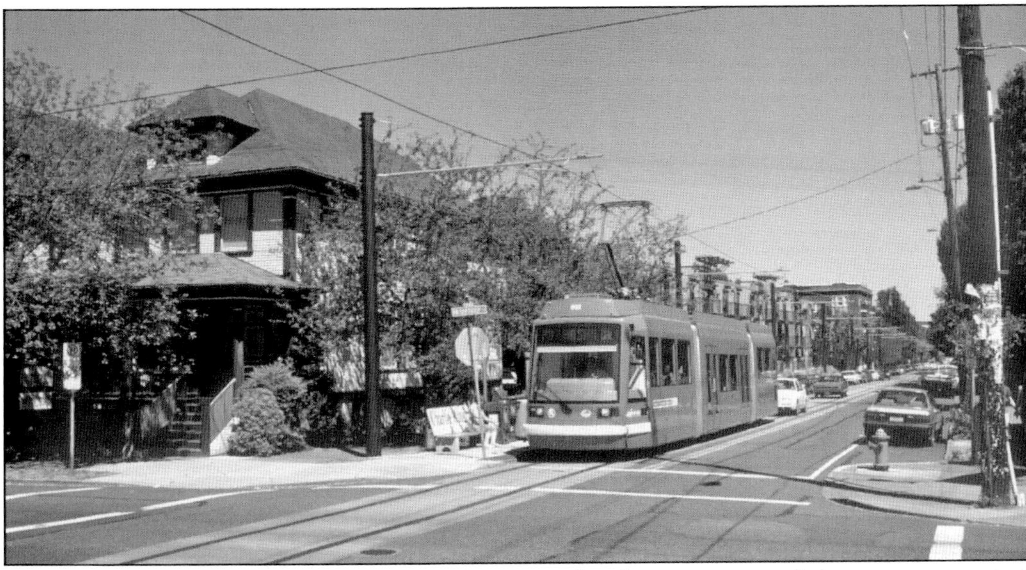

Today's city-operated Portland Streetcar line is said to have reinvented the streetcar, so it is appropriate that 2001-built Skoda car No. 002 is westbound on Northwest Northrup Street at Twenty-first Avenue in territory once served by Willamette Heights line trolleys. The destination sign has already been changed to read "Portland State Uni." for the trip back east and south in this July 29, 2002 picture. (Photograph by Steve Morgan.)

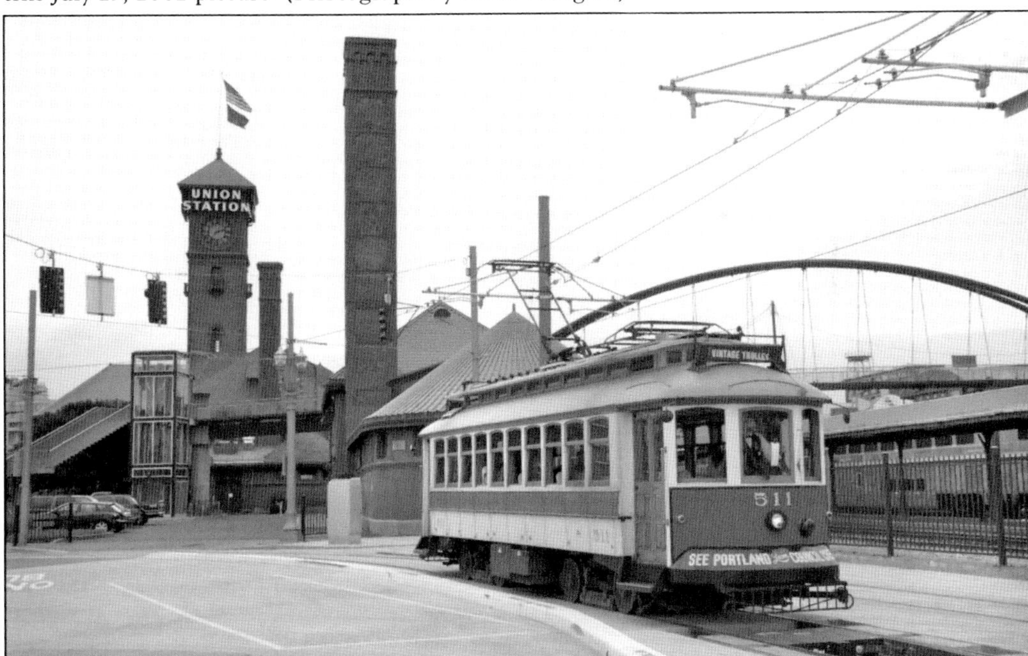

Operator Neal Berlin pilots Vintage Trolley (VT) No. 511 past Union Station at 2:35 p.m. on September 13, 2009, the first day of VT service on the new transit mall tracks running between Union Station and Portland State University. On August 23, 2009, tighter headway on the Steel Bridge brought to a close Vintage Trolley's original line (1991–2009) between Lloyd Center and the Galleria. (Photograph by Steve Morgan.)

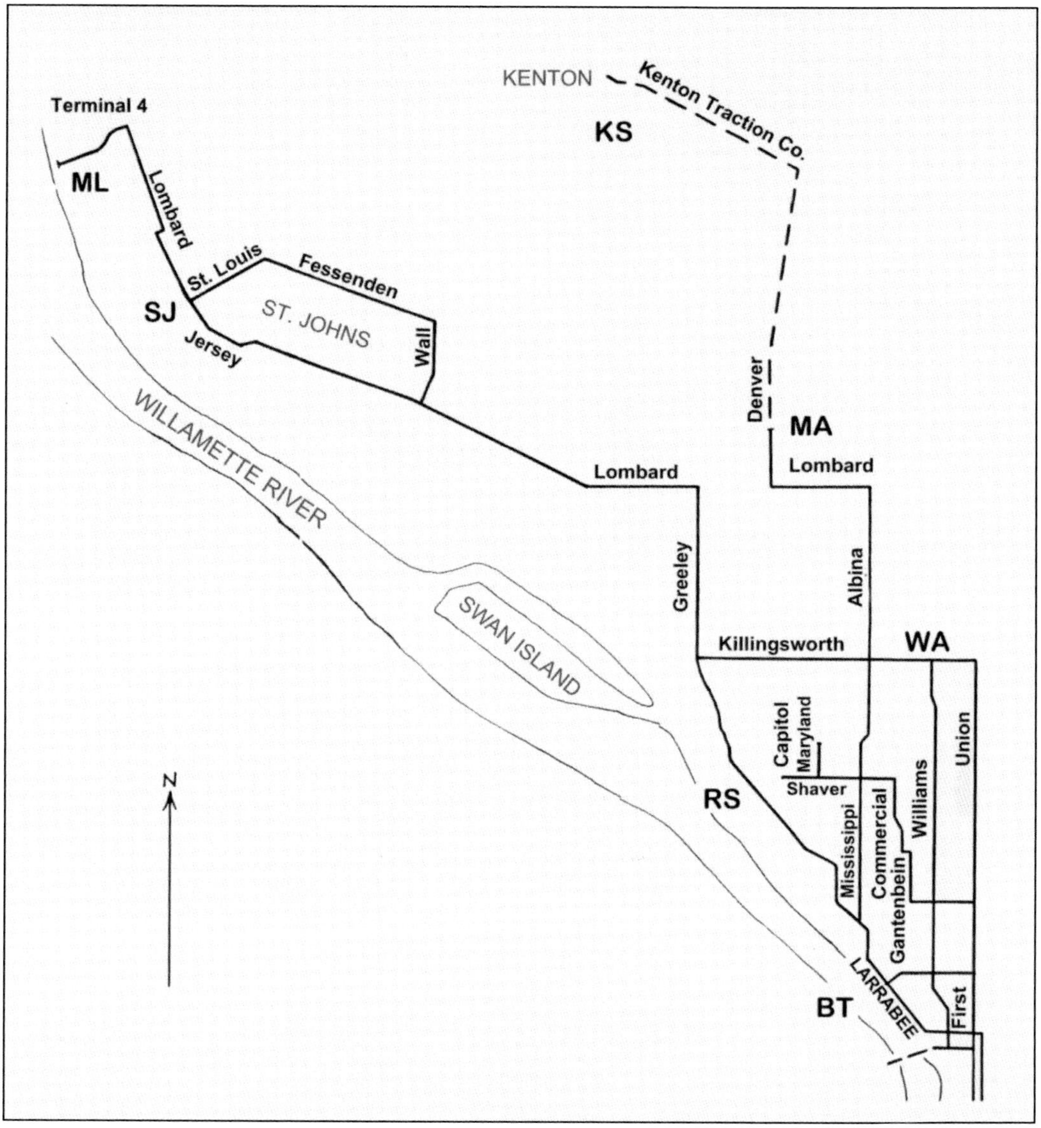

Lines in North Portland included the following: Albina, 1889–1892; Bridge Transfer (BT), 1915–1947; Kenton (K), 1909–1912; Kenton Stockyards (KS), 1909–1928; Lower Albina (L), see MA; Mississippi Avenue (MA), 1892–1940; Municipal Terminal (ML), 1920–1929; Russell Shaver (RS), 1903–1936; St. Johns (SJ), 1889–1937; Upper Albina (U), see WA; and Williams Avenue (WA), 1892–1937. This map shows lines during the 1920s, by which time several had disappeared or been renamed. There were two Kenton lines. One was a stub running from the end of the Mississippi Avenue line that was merged into that line in 1912. A separate line from Kenton to the stockyards was operated by Kenton Traction from 1909 to 1928. The Lower and Upper Albina lines eventually came to be known as the Mississippi Avenue and Williams Avenue lines.

Three

To Albina, St. Johns, and Kenton

North Portland's colorful neighborhoods were mostly unplatted farmland before the arrival of the streetcar. Street railways running out the Portland Peninsula helped develop the once separate towns of Albina, St. Johns, and Kenton.

St. Johns was established near the tip of the Peninsula in 1868 by developer James "Saint" Johns. A beautiful suspension bridge was built across the Willamette at St. Johns in 1931, and the area had become an important shipping and shipbuilding center by World War II.

Albina was founded in 1887 on the bluff above the Oregon Railway and Navigation Company yards, where many of its residents worked. Its politics were controlled by former governor George Williams and an Englishman named Edwin Russell, whose names would live on in trolley line designations.

In 1909, Chicago-based Swift and Company established the town of Kenton near the Columbia River on the Lower Peninsula. The Kenton Traction Company operated a trolley shuttle between the company town and Swift's meat packing plant.

A steam motor line provided the first mechanized transit in North Portland, reaching St. Johns in 1889. In November of that same year, the first electric street railway in the state inaugurated service to Albina. The remainder of the route to St. Johns was electrified in 1903.

Two more lines were built in North Portland. The Russell Shaver line began running to the Overlook neighborhood in 1903, and the city's last new line, the Municipal Terminal stub, started in 1920. The onset of the Great Depression ensured that no more streetcar lines would be built. Rail transit was gone in North Portland from September 14, 1940, until the MAX yellow line began operating May 1, 2004.

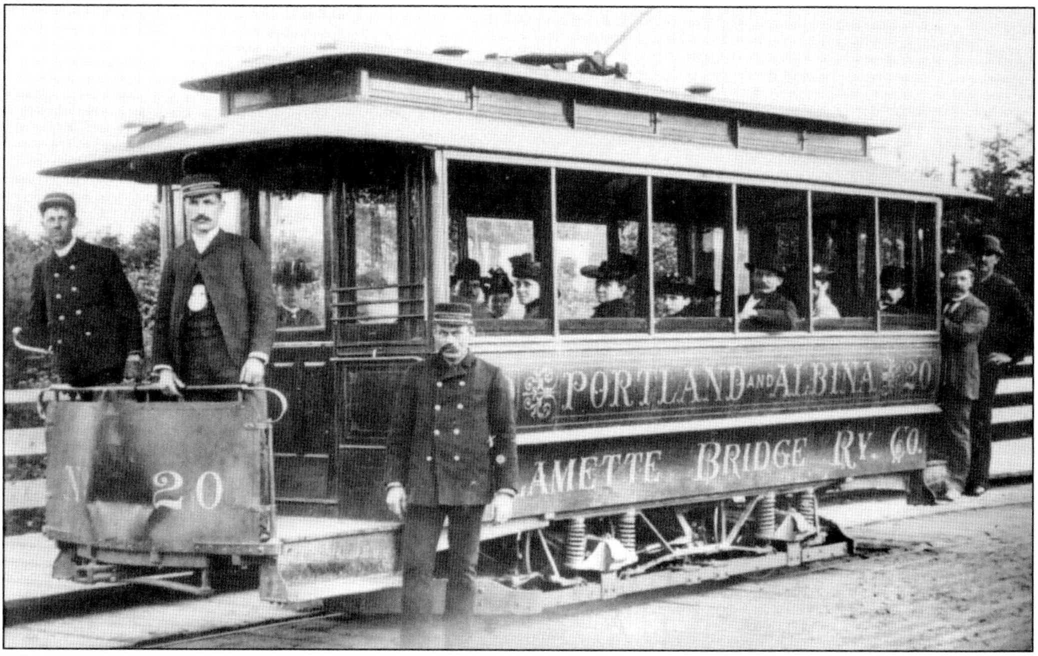

The first electric streetcars in the state began running over the lower portion of the St. Johns route in November 1889. Service was provided from Third and G Streets in Portland to North Stanton and Commercial Streets in Albina. Jack Workman, who was motorman on the first run, is seen holding onto the dashboard of No. 20 on the Slough Bridge near present day North Interstate and Tillamook Streets.

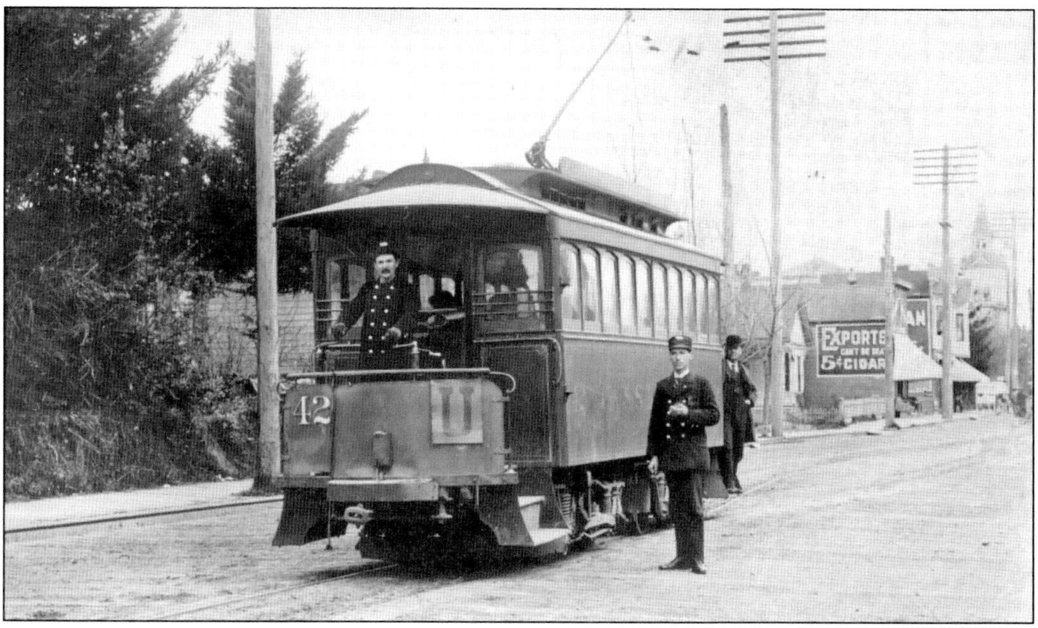

By 1892, Willamette Bridge successor City and Suburban Railway had divided the Albina electric into two lines: Lower Albina (L) and Upper Albina (U). Bombay-roofed car No. 42 is seen here on North Williams Avenue on the U line. Motorman Charles Love took many such photographs for proud crews like this. (Photograph by Charles Love.)

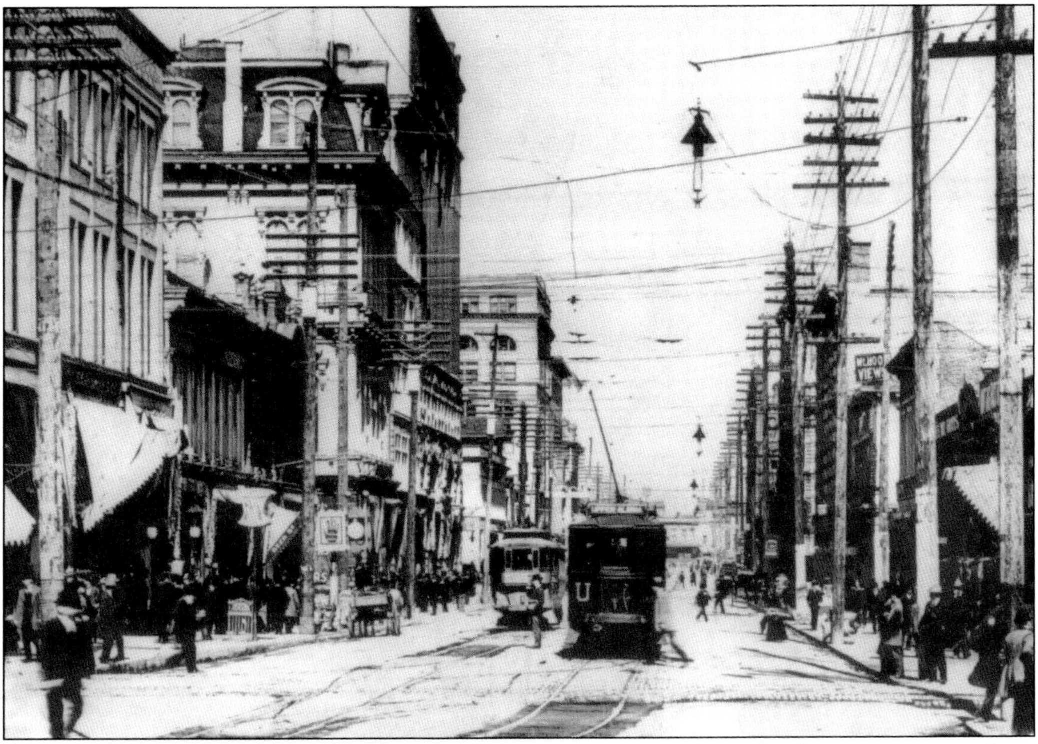

By the late 19th century, Portland's shopping district had shifted to Third Avenue, as seen here on Southwest Third Avenue at Morrison Street near the downtown terminus of the Upper Albina line. The tall Dekum Building in the background is the only structure surviving today. Streetcar platforms are now enclosed, as evidenced by City and Suburban Railway Upper Albina car No. 37 and the portable vestibule on the passing trolley.

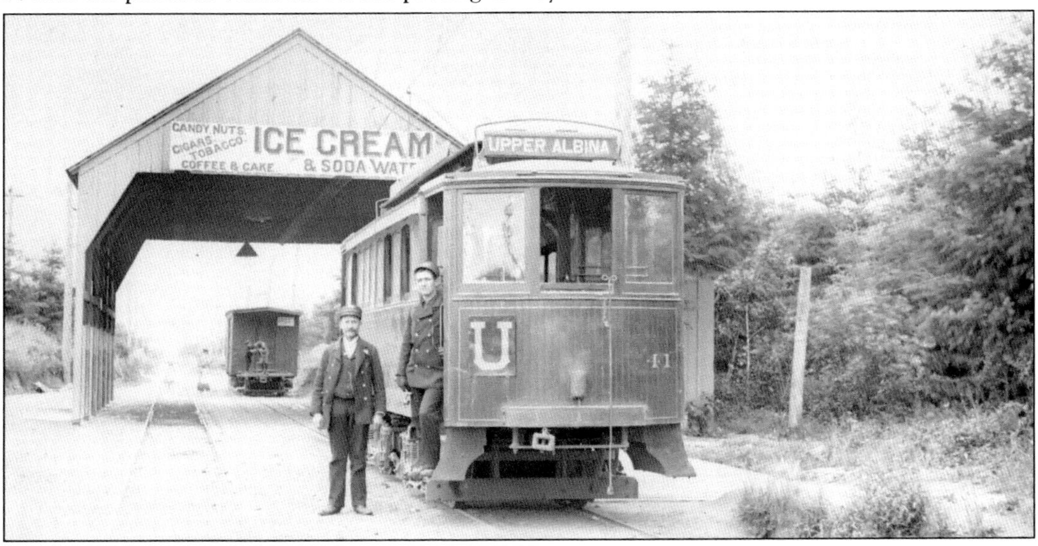

The City and Suburban Railway's Piedmont transfer station was located at what became North Killingsworth and Moore Streets. Riders transferred here between Upper Albina trolleys and St. Johns steam trains. Waiting passengers could purchase candy, cigarettes, and ice cream. In the background, children are playing on a boxcar that may have served as a waiting room.

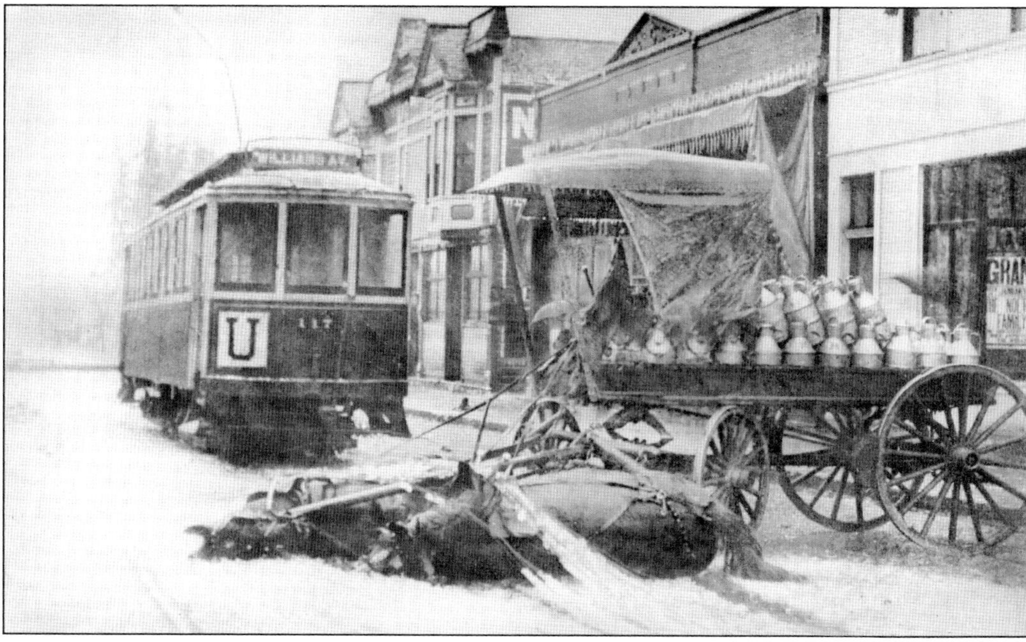

On the morning of January 28, 1907, Portland Railway car No. 117 was delayed when a silver thaw caused telephone poles to collapse along 15 blocks in Upper Albina, bringing down trolley and telephone wires and killing two horses. The dairy wagon had stopped to make a delivery on North Williams Avenue at Page Street when a 600-volt trolley wire dropped onto the team, killing them instantly. (Courtesy Mark Moore.)

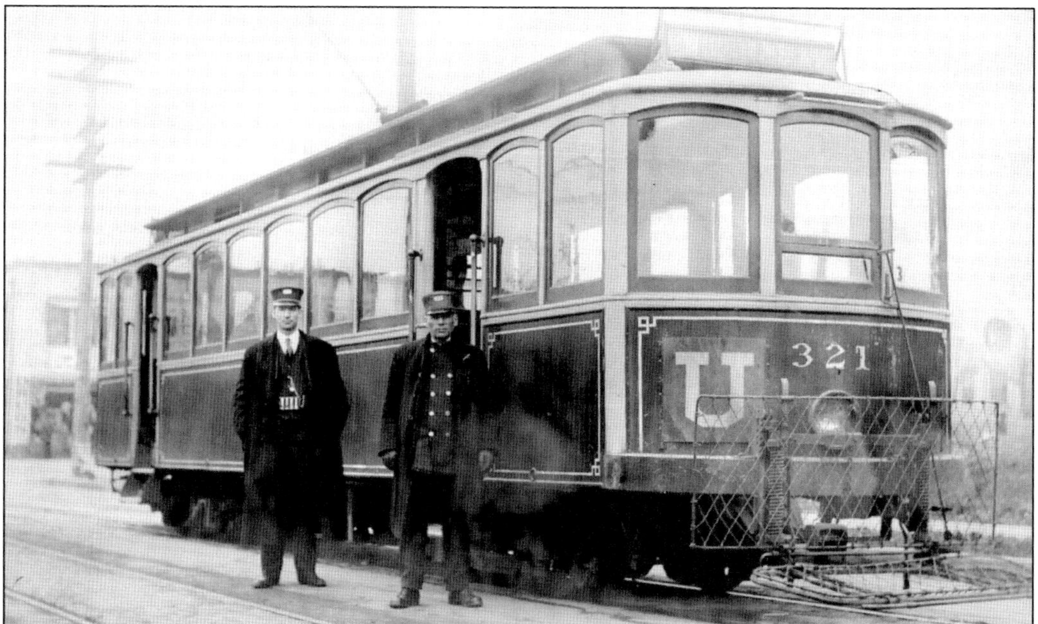

The crew of Fuller *Standard car* No. 321 is waiting on North Killingsworth Street near the Piedmont carbarn ready for Williams Avenue line duty. We are now in the Portland Railway Light and Power Company years. In 1913, PRL&P added Nelson safety fenders, like the one seen here, to most of its fleet. The building in the background is a drugstore. (Courtesy Mark Moore.)

Transfers incorporating maps, like this one for the Mississippi Avenue line, were introduced in August 1936. The punches indicate that a passenger boarded a southbound car on North Lombard and Albina Streets at 8:00 a.m. Boxes were also provided for special riders and circumstances, such as emergencies, students, and cars returning to the barn. The ND space was for next day, meaning between midnight and 5:00 a.m.

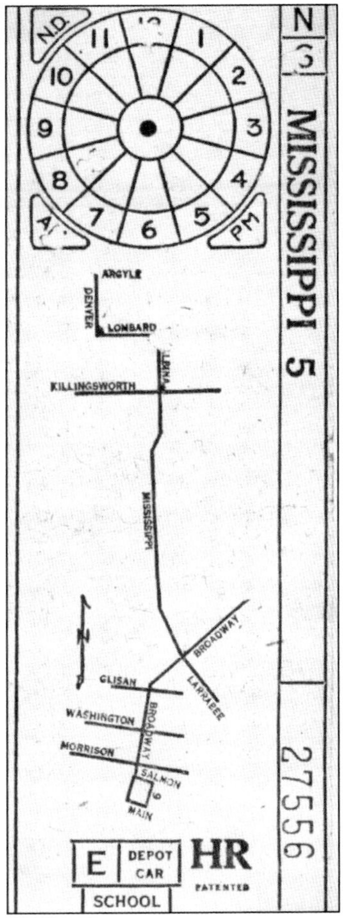

Mississippi Avenue car No. 315 waits at North Denver and Kilpatrick Streets in the company town of Kenton around 1912. No. 315 was built in 1903 by the first Portland Railway Company as part of their Fuller Standard series. Smokers—including cigar-smoking Franklin Fuller, company president—favored these large, end compartments because smoking was prohibited in the main part of the car. (Courtesy Mark Moore.)

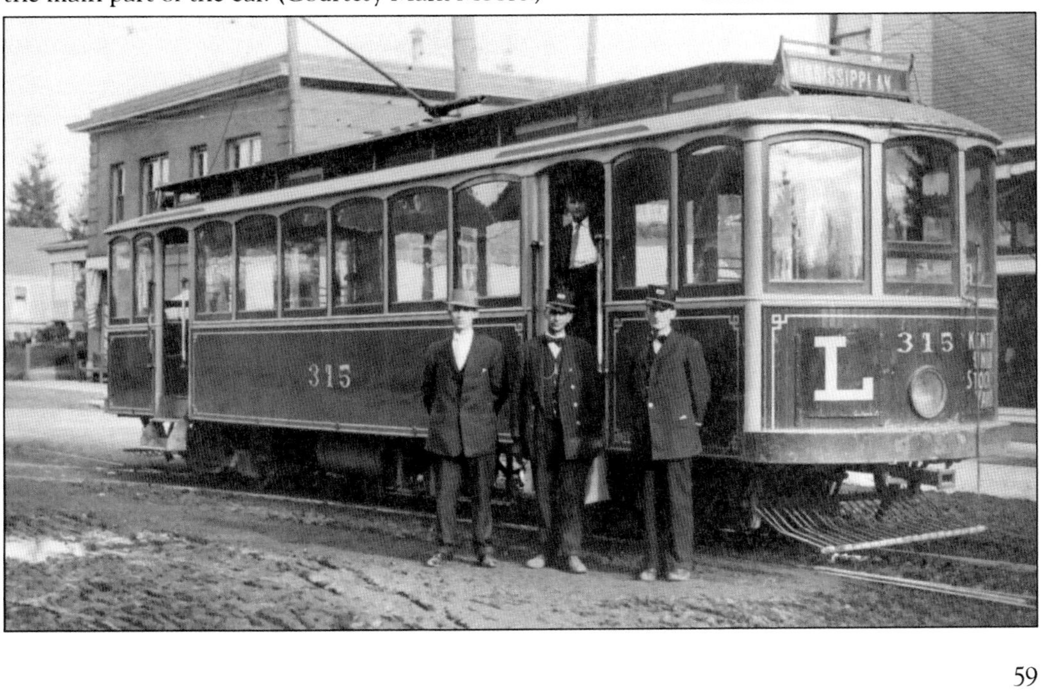

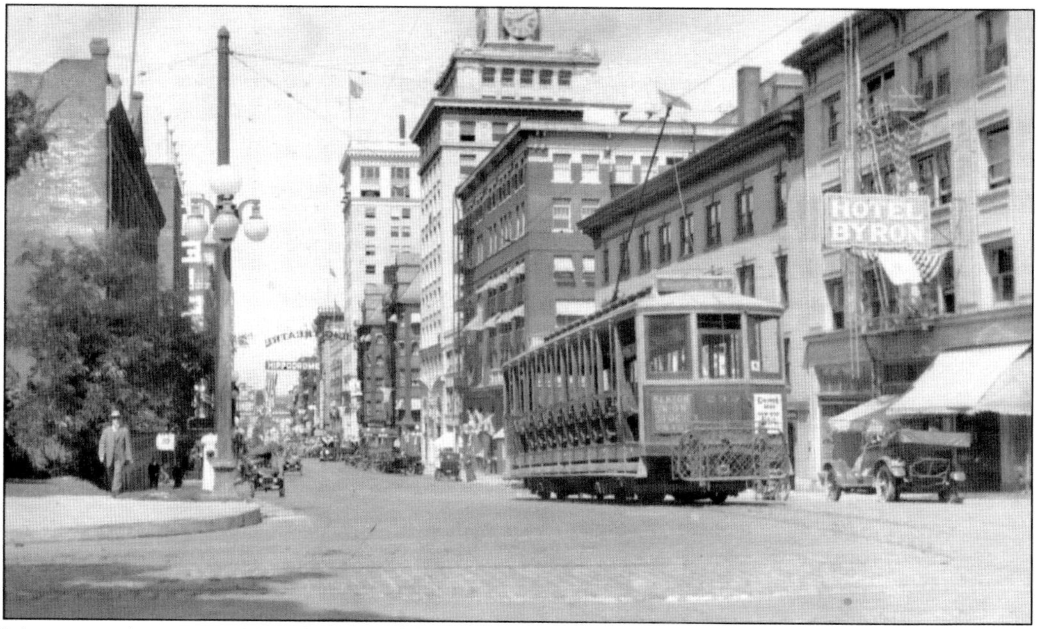

Mississippi Avenue car No. 239 is northbound on Southwest Broadway approaching Salmon Street around 1916. No. 239, one of 25 open cars built by the City and Suburban Railway in 1903, was nearing retirement when this picture was taken. In fact, most open "breezers," like this one, were in storage by 1919. The building with the clock tower is the Jackson Tower, built as headquarters for the *Oregon Journal* newspaper in 1912. (Courtesy Mark Moore.)

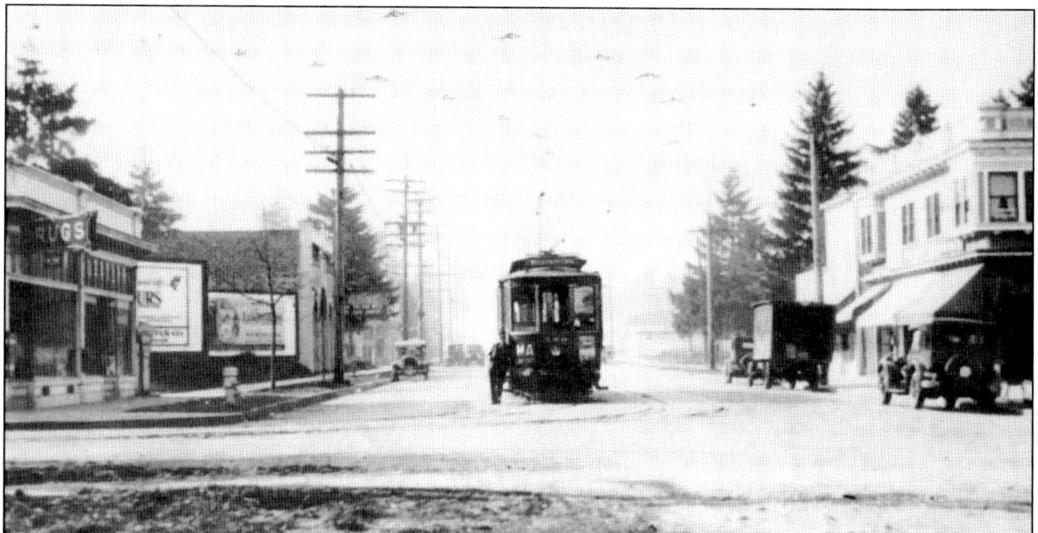

Things seem pretty quiet as the motorman leans against Mississippi Avenue car No. 590 in this 1920s scene taken at North Albina Avenue and Lombard Street. Mississippi Avenue cars alternated between this terminus and North Denver Avenue and Argyle Streets in Kenton. Rush hour trippers turned back at North Albina Avenue and Ainsworth Street. Businesses in this typical streetcar commercial district include a drugstore and market.

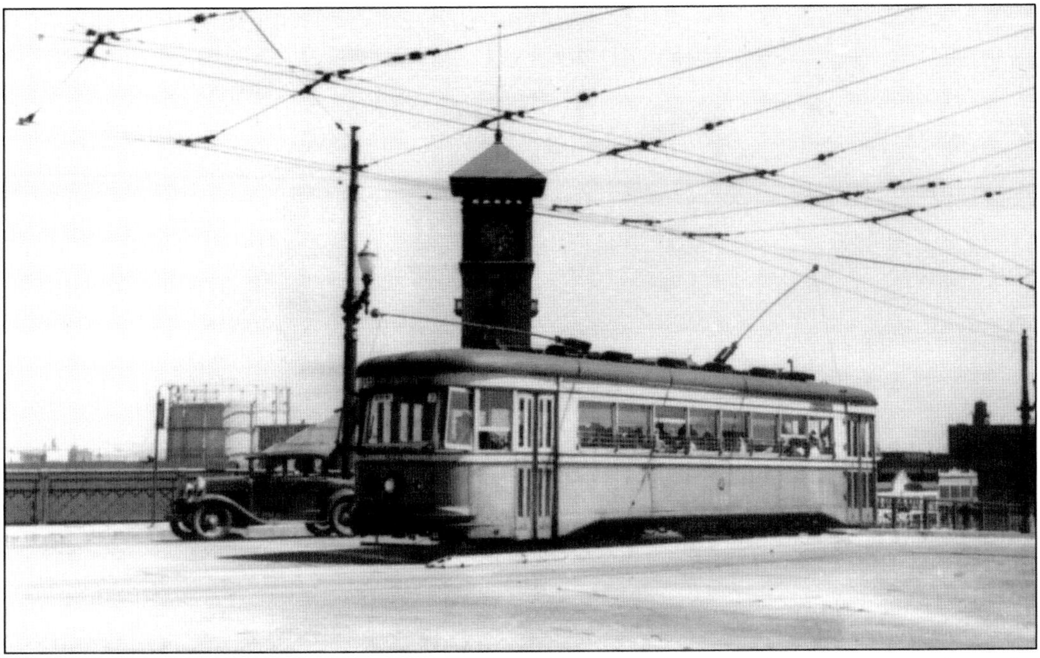

Portland Traction Mississippi Avenue car No. 812 is seen here on the west approach to the Broadway Bridge with the Union Station tower looming in the background. Portland's last order for new streetcars, in 1932, was for 15 Brill Master Units like this. They were assigned to the Broadway line and quickly garnered the nickname "Broadways," although they also appeared on other remaining lines, including Alberta and Mississippi and Twenty-third Avenues.

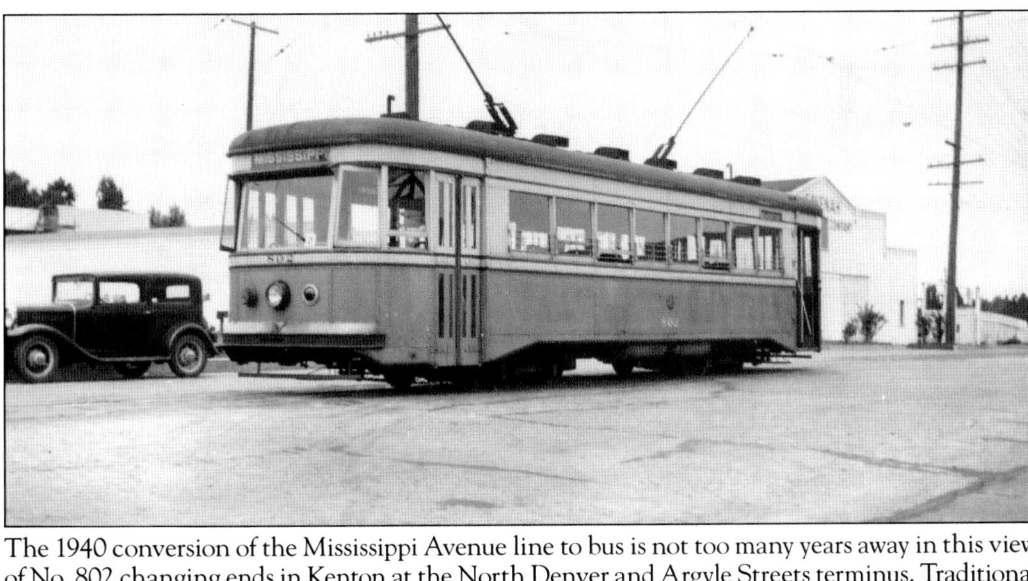

The 1940 conversion of the Mississippi Avenue line to bus is not too many years away in this view of No. 802 changing ends in Kenton at the North Denver and Argyle Streets terminus. Traditional maroon and cream colors were not used on the *Broadways* at first; they arrived in Portland Traction's new livery with gray bodies, ivory trim, a dark green belt line, and black roofs.

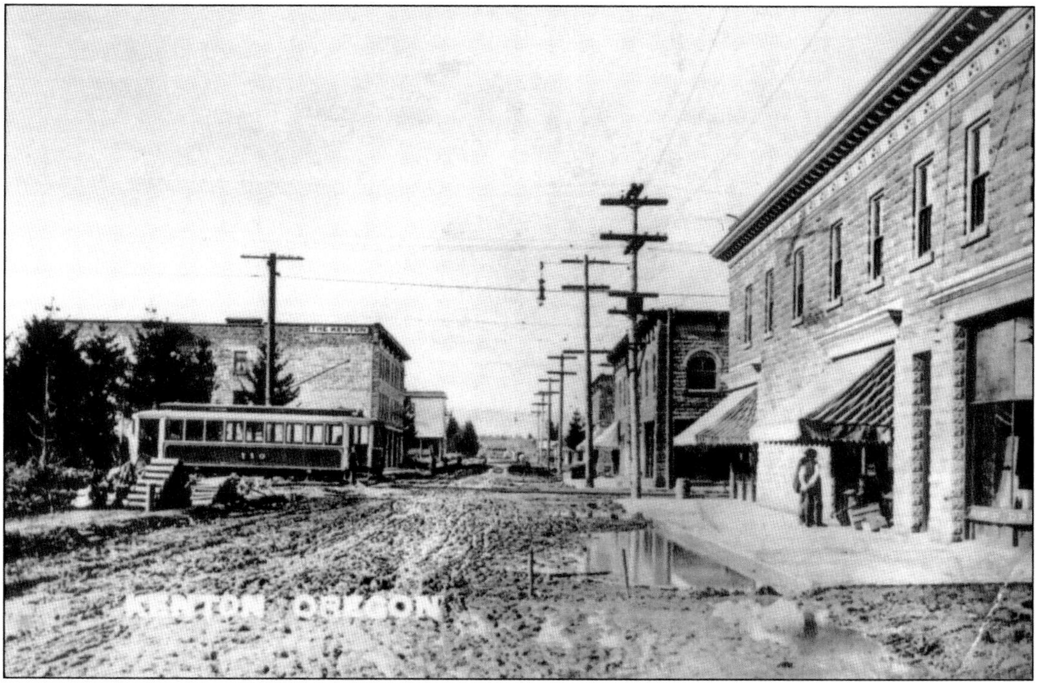

Kenton Traction Company, a Swift Meat Company subsidiary, operated a stub line from the company town of Kenton to the stockyards and packing plant 2 miles to the north. Service was provided by half a dozen older trolleys leased from PRL&P. No. 110 is seen here on muddy North Denver and Kilpatrick Streets in Kenton on December 10, 1910. Swift's enterprise became the largest livestock exchange on the Pacific Coast.

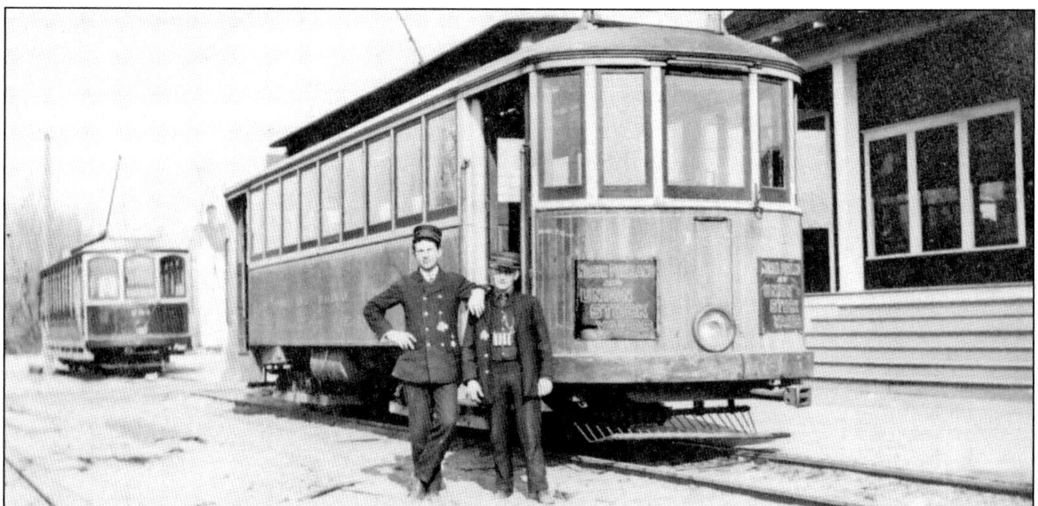

From September 15, 1909, until December 1928, Kenton Traction Company operated a stub line from Kenton to Swift's "Packingtown" on what is now North Marine Drive. Trolleys leased from PRL&P included former C&S standard No. 137 and open car No. 251, seen here in front of the Exchange Building at the stockyards. Note the St. Patrick's Day shamrocks worn by the crew. (Courtesy Mark Moore.)

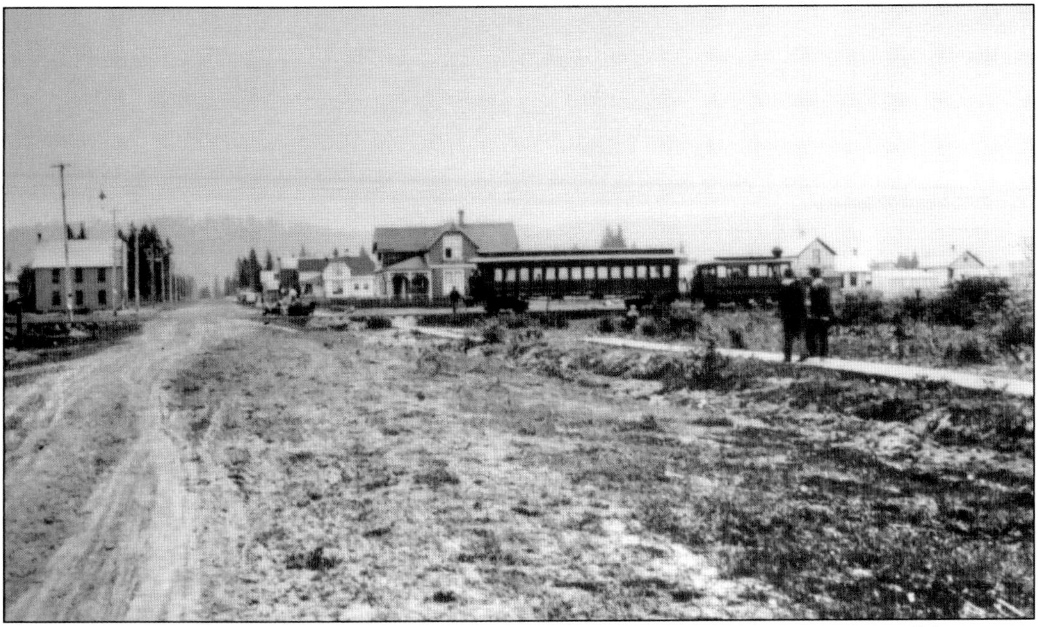

Steam streetcars were the first to serve St. Johns, reaching Portsmouth Station in 1889 and downtown St. Johns in May of the following year. A Willamette Bridge Railway "dummy" engine pulling a locally built Columbia Car and Tool coach is seen here northbound at the muddy intersection of North Portsmouth and Lombard Streets. Steam dummy engines muffled undesirable locomotive sounds inside streetcar-like wooden bodies.

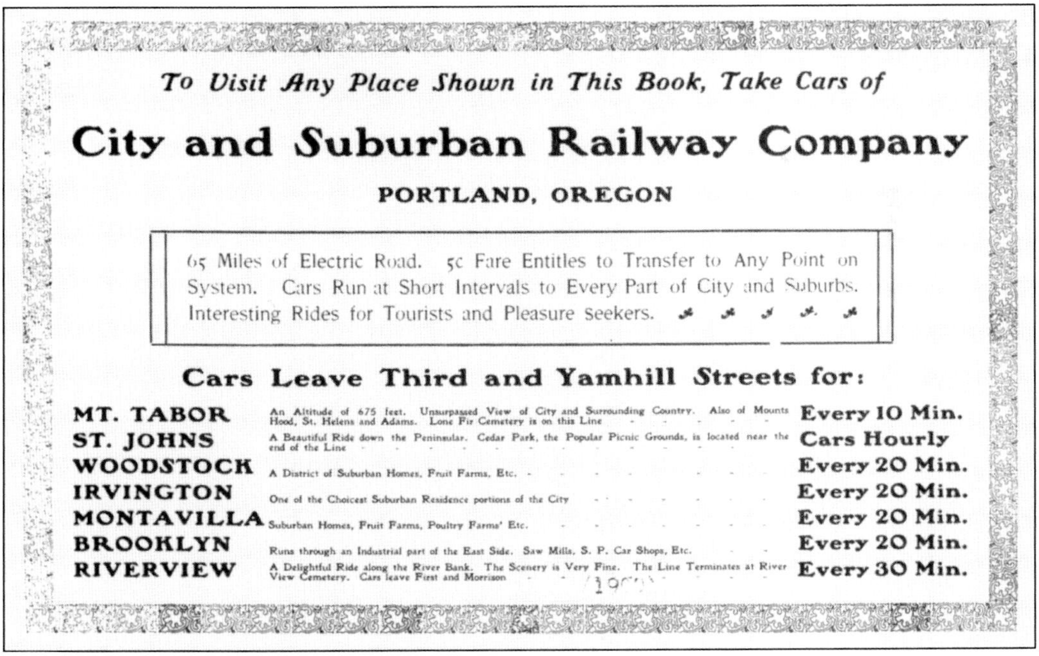

The St. Johns line was not yet one of the "Electric Roads" mentioned in this 1900 advertisement, but it is promoted as "a beautiful ride down the Peninsular," allowing access to nearby Cedar Park. By the time of their merger in 1904, the City and Suburban Railway had 74 miles of line, and competitor Portland Railway had 30 miles.

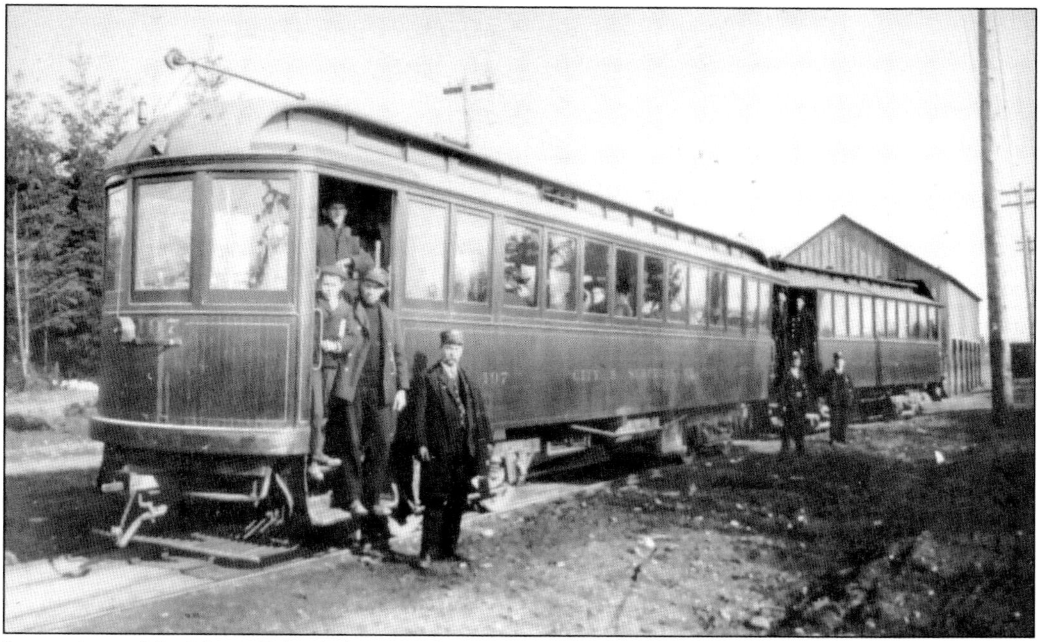

Interurbans, like No. 197, built for St. Johns service after electrification in 1903, were too big to run downtown until bridges could be strengthened and a longer loop track built. The Piedmont transfer station, seen above, remained in use for two more years. In 1905, a newspaper reflected rider dissatisfaction when it complained that this "transfer nuisance" should be abated and through service provided from Portland to St. Johns.

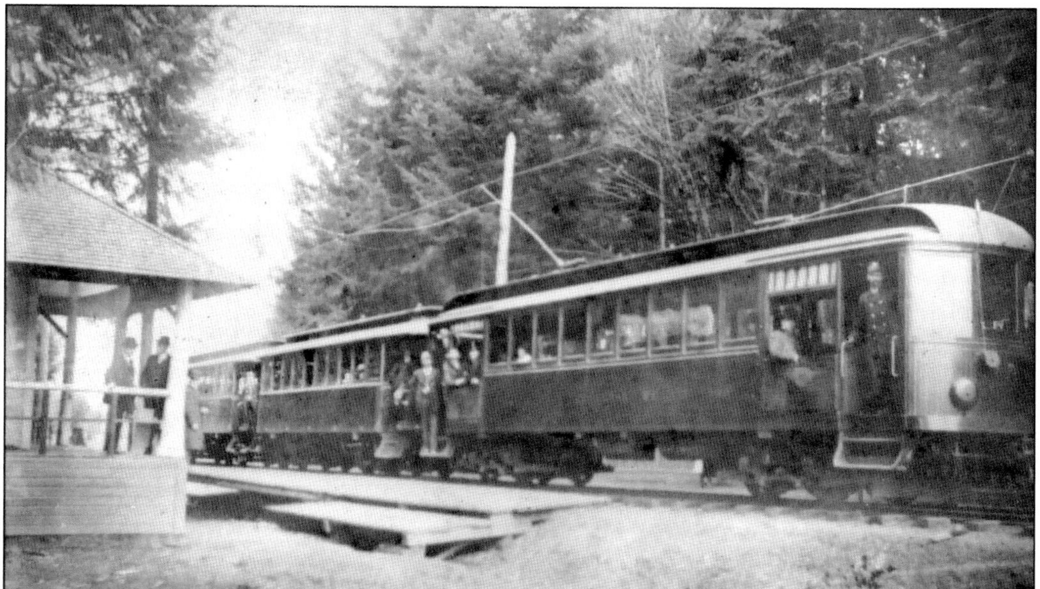

This rare shot of a three-car St. Johns train shows No. 199 with two former Pullman steam train trailers at Cedar Park station on North Fessenden Street about 1904. The first two St. Johns cars featured open sections, as seen here. These proved unpopular and were soon enclosed. The five cars in this series began working the St. Johns line in 1903 when the steam trains were finally discontinued.

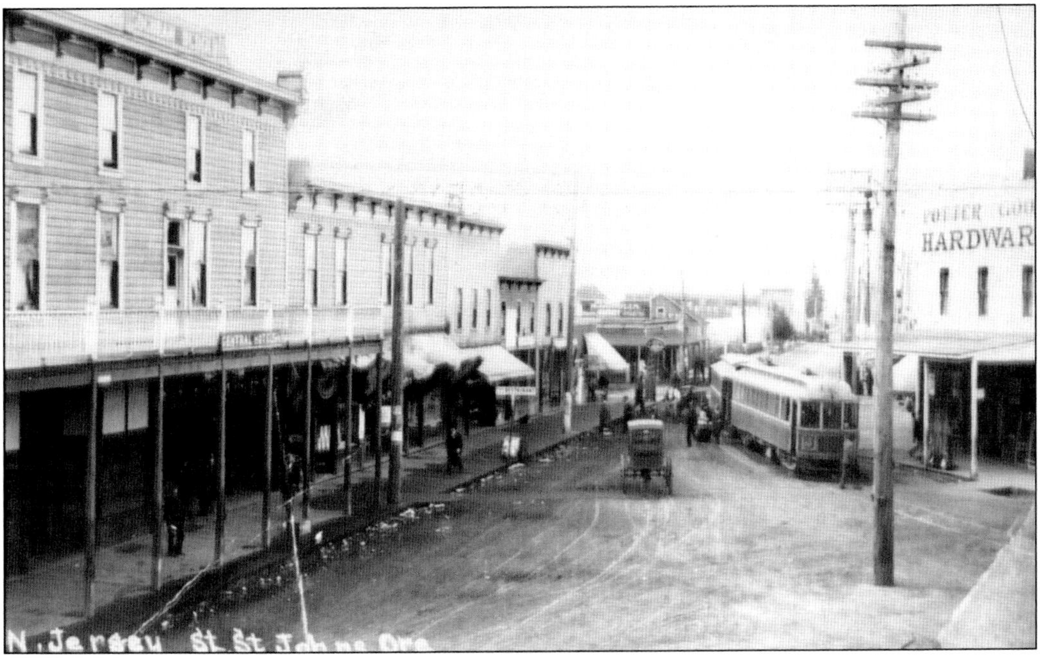

A two-car train headed by No. 197 is about to depart downtown St. Johns in this *c.* 1906 view taken at the North Jersey and Philadelphia Streets terminus. The Central Hotel, at left, and Potter Good Hardware, at right, would soon be modernized, losing their western-style porches and raised wooden sidewalks.

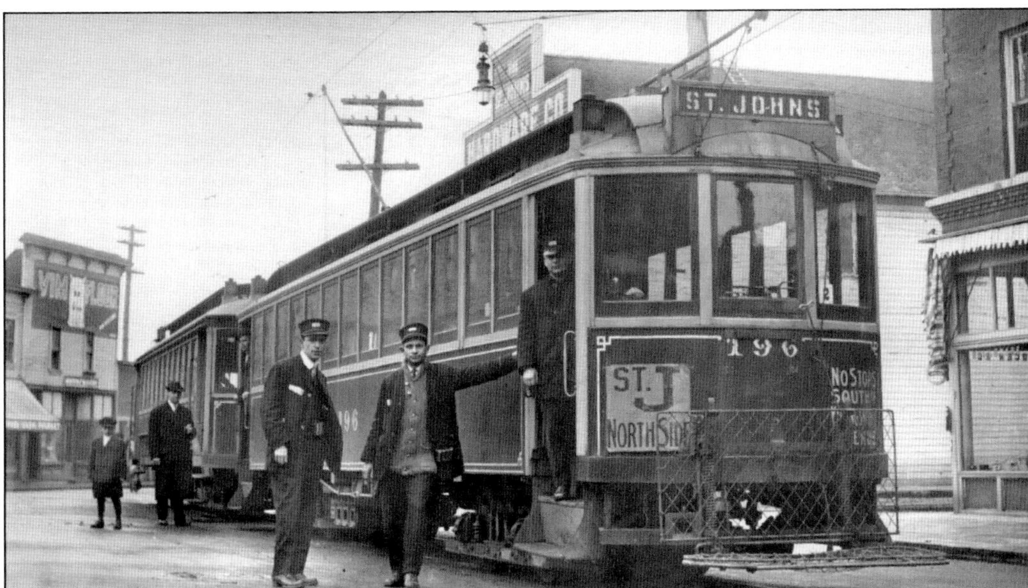

St. Johns car No. 196 and trailer 276 pose at North Philadelphia and Jersey Streets about 1913. Alongside are conductors Gustave Nelson, Howard Shafer, and motorman W. Frank Allman. The St. Johns Hardware Company is to the right, and a market advertising "Vim Flour" is in the background. Until the loop through St. Johns was completed, trains alternated between north side (North Fessdenden Street) and south side (North Lombard Street) terminals.

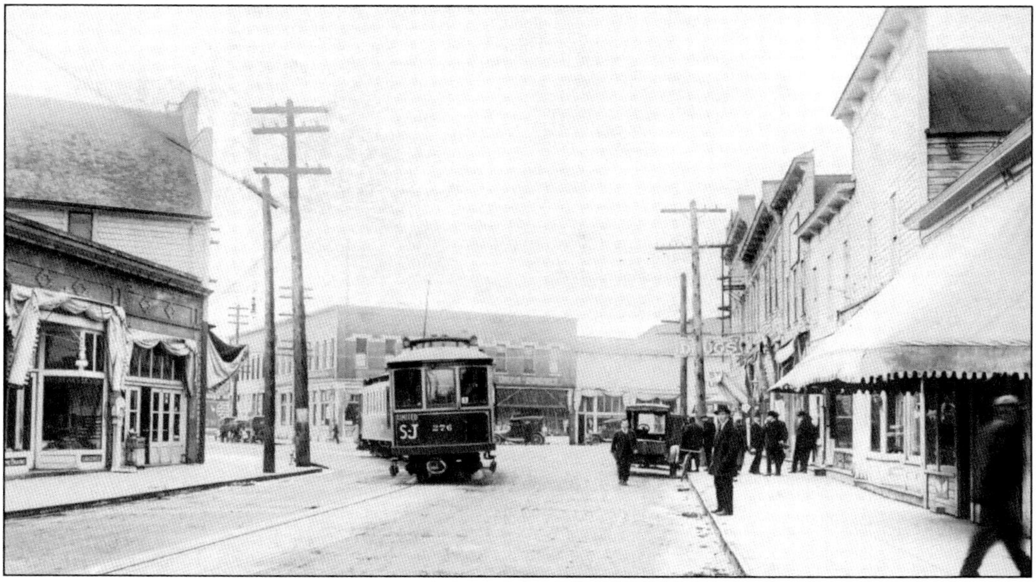

When this picture was taken in St. Johns (SJ), limited trains like this could finally run directly into downtown Portland. Bridges had been strengthened and curves adjusted so that the long SJ trains could cross the Willamette River bridges and the last portion of the loop around St. Johns had been completed. From June 1911, trains ran over the complete Wall Street loop in Saint Johns. (Courtesy Mark Moore.)

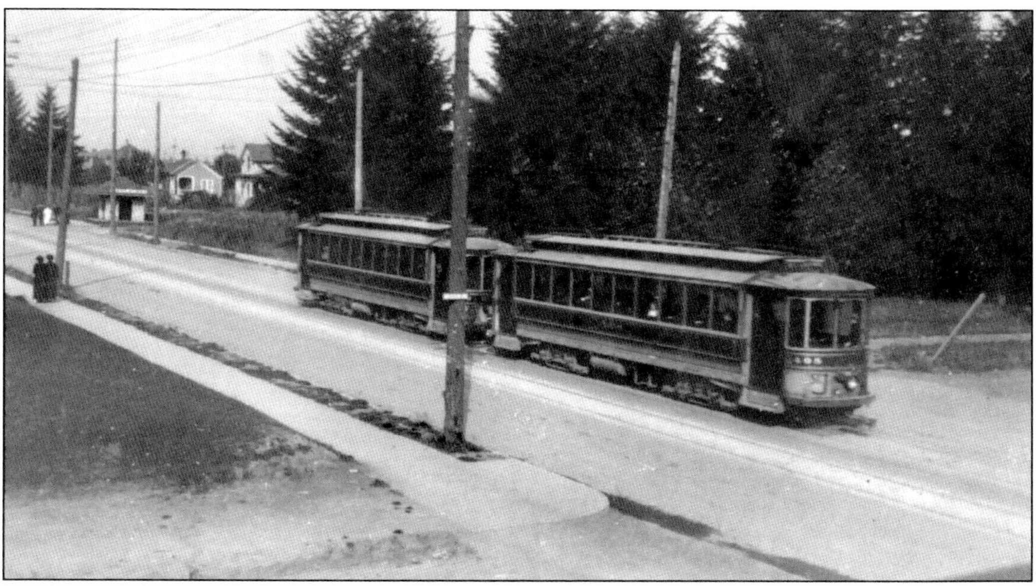

Portland Railway, Light and Power ordered a series of trolleys that looked quite different from the interurbans used previously on the St. Johns run. They featured multiple-unit operation, meaning the motorman at the front of a train controlled the speed and braking of all cars. Paired car Nos. 408 and 409 are approaching North Albina station at North Killingsworth and Missouri Streets on October 22, 1909. (Courtesy Mark Moore.)

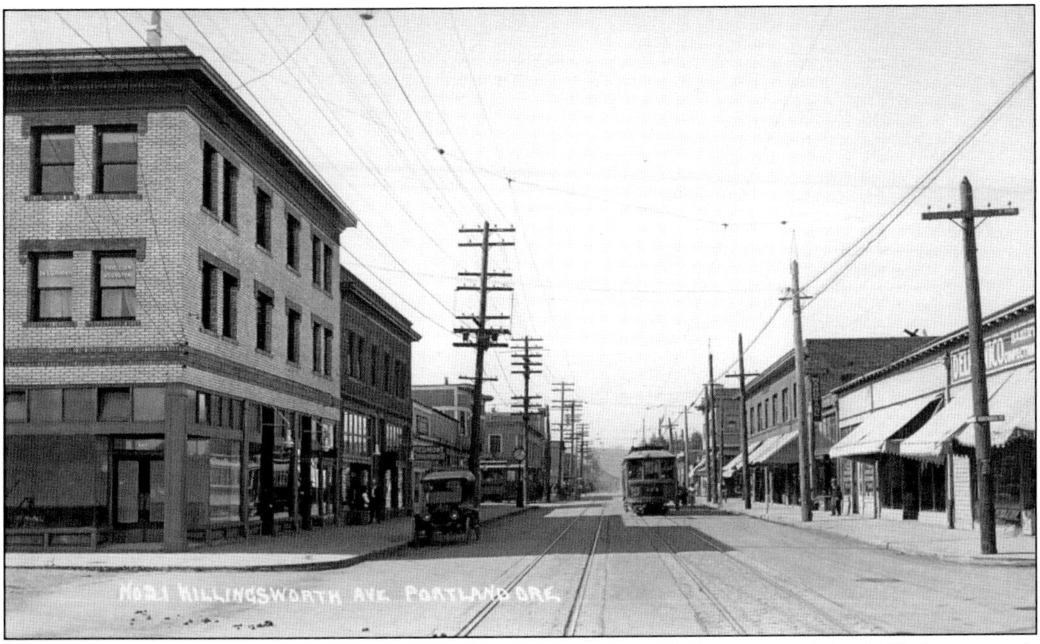

St. Johns car No. 274 is traversing the Piedmont commercial district on North Killingsworth Avenue around 1911. In the background, a Lower Albina line streetcar is waiting to cross on North Albina Street. Stores in view include Piedmont Furniture on the left and Nichols Hardware on the right. No. 274 is heading to Union Avenue, where it will turn south on a new route downtown. (Courtesy Mark Moore.)

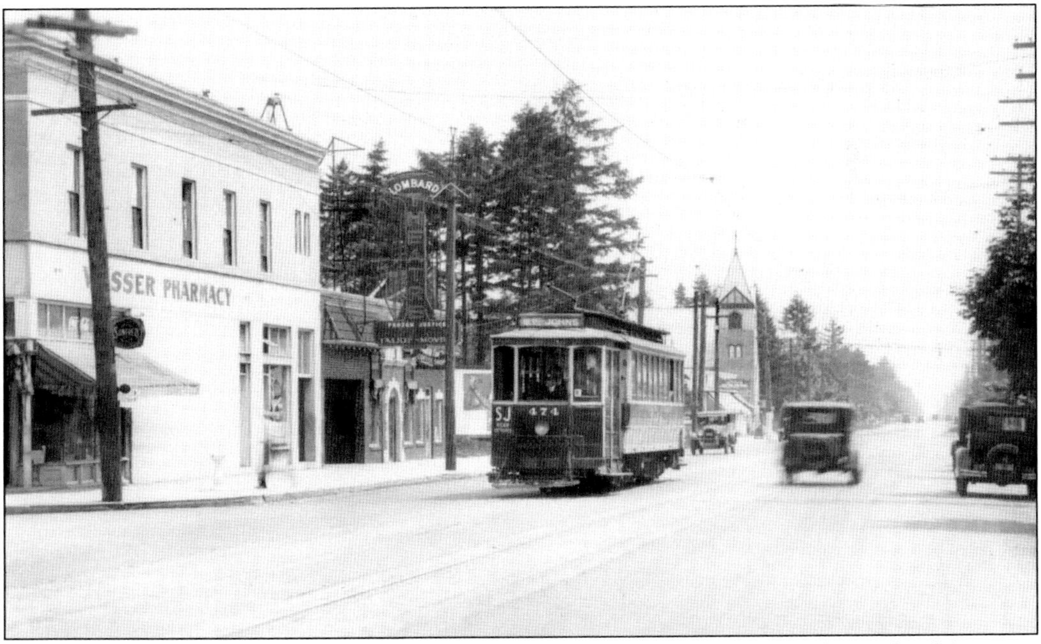

St. Johns line No. 474 is westbound next to the Wasser Drug Store on North Lombard Street at Peninsular in 1934. It has just passed the Lombard Theater, a neighborhood movie house, which is showing the 1929 Paramount "talkie" *Frozen Justice*.

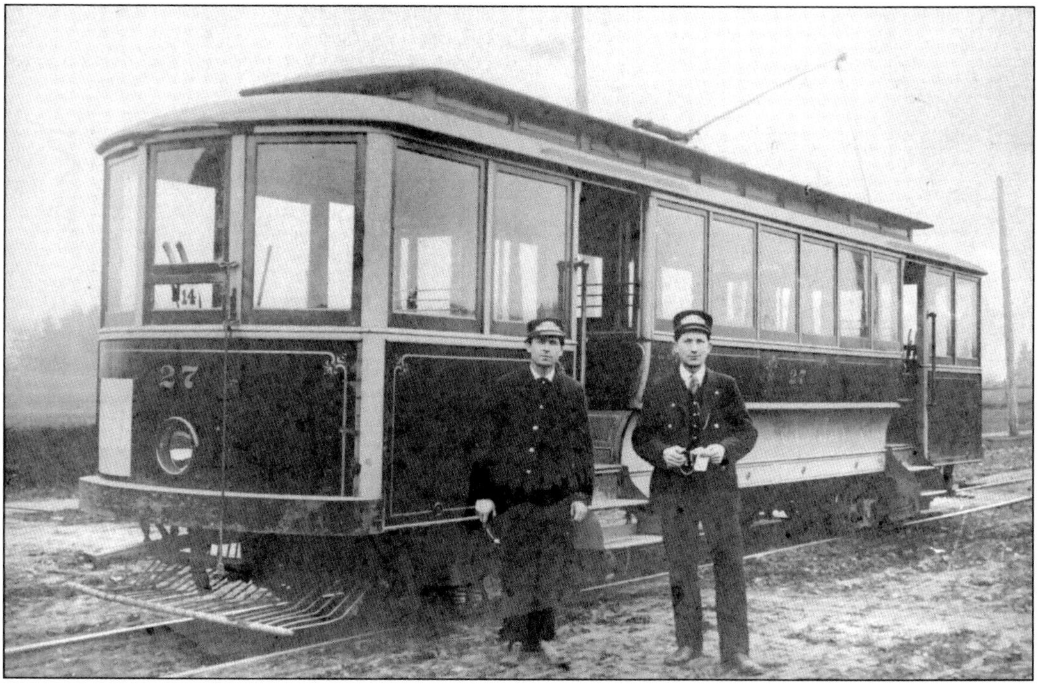

Between 1896 and 1904, rivals City and Suburban Railway and Portland Railway (the first of three companies with that name) provided most streetcar service in Portland, sometimes with competing lines. Portland Railway car No. 27, seen here with an "Albina" dash sign, may be on the new Russell Shaver line. (Courtesy Mark Moore.)

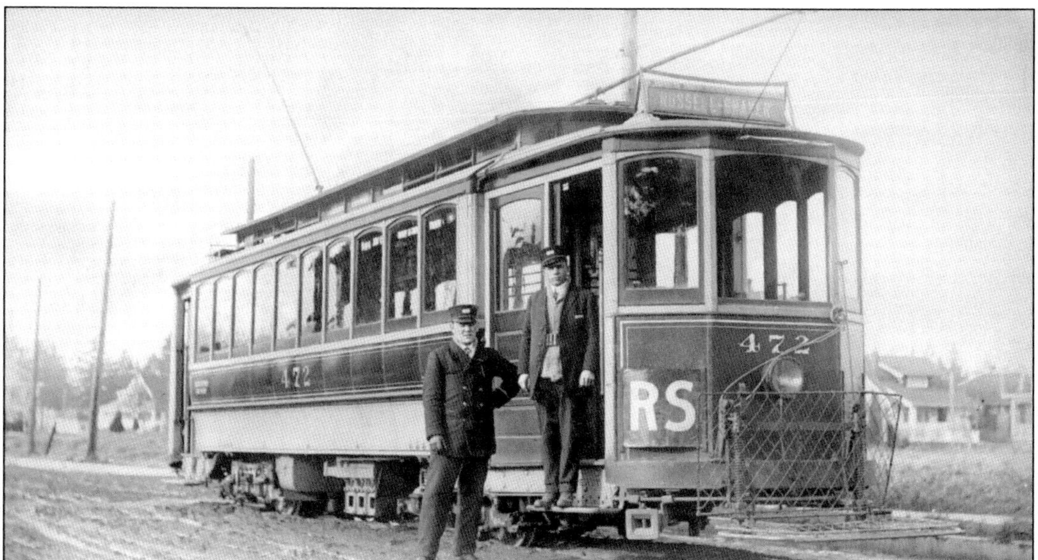

Russell Shaver car No. 472 is at the northern terminus on North Shaver Street at Concord Avenue in Overlook. Service on this line began in August 1903. In 1912, a short stub line also operated nearby from Shaver to Prescott on Maryland Avenue. Russell Shaver went downtown until 1909, when it became a crosstown line running over former East Side Line tracks to Southeast Grand Avenue and Hawthorne Boulevard.

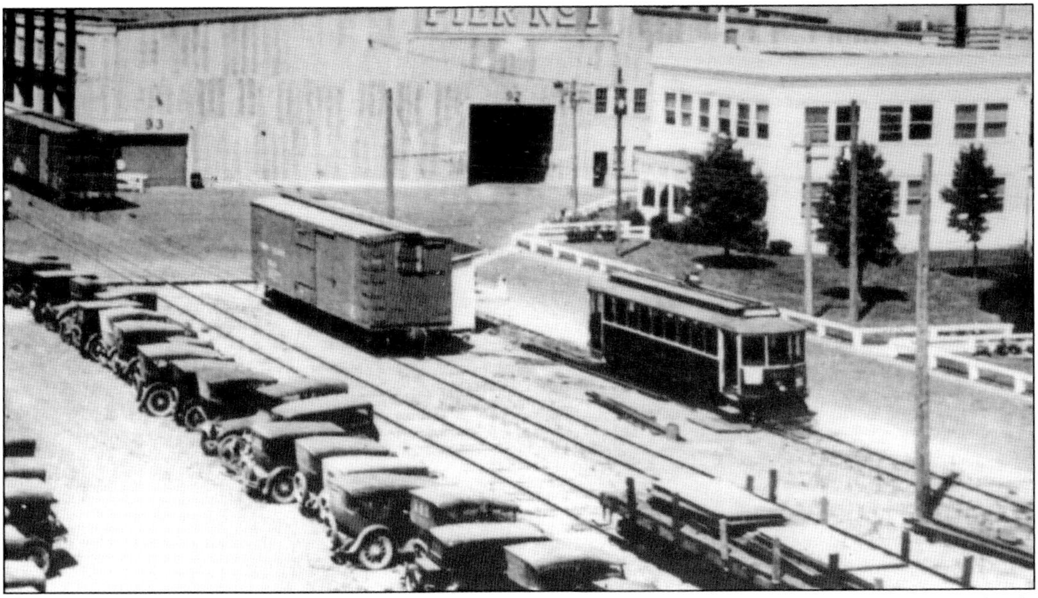

The last entirely new streetcar line was the Municipal Terminal line, a stub operation built for the Commission of Public Docks in 1920 to serve Terminal No. 4 north of St. Johns. The route, which operated until October 1929, ran from North Jersey and St. Louis Streets to Pier 1, Terminal 4, on Terminal Road. This only known Municipal Terminal photograph shows No. 107 at Pier 1 about 1926.

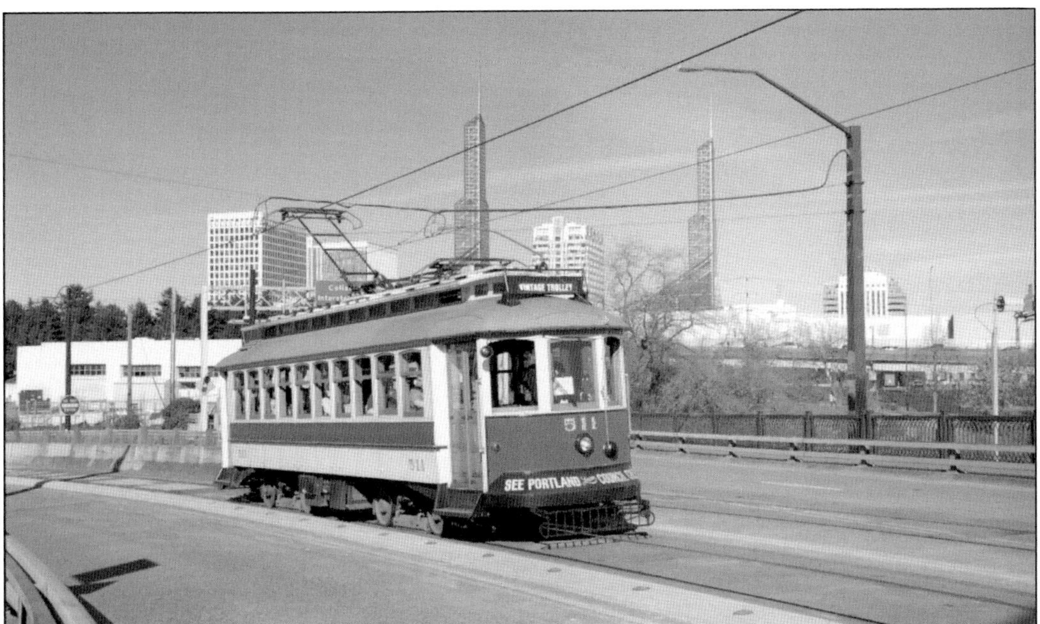

Although MAX light rail now runs through North Portland, the closest thing to a new streetcar line in that district was Vintage Trolley (VT), albeit with replica Council Crest cars. Gomaco-built car No. 511 is inbound the Steel Bridge on April 19, 2009, four months before the end of VT service on this route after nearly 18 years. The Oregon Convention Center spires are in the background. (Photograph by Steve Morgan.)

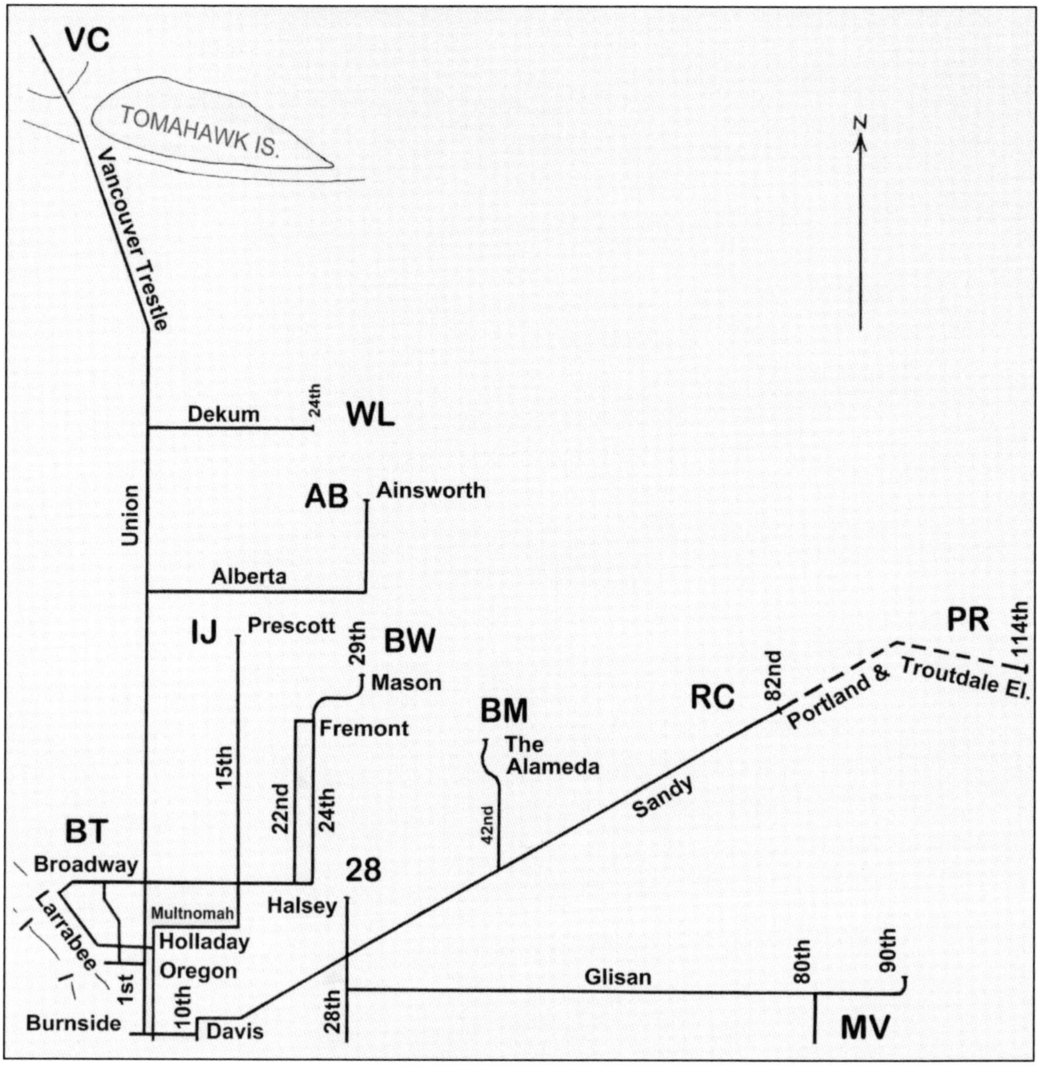

Lines in Northeast Portland included the following: Alberta (AB), 1905–1948; Beaumont (BM), 1911–1936; Broadway (BW), 1903–1948; East Ankeny (EA), 1892–1913; East Side, 1907–1909 and 1914; Irvington (IV), 1890–1940; Irvington-Jefferson (IJ), 1914–1933; Montavilla (MV), 1892–1948; Parkrose (PR), 1911–1927; Rose City (RC), 1907–1936; 28th Avenue (28), 1913–1936; Union Avenue, 1909–1914; Vancouver (VC), 1888–1940; and Woodlawn (WL), 1900–1937. This map shows lines during the 1920s. Union Avenue was a short turn (tripper) on the Alberta line. Dash signs for Union Avenue also appeared on the East Side line. The Alberta line was originally known as the Union Avenue and Vernon line. (Note: the Montavilla and Bridge Transfer lines, parts of which ran in Southeast, is covered in chapter 5.)

Four

To Vancouver, Irvington, and Rose City Park

Northeast Portland was first served by steam railroads and a horsecar line. East Portland ordinances forbidding steam trains caused the Willamette Bridge Railway to begin with a horsecar line along what is now Northeast and Southeast Grand Avenue in March 1888. That November, a group of investors headed by Frank Dekum completed a narrow-gauge steam railroad from East Portland to the Columbia River.

During the next few months, forest was cleared for two prominent developments. Piedmont was nestled alongside the Vancouver line on present-day Martin Luther King Boulevard, and Woodlawn was located adjacent to the Portland and Vancouver yard on Northeast Dekum Street.

In 1890, the Willamette Bridge Railway opened an electric line to Northeast Fifteenth Avenue and Hancock Street in Albina. It served Holladay's Addition and Irvington, which contained more than 140 upper-middle-class homes by the early 1900s.

The Vancouver line was purchased by the Portland Consolidated Street Railway in 1892 and promptly electrified. Successor Portland Railway created a separate Woodlawn line in 1900. In 1905, a new line was built out of Northeast Alberta Street to the Vernon neighborhood.

Hartman and Thompson opened the largest residential district in Portland in 1907. Transport to the Rose City Park development was provided by the Rose City line on Northeast Sandy Boulevard. The realtors added a stub line to Parkrose in 1911.

Northeast Portland's most exclusive neighborhood appeared in 1909. The Alameda set out to be an equivalent to Arlington Heights and Kings Heights in the West Hills. It was reached by the Broadway line, which started running out Northeast Twenty-fourth Avenue in 1903, and the Beaumont line, a stub service on Northeast Forty-second that began in 1911.

Car lines in Northeast Portland remained much the same until supplanted by buses in 1936. The area's last streetcars, before the arrival of light rail in 1986, ran during the summer of 1948.

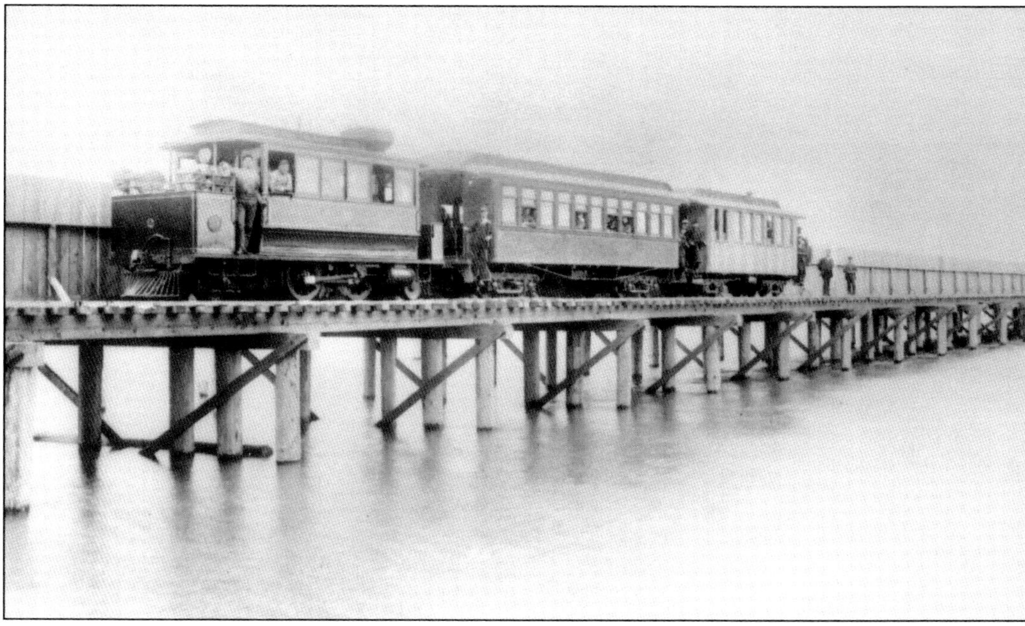

Portland and Vancouver Railway steam dummy No. 2 is seen on the Columbia Slough trestle with two coaches about 1889. It was company practice to couple a freight car onto the rear of the train to haul beer from the Vancouver Brewery. This occasionally provided refreshment for passengers. The ride began on an 8,000-foot trestle across bottomlands and ended up zigzagging over the trestles in East Portland.

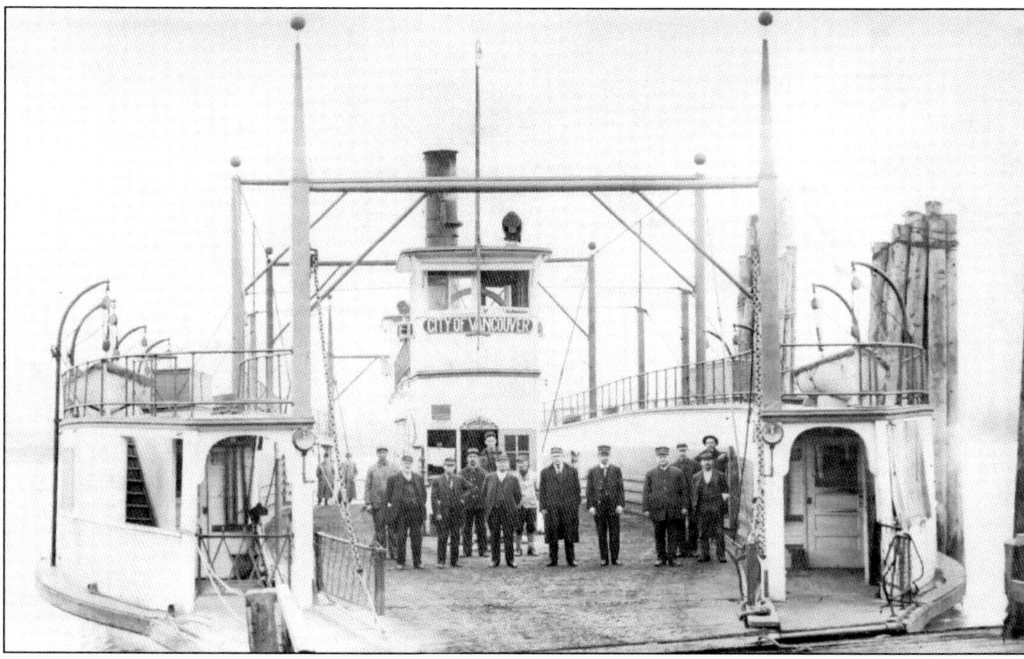

The ferry *City of Vancouver* is at the Vancouver ferry slip about 1910. The 460-ton steam-powered wooden side-wheeler had a beam of 55 feet. This second of two ferries owned by the traction company made the connection between Portland and Vancouver, Washington, until the Interstate Bridge was completed in 1917.

...TIME TABLE...

PORTLAND RAILWAY COMPANY

Single Fares Entitle Passengers to Free Transfers to Other Divisions, within the City Limits

Cars run from 6 A. M. to 12 P. M. on Week Days and from 8 A. M. to 12 P. M. on Sundays, as follows:

SUBJECT TO CHANGE WITHOUT NOTICE

FIRST STREET AND WILLAMETTE HEIGHTS

Cars leave corner First and Washington Streets for Willamette Heights every hour, and every ten minutes thereafter, connecting with cars at Thirteenth Street.

Cars leave Willamette Heights for First and Washington Streets at seven minutes past every hour, and every ten minutes thereafter.

THIRTEENTH STREET

Cars leave Montgomery Street at six minutes past the hour, and every ten minutes thereafter, connecting at Washington Street with Willamette Heights cars.

FIRST AND THURMAN STS., (Via Sixteenth St.)

Cars leave First and Washington Streets for Thurman Street five minutes after the hour, and every ten minutes thereafter.

Cars leave Sixteenth and Thurman Streets for First and Washington Streets every hour and every ten minutes thereafter.

GLISAN STREET AND HAMILTON AVE. (Second St. Line)

(THE METROPOLITAN R. R. CO.)

Cars leave corner Second and Washington Streets (connecting with Willamette Heights cars) for Hamilton Ave. nine minutes after the hour, and every ten minutes thereafter. The cars leaving nine and thirty-nine minutes past the hour connect with the Cemetery cars at Hamilton Avenue.

Cars leave Hamilton Avenue for down town on the hour, and every ten minutes thereafter. Cemetery cars leave Riverview Cemetery every hour and half hour.

PORTLAND AND VANCOUVER DIVISION

LEAVE PORTLAND

Corner of First and Washington Streets, as follows:

*W 6 00	11 40	W 5 20
* 6 20	W12 00	5 40
*W 6 40	12 20	W 6 00
* 7 05	W12 40	6 10
*W 7 20	1 00	W 6 40
7 40	W 1 20	W 7 00
W 8 00	1 40	W 7 30
8 20	W 2 00	W 8 00
W 8 40	2 20	W 8 30
9 00	W 2 40	W 9 00
W 9 20	3 00	W 9 30
9 40	W 3 20	W10 00
W10 00	3 40	W10 30
10 20	W 4 00	†W11 00
W10 40	4 20	†W11 30
11 00	W 4 40	W12 05
W11 20	5 00	

LEAVE VANCOUVER

as follows:

* 6 45	12 05	5 25
* 7 25	12 45	6 05
8 05	1 25	6 40
8 45	2 05	†11 15
9 25	2 45	
10 05	3 25	
10 45	4 05	
11 25	4 45	

W — Woodlawn only.

* Daily except Sunday.

† Wednesday and Saturday only for Vancouver.

Light type, A. M.

Heavy type, P. M.

WAITING ROOM, WASHINGTON STREET, NEXT TO FIRST

When the Portland Railway Company published this 1891 timetable in the *R. L. Polk Directory*, up to 16 trains a day were running between Portland and Vancouver, Washington. Daily service began at 6:35 a.m. and ended at 9:30 p.m. On Wednesdays and Saturdays, trains ran until 11:30 p.m. Fare was 25¢, and the trip, including ferry, took approximately 45 minutes. The Sunday *Oregonian* quoted passengers as saying that trains were "spinning along the road at the rate of about fifteen miles per hour." There were 13 stops along the 8-mile line, including a station at Woodlawn. On the eve of electrification in 1893, the company had six passenger cars, two regular engines, and a third locomotive for work trains.

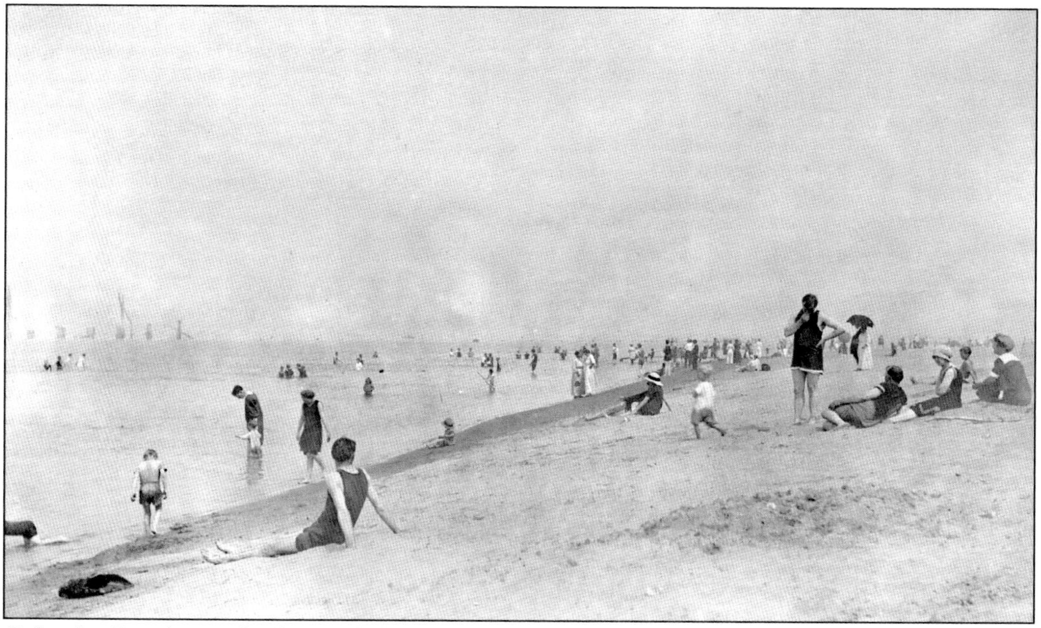

Columbia Beach was the first park developed along the Vancouver line. In 1916, PRL&P opened the 5,800-foot-wide bathing beach on what is now Tomahawk Island. It also offered camping, picnicking, and an athletic field. This island, 7 miles from downtown Portland, would later become the site of the ill-fated Lotus Isle amusement park, which competed with Jantzen Beach Park on nearby Hayden Island from 1929 to 1932.

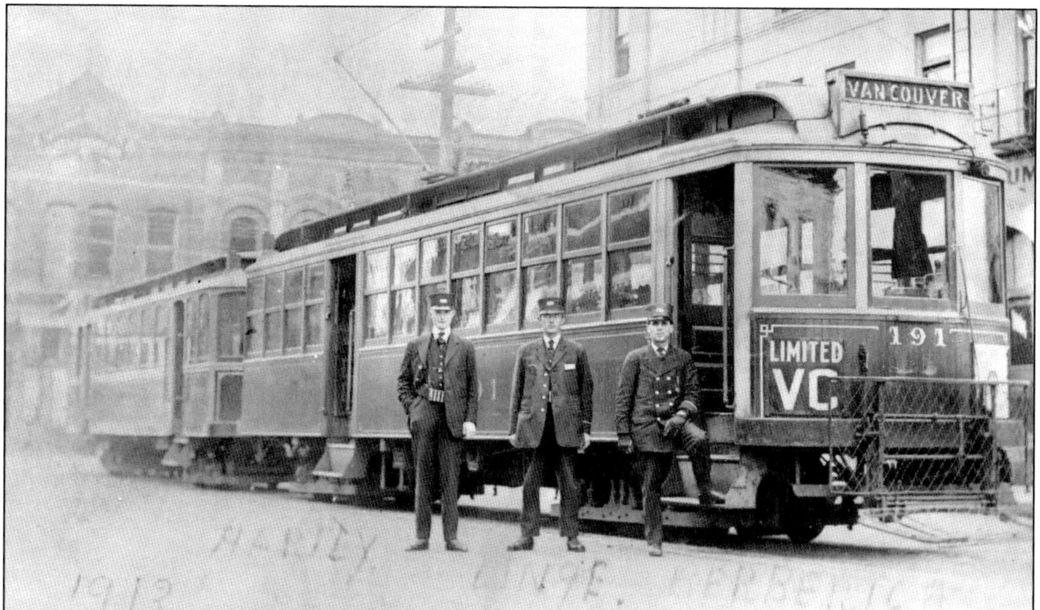

Conductors Fred Hartley (left), Linge (center), and motorman Joseph Berberich pose with Vancouver Limited No. 191 and trailer at the Third and Main Street terminal in Vancouver. Limiteds made no stops south of Northeast Stafford Street. Until the 1920s, a typical Vancouver line train consisted of a 191 class *Vancouver* pulling a trailer. The *Vancouvers* were narrow-gauge combines when built in 1906, but their freight compartments were used mainly by smokers.

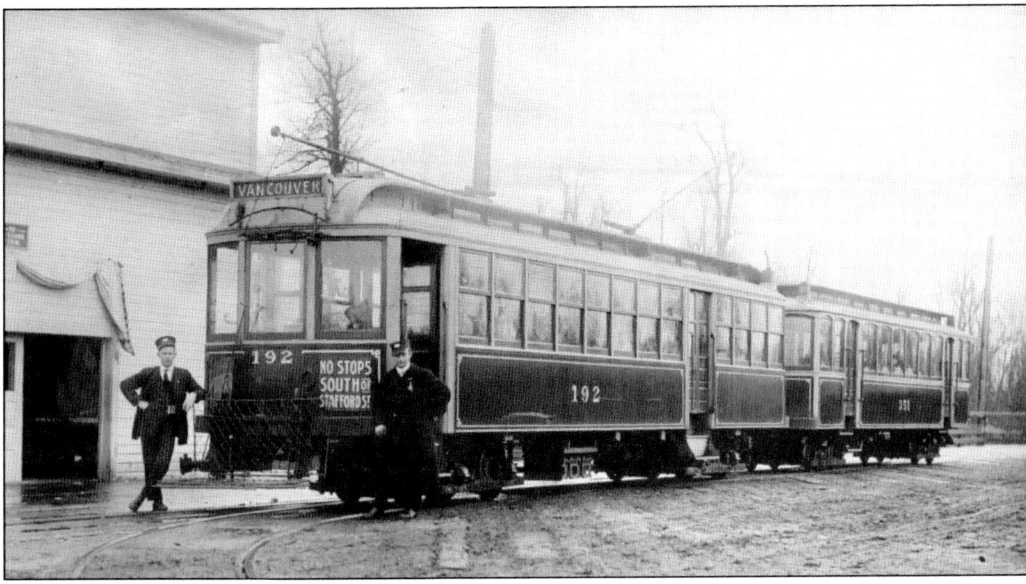

Car No. 192 and trailer 351 are waiting at Hayden Island Station on the Vancouver line. The sign on the station reads "To Vancouver 0.7 m." This stopping point offered a lunch counter. It is interesting to note that these interurban cars feature marker lights and a roof-mounted air whistle.

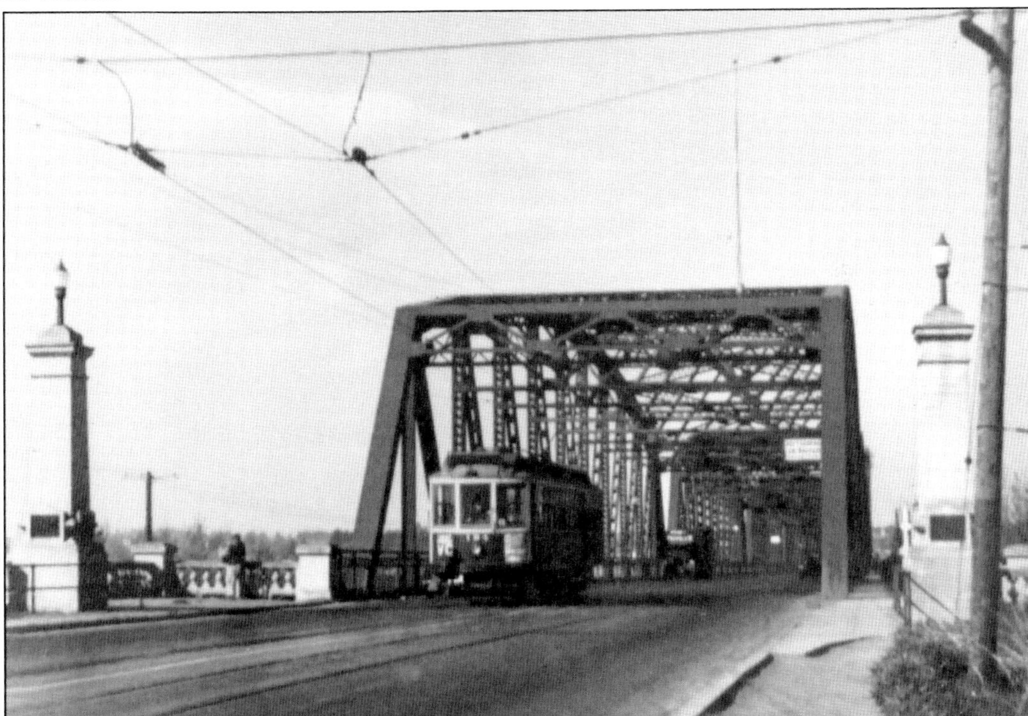

Vancouver line car No. 194 is crossing the lightly traveled Interstate Bridge during the 1930s. By this time, the 5¢ bridge toll had been dropped. The steel truss bridge was designed by the firm of Waddell and Harrington in Kansas City, Missouri, in 1915 and built in 1917. Multnomah County Oregon and Clark County Washington issued bridge construction bonds.

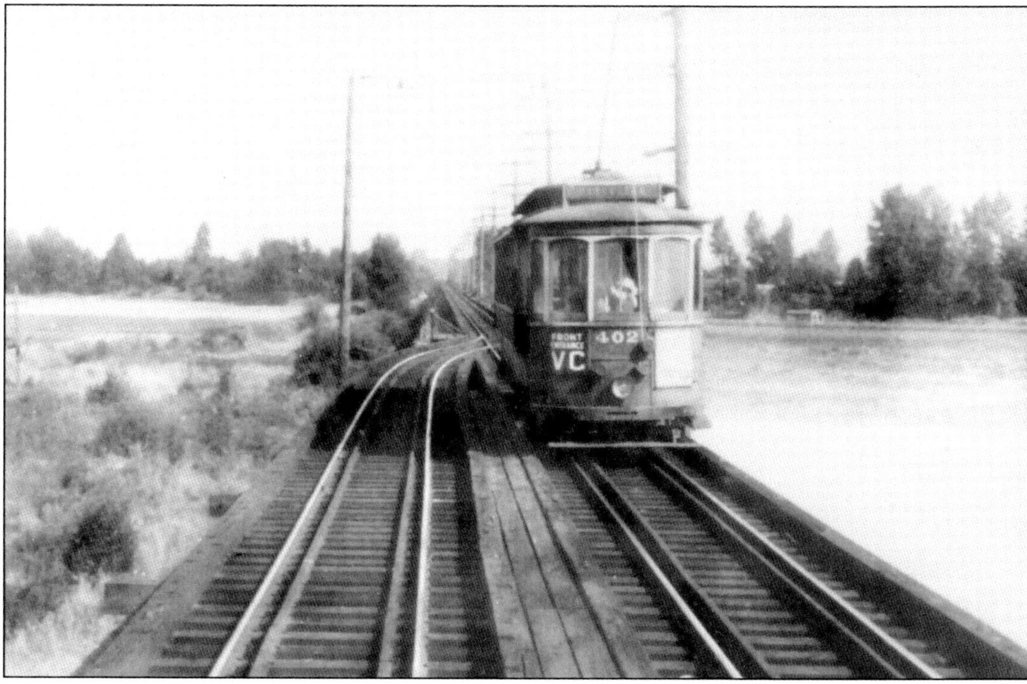

Vancouver line No. 402 zips past the passing track on the trestle near North Columbia Boulevard in the late 1930s. This car was from a group of 40 purchased from the American Car Company in 1907 and mainly run in two-car multiple-unit trains. In 1925, these trolleys were upgraded with two additional motors, but excessive platform overhang and soft springs gave them a rough ride.

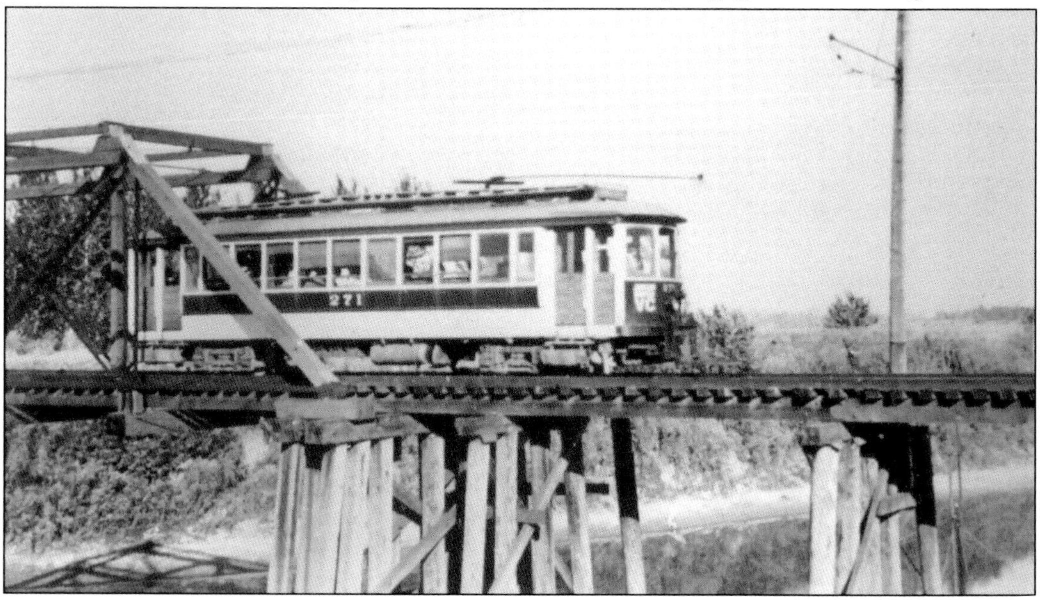

Vancouver car No. 271 is crossing the trestle parallel to and just east of Northeast Union Avenue near Faloma Station on the Vancouver line. According to a great-great grandson of Mr. Love, the station's name was derived from the first two letters of the last names of three landowners in the vicinity: Captain Farnsworth, who piloted the riverboat *Calliope*; Captain Lewis Love, also a river pilot; and steamboat engineer Maier.

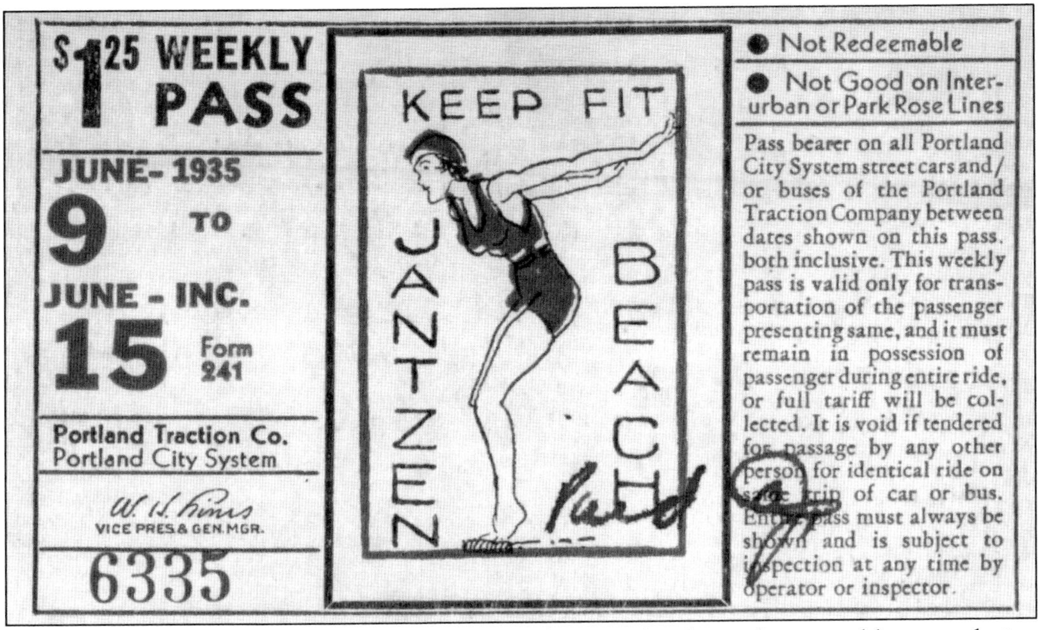

Advertisements for Jantzen Beach Amusement Park were a familiar sight on weekly passes during summertime in the 1930s. The traction company enthused, "Vancouver cars will take you within a short distance of the park entrance." The 123-acre park on Hayden Island was heralded as a million dollar playground when Jantzen Woolen Mills opened it on May 26, 1928. It closed on Labor Day 1970 after years of dwindling revenues.

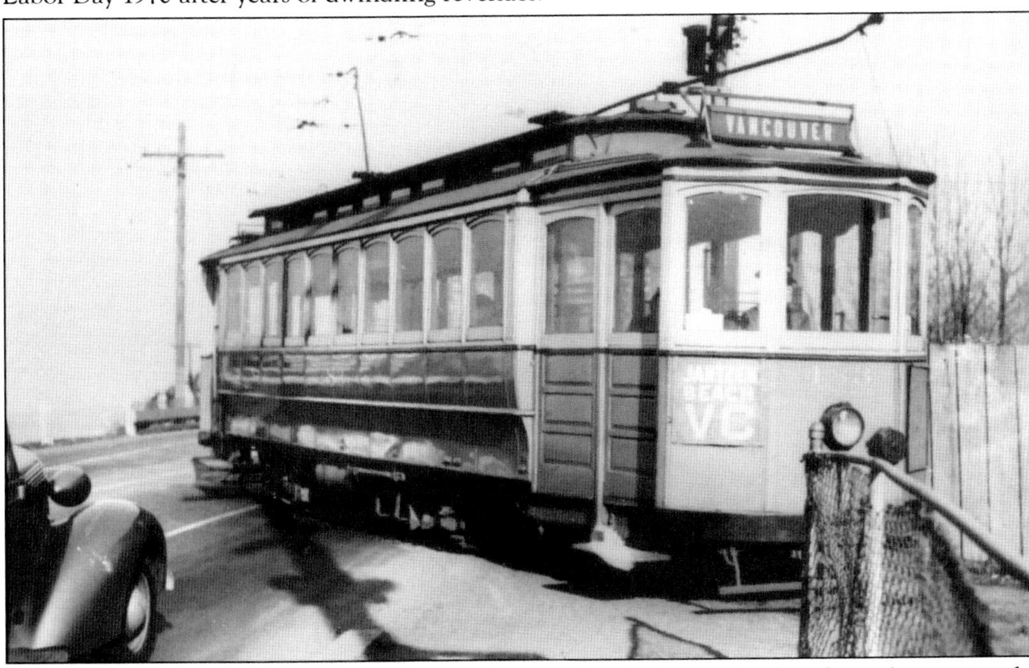

Highway traffic waits as No. 483 pulls into Jantzen Beach during the last days of operation for the Vancouver line. The trolley appears to have recently received a new coat of green and cream paint, which may be one reason that this car was saved for possible operation on other lines when Vancouver line streetcars stopped running September 3, 1940.

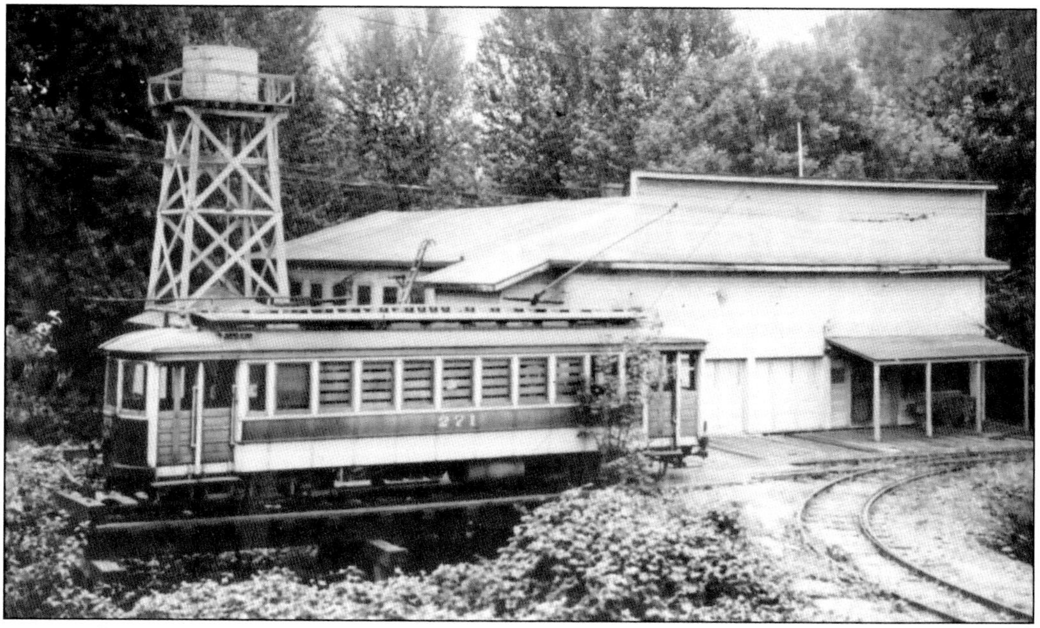

In 1939, former Council Crest open car No. 271 was briefly saved from the scrapper's torch when it was remodeled as a trestle repair car (note the boarded windows). It was kept on a spur next to the old Hayden Island station on the island loop. This building had ceased being a station and lunch counter after the Interstate Bridge opened in 1917. The track on the right led to the Interstate Bridge.

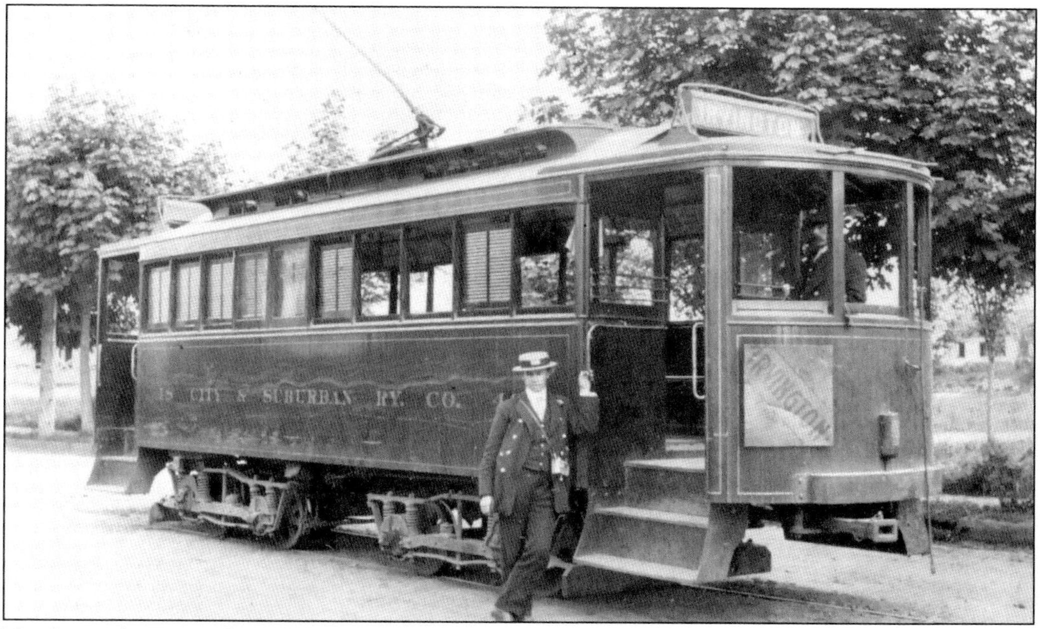

Not long after it was built from spliced horsecars in 1901, City and Suburban Railway car No. 48 is seen at the northern end of the Irvington line on Northeast Fifteenth Avenue and Tillamook Street. The jaunty conductor is wearing a straw hat and has a portable fare register slung over his shoulder. New home construction is well under way along the Irvington line, which began running in 1890.

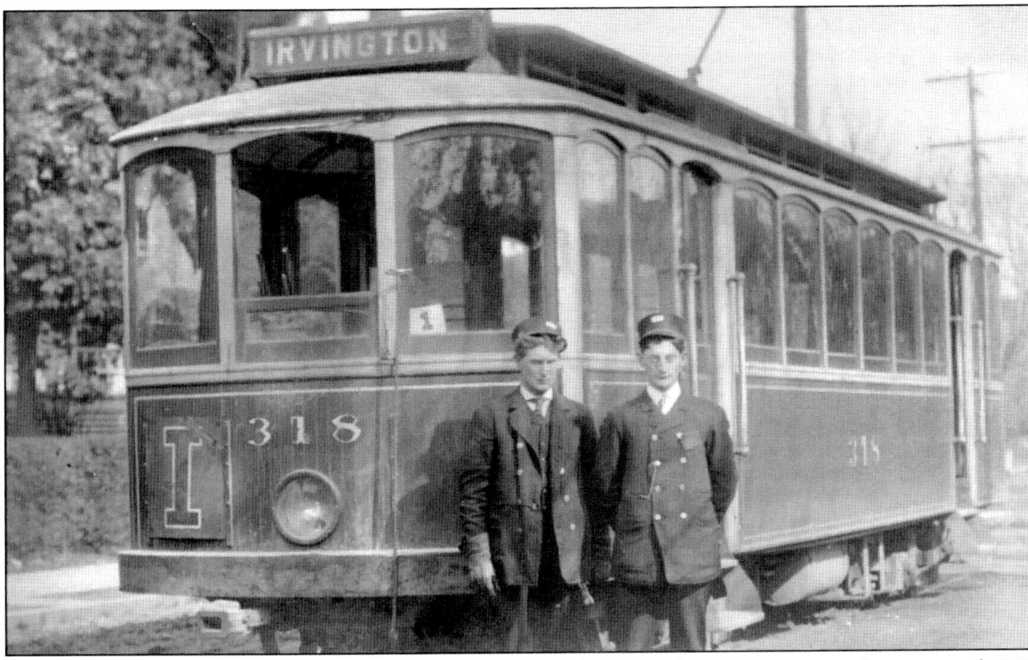

Fuller *Standard* No. 118 had been renumbered 318 by the time this picture was taken around 1911 at the end of the Irvington line on Northeast Fifteenth Avenue at Siskiyou Street. The neatly uniformed young PRL&P car men include a gloved motorman. (Courtesy Mark Moore.)

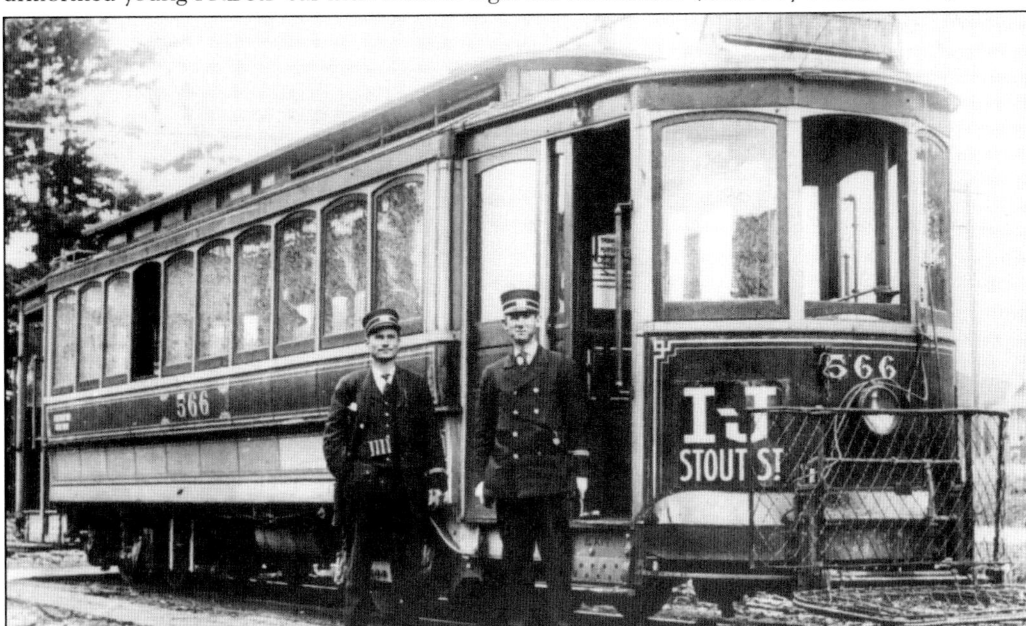

Nicely detailed Portland Railway, Light and Power car No. 566 is waiting for riders at the muddy new Northeast Fifteenth terminus in 1914. In February, the Irvington line was combined with the Jefferson Street line in Southwest Portland to form the Irvington-Jefferson line (IJ) operating via the Steel Bridge from Northeast Fifteenth Avenue and Prescott Street to Southwest Jefferson and Stout Streets, and also to Southwest Chapman and Mill Streets.

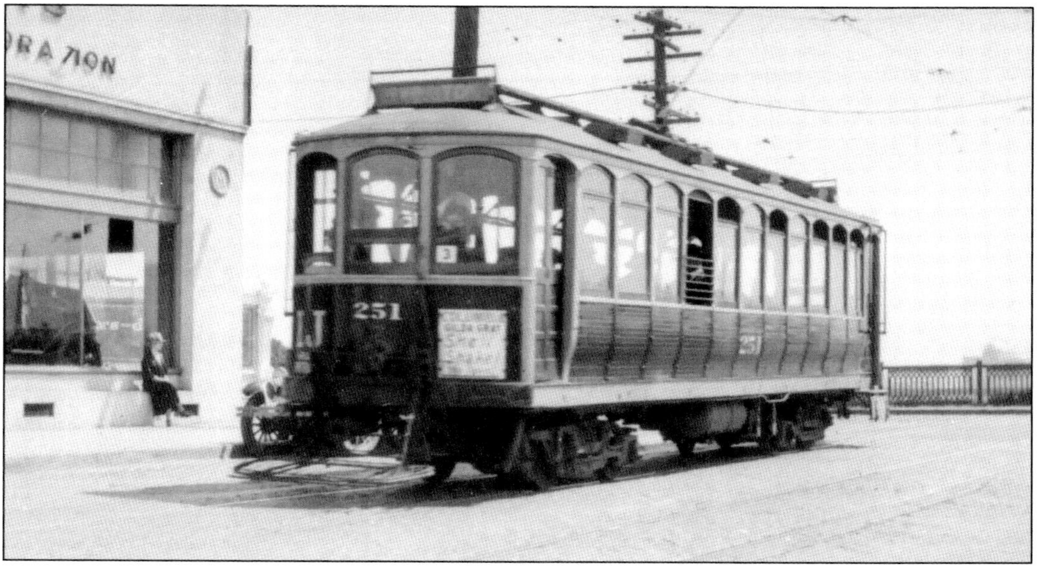

Irvington-Jefferson car No. 251 is turning onto North Williams at Oregon Street in 1925, having just crossed the Steel Bridge. No. 251 was originally a center aisle open car built by the first Portland Railway Company in 1901. The 10 cars in this class continued to be known as "pneumonia cars" after the hasty 1919 conversion to closed cars left them without bulkheads or heaters.

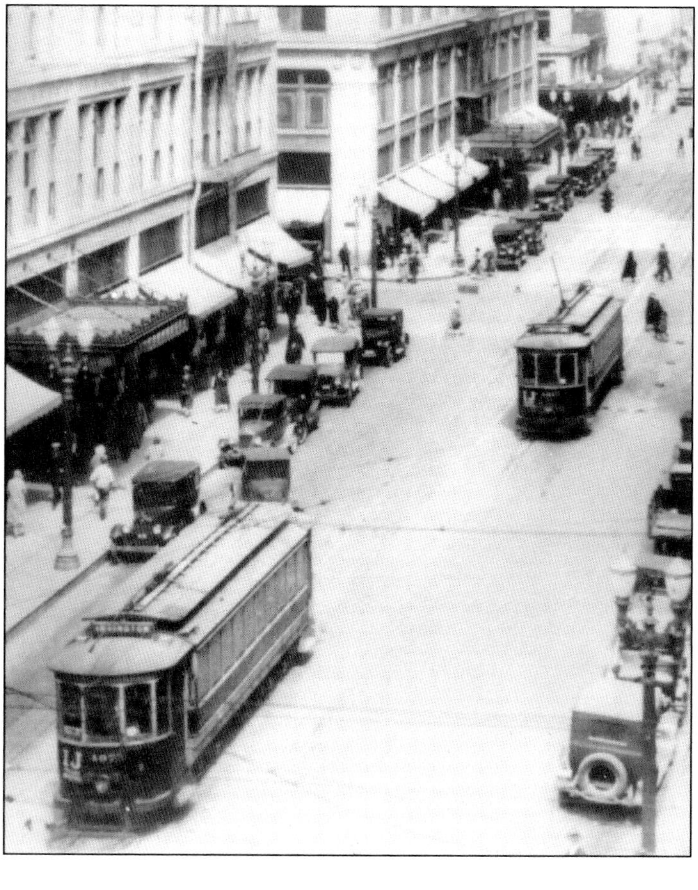

Irvington-Jefferson car Nos. 406 and 407 pass on Southwest Fifth Avenue at Alder Street in downtown Portland in 1926. Until 1928, the IJ line had two western terminals: one at Southwest Chapman (now Eighteenth Avenue) and Mill Streets and another at Southwest Jefferson and Stout Streets (now Twentieth Avenue). In 1933, Portland Traction Company removed the Jefferson Street portion of the route. The Meier and Frank and Lipman Wolfe department stores are in the background.

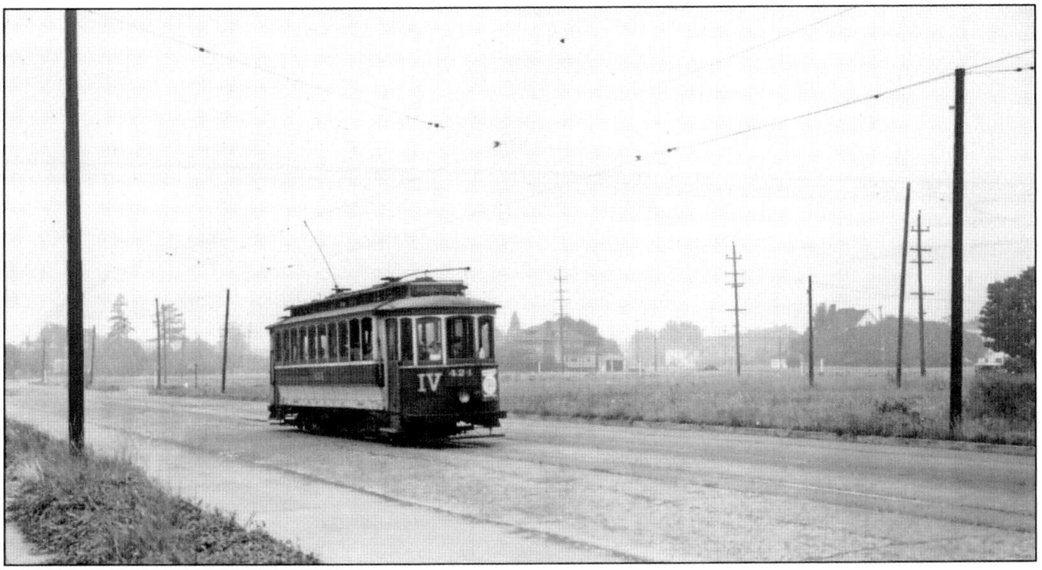

No. 424 is eastbound on the line once more called Irvington on Northeast Multnomah near Northeast Fifteenth Avenue during the early 1930s. Today this location would be in the middle of the Lloyd Center. Between 1923 and 1933, Ralph Lloyd acquired most of Holladay's Addition for his proposed Eastside Civic Center; however, the Depression intervened, and the property remained vacant until Lloyd Center was built in 1960.

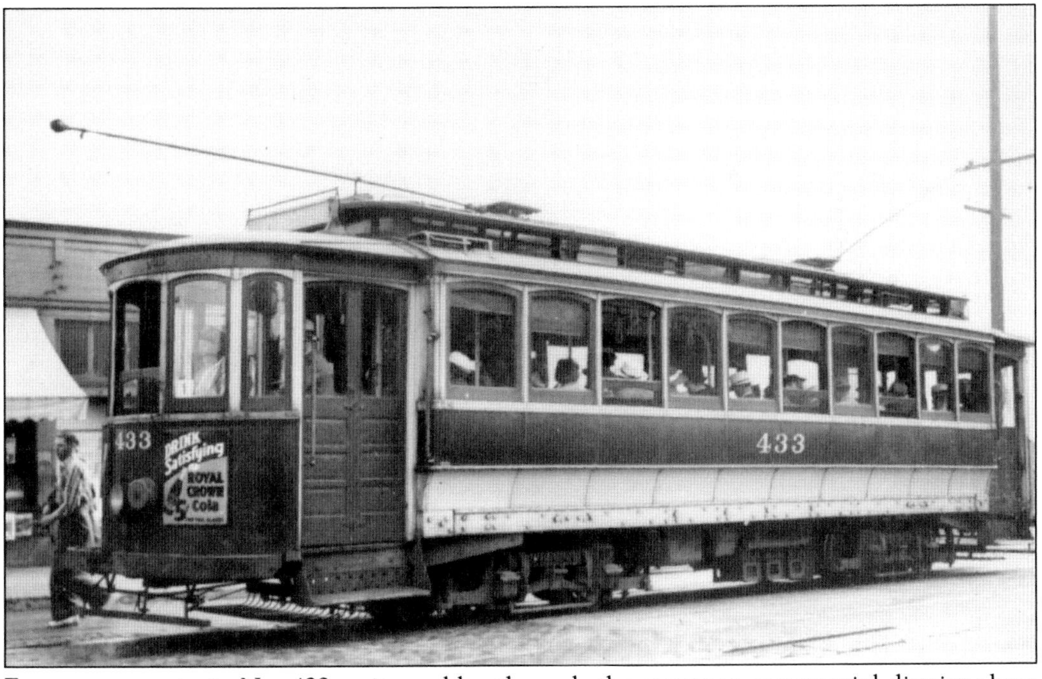

Few seats remain in No. 433 as it rumbles through the streetcar commercial district along Northeast Fifteenth Avenue near Broadway during the Great Depression. It may be rush hour, or perhaps this veteran Irvington line trolley is crowded with Sunday churchgoers. The Irvington line converted to gas bus in 1940.

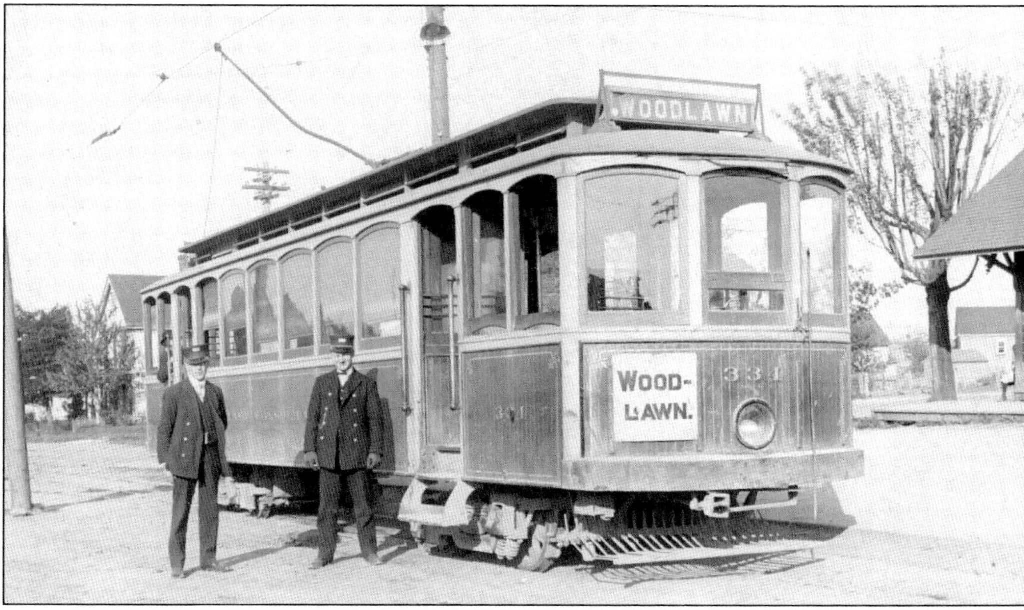

Portland Consolidated Railway No. 334 is waiting by Woodlawn Station on what is now Northeast Dekum Street and Seventh Avenue about 1904. Trolley service to this point was inaugurated in 1900 and extended to Northeast Thirteenth Avenue in 1912 and to Twenty-fourth Avenue in 1913. The Portland and Vancouver Railway built ornate stations at Woodlawn and at the Vancouver ferry landing for its steam motor line in 1888. (Courtesy Mark Moore.)

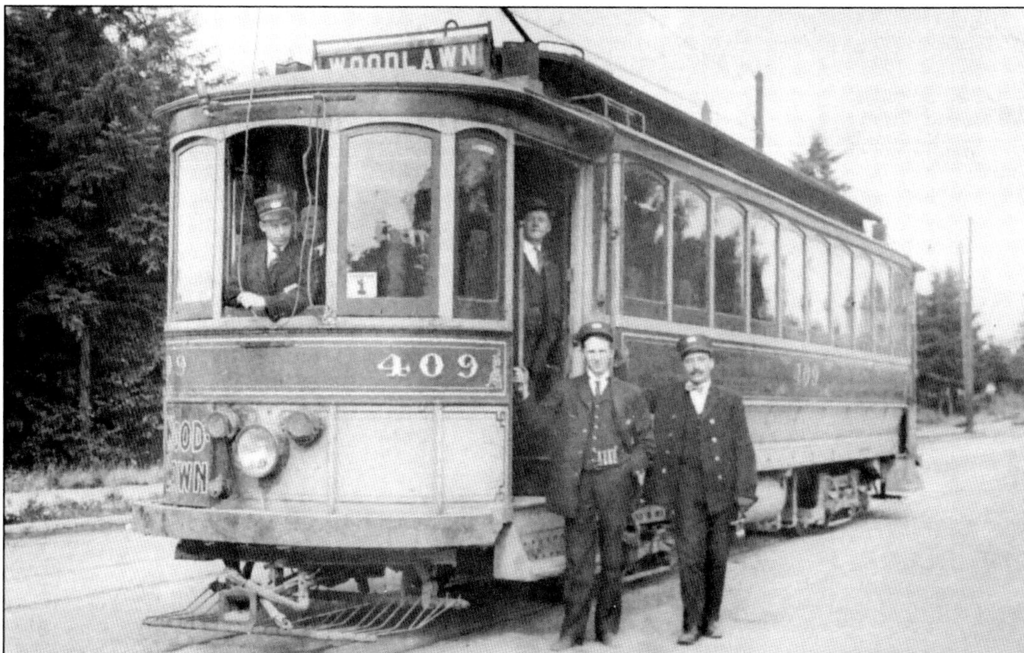

Car No. 409 is lying over at the new eastern terminus of the Woodlawn line at Northeast Thirteenth Avenue and Dekum Street around 1912 with too many crewmen. The conductor is Mr. Trout; the motorman (holding the controller handle) is not identified. Perhaps the third car man (with the trolley rope in hand) is riding to work at the Piedmont carbarn.

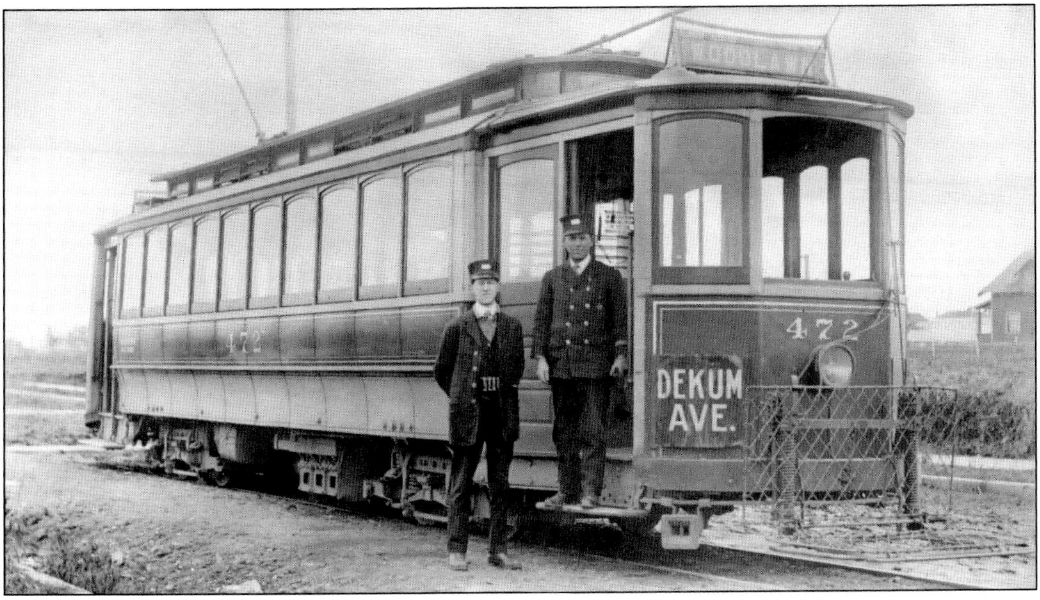

Conductor George Race and motorman Carleton Walker pose with No. 472 at the final terminus of the Woodlawn line on Northeast Dekum Street at Twenty-fourth Avenue around 1913. In 1934, after Portland car lines had been converted to one-man operation, a motorman was robbed while changing ends here. His two armed assailants escaped in a stolen automobile with $11. Three years later, Woodlawn became a bus line.

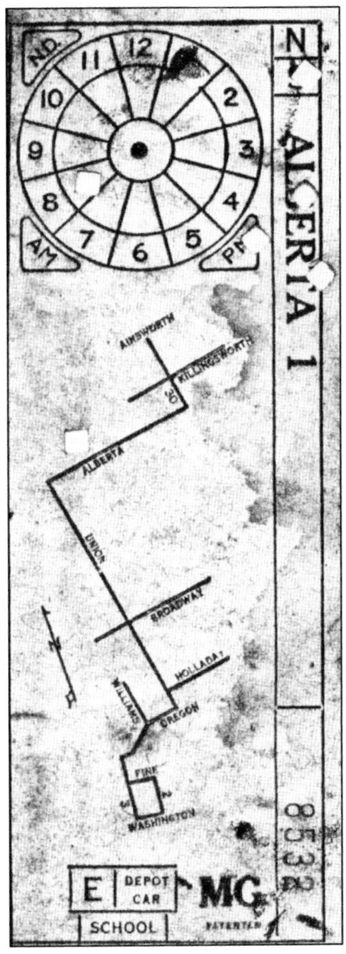

Portland Railway opened the Alberta line as a branch on Northeast Alberta Street from Northeast Union (now MLK Boulevard) to Twenty-second Avenue on July 19, 1905. In June 1908, an extension was built to Northeast Thirtieth Avenue, and in March 1909, a final leg was completed to Ainsworth Street. The route remained essentially the same over the years, except during bridge construction. Streetcar operation was discontinued August 1, 1948.

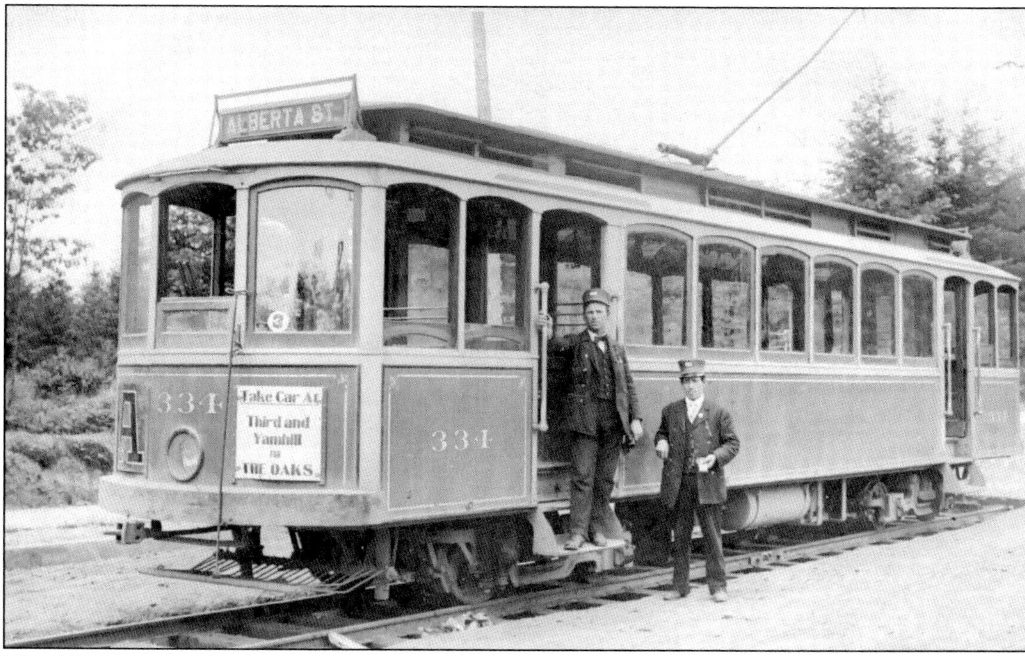

The Alberta Street line served the Vernon neighborhood, which is centered on Northeast Fifteenth Avenue between Northeast Alberta and Ainsworth Streets. No. 334 appears to be at the original Vernon end of the line on Northeast Alberta Street and Twenty-fourth Avenue about 1907. The dash sign encourages riders to "Take Car At Third and Yamhill for THE OAKS" amusement park. (Courtesy Mark Moore.)

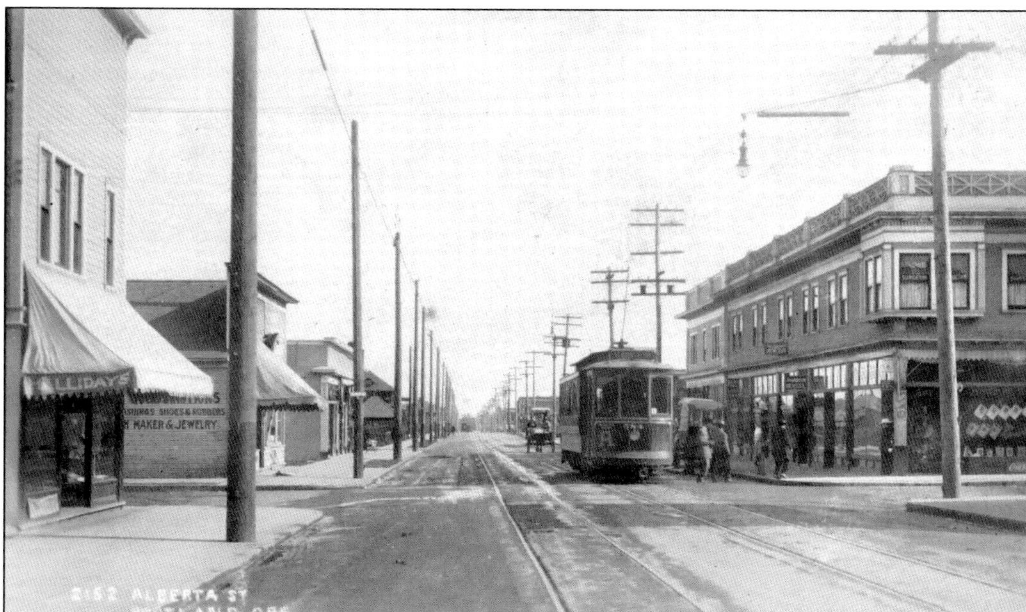

This postcard shows Alberta Street line No. 584 in the Vernon commercial district on Northeast Alberta Street at Seventeenth Avenue about 1912. Businesses in view include Halliday's market, a jewelry store, a boot maker, Alberta Realty, Vernon Drug, Vernon Social Club, a dentist, a doctor, a pool hall, a lunch counter, and a grocery store.

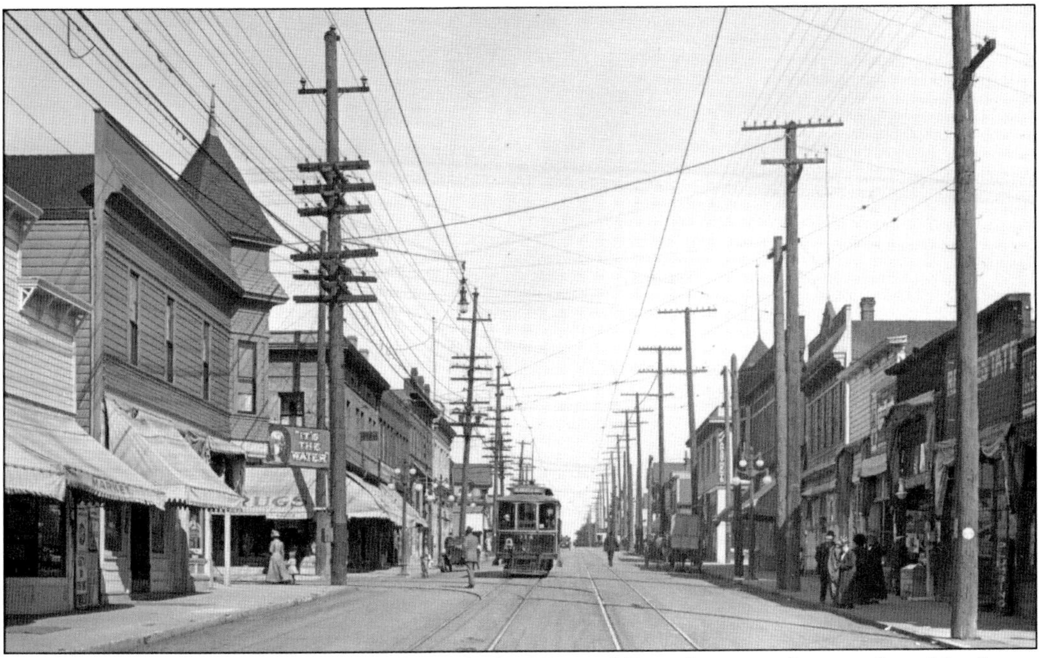

Alberta car No. 314 is rolling south through the Upper Albina business district along Northeast Union Avenue (now MLK Boulevard) at Northeast Russell Street on a sunny morning in the early 1910s. On the left are Russell Drugs, which housed physician and dentist offices, and a turreted building sporting an illuminated Olympia Beer sign. On the other side of the street are a realtor, bicycle shop, plumber, news dealer, and apartments.

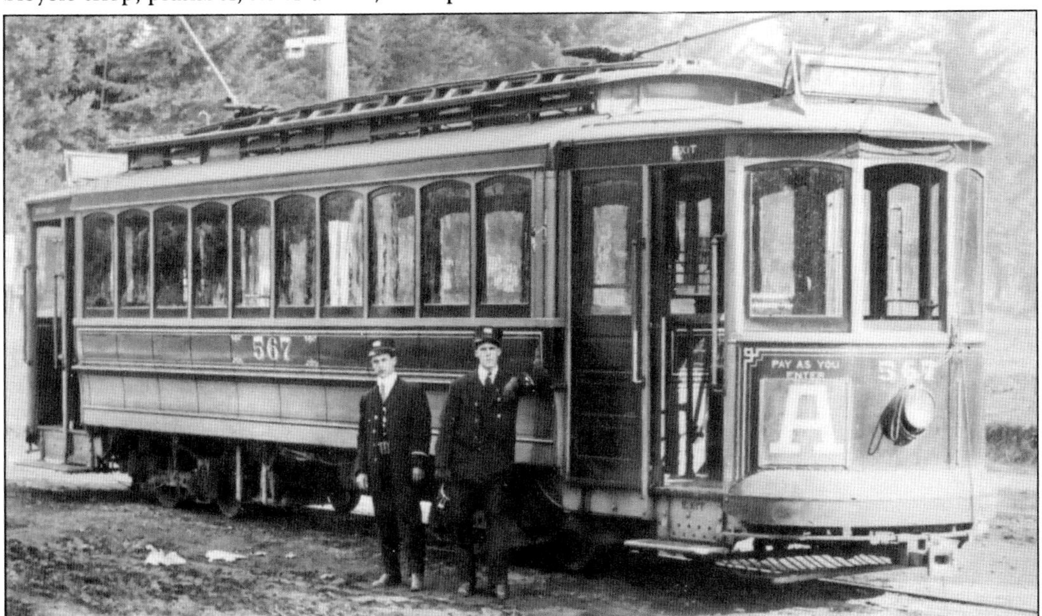

No. 567 is lying over at the undeveloped northern end of the Alberta line at Northeast Thirtieth Avenue and Ainsworth Street about 1912. The crew consists of conductor Hall and motorman John Lentz. Their car was less than two years old when this picture was taken and still sports the beautiful pinstripes applied by American Car Company craftsmen in St. Louis, Missouri.

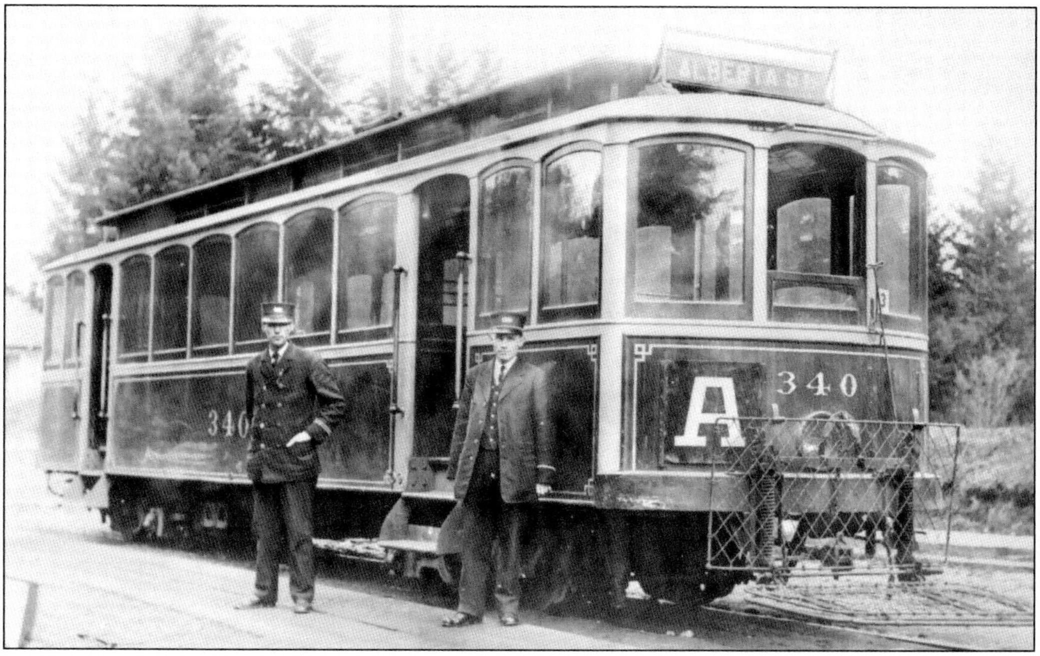

Motorman Clyde Graham and conductor Charles Dahlen are standing next to Alberta Street line car No. 340 at the northern terminus on Northeast Thirtieth Avenue and Ainsworth Street in 1913. During the next decade, these Fuller *Standard* cars would be replaced by newer equipment on most lines. Final retirement for the locally designed series came in 1933.

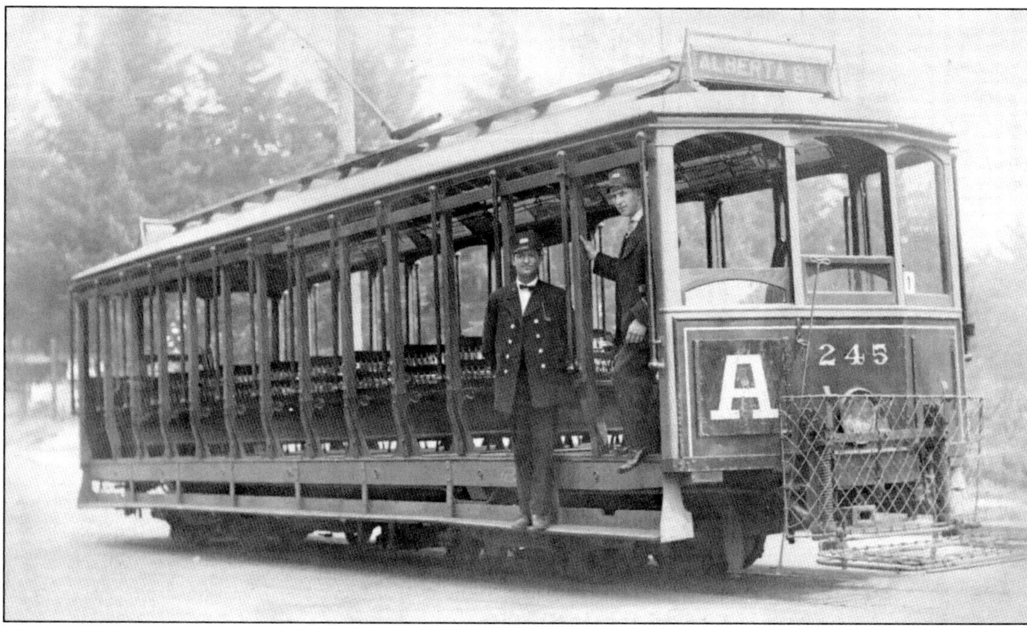

The neighborhood is still young in this 1913 view at the end of the Alberta line on Northeast Thirtieth and Ainsworth Streets. Crewmen Harry Bloom and one of the Lecuyer brothers have changed ends on their handsome center aisle open car. No. 245 was one of a series of cars from the Portland Railway shops that gained national attention when featured in a 1904 *Street Railway Journal* article.

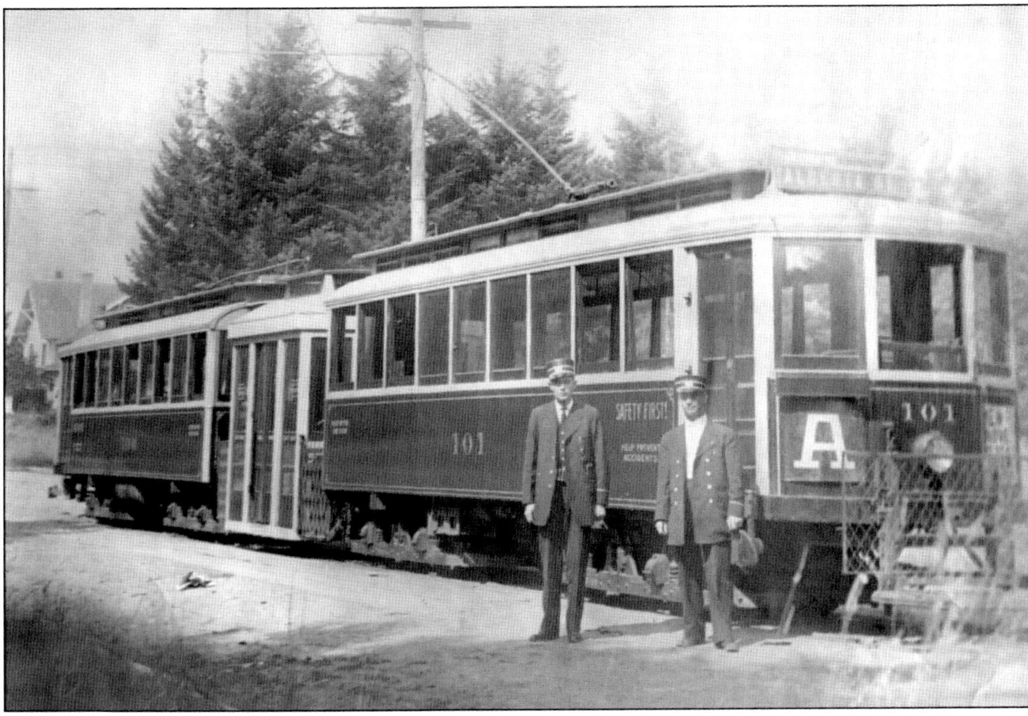

Articulated car No. 100–101 is at Northeast Thirtieth Avenue and Ainsworth Street during its single year of service on the Alberta line in 1914. PRL&P's articulated car was nicknamed "The Dragon." One platform on each car was replaced by a conductor's cab through which passengers entered and exited. The experimental unit became one of a kind after slow boarding and acceleration soured management on the idea of center entrance cars in general.

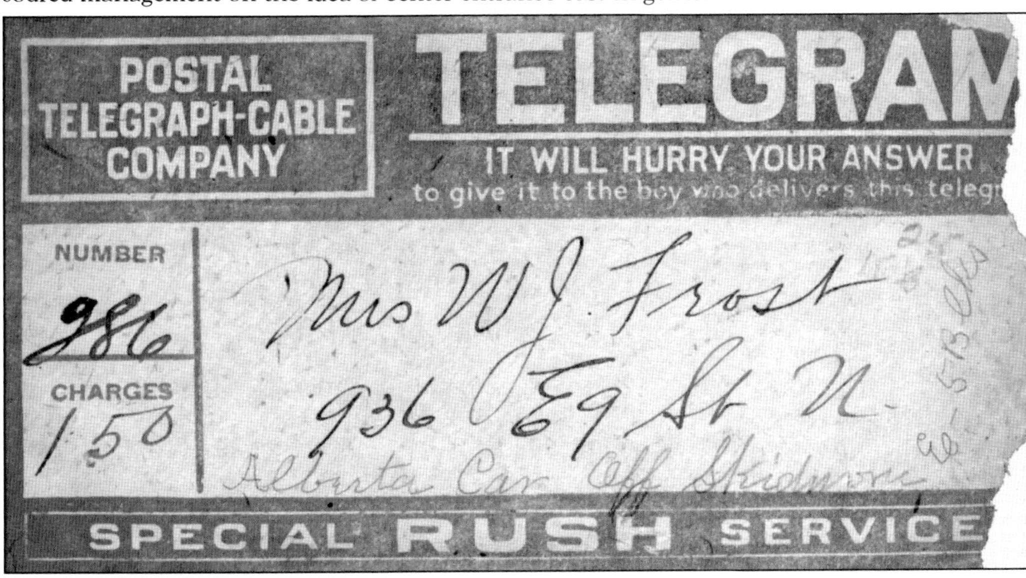

In an era when they delivered telegrams, streetcars were a vital part of the communication system. This 1919 Postal Telegraph Company special rush message from Boston, Massachusetts, went to its North Portland destination via an Alberta line trolley, as per the directions penciled beneath the address: "Alberta Car Off Skidmore, E–5 blks."

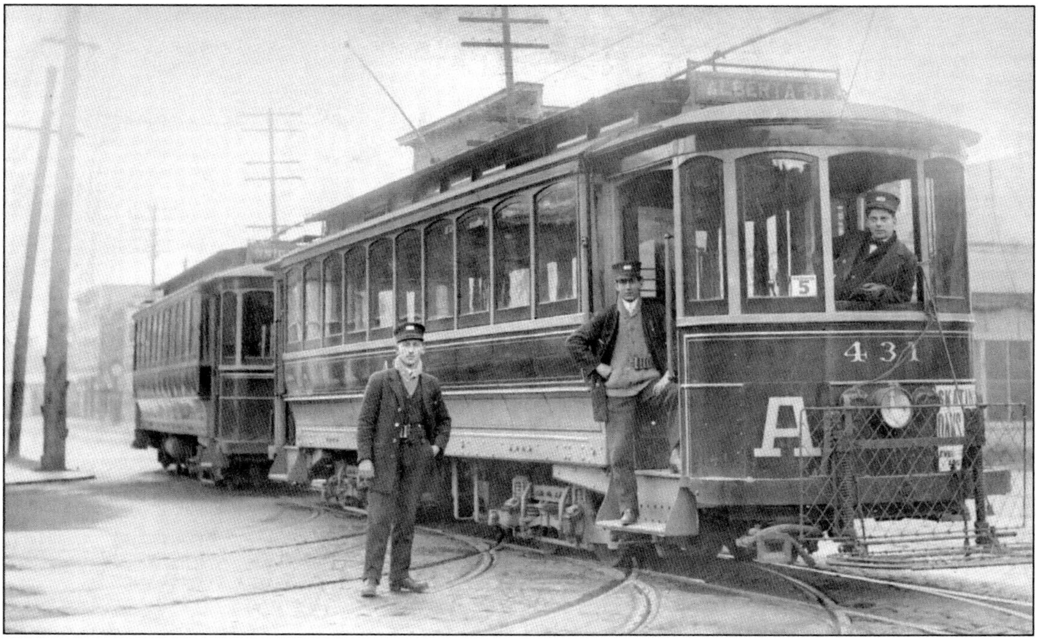

Two Alberta Street line trolleys appear to be lined up for multiple-unit operation near the Piedmont carbarn on North Killingsworth Street. The No. 400s operated in pairs on the St. Johns and Vancouver lines but were generally operated singly elsewhere. During the 1910s, they were also assigned to Mount Tabor, Sunnyside, Alberta, and Woodlawn. The second car's sign reads, "Union Avenue," a tripper service on the Alberta run.

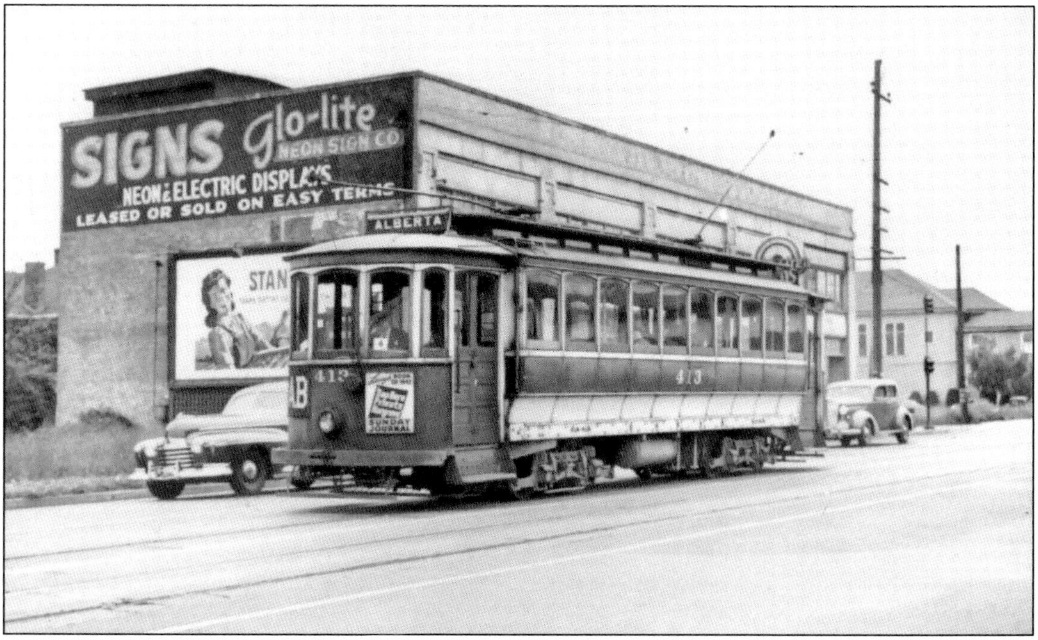

Inbound Alberta line car No. 413 is on Northeast Union Avenue (now MLK Boulevard) between Northeast Wasco Street and Multnomah Boulevard passing in front of a sign for the Glo-lite Neon Sign Company. Glo-lite had gone out of business by the time this picture was taken in 1942. After World War II, it seemed that both neon signs and streetcars would go the way of the dinosaur.

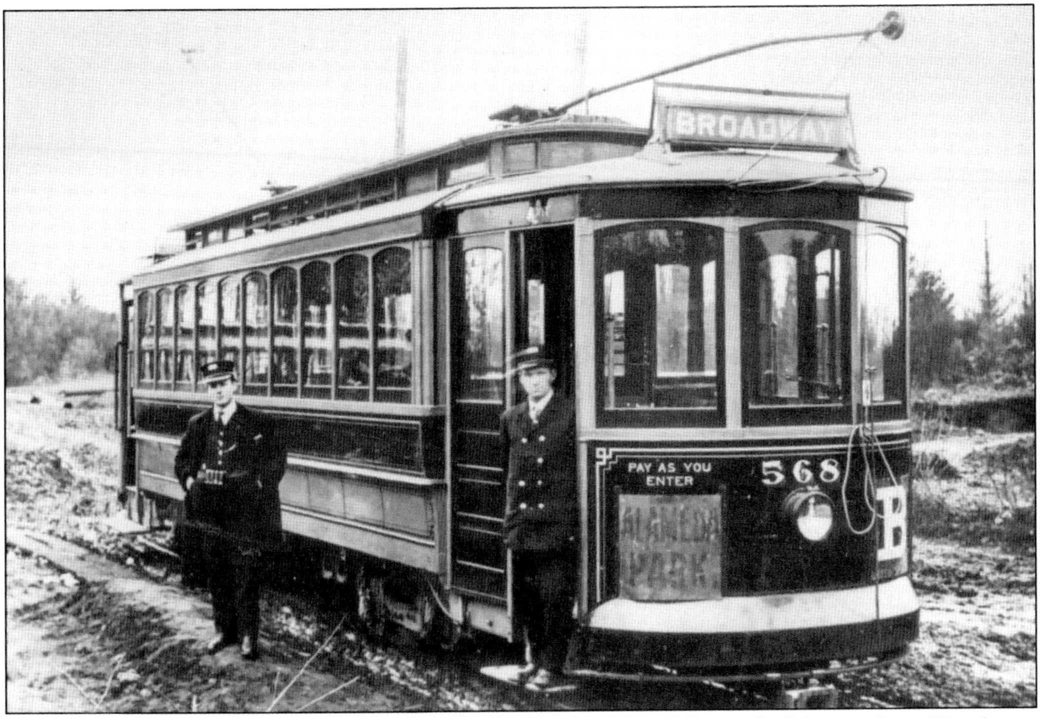

The Broadway Line began in 1903. Brand-new car No. 568 is at the end of the track on Northeast Twenty-ninth Avenue and Mason Street in a still-fresh Alameda Park around 1911. In February 1910, the Broadway line reached its northernmost terminus in an effort to develop real estate. Development quickened after the completion of the Broadway Bridge in 1913.

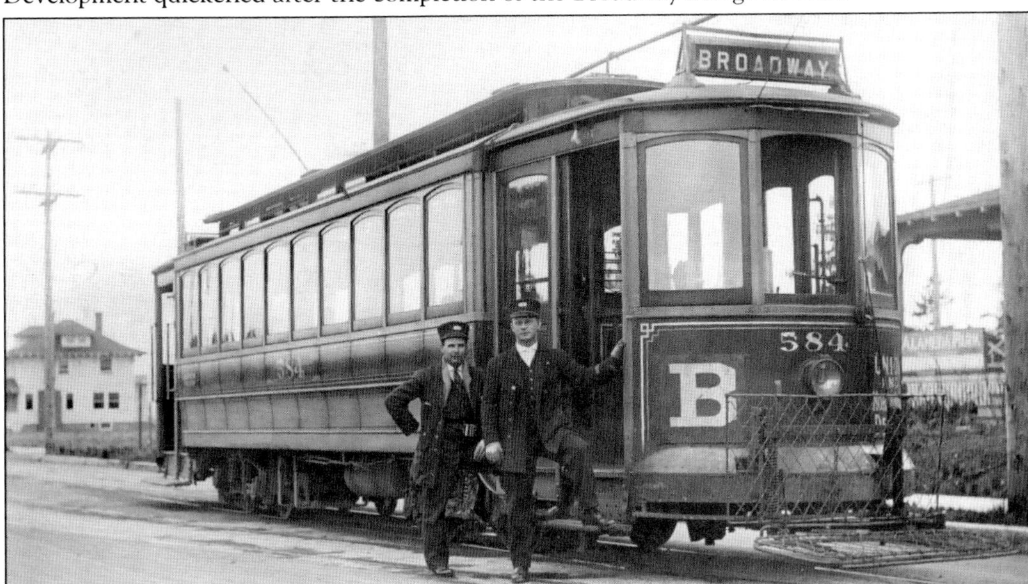

Everett Prichard and Guy Rinehart pose with No. 584 about 1913. Their *Broadway* line car is waiting in front of the Alameda Park Tract Office at the Northeast Twenty-ninth Avenue and Mason Street terminus. The partially obscured dash sign reading "Union and North Bank Depots" refers to the train stations in Northwest Portland.

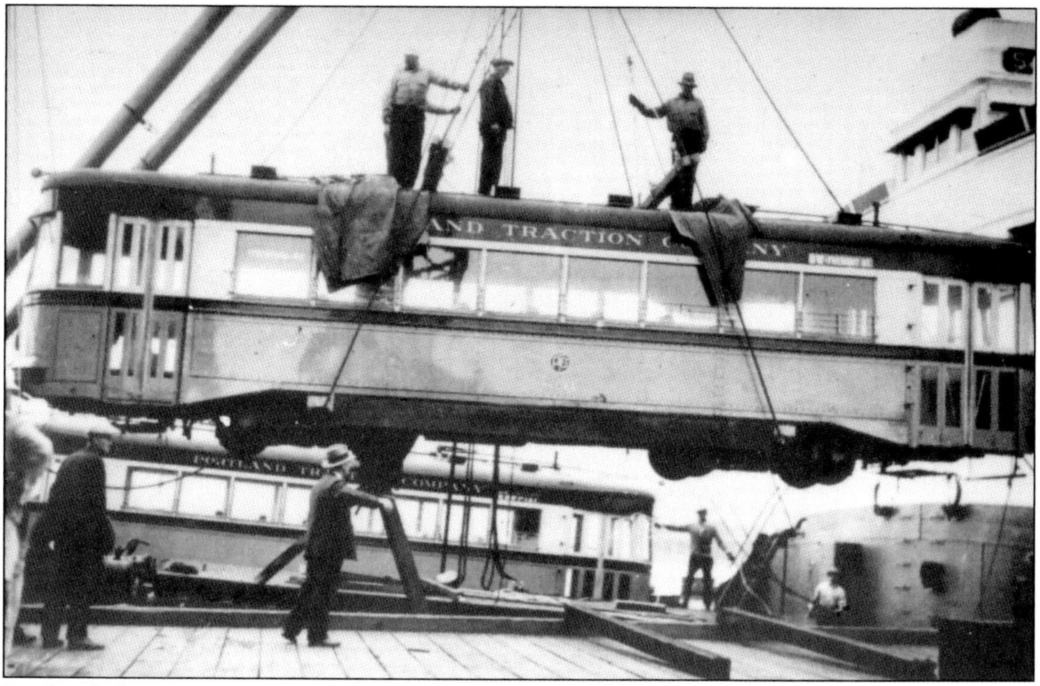

Portland's first new streetcars in 14 years, and, ironically, its last, arrived on April 30, 1932, aboard the steamship *San Clemente*. These handsome streamliners, which the press heralded as the "Newest Thing in Streetcars," wore the French grey, hunter green, and ivory livery of the new Portland Traction Company. As a result of their primary assignment on the Broadway line, they were soon nicknamed the "Broadways."

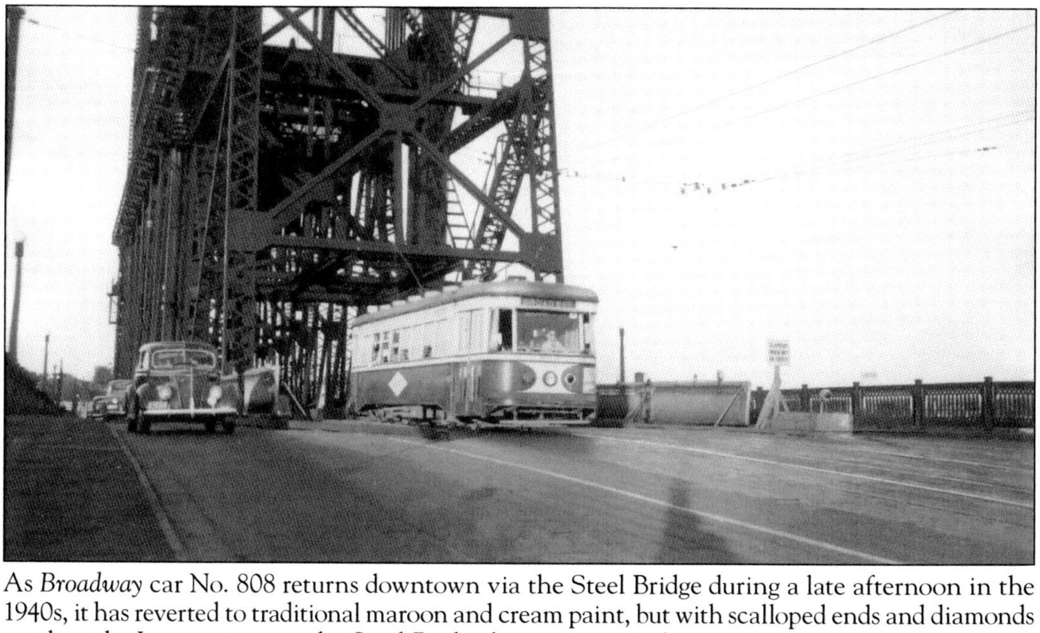

As *Broadway* car No. 808 returns downtown via the Steel Bridge during a late afternoon in the 1940s, it has reverted to traditional maroon and cream paint, but with scalloped ends and diamonds on the side. In recent years, the Steel Bridge has once again become a streetcar connection, as Tri-County Metropolitan Transportation District (Tri-Met) light rail trains and Vintage Trolley reproduction Council Crest cars roll across the river.

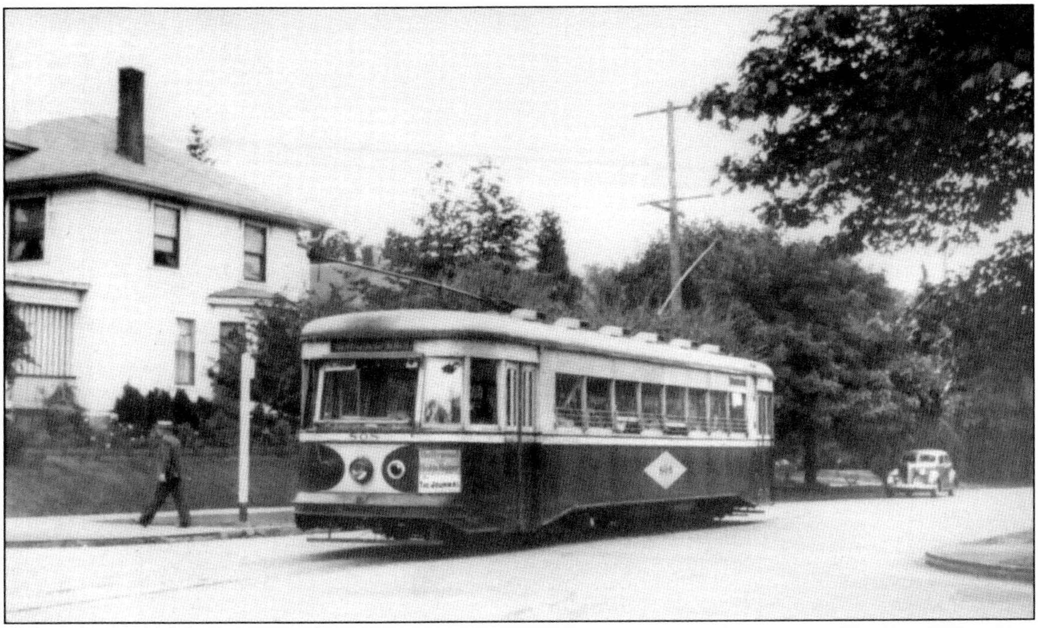

Broadway No. 808 has paused to let a gentleman cross a street in Irvington. Portland Traction Company claimed an 8.7% increase in revenue due to the higher speed, greater comfort, and improved appearance of the *Broadway* cars. A *Transit Journal* article reported more riders in spite of the fact that the Broadway line connected downtown with "a high class residential district where most families have at least one automobile."

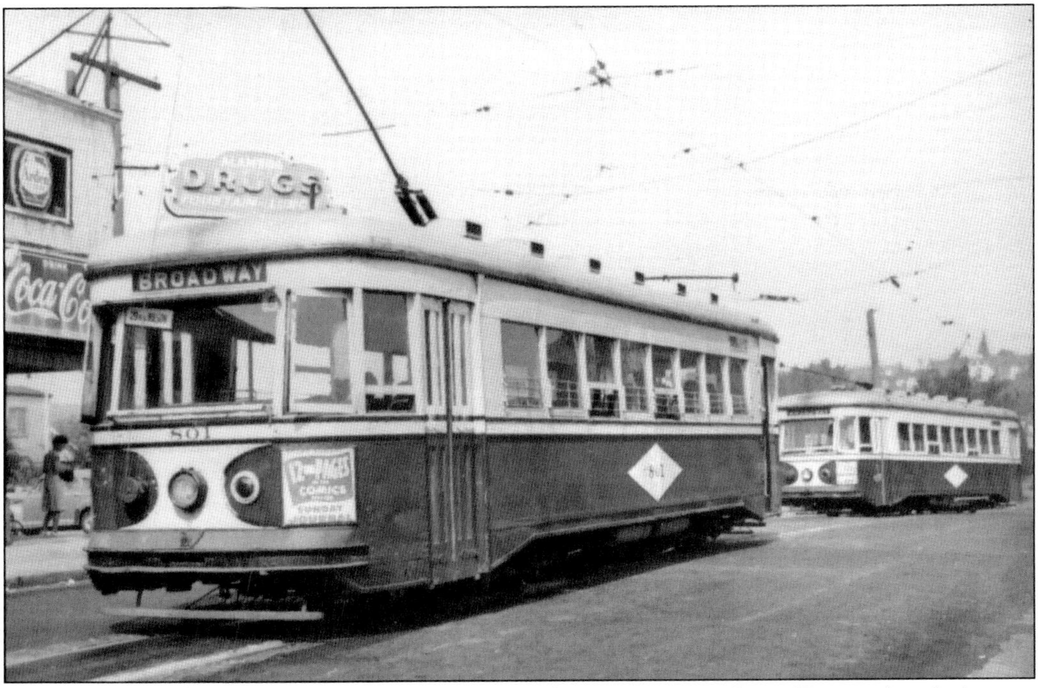

Outbound and inbound *Broadway* cars pass Alameda Drugs on Northeast Twenty-fourth Avenue and Fremont Street. Homes in Alameda can be seen on the hillside in the background. It is during the 1940s, when drugstores had fountains and lunch counters.

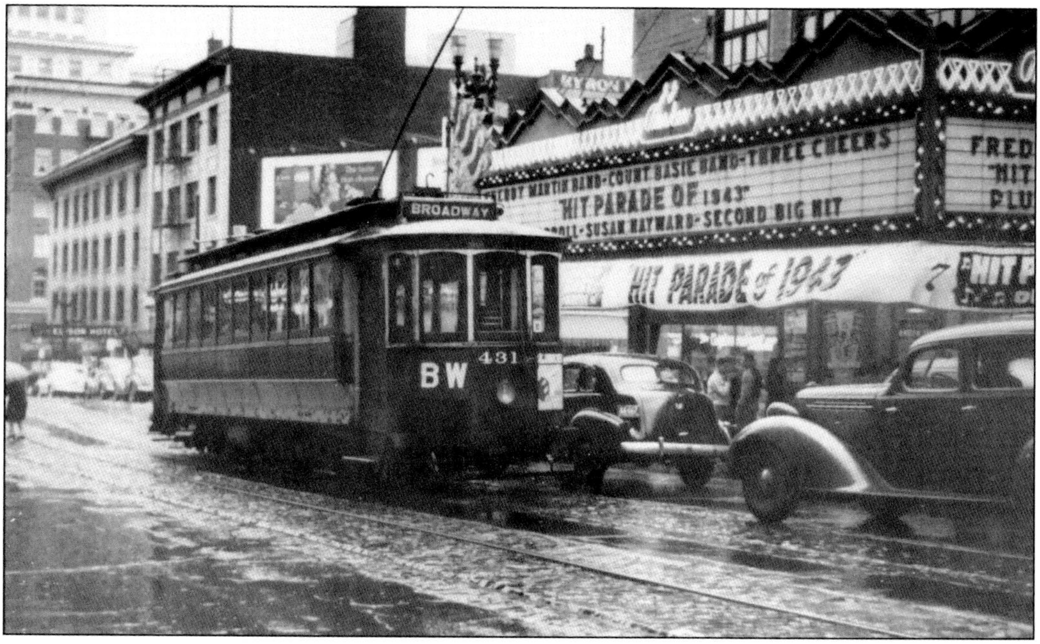

During World War II, every streetcar was needed, so the old wooden cars did not completely disappear from a Broadway line dominated by newer streamlined trolleys. An example is Broadway line tripper No. 431, seen trundling northward through a typical Portland downpour on Southwest Broadway and Salmon Street. The Broadway Theater is showing *Hit Parade of 1943*.

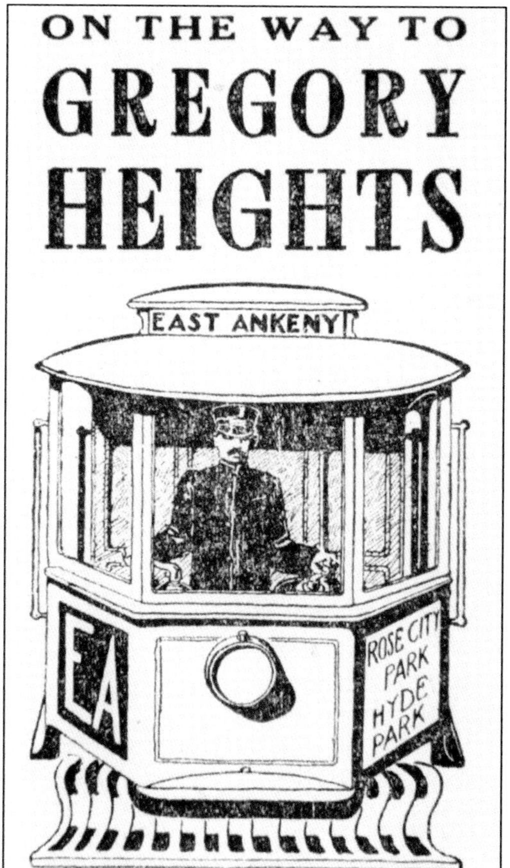

The line to Rose City Park began as an extension of the East Ankeny (EA) line around 1907 when EA had alternating terminals on Northeast Twenty-eighth Avenue at Sandy Boulevard and Northeast Glisan Street at Thirty-ninth Avenue. The Gregory Investment Company placed this drawing in a February 10, 1909, advertisement in the *Portland Telegram*. Their office was in Gregory Heights, a new development just east of Rose City Park.

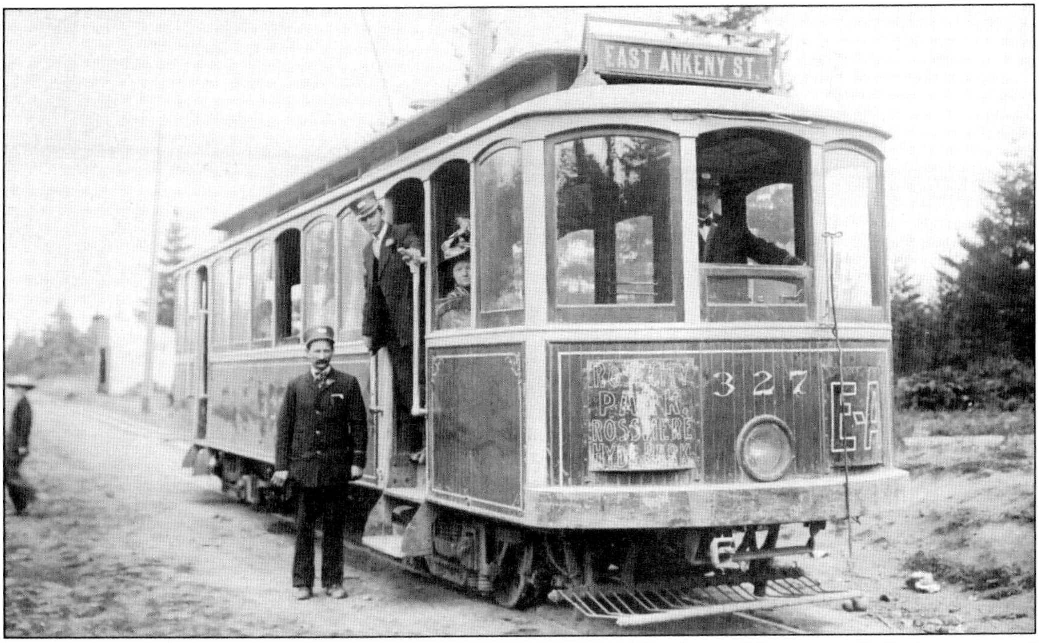

East Ankeny Street line No. 327 appears to be headed for Northeast Twenty-eighth Avenue and Sandy Boulevard in a picture taken in 1911. At that time, the line alternated between terminals on Northeast Twenty-eighth Avenue at Sandy Boulevard and Northeast Glisan Street at Thirty-ninth Avenue. The dash sign reading "Rose City Park, Rossmere and Hyde Park" refers to new tracts located on the north side of Sandy. (Courtesy Mark Moore).

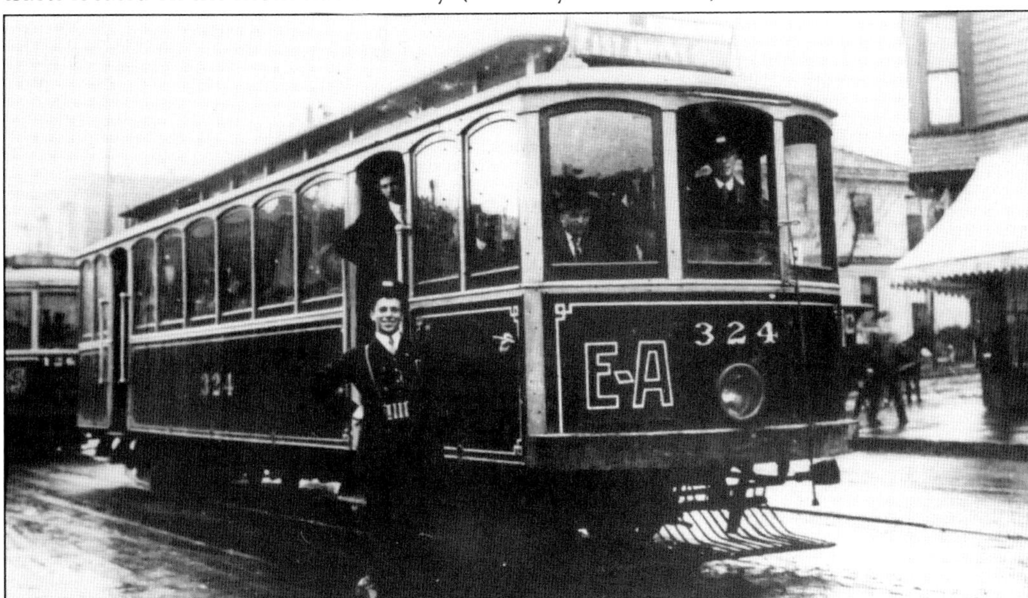

East Ankeny Street line PRL&P Fuller *Standard* No. 324 and Russell Shaver car No. 126 seem to be waiting on Southeast Grand Avenue near Ankeny Street in the 1910s. In October 1909, Russell Shaver cars took over part of the old East Side line and began running south on Grand Avenue to Southeast Hawthorne. East Ankeny line cars used Grand Avenue on their way to the Morrison Bridge.

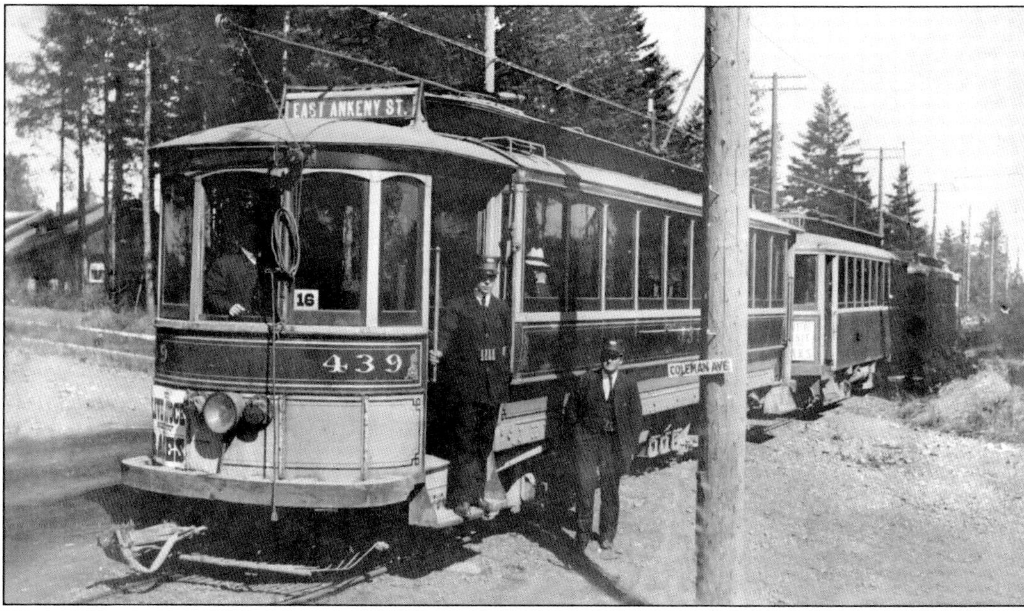

These East Ankeny/Rose City Park trolleys on Northeast Sandy Boulevard and Coleman Avenue (now Northeast Sixty-second) are waiting for passengers from the Portland Country Club racetrack. The track was used by horses, bicycles, and automobiles over the years. Last known as Rose City Speedway, it closed in 1926 to be replaced by Rose City Golf Course. From 1908–1914, it was served by a spur to Northeast Brazee Street.

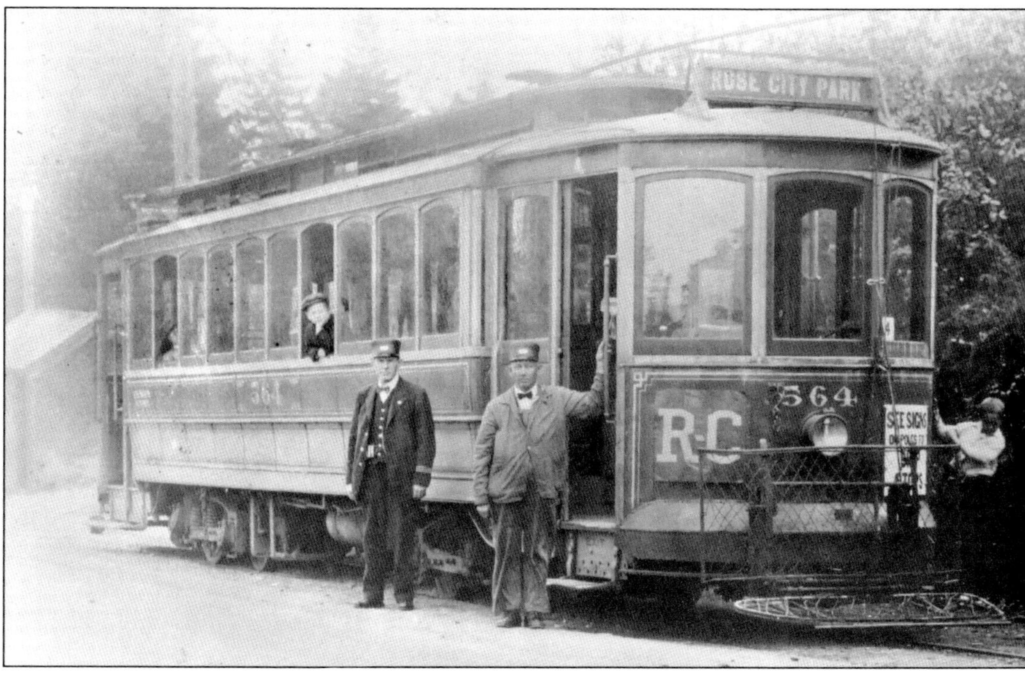

Rose City Park No. 564 is lying over at the eastern terminus of the line on Northeast Sandy Boulevard around 1917. While the crew strikes a serious pose, a young boy plays on the newly installed safety fender. The sign on the dash advising riders to "see signs on poles for skip stops" refers to a World War I conservation measure in which streetcars did not make all stops.

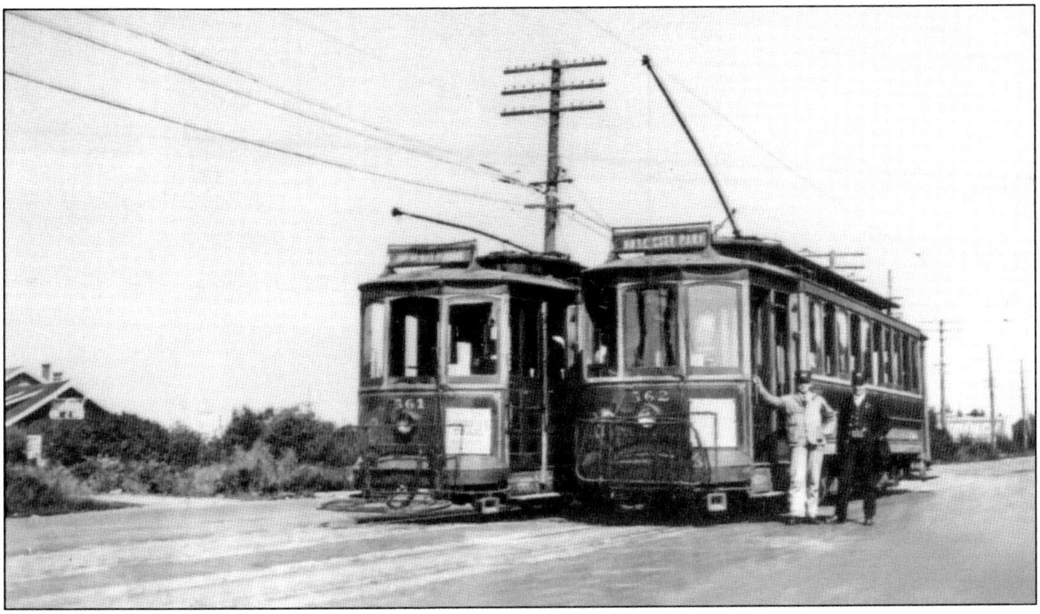

Inbound car No. 562 meets outbound car No. 561 at what appears to be the later eastern terminus of the Rose City (RC) Park line at Northeast Sandy Boulevard and Eighty-second Avenue. In 1912, the RC line was extended to this final eastern terminus. Note the motorman dressed like a railroad engineer.

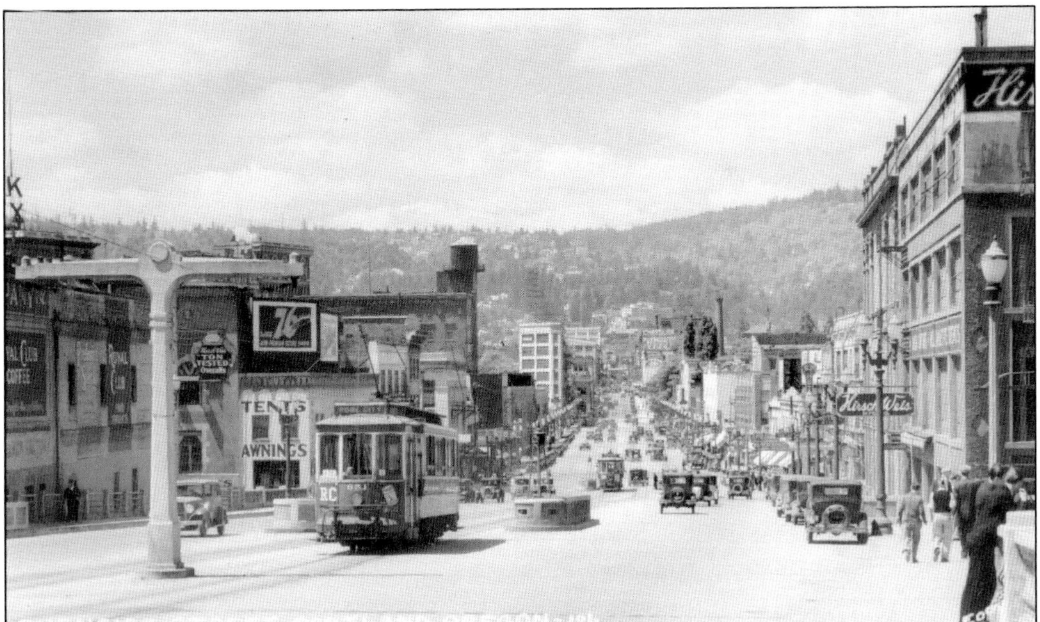

Rose City line car No. 651 heads down the west ramp of the Burnside Bridge around 1930. Rose City line streetcars will continue to operate for just six more years. The second Burnside Bridge was completed on May 28, 1926. It was the only Willamette River bridge in Portland to have been designed by an architect, and it originally included ornate concrete trolley poles. (Photograph by R. C. Eddy; courtesy Mark Moore.)

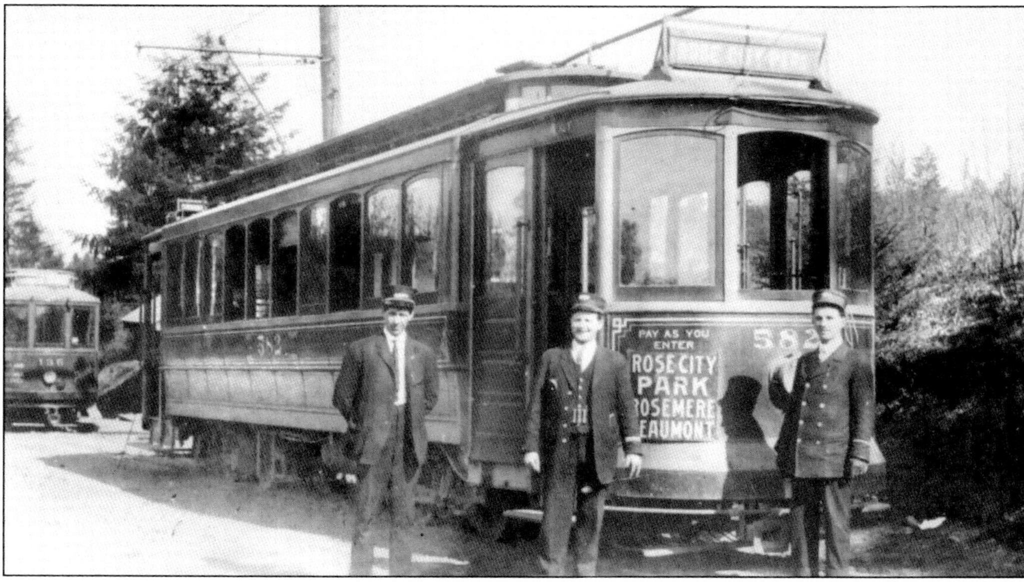

These crewmen are posing during a meet at Northeast Sandy Boulevard and Northeast Sixty-seventh Avenue about 1917. In the foreground is Rose City Park line car No. 582. Behind it is Parkrose shuttle No. 136. The Portland and Troutdale Electric Railway bought two cars from PRL&P and painted them green with silver trim. The Rose City Park line began operating in 1907. Parkrose started runs five years later. (Courtesy Mark Moore.)

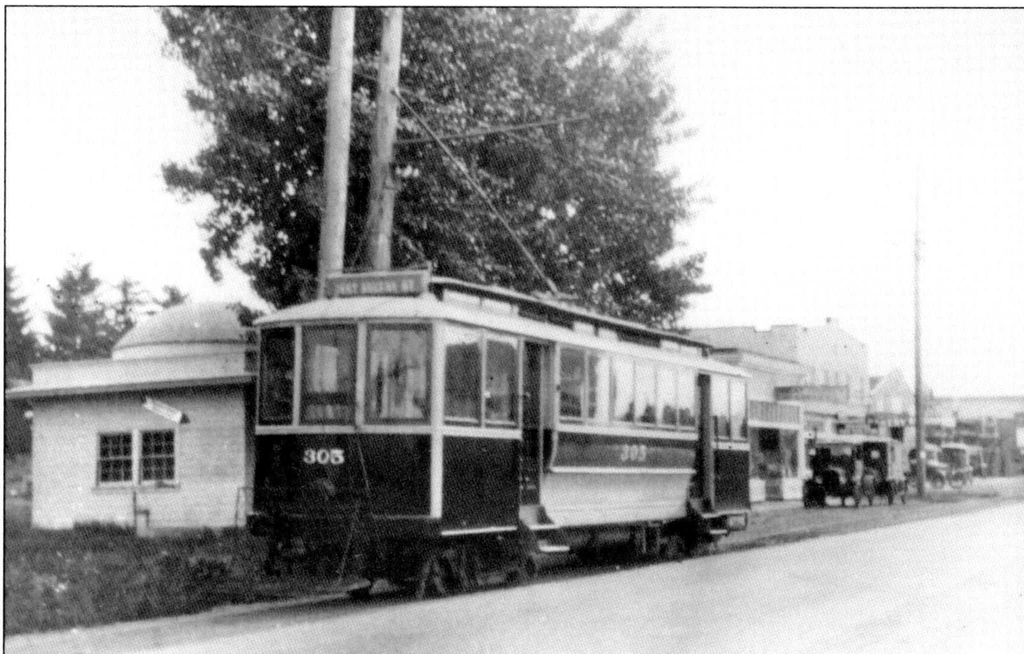

Substitute car No. 305, displaying an East Ankeny roll sign, is at the Parkrose station on Northeast Sandy Boulevard near present-day 122nd Avenue in 1923. The Portland and Troutdale Electric Railway, owned by realtors Thompson and Hartman, operated the Parkrose line from November 7, 1911, until October 1927. It was a stub connecting with Rose City cars at Northeast Eighty-second Avenue. Tracks ran beside Northeast Sandy Boulevard. (Courtesy Mark Moore.)

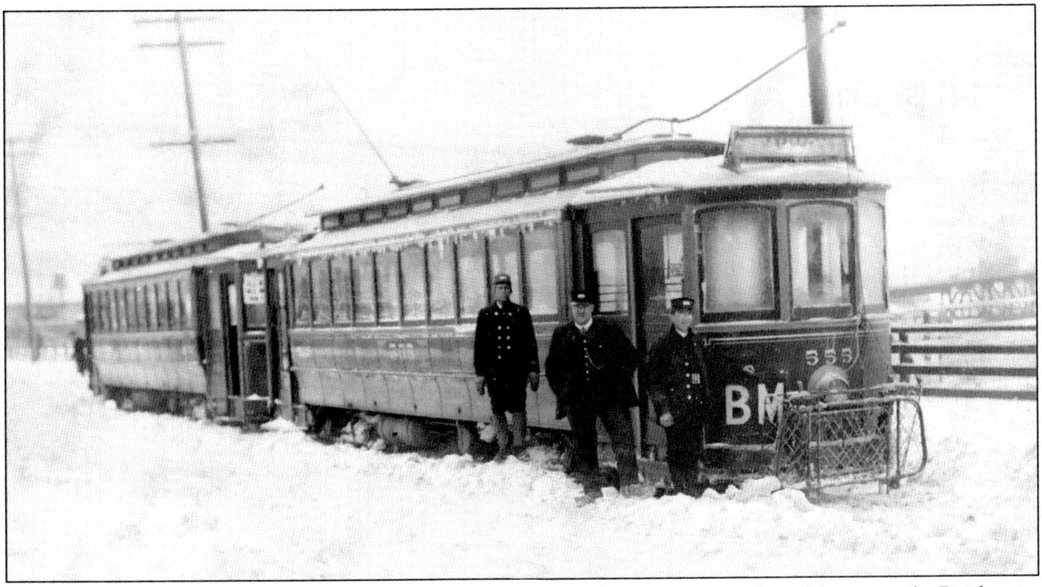

Beaumont No. 555 and a Rose City Park car are stuck in snow on the old Burnside Bridge in February 1916. Beaumont began as a stub line from Northeast Forty-second and Sandy Boulevard to Northeast Forty-first Avenue and Alameda Drive in 1911. In 1914, Beaumont trolleys began running downtown and continued to do so until replaced by gas buses in December 1936, when Northeast Forty-second Avenue was widened and the poles removed.

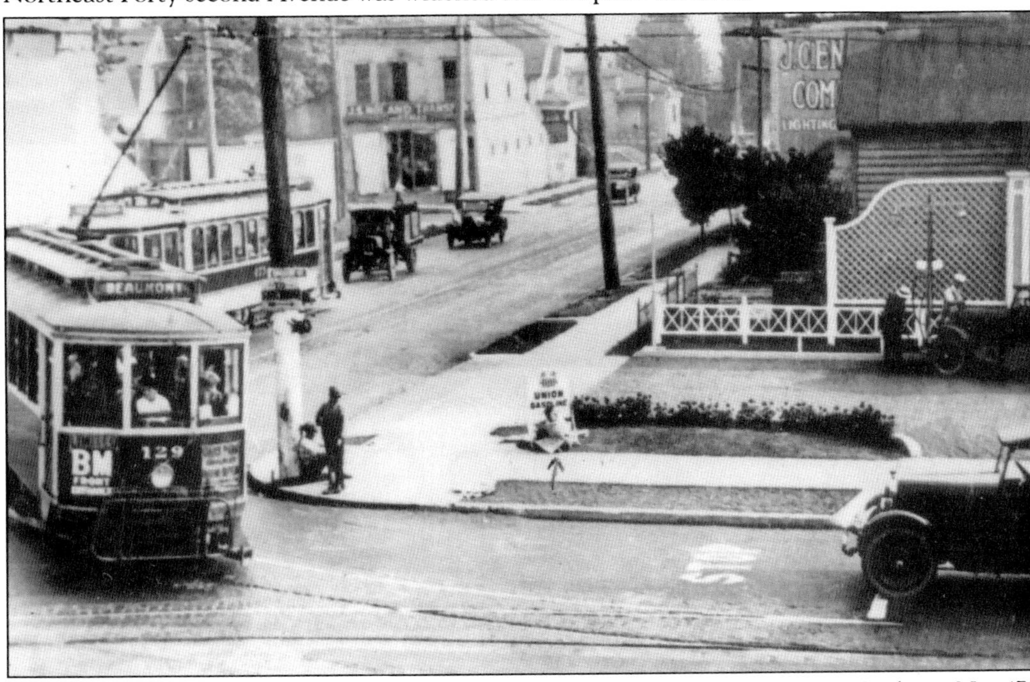

One-man rush hour Beaumont line limited No. 129 is about to pass Rose City Park car No. 473 at the corner of Northeast Union Avenue and Oregon Street during an evening in September 1924. The new Burnside Bridge is under construction, and these two lines have been rerouted. The newsboy in front of the Union Gasoline sign is Larry Griffith, who would become a lifelong activist for restoration of street railways.

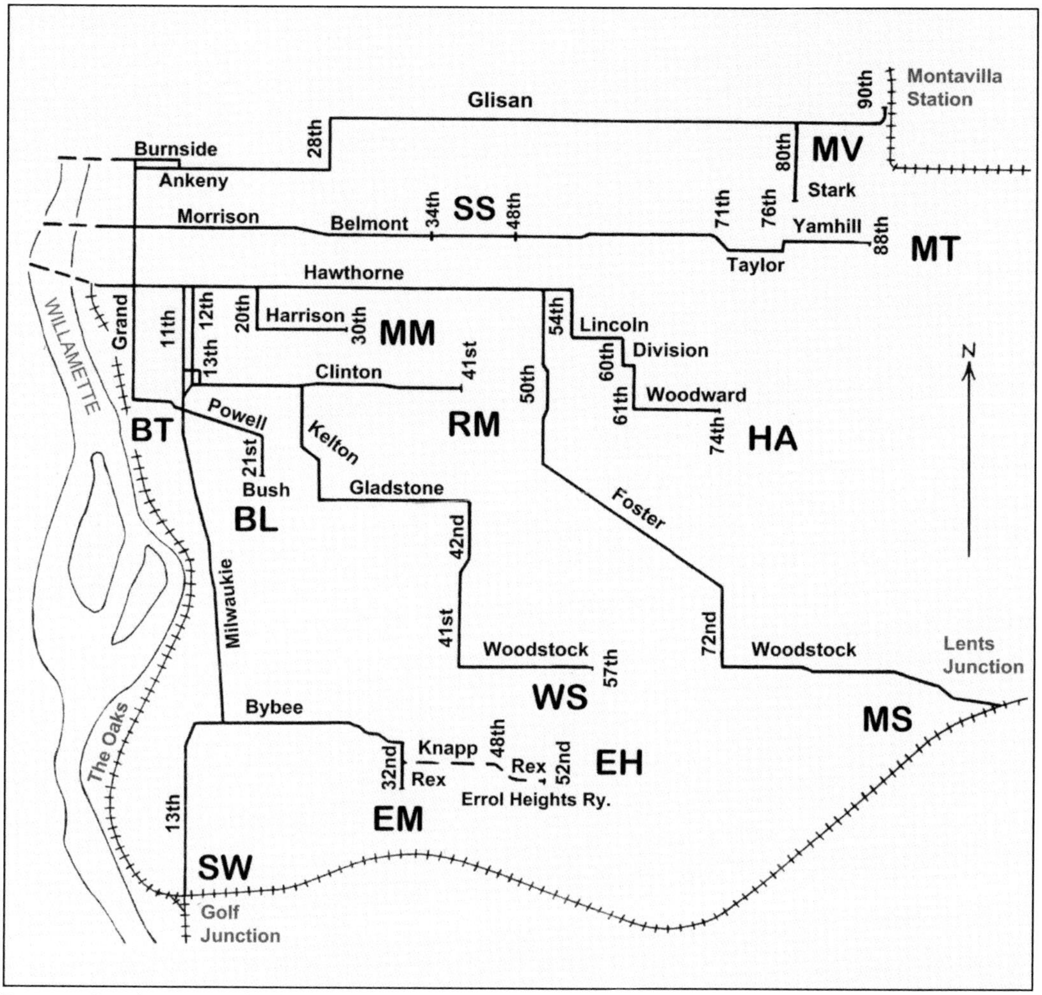

Lines in Southeast Portland included the following: Brooklyn (BL), 1901–1927; Bridge Transfer (BT), 1915–1947; East Ankeny (EA), 1892–1913; East Side, 1907–1909 and 1914; Eastmoreland* (EM), 1912–1926; Errol Heights* (EH), 1913–1929; Hawthorne* (HA), 1889–1936; Murraymead* (MM), 1913–1936; Mount Scott* (MS), 1892–1936; Mount Tabor (MT), 1888–1948; Montavilla (MV), 1892–1948; Richmond* (RM), 1908–1936; Sellwood* (SW), 1891–1940; Sunnyside (SS), 1909–1933; Waverly-Richmond (WR), 1889–1908; Waverly-Woodstock (WW), 1890–1908; and Woodstock* (WS), 1908–1936. This map shows only those lines still in existence during the 1920s. Some began as interurbans but evolved into suburban lines, using regular streetcar rolling stock and practices. They were from two different divisions according to whether their tracks were narrow gauge (42 inches wide), or standard gauge (56.5 inches wide). Standard gauge lines above are indicated by an *. Long interurban lines (not covered in this book) are indicated by track symbols.

Five

To Mount Tabor, Mount Scott, and Sellwood

Street railways played a substantial role in the eastward shift of population that followed completion of the Morrison Bridge in 1887. In March 1888, Willamette Bridge Railway horsecars began running across the bridge. That July, Mount Tabor Steam Motor line trains launched operations from Southeast Grand Avenue to Southeast Thirty-fourth Avenue and Belmont Street in Sunnyside.

During the fall of 1889, the competing Mount Tabor Street Railway inaugurated steam service on Southeast Hawthorne Boulevard from Southeast Grand Avenue to Southeast Fifty-fourth Avenue. In 1892, the Mount Scott line along Southeast Foster Road and Southeast Woodstock Street was added to the community of Lents. More line building brought streetcars to Montavilla later that year.

The Waverly and Woodstock Electric Railway opened a forked route to the neighborhoods of Richmond (at Southeast Forty-first Avenue and Clinton Street) and Woodstock (at Southeast Fifty-seventh Avenue and Woodward Street) in 1891. About 1902, the nearby Brooklyn line was completed out Southeast Powell Boulevard to Southeast Twenty-first Avenue and Bush Street in the German immigrant Brookland neighborhood.

In 1903, when the east side railway's tracks to Oregon City were relocated, the old right-of-way changed from an interurban stop to a streetcar line. The Sellwood line terminated near the gates to Garthwick on Southwest Thirteenth Avenue and Ochoco Street.

Trolleys served two Southeast neighborhoods carved out of land belonging to Portland businessman and Mayor William Ladd. Ladd's Addition (1891), bordering Southeast Hawthorne from Southeast Twelfth to Southeast Twentieth Avenues, was patterned after the diagonal streets of Washington, D.C. Ambitious Eastmoreland (1910) included a golf course and a college.

A final group of lines appeared from 1903 to 1915. Eastmoreland, Errol Heights, and Murraymead were stub lines. Bridge transfer was a crosstown service intersecting other lines. In 1948, the last two streetcar lines in Southeast Portland were Montavilla and Mount Tabor.

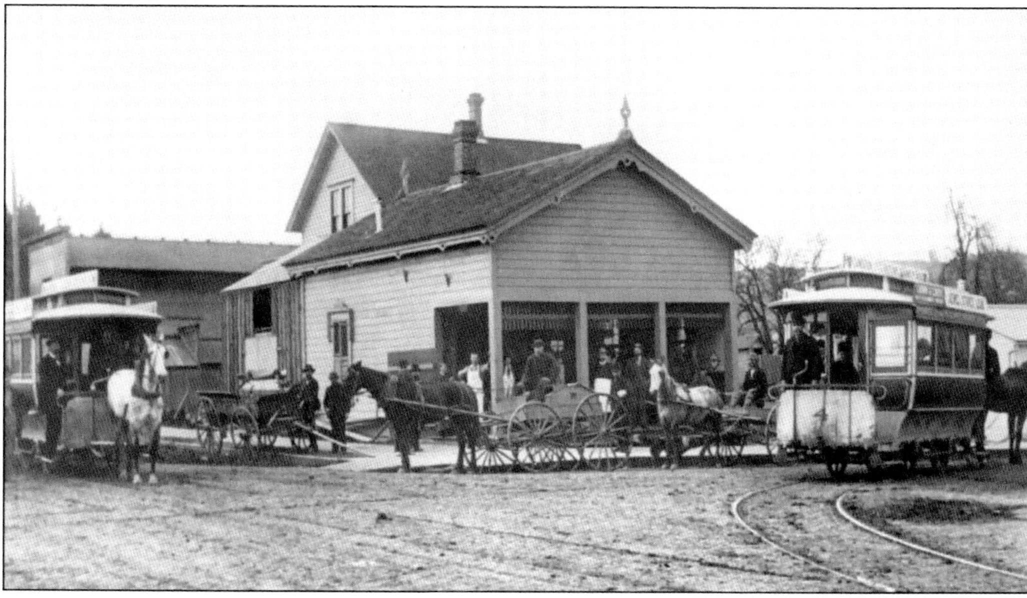

The photographer was standing on the corner of Fifth and N streets (now Southeast Grand Avenue and Morrison Street) in East Portland when he took this picture of the first eastside streetcar line about 1888. Willamette Bridge Railway horsecar No. 4 is turning west toward the new Morrison Street Bridge, while another horsecar is traveling up Fifth Street. This was the precursor to the East Side Line. (Courtesy Mark Moore.)

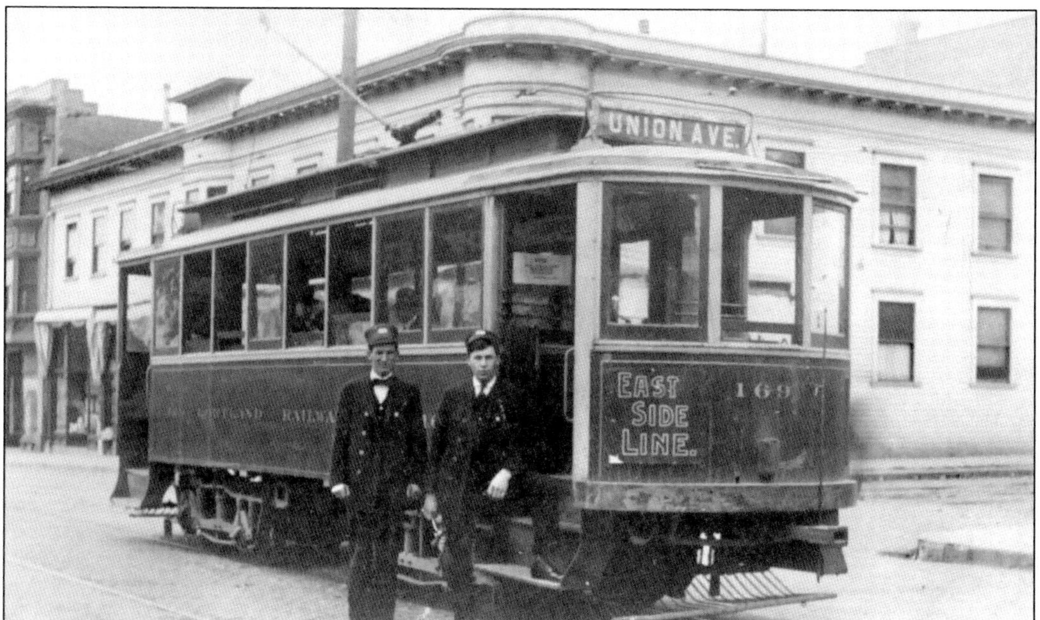

No. 169 is on Northeast Union Avenue under the command of Robert McKee and Harry Alterstrom. The first East Side line operated along Grand Avenue from Northeast Holladay Street to Southeast Hawthorne Avenue between 1907 and 1909, when it merged with the Russell Shaver line. A second East Side line ran during 1914 on North Larrabee Street, North Holladay Avenue, and Northeast Union Avenue, sharing tracks with the Alberta line.

The Mount Tabor (MT) line began as a steam dummy to Southeast Belmont Street and Thirty-fourth Avenue in 1888. The line was extended to Southeast Sixty-ninth Avenue in 1889. In 1912, a second fare stub service was added from there to Southeast Eighty-eighth Avenue and Yamhill Street. A year later, it merged into MT. Westside terminals varied over the years, ending with the Hall Street loop. MT converted to bus August 15, 1948.

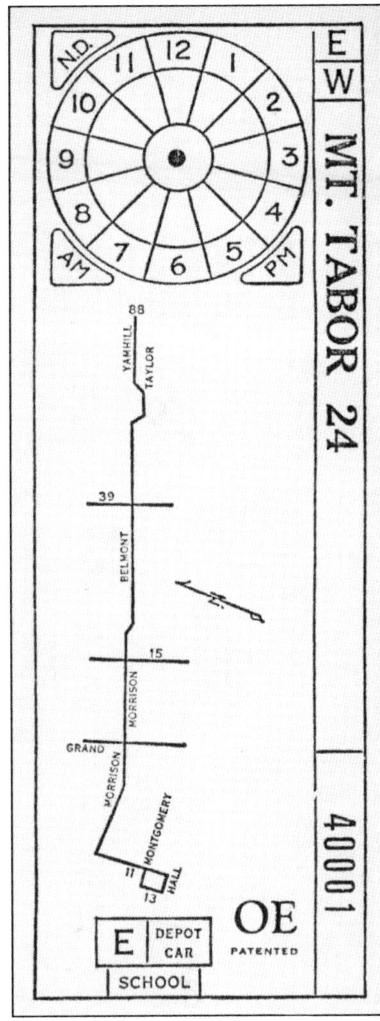

City and Suburban Railway steam motor No. 4 and coach 11 (still lettered for predecessor Willamette Bridge Railway) have reached the eastern end of the Mount Tabor steam line at present-day Southeast Sixty-ninth Avenue and Belmont Street around 1890. The terminal was located next to the railway shops and yard on Mount Tabor. When it opened in 1888, this was Portland's first steam dummy line. (Courtesy Mark Moore.)

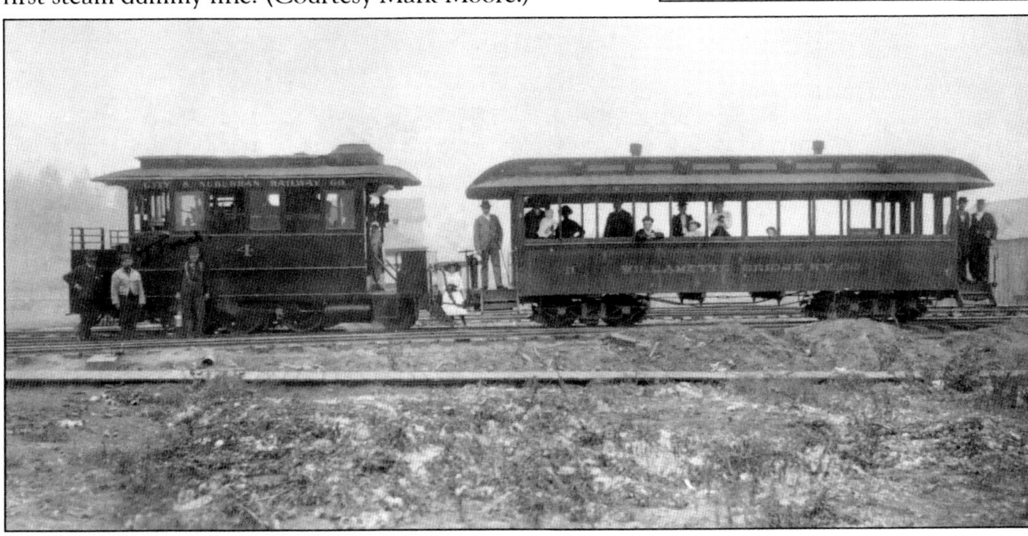

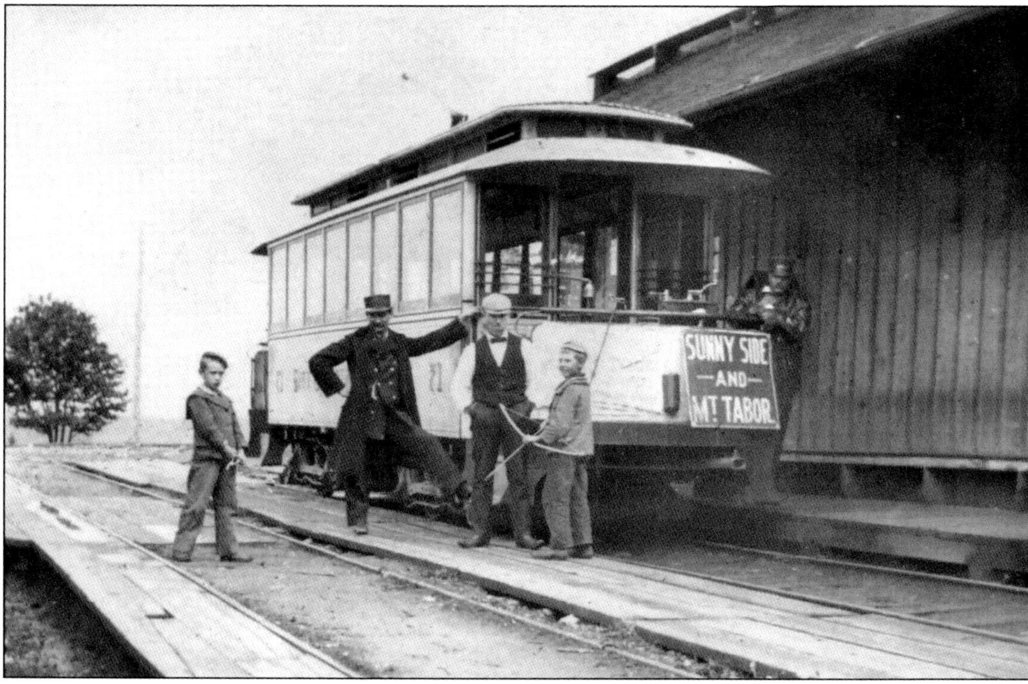

Bow-and-arrow-toting boys greet one of the first trolleys, City and Suburban Railway white and gold Pullman No. 71, at the end of the Mount Tabor line on Southeast Sixty-ninth and Belmont Streets in the 1890s. The building next to the car was a locomotive shed until the route was completely electrified in 1896. The line ran between Buckman, East Portland's earliest suburb, and Sunnyside. In between was Lone Fir Cemetery.

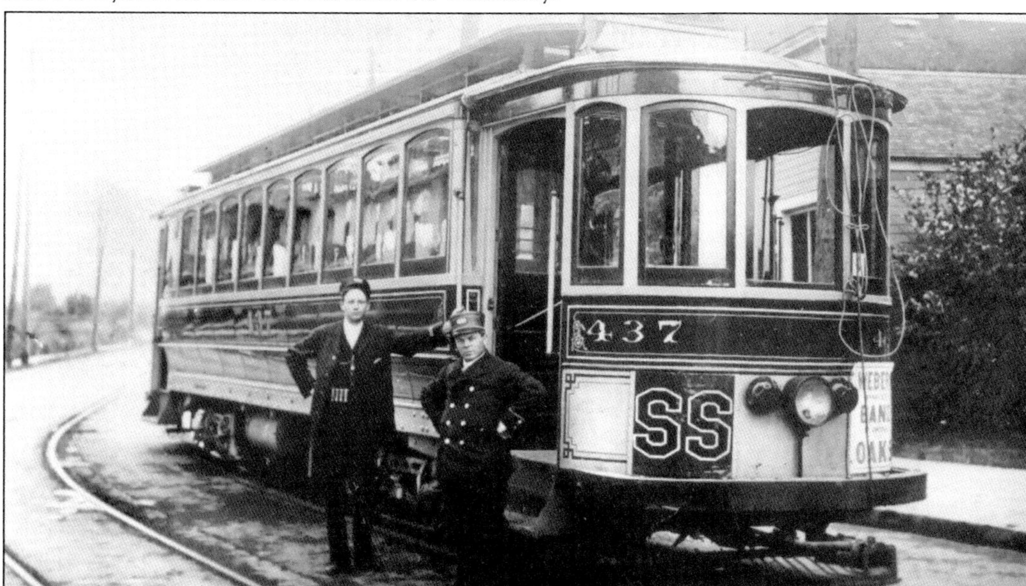

The crew seems impatient to get back on their new 1907 trolley resplendent in gleaming maroon and cream paint with fancy pinstripes. Sunnyside trippers and owls (late-night cars) turned back here at Southeast Thirty-ninth Avenue and Belmont Street. The dash sign advertises an appearance at Oaks Park by John Weber and his Prize Band of America, a popular brass band of the era.

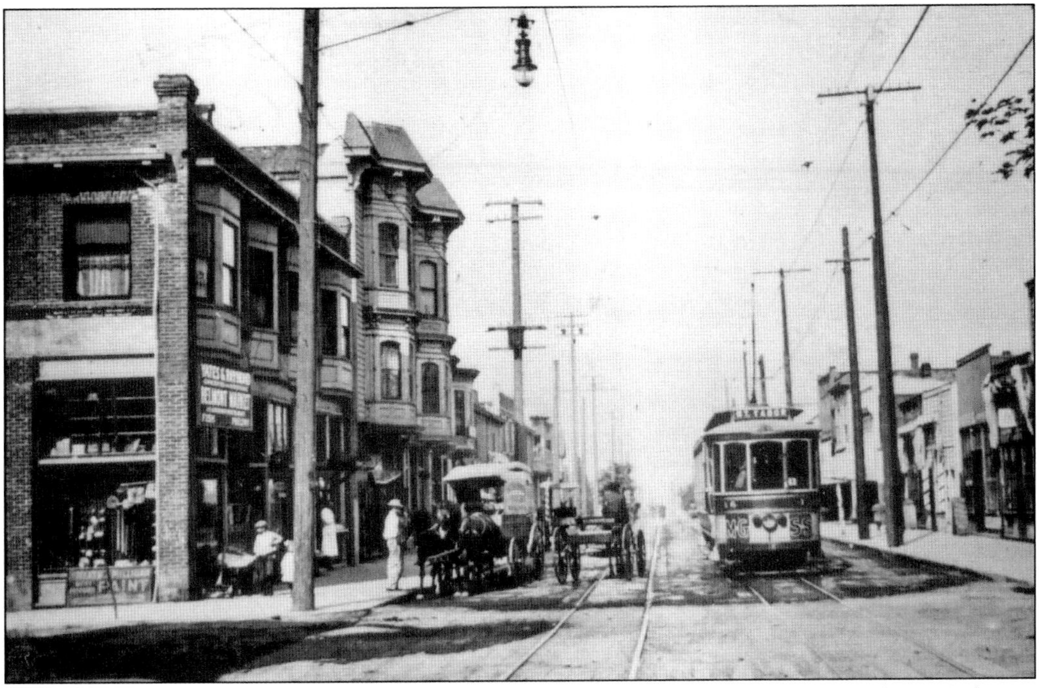

Mount Tabor–Sunnyside–Montgomery line car No. 436 is heading east on Southeast Belmont Street at Thirty-fifth Avenue in the Sunnyside commercial district around 1908. The wagons in the street next to the trolley are delivering goods to the Yates and Raymond Belmont Market on the corner, a neighborhood purveyor of everything from fish and poultry to paint.

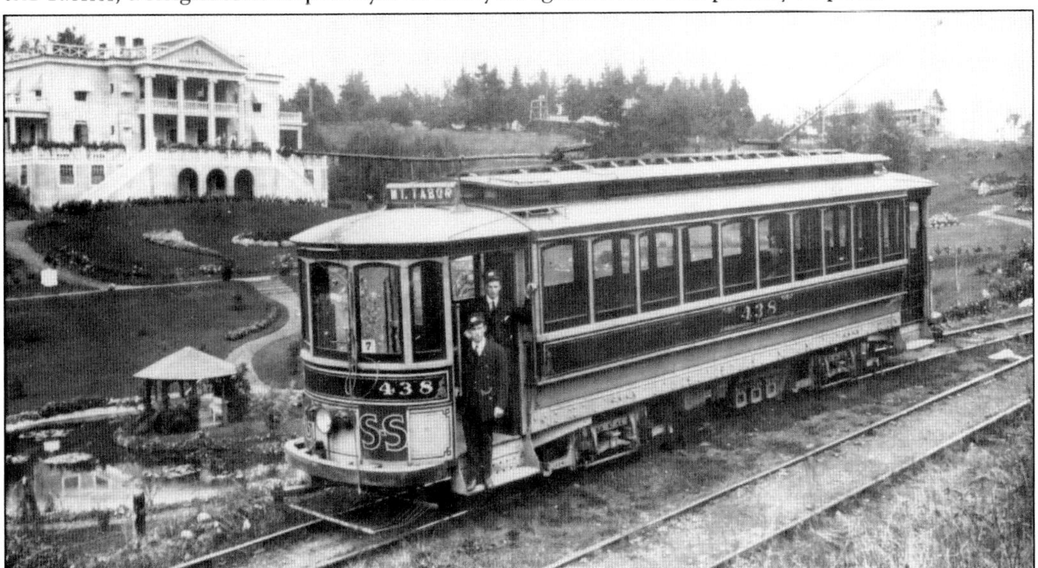

Mount Tabor–Sunnyside car No. 438 poses on Southeast Belmont Street near Southeast Sixty-sixth Avenue about 1910. The building in the background is a replica of the Massachusetts State House built for Portland's 1905 Lewis and Clark Exposition. It was moved to Mount Tabor, where it served as the Crystal Springs Sanitarium and then as the home of Benage Josselyn, PRL&P president. The 27-room mansion was razed in the 1940s. (Courtesy Mark Moore.)

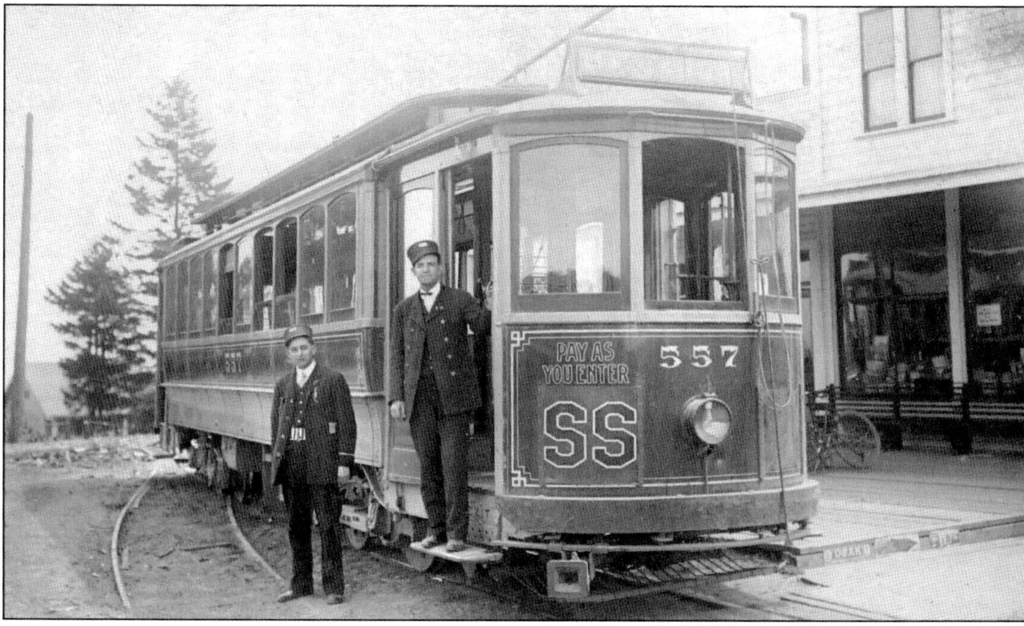

Pots, pans, and other kitchenware are stacked in the storefront window behind Mount Tabor–Sunnyside car No. 557 at the Southeast Sixty-ninth and Belmont Streets terminal around 1911. Sunnyside began as a "short-turn" run to Southeast Thirty-ninth on the Mount Tabor line in October 1909. The Portland Electric Power Company extended the line to Southeast Forty-eighth during the 1920s. The Sunnyside line was merged into the Mount Tabor line in 1933.

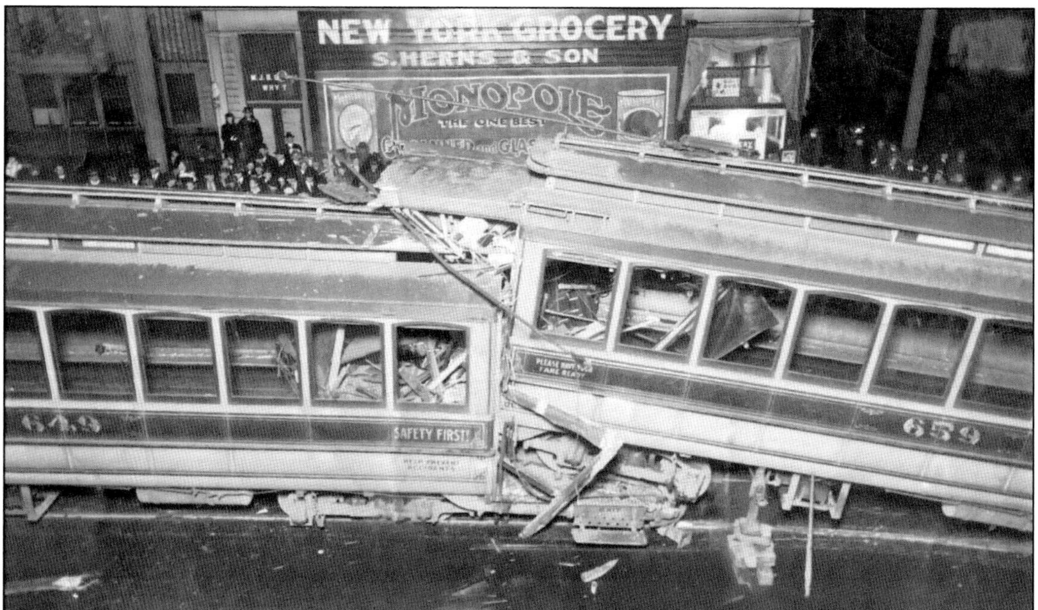

This collision took place at Southwest Eleventh Avenue and Morrison Street in 1915. Empty Sunnyside No. 649 (with the ironic "Safety First!" sign) slipped its brakes at Southwest Thirteenth and Hall Streets, traveled down Thirteenth Street to Montgomery Street, east to Eleventh Street, then north where it hit standing Mount Tabor car No. 659. The trolleys rose in the air on impact and then crashed down on each other, seriously injuring several passengers.

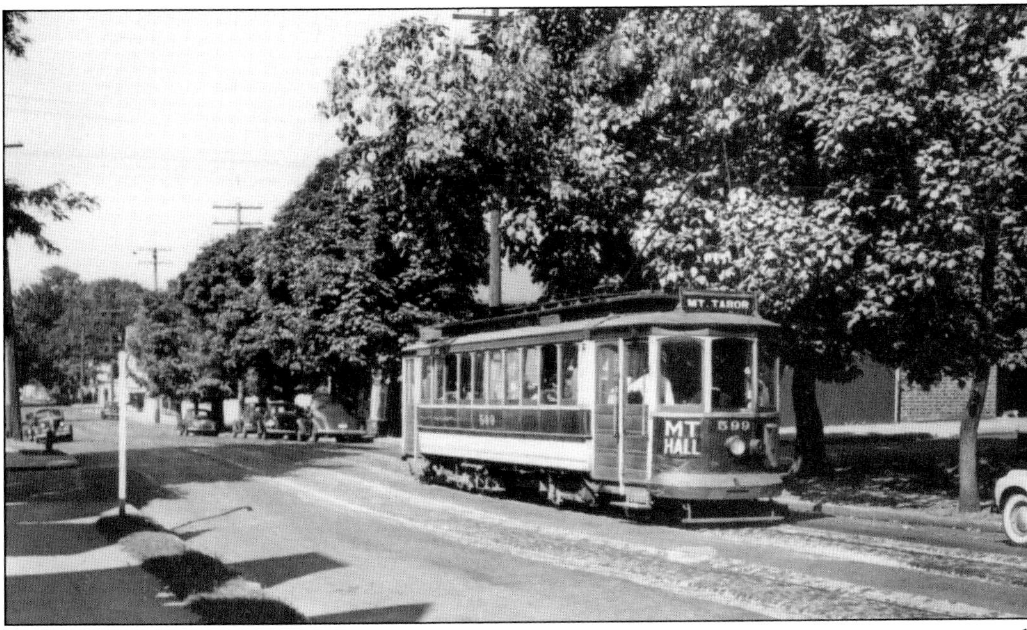

Mount Tabor No. 599 rolls westward along the bricks of Southeast Morrison Street near Seventeenth Avenue in the Buckman Neighborhood on a quiet 1940s morning. The neighborhood is named for 19th century orchardist and city council member Cyrus Buckman. The trolley has left Lone Fir Cemetery three blocks behind and is now three blocks south of historic Buckman Elementary School.

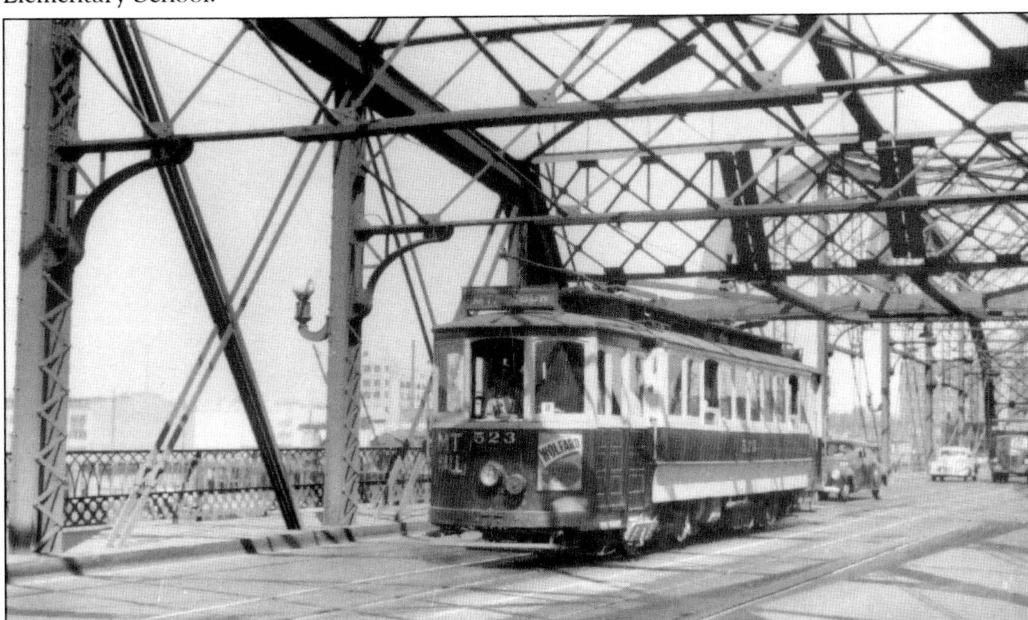

Mount Tabor car No. 523 is westbound on the old Morrison Bridge in the 1940s. Rail historian Bill Hayes recalled that a ride on the line "had a lot to offer, going from the lush greenery of Mount Tabor, past the lovely large homes of the well-to-do . . . down into the more workaday neighborhood of Sunnyside, then downhill to the river and across the old Morrison Bridge into the busy downtown."

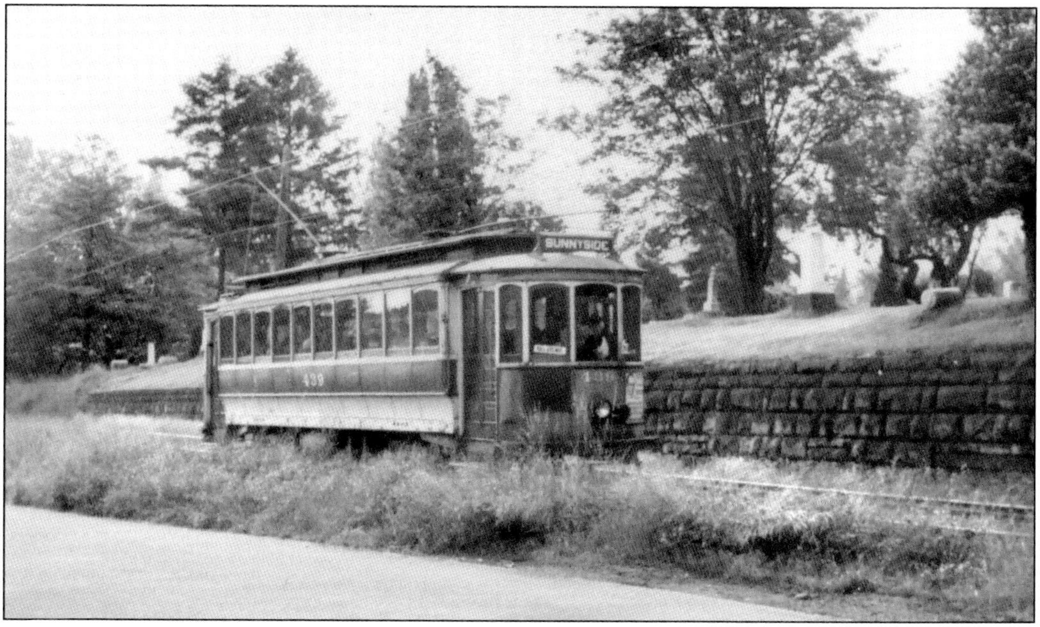

Tired-looking Sunnyside tripper No. 439 is heading east on a private right-of-way next to Lone Fir Cemetery on Southeast Morrison Street in the late 1940s. As indicated by the sign in the window, the car is bound for Southeast Forty-eighth Avenue. When Lone Fir Cemetery was established, it was considered far out of town. Pioneers from the first burial ground in Portland were relocated here when downtown land became valuable in the 1860s.

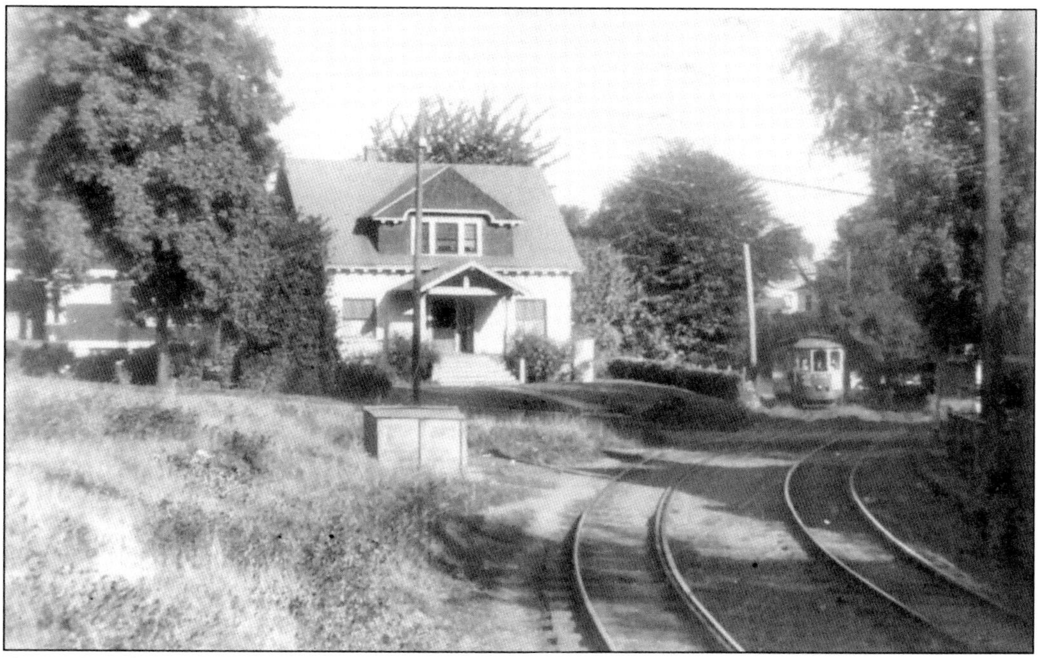

A No. 520 class Mount Tabor line trolley has just entered the private right-of-way from Southeast Belmont Street near Southeast Twenty-seventh Avenue on an afternoon in the 1940s. There were several short, private rights-of-ways along the line, whose tracks preceded most area homes. (Photograph by Charles E. Hayden.)

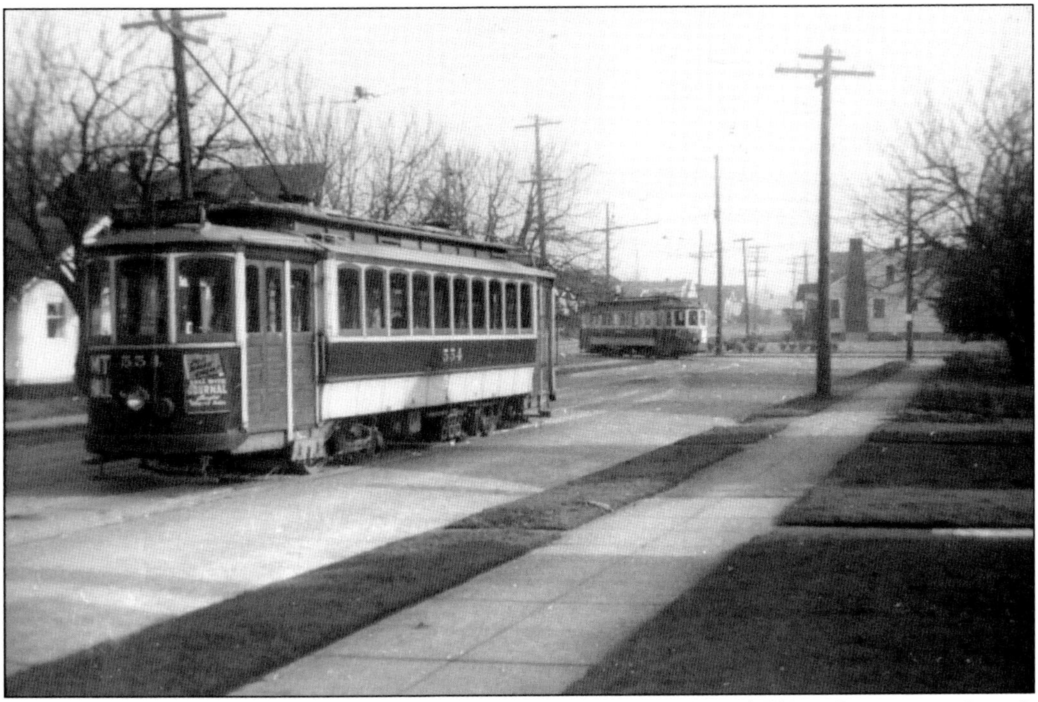

The shadows are gathering around Mount Tabor line car Nos. 554 and 553 as they approach each other at the passing track on Southeast Yamhill Street and Eightieth Avenue about 1946. This area is four blocks south of Montavilla and the terminus for the Montavilla car line. The Mount Tabor terminus is eight blocks farther east at Southeast Eighty-eighth Avenue and Yamhill Street. (Photograph by Charles E. Hayden.)

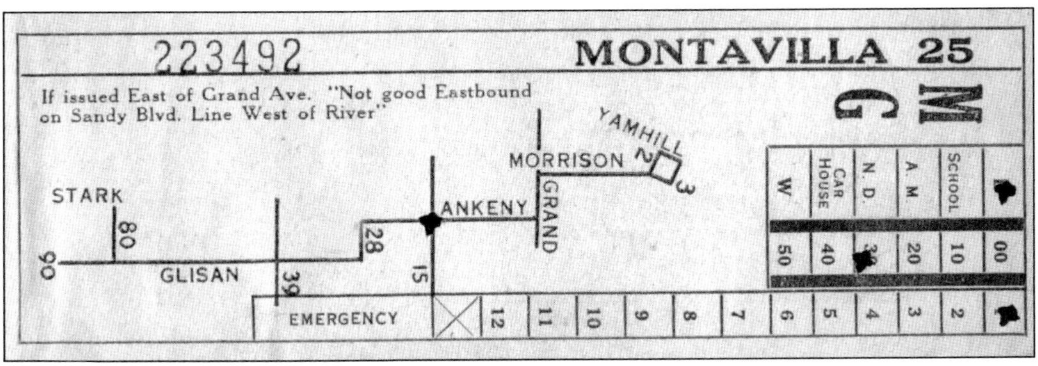

The Montavilla line began on July 26, 1892, as a projected line to Fairview. Service was provided to Northeast Glisan Street and Eighty-second Avenue. In 1900, the eastside terminus was relocated to Southeast Eightieth Avenue and Stark Street in Montavilla. A 1911 stub line extension out of Northeast Glisan Street to Ninetieth and Irving Streets became one of two alternating terminals two years later, as illustrated by the reversed map on this transfer.

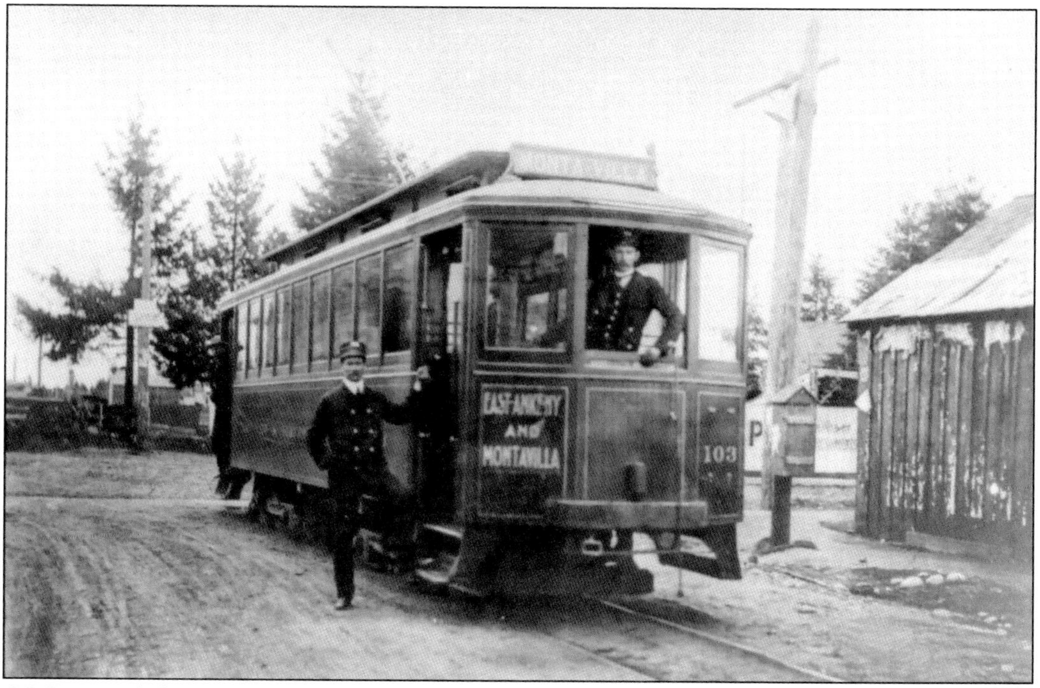

C&S opened the Montavilla line as an extension of its East Ankeny line, which was built at the same time. This picture dates from 1900, when the eastern end of the line was rerouted down Southeast Eightieth Avenue to Stark Street, traversing a tract known as Mount Tabor Villa. The name was shortened to "Mt. Ta. Villa," and then to "Monta.Villa" on destination signs (above), a designation soon adopted by the community.

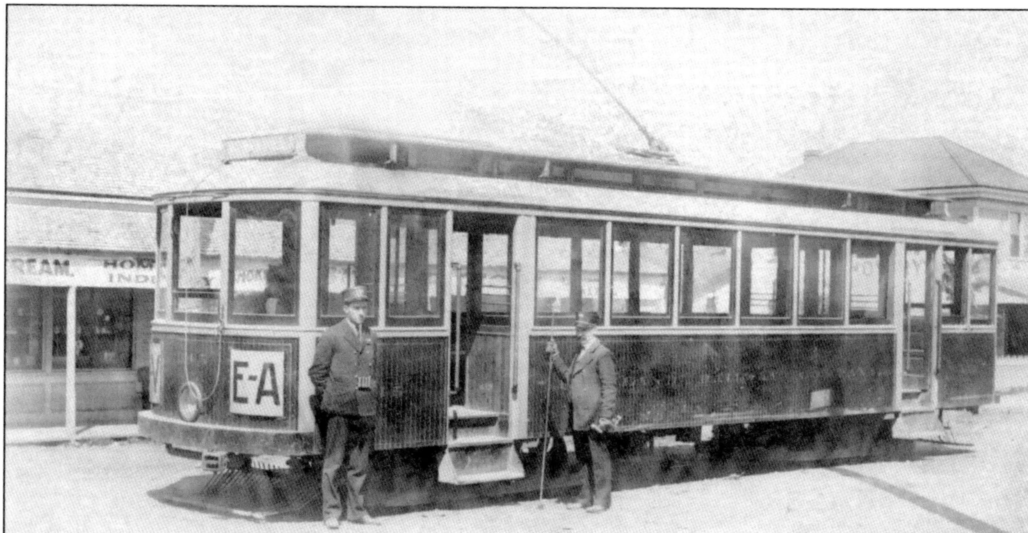

A lone passenger has boarded Montavilla–East Ankeny car No. 345 in front of an ice cream shop near Southeast Eightieth Avenue and Stark Street in Montavilla. The eager motorman holds a switch iron in one hand and the controller handle in the other. By the time this c. 1905 photograph was taken, the City and Suburban Railway had become part of the second Portland Railway Company. (Courtesy Mark Moore.)

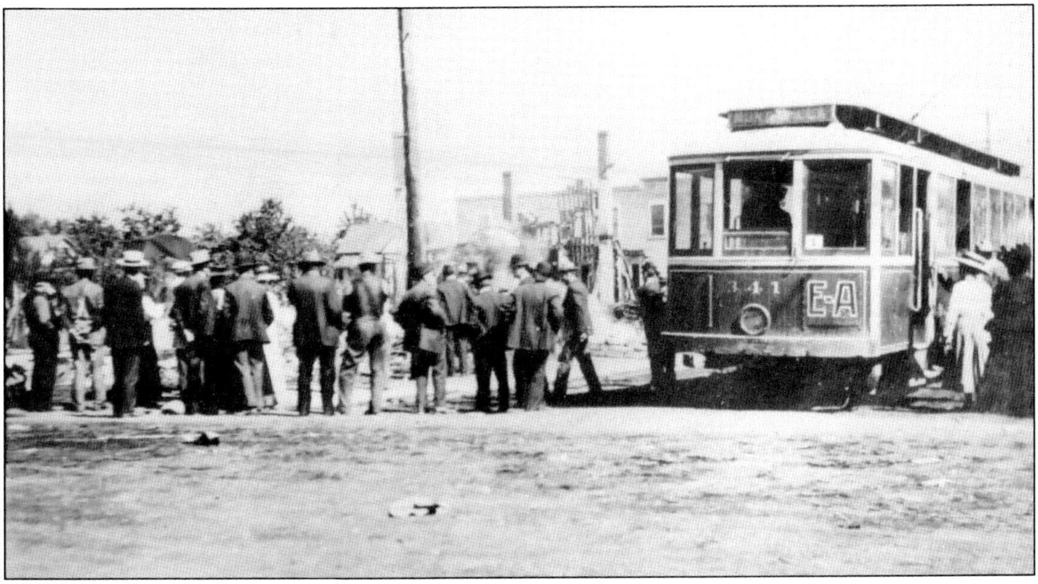

PRL&P Montavilla line car No. 341 boards passengers at the end of the Montavilla line on Southeast Eightieth and Stark Streets the day after fire destroyed Dickson's Drug Store. The five-month-old store at this corner was destroyed in a fireworks explosion July 4, 1910. It was rebuilt. The former Portland Railway Fuller *Standard* trolley dates from 1903.

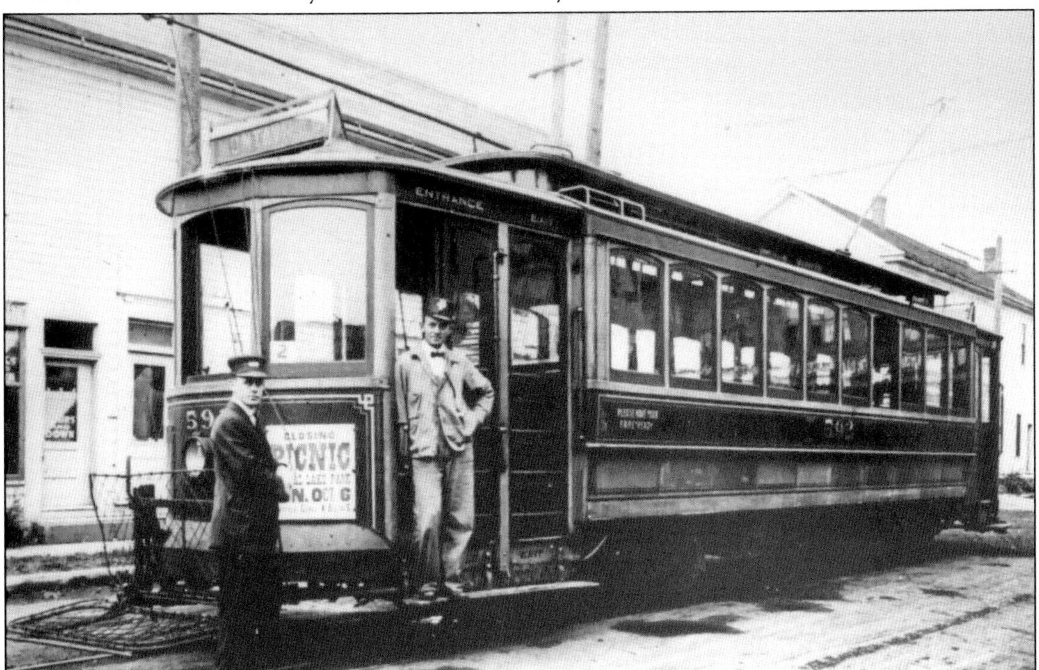

A motorman dressed in engineer garb leans casually against a door in the large pay-as-you-enter vestibule of car No. 592 at Southeast Eightieth Avenue and Stark Street in Montavilla in 1912. The dash advertisement announces the October closing picnic for the Knights and Ladies of Security, a Kansas-based fraternal beneficiary society. In the years leading up to World War I, fraternal organizations were growing as rapidly as street railways.

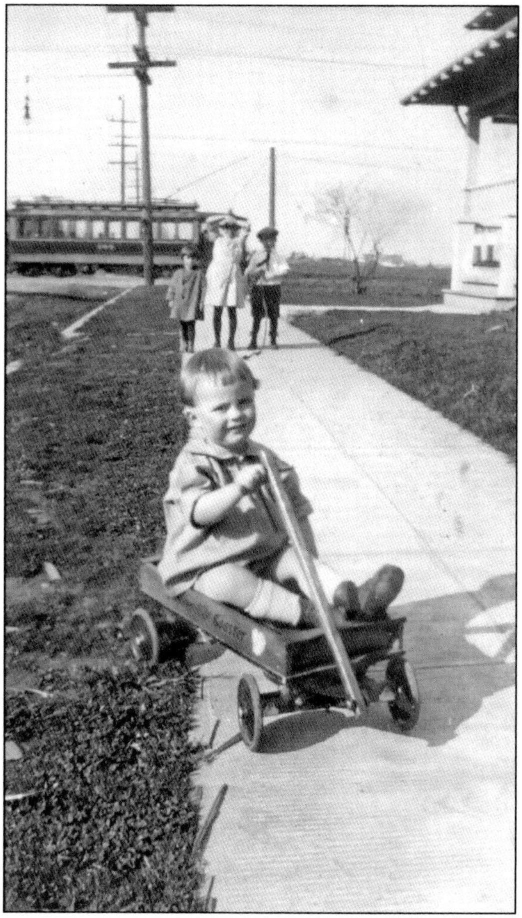

The boy in the wagon is Ronald Million, a young member of a family of PRL&P car men. His father worked at the Ankeny division for many years. In the background, as if on cue, a Montavilla line trolley is passing at the corner of Northeast Eighty-second Avenue and Glisan Street. It is 1924, and the Million family's bungalow is one of the first houses in the neighborhood.

A trolley car numbered in the 430s is waiting next to the Montavilla interurban station on Northeast Ninetieth Avenue off Glisan Street. This was the northernmost of the two Montavilla line terminals, the other being at Southeast Eightieth Avenue and Stark Street. The depot was built by the Mount Hood Railway, which became part of PRL&P in 1914. Until 1927, interurbans bound for Bull Run used the tracks at the right.

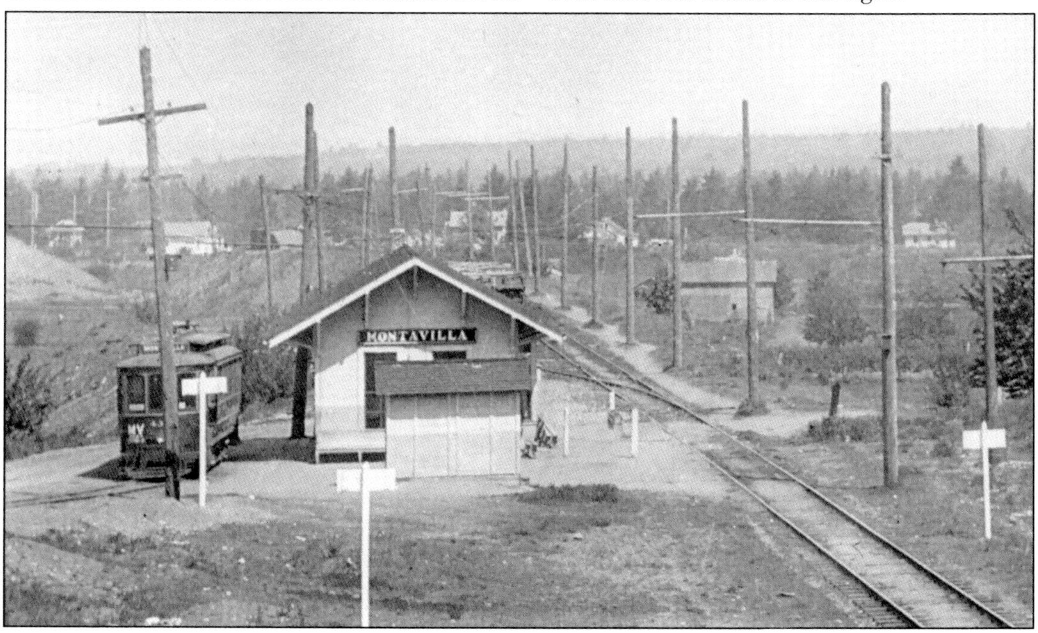

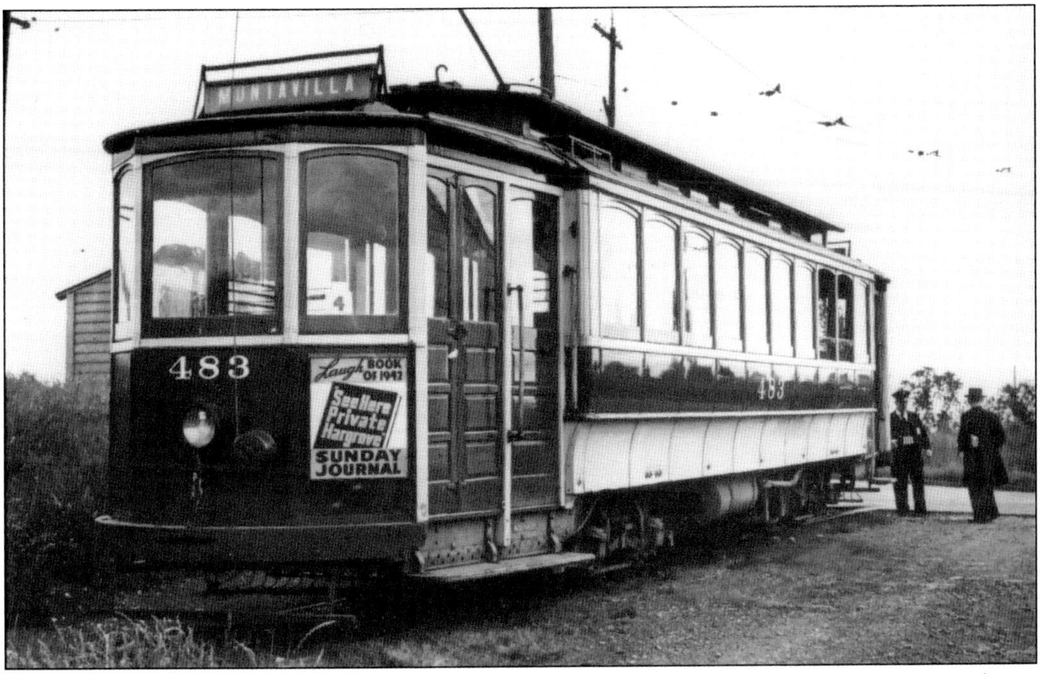

Newly painted Portland Traction car No. 483 is waiting at the Montavilla terminal on Northeast Ninetieth Avenue and Glisan Street in 1942. W. C. Coovert, 64-year-old motorman, suffered a sprained ankle in a freak accident here in 1936. He forgot to set the brakes, and as he left the car to change poles, it began to roll, knocking him down. The trolley finally stopped 8 feet off the end of the tracks.

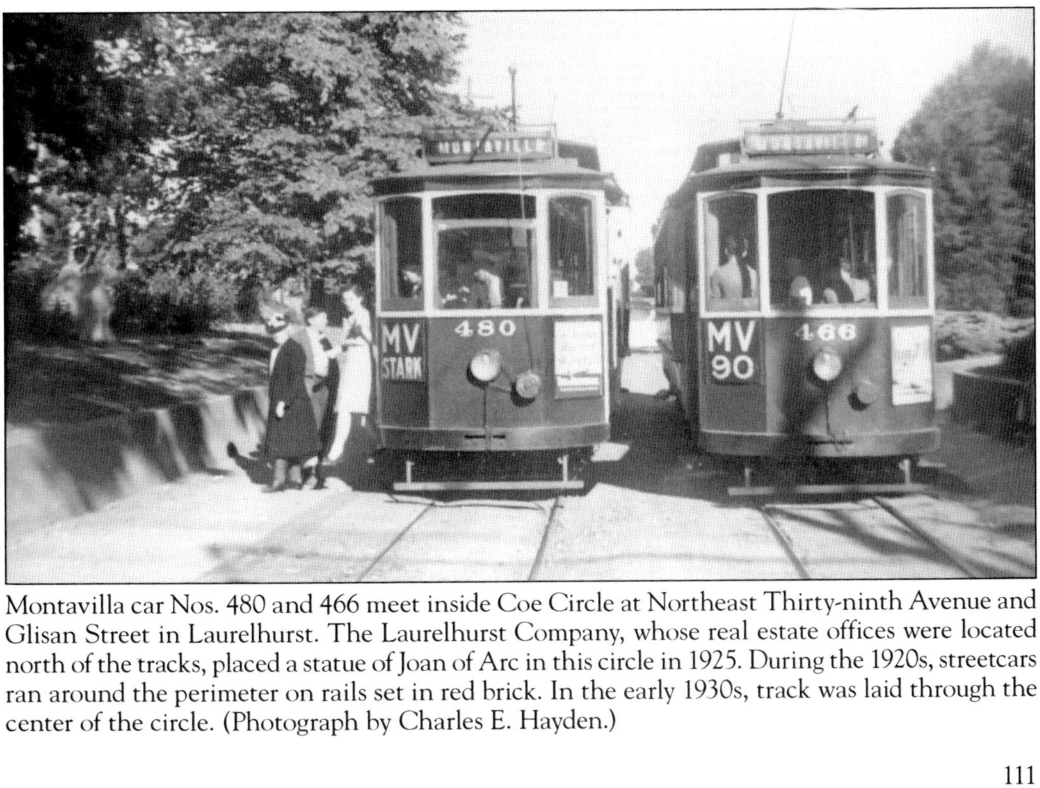

Montavilla car Nos. 480 and 466 meet inside Coe Circle at Northeast Thirty-ninth Avenue and Glisan Street in Laurelhurst. The Laurelhurst Company, whose real estate offices were located north of the tracks, placed a statue of Joan of Arc in this circle in 1925. During the 1920s, streetcars ran around the perimeter on rails set in red brick. In the early 1930s, track was laid through the center of the circle. (Photograph by Charles E. Hayden.)

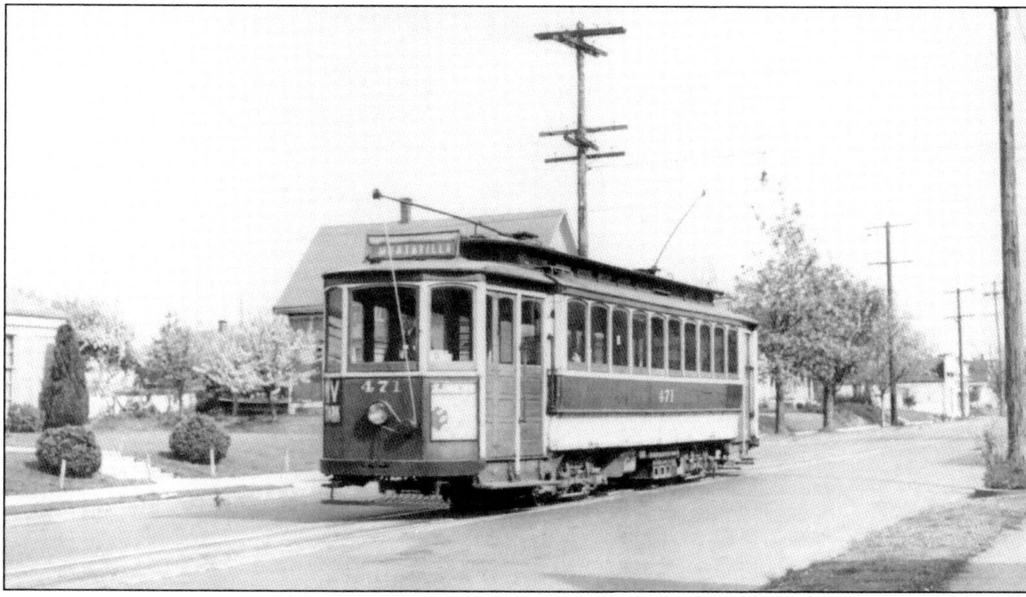

No. 471, which gained a reputation for being involved in fender benders with automobiles, is running past the old Montavilla branch library on Southeast Eightieth Avenue on its way to the Stark Street terminal in Montavilla. The veteran trolley was retired in 1947 after colliding with a bulldozer that was backing out of a fill on Northeast Glisan Street.

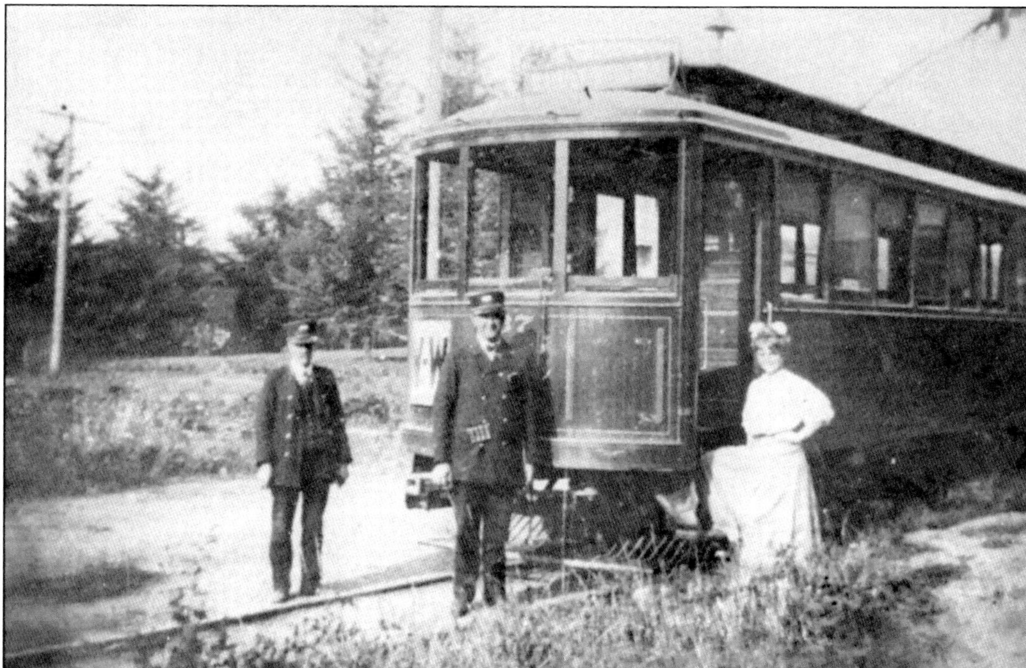

A pretty lass poses with the crew of Portland Railway's Waverly-Woodstock line car No. 137 around 1905. The first trip was made August 29, 1890, with alternate terminals at Southeast Forty-first Avenue and Gladstone Street in Woodstock and Southeast Forty-first Avenue and Clinton Street in Richmond. The Waverly-Richmond portion of the line had opened the previous December. The two branches forked at Southeast Twenty-sixth Avenue in Waverly.

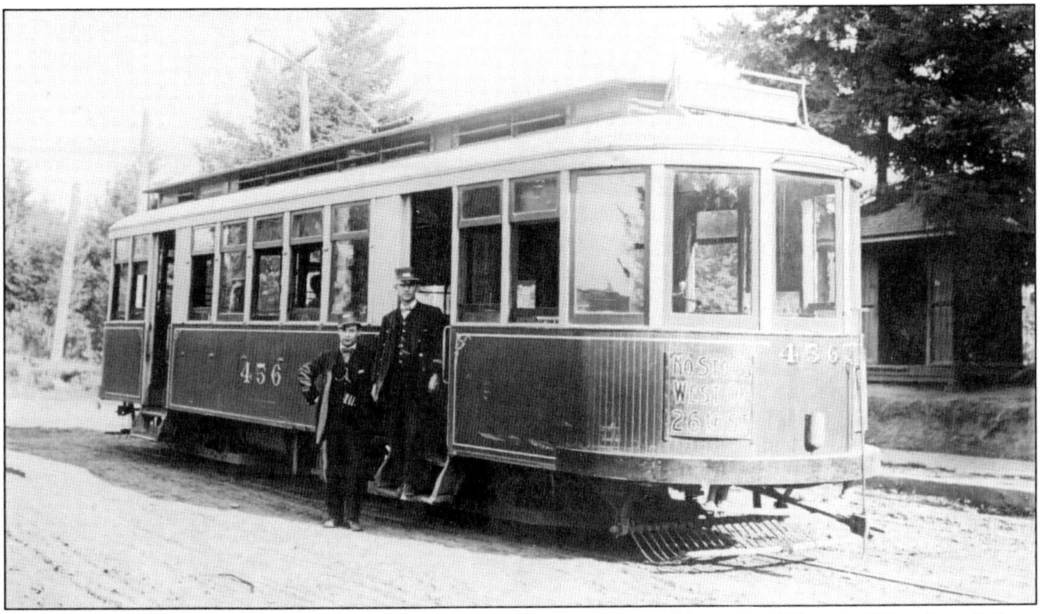

This is an uncommon view of PRL&P *Toronto* class car No. 456 on the Waverly-Woodstock line before it was re-gauged and broken into separate Richmond and Woodstock lines in December 1908. The line was built by the Thompson-Houston Electric Company for the Waverly-Woodstock electric railway. PRL&P decided it would be more efficient for Waverly-Woodstock to become part of the standard-gauge division operating from the Sellwood carbarn. (Courtesy Mark Moore.)

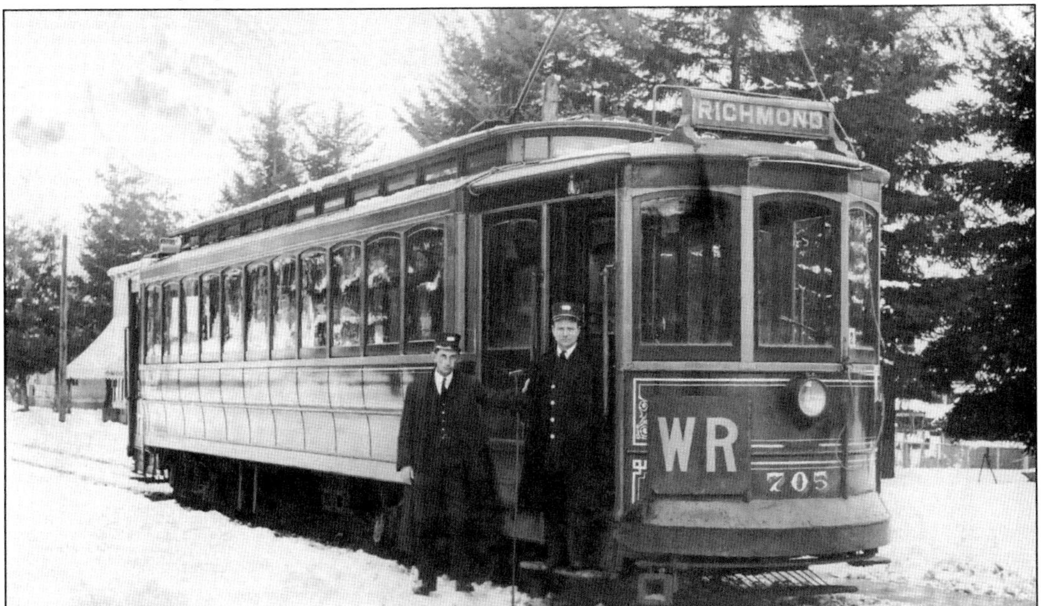

The crew of new standard-gauge Waverly-Richmond line car No. 705 is getting ready to head back through the snow from the Southeast Forty-first Avenue and Clinton Street terminus in Richmond during the 1910 Christmas season. The motorman holds a switch iron in readiness for the switch at Southeast Thirty-seventh Avenue. The awning of a grocery store can be seen in the background. (Courtesy Mark Moore.)

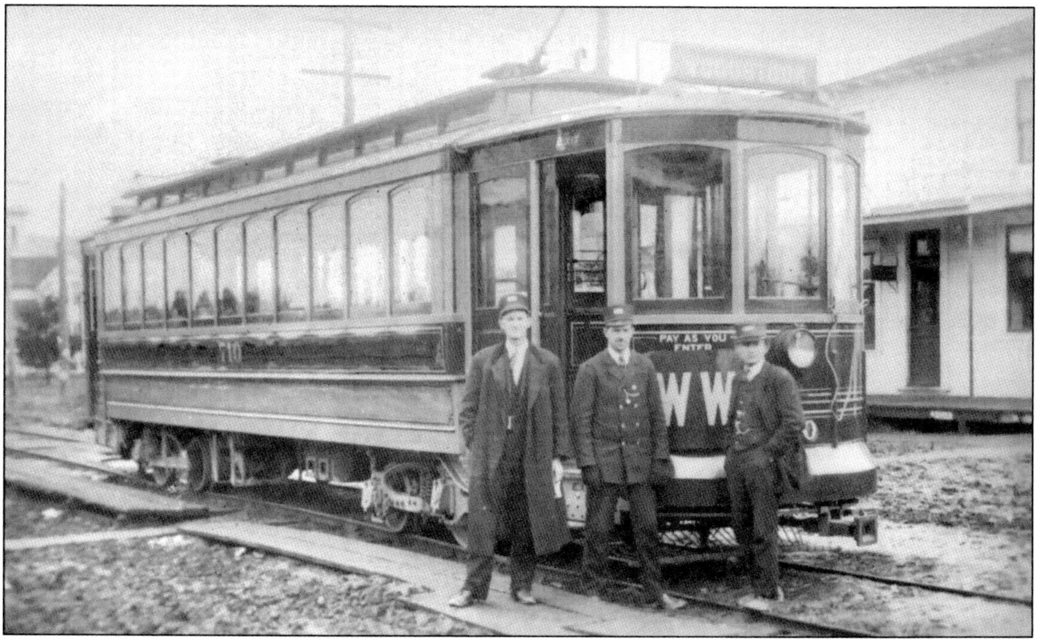

Woodstock car No. 700 is thought to be at the earlier Woodstock line station at Southeast Forty-sixth Avenue and Woodstock Street around 1911. The old Waverly–Woodstock dash signs are still being used on the now separate standard-gauge Woodstock line. Note the wooden plank sidewalks on a very muddy Southeast Woodstock Street and the school or church bell tower in the left background.

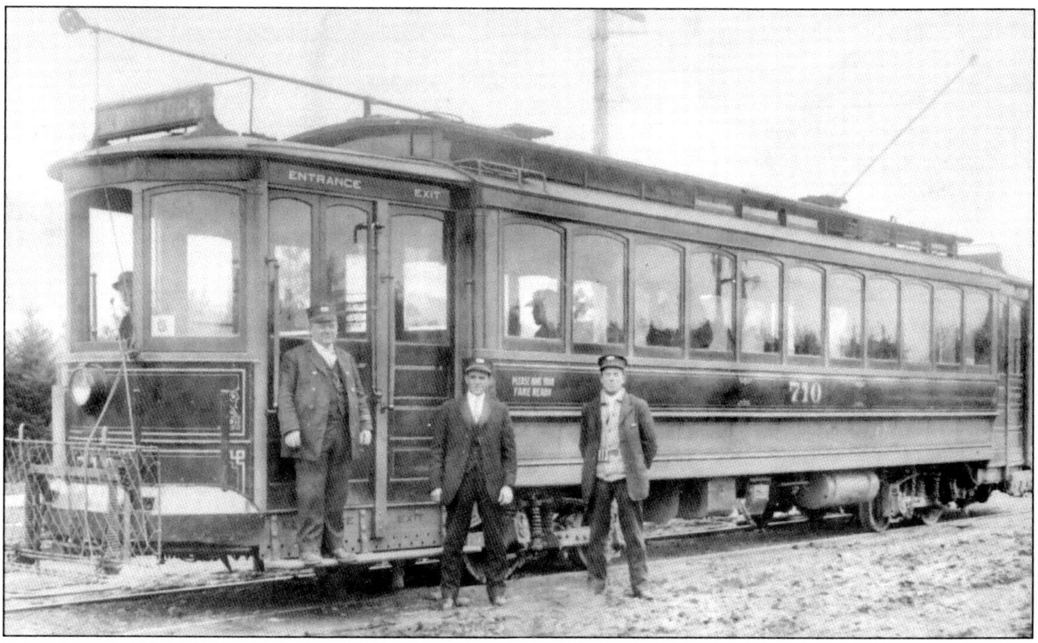

Woodstock line car No. 710 is at the new eastern terminus of the line on Southeast Fifty-seventh Avenue and Woodstock Street about 1913. Like many Portland streetcars, No. 700 was equipped with Brill maximum traction trucks. Bill Hayes recalled the special sound their combination of large driving wheels and smaller pony wheels made as they rolled over the tracks at busy intersections.

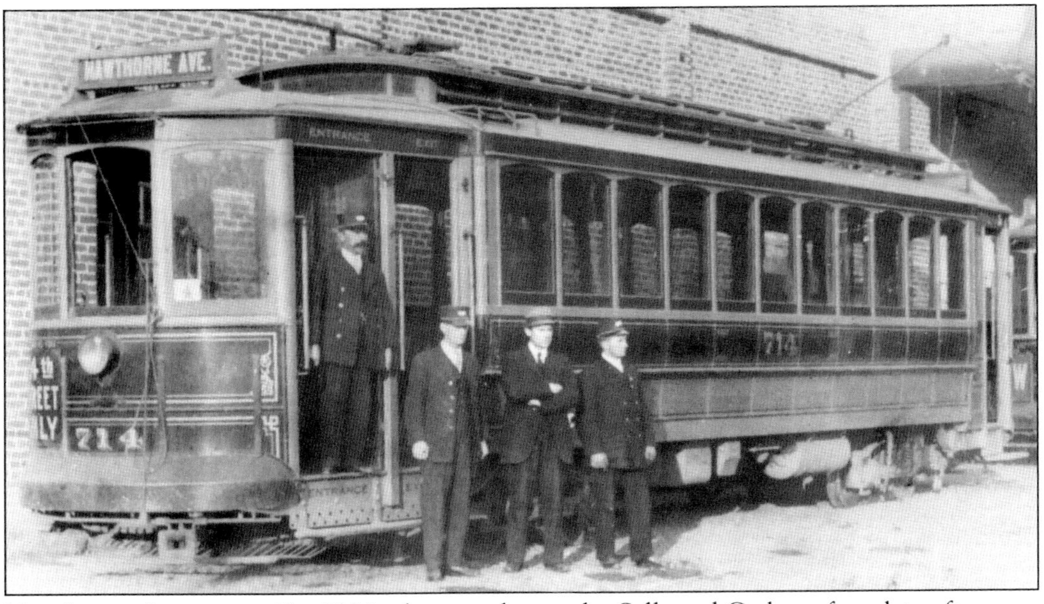

Hawthorne Avenue car No. 714 is about to depart the Sellwood Carbarn for a late afternoon rush hour stint. The year is about 1912, before Nelson safety fenders and trolley retrievers were installed. The Hawthorne Avenue line started as a steam dummy operation. Electrification on this standard gauge route began in 1891. The dash sign reads "54th Street Only," signifying that this is a rush hour tripper.

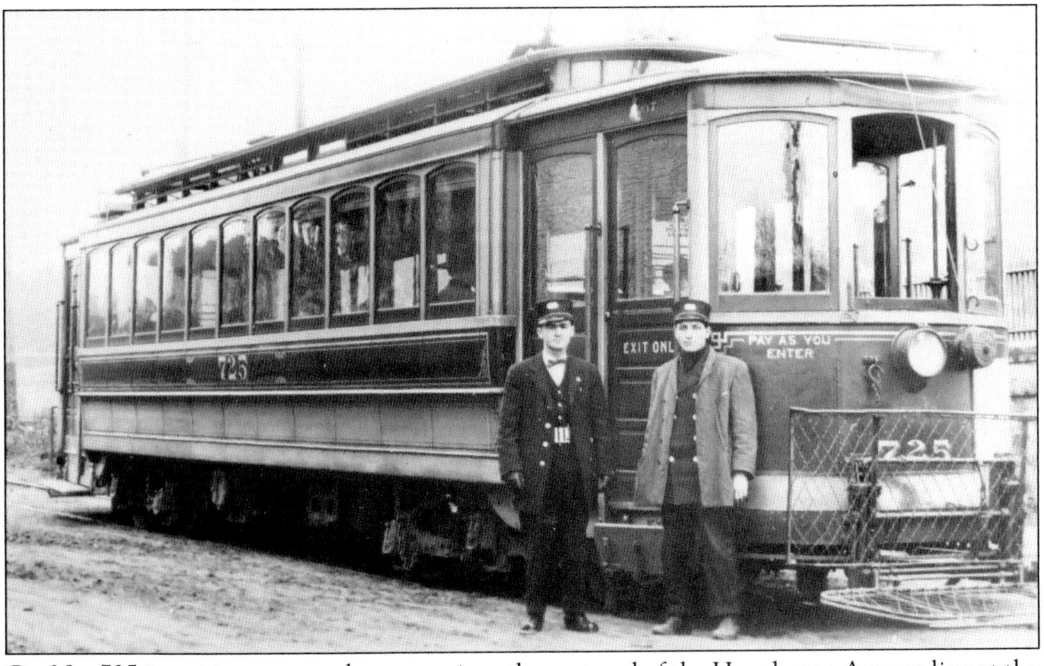

Car No. 725 is waiting next to the reservoir at the east end of the Hawthorne Avenue line at the Southeast Sixtieth and Division terminal in 1913. That year the line was extended to present-day Southeast Woodward Street and Seventy-fourth Avenue. Some veteran streetcars were saved from the scrapper's torch to become beach cabins or diners, but No. 725's retirement proved less glamorous; in 1937, it began a new career as a chicken coop.

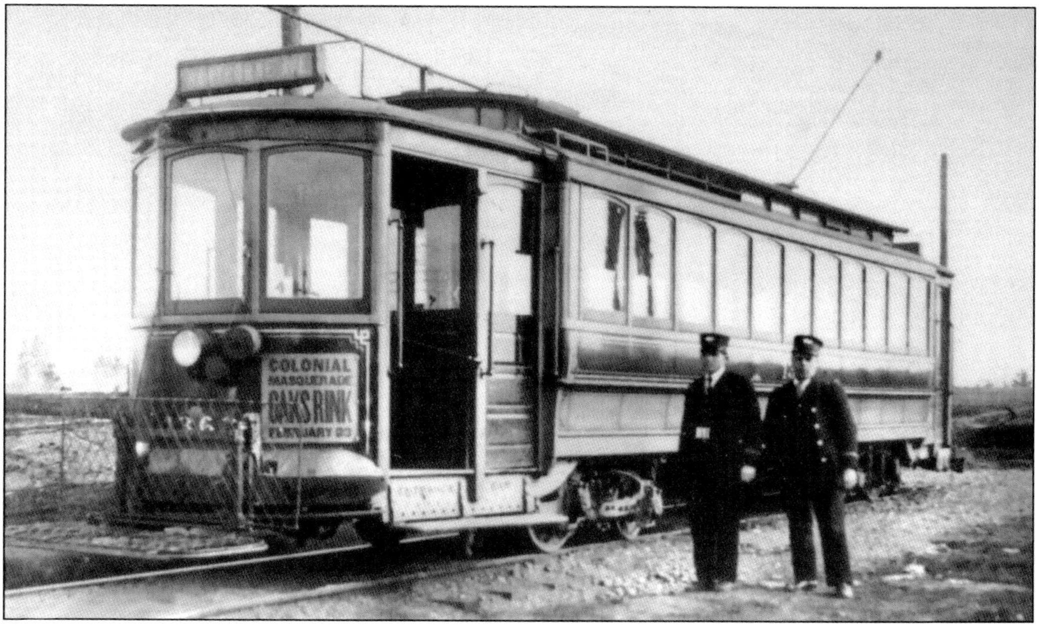

No. 1363 sits in a barren landscape at the new Hawthorne Avenue line terminus on Southeast Woodward Street at Seventy-fourth Avenue around 1918. This 1907 vintage car was among PRL&P's final group of standard-gauge suburbans. Today the last surviving car of this class, No. 1351, is a novelty store at Lincoln City on the Oregon Coast. The dash sign promotes a Colonial masquerade at The Oaks roller skating rink.

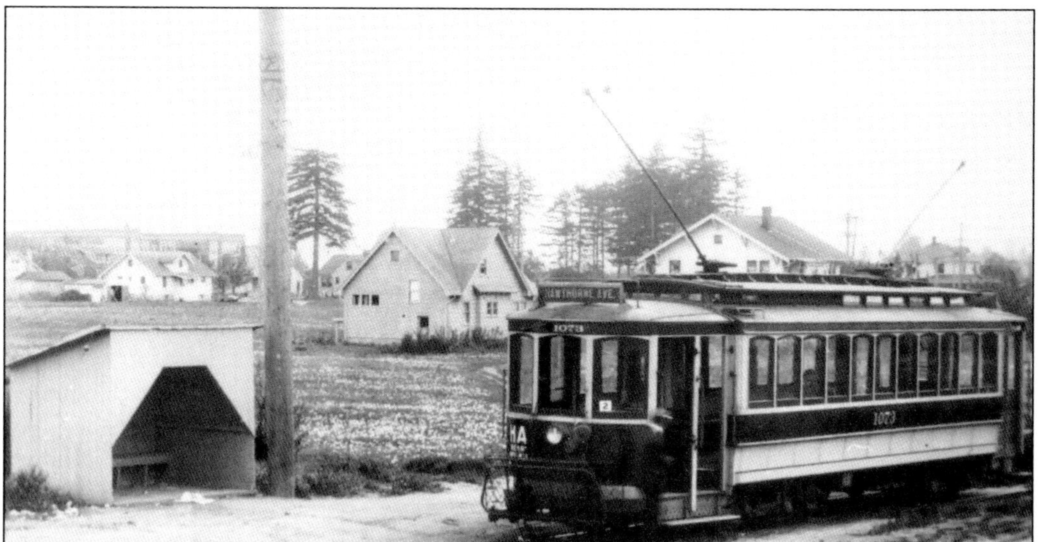

Hawthorne car No. 1073 is changing ends at Southeast Woodward Street and Seventy-fourth Avenue in the late 1920s. Not many houses obstruct the view of Kellogg School in the background, a lack of development that served Bill Hayes well when he was a schoolboy. Motorman Jimmy Tharp and conductor "Hazelnut" Hazelett allowed him to man the controls on their big class 700 car from here to the passing track at Southeast Sixty-seventh Avenue.

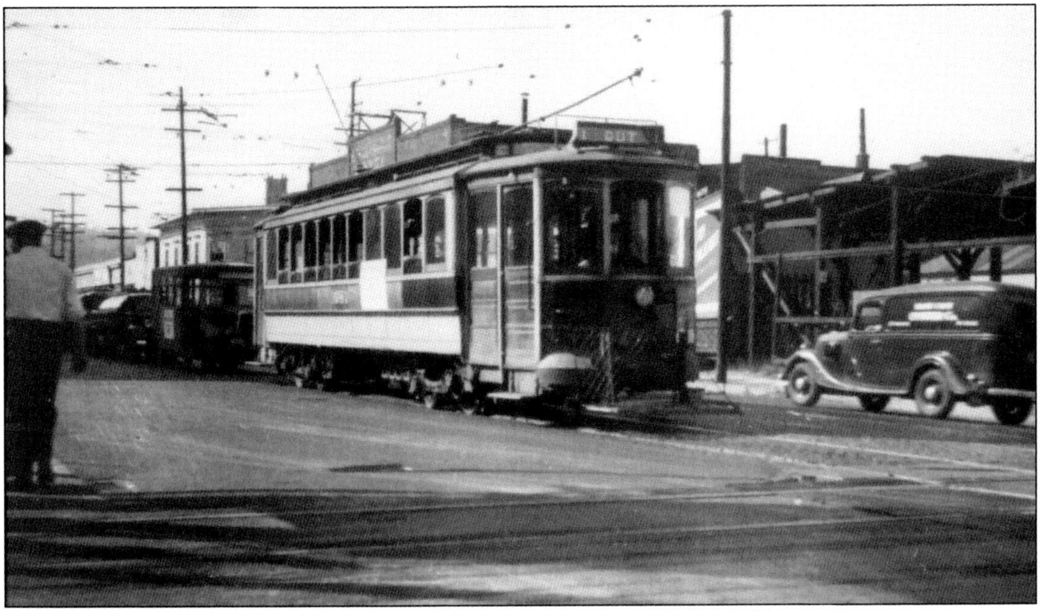

The "Out" on the roll sign means that No. 1081, seen here surrounded by trucks, vans, and a bus on Southeast Hawthorne Boulevard at Southeast First Avenue, is a rush hour tripper en route to the Sellwood carbarn. It is probably 1936, the year all remaining standard-gauge city cars, except for those working the Sellwood line, will be out of service.

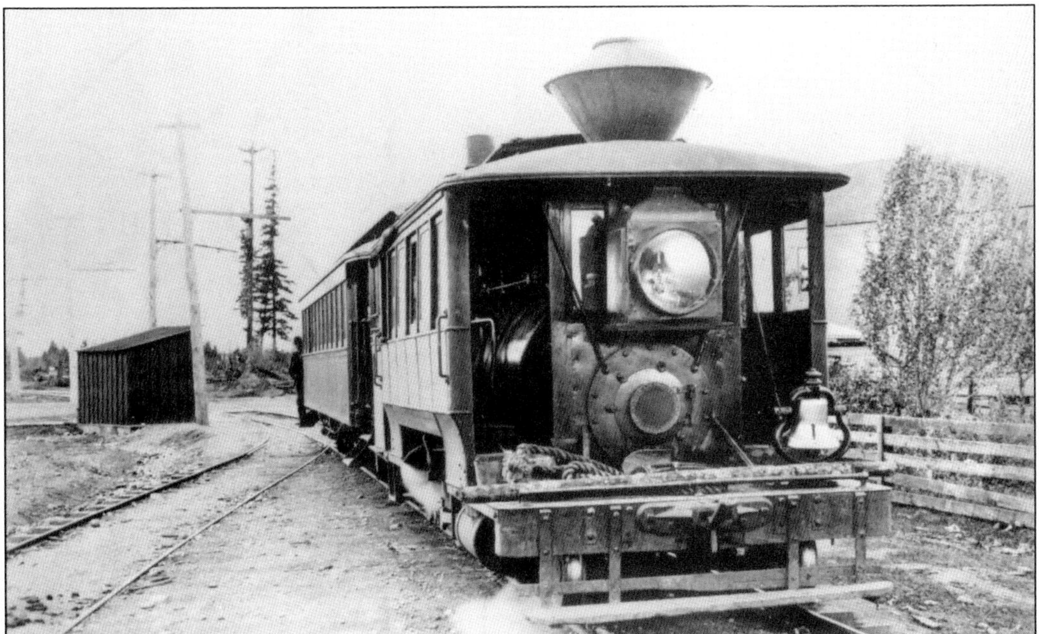

In 1892, Portland, Chicago, and Mount Scott Railway steam dummies like this one began running from Southeast Fiftieth Avenue and Hawthorne Boulevard to the community of Lents near Mount Scott. (Chicago was a small development south of Southeast Foster Road.) Although electrification had begun the year before on the Hawthorne line, the Mount Scott run remained steam until taken over by the Oregon Water Power and Railway Company in 1903.

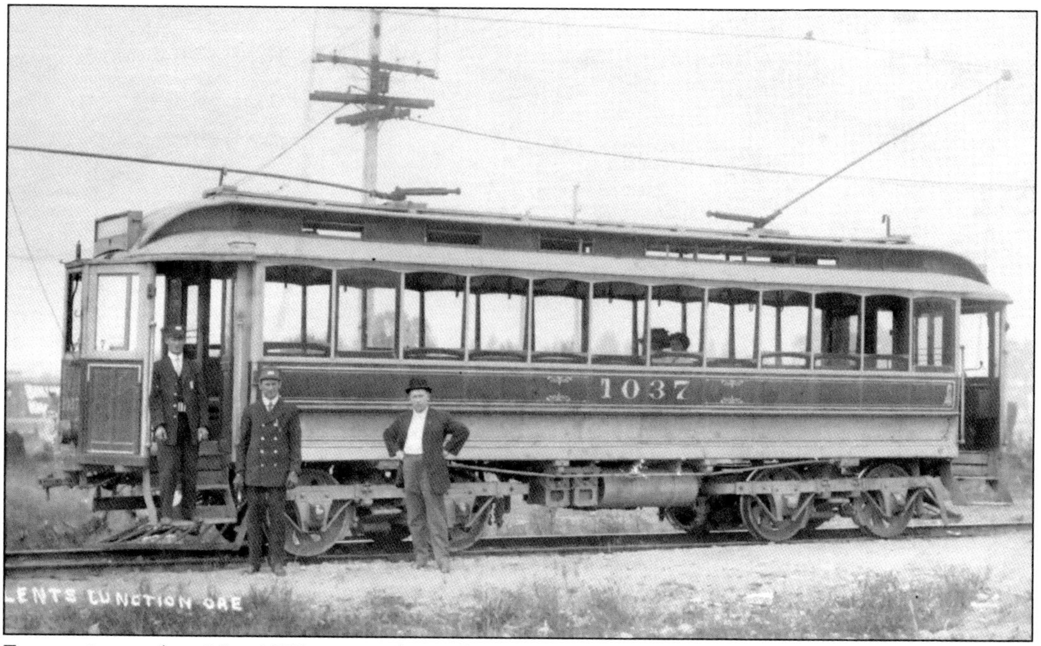

Former interurban No. 1037 was working the Mount Scott line during this hot day in the early 1900s. Built as one of the east side railway's named cars (probably Rose) in 1892, it was No. 37 during the Oregon Water Power years, and then renumbered again by PRL&P. The car was transferred to Salem in 1911 but returned for duty on the Murraymead line in Southeast Portland in 1914. (Courtesy Mark Moore.)

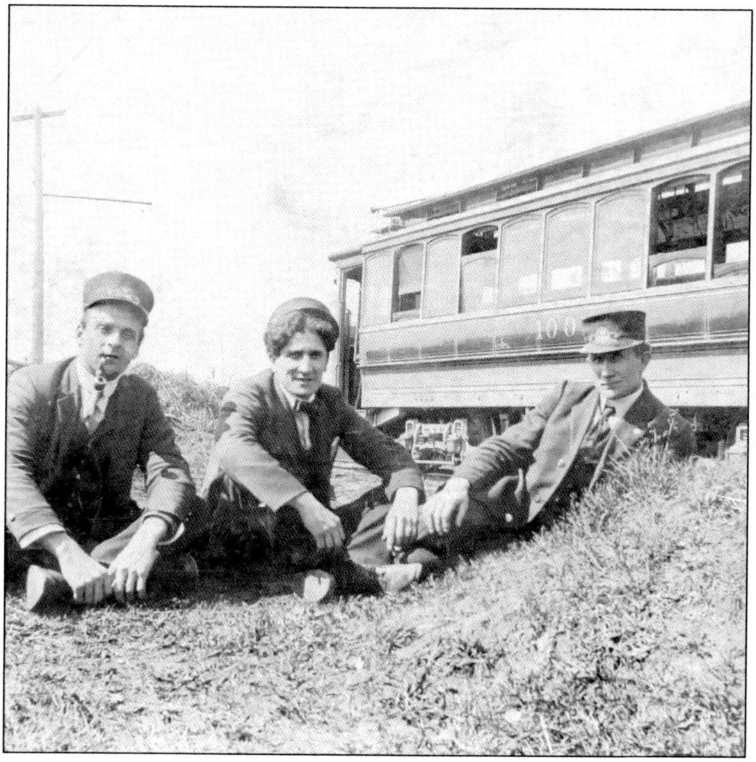

Crewmen Reck (left), Drake (center), and Seavey take a break next to brand-new Mount Scott car No. 1001 at Lents Junction near present-day Southeast Foster Road and 102nd Avenue. Pipe-smoking motorman Albert A. Reck went to work for Oregon Water Power and Railway in 1906 and retired from Portland Traction in 1954 at the age of 77. The last interurban rolled into the barn four years later. (Courtesy Mark Moore.)

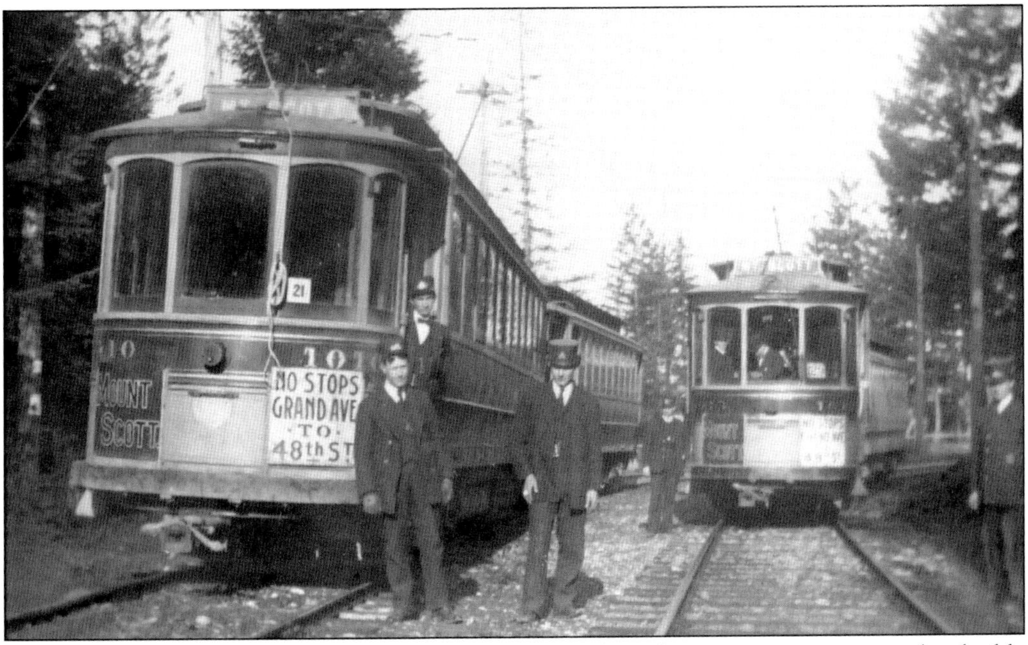

Nos. 1010 and 1015 head up two multiple-unit Mount Scott line trains meeting on the double track at Southwest Ninety-fourth Avenue near Lents Junction. Both trains are limited rush hour runs and carry dash signs warning that they make no stops until Southeast Forty-eighth Street (now Avenue). Mount Scott streetcars ran out Southeast Hawthorne Boulevard from Southeast Grand to Southeast Fiftieth Avenue, before turning toward Lents. (Courtesy Mark Moore.)

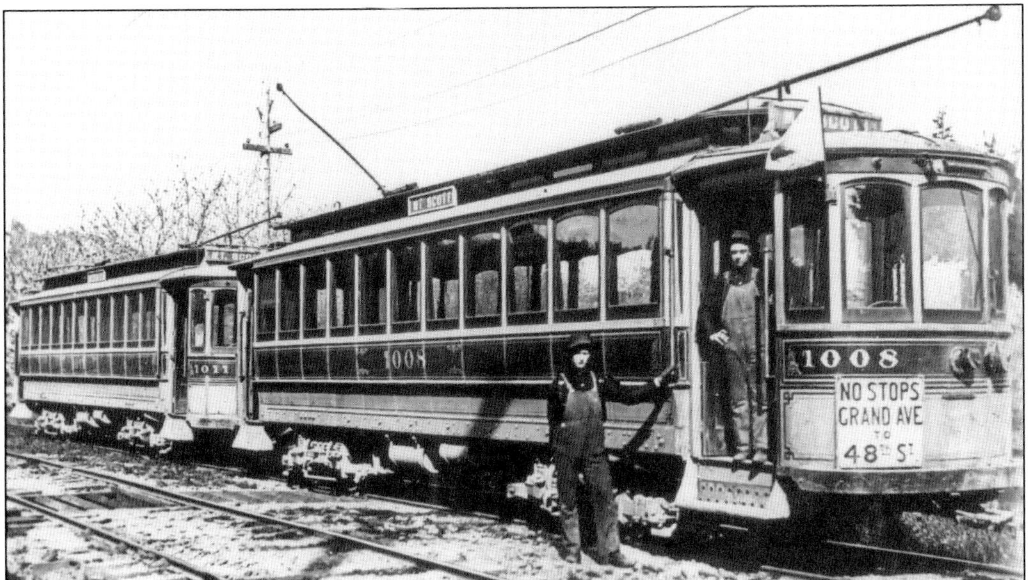

Two "Yellow Jackets" (so named because their yellow and maroon colors were such a change from the sedate livery worn previously by OWP rolling stock) are running extra on the Mount Scott line with shop crew. The cars are thought to be at Golf Junction, near Southeast Thirteenth Avenue and Ochoco Street about 1910. Note the side-facing destination signs, the white extra flags, and the lack of permanent headlights.

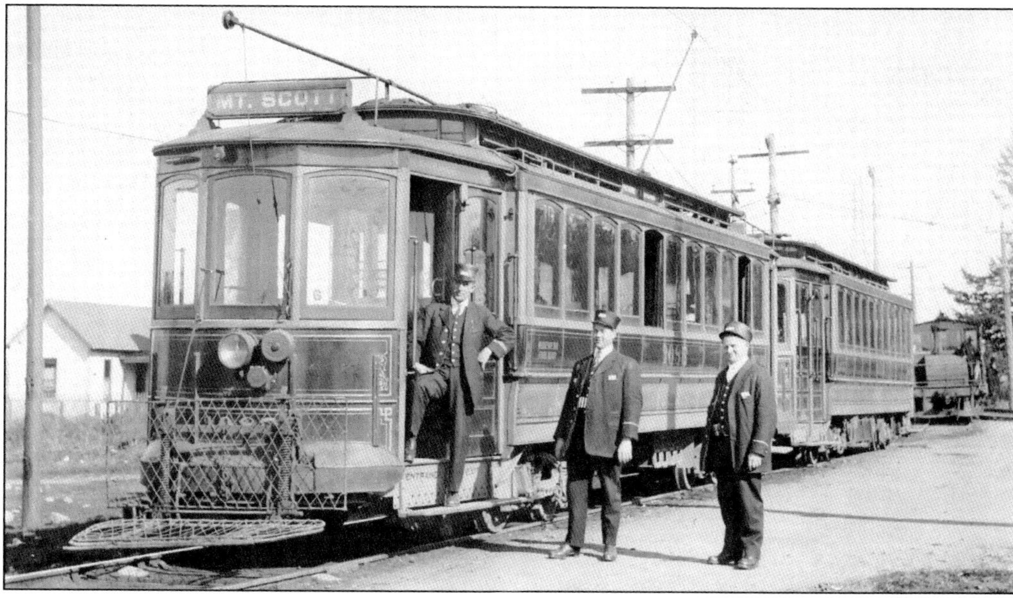

A two-car Mount Scott line train headed up by No. 1085 is being followed by a steeple cab freight locomotive at Lents Junction in a photograph taken just before train gates were installed on two-car trains in 1914. Electric freight trains pulled by steeple cabs were a frequent site on the standard-gauge lines, hauling wood and produce to businesses throughout Southeast Portland. (Courtesy Mark Moore.)

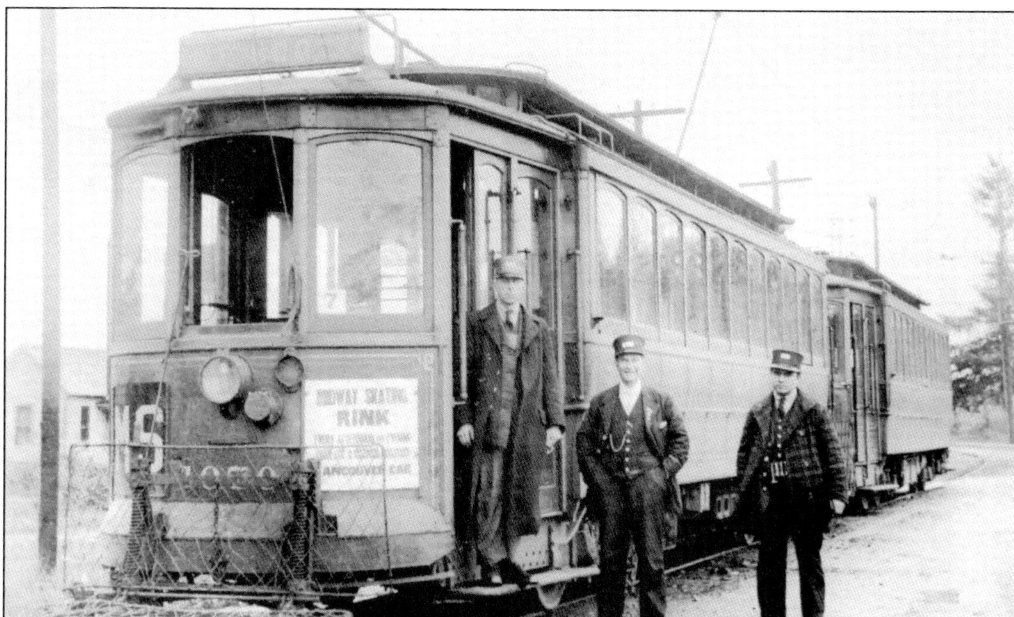

Close examination reveals that train gates have been installed between Mount Scott line car No. 1070 and its sister. In 1914, PRL&P equipped all of its two-car trains with collapsible safety gates to avoid accidents where people might fall between cars while attempting to board. As trains rounded a curve, the gates would automatically fold up on one side and open out on the other. (Courtesy Mark Moore.)

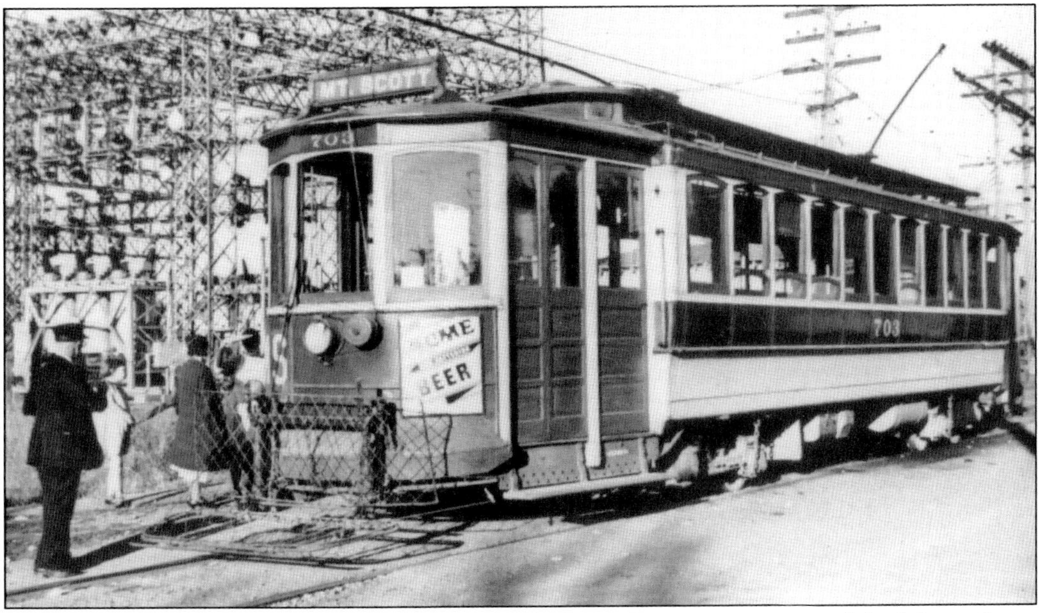

Car No. 703, seen here next to the substation at the Lents Junction terminus of the Mount Scott line, was normally found on the Richmond line. After 1928, the traditional two-car Mount Scott line trains were split up and operated singly. The dash sign promoting "non fattening" Acme Beer was part of a 1930s advertising campaign, which helps date this picture.

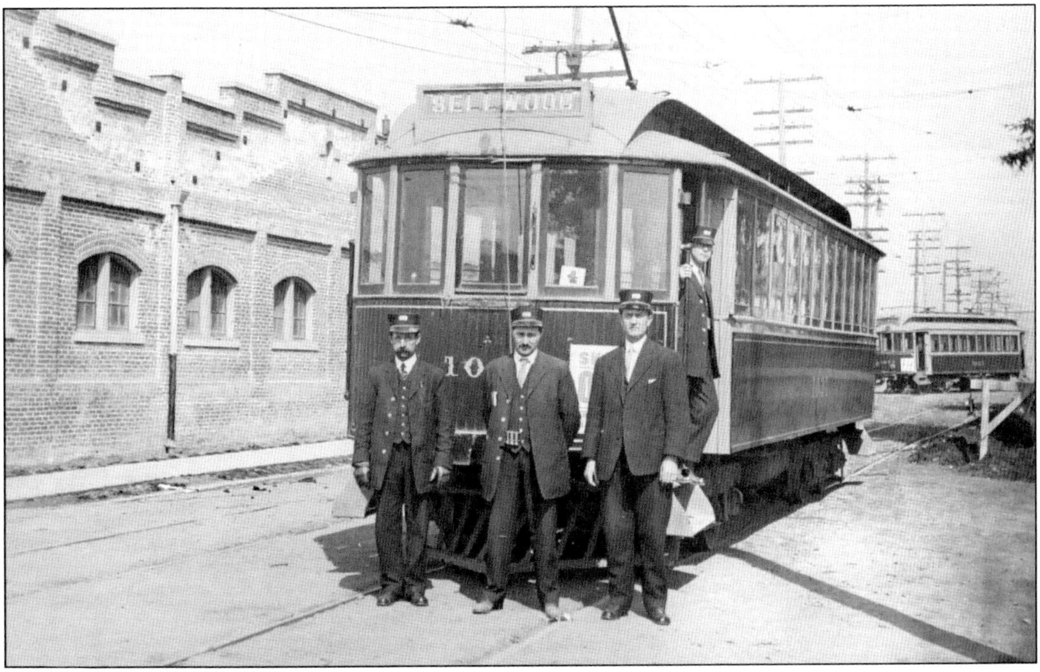

Sellwood line crewmen pose with former interurban No. 1031 at the Sellwood carbarn on Southeast Thirteenth Avenue and Ochoco Street. The Sellwood line had its beginnings in the East Side Railway's interurban venture to Oregon City in 1891. It became a separate city line in 1903 when OC cars were rerouted closer to the river. One wall of this 1911 vintage carbarn survives today in a condominium complex. (Courtesy Mark Moore.)

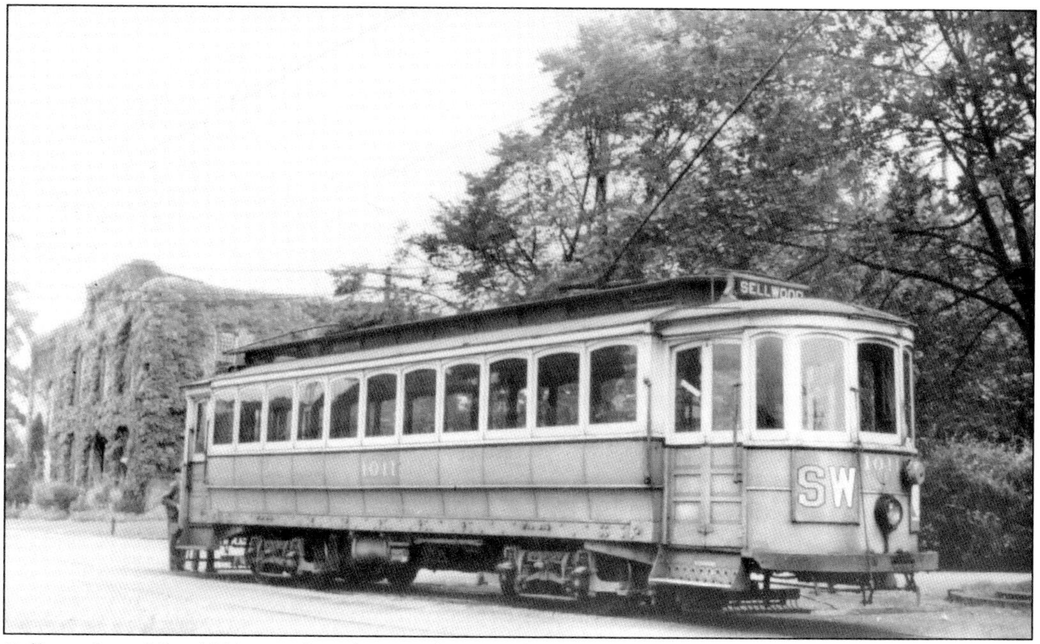

Sellwood car No. 1011 is at Southeast Thirteenth Avenue and Ochoco Street just before it was retired in 1939. The Sellwood line was unique in many ways: it outlasted other standard-gauge city lines, it was the only line with a carbarn as the outer terminal, and often no two cars on the line seemed to be of the same type. The ivy-covered Sellwood substation in the background remains today.

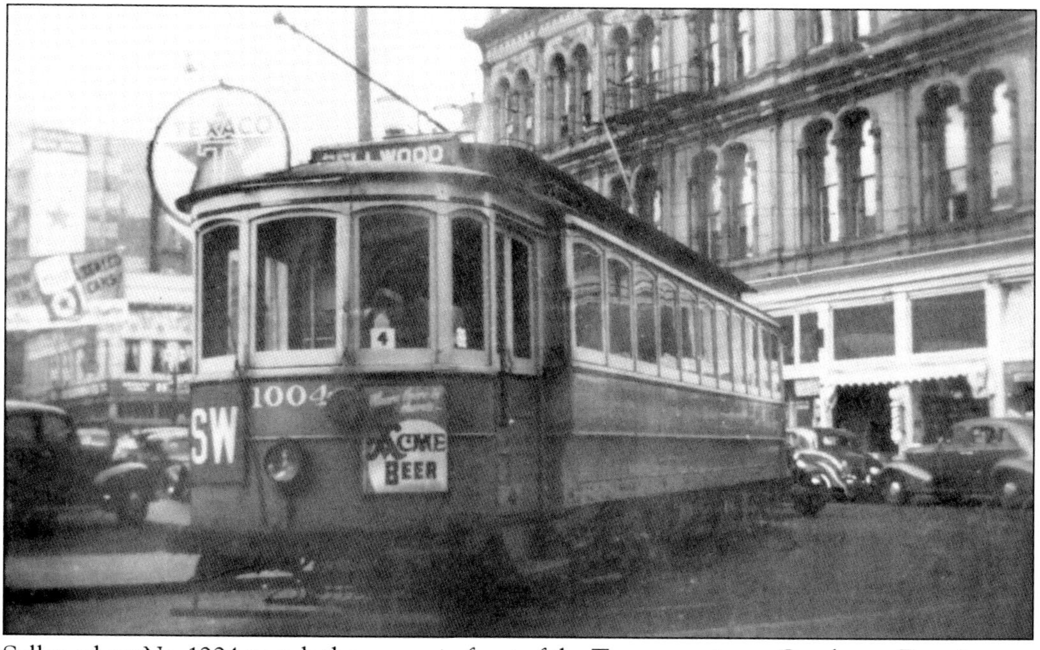

Sellwood car No. 1004 rounds the corner in front of the Texaco station at Southwest First Avenue and Alder Street in downtown just before the demise of the line in 1940. This former yellow jacket is now more of a green hornet with its 1930s cream and green colors. Today MAX light rail trains travel through this area, which was cleared for ramps to the new Morrison Bridge in 1958.

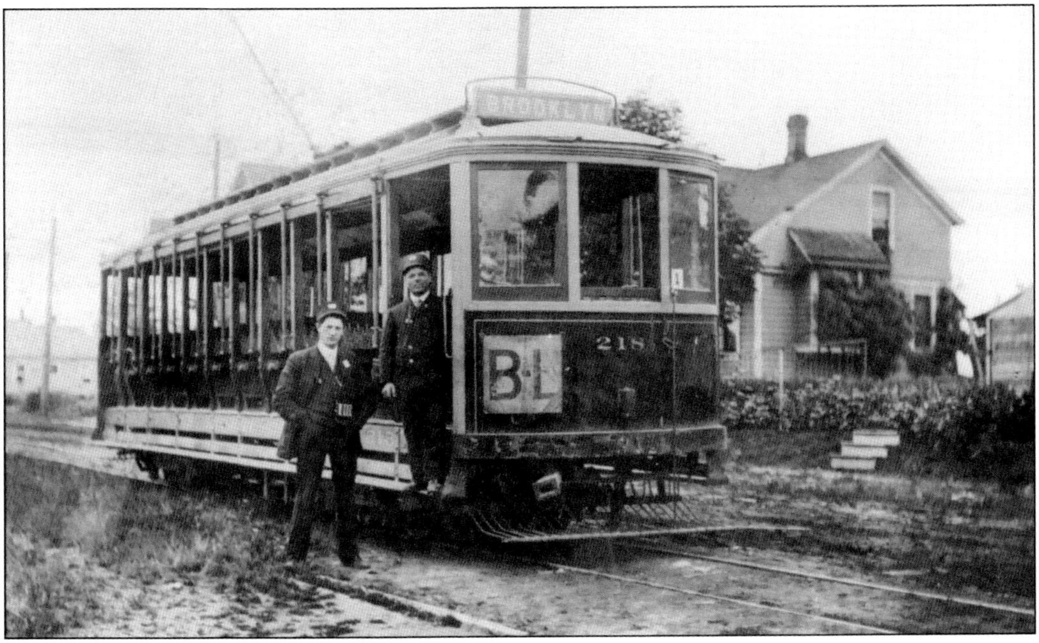

From 1901 to 1927, the Brooklyn line ran out Southeast Powell Boulevard to Twenty-first Avenue and Bush Street in the German immigrant neighborhood of Brookland. The high steps on open cars like No. 218 were a challenge for women wearing the hobble skirts that were then vogue. In 1909, to make things even more difficult, the *Portland Telegram* advised that "no really young and attractive woman ever gets off a streetcar backward."

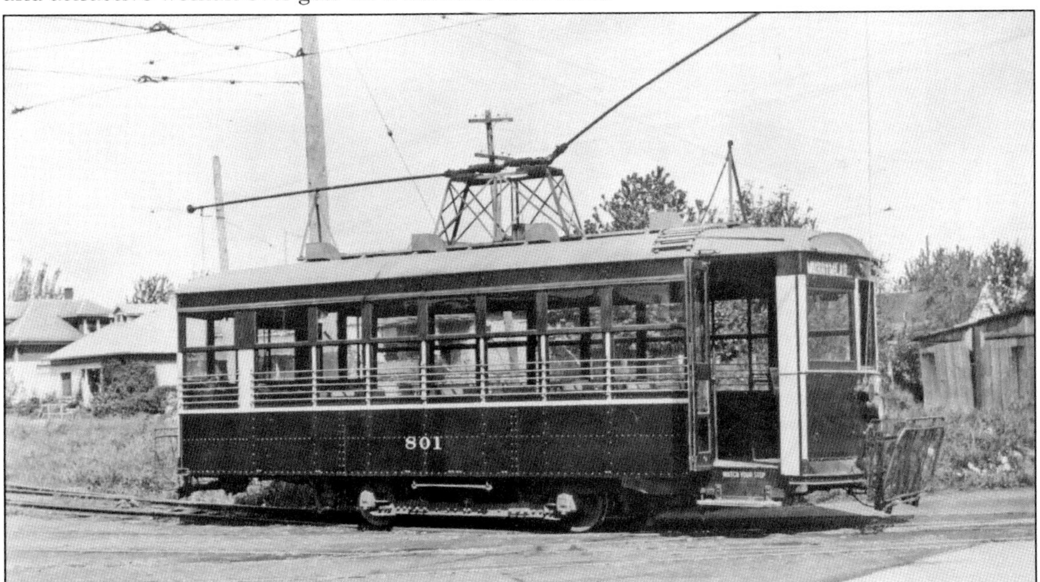

Like most stub lines, Murraymead came about through an agreement with a developer. It ran an L-shaped route through Colonial Heights from Southeast Twentieth Avenue and Hawthorne Boulevard to Southeast Thirtieth Avenue and Harrison Street from June 1, 1913, to August 30, 1936. Standard-gauge Birney Nos. 801 and 802 were assigned to Murraymead after World War I. No. 801, seen here at the Sellwood carbarn, survives today in a Portland restaurant.

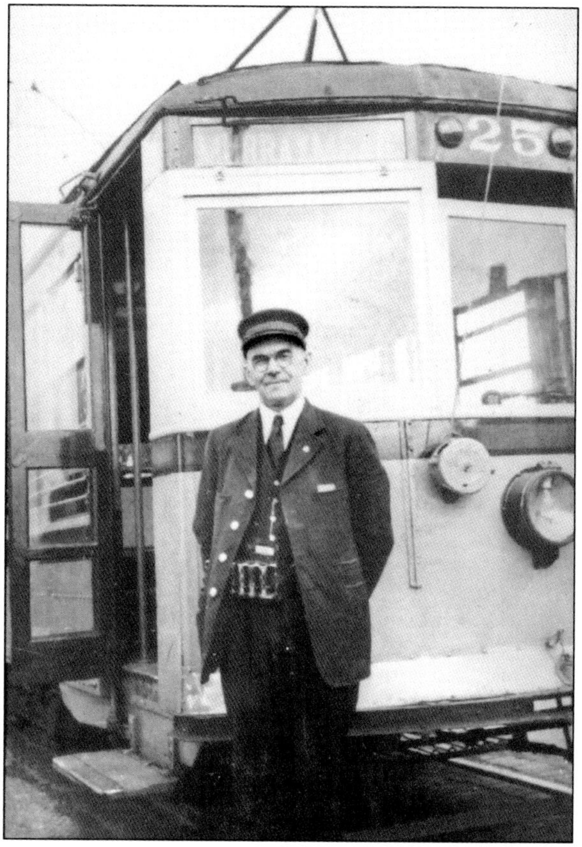

Birney No. 25 is seen at Southwest Twentieth Avenue and Hawthorne Boulevard at the northern end of the Murraymead stub line wearing Portland Traction's gray and green. In 1932, after the new *Broadway* cars took the numbers 800–814, the standard-gauge Birneys were renumbered from 801–802 to 24–25. This lightly traveled short line was a good run for motormen with "lots of whiskers" to bid in before retirement.

This photograph of Yellow Jacket No. 1001 at Southeast Milwaukie Boulevard and Bybee Street is thought to have been taken on the first day of service for the Eastmoreland stub line in March 1912. The Ladd Estate Company built the line from Southeast Bybee Avenue and Milwaukie Street to Southeast and Thirty-second Avenue and Rex Street near the Reed College campus.

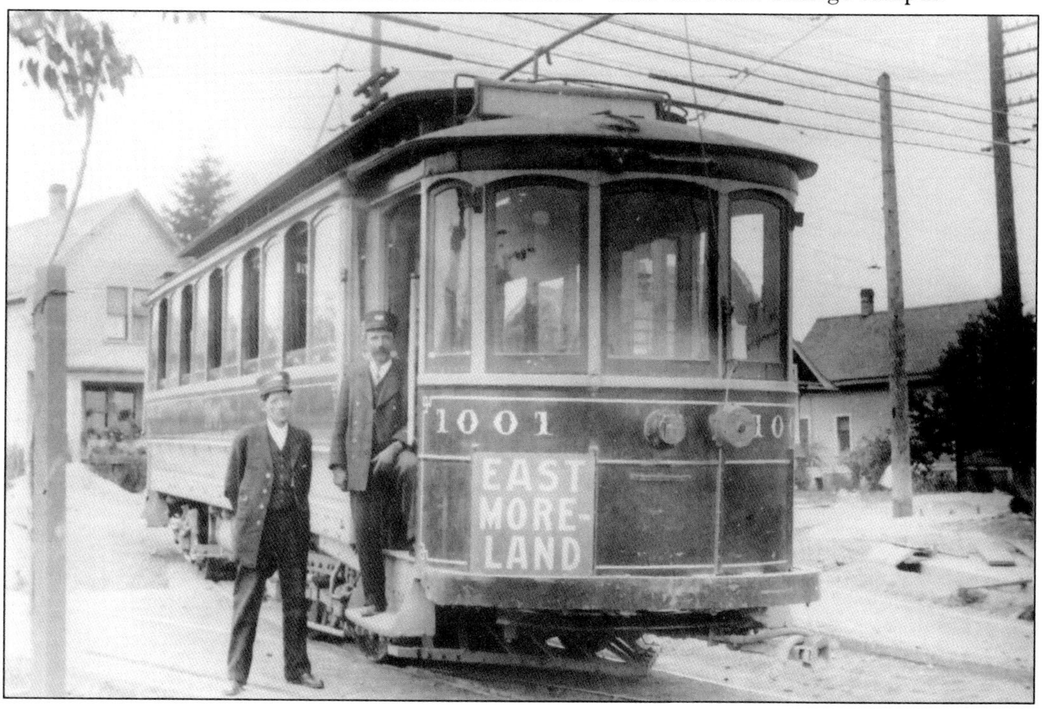

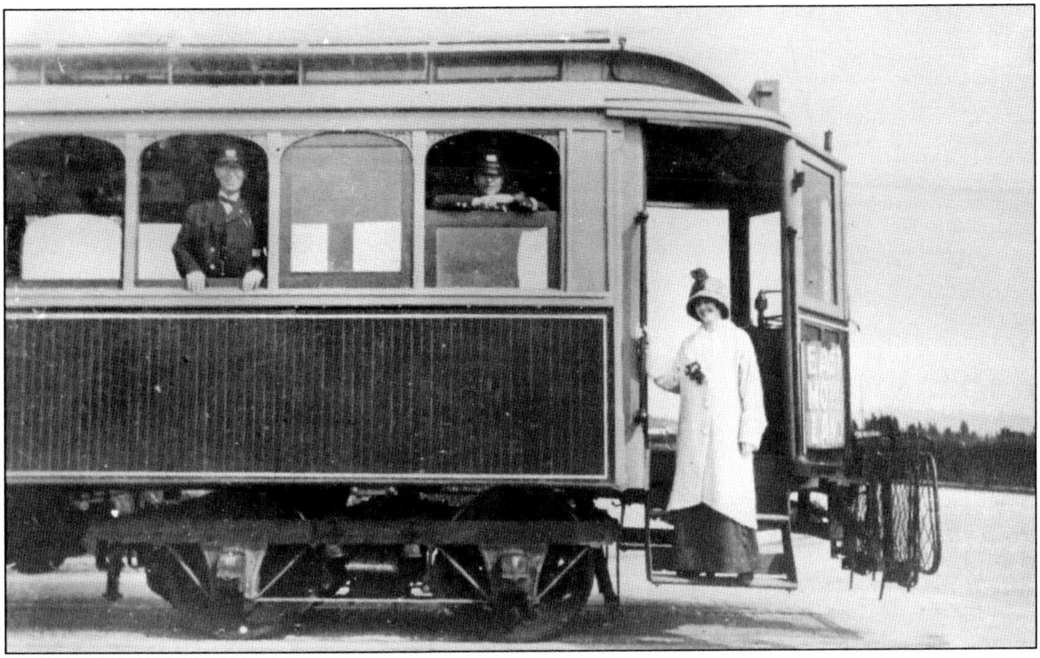

A woman poses on the steps of Eastmoreland line car No. 1042 around 1913 at what appears to be the end of the line on Southeast Thirty-second Avenue and Rex Street. Pioneering No. 1042 was locally built in 1892 by the Columbia Car and Tool Works as the East Side Railway's Alva. It became a work car before retirement in 1926, the year the Eastmoreland line was converted to bus.

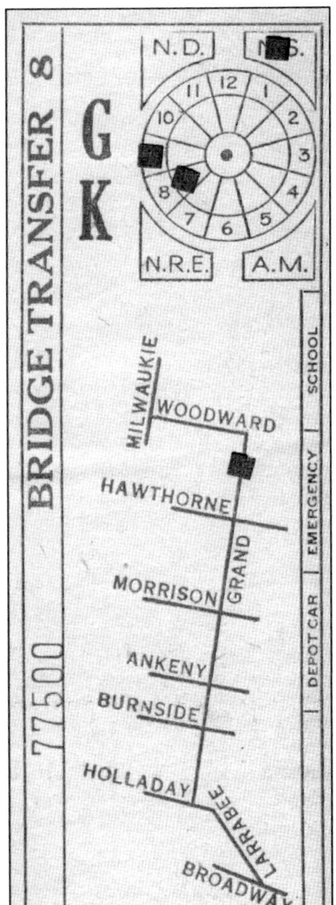

The Bridge Transfer (BT) line was created January 1, 1915, by adding the route used by the second east side line to the southern portion of the Russell Shaver line. In June 1927, the Brooklyn line was merged with Bridge Transfer as an alternate southern terminus. In 1934, BT was reduced to the route illustrated on this upside-down transfer map. Conversion to bus came twice, in 1940 and 1947.

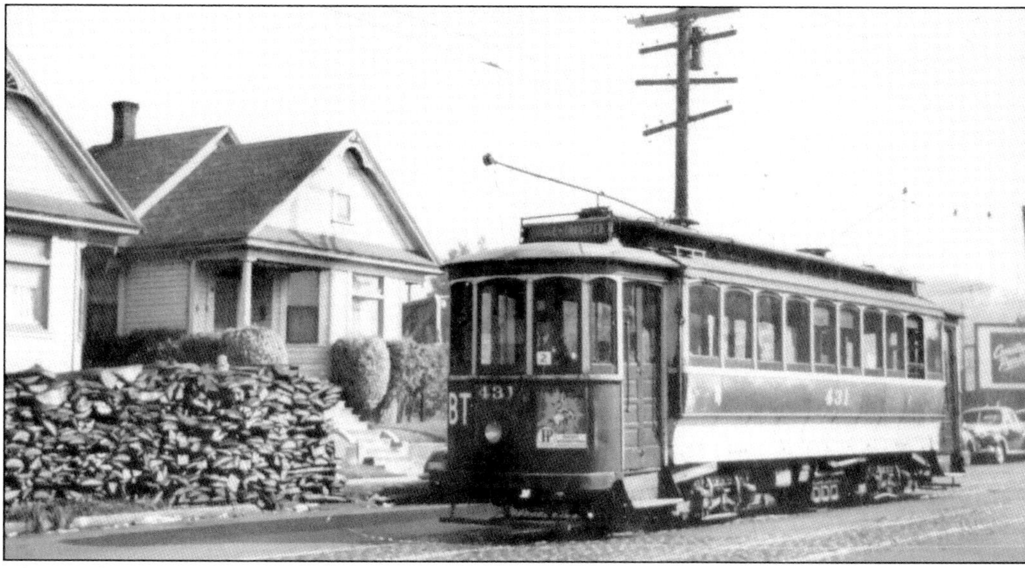

The Bridge Transfer line served as a link between car lines crossing Willamette River bridges (Broadway, Steel, Burnside, Morrison, and Hawthorne). This view shows Bridge Transfer No. 431 westbound on Northeast Holladay Street during the 1940s. The wood for home heating stacked at curbside was once a common sight in Portland.

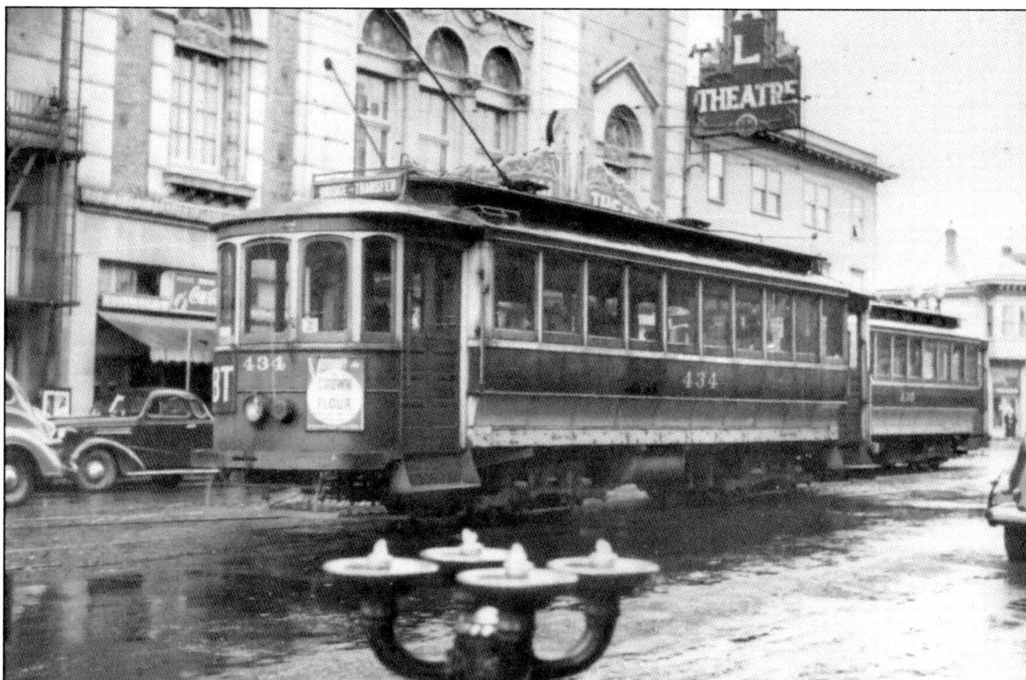

Bridge Transfer line car Nos. 434 and 430 are passing in front of the Oriental Theater on Grand Avenue between Southeast Morrison and Belmont Streets. The exuberant Italian Renaissance–style theater opened December 31, 1927. Sadly, the city's largest movie palace, seating 2,750, was demolished in 1970. One of the classic Benson bubbler drinking fountains that lumber baron Simon Benson began donating to the city in 1912 is in the foreground.

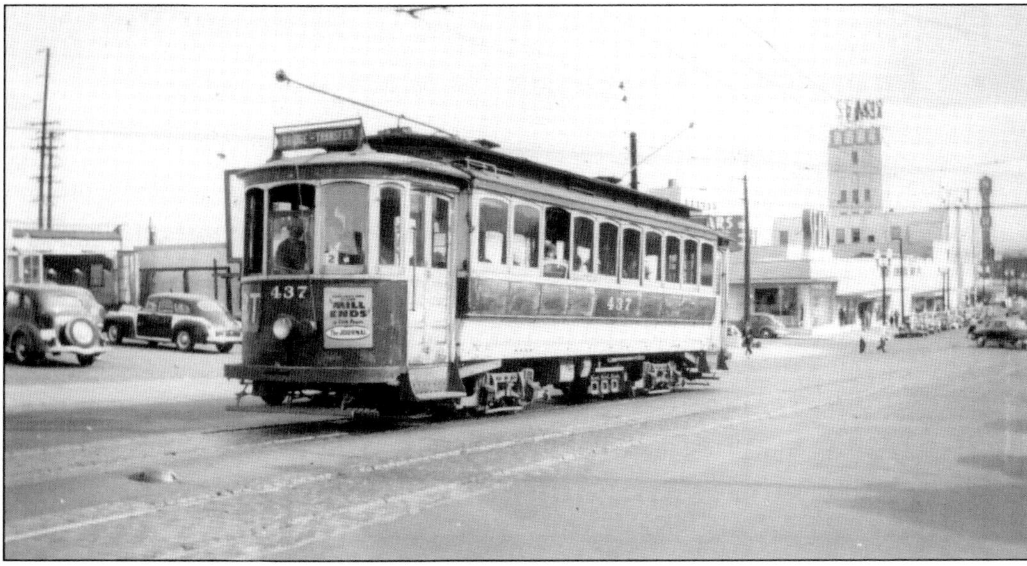

Car No. 437 hums north on Northeast Grand Avenue with the Sears store in the background. The eastside's crosstown trolley line was converted to bus on March 23, 1940, but returned to operation during World War II when the rails were chipped back out of the pavement. The BT was gone again December 27, 1947. Then, in 2008, funding was approved for a new line along much of the old route.

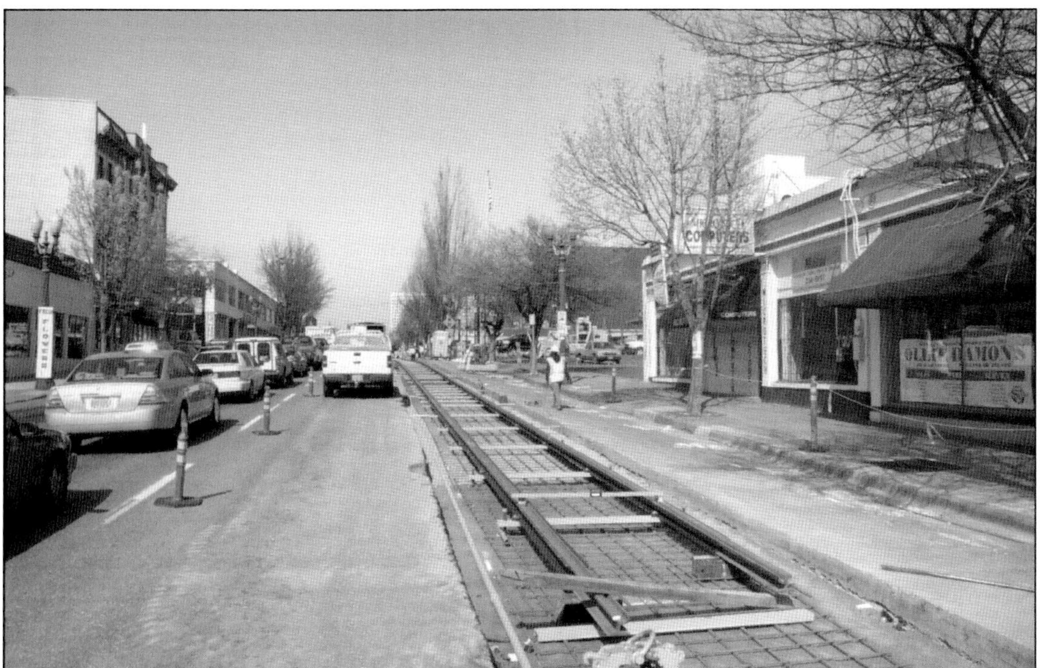

In 2010, work was under way to return streetcars to southeast Portland. The new Portland streetcar line will extend from the Pearl District to the Oregon Museum of Science and Industry via the Broadway Bridge and the Lloyd District, reviving much of the former Bridge Transfer line. This March 23, 2010, photograph shows track being laid on Southeast Grand Avenue at Pine Street. (Photograph by Steve Morgan.)

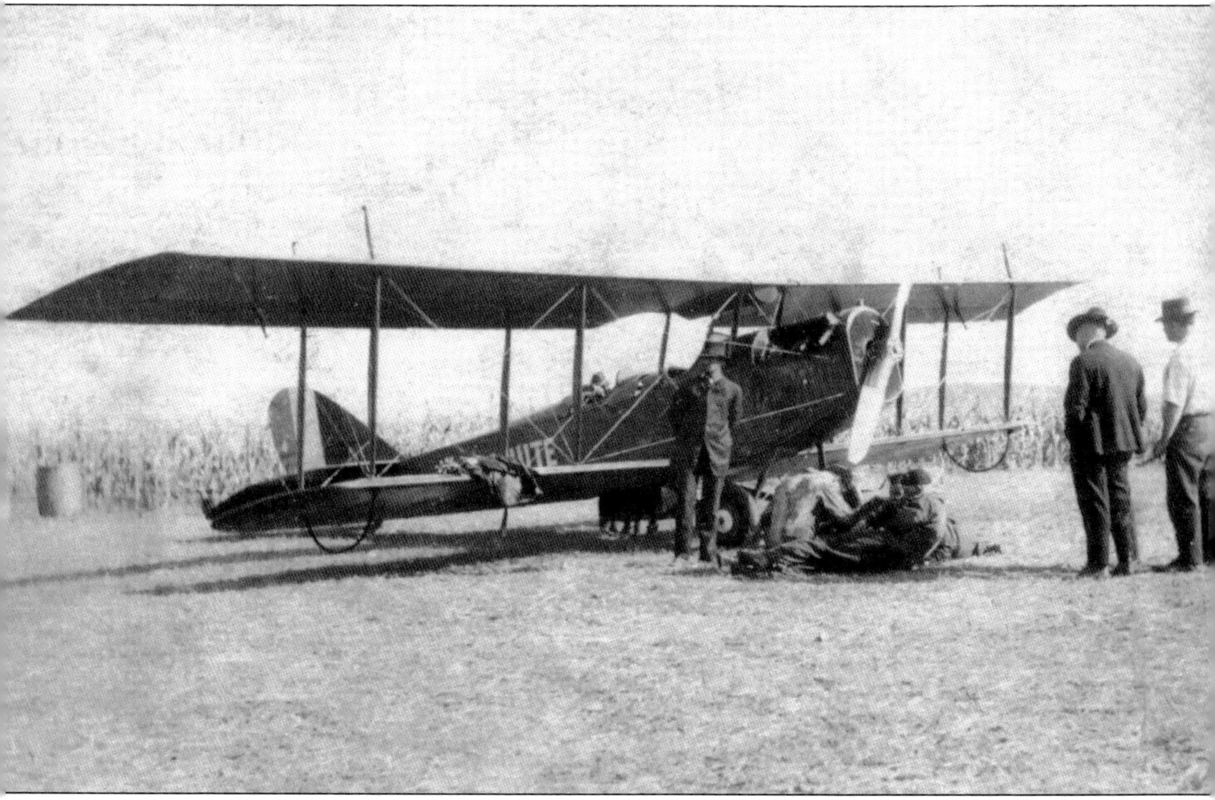

Following World War I, pilots in their surplus "Jennies" barnstormed the countryside staging aerial stunt shows and giving willing passengers rides. Wing-walkers and parachutists were part of many shows. Several interested onlookers watch an unidentified barnstorming crew repack its parachutes in this 1917 photograph, taken at what would become known as Franing Field. It was shows like these that planted the seed of interest in many future pilots. (Courtesy of Quad City International Airport (QCIA).)

On the Cover: The dedication of the Quad City Airport's new terminal complex in October 1954 brought several thousand spectators to the ceremonies. Visitors could explore the terminal and control tower and view the displays of aircraft on the ramp. One of the big crowd-pleasers was the chance to explore a United Air Lines DC-6B, flown in especially for the ceremony, as only the two-engined Convair was used to service Moline. (Courtesy of QCIA.)

IMAGES
of Aviation

QUAD CITY INTERNATIONAL AIRPORT

David T. Coopman

ARCADIA PUBLISHING

ISBN 978-0-7385-8371-6

Published by Arcadia Publishing
Charleston, South Carolina

Printed in the United States of America

Library of Congress Control Number: 2010931877

For all general information, please contact Arcadia Publishing:
Telephone 843-853-2070
Fax 843-853-0044
E-mail sales@arcadiapublishing.com
For customer service and orders:
Toll-Free 1-888-313-2665

Visit us on the Internet at www.arcadiapublishing.com

This book is dedicated to all past and present members of the aviation community and the passengers who have helped make Quad City International Airport what it is today.

Contents

Acknowledgments 6

Introduction 7

1. Framing Field: 1922–1934 9
2. Moline Airport: 1935–1952 33
3. Quad City Airport: 1953–1984 63
4. Quad City International Airport: 1985–Present 97

ACKNOWLEDGMENTS

This historical overview of the Quad City International Airport could not have been completed without the assistance of many people connected to commercial and private aviation. My deep gratitude goes to QCIA's director of aviation, Bruce Carter, AAE, and marketing representative Cathie Rochau, for allowing me total access to the airport's archive of photographs and articles; Kris Streed Crawford, for sharing Dr. Warren Streed's collection of aviation photographs and memorabilia; Ken Roberts, for photographs from the collection of early Monocoupe racer and airport manager Vern Roberts; the family of longtime United Airlines manager Richard Shrader, for access to his early photographs; and to Arcadia Publishing editor Ted Gerstle, for his valuable assistance and constant encouragement for this project.

Thanks to Richard Haney, William Hansen, Chuck Hoaglund, John Lartz, Fred Marzolph, Mack McAdams, Jerry Reeser, Ralph Stephenson, Anita Sundin, Earl "Buck" Wendt, the *Dispatch/ Argus*, the Rock Island County Historical Society Library, and Sacred Heart Church (Moline) for assistance with research and photographs.

Credit for some of the photographs in the QCIA archives belongs to commercial photographers Raymond Utke, William Schultz, and H.K. Williams. Images not credited are those from the personal collection of the author.

INTRODUCTION

The history of the Quad City International Airport begins as early as 1919, when the first airplane wheels touched ground in a flat pasture that would eventually become the airport. That pasture, known as Franing Field, was selected as a control point for the first coast-to-coast flights of Army airplanes. It would not be long before barnstormers began using the field to perform daring aerobatics and give brave individuals rides over the city.

Credit for creating the Moline Airport goes to several local aviation enthusiasts. Gustaf DeSchepper, the first Moline resident to receive a pilot's license, joined with his flying instructor, J. Wesley Smith, to create a flying service. In 1922, the duo leased space on a farm near Moline's present-day Fifty-third Street and Avenue of the Cities. There they soloed two more enthusiasts, Floyd Ketner and Dr. C.C. Sloan, both of whom joined them in the company. With the city closing in around that farm, they leased 30 acres of land at Franing Field, erected a hangar, and began to give pleasure rides and deliver freight.

Wesley Smith moved east in late 1922 to take a position with another aviation enterprise. Earl "Rusty" Campbell, who had given airplane rides from another farm in Moline two years earlier, was invited to join the flying service. He arrived in 1923. The men then created the Campbell-DeSchepper Airplane Company to repair and sell airplanes, give rides, and fly freight. It would also continue to further develop the airport by leasing 200 additional acres.

With interest in aviation growing all across the country, Henry Ford wanted to demonstrate the safety and reliability of airplanes. Modeled after the Glidden Tour for automobiles, Ford created the National Air Tour. The Moline field was chosen as a control point for the first tour in 1925. It would serve in that capacity for three more tours between 1926 and 1929. With each visit of the tour, ever-larger crowds turned out to watch the planes land and take off.

As airmail routes began their further evolution, the Campbell-DeSchepper Airplane Company proposed to bring airmail service to Moline. With the full support and financial backing of the Moline Association of Commerce, airmail service began on May 12, 1926. Twice each day, planes of National Air Transport (NAT) would stop on their trips between Chicago and Dallas. Before the end of the year, NAT began flying passengers, as well as mail and express freight.

The Moline Association of Commerce constantly aided the continued development of Moline Airport. The association saw the benefits of the airport for area citizens and businesses and for the overall prestige of the community. By December 1926, the civic group had paid for the installation of boundary, obstacle, approach, and flood lighting. The airport was now equipped to handle day or night flights.

Over the next several years, as more flight operations were occurring at the airport, it was apparent that the sod landing areas needed to be upgraded. Spring rains made landings and takeoffs nearly impossible at times. Hard-surfaced runways were needed for the larger, heavier commercial aircraft. A movement was begun to have the city take over ownership of the airport. In July 1929, voters elected, by a margin of 3 to 1, to do just that. But a misplaced decimal point on the ballot nullified that vote.

In May 1930, United Air Lines (renamed United Airlines in the mid-1970s) purchased National Air Transport and began serving Moline under the new name. It was now very important that the airport, especially the runways, continued to be upgraded. Unfortunately, this was during the Depression, and at times the airport barely survived financially. A second vote in 1932 to approve city ownership of the field failed, but in 1935, Moline finally took ownership.

This was a timely period for Moline, as the federal government was creating make-work projects to aid the depressed economy. The Works Progress Administration (WPA) began a three-year task of leveling the field and paving the runways. In 1939, with city and WPA funds, a new hangar building was erected that included a passenger waiting area, office space for the airline, a US Weather Bureau, and a Civil Aeronautics Authority office.

Following World War II, the concept of a regional airport was taking form. Illinois communities felt that Moline, with an airport in place and growing, was ideally suited to serve as a Class IV air carrier airport. Davenport, Iowa, was developing a new airport north of town at Mount Joy, which the city wanted to be designated the region's primary airport. Several years of cross-river community bickering, engineering studies, and hearings before the Civil Aeronautics Administration finally ended in the awarding of Class IV status to the Moline field. Helping save Moline's bid was the Illinois Airport Authority Act, which had authorized the creation of local airport authorities with separate taxing and bonding powers. In November 1947, county voters approved the purchase and operation of the airport, now to be known as the Quad City Airport. The seven largest county townships comprise a governmental unit known as the Metropolitan Airport Authority (MAA).

In 1954, a $3 million expansion program culminated in the dedication of a totally new, modern terminal building. A remodeling project in 1961 added second-floor additions to both the east and west wings and a 120-foot addition to the main floor that enlarged the restaurant and added an automated baggage system. Another addition added passenger boarding lounges and a larger baggage claim area in 1969.

As airline and civilian aircraft traffic continued to increase, runways were lengthened or totally rebuilt, along with taxiways and larger aircraft aprons. The south side of the airport property was redeveloped for general aviation, beginning in 1975 with the construction of a new Federal Aviation Administration (FAA) control tower. Private aircraft T-hangars and corporate aircraft hangars and facilities were all moved to this new location.

Continued passenger growth and an increase in the number of airlines using the airport called for further modernization. A new $5.3 million terminal was dedicated in May 1985. It featured larger ticketing areas, larger main waiting lounges, a new and expandable baggage claim area, and two concourses—one for boarding jets via jetways and one for commuter airlines.

During 1986, the Quad Cities was granted US Customs port-of-entry status. This allowed airfreight to clear customs at the Quad City Airport. Corporate aircraft arriving from outside of US boundaries could also have its passengers cleared. In 1997, the airport name was changed to Quad City International Airport (QCIA) to reflect that status.

The new terminal that opened in 1985 was doubled in size in 2000, at a cost of $17 million, to accommodate expected passenger growth for the new century. Most of the changes were on the airfield side of the terminal: more gates and larger waiting areas that offer passengers wide panoramas of the runways.

Although the terrorist attacks of September 2001 greatly changed the airline business, passenger service has continually grown at Quad City International Airport. Offering flights to many popular destinations through domestic and international connections has made QCIA the third largest airport for passenger traffic in the state of Illinois.

One

Franing Field
1922–1934

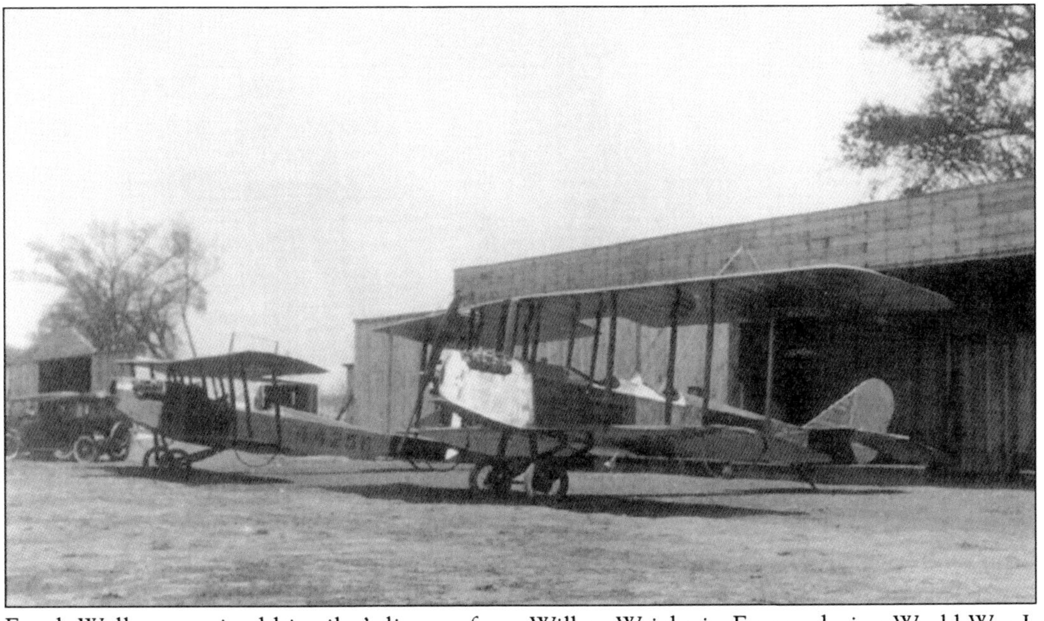

Frank Wallace received his pilot's license from Wilbur Wright in France during World War I. Returning to Bettendorf, Iowa, after the war, he established Wallace Field in 1919. The field was actually the first airport in the area, with sales and several excellent repair businesses. It was located at present-day Thirty-fifth and State Streets, where it remained until 1935 when the field was crowded out by industry. (Courtesy of QCIA.)

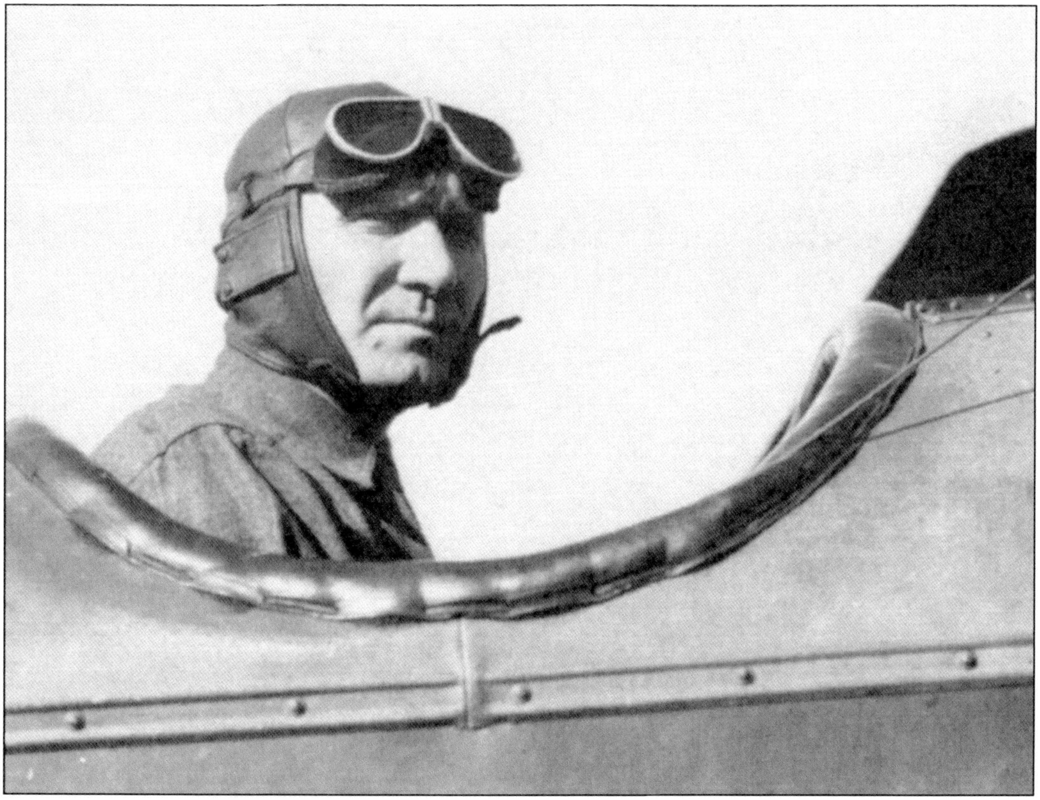

Gus DeSchepper received his flight instruction at Wallace Field in Bettendorf, Iowa, and was the first Moline resident to receive a private pilot's license. He was the moving force behind the establishment of the airport at Franing Field. After Rusty Campbell replaced Wesley Smith in the fledgling airport operation, he and Campbell formed the Campbell-DeSchepper Airplane Company to sell and service airplanes and operate the airport. (Courtesy of QCIA.)

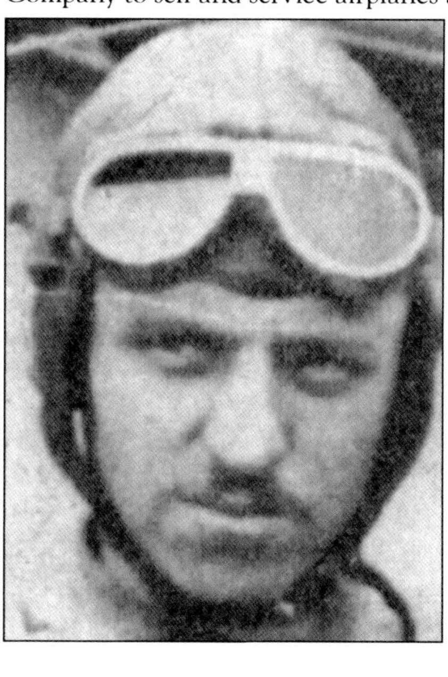

Floyd Ketner was the second civilian pilot from Moline to receive a pilot's license, and one of the original four pilots who created the airport in Moline. Besides repairing and selling airplanes, he experimented in aircraft design. Ketner modified and built a monoplane he hoped would be successful. Rusty Campbell flew it and told him it was unsafe. Ketner did not listen and was killed when the plane crashed. (Courtesy of QCIA.)

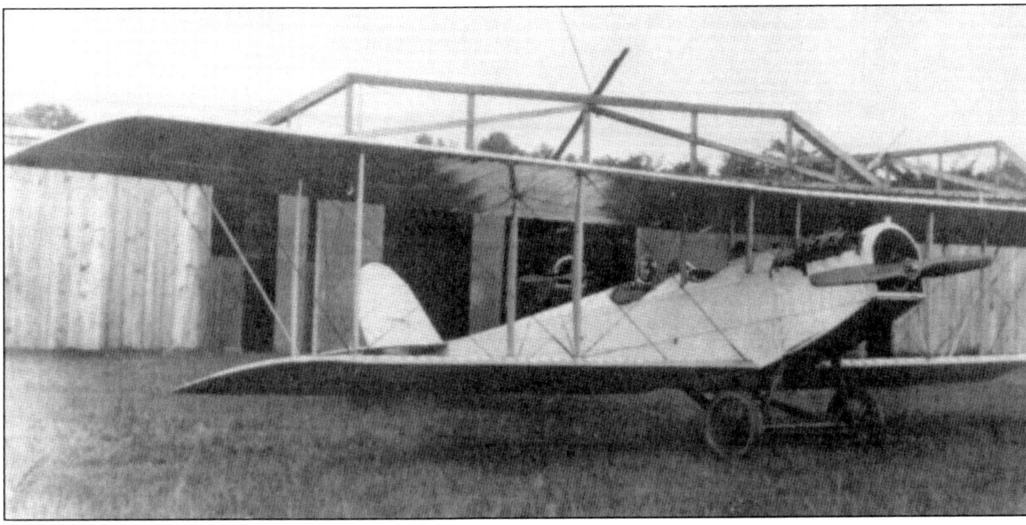

After learning to fly from Wesley Smith at the Colona Avenue field, Dr. C.C. Sloan became one of the original organizers of the Moline Airport at Franing Field. This photograph shows the doctor in his Canadian-built JN4 Can Jenny. The latticework above the wing on Sloan's plane is not part of the plane. It is part of the roof structure of the airport's first hangar. (Courtesy of QCIA.)

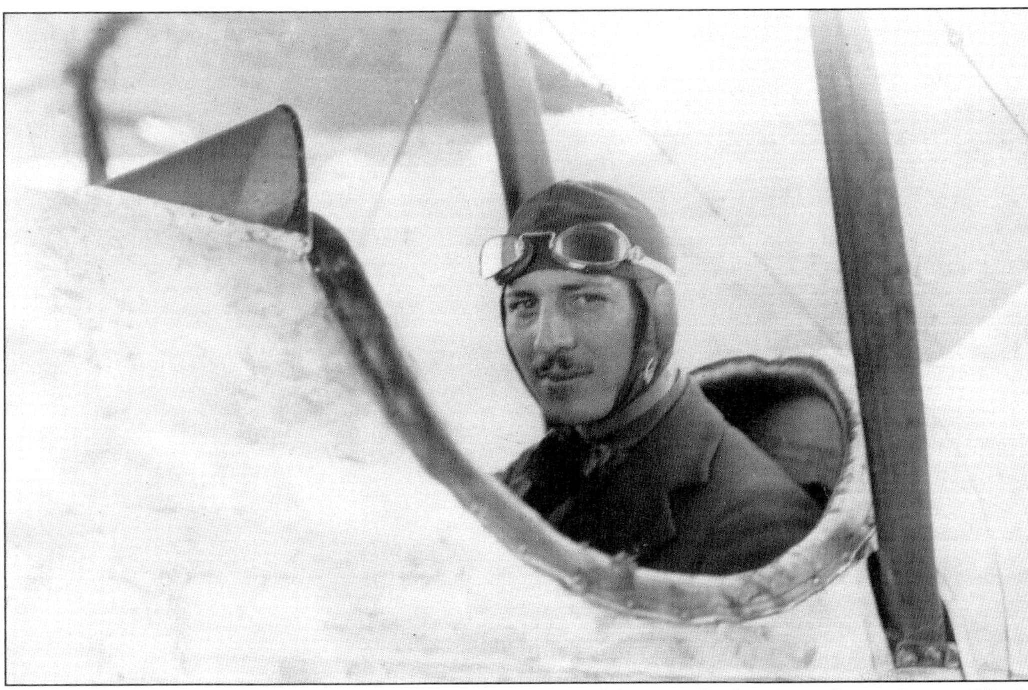

J. Wesley Smith was a native of Geneseo, Illinois, and flew with the Canadians during World War I. After the war, he taught Gus DeSchepper, Floyd Ketner, and Dr. C.C. Sloan how to fly and joined them in developing an airport at Franing Field. When Smith took a job in Washington, DC, he asked Earl "Rusty" Campbell to take his place as manager of the budding Moline Airport. (Courtesy of QCIA.)

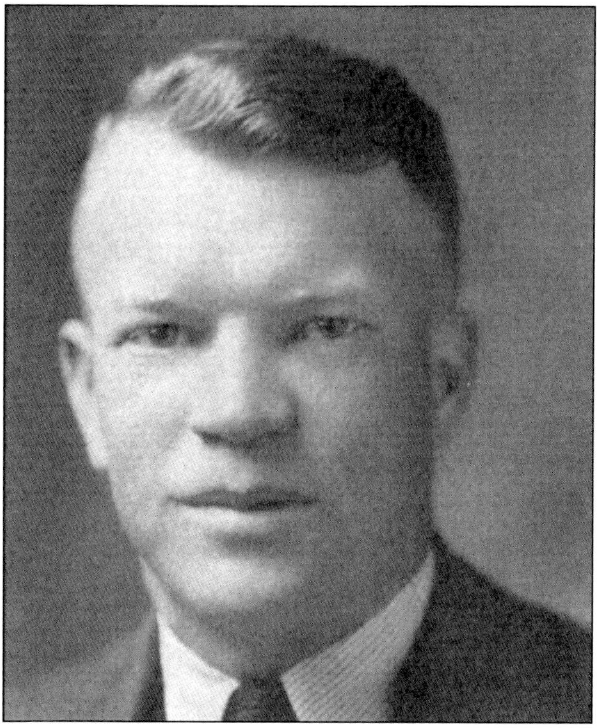

Iowa native Earl "Rusty" Campbell was a flight instructor during World War I. Following the war, he barnstormed the Midwest, giving sightseeing rides. Campbell was asked to manage Franing Field when Wesley Smith took a job elsewhere. Campbell aggressively set to work creating Campbell-DeSchepper Airplane Company and building up the airport. He was most responsible for bringing National Air Transport and its airmail route into Moline. (Courtesy of QCIA.)

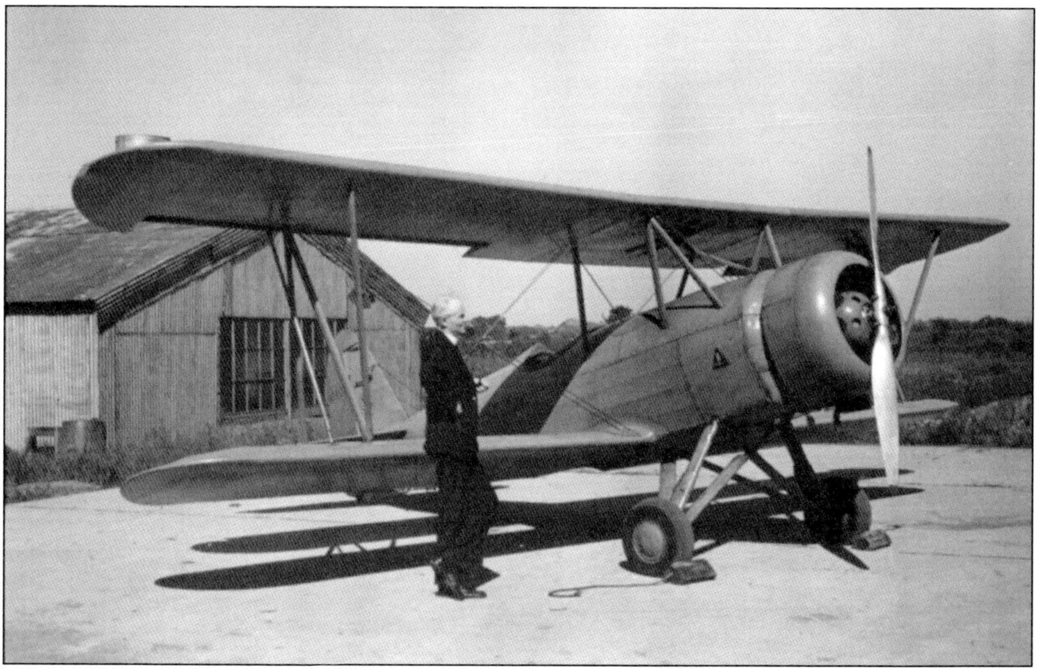

Rev. John Culemans came to Moline to establish Sacred Heart Church for Flemish-speaking Belgians. He took lessons from fellow Belgian Gus DeSchepper in 1925, and flying became his hobby. As chairman of the Association of Commerce aviation committee, Rev. Culemans was probably most responsible for the city's purchase of the airport. When his Travel Air was destroyed in a hangar fire, his parishioners bought him a new airplane. (Courtesy of Sacred Heart Church.)

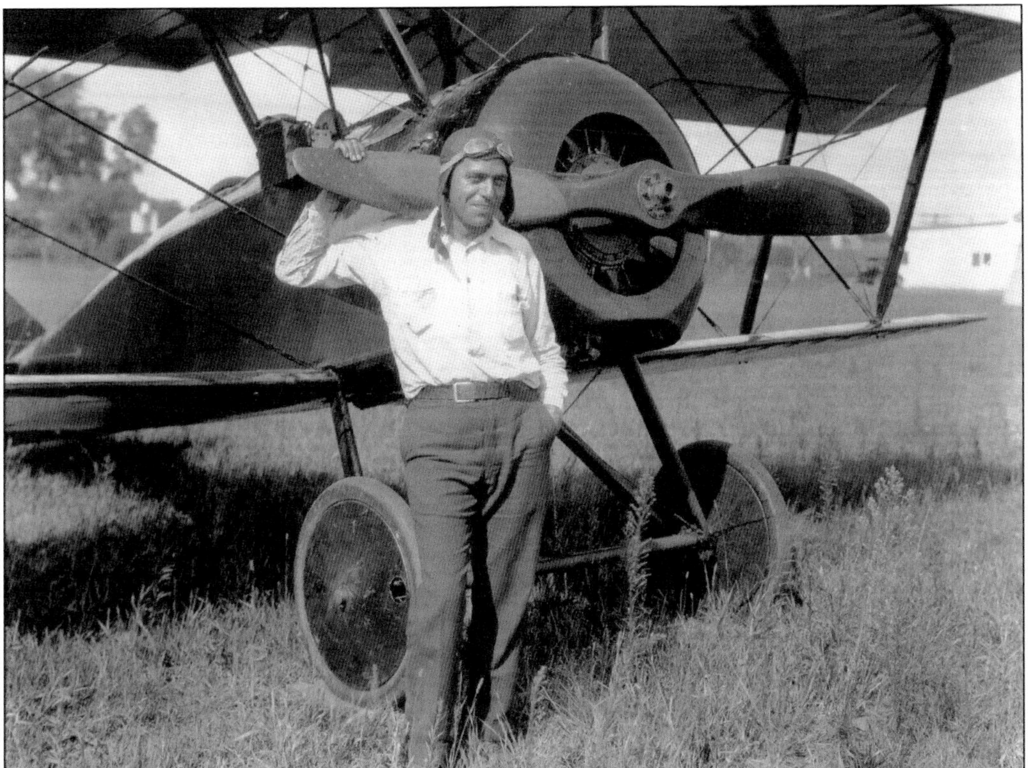

Roy "Stub" Quimby arrived at Moline in 1923 as a mechanic for Rusty Campbell. Having many hours of flight time as an airplane passenger, Quimby finally learned to fly and became a test pilot for the Mono Aircraft Company. He was also a member of the Mono racing team. When Mono Aircraft was sold and moved to St. Louis, Quimby became foreman of the International Harvester Company experimental department. (Courtesy of Ken Roberts.)

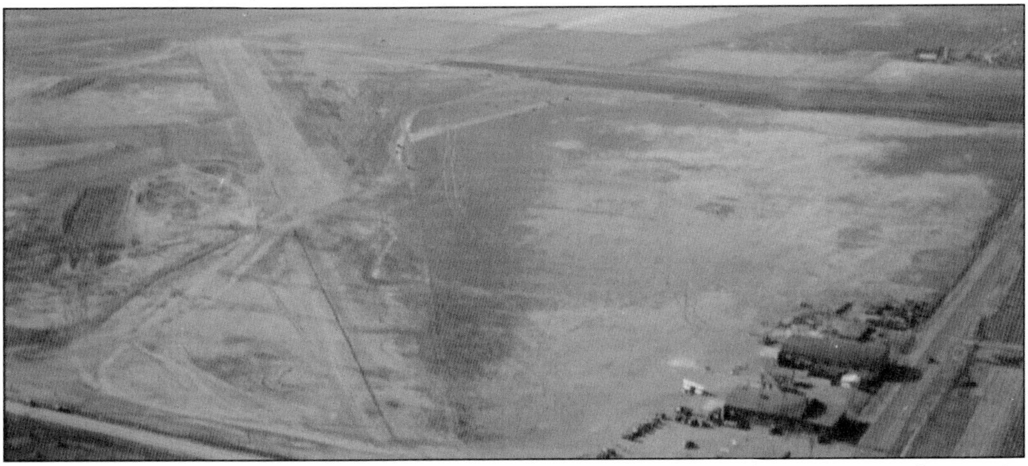

Looking southwest, this aerial photograph from around 1925 shows the airport as pilots might have seen it while circling for a landing. While there is a rudimentary northeast-southwest runway, pilots could land or take off into favorable wind conditions anywhere on the field. The large expanse of flat farmland gives proof that Framing Field was a good location for an airport and offered plenty of room for expansion. (Courtesy of QCIA.)

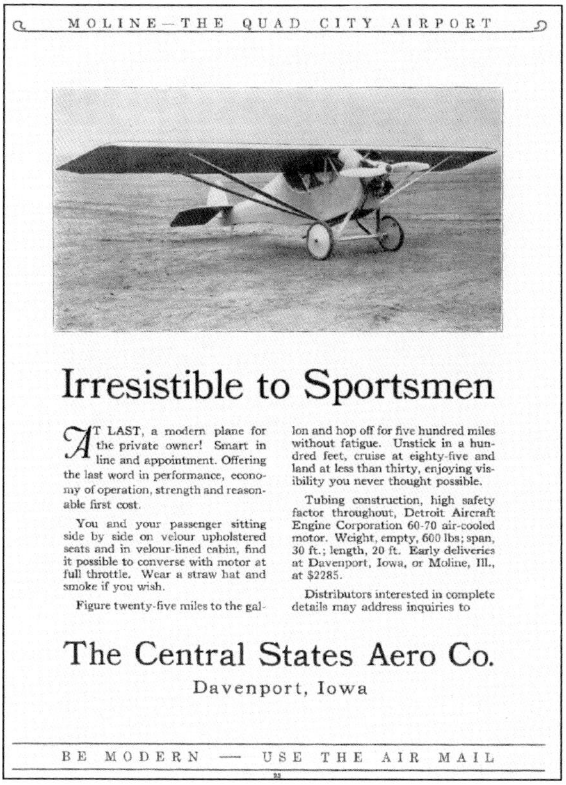

When Moline was chosen as a stop along the first National Air Tour, the Campbell-DeSchepper Airplane Company published a booklet describing the city and the airport. It was sent to the chambers of commerce of Dearborn and all the stops along the tour. Central States Aero used the publication to show off its new Monocoupe. Campbell and DeSchepper referred to the field as "the Quad City Airport."

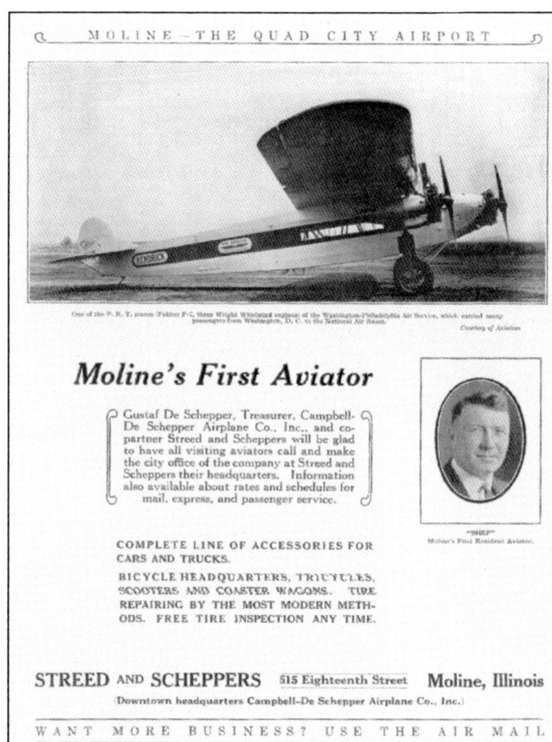

In the booklet distributed to competitors of the National Air Tour, Gus DeSchepper and partner Richard Streed invited fellow aviators to make the offices of Streed and Scheppers their headquarters while at Moline. The tire and bicycle shop in downtown Moline also served as the city office of the Campbell-DeSchepper Airplane Company. The aircraft in the advertisement is a Fokker F-7 trimotor.

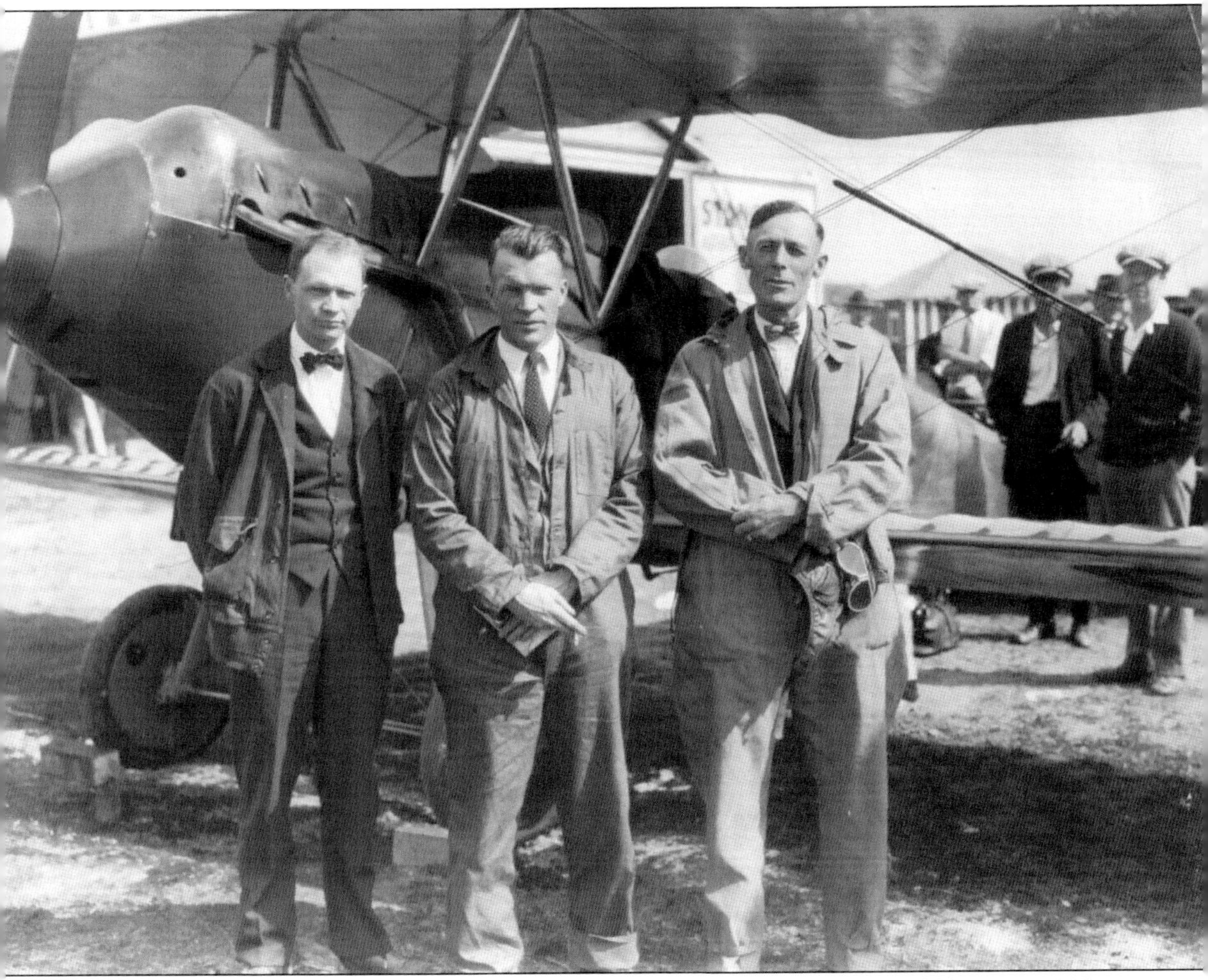

The National Air Tour, sometimes referred to as the Ford Reliability Tour, was held between 1925 and 1931. Its purpose was to promote aircraft technology and safety and to encourage cities to build airports or improve those that already existed. Starting and finishing in Dearborn, Michigan, the tour would visit 12 Midwestern cities in six days. Somewhat like an automobile rally, dozens of airplanes took to the air, and each pilot who kept a certain percentage of an 80-miles-per-hour schedule, regardless of weather or engine trouble, would receive a perfect score and have his name engraved on the Edsel Ford Trophy. There was no prize money. The tour visited Moline four times during the seven years it was held. In this 1925 photograph, Moline pilot Rusty Campbell (center) poses with *Moline Dispatch* aviation editor W.B. Mueller (left) and mechanic S.A. McGinnis. Mueller was a passenger on the Chicago-Moline leg of the tour. Campbell and his plane, a Travel Air A, was the first to land, and he received a perfect score. (Courtesy of QCIA.)

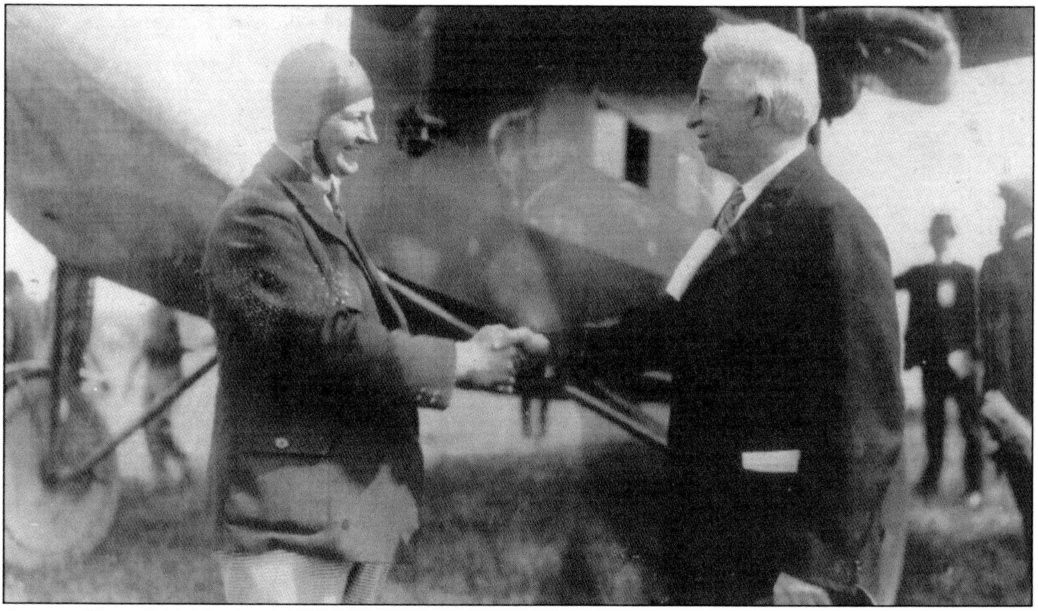

Anton "Tony" Fokker gained renown with his airplane designs for the Germans during World War I. After the war, he established an aircraft company in the Netherlands and after moving to the United States in 1922 started an American branch. As part of the 1925 National Air Tour, Fokker brought his trimotor Fokker F.VIIA into Moline. He is seen on the left, greeting Ralph Cram, publisher of the Davenport *Democrat*. (Courtesy of QCIA.)

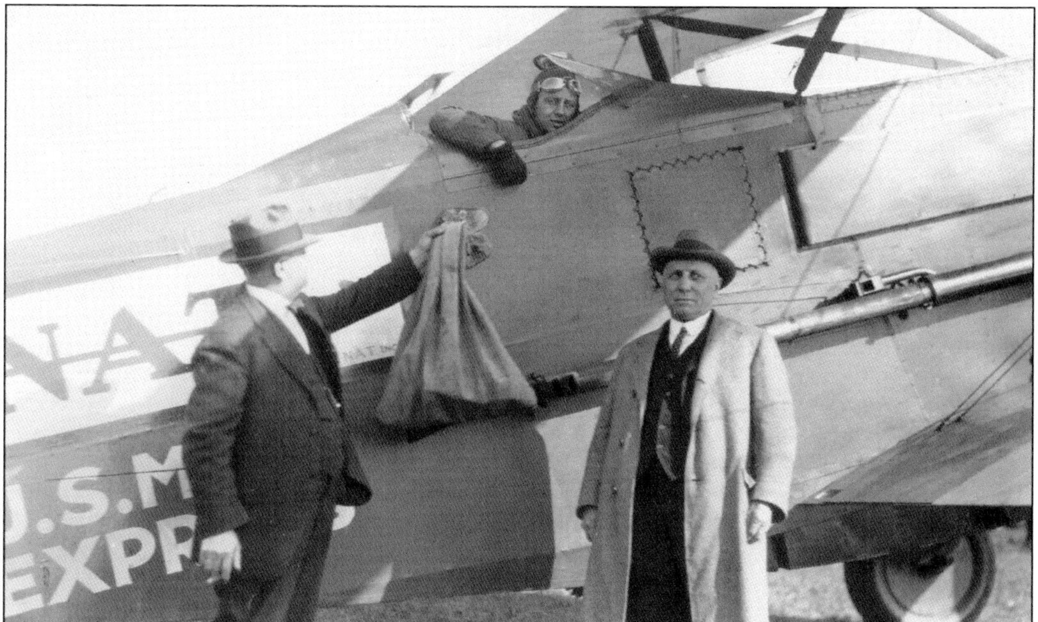

Through the efforts of Rusty Campbell and the Association of Commerce, National Air Transport made the first airmail flight, from Chicago into Moline, on May 12, 1926. Moline postmaster George Carlson (left), accompanied by Rock Island postmaster Hugh McDonald, hands pilot Paul Johnson the first bag of mail bound for Kansas City. National Air Transport would later become part of United Air Lines. (Courtesy of Rock Island County Historical Society.)

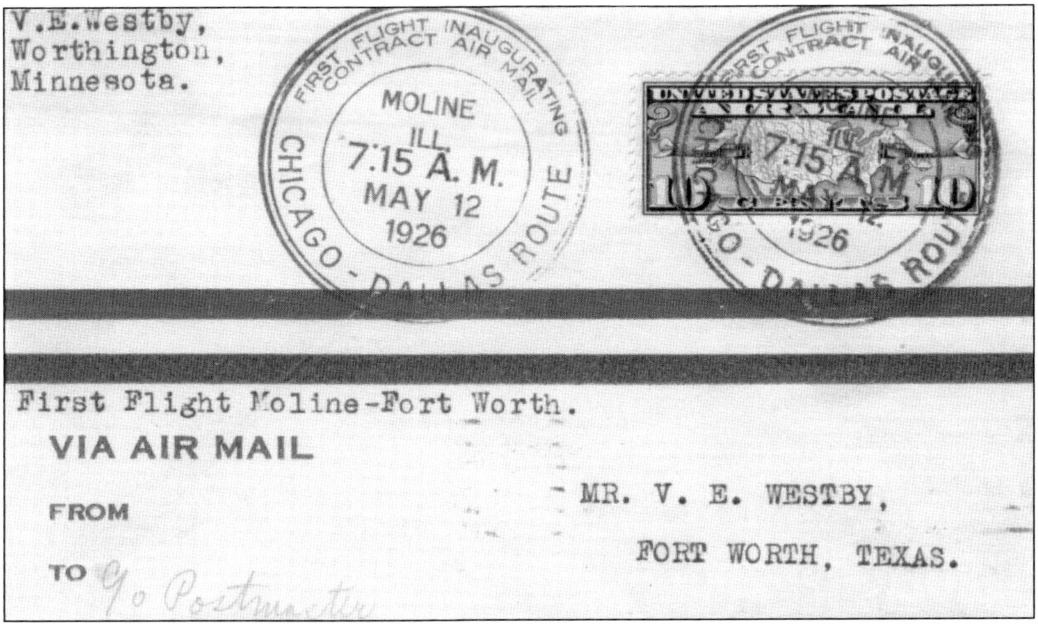

Collecting first-day covers has been a popular hobby for many years. Probably the most important part of a cover is the postmark, as it verifies the date of the event and/or the date of cancellation of a particular stamp design released by the post office. Note the date and time stamp on this envelope. Although not shown, the envelope was cancelled again at Fort Worth at 6:00 p.m. the same day.

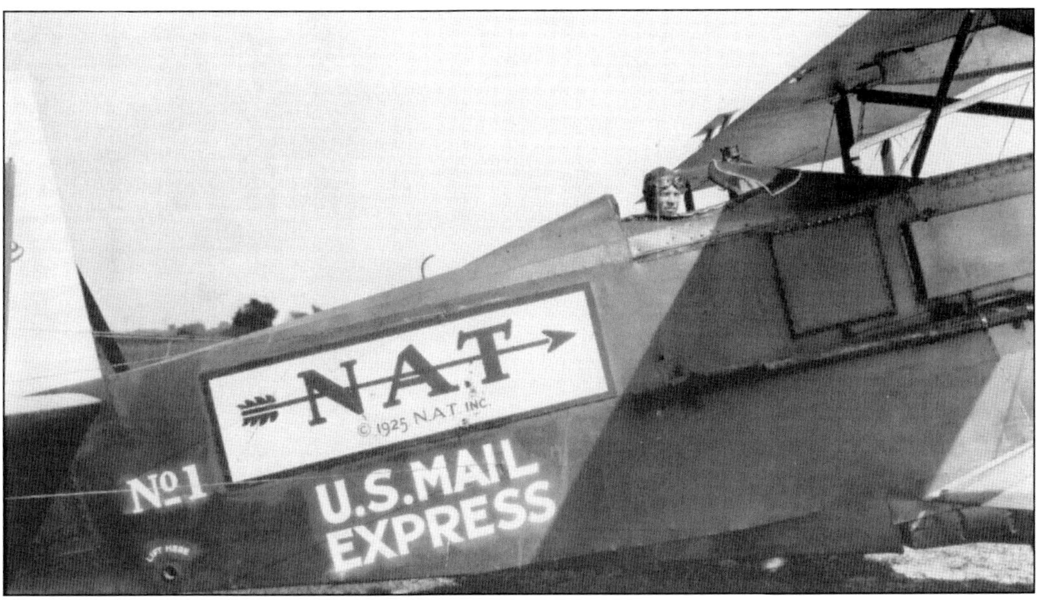

It was partly due to Rusty Campbell's diligent efforts that National Air Transport established the airmail route through Moline. The Campbell-DeSchepper Airplane Company waived fees for using the field and supplied hangar space and mechanics for the airline's use. Campbell also served as a substitute pilot as needed. This 1926 photograph shows Campbell posing in the cockpit of one of NAT's Curtiss "Carrier Pigeon" mail planes. (Courtesy of QCIA.)

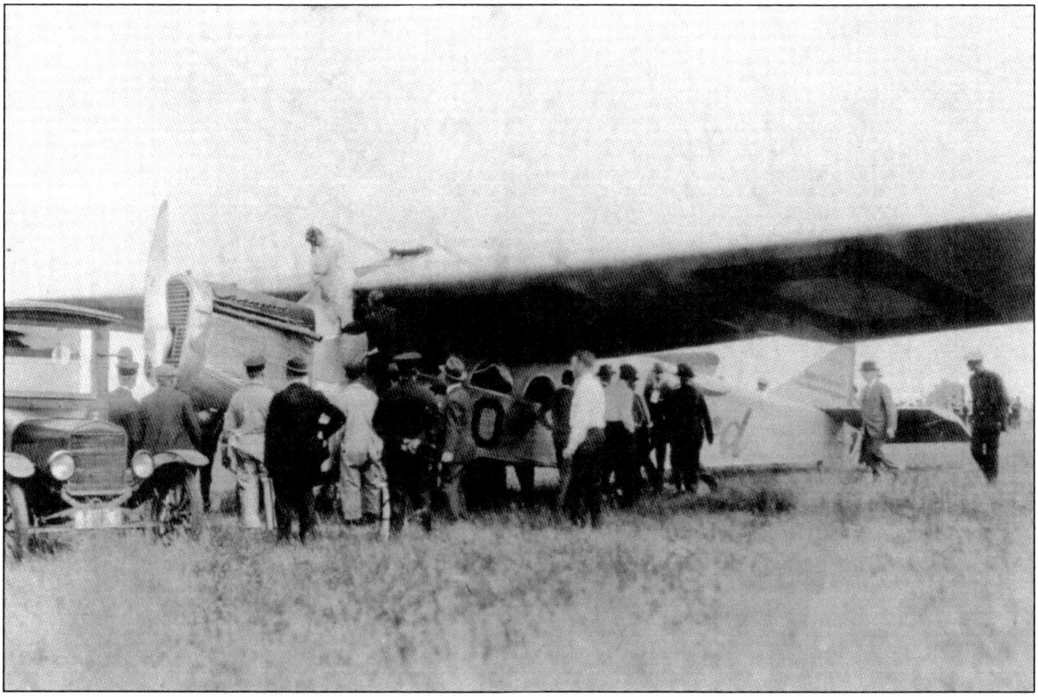

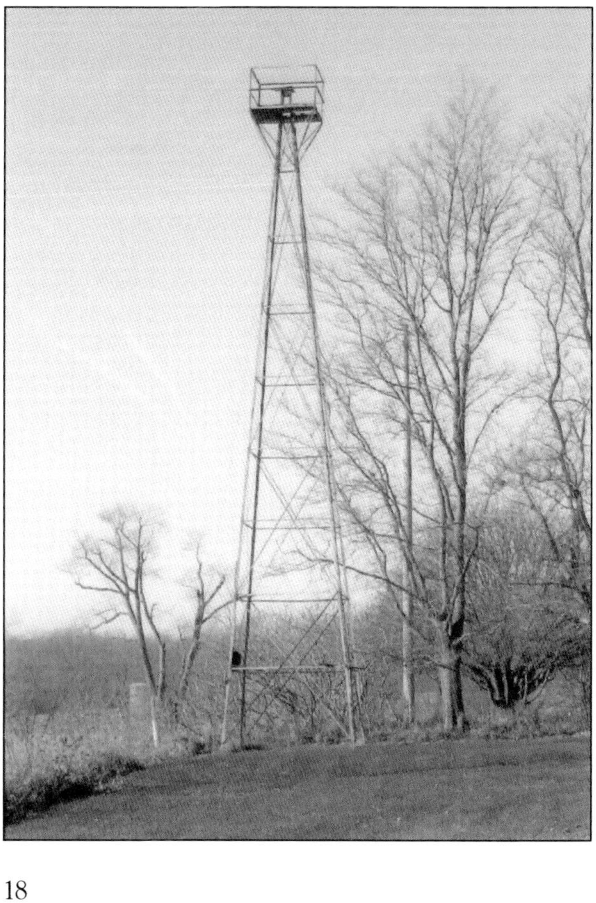

Spectators crowd around the forerunner to the Ford Tri-Motor at the 1926 National Air Tour stop at Moline. This was the Ford-Stout 2-AT Mono-Motor transport, the first all-metal aircraft to receive airworthiness certification in America. The plane could carry nine passengers and was flown by one pilot, who sat in an open cockpit. The Mono-Motor's pilot, S.L. Manning, can be seen standing in that cockpit. (Courtesy of QCIA.)

To allow pilots to safely fly mail at night, the Department of Commerce began building a network of beacons to guide pilots to their airport destinations. According to the *History of Public Works in the United States 1776–1976*, the Airways Division installed the first beacon in 1926 near Moline. The original tower still stands along old Illinois Route 2, between Rapids City and Hillsdale. (Courtesy of Rock Island County Historical Society.)

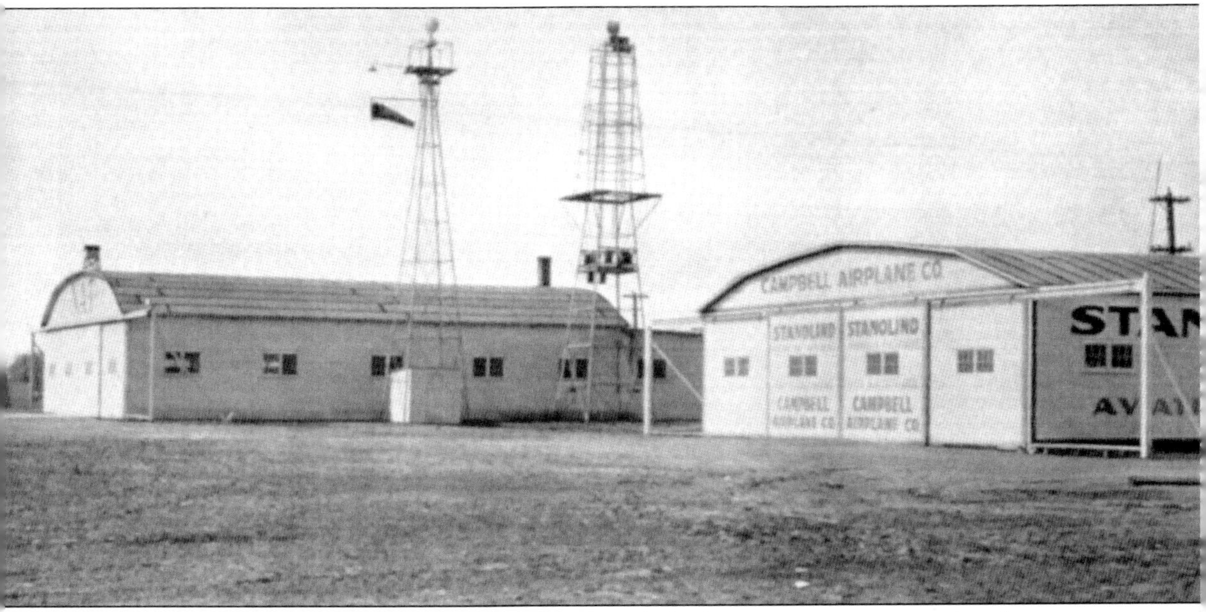

In 1926, a French inventor conceived a crimson-colored light that created an intense glow designed to pierce a fog bank 400 feet deep. That light was reported to be visible from the air for up to 60 miles. The structure consisted of 32 neon tubes, each 10 feet long, with the tubes mounted on a tower 55 feet tall. This photograph shows those tubes assembled on the tower to the right. The Moline Airport was the first landing field in the United States to install this fog-penetrating beacon. The airport may also have been the first to take it out of service, as it failed to work. It was replaced, near the end of 1926, with the type of beacon that the Department of Commerce Airways Division was installing to aid pilots in night flying. (Courtesy QCIA.)

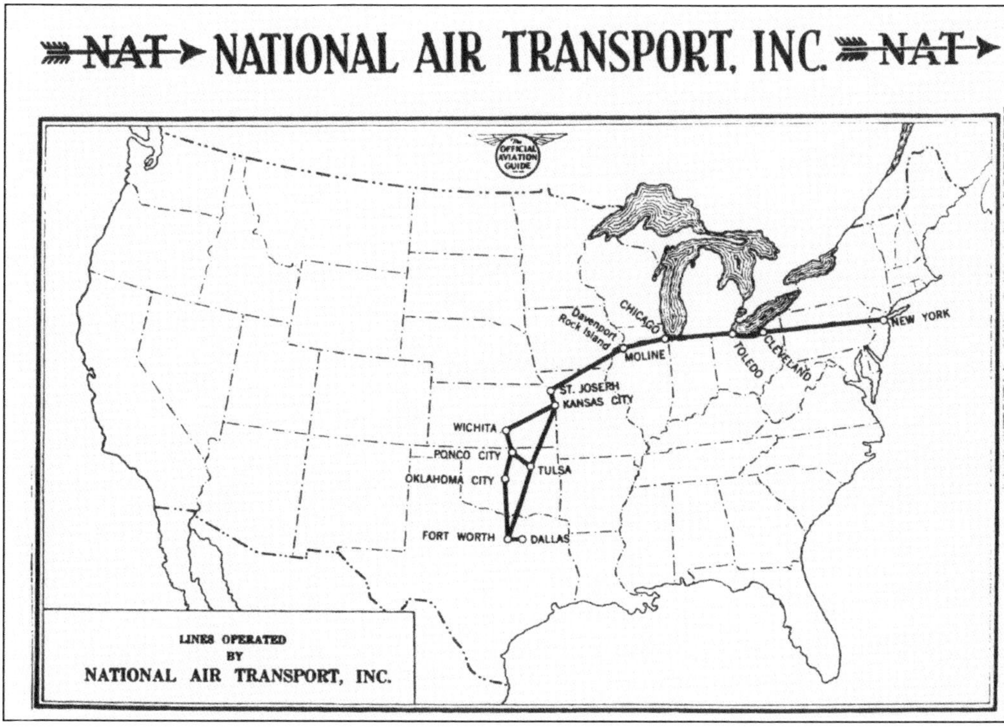

National Air Transport was awarded the Chicago-Dallas airmail route by the Post Office Department in late 1925 and began flying it on May 12, 1926. Wanting to expand its reach, the airline successfully bid on the New York–Chicago airmail route and began flying that segment in 1927. This map shows the routings that NAT used for mail and would eventually use to start its passenger service. (Courtesy of QCIA.)

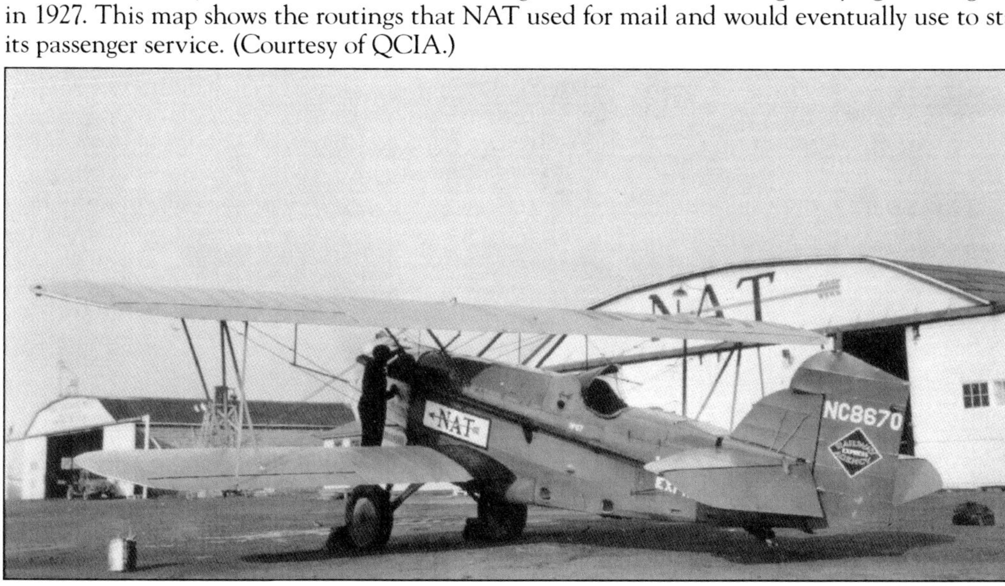

A National Air Transport "Moline Division" mail plane, shown here in this 1927 photograph, is serviced for a trip. The Curtiss Carrier Pigeon was powered by a 12-cylinder Liberty engine and could carry 1,000 pounds of mail or freight at 120 miles per hour. It is possible this was one of the standby planes kept at the airport and flown by Moline pilots Rusty Campbell and John Cable. (Courtesy of QCIA.)

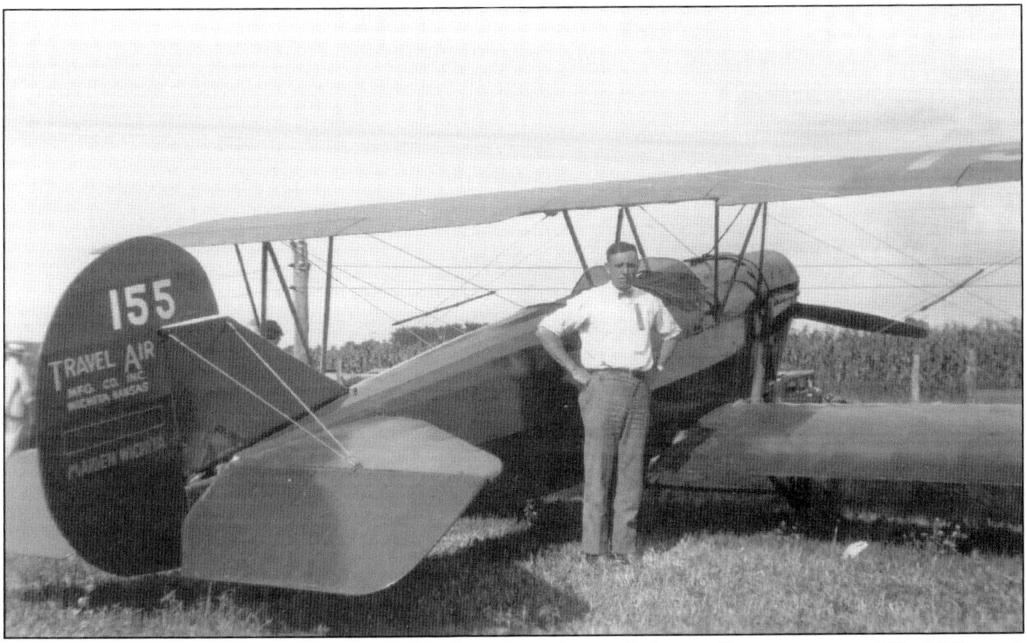

Beryl "Pat" Miller was a member of the first squadron of Army flyers to enter World War I. After the war, he barnstormed as both a pilot and a stuntman. In 1927, Rusty Campbell asked Miller to come work as a mechanic at Franing Field. Miller worked at the airport for 50 years, taught flying, supervised buildings and grounds, and was assistant manager during World War II. (Courtesy of QCIA.)

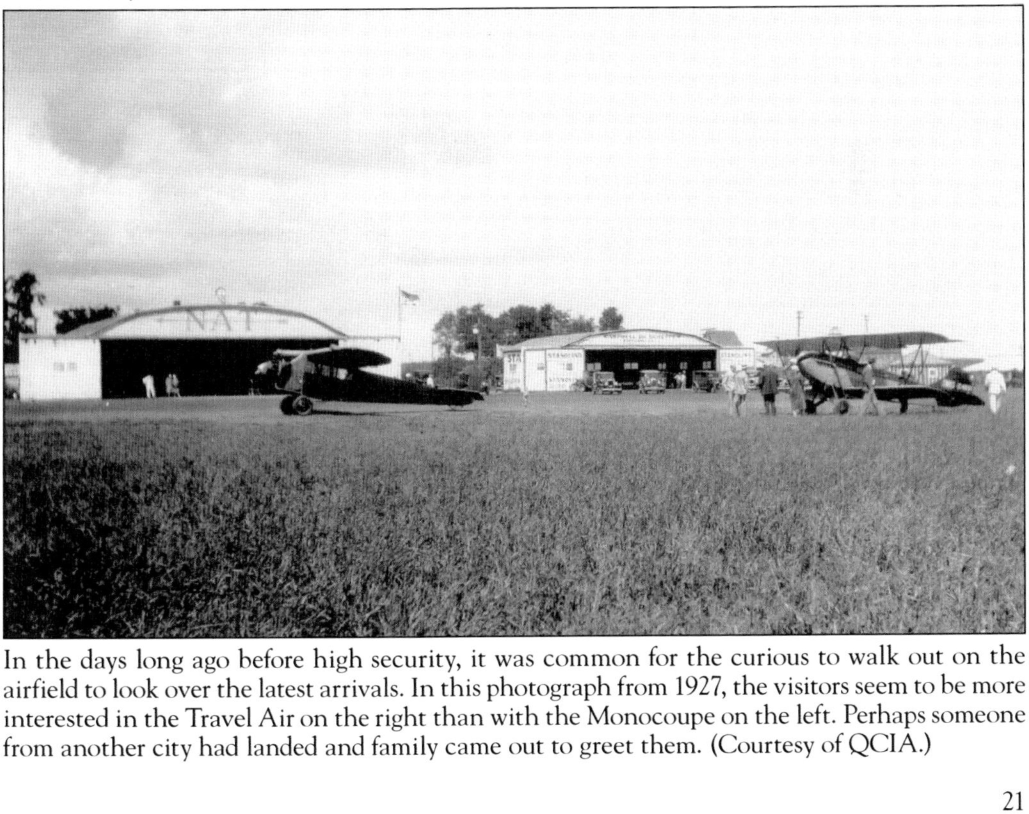

In the days long ago before high security, it was common for the curious to walk out on the airfield to look over the latest arrivals. In this photograph from 1927, the visitors seem to be more interested in the Travel Air on the right than with the Monocoupe on the left. Perhaps someone from another city had landed and family came out to greet them. (Courtesy of QCIA.)

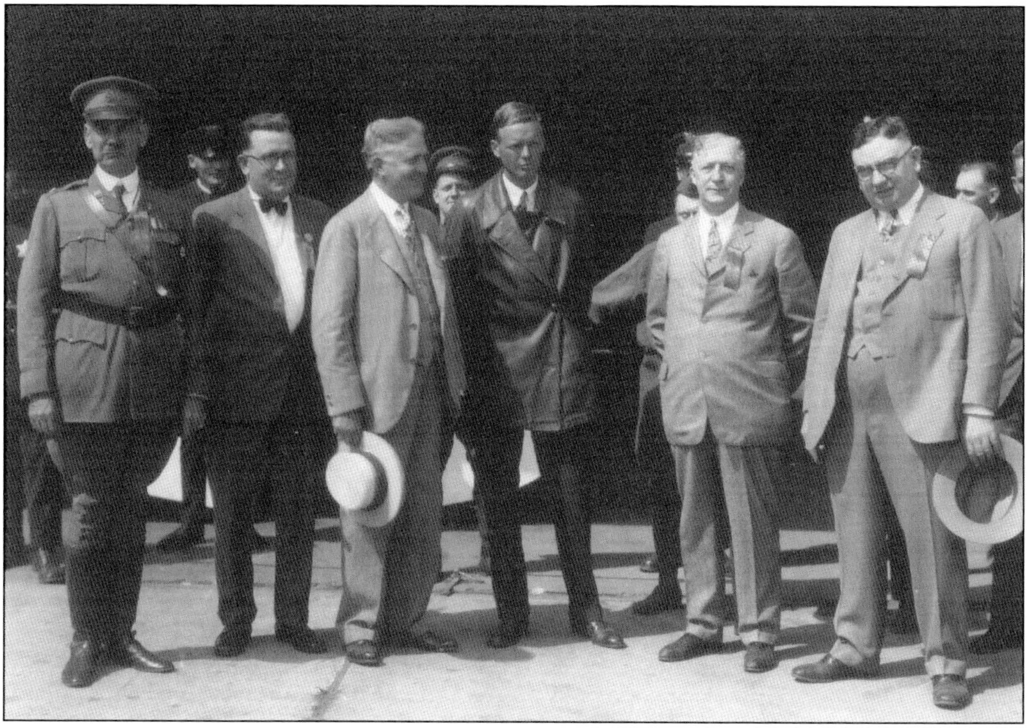

Just three months after his historic solo flight across the Atlantic Ocean, Col. Charles Lindbergh flew his *Spirit of St. Louis* into Franing Field for a visit. In this photograph of the greeting service are, from left to right, Col. D.M. King, arsenal commandant; John Siefken, mayor of East Moline; Claude Sandstrom, mayor of Moline; Lindbergh; Louis Roddewig, mayor of Davenport, Iowa; and Chester Thompson, mayor of Rock Island. (Courtesy of QCIA.)

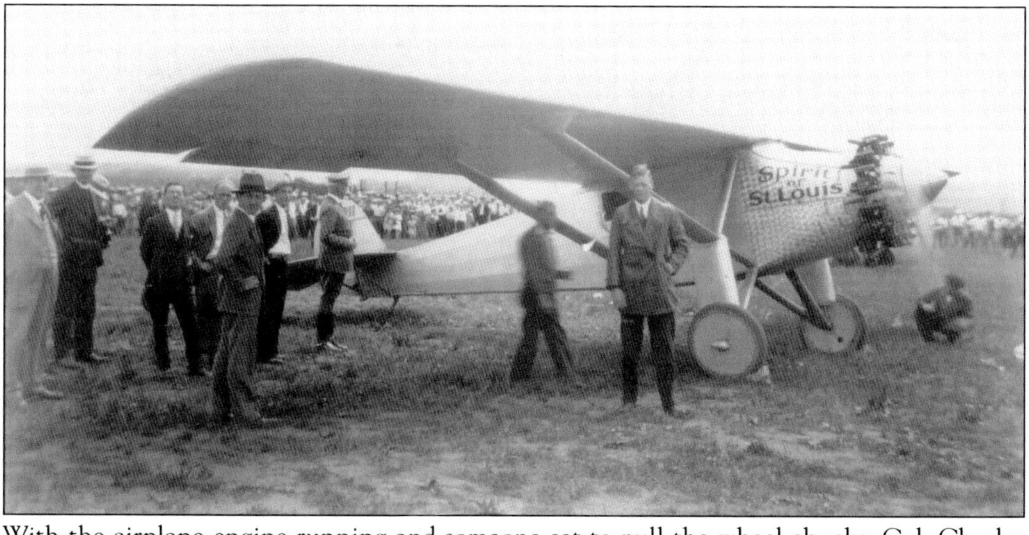

With the airplane engine running and someone set to pull the wheel chocks, Col. Charles Lindbergh poses for the *Moline Dispatch* photographer. Newspaper accounts noted that a crowd of 50,000 people turned out to see "Lindy" arrive on August 19, 1927. A dinner was held in his honor at Augustana College. The next day, another large crowd of several thousand was on hand to see him off. (Courtesy of QCIA.)

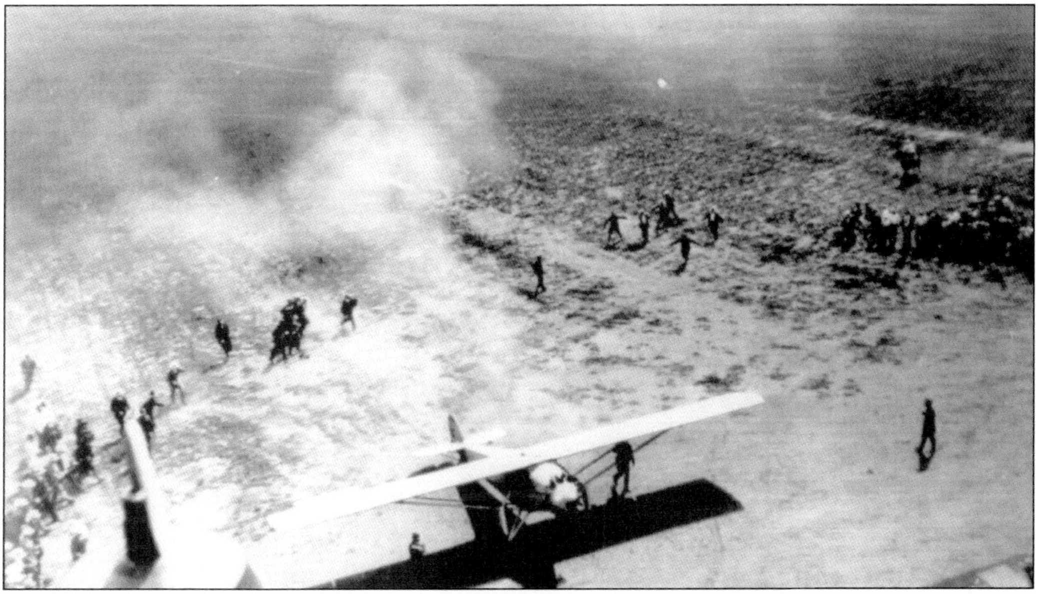

The *Moline Dispatch* took this photograph as Lindbergh revved his engine in preparation for taking off. Bystanders have moved away from behind the plane, as Lindbergh's prop wash creates a cloud of dust. A close inspection of this photograph reveals several spectators have arrived at the airport on horseback. Evidently the horses do not seem bothered by all the commotion. (Courtesy of QCIA.)

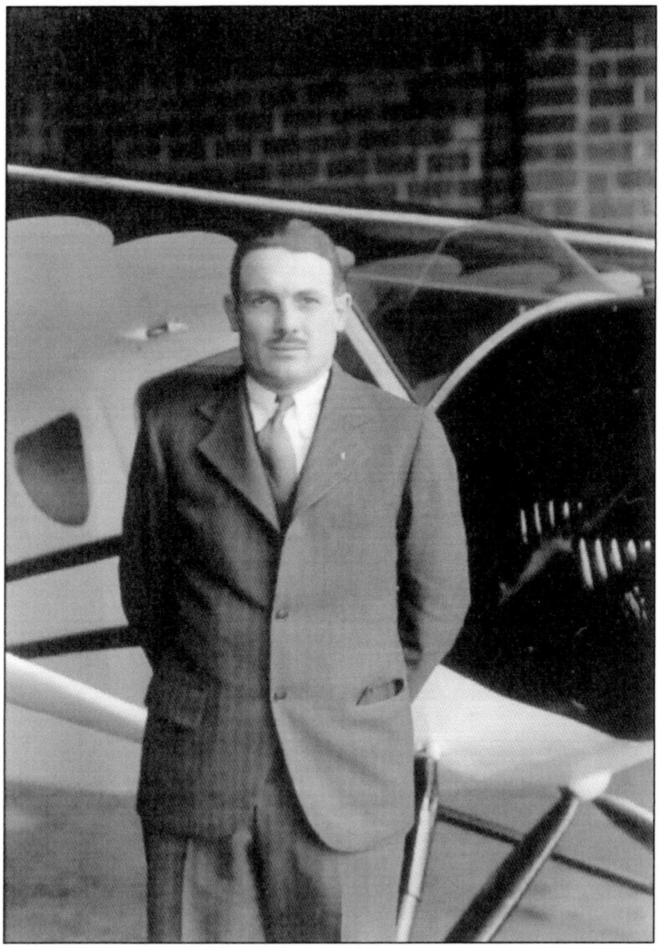

Don Luscombe purchased an old Curtiss Jenny and learned to fly. Not liking the open draftiness of the plane, he envisioned a closed-cabin airplane with side-by-side seating. Thus was born the Central States Aero Company in 1927. With money from the Velie Motor Company, Luscombe reorganized Central States into the Mono Aircraft Company. He would later form another company to build the first all-metal light airplane. (Courtesy of Kris Streed Crawford.)

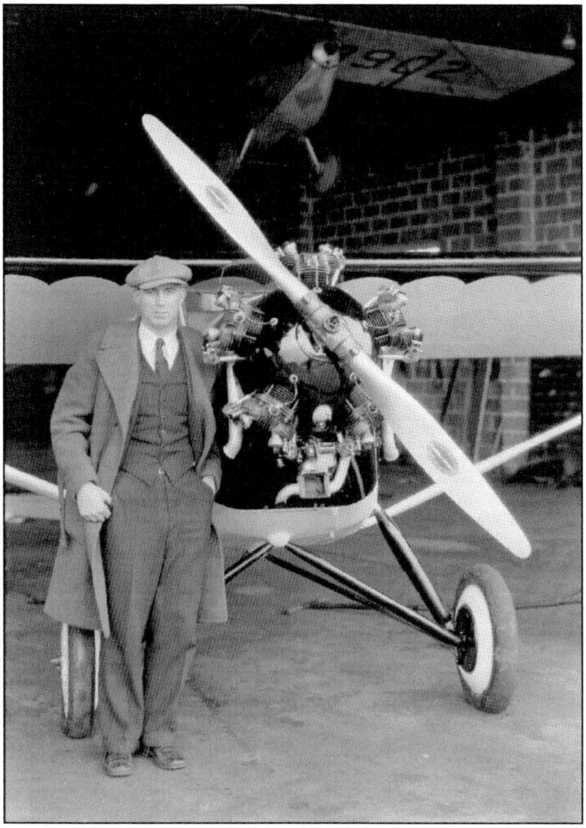

Iowa farm boy Clayton Folkerts was a self-taught airplane designer, builder, and pilot. His most famous design was the Monocoupe, manufactured by Central States Aero in Bettendorf and later in Moline. It featured side-by-side seating and an enclosed cockpit. By 1930, that plane dominated air races. The Monocoupe 90, a streamlined version of the original, was also created by Folkerts and remained in production from 1930 until 1950. (Courtesy of QCIA.)

The Velie Carriage Company was formed in 1901. By 1908, it was evident that automobiles would replace carriages, and the company began manufacturing cars. When Central States Aero Company began using Velie's five-cylinder radial aircraft engine, Velie purchased the company and renamed it Mono Aircraft. The three stages of Velie transportation are shown posed at the Mono Aircraft hangar. (Courtesy of Rock Island County Historical Society.)

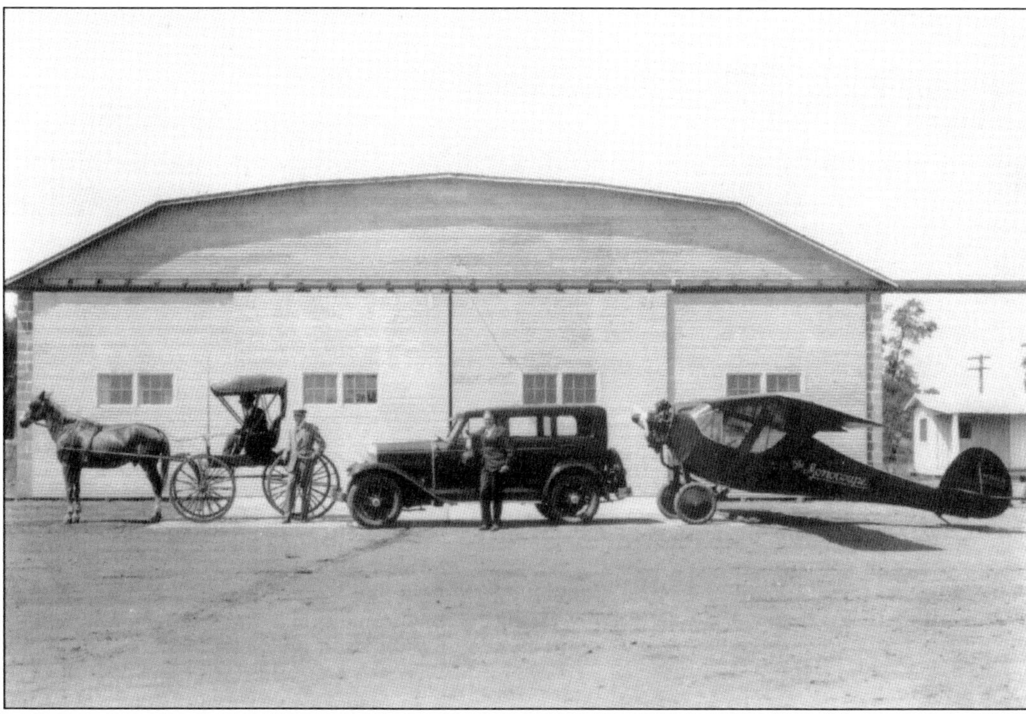

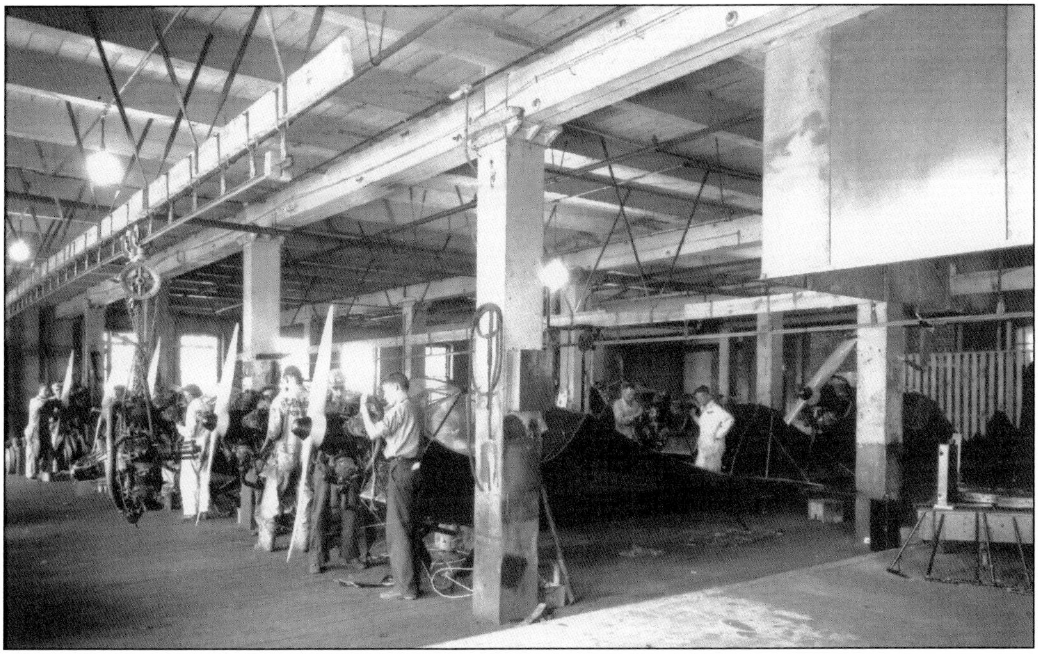

Don Luscombe's Central States Aero Company began building the Clayton Folkerts–designed Monocoupe in early 1927, in a small building at Wallace Field in Bettendorf. As the plane's features became known, that facility became inadequate for any volume of production, and the operation was moved to downtown Bettendorf. Velie Motor Corporation began providing an improved engine for the airplane. The company became known as Mono Aircraft Company in January 1928, when Velie purchased the business. Production was moved to the Velie plant on Third Avenue in Moline. Wings, fuselage, and engine were completed at the downtown factory. Wings were attached and the aircraft test flown at the Moline Airport facility. The company was sold to interests in St. Louis in late 1929, after the death of both Willard Velie and his son. (Both, courtesy of Rock Island County Historical Society.)

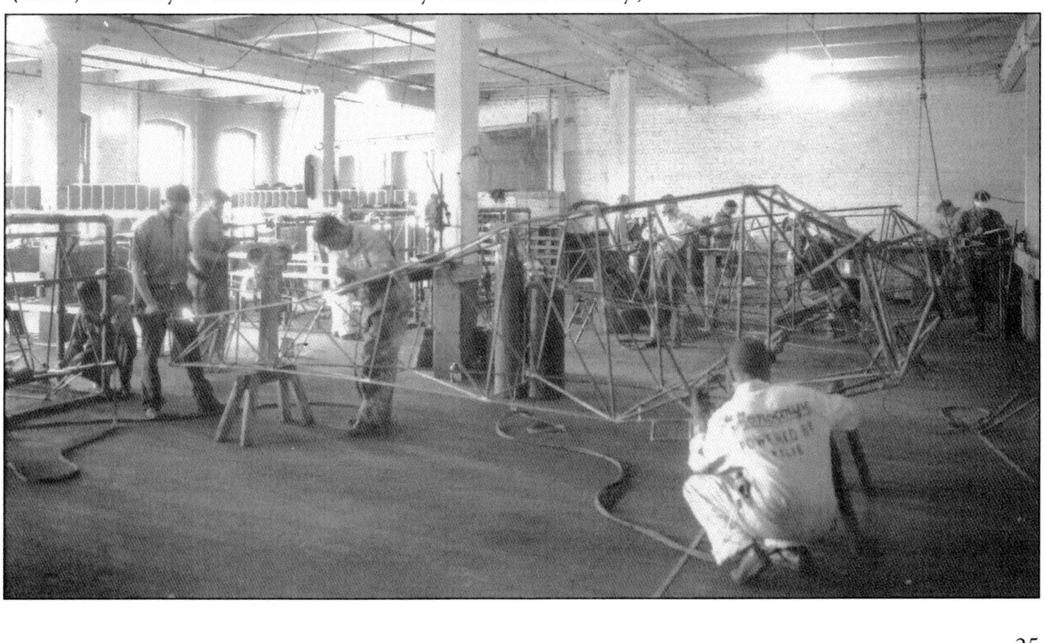

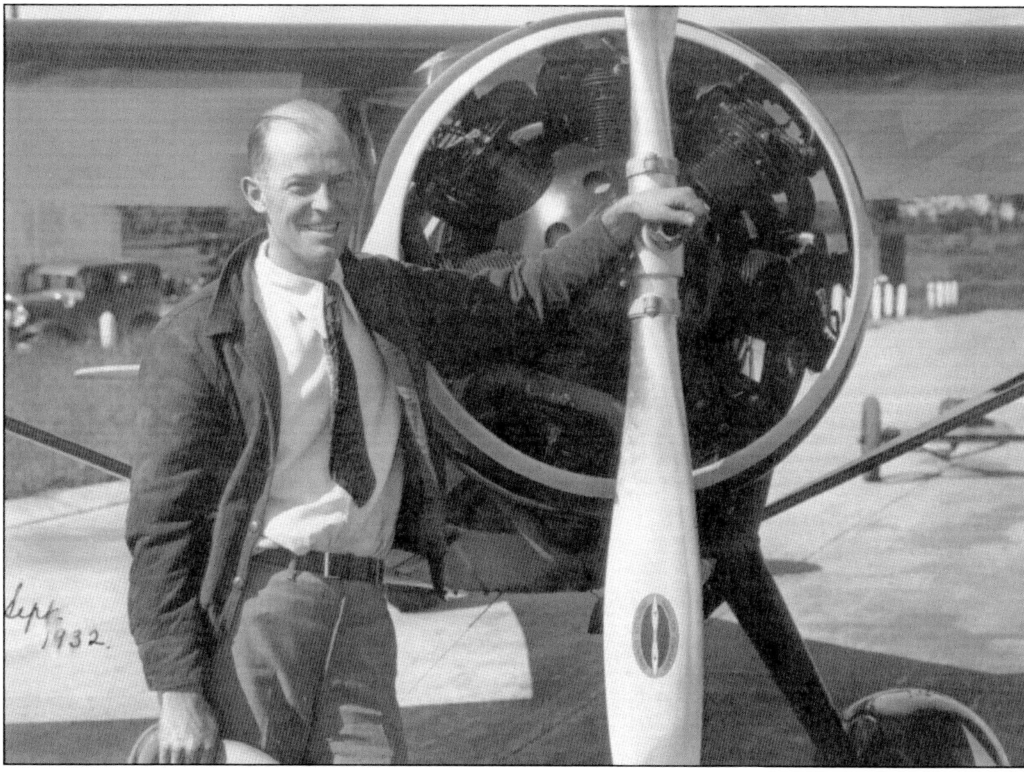

Early barnstormer Vern Roberts became the idol of Charles Lindbergh, who watched Roberts perform his daring stunts over Lindbergh's home state of Minnesota. Roberts came to Moline in 1927 and became the chief test pilot for Mono Aircraft and head of its racing team. A winner of many national air races, Roberts was named manager of Moline Airport upon the death of former manager Rusty Campbell. (Courtesy of Ken Roberts.)

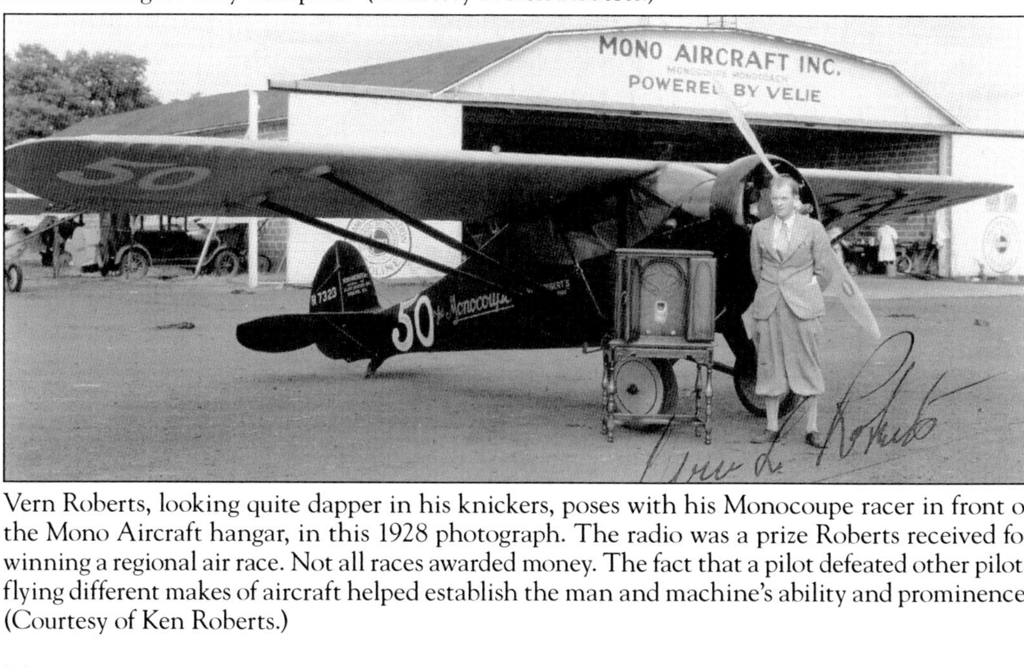

Vern Roberts, looking quite dapper in his knickers, poses with his Monocoupe racer in front of the Mono Aircraft hangar, in this 1928 photograph. The radio was a prize Roberts received for winning a regional air race. Not all races awarded money. The fact that a pilot defeated other pilots flying different makes of aircraft helped establish the man and machine's ability and prominence. (Courtesy of Ken Roberts.)

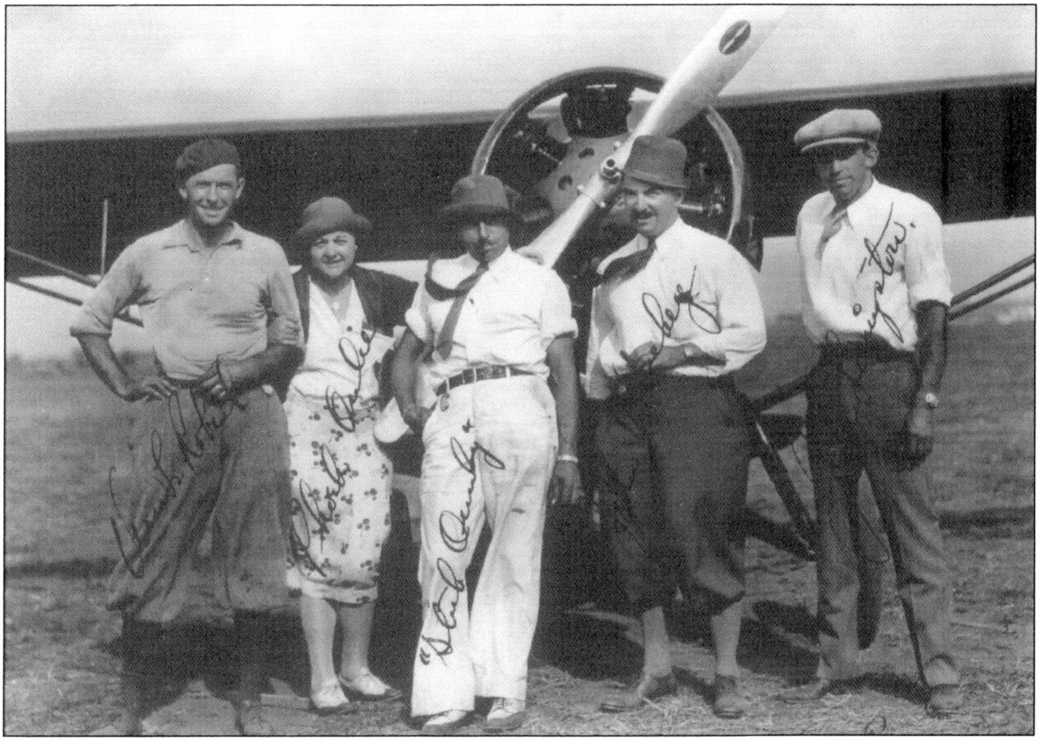

Mono Aircraft Company gained strong sales thanks to the winning reputation of its airplanes. Regional and national races were consistently being won by pilots in their Monocoupes and by members of the company's own racing team. It was not unusual for the aircraft to win first place in each race event. Members of the late-1920s team are, from left to right, Vern Roberts, Phoebe Omlie, Roy "Stub" Quimby, John Hinchey, and John Livingston. (Courtesy of Ken Roberts.)

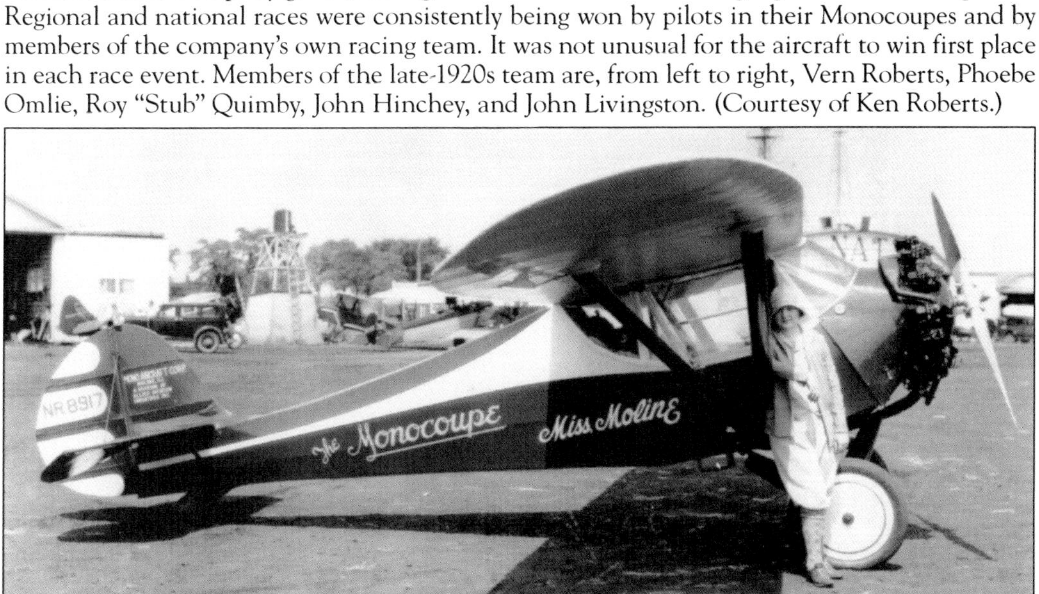

Phoebe Omlie raced and set numerous flying records in her Velie Monocoupe. She was the first woman to earn a transport pilot's license and the first to receive an aircraft mechanic's license. In 1928, Omlie flew for the Mono Aircraft Company, as a member of its racing team. She set a world's altitude record for females at 25,400 feet over Moline. Her plane was the *Miss Moline*. (Courtesy of QCIA.)

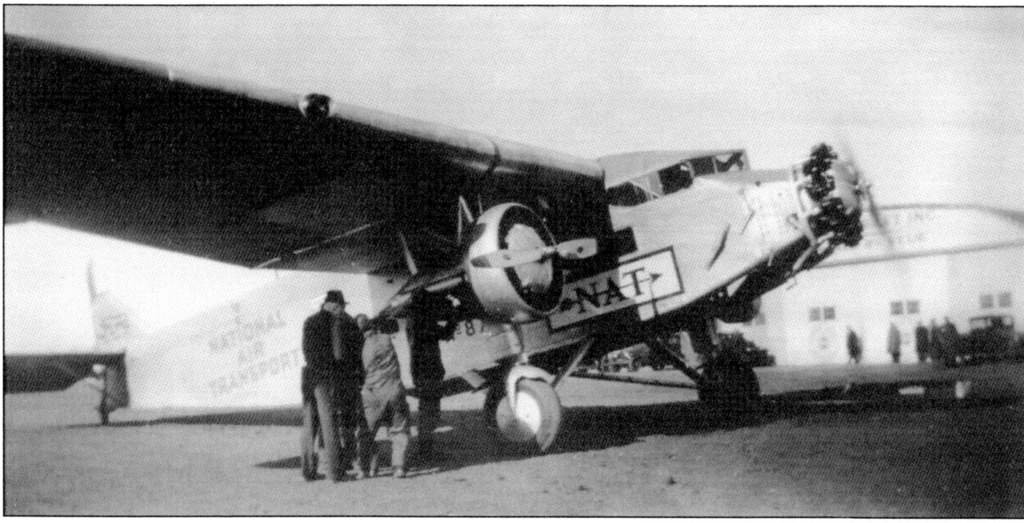

The Ford Tri-Motor began life in a design by the Stout Metal Airplane Company in the very early 1920s. The original Stout designs created an airplane with only one engine and an open cockpit. Henry Ford purchased the Stout firm in 1925 and had the craft redesigned to include the addition of two more engines. Ford touted it as "the safest airplane in the world," due to its all-metal construction. The Ford Tri-Motor above is the model 5-AT. It could carry up to 13 passengers. A unique feature of this model was the drop-down cargo holds below the lower inner wing. The photograph was taken during the 1929 National Reliability Tour's stop at Moline. In the photograph below, the drop-down cargo hold can plainly be seen. The two gentlemen in the foreground are unidentified. (Both, courtesy of QCIA.)

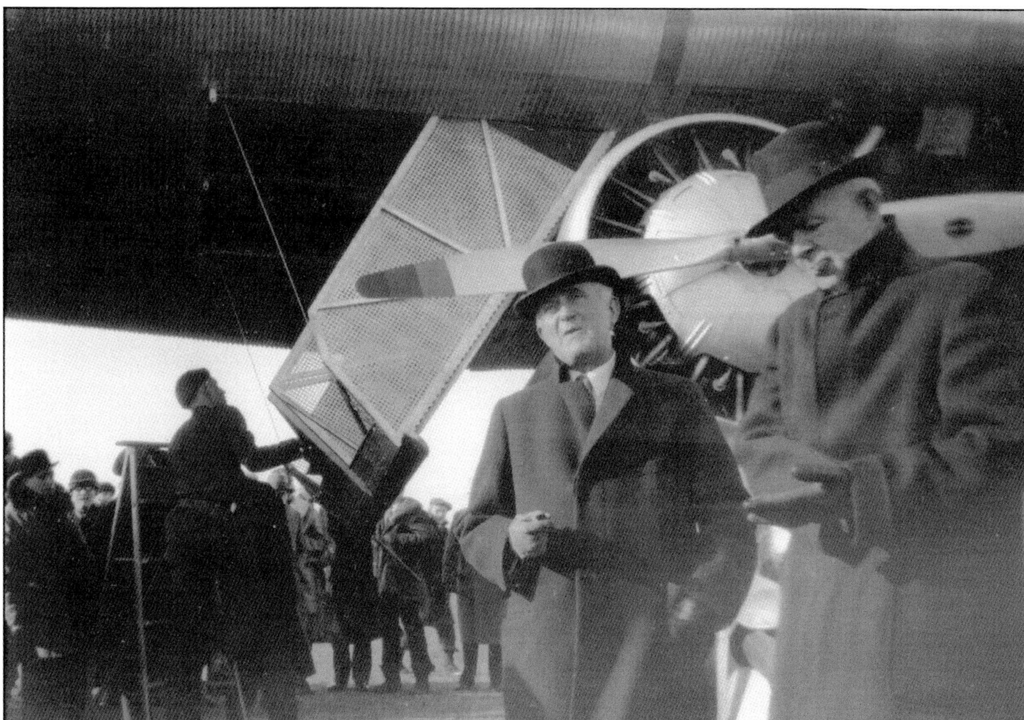

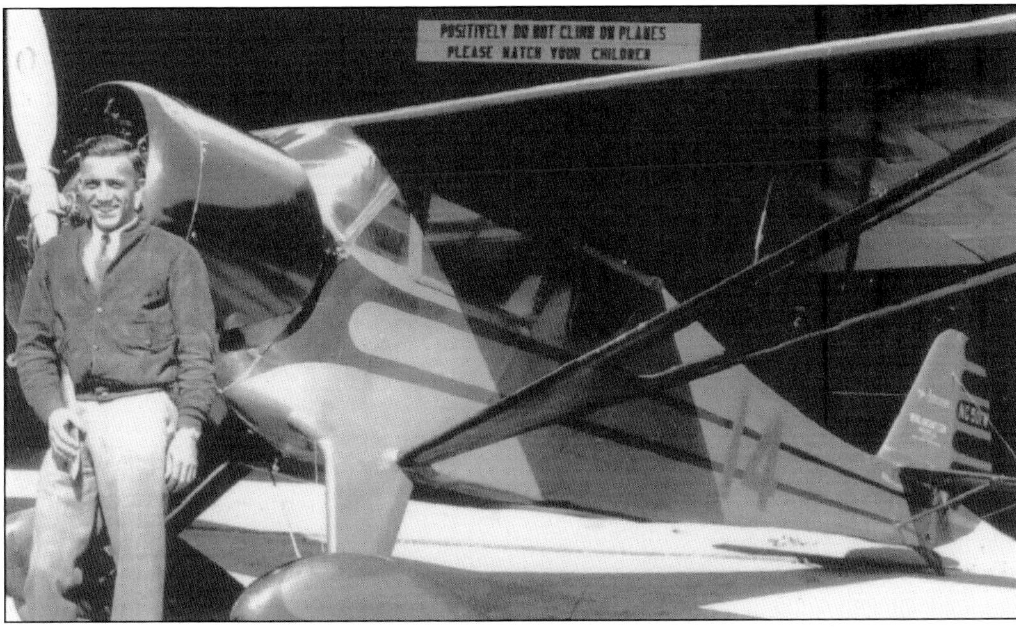

Although he managed airports at Waterloo, Iowa, and Monmouth, Illinois, John Livingston was seen often at Franing Field as a member of the Monocoupe racing team. He flew Monocoupes and Wacos in 137 races, never finishing lower than third place. Author Richard Bach, a former Iowa Air Guard pilot, credits Livingston as the man who inspired him to write the best-selling novel *Jonathan Livingston Seagull.* (Courtesy of Ken Roberts.)

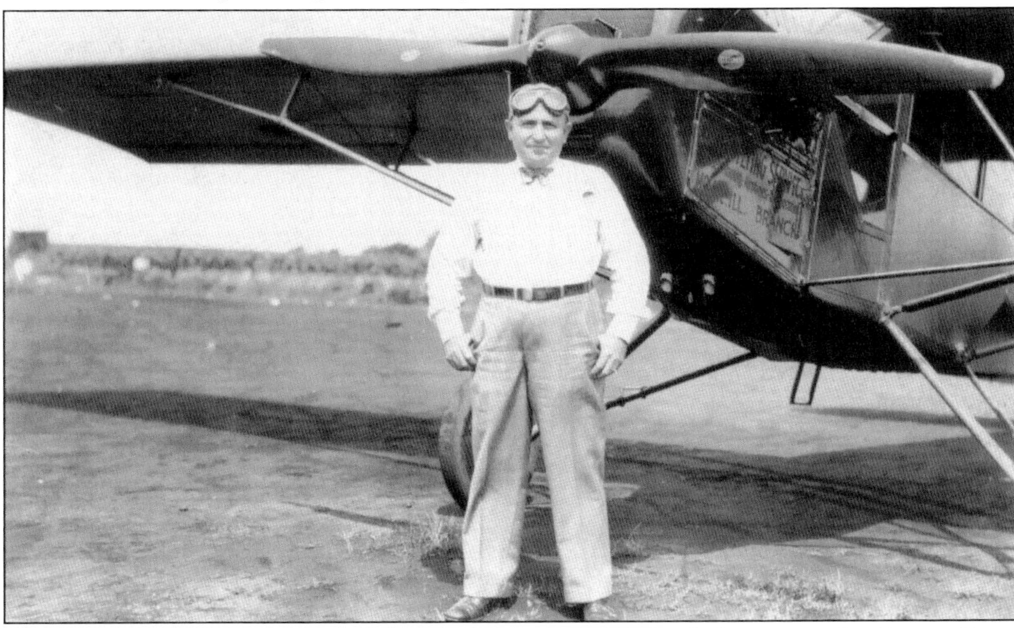

Gabe Mosenfelder was photographed in front of a Curtiss-Robin belonging to the Curtiss Flying Service, Moline branch. Curtiss set up operations at many airports around the country to sell and service its aircraft, repair other makes, and provide flying lessons and charters. Mosenfelder was one of several local aviators utilized by Curtiss to pilot those charter flights. (Courtesy of Kris Streed Crawford.)

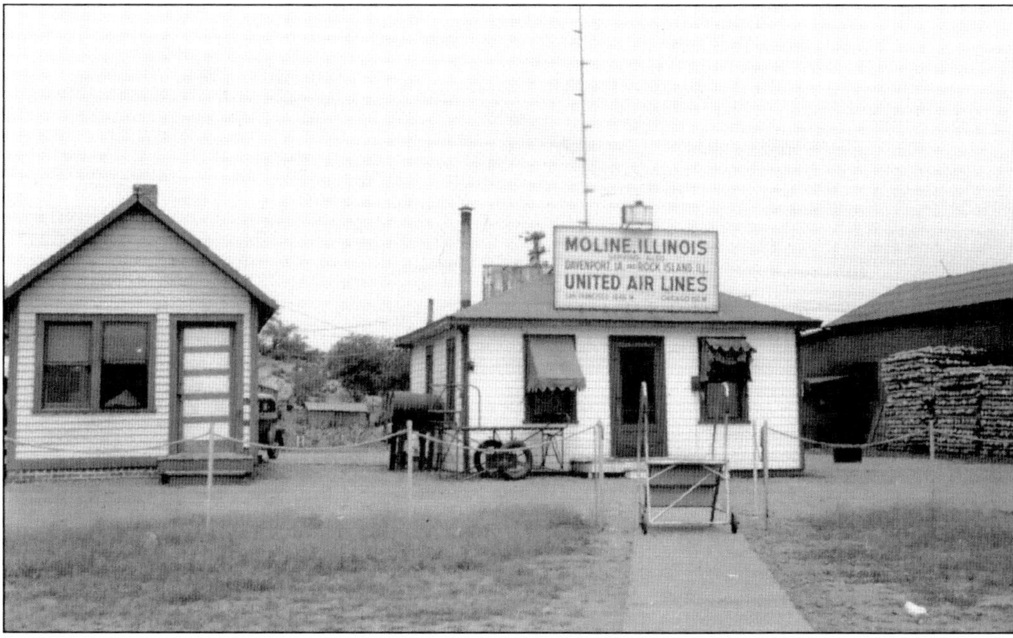

Looking nothing like terminals of today—or even of the last 70 years—this was the United Air Lines office and passenger terminal in 1932. The field had yet to have paved runways, as witnessed by the grass and dirt in the foreground. At least passengers had the luxury of a concrete walkway to the loading door. A mobile stairway sits on the walkway. (Courtesy of QCIA.)

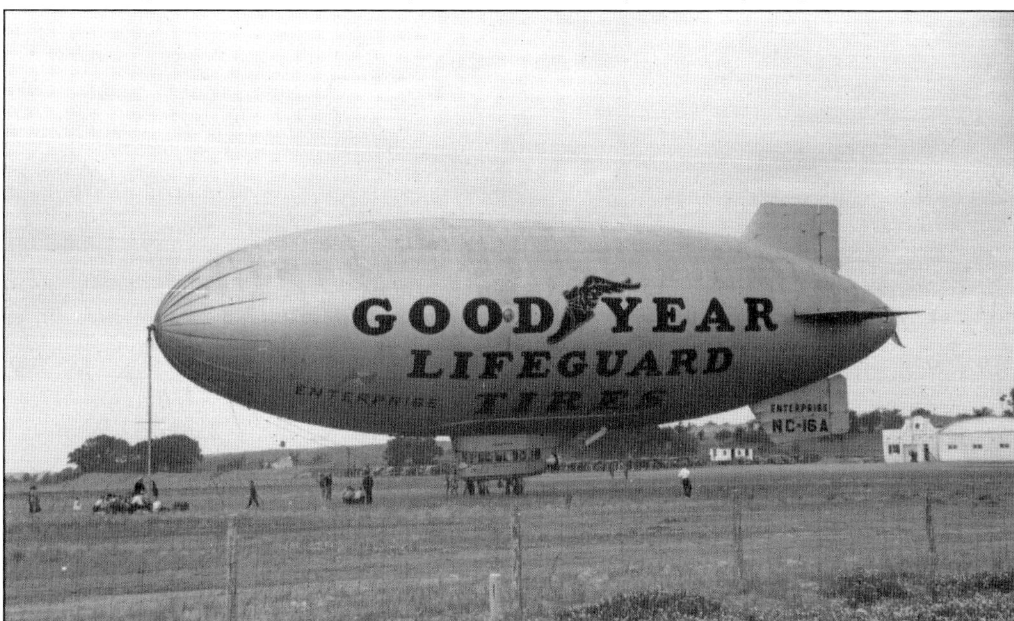

Richard Streed and airport founder Gus DeSchepper were partners in Streed and Scheppers, a tire, bicycle, and automotive parts business. In support of its dealers, the Goodyear Tire and Rubber Company would have one of its fleet of blimps visit dealers' cities to promote the company's line of products. Streed and DeSchepper arranged to have the blimp visit Moline in the early 1930s. (Courtesy of Kris Streed Crawford.)

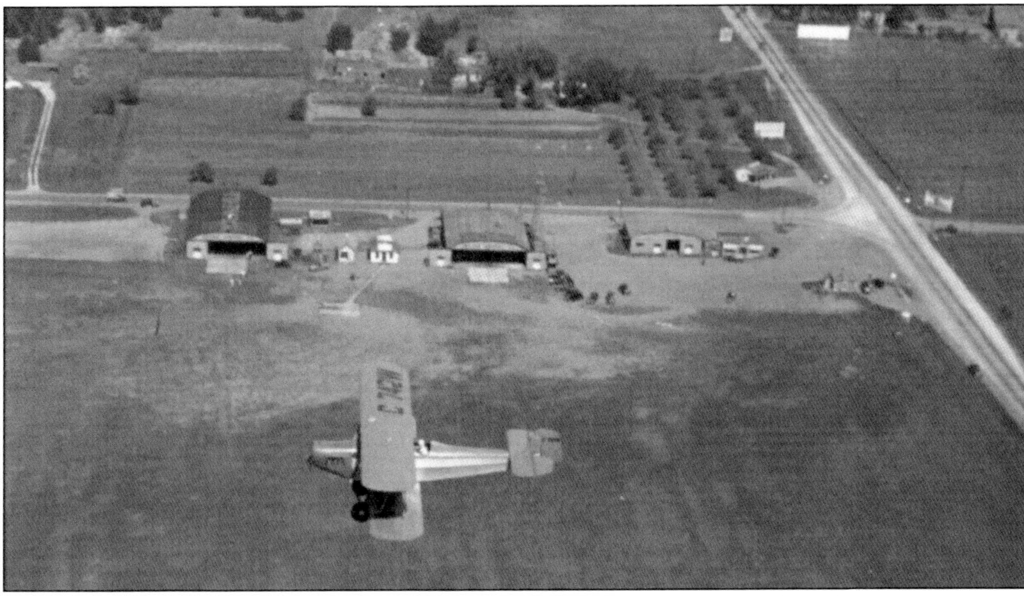

A great aerial from the early 1930s, looking north, captures a Curtiss JN-4D biplane as it passes over Franing Field. Although Campbell-DeSchepper Airplane Company had built up the facilities with three hangars and several small buildings for ancillary services, the airfield itself was still just a flat, level pasture. As seen here, patrons and the curious could easily access the field. (Courtesy of QCIA.)

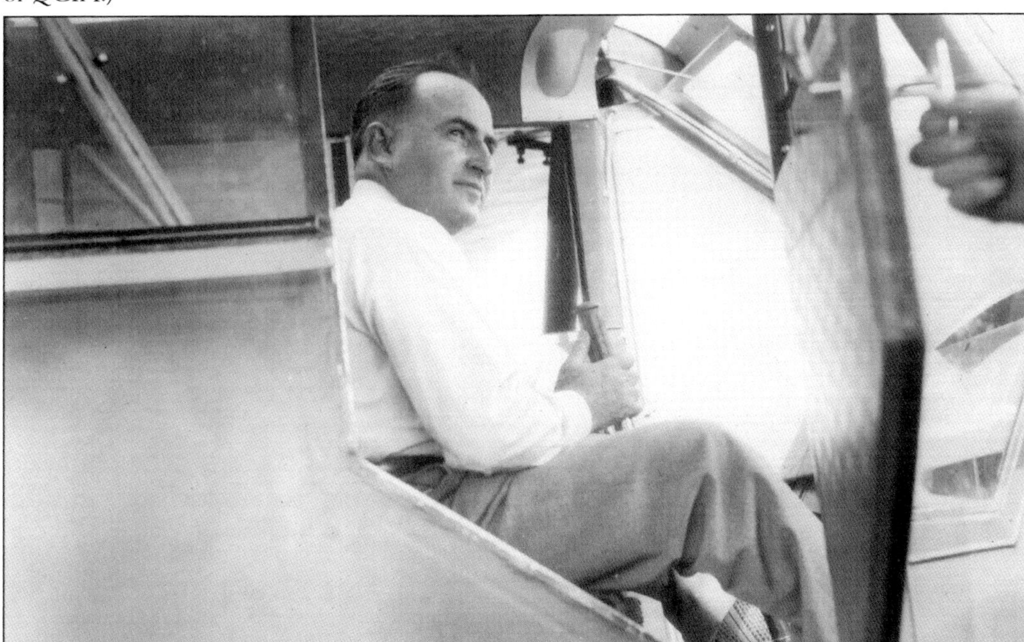

Rock Island clothing store owner Gabe Mosenfelder is seated at the controls of his own Curtiss-Robin aircraft. One of the biggest local enthusiasts of aviation, it has been said that on occasions when the Moline Airport was in financial trouble, it was Mosenfelder who provided the money to keep the field afloat. Over the years, he owned three airplanes and flew many others belonging to other local pilots. (Courtesy of QCIA.)

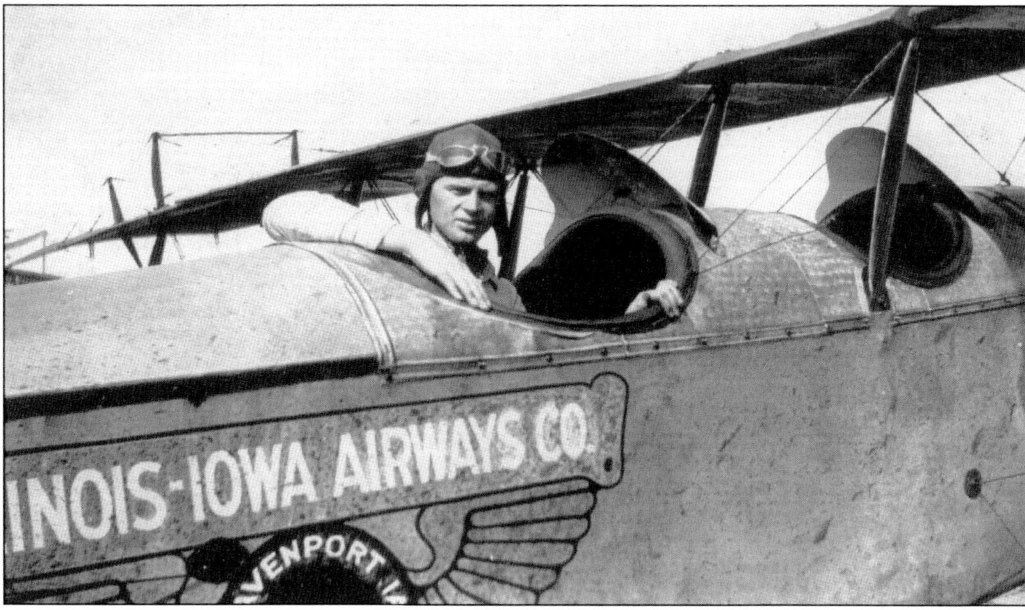

Moline dentist Dr. Warren Streed poses in the cockpit of the Illinois-Iowa Airways Company's Curtiss Jenny. Illinois-Iowa Airways operated a flight school, sold new and used airplanes, and performed repairs and modifications. Streed and other local pilots would occasionally take the controls of the firm's airplane to fly express freight or passengers for the company. (Courtesy of Kris Streed Crawford.)

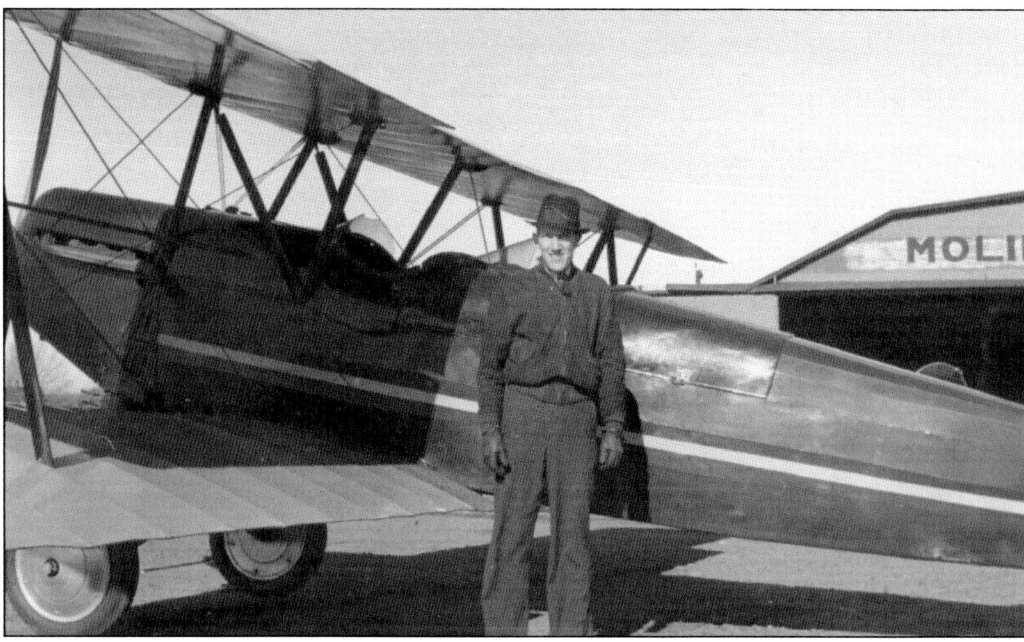

Ken Lee stands in front of Dr. Warren Streed's Travel Air. The aviation bug bit Lee when he assisted Red Webster in rebuilding a Jenny in 1926. Webster repaid Lee's labor by giving him flying lessons, and Lee then went on to teach many others. He and one of his students, Harold Eddington, purchased a Stinson Cabin plane and went into business giving rides, charters, and freight hauling. (Courtesy of QCIA.)

Two

Moline Airport 1935–1952

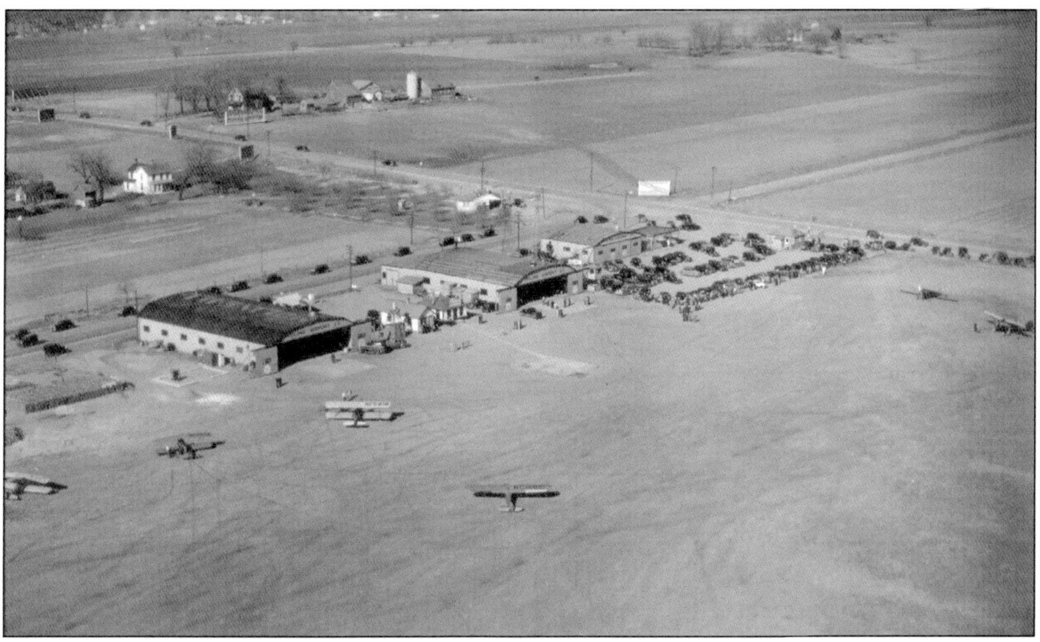

Judging from the cars in the parking lot, along the hard road to Milan and Route 150, some sort of impromptu air show is evidently in progress on a late fall day in 1935. The Campbell-DeSchepper name on the hangars has been replaced by Moline Airport Company titles. The white outline of the pump house foundation can be seen just left of the hangar on the left. (Courtesy of QCIA.)

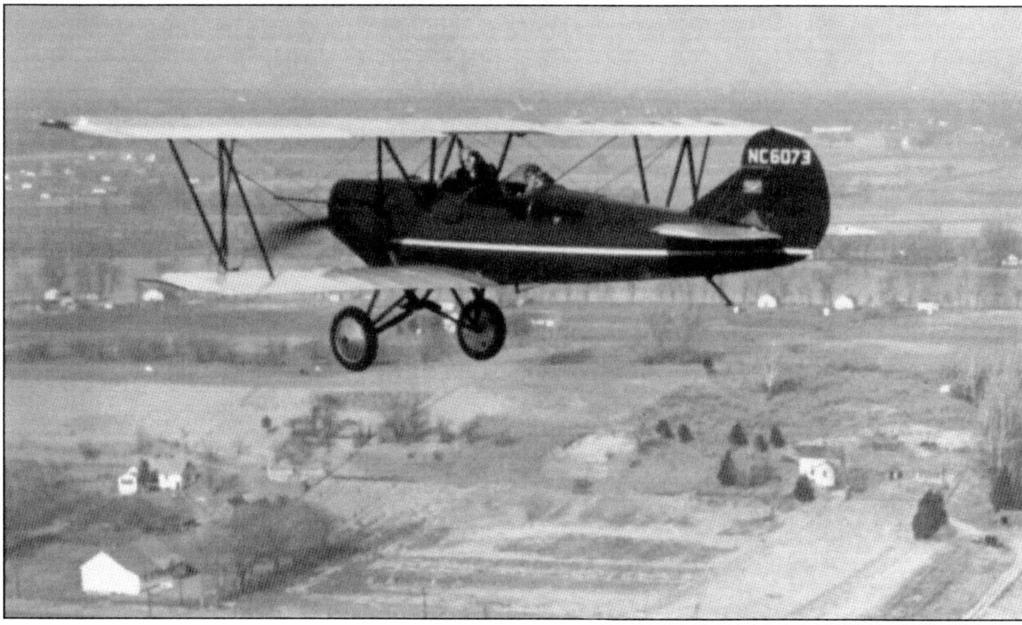

This air-to-air photograph from 1935 captures Dr. Warren Streed as he pilots his Travel Air 2000 over farmland near the Rock River and Moline Airport. The river is just off to the right. This airplane was equipped with a Wright OXX6 engine for increased horsepower. Streed would later become one of the founding members of the Quad City Airmen's Association and an airport commissioner. (Courtesy of Kris Streed Crawford.)

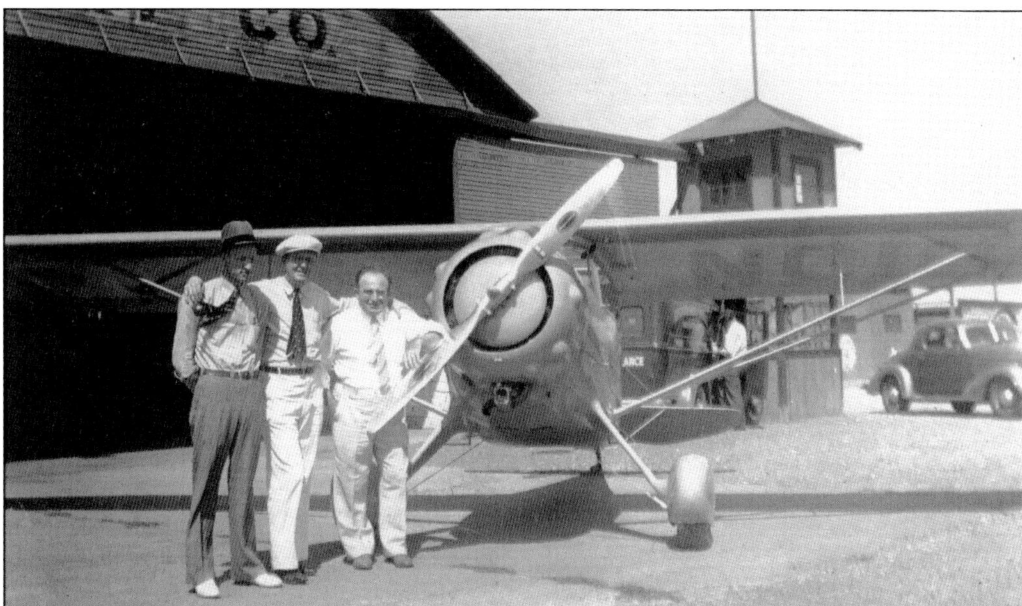

Photographed at Moline before leaving for the 1935 National Air Races in Chicago are, from left to right, William Ziegler, Louis "Red" Webster, and Gabe Mosenfelder. Both Ziegler and Webster were pilots and noted automobile and aircraft mechanics. Webster was also a flight instructor and taught several hundred Civil Air Patrol cadets at the Moline field during the course of World War II. (Courtesy of Kris Streed Crawford.)

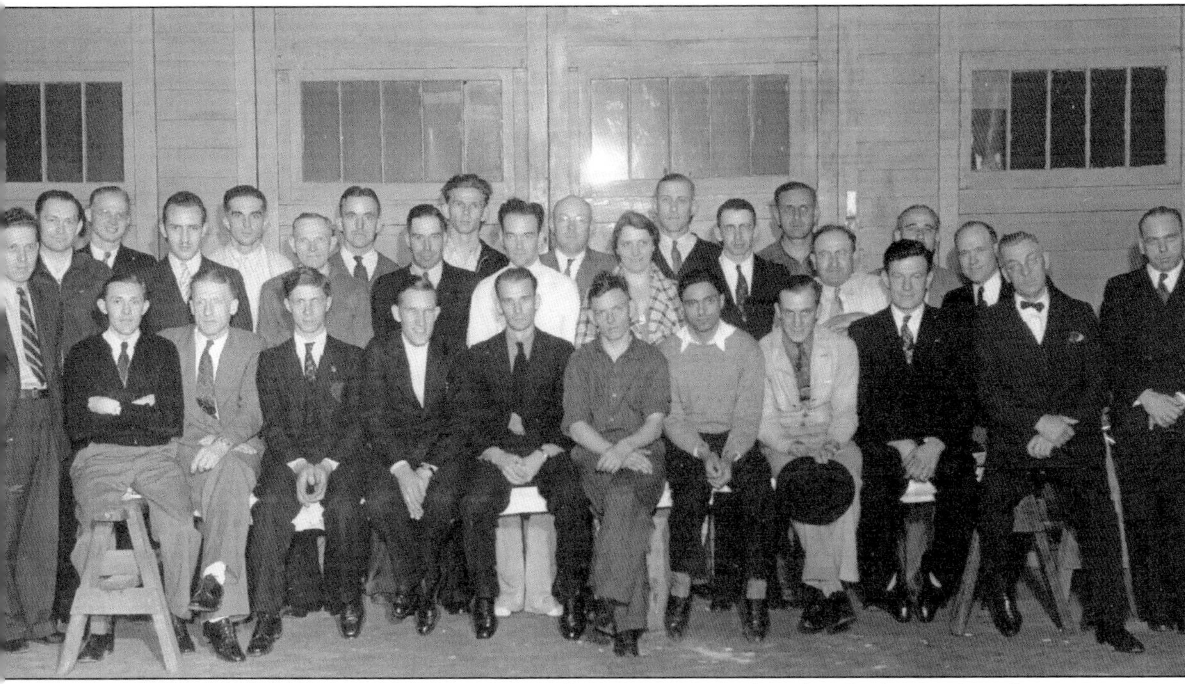

The Quad City Airmen's Association was formed in May 1935, with 21 local pilots and mechanics recorded as charter members. Its stated purpose was to seek harmony and unity among the pilots of the Quad City area and to study the various phases of aviation. Harmony and unity was probably a good idea, as this was the period when officials of Davenport and Moline began sparring over the issue of which city would receive the Class IV, or air carrier, airport designation. The association's meetings would entail courses of study on the latest developments in aviation, with suitable speakers or instructors. Members at this 1936 meeting are, from left to right, (seated) Ken Lee, Bill Ziegler, Des Erickson, Ralph Oakley, Ray Laverenz, Paul Bloom, Jim Corelis, Ed Greim, Clarence Paustian, and G.F. Jontz, speaker; (standing) George Dickson, Vern Aten, Dr. Warren Streed, Herb Schlicting, Delbert Clayton, George Willecke, Ed Andreson, Floyd Adams, Dwight Carlson, Joe Mieser, Glen Phelps, Ada Phelps, Ed Schmidt, Al Fankhauser, Pat Miller, Gabe Mosenfelder, Clyde Shoemaker, Harold Mills, and Roy Quimby. (Courtesy of QCIA.)

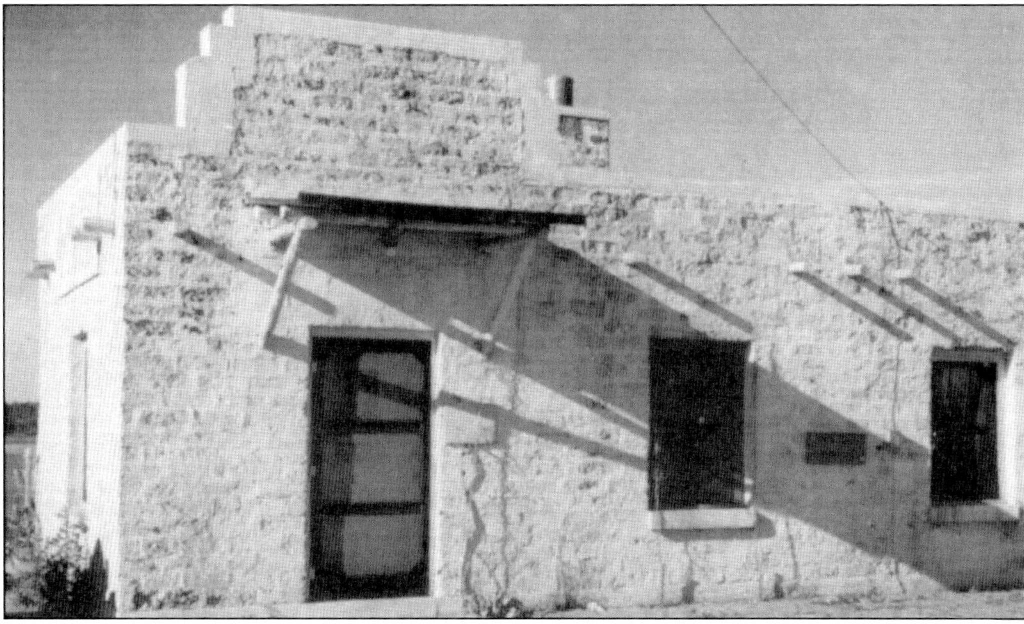

Looking more like it belongs somewhere in the Southwest, this was the first US Weather Bureau office built on the grounds of the airport. Erected in 1936, the building was of rather interesting construction. Instead of wood or concrete, it used emulsified asphalt blocks and was supposedly the only building in the country constructed of this material. The US Weather Bureau moved to the new hangar-terminal building in 1939. (Courtesy of QCIA.)

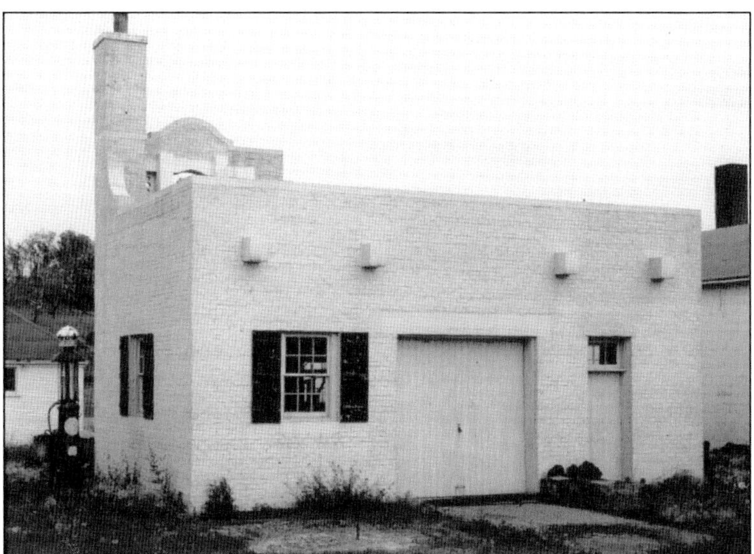

Another airport building with a Southwestern look is this pump house. Built in the mid-1930s, it served several functions at various times. It housed the pump and plumbing for the airport's water well. For a period of time, the building was the collection point for airmail and later was the first fire station. It is the only original building remaining on airport property. (Courtesy of QCIA.)

Another famous visitor to Moline Airport was Amelia Earhart, seen here in a hangar in October 1936. Her appearance was for an address to the Moline After Dinner Club at the LeClaire Hotel. Afterwards, she met with the Quad City Airmen's Association, answered questions, and talked about her new Lockheed Electra 10E airplane, which she would be flying when she went missing in July 1937. (Courtesy of QCIA.)

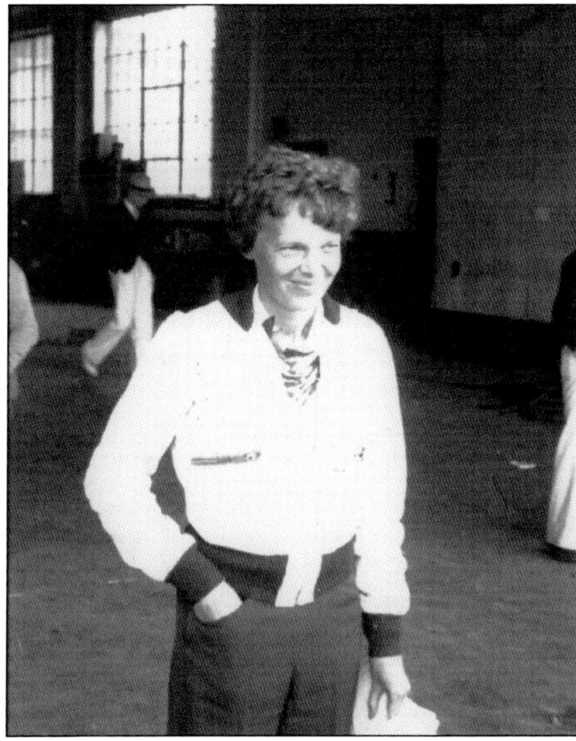

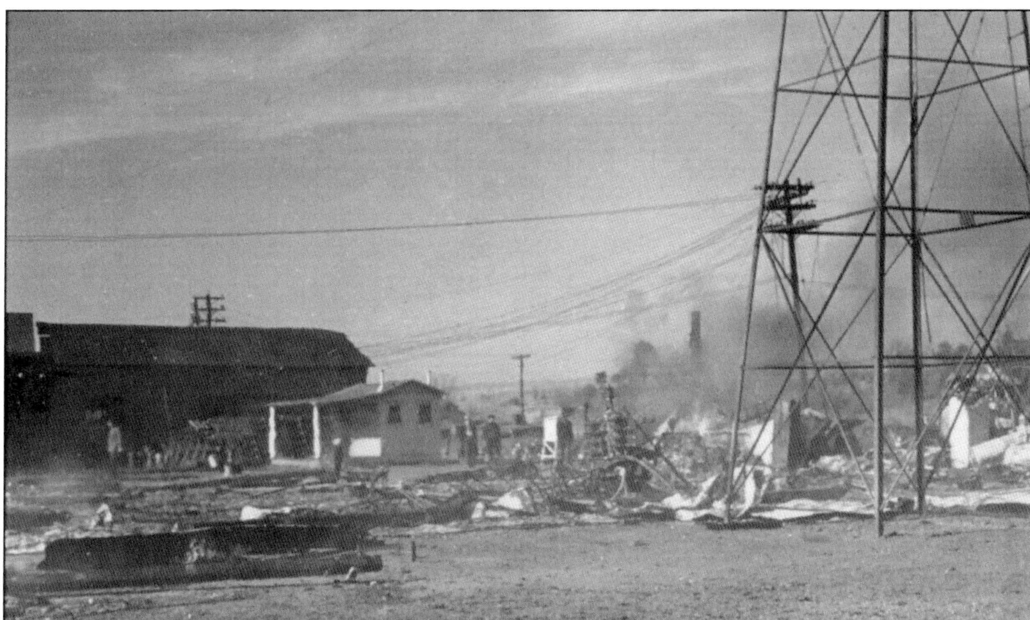

This November 1937 photograph displays the smoldering ruins of the hangar used by United Air Lines. The fire began above a false ceiling in the hangar and had already ignited the roof before mechanics discovered the fire. The blaze destroyed one airplane, but four were pushed to safety. The field's beacon and weather apparatus towers were not harmed, but the airline's tools, spare parts, and radio equipment were destroyed. (Courtesy of QCIA.)

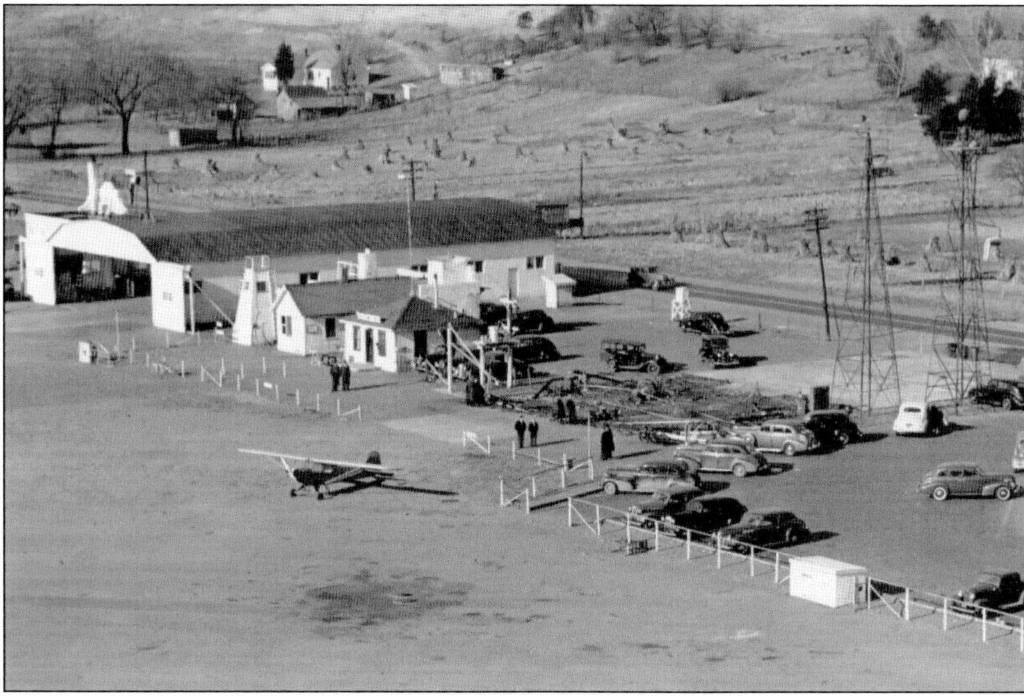

This photograph, taken days later with only the steel debris left at the site, indicates how thorough the destruction was. There is nothing left but the concrete floor. It was discovered that the fire was the result of arson. The owner of the airplane destroyed in the fire wanted the insurance money to purchase a better plane. A temporary Quonset-style hangar was erected in its place. (Courtesy of QCIA.)

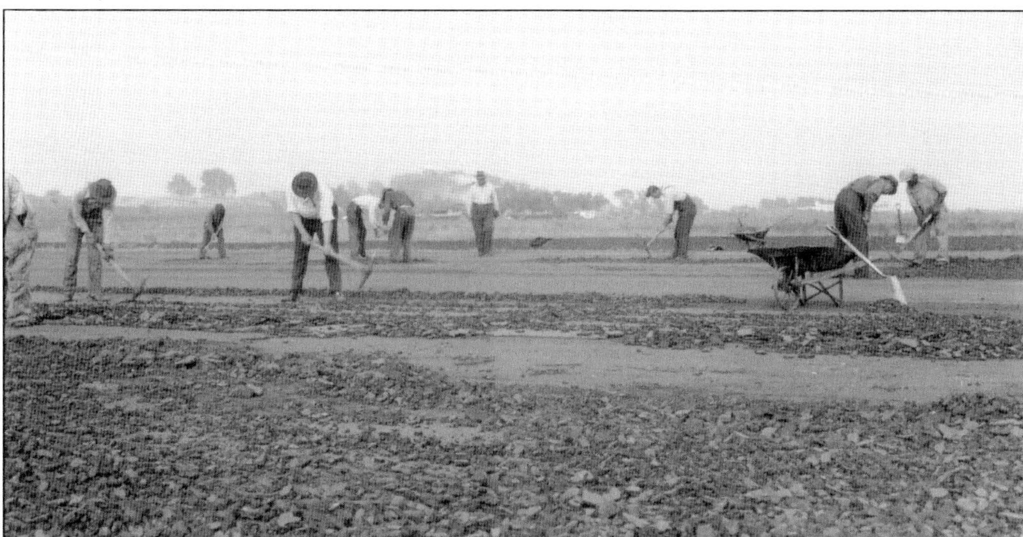

Laborers hired by the Works Progress Administration (WPA) spent three years leveling Moline Airport to get it ready for runway and taxiway paving. A surplus narrow-gauge railroad was purchased and installed at the field to haul fill from several nearby hills. These men are fine-grading a runway surface in preparation for its layer of asphalt paving. The WPA put over 400 men to work on the various airport projects. (Courtesy of QCIA.)

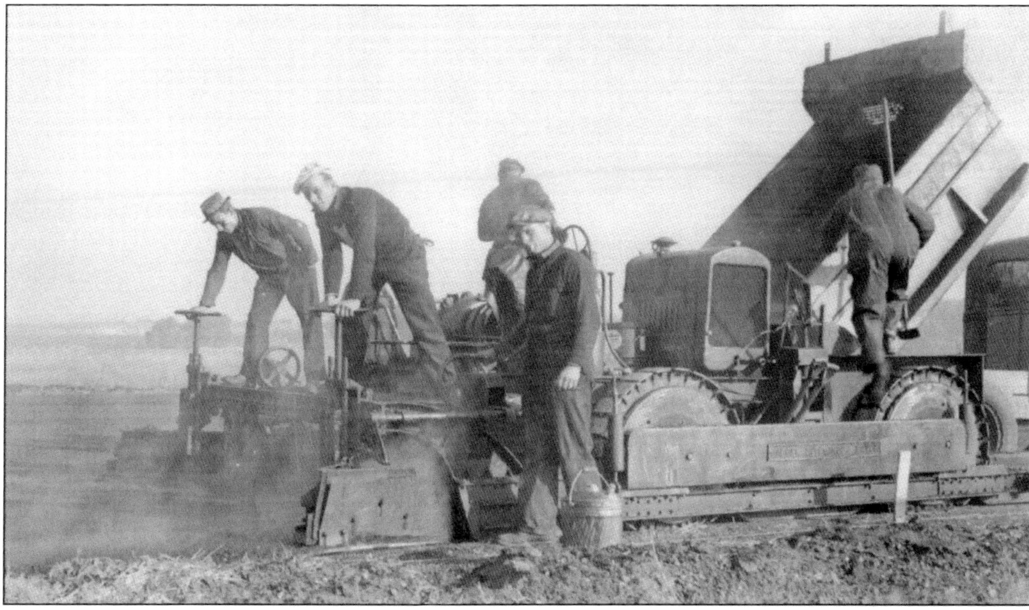

Once the City of Moline took ownership of the airport, the paving of runways could finally begin. The Works Progress Administration (WPA) hired 450 men to grade and level the field. By 1938, over 480,000 cubic feet of earth had been moved and 215,000 square yards of four-inch thick asphalt had been laid for the runways. This 1938 photograph shows the men and a paver at work. (Courtesy of QCIA.)

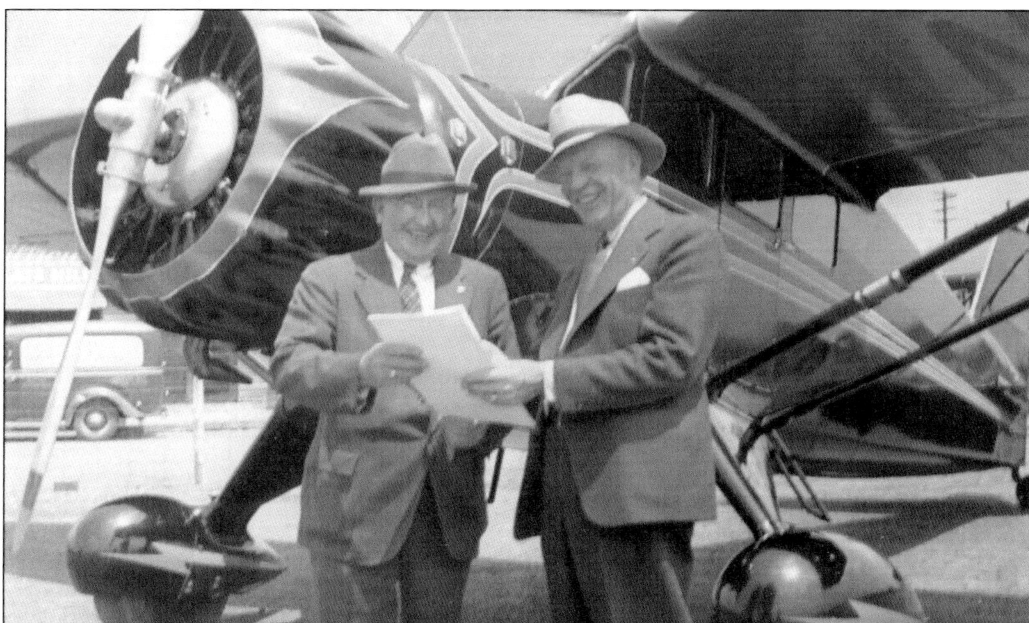

Two of the moving forces behind Moline Airport, Gabe Mosenfelder (left) and Rusty Campbell, are shown with the gull-winged Stinson owned by Ken Lee and Harold Eddington. Lee and Eddington used this plane for rides, charters, and freight hauling. Campbell left Moline in 1930 but returned in 1938 to operate the airport for the city. This photograph was taken in 1938, shortly before Campbell's death. (Courtesy of Kris Streed Crawford.)

MOLINE AIRPORT MOTEL

NOTHING LIKE IT ANYWHERE

Just North of Moline Airport on U. S. 6, U. S. 150, State Route 92

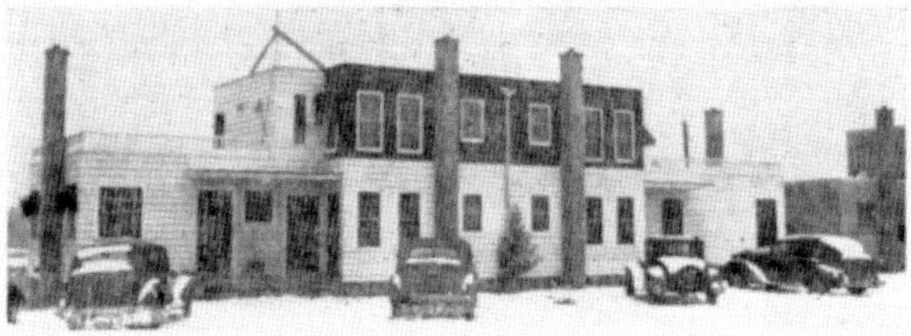

ONE OF SIX APARTMENT BUILDINGS IN OUR COURT

Complete Apartment Motel with private bath, toilet, kitchenette with 6 ft. refrigerator, 4-burner gas cook stove, bake oven, dinette set, dishes, etc.; twin beds, innerspring mattress . . . Plenty of closet space—each apartment with individual entrance . . . Just like home . . . . Located between the large airfield and beautiful Rock River . . . . Heated in Winter . . . Reasonable Prices. PHONE—MOL. 4531

Built in the mid-1930s to take advantage of the growing airport, the Moline Airport Motel was located on the west side of Route 150, near the Rock River Bridge. Probably designed for the business traveler, each room was outfitted like a small apartment. Interestingly, it touted that it was heated in the winter. The motel was demolished in the late 1950s to make way for interstate highway construction.

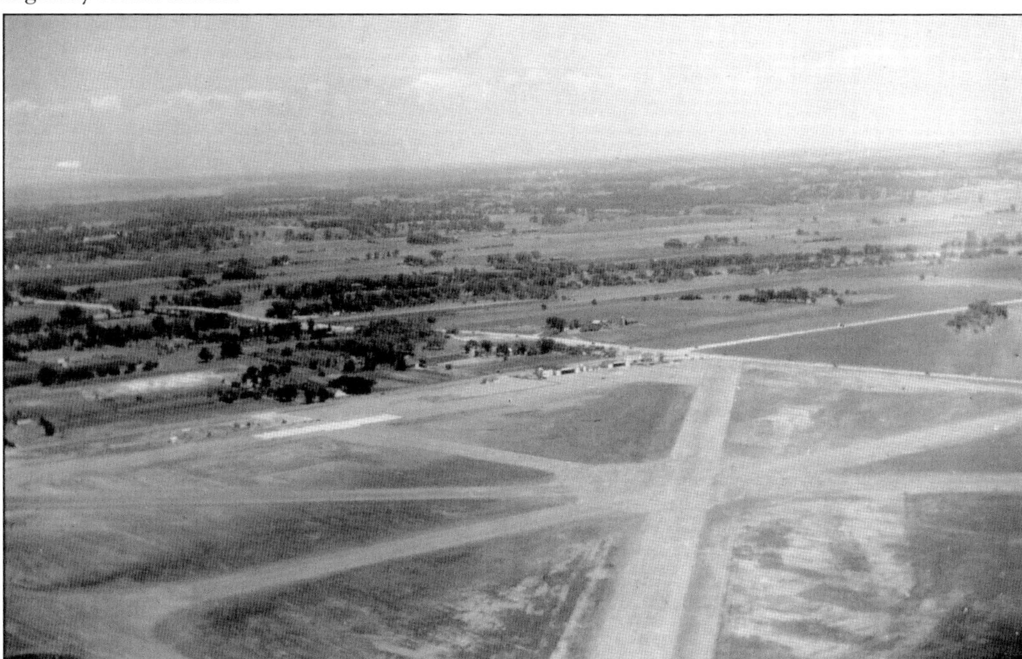

This view looking northeast shows the runway patterns of the Moline Airport in the late 1930s. It appears that this photograph was taken shortly before construction began on the new hangar/terminal, as witnessed by the concrete apron and cleared area at left center. The photograph also provides an excellent view of the Rock River valley and southern Moline, long before development came to that area. (Courtesy of QCIA.)

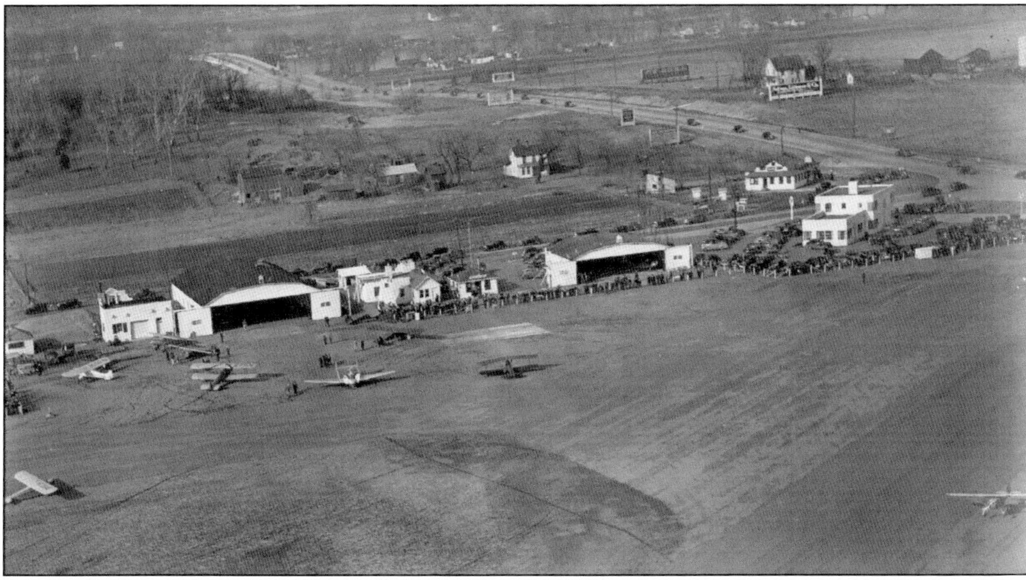

Airplanes and spectators gathered for an air show in late 1937. All of the buildings that made up Moline Airport by this time are now complete, with the addition of the two-story structure on the right. It contained a service station, restaurant, and apartments for the airport manager and resident mechanic. Significant amounts of the taxiway areas and runways have been paved with asphalt. (Courtesy of QCIA.)

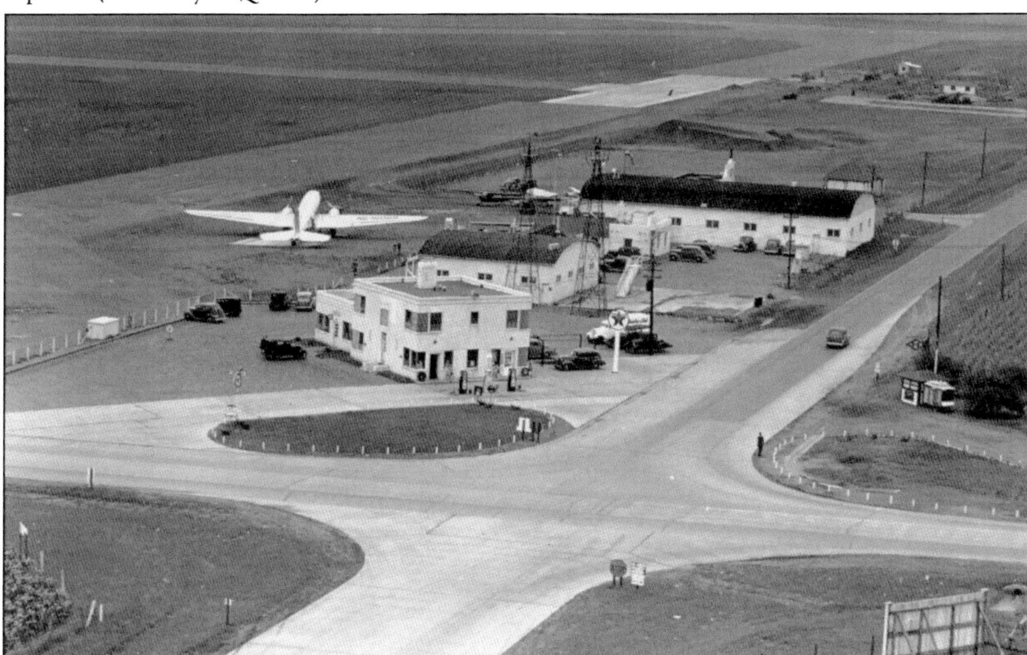

Another angle of Moline Airport's facilities in late 1937 shows some of the site preparation for the planned new hangar-terminal complex. The view is rather deceiving, as the location for the new building location appears closer than it really was. The distance between the old Mono Aircraft hangar and the new hangar was nearly one-half mile. This photograph also provides a great view of the recently built service station-restaurant. (Courtesy of QCIA.)

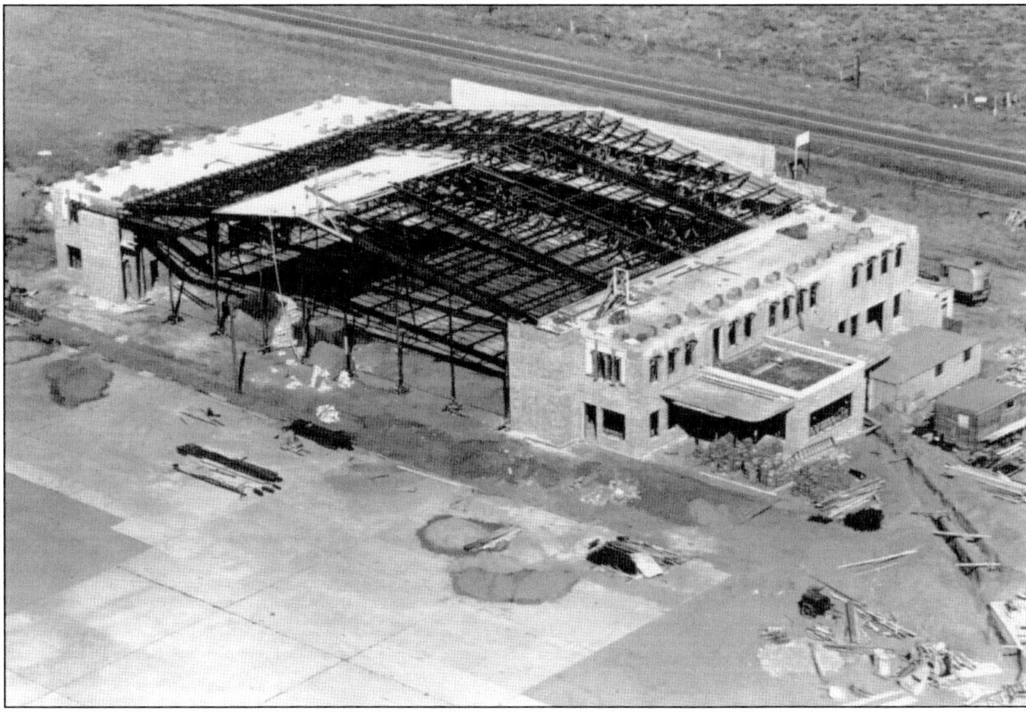

The voters of Moline, through the urgings of the Association of Commerce, passed a $175,000 bond referendum that enabled the construction of this combination hangar, shop, and terminal building. The referendum's passing provided the materials, and monies from the Works Progress Administration paid for the labor and insured that men hired for airport projects would continue to receive a paycheck. This photograph from late 1938 captures the construction activity. (Courtesy of QCIA.)

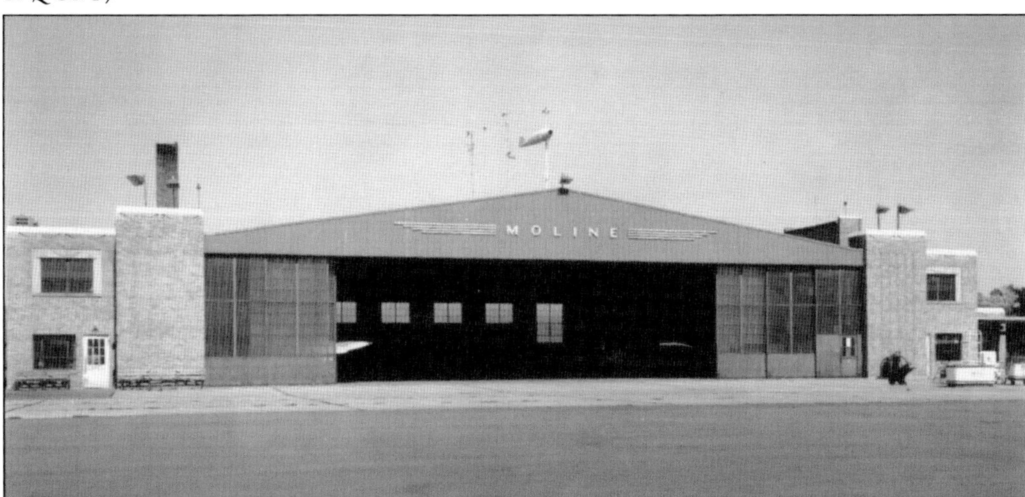

An airport publicity photograph depicts the new hangar-terminal building in its completed form. Airport administrative offices, facilities for both the US Weather Bureau and the Civil Aeronautics Authority, and the United Air Lines office and passenger waiting area surround the hangar space and repair shop. The airline ticket office and passenger area is on the far right of the building. (Courtesy of QCIA.)

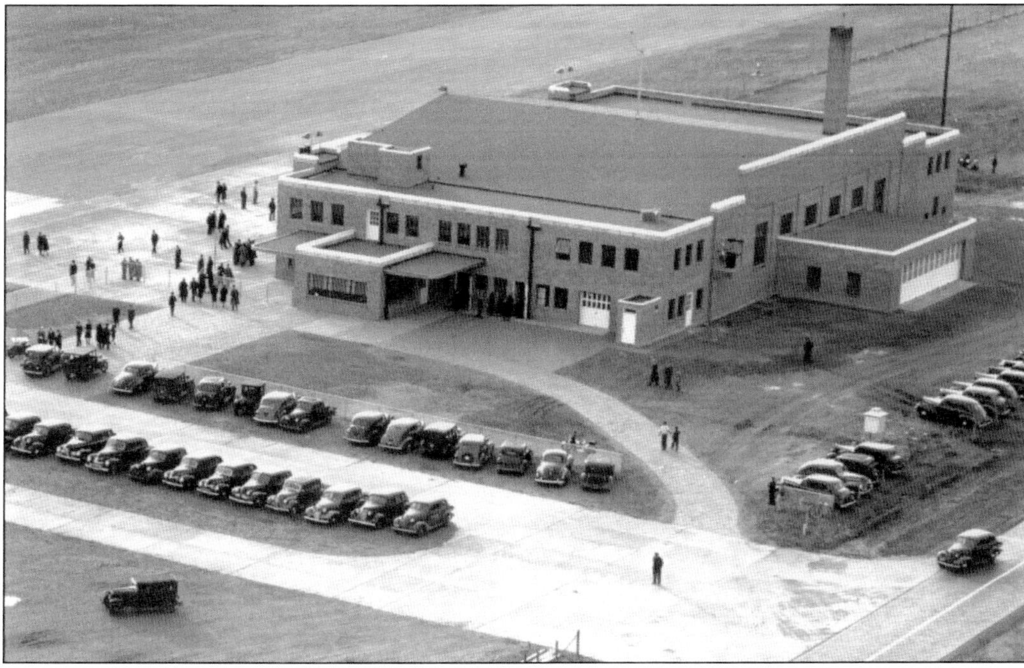

This view of the hangar-terminal building was taken during the open house for representatives of the city and various civic organizations. The airline passenger terminal is clearly seen from this angle. Access to the roof allowed for meteorological observations by both weather bureau and airline personnel. There were several antennae on the roof for both the CAA communication center and the airline's communication radio. (Courtesy of QCIA.)

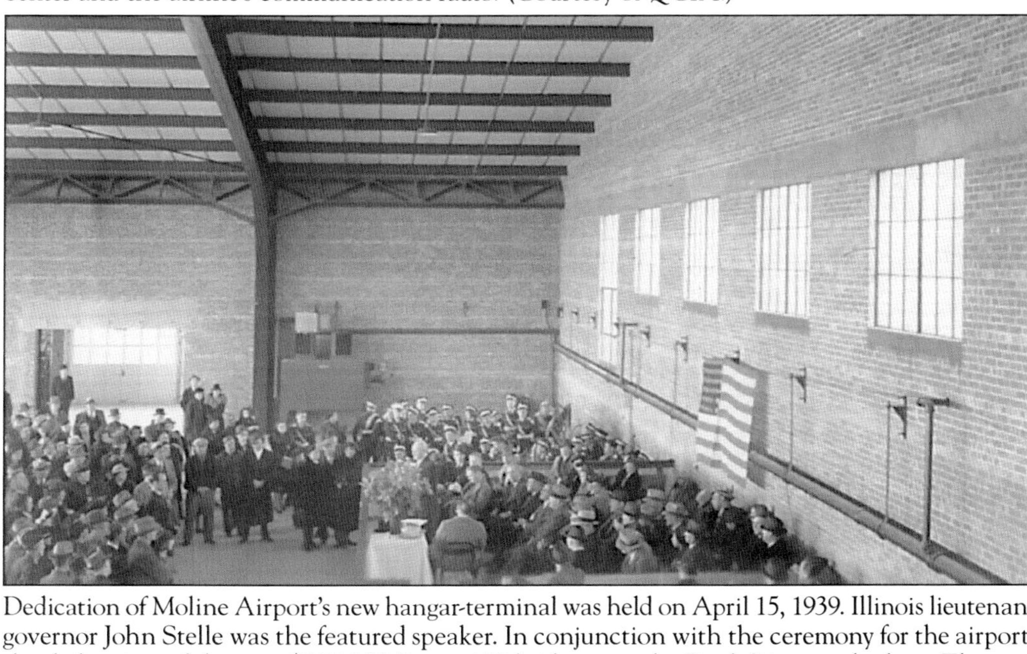

Dedication of Moline Airport's new hangar-terminal was held on April 15, 1939. Illinois lieutenant governor John Stelle was the featured speaker. In conjunction with the ceremony for the airport, the dedication of the new $500,000 Route 150 bridge over the Rock River took place. The new bridge was the last link in the newly improved highway from downtown Moline to the airport. (Courtesy of QCIA.)

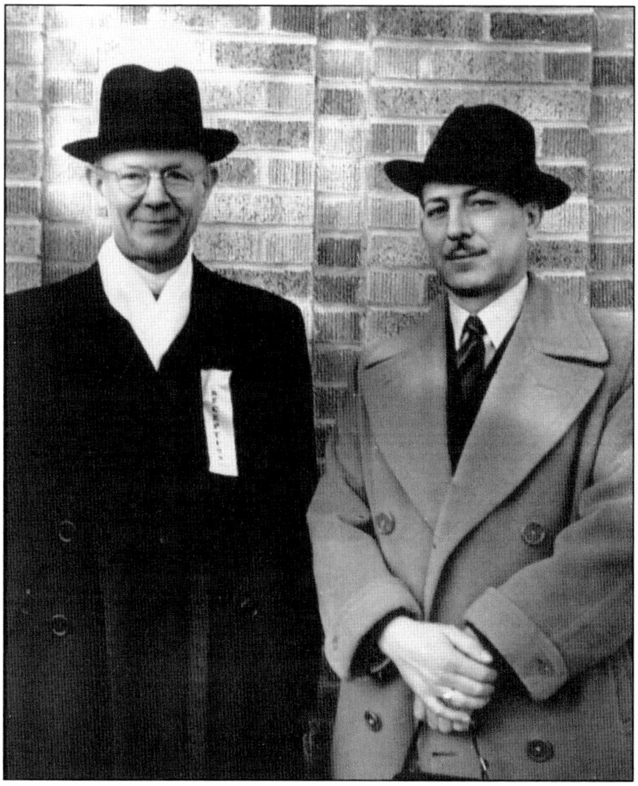

Two of the men highly responsible for Moline Airport are captured together in this 1939 photograph. Rev. John Culemans (left) and J. Wesley Smith were honored at the dedication of the new hangar-terminal building. Culemans was chairman of the Association of Commerce aviation committee and championed the airport at every turn. Smith was one of the original organizers and investors in the airport at Franing Field. (Courtesy of QCIA.)

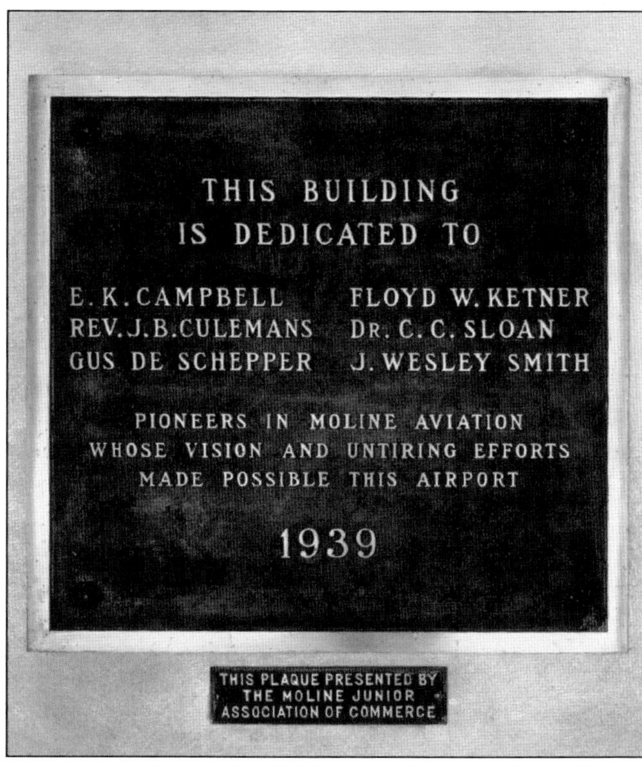

During the dedication of the hangar-terminal building on April 4, 1939, this plaque was presented to honor and recognize the six men most responsible for creating Moline Airport. It seemed only fitting that the plaque was moved to each of the new terminal buildings, as the new structures were extensions of the dreams, labor, and persistence of those men. (Courtesy of QCIA.)

Shortly after the new hangar-terminal building was erected, the Association of Commerce had this brochure printed and sent to chambers of commerce and airports across the country. With rumblings beginning to be heard from officials in Davenport, Iowa, that they wanted to have the main air carrier airport located in their city, the association hoped to show off the modern facilities and benefits of Moline Airport. The brochure touted every amenity the airport offered aviators and indicated the close distances to the various cities' business districts. It noted that the airport served the Rock Island Arsenal, the nation's largest war plant, and promoted the easy connections and five daily stops offered by United Air Lines. It was an all-out effort to impress the business and private aviation communities that Moline Airport was first-rate in every way. (Both, courtesy of QCIA.)

MOLINE
Municipal Airport

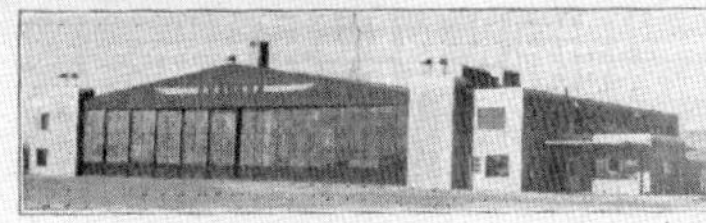

A 208-acre all weather field with 215,000 square yards of paved runways. Approved by Federal Civil Aeronautics Authority for operations by all types of land planes.

Five daily schedules on mid-continent coast-to-coast route of United Air Lines.

New $100,000 heated hangar, shops and administration building with Federal weather bureau and CAA Communications Station service.

A $1,000,000 airport offering complete accommodations for private planes day and night.

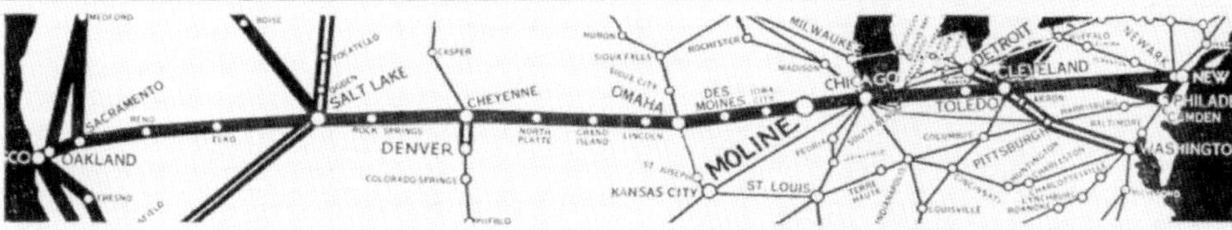

Recognized as one of the finest ports in the United States the Moline Muncipal Airport was completed at a cost of over $1,000,000 by the city of Moline and the United States Government. This cost includes 208 acres of land, four hard-surface runways, taxi strips, a modern $100,000 heated hangar, shops and administration building and every facility to serve the needs of modern transportation.

Located three miles south of Moline on a 4-lane concrete highway from the heart of the business district, and within a fifteen minute drive from the business district of Rock Island and Davenport, Iowa, the port is easily accessible to a population of over 160,000. The field also serves the government's largest war plant, the Rock Island Arsenal, and is used frequently by army and navy planes.

In the 4-year development of the airport 480,000 cubic yards of dirt were moved to produce the proper grade for the field. The modern runways are 100 feet wide and equivalent to twenty-one miles of hardsurfaced highways. Gravel shoulders 50 feet wide are equal to 18½ miles of graveled highways, and give the runways a usable width of 200 feet. The length of the runways are: Southwest-northeast 3850 feet; southeast-northwest 4040 feet; north-south 3025 feet and east-west 3000 feet.

The entire field, exclusive of the paved runways, is a gravel top satisfactory for the landing of the average plane the year around.

The airport is bounded by white marker lights of the knock-over type. Green range lights for traffic control are located at the end of each of the four runways. The port is served by the directional beacons and radio range stations of the mid-continent route, New York to San Francisco.

An office, with full personnel, of the United States Weather Bureau is located on the port and renders complete 24-hour service to all private flyers and transport lines.

A Civil Aeronautics Authority Airways Communication station is maintained at the airport to serve the needs of all pilots. This office assembles weather reports through teletype service from 550 similar branches throughout the United States and makes such information available to pilots at all times.

The Moline port is an important base on the mid-continent trans-continental airway maintained by the United States Government. The giant Mainliners of the United Air Lines operating on this shortest coast-to-coast route use the Moline Muni-

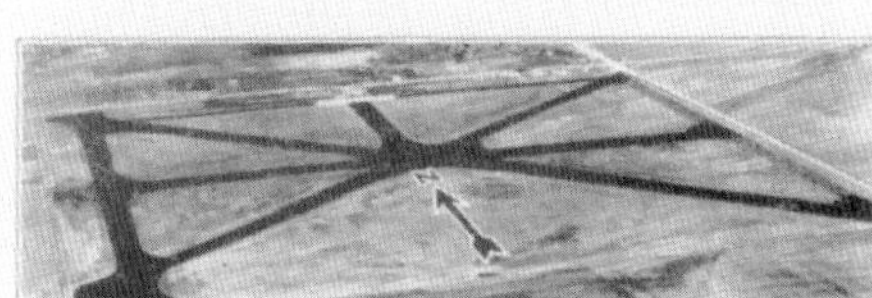

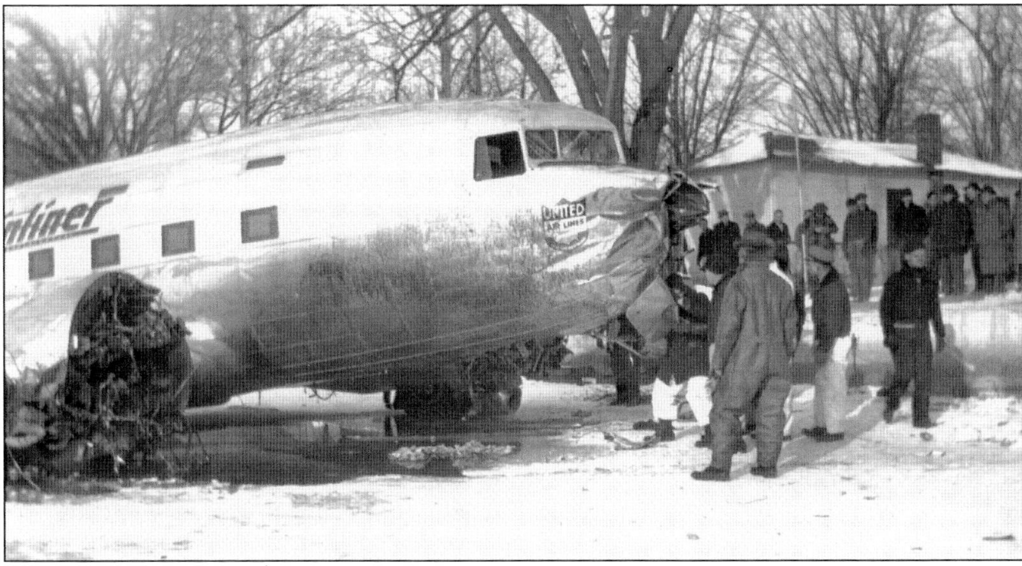

This plane developed problems with an engine over Iowa City during the early morning of January 12, 1940, and turned back to land at Moline. During a missed approach, the second engine lost power, and the pilots made a forced landing on the frozen Rock River, just west of the Route 150 bridge. The pilot missed the bridge and dropped the plane onto the ice with its wheels up. Sliding downriver, a wing clipped a tree and spun the plane into a concrete wall. While the fuselage was undamaged, the nose received the brunt of the collision with the wall. No one on board received any serious injuries. United mechanics removed the wings, loaded the plane on a trailer, and trucked it to a repair facility in Cheyenne, Wyoming. (Above, courtesy of Fred Marzolph/Earl Wendt; below, courtesy of the Richard Shrader family.)

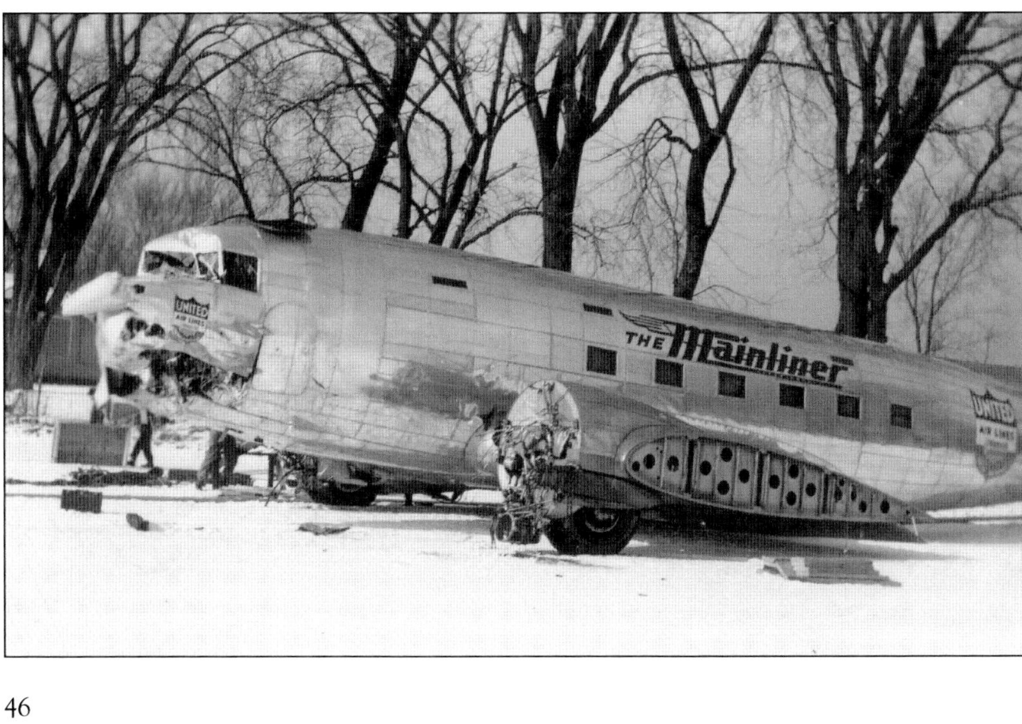

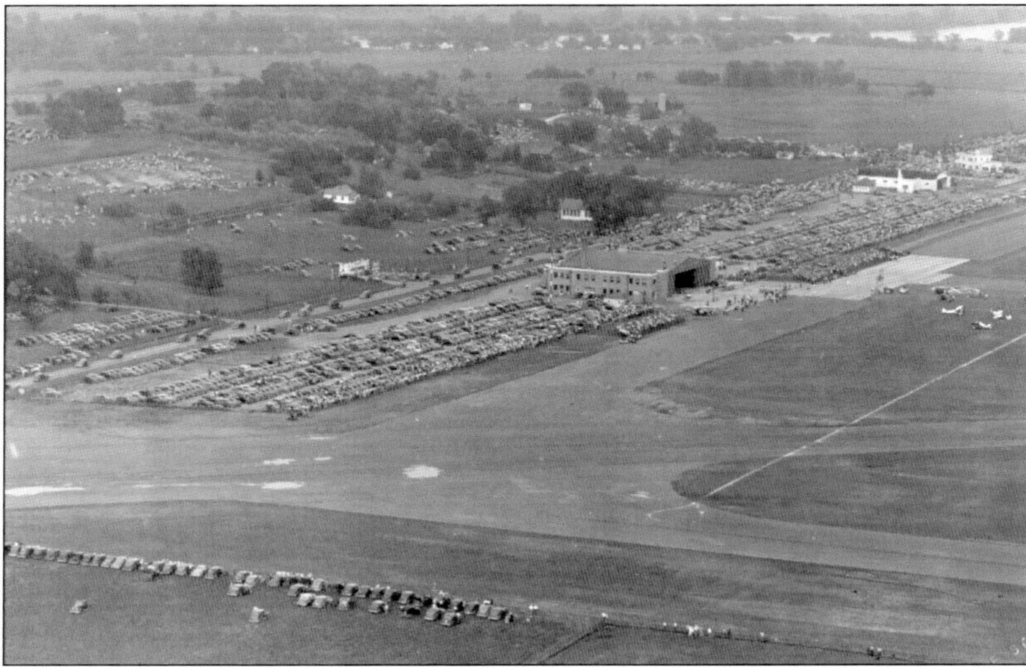

The airport staged an air show in 1940. From the number of vehicles parked along the roads and around the perimeter, it appears that most of Moline attended. A close look at the old airport complex shows only the large hangar, pump house, former US Weather Bureau building, and the corner gas station-restaurant-apartment building. The former airport office and airline terminal building have been torn down. (Courtesy of QCIA.)

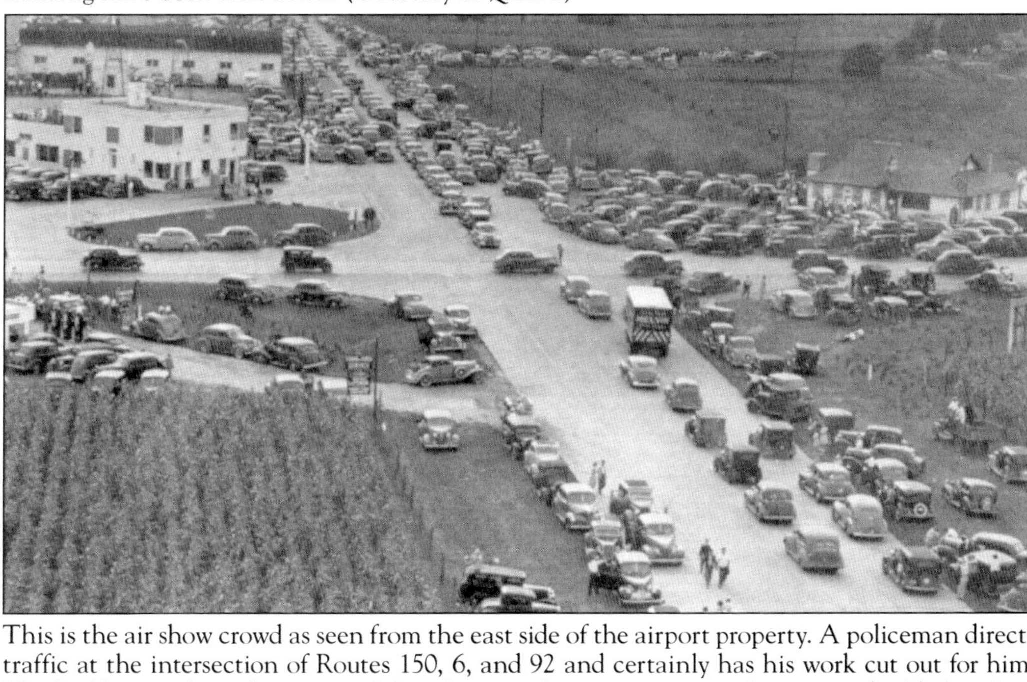

This is the air show crowd as seen from the east side of the airport property. A policeman directs traffic at the intersection of Routes 150, 6, and 92 and certainly has his work cut out for him. The building at the right center of this photograph was a restaurant known as the Skyline Inn. Opened in the mid-1920s, it still exists today in the same basic structure. (Courtesy of QCIA.)

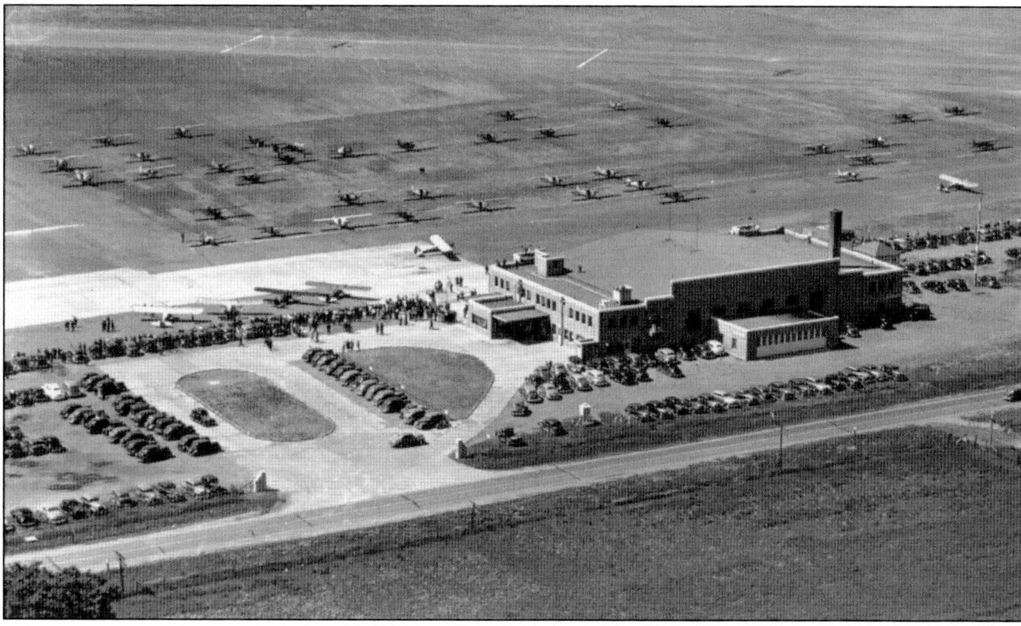

The Quad City Airmen's Association hosted a fly-in breakfast and air show in 1941 that brought visiting aviators from 30 cities and over 100 airplanes to the airport. Aircraft provided both static and flying displays. Over the years, the association hosted many such events at the Moline Airport and took part in fly-in visits to many other airfields around the Midwest. (Courtesy of QCIA.)

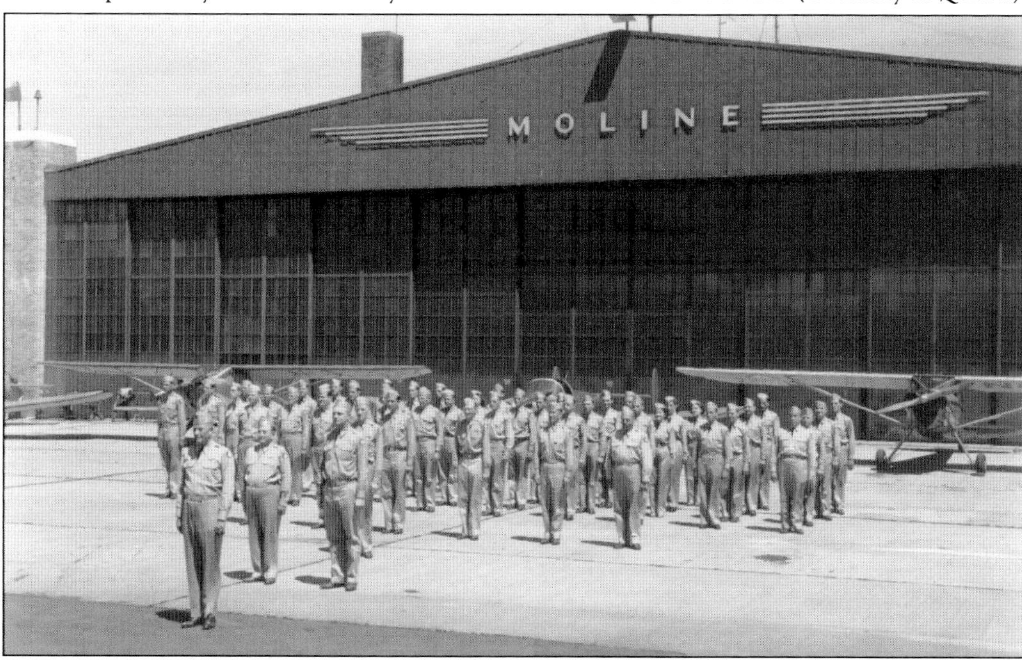

Organized during World War II, the Moline squadron of the Civil Air Patrol (CAP) was made up of mostly private pilots who owned their own planes. Volunteers had to take required courses in military procedures, including military drill, airport protection, guard duty, navigation, and radio code, and were on call for any duty. No private pilot was allowed to fly unless he belonged to the CAP. Vern Roberts was squadron commander. (Courtesy of QCIA.)

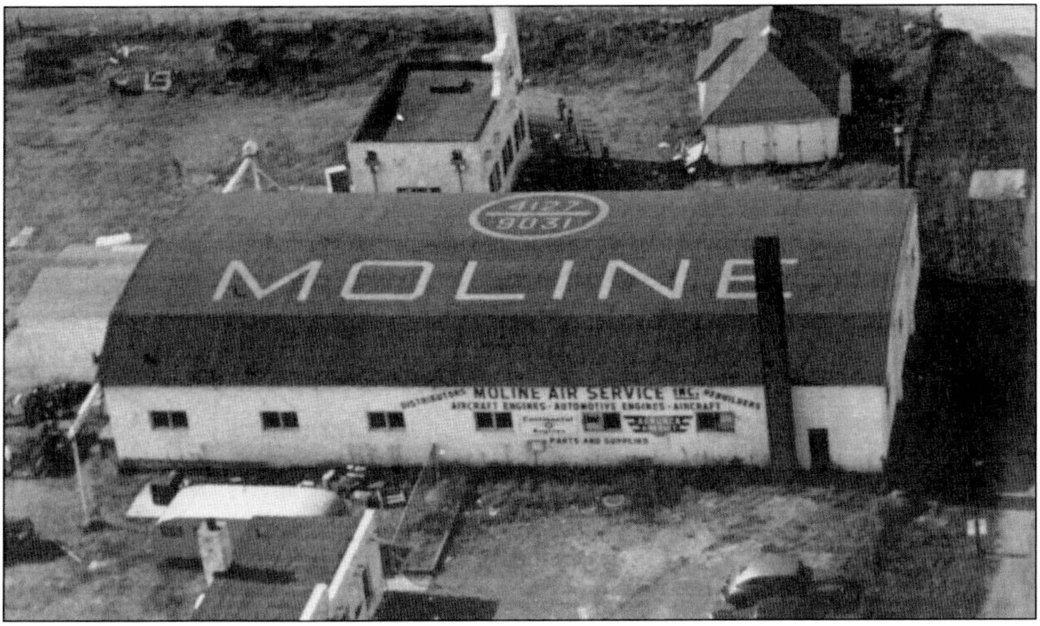

Early navigation was done primarily by watching the ground. Pilots would follow roads, railroad tracks, rivers, or any other discernible landmark. Names of towns and distances to landing fields would often be painted on the roofs of large barns and buildings to aid pilots. This leftover signage from earlier days at Moline identifies the field and gives its location in latitude (41 27) and longitude (90 37). (Courtesy of QCIA.)

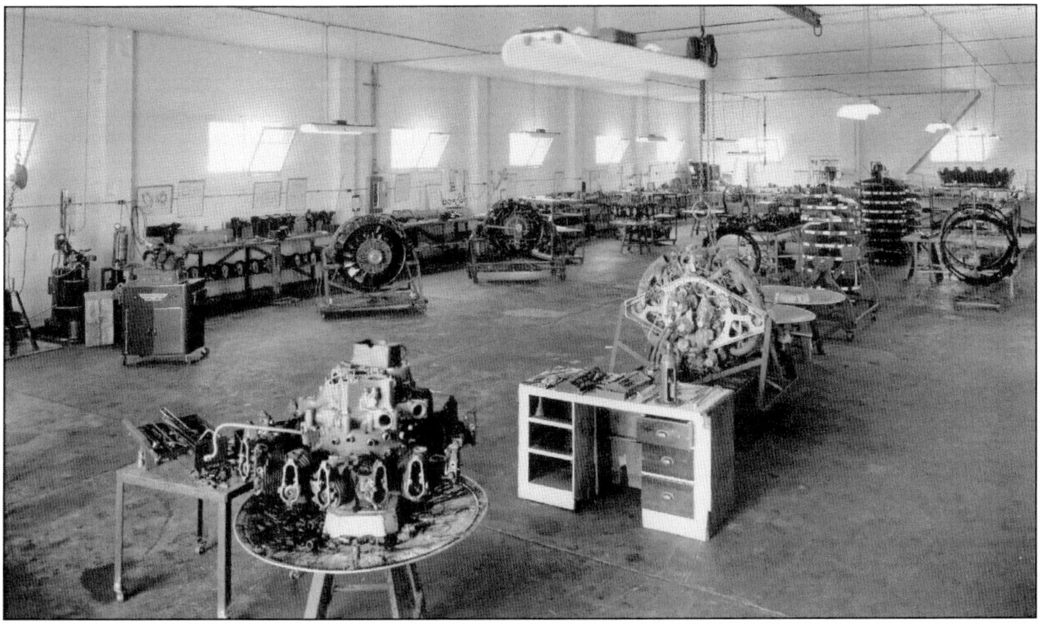

Airport manager Vern Roberts, with the help of area civic leaders, created Moline Air Service in 1942 to provide better wartime service at the airport and to train cadet pilots. The city also contracted the company to manage the airport. Moline Air Service trained over 1,000 cadet pilots during the war years and also rebuilt nearly 600 radial aircraft engines that were used to power tanks during the war. (Courtesy of QCIA.)

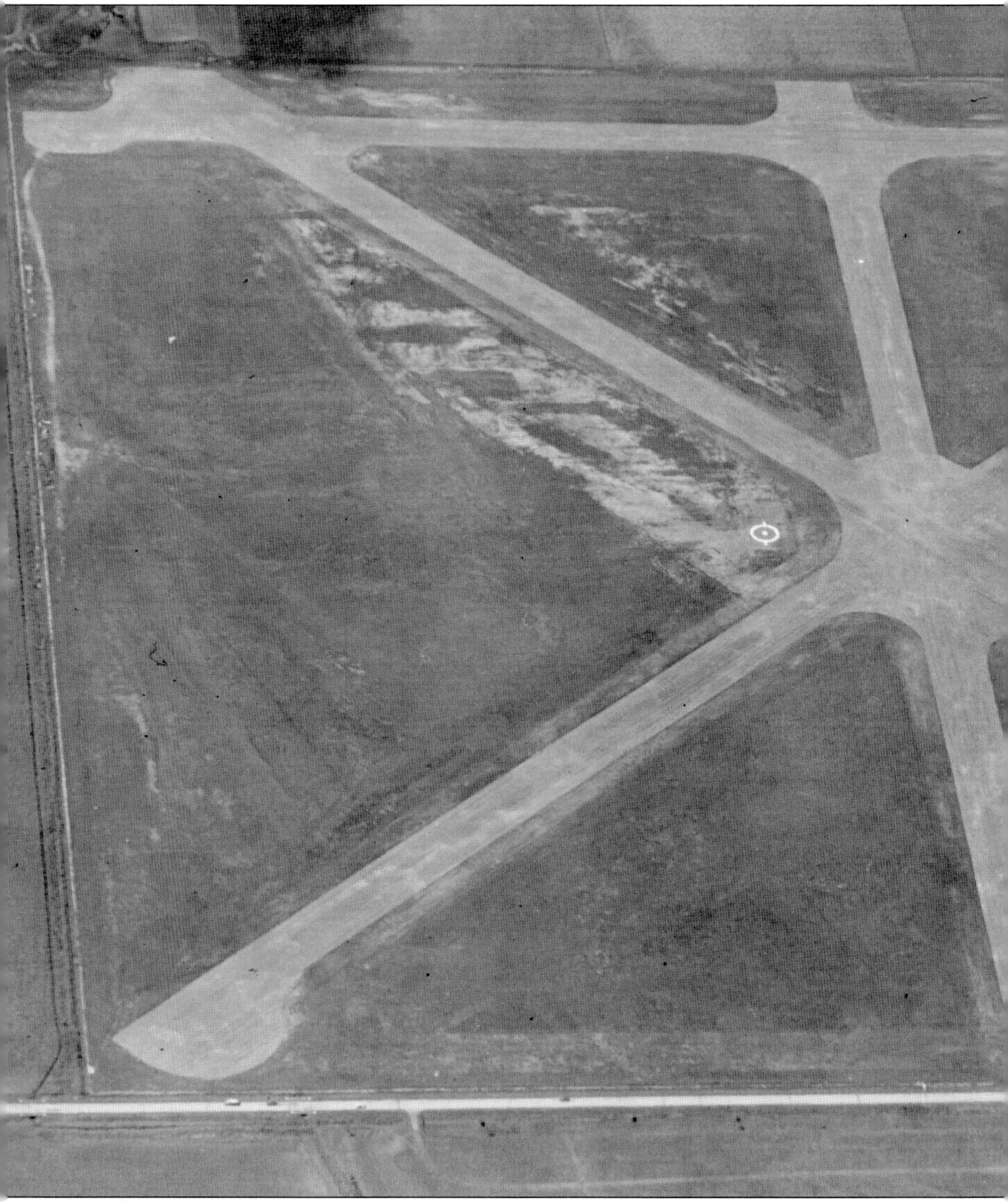

Looking west, this photograph illustrates Moline Airport's layout in 1944. Route 150 is at the bottom of the photograph, and Route 92 (Airport Road) is seen on the right. The new hangar-terminal is at the right center. Many buildings of the original complex, seen in the lower right, were gone by this date. Only the service station-restaurant-apartment building, the pump house,

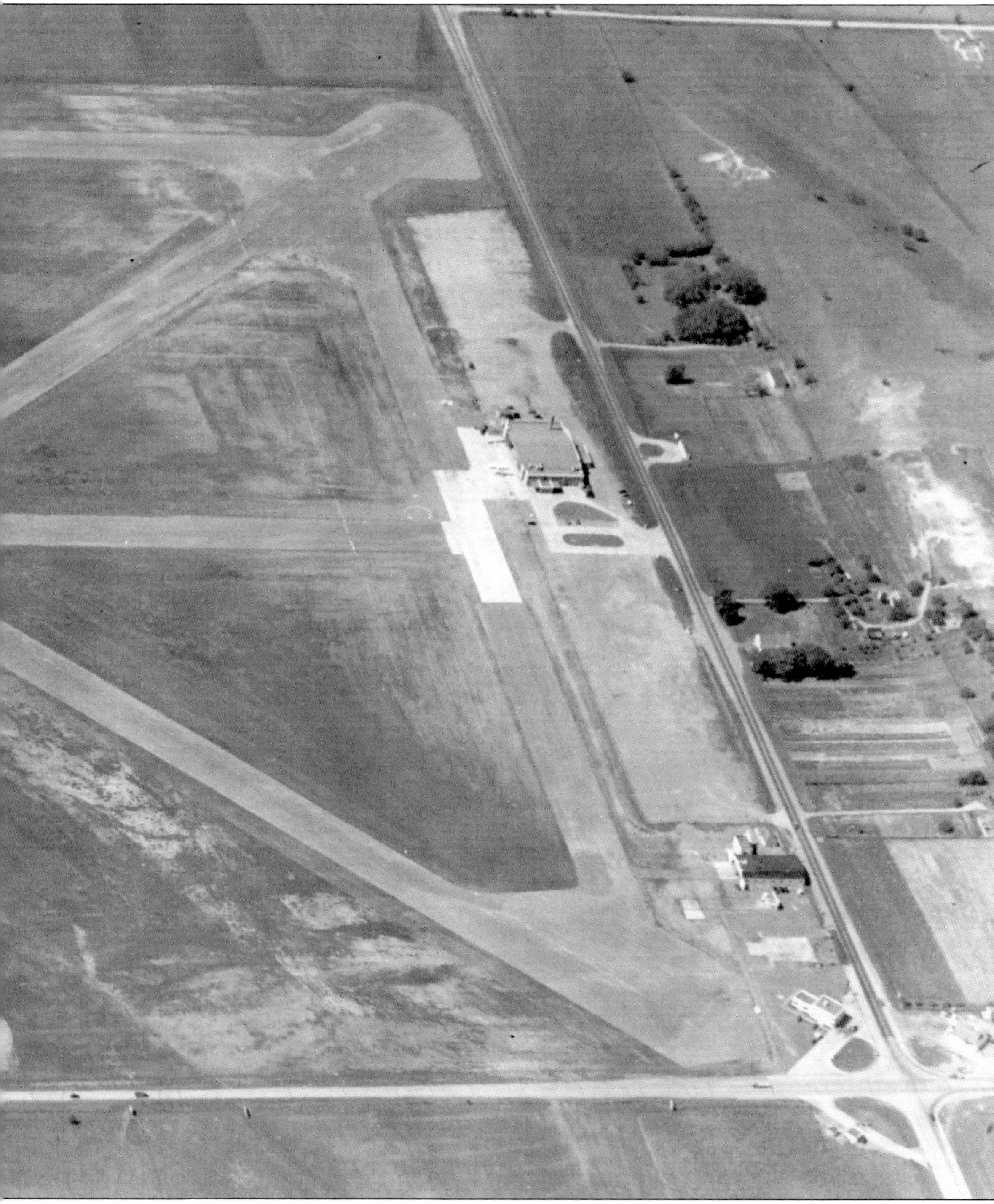

and the former Mono Aircraft Company hangar remain. It is interesting to note that the east end of the east-west runway and the southeast end of the southeast-northwest runway had no connecting taxiways. Planes had to back-taxi from those runway ends to get to the terminal or to those runway ends for their takeoff positions. (Courtesy of QCIA.)

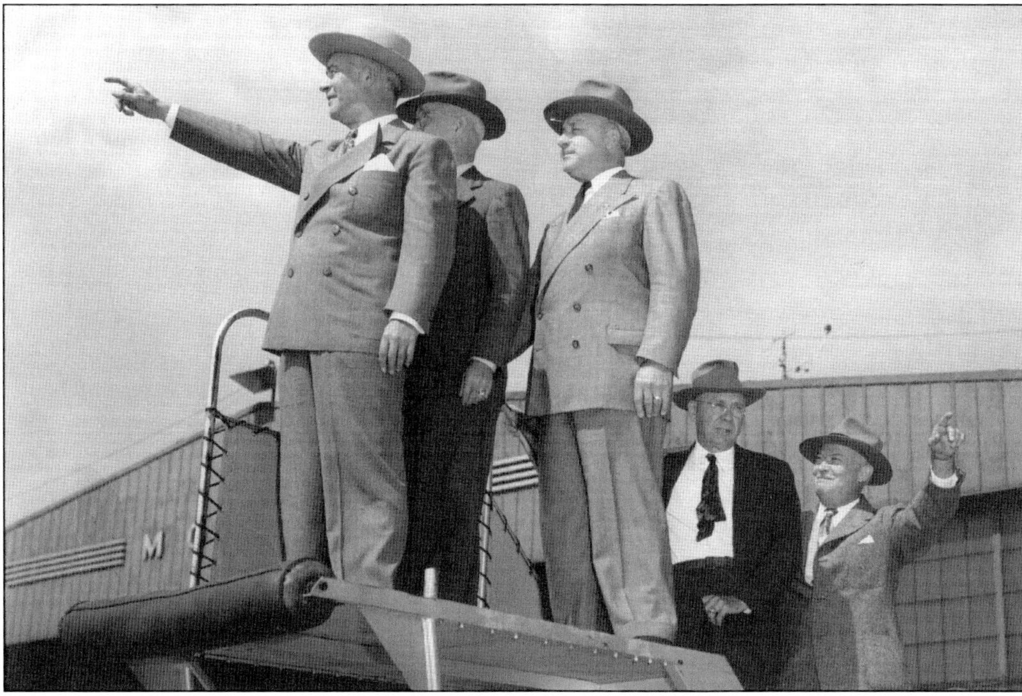

Ready to welcome Braniff Airway's first flight into Moline in 1944 are, from left to right, Gov. Dwight Green, aviation committee chairman C.R. Rosborough, state senator Charles Carpentier, Moline mayor Ezra Sohner, and airport manager Vern Roberts. There seems to be a little confusion over which direction the flight would arrive. A good bet would be to pay attention to the airport's manager. (Courtesy of Ken Roberts.)

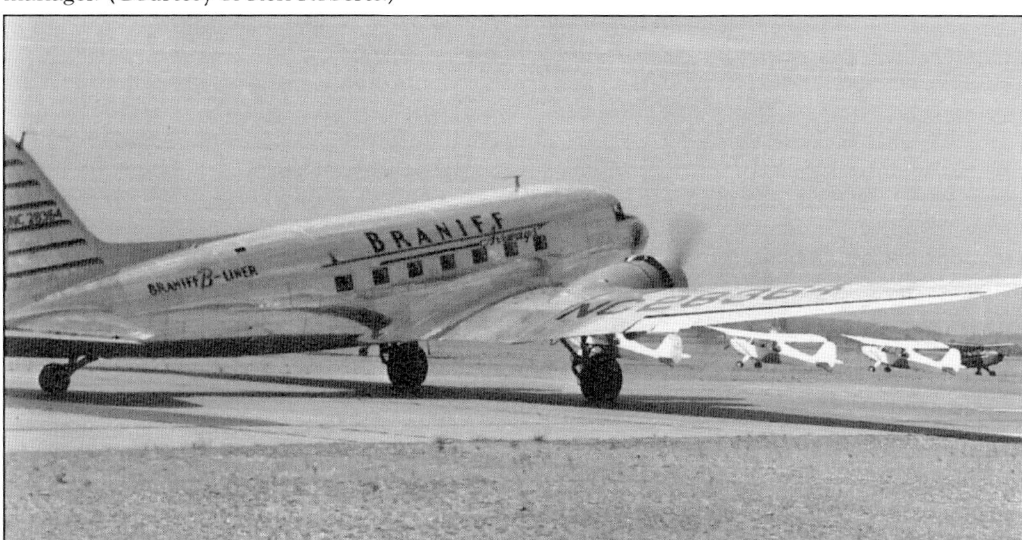

Braniff Airways began an expansion by offering service to intermediate cities along its route network. It inaugurated its Moline service in March 1944 as a stop on its direct Chicago–Kansas City route. This opened up destinations to the southwest and beyond for Quad City passengers. Braniff DC-3 "B-Liners," like this one, initially flew one outbound trip in the morning and a return trip in the early evening. (Courtesy of QCIA.)

Shortly after Braniff Airways started service to Moline in March 1944, the airline added Burlington, Iowa, to its system, and Topeka was added in November. This advertisement lists Braniff's schedule through Moline and also provides travelers with a route map. (Courtesy of QCIA.)

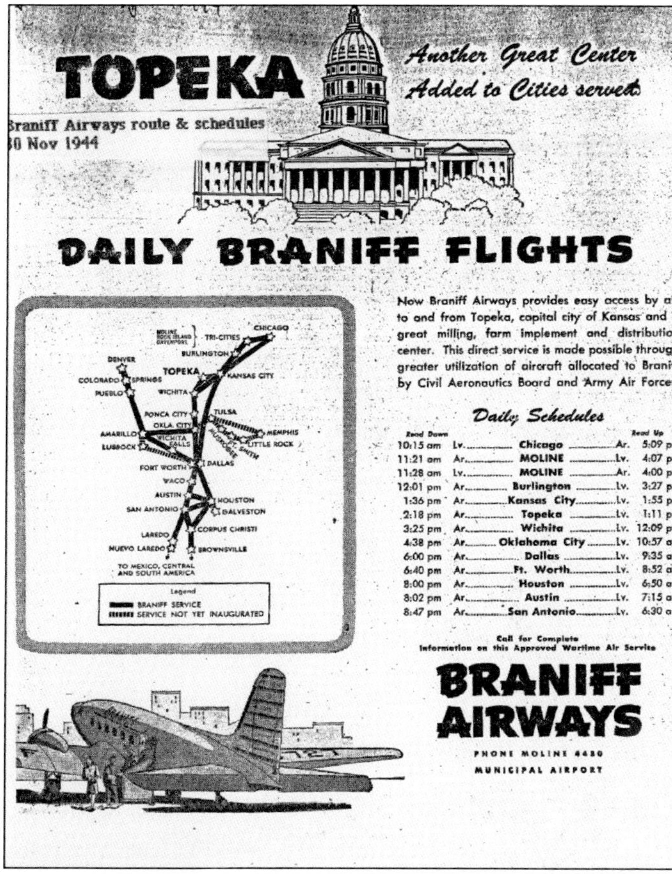

This Trans-Luxury Airlines DC-3 was flying military personnel in August 1946. After leaving Chicago, the pilot shut down the left engine and started an emergency landing at Moline. On a missed approach, the left wing struck the ground, and the plane cartwheeled, breaking in two and destroying the cockpit. Both pilots were killed, but 23 others escaped with minor injuries. (Courtesy of QCIA.)

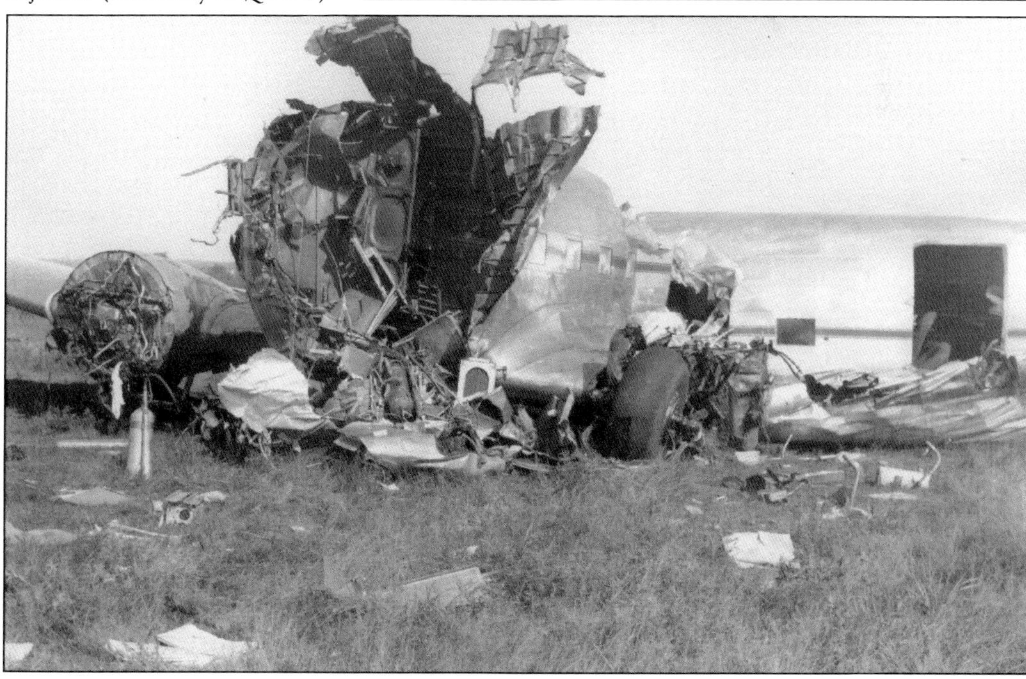

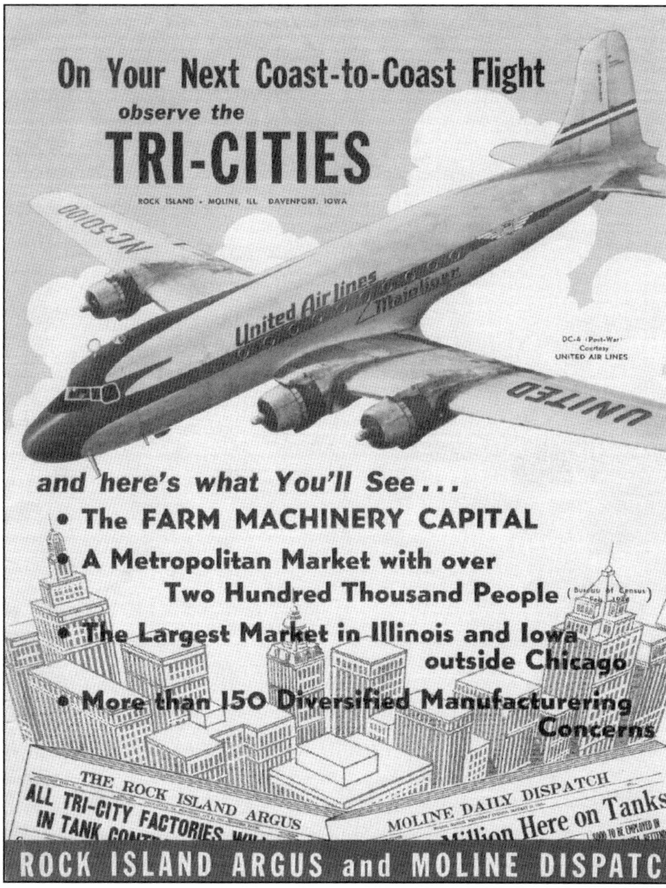

As part of a 1946 campaign that promoted the Tri-Cities (the area would become the Quad Cities later in the 1940s), this advertisement was placed in a number of large-city newspapers. Evidently passengers were to "see" what was promoted in the advertisement from 20,000 feet in the air. One thing was definite: with eight large implement plants, it *was* the "farm machinery capital."

Famous aviators Clarence Chamberlain and Jackie Cochran visited the Quad City Airport in the late 1940s on a speaking tour. Chamberlain was the second person to pilot a plane across the Atlantic and the first to carry a passenger. Cochran was a racing pilot and director of the Women Airforce Service Pilots, who ferried military planes during World War II. (Courtesy of QCIA.)

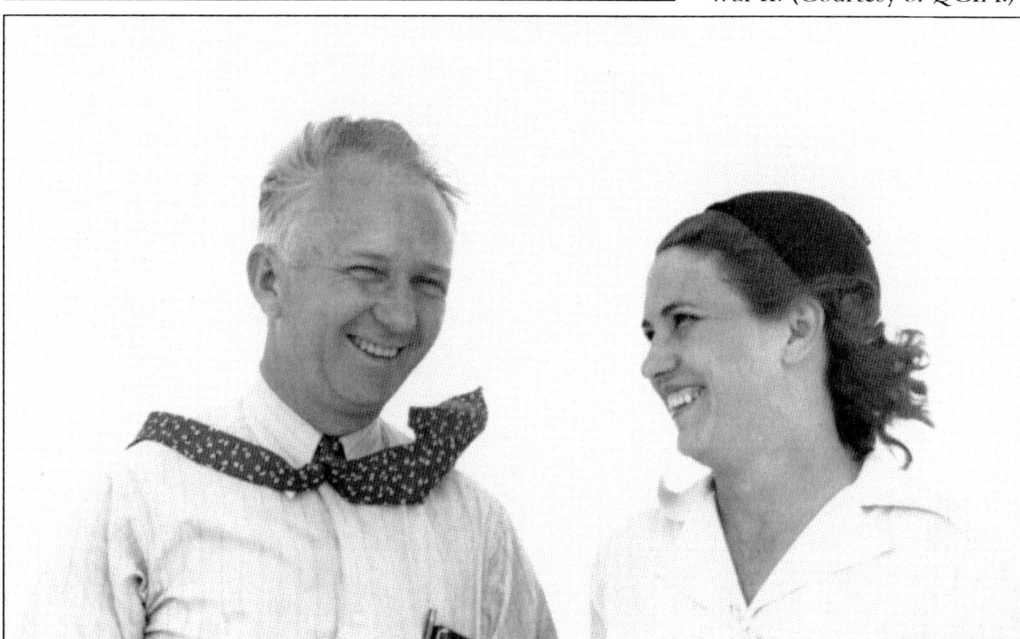

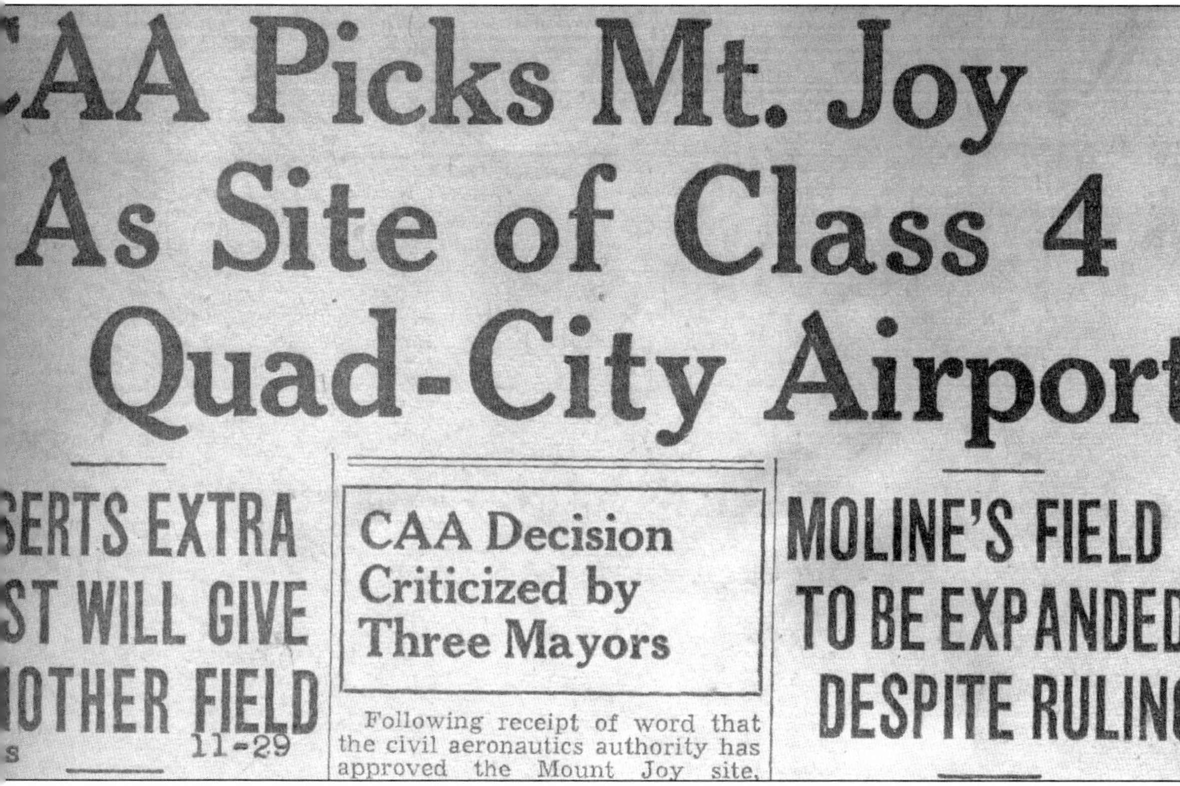
CAA Picks Mt. Joy As Site of Class 4 Quad-City Airport

SERTS EXTRA ST WILL GIVE IOTHER FIELD

S 11-29

CAA Decision Criticized by Three Mayors

Following receipt of word that the civil aeronautics authority has approved the Mount Joy site,

MOLINE'S FIELD TO BE EXPANDED DESPITE RULING

In early 1944, the Civil Aeronautics Administration (CAA) held general discussions with Moline and Davenport regarding area aviation and airport development. Davenport was in the early stages of planning a new airport at Mount Joy and wanted its airport designated as a Class IV, or air carrier, airport. Moline brought up the need for resurfacing its runways and taxiways, a project that would easily bring the airport up to Class IV status. The CAA stated that the area needed only one air carrier airport. A 1945 survey funded by both cities favored Davenport over Moline. However, the CAA refused to allocate funds to either city until surveys of both sides of the river had been completed. Effort was made in mid-1946, at Davenport's urging, to move Moline Airport from Chicago CAA authority to Kansas City authority, as that office was more partial to the Davenport site. That ploy did not work. In another survey completed in 1947, the CAA gave the nod to the Mount Joy site, although it was later determined that several key issues in the survey were in error.

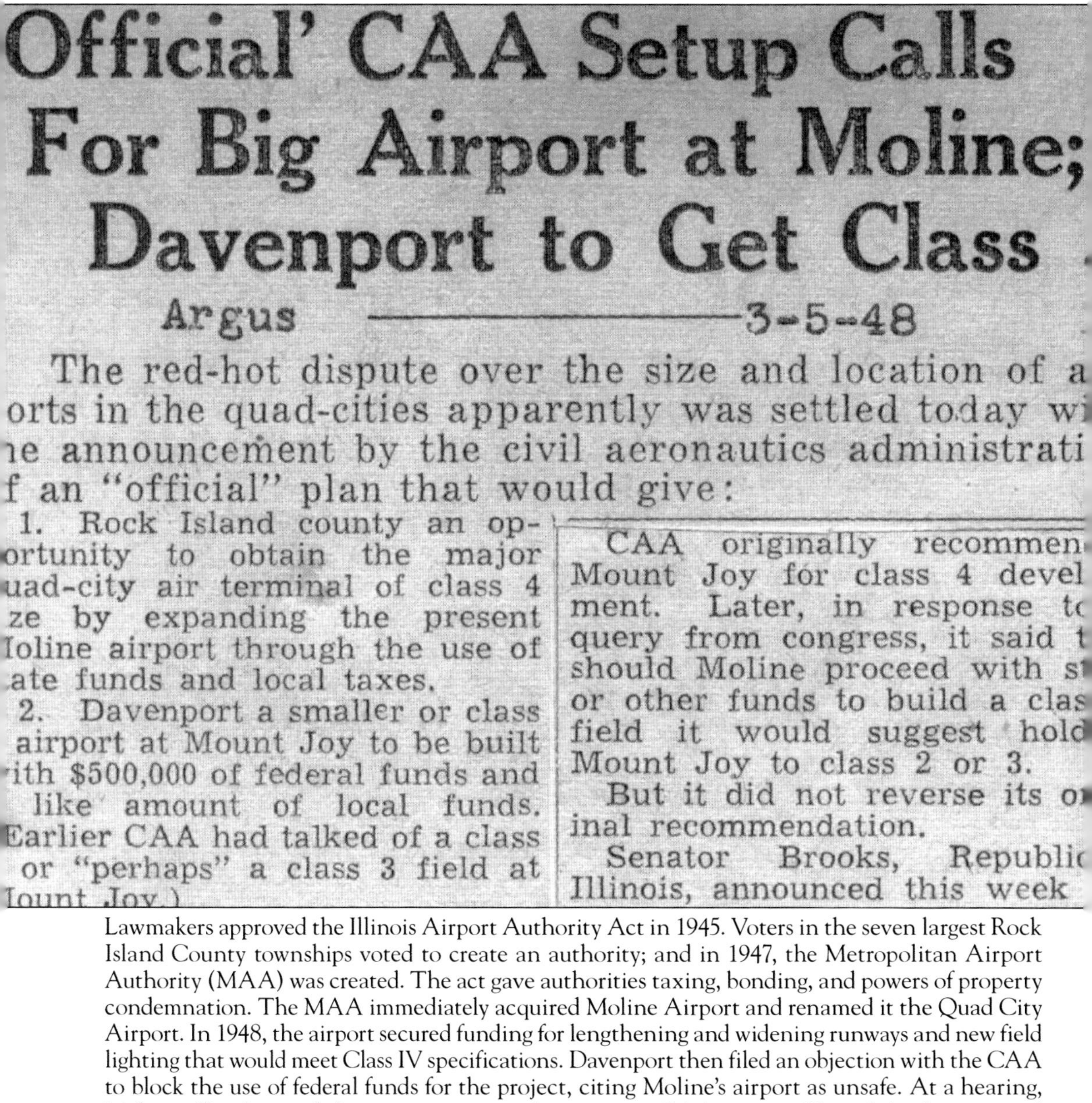

Official' CAA Setup Calls For Big Airport at Moline; Davenport to Get Class

Argus ——————— 3-5-48

The red-hot dispute over the size and location of a
orts in the quad-cities apparently was settled today wi
ne announcement by the civil aeronautics administrati
f an "official" plan that would give:

1. Rock Island county an op-
ortunity to obtain the major
uad-city air terminal of class 4
ze by expanding the present
Ioline airport through the use of
ate funds and local taxes.

2. Davenport a smaller or class
airport at Mount Joy to be built
ith $500,000 of federal funds and
like amount of local funds.
Earlier CAA had talked of a class
or "perhaps" a class 3 field at
Iount Joy.)

CAA originally recommen
Mount Joy for class 4 devel
ment. Later, in response t
query from congress, it said t
should Moline proceed with st
or other funds to build a clas
field it would suggest hold
Mount Joy to class 2 or 3.

But it did not reverse its o
inal recommendation.

Senator Brooks, Republic
Illinois, announced this week

Lawmakers approved the Illinois Airport Authority Act in 1945. Voters in the seven largest Rock Island County townships voted to create an authority; and in 1947, the Metropolitan Airport Authority (MAA) was created. The act gave authorities taxing, bonding, and powers of property condemnation. The MAA immediately acquired Moline Airport and renamed it the Quad City Airport. In 1948, the airport secured funding for lengthening and widening runways and new field lighting that would meet Class IV specifications. Davenport then filed an objection with the CAA to block the use of federal funds for the project, citing Moline's airport as unsafe. At a hearing, Moline officials noted that its airport met then current CAA criteria. United Air Lines stated that should Mount Joy receive Class IV status, it planned to stay at Moline. The CAA reversed its decision and gave Moline the Class IV airport. The Illinois side already had the developed airport, population, and the financial wherewithal. Davenport did not. As one newspaper put it, "It came down to the three Ps: population, politics, and practical considerations."

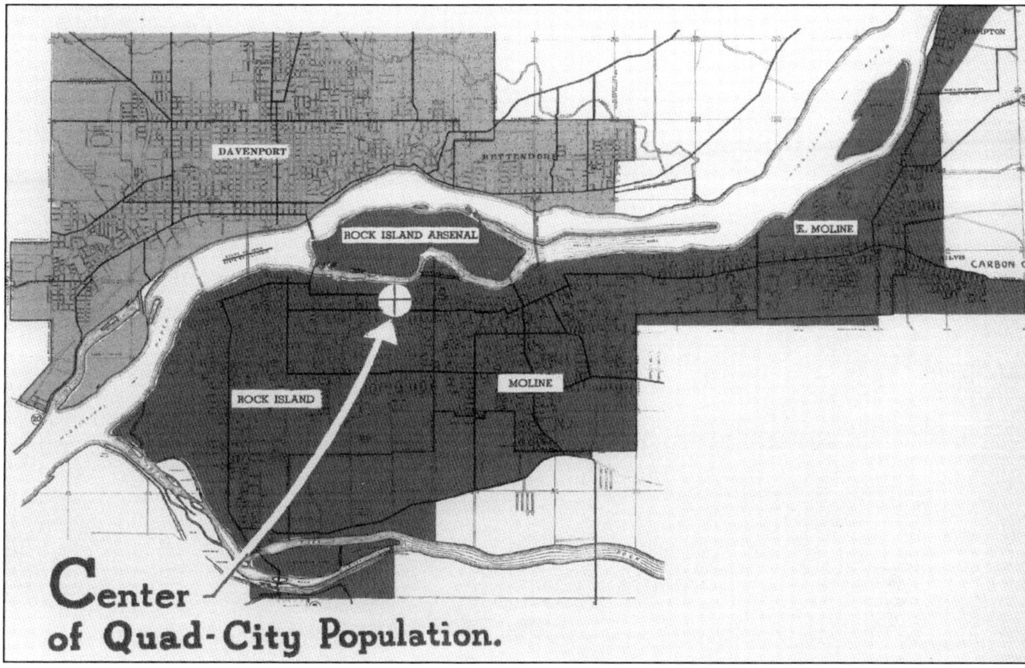

Before the Civil Aeronautics Administration (CAA) made its decision on which city would receive the nod for a Class IV airport, it demanded surveys of both sides of the river. The chamber of commerce provided this map, proving that the center of population for the Quad Cities was in Rock Island at about Fifth Avenue and Thirty-eight Street. The survey also revealed there were more industrial users of aviation on the Illinois side.

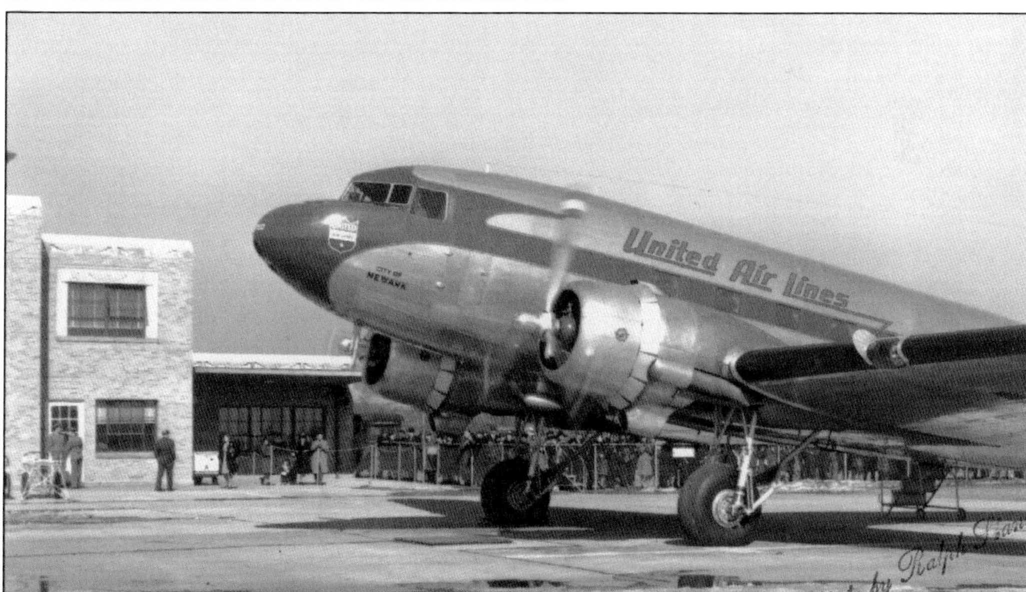

A contingent of people is behind the fence, beyond the DC-3. No doubt the pilot wondered why so many were waiting for his arrival. Actually they were not waiting for this plane. They were there to greet the arrival of the first United Air Lines DC-4 into Moline. A mix of DC-3 and DC-4 aircraft would serve the airport until replaced by Convairs in 1953. (Courtesy of QCIA.)

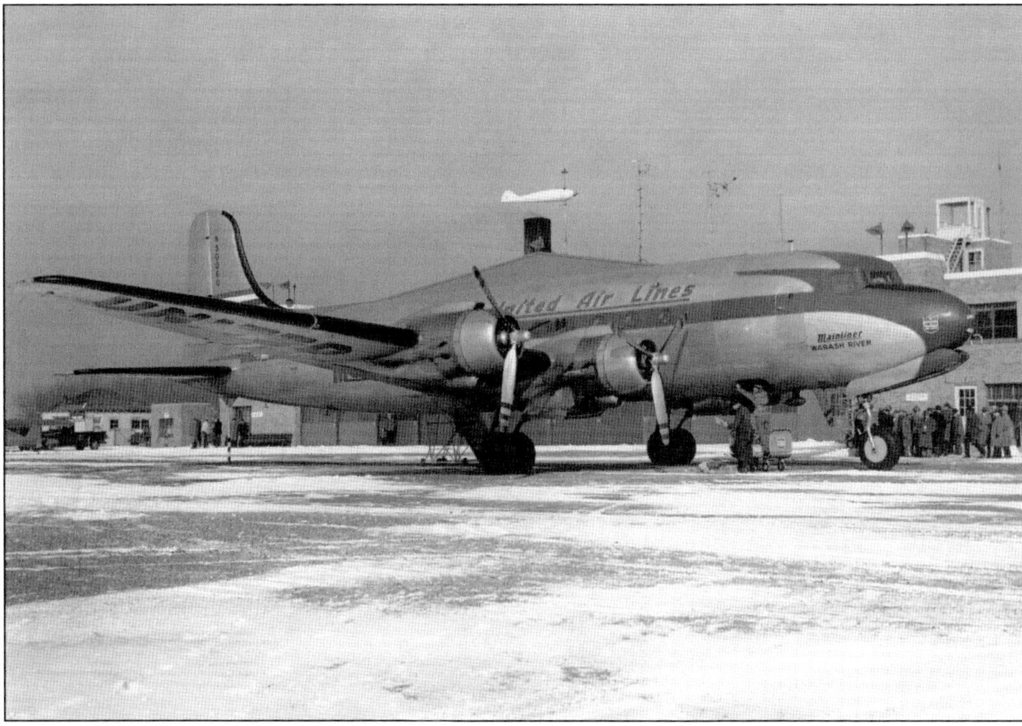

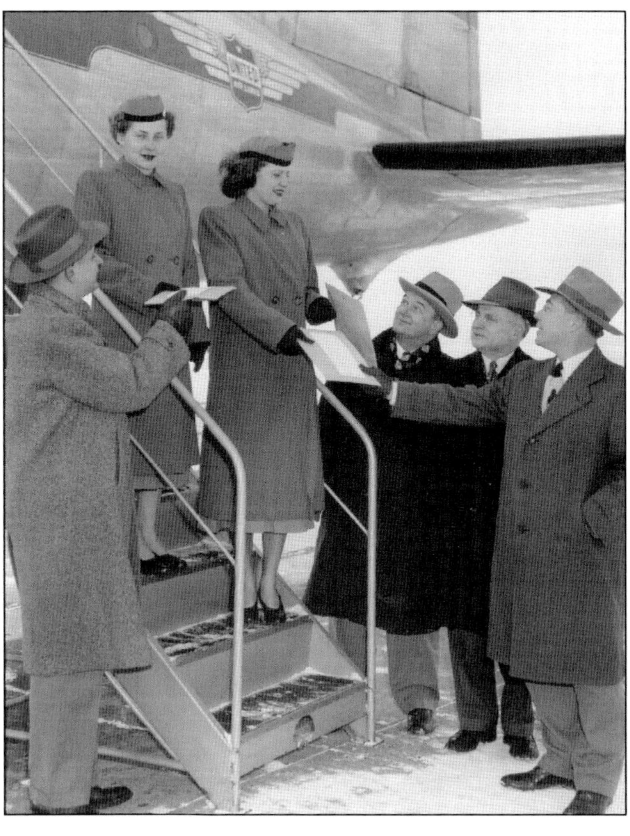

Mainliner *Wabash River* inaugurated DC-4 service to Moline in February 1950 and was welcomed by officials from the Quad Cities. The plane carried twice the number of passengers as the DC-3 and had a crew of five. It would not replace the smaller DC-3 at Moline but would be used on three westbound and three eastbound flights per week. (Courtesy of QCIA.)

Officials present materials about their cities and the airport for distribution at each stop along the DC-4's route. From left to right are Sam Skafidas, chairman of the East Moline-Silvis Association of Commerce; stewardesses Dolores Tiesner and Shirley Marquardt; Leslie Johnson, airport commission chairman; Clarence Bendle, chairman of the Moline Association of Commerce; and K.R. Popplewell, chairman of the Rock Island Chamber of Commerce. (Courtesy of QCIA.)

At airports without control towers, pilots called their airline station on a company frequency prior to landing to receive the latest weather conditions at the field. Although this photograph is a bit staged, it illustrates how it was done. Station manager Dick Shrader would check with the weather bureau and also make his own check of the at-the-moment conditions, then relay that information to the radio operator. (Courtesy of Richard Shrader family.)

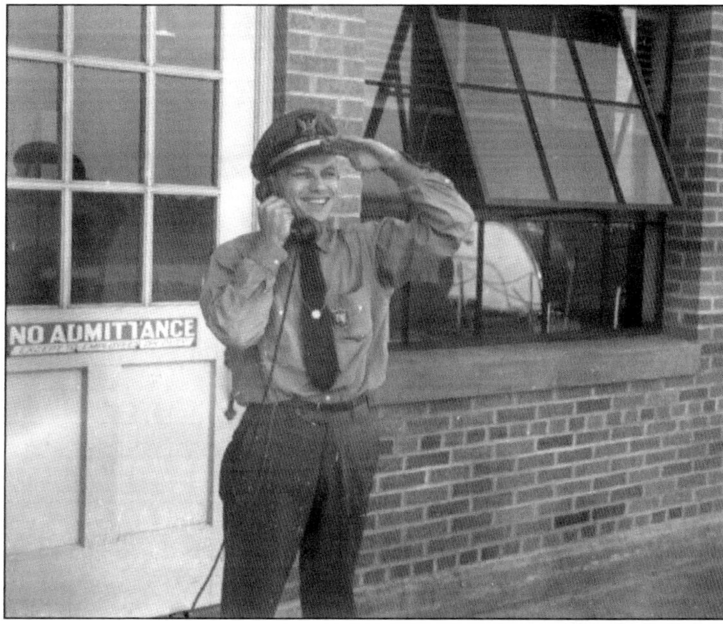

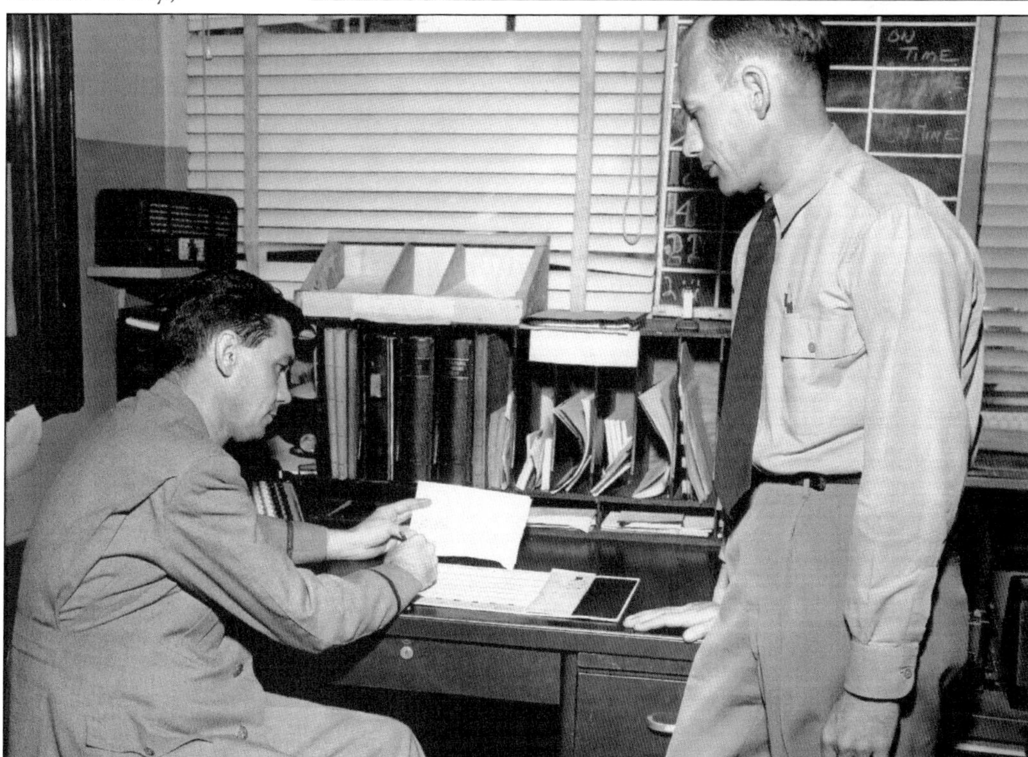

United Air Lines senior agent Bob Deamer (left) and station manager Dick Shrader review a load dispatch for the next airport along the route of a departing flight. The dispatch would give the airline load planner at the next station the number of passengers, plane's weight and balance, and cargo information, allowing him to determine available space for baggage and freight at his stop. (Courtesy of Richard Shrader family.)

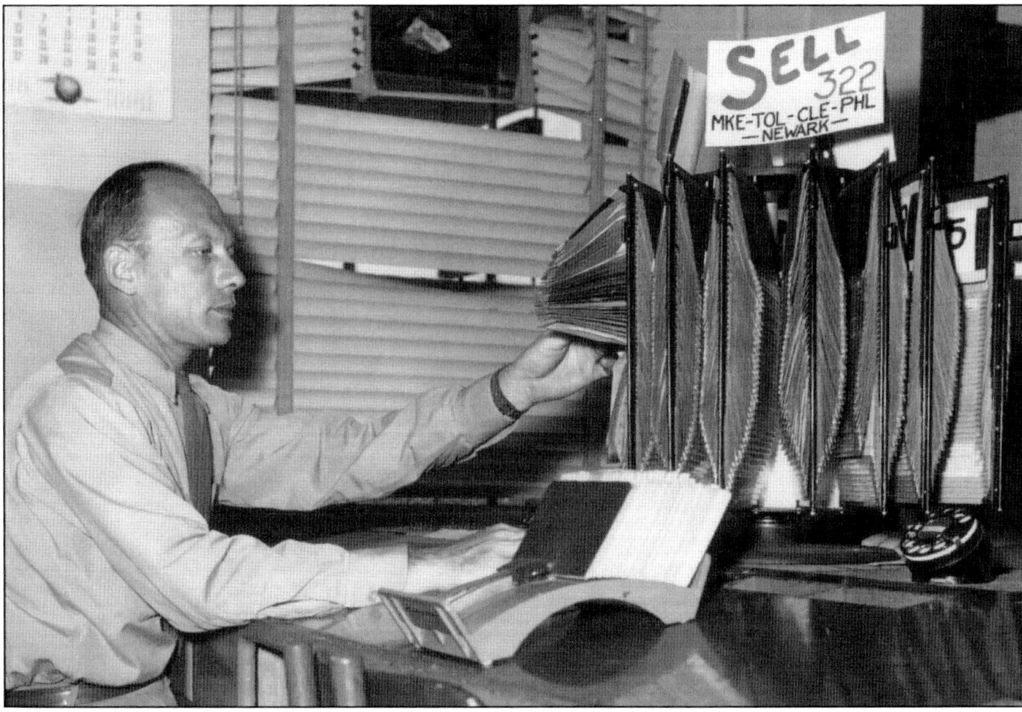

Before computers, passenger reservations were marked on a card, and the ticket agent would call a central booking office that would enter the reservation, then confirm with the agent. Dick Shrader received a reward for suggesting a plan that would allow a city airline office to control seating on flights that originated from that particular city. The plan saved an average of 15 of these reservation transactions per trip. (Courtesy of Richard Shrader family.)

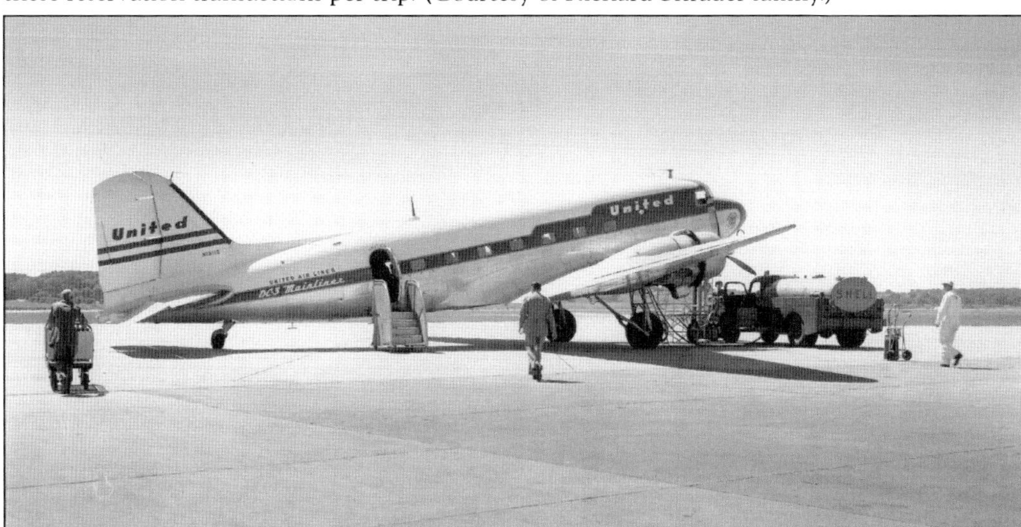

This DC-3 is being prepared for the next destination along its route. At the front of the aircraft, the plane is being refueled while a ramp agent loads freight with a fork truck. A customer service agent walks toward the plane with passenger and load information as another ramp agent rolls baggage toward the waiting plane. This scene was repeated eight times a day in 1950. (Courtesy of Richard Shrader family.)

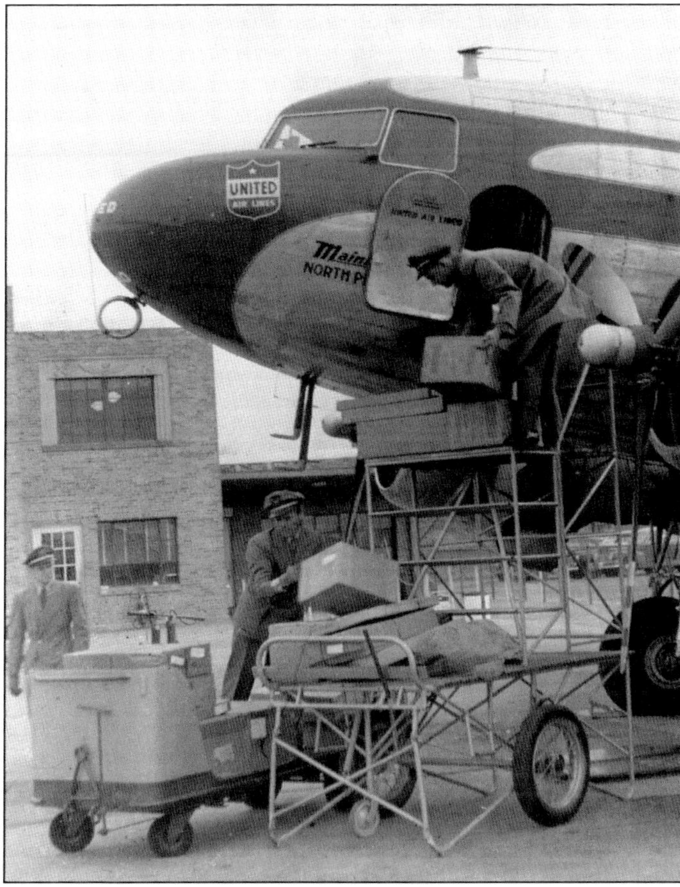

United agents stack and load freight and airmail into the cargo hold of this DC-3. Agents not only had to lift and reach, but the man on top of the platform had to make sure he did not lose his balance. A pilot would oversee another agent inside the cargo hold to make sure the load was evenly distributed. (Courtesy of Richard Shrader family.)

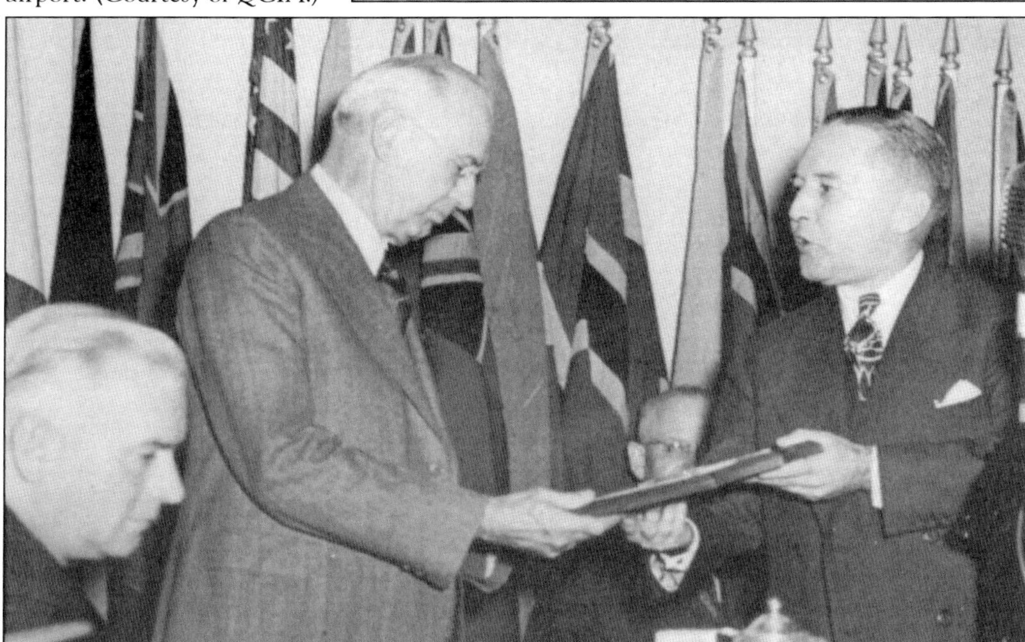

William Patterson (right), United Air Lines president, presents Moline mayor Ezra Sohner with a plaque marking the 25th anniversary of airmail in 1951. Former Illinois governor Dwight Green (left) proposed and championed the Airport Authority Act, which led to the creation of the Metropolitan Airport Authority, owner of the airport. (Courtesy of QCIA.)

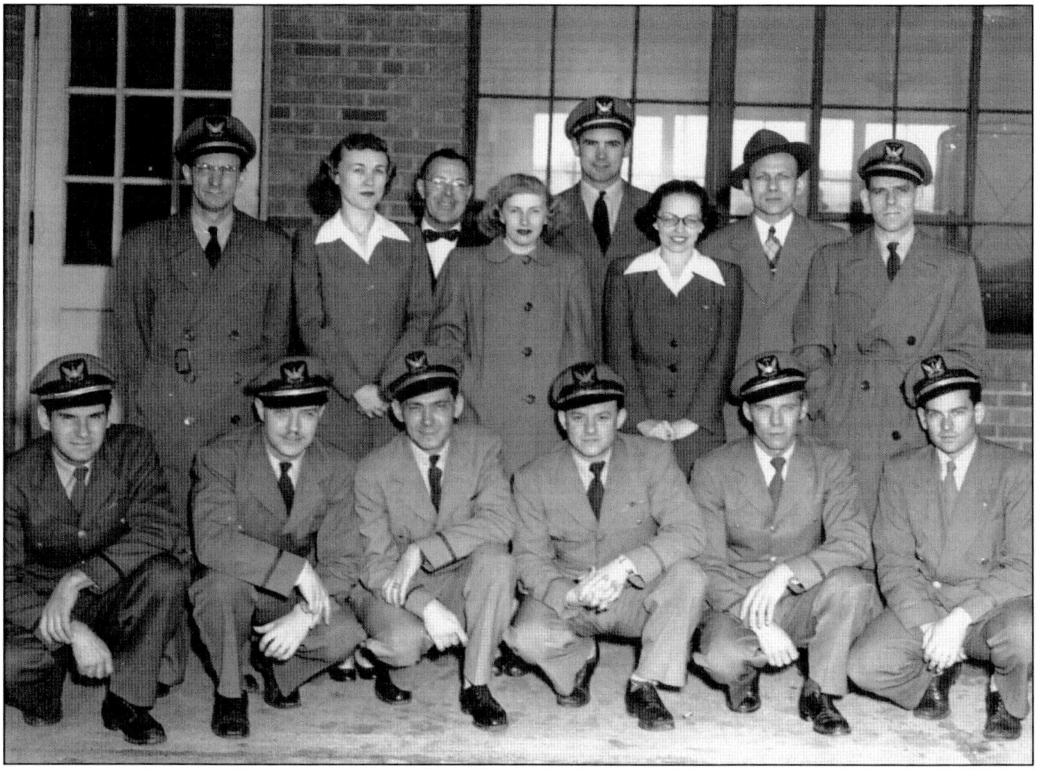

United Air Lines sales and customer service agents pose for this photograph in observance of the airline's 25th anniversary at Moline Airport on March 12, 1951. Pictured from left to right are (first row) Edward Moylan, Arnold Groth, Keith Morrison, James Hall, Lewis Waterstedt, and Hartwell Steele; (second row) Jess Cowan, Daphne Pearson, Donald Fuelscher, Elaine Boruque, Frank Murdock, Mary Fay, Richard Shrader, and Robert Deamer. (Courtesy of Richard Shrader family.)

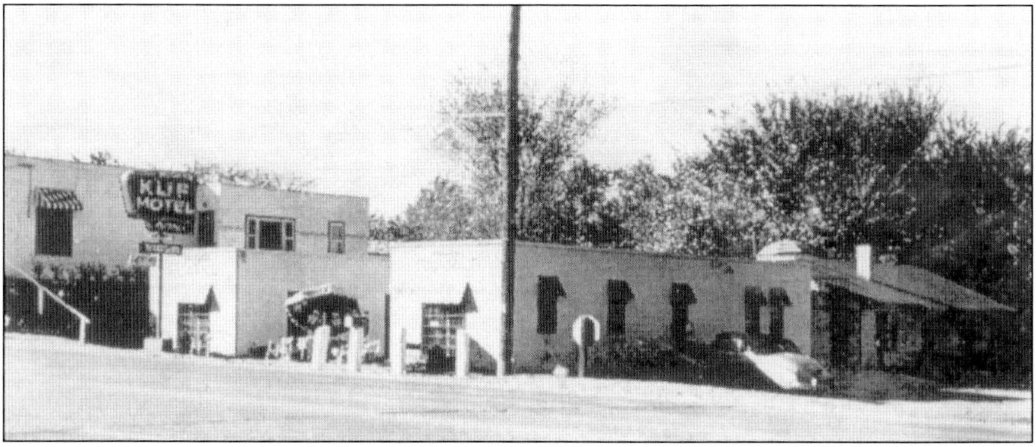

As the airport became busier, it was only natural that related enterprises like restaurants and motor courts would begin to locate near the field. This photograph from 1951 shows one such business, the Klif Motel. Located just north and east of the airport along Route 150, it advertised itself as ultramodern and included air-conditioning and television. The Klif moved to Coal Valley in the early 1960s to make way for Interstate 80.

Three

Quad City Airport 1953–1984

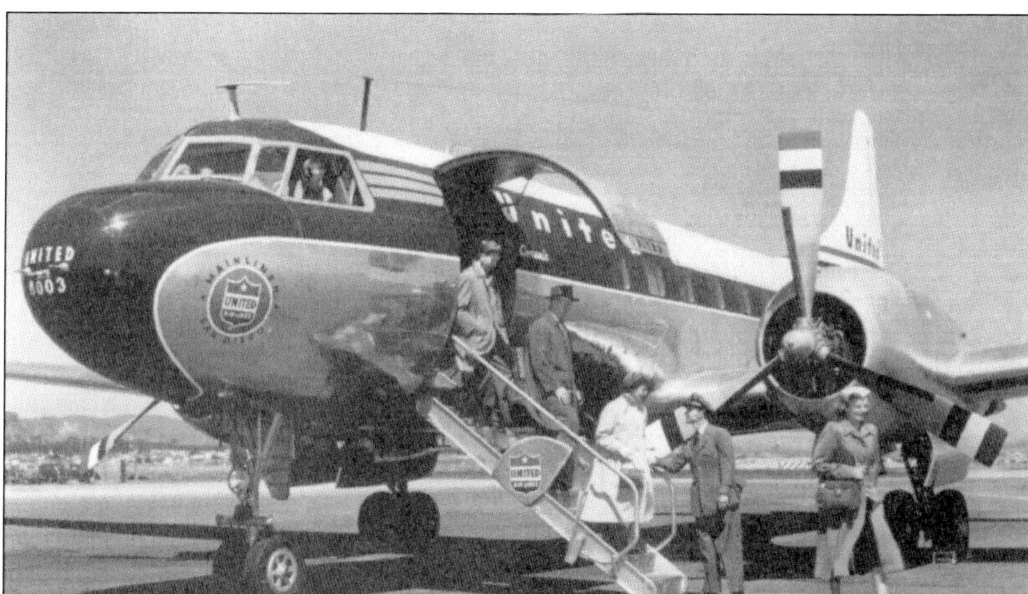

United introduced the Convair 340 to its Chicago–Moline–Cedar Rapids–Des Moines–Omaha route on January 27, 1953. The airplane was designed to replace the Douglas DC-3 and DC-4 aircraft that routinely served Moline. It carried 44 passengers and utilized self-contained boarding stairs. In the late 1950s, DC-6B four-engined aircraft began replacing the Mainliner Convairs that served the Moline routes. (Courtesy of QCIA.)

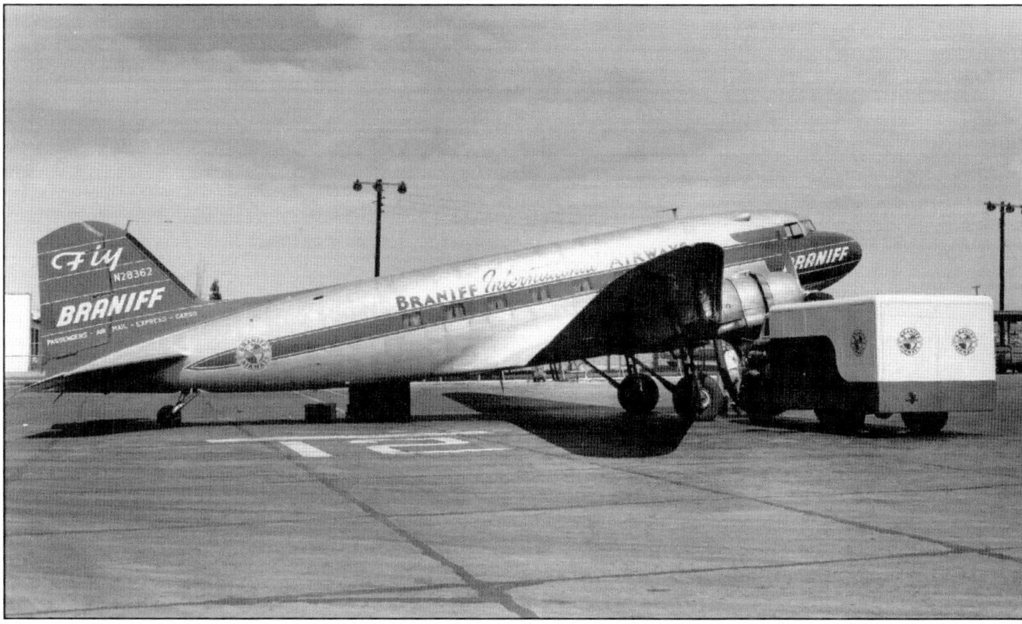

Although this photograph was not taken at Quad City Airport, the DC-3 pictured displays Braniff Airways' new design scheme. By late 1954, the airline was flying four trips per day at Moline. Throughout Braniff's tenure here, its passenger count was considered very good. The airline constantly tried to drop service at Burlington, Iowa, due to low ridership, but the CAA would not allow it. (Courtesy of QCIA.)

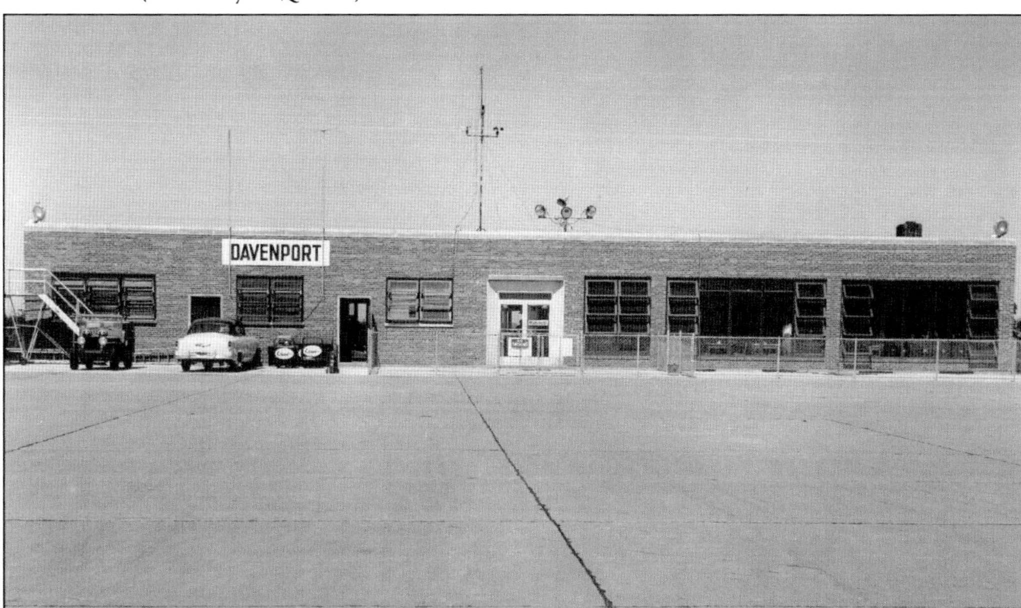

With the fight between Moline and Davenport over which city would have the larger air-carrier airport settled in Moline's favor, Davenport set about constructing its new field. Davenport Municipal Airport would now be located a few miles north of the city at Mount Joy, replacing Cram Field, which had been in operation since 1926. This 1953 photograph shows the Mount Joy airport's terminal from the airfield side. (Courtesy of QCIA.)

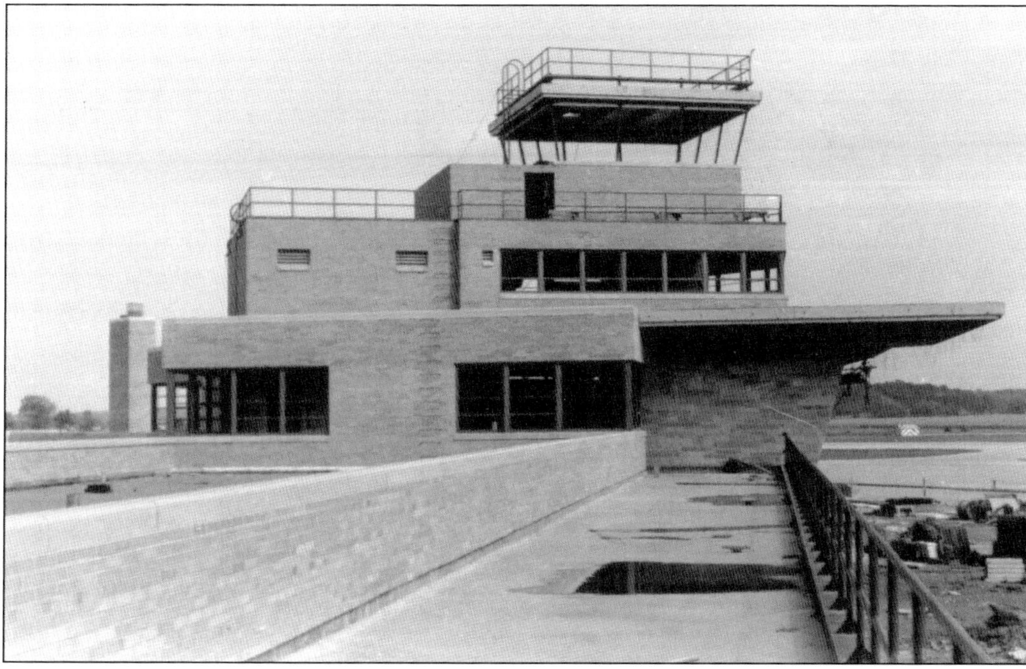

With the number of flights and passengers constantly increasing, the Metropolitan Airport Authority (MAA) authorized $510,000 to build a new terminal. Taken from the roof of the west wing and looking east, this photograph shows that the exterior work on the new terminal construction is fairly complete by early 1954. The wing wall in the left foreground would form the basis for a second floor addition added later. (Courtesy of QCIA.)

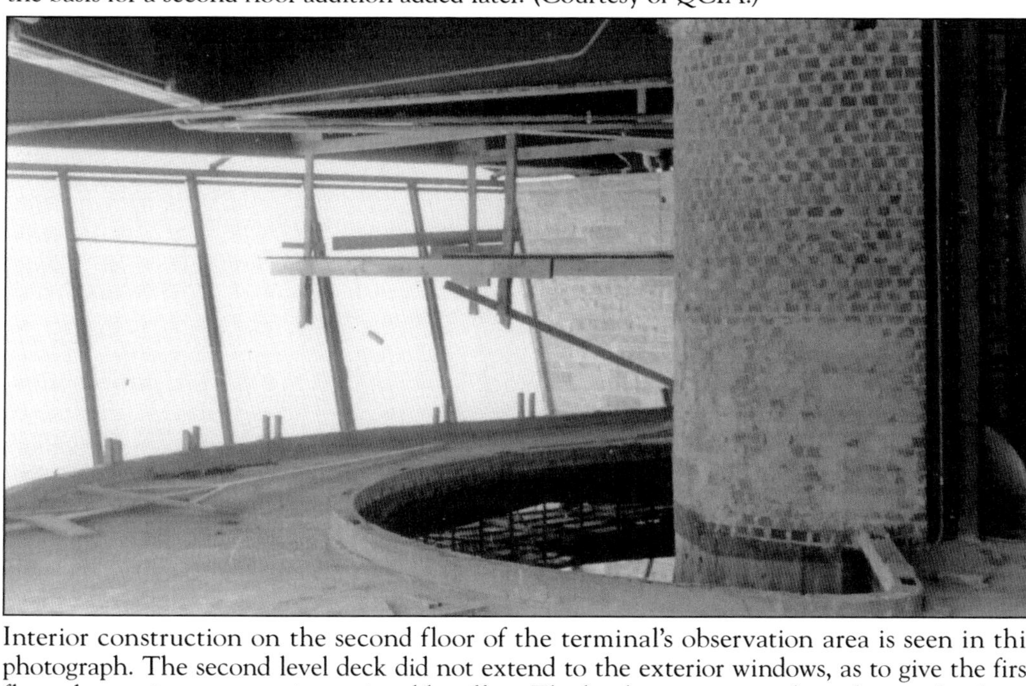

Interior construction on the second floor of the terminal's observation area is seen in this photograph. The second level deck did not extend to the exterior windows, as to give the first floor observation area an airy, atrium-like effect. The brick structure on the right was the three-story central elevator shaft. (Courtesy of QCIA.)

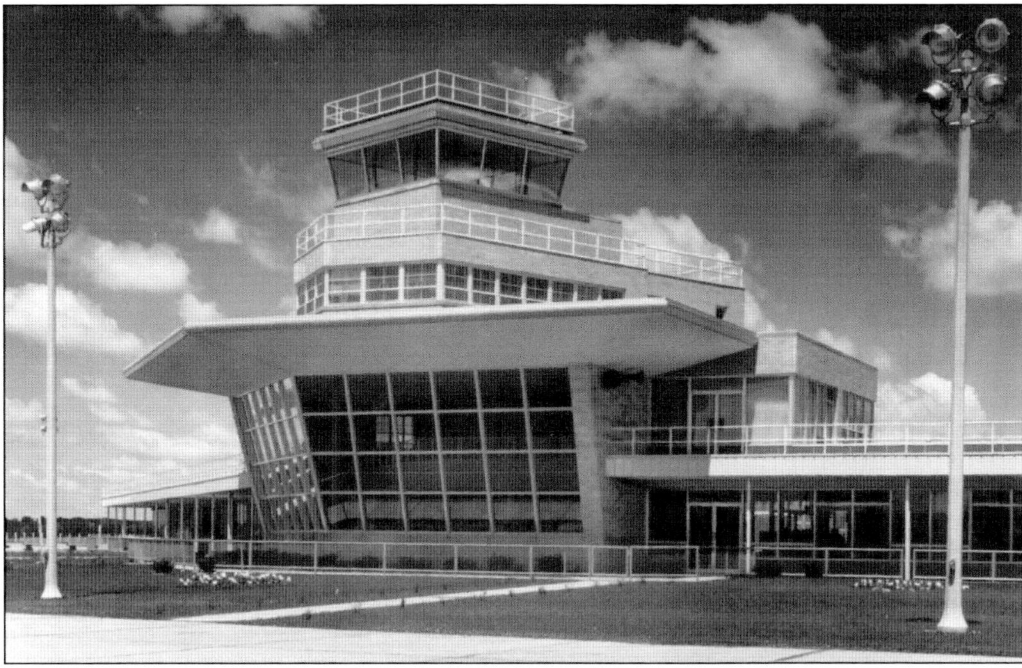

This beautiful new terminal, dedicated in September 1954, completed a $3 million modernization program at the Quad City Airport. Designed by Swanson and Maiwald Architects, the building was essentially a center tower section with two wing sections that formed a rather flat U-shape. Each wing section was expandable in length and could accommodate the addition of a second level, as future needs dictated. (Courtesy of QCIA.)

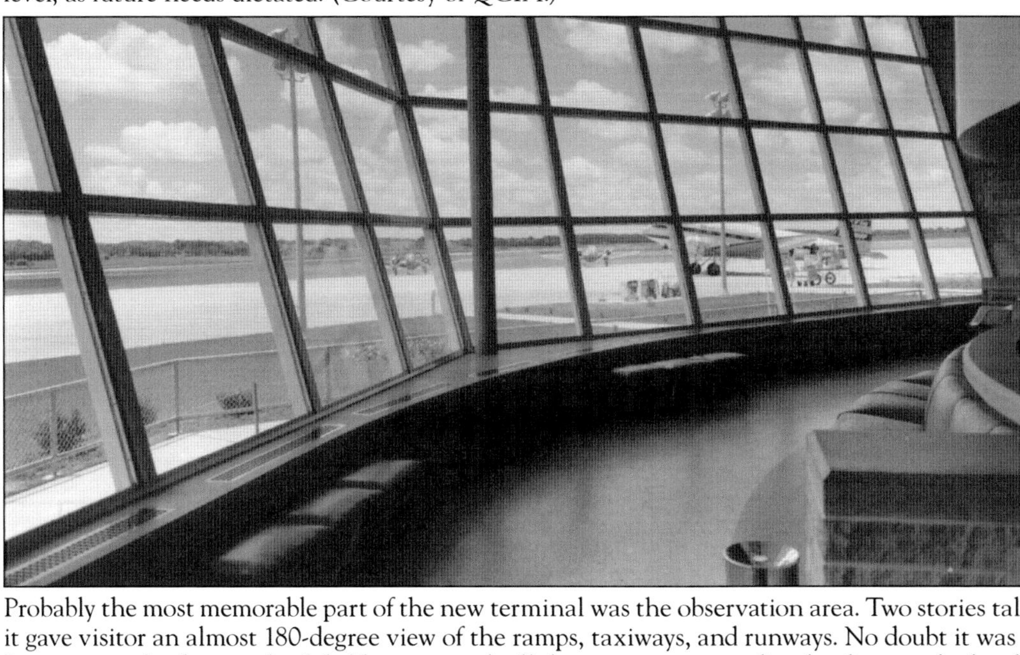

Probably the most memorable part of the new terminal was the observation area. Two stories tall, it gave visitor an almost 180-degree view of the ramps, taxiways, and runways. No doubt it was a favorite spot for thousands of children to watch all the activity surrounding landings and takeoffs or the loading or unloading of passengers and baggage. It also served as an excellent location for political press conferences. (Courtesy of QCIA.)

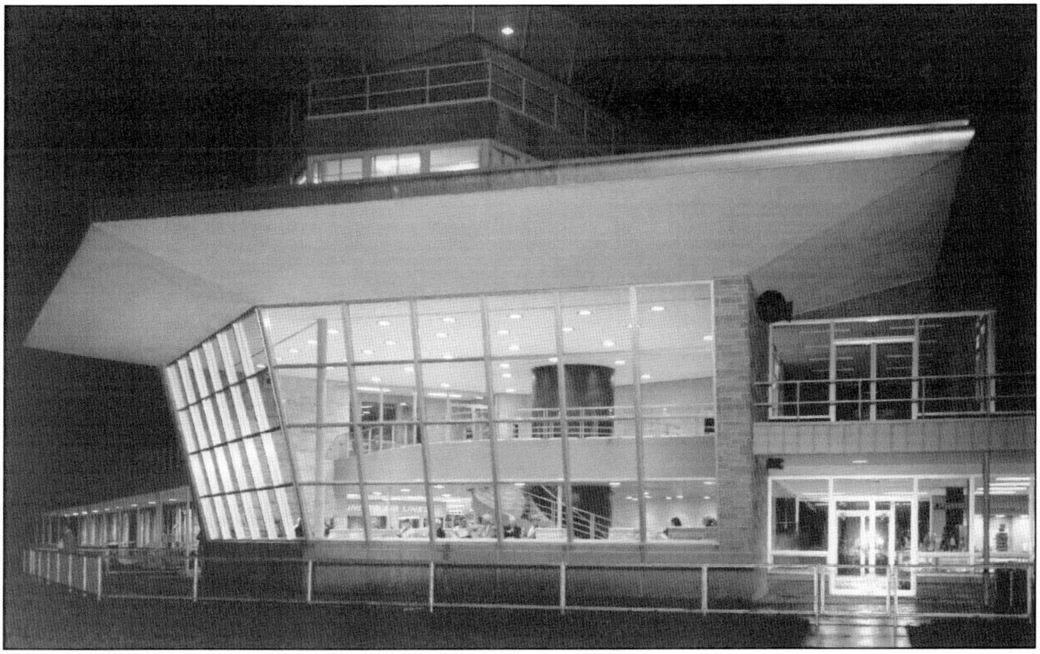

A nighttime photograph from the aircraft apron provides this beautiful view of the terminal's central observation area. Through the glass can be seen the United Air Lines ticket counter to the left of the spiral stairway and the rental car counter to the right. A gift shop is located through the ground floor doors to the extreme right of this photograph. (Courtesy of QCIA.)

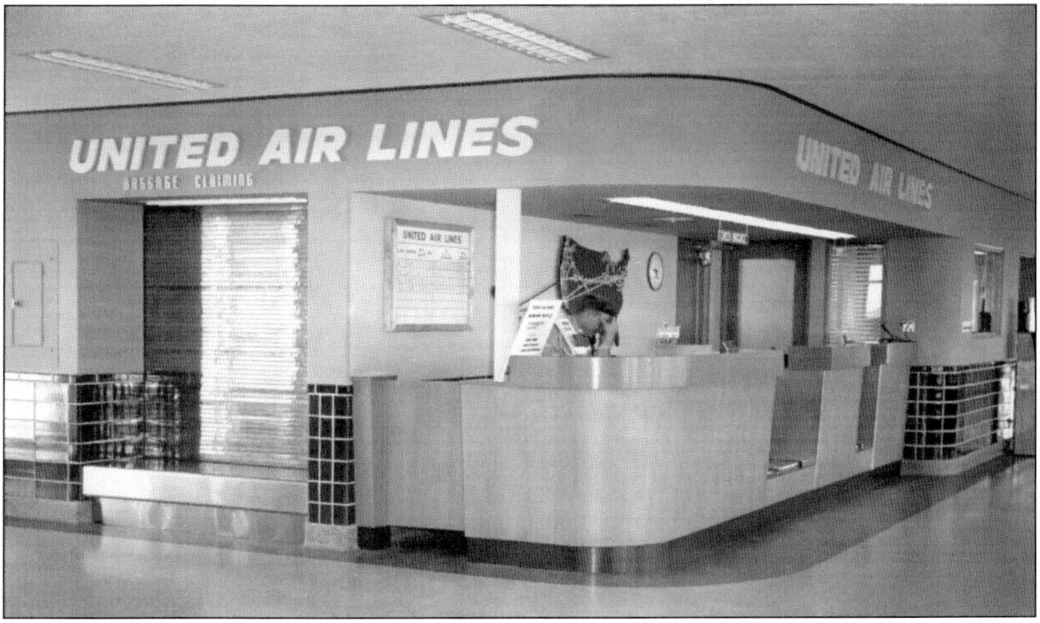

The United Air Lines counter had four positions to quickly assist passengers with check-in or the sale of tickets. Note the baggage-claiming window. Knowing how passengers gang up on the baggage claim areas today, it is somewhat difficult to imagine the passengers waiting patiently and orderly for their luggage back in the 1950s. Perhaps it was a more civilized period. (Courtesy of QCIA.)

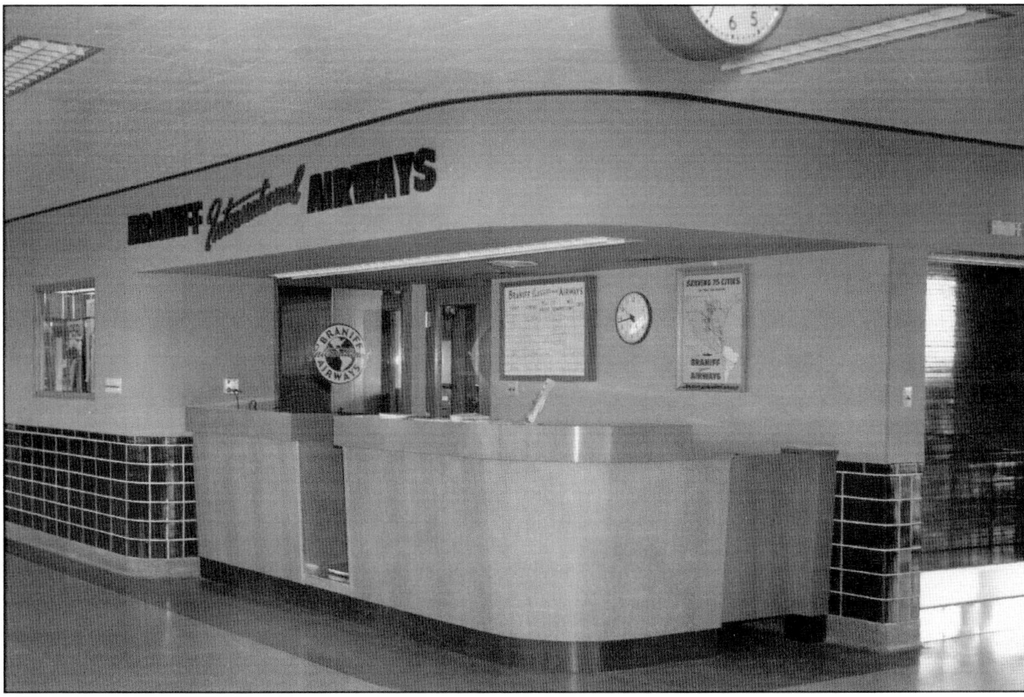

Braniff International Airways' counter had three positions for check-in and ticketing. A schedule board is on the wall. Unlike video monitors in today's terminals that provide flight information, that information is handwritten on the board. Braniff's baggage-claim window, similar to that of United, must have been crowded when passengers retrieved luggage. (Courtesy of QCIA.)

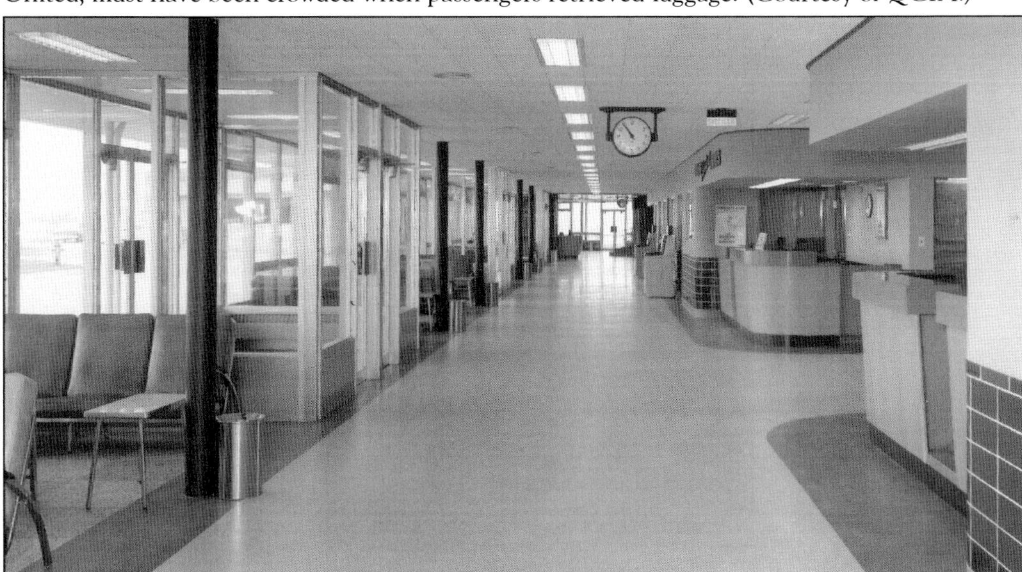

Looking east in the main passenger concourse, the new terminal reflected the style of that time. Passengers waited for their flights across from the airline counters on the right. The first ticketing position on the right was originally built for Ozark Airlines, but that airline had moved operations to Davenport in a dispute over airport usage charges shortly before the terminal opened, and the counter was left vacant. (Courtesy of QCIA.)

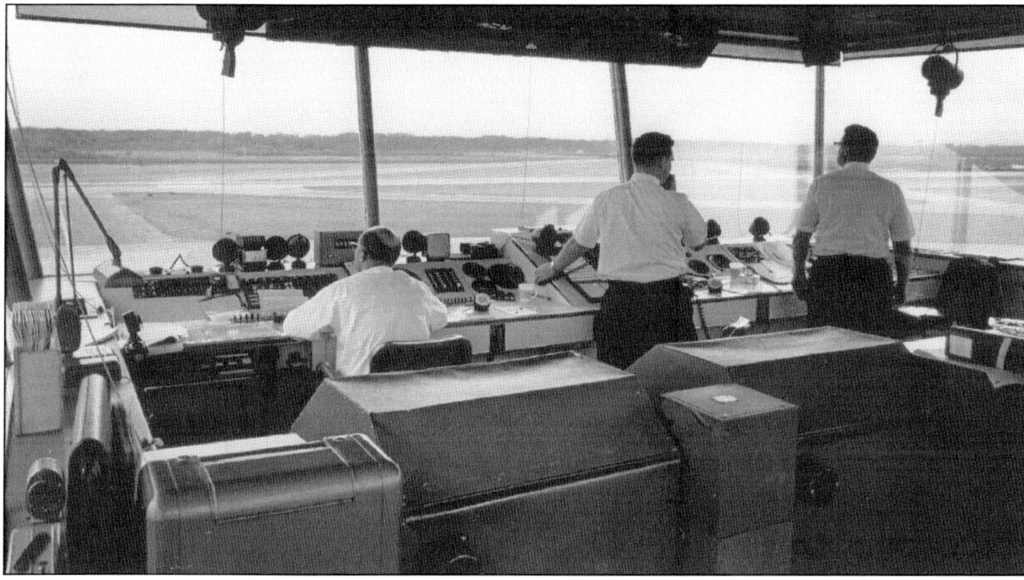

The terminal's crown was the Civil Aeronautics Administration control tower. It directed all aircraft operating on or near the airport. In this photograph, Harry Beard (left) provides weather information and advisories to departing and passing aircraft. Dale McClain (center) handles aircraft approaching the airport for a landing and those on the ground. Gene Neppl (right) is the local and departing aircraft traffic controller. (Courtesy of QCIA.)

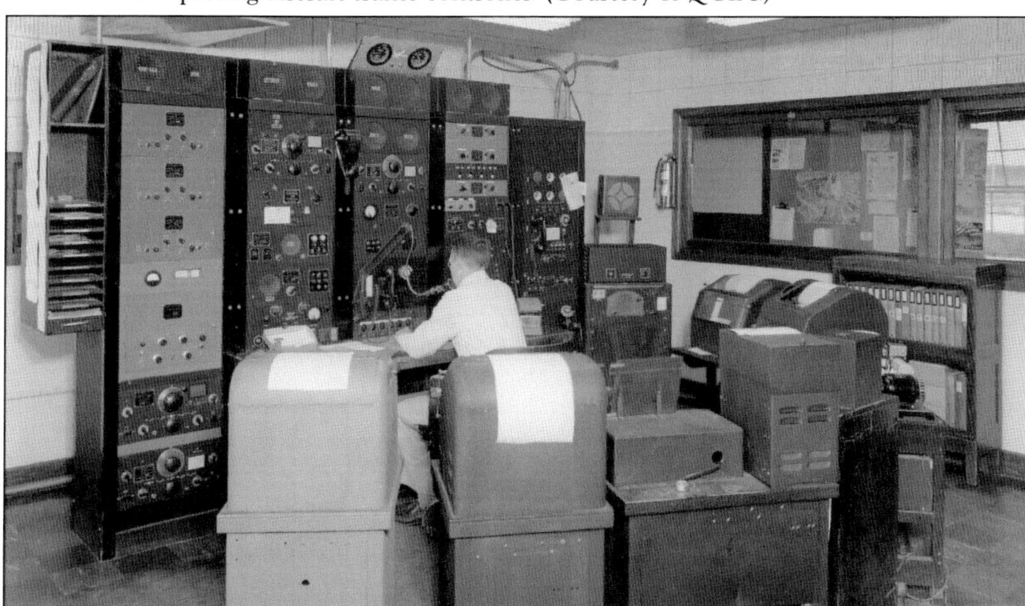

Aircraft communications, weather broadcasts, and flight assistance services emanated from this Civil Aeronautics Administration control center. Master radios for the control tower and monitors for the navigational equipment, radio markers, and instrument landing system were located here. The teletype machines provided reports to and from US Weather Bureau offices. Although much of this equipment was added in 1954, the center was located in the former hangar-terminal building. (Courtesy of QCIA.)

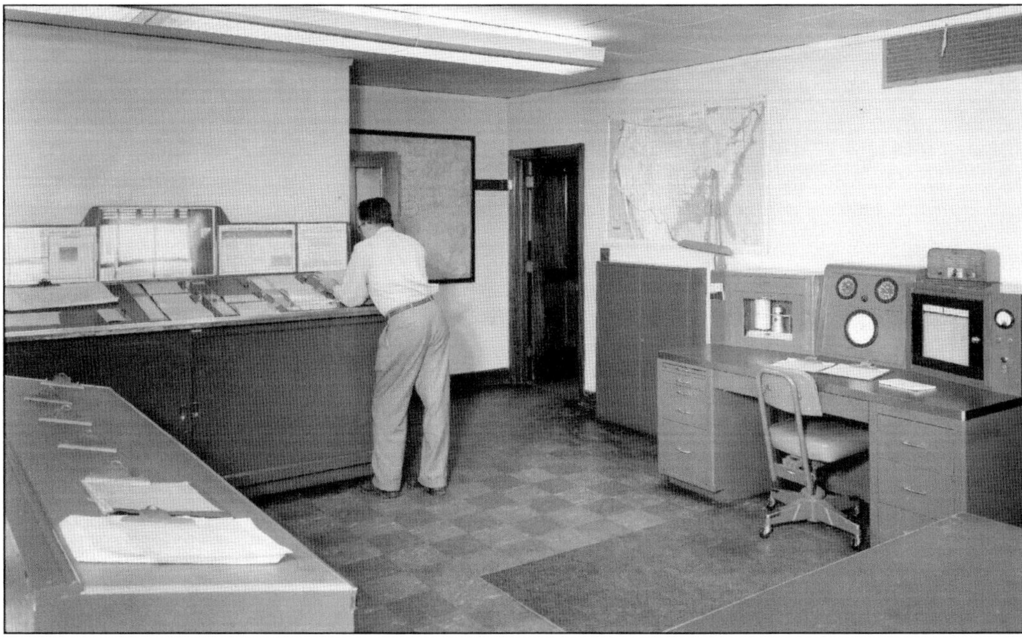

This was the US Weather Bureau station at Quad City Airport in 1954. Before the days of weather radar, satellites and computers, hourly observations and reports from other weather stations helped the meteorologists interpret the weather patterns and compile maps that pilots consulted before planning their flight routing. The technology of the day sits on the desk to the right. The bureau was located in the 1939 terminal building. (Courtesy of QCIA.)

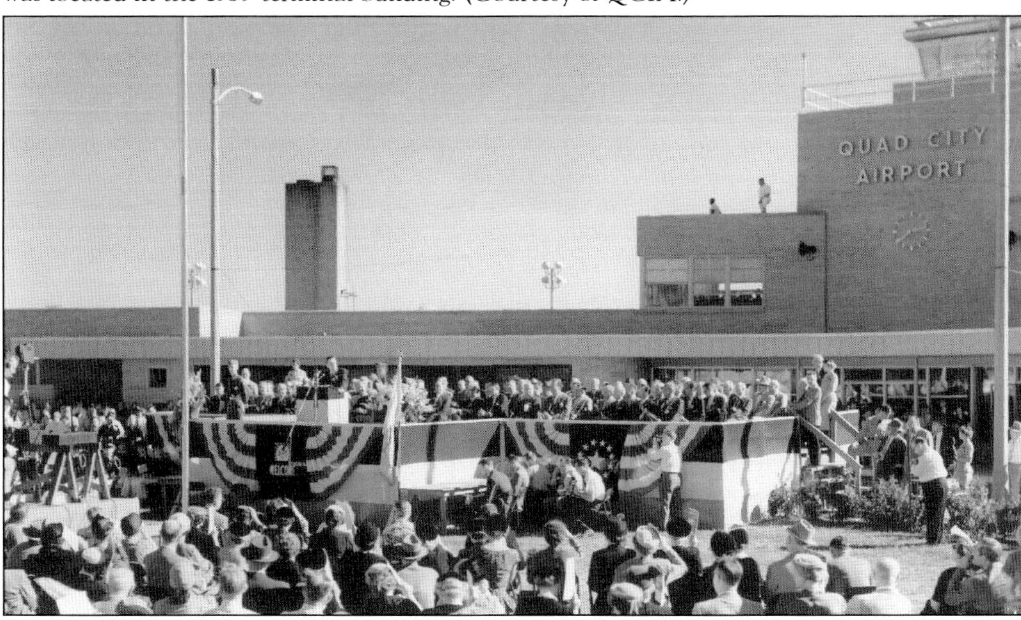

The dedication of the Quad City Airport on September 26, 1954, drew a large crowd of spectators. Officials of the Metropolitan Airport Authority (MAA); Illinois state government; Braniff, Ozark, and United airlines; local mayors; and members of the Moline Association of Commerce, who worked diligently over the years to secure the airport for Moline, were all present on the stage. Rock Island's WHBF radio broadcast the dedication address. (Courtesy of QCIA.)

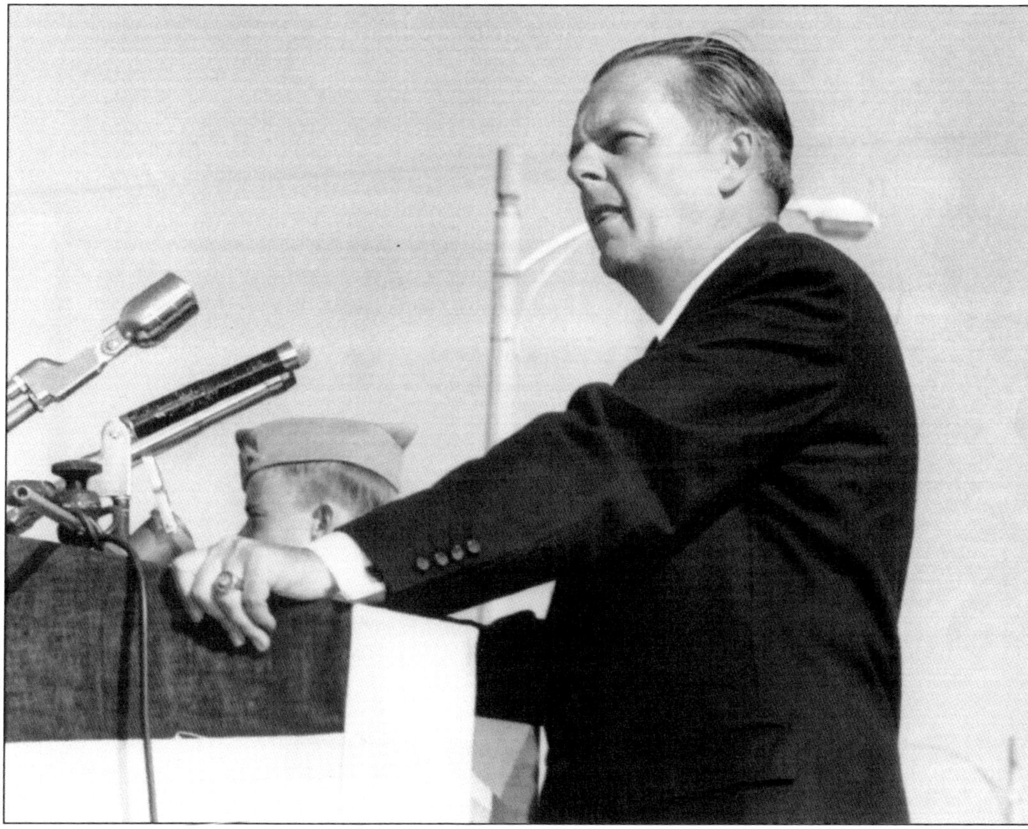

The keynote speaker at the terminal dedication was Illinois governor William Stratton. He congratulated the local citizens for passing the referendum that created the Metropolitan Airport Authority and praised former and current congressmen for their hard work on behalf of the airport. Stratton was also quick to point out that the state's engineering assistance and financial participation had aided the community in growing the airport. (Courtesy of QCIA.)

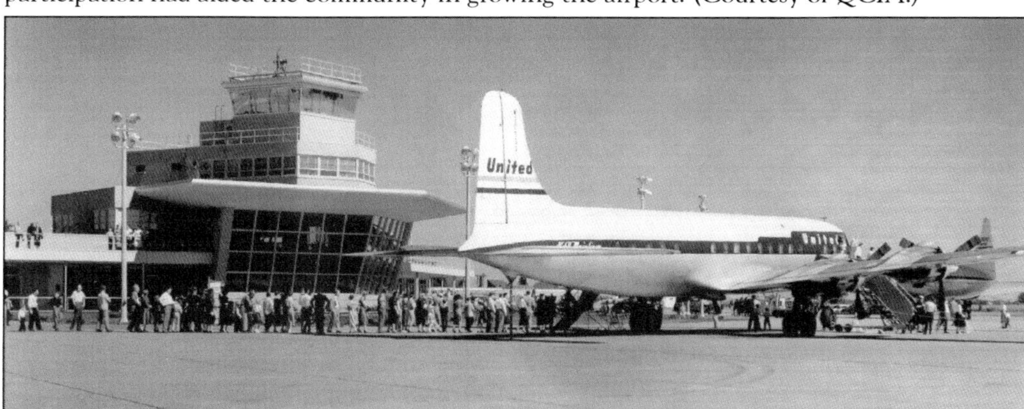

A steady stream of spectators lines up to tour the United Air Lines DC-6B during terminal dedication activities. The visitors could also step aboard a United Convair parked just ahead of the DC-6B. Note the spectators on the terminal's second-story outside observation deck, an activity long since gone because of security rules. This photograph offers an opposite view from that of this book's cover image. (Courtesy of QCIA.)

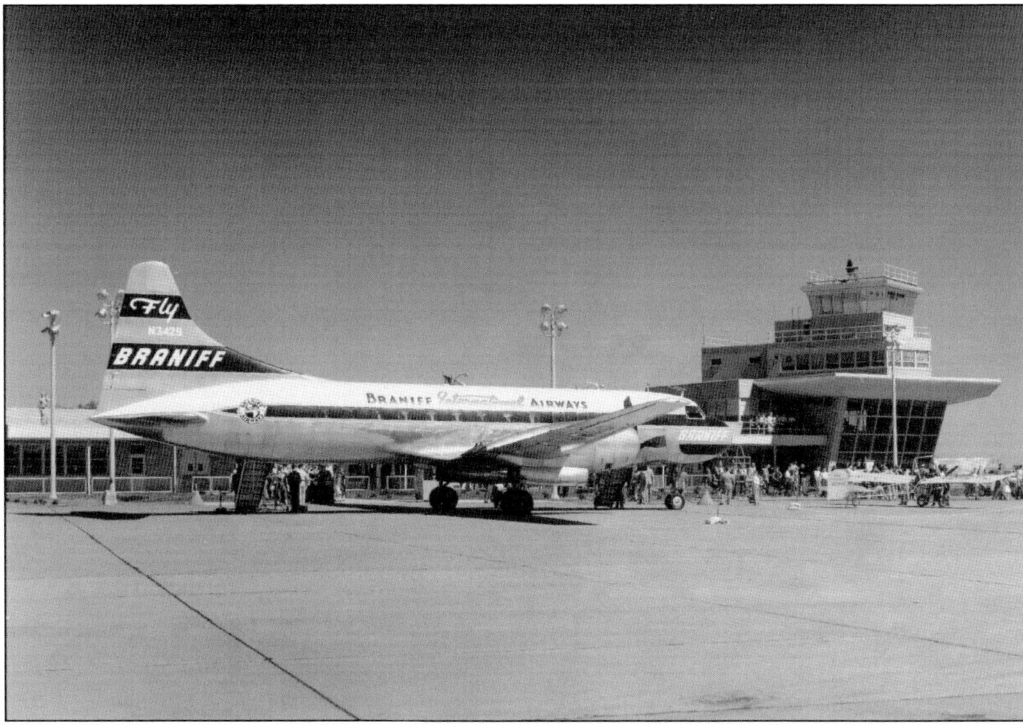

Braniff International Airways put one of its new Convair 340 aircraft on display at the Quad City Airport's 1954 terminal dedication. Braniff was still using DC-3 aircraft to service Moline at this time, but the Convair would replace all of the airline's DC-3s by 1956. In front of the Braniff plane was a replica of a 1910 French Bleriot monoplane, the first plane to cross the English Channel. (Courtesy of QCIA.)

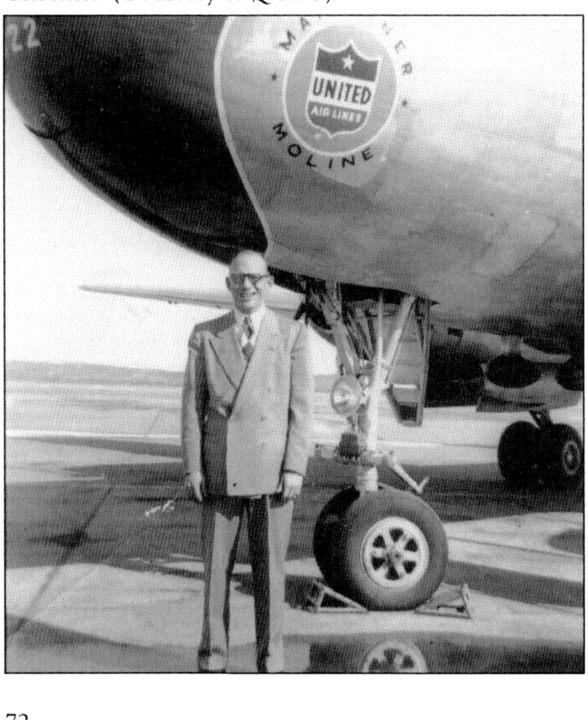

United Air Lines named its aircraft after the cities the airline served or prominent geographical features along their routes. Station manager Dick Shrader proudly poses with *Mainliner Moline*, one of the Convairs that served Quad City Airport. Earlier, a DC-3 was christened with that name, and later a DC-7 carried the name as well. (Courtesy of Richard Shrader family.)

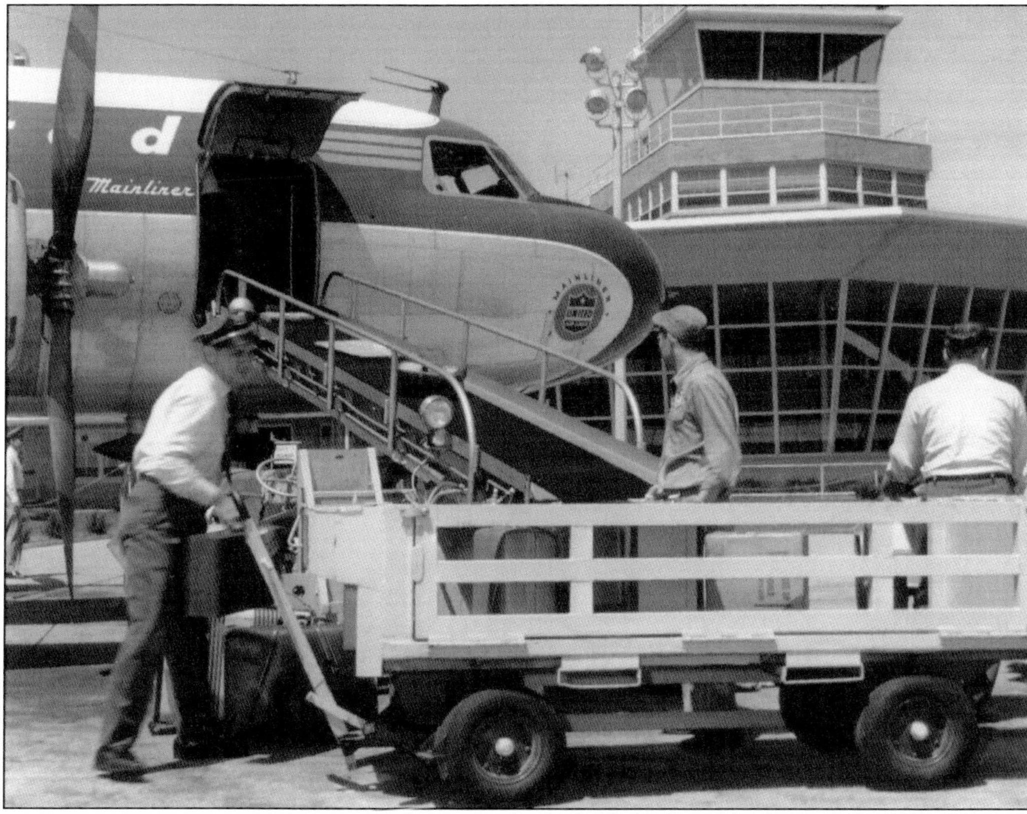

OSHA might now approve of loading baggage in this manner. By the early 1950s, United ramp agents at Moline were using conveyors to transfer freight and baggage into and out of the aircraft. One thing that made loading easier was that the nose-high DC-3s had been phased out in favor of the level-sitting Convair. (Courtesy of Richard Shrader family.)

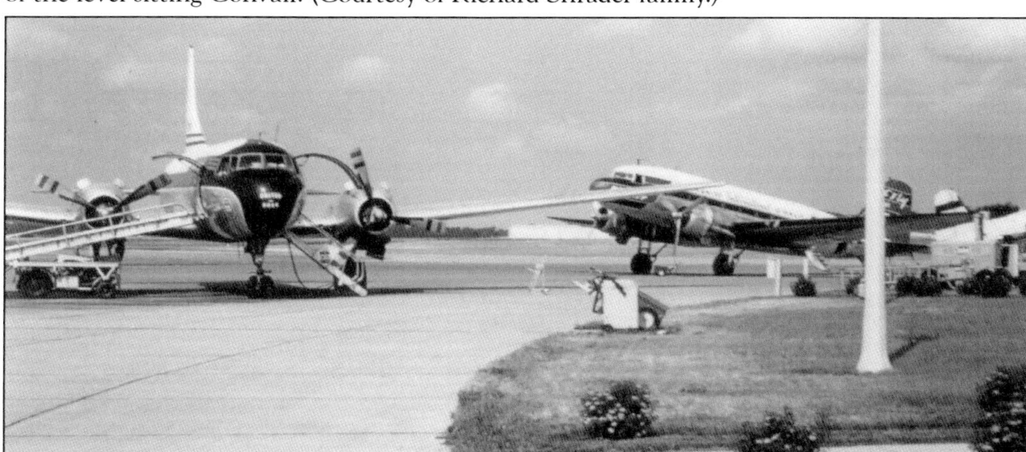

A photograph from mid-1957 captures aircraft of the three airlines serving Moline on the ramp at one time. United to the left, Braniff in the center, and Ozark, with its tail peeking out above the Braniff's wing, on the extreme right. Customarily, passengers board on the left of the aircraft. However, it appears from its parking position that the Ozark DC-3 loads from the right side. (Courtesy of QCIA.)

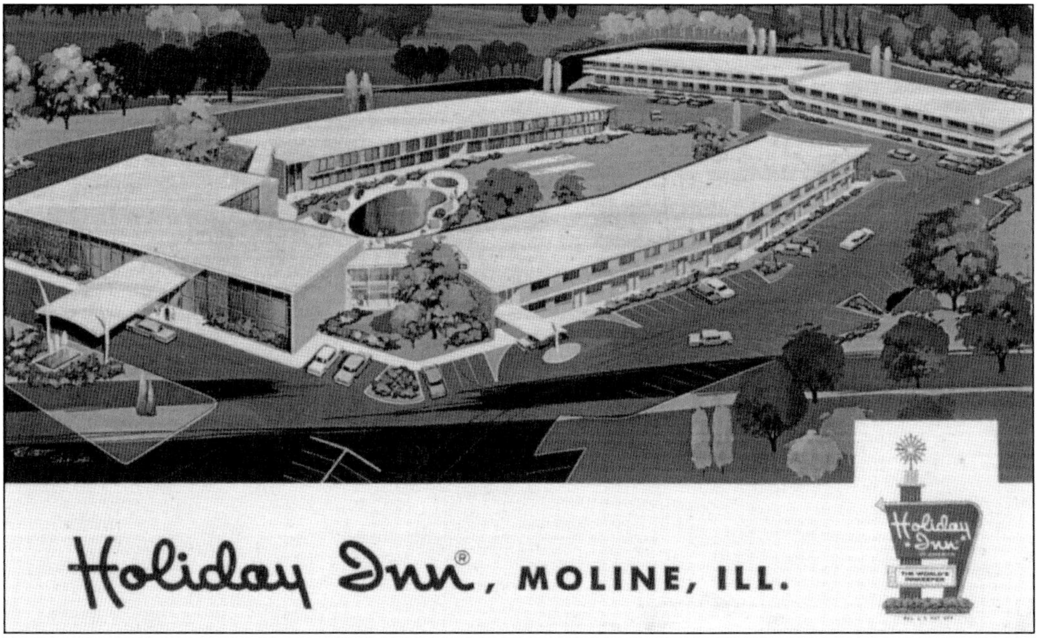

In the late 1950s, Holiday Inn took advantage of available land along Route 150 between the Quad City Airport and the Rock River to build this motel. With ever-increasing passenger arrivals at the airport and construction of Interstate 80 within several hundred yards to its north, this was a perfect spot for the complex. It has since undergone two enlargements, been enclosed, and had a convention center added.

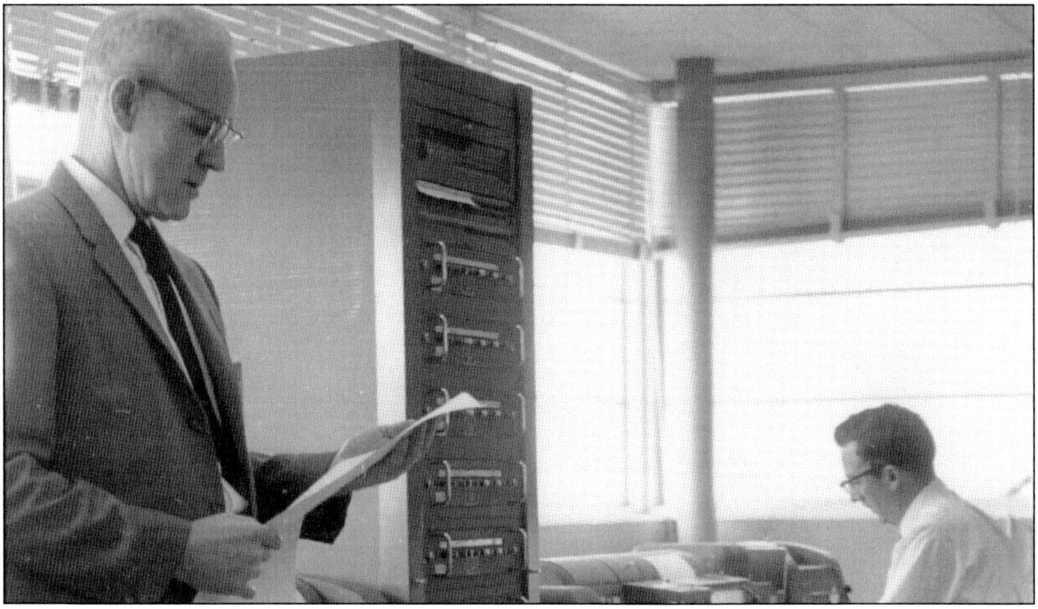

When the new terminal was built in 1954, the offices of the US Weather Bureau remained in the 1939 hangar-terminal building. When the second floor addition was added in 1961, the US Weather Bureau office moved into the new terminal. William Joerin (left), chief meteorologist, examines incoming data while George Overgard dispatches the latest Quad City weather information to other weather offices over the weather bureau network. (Courtesy of QCIA.)

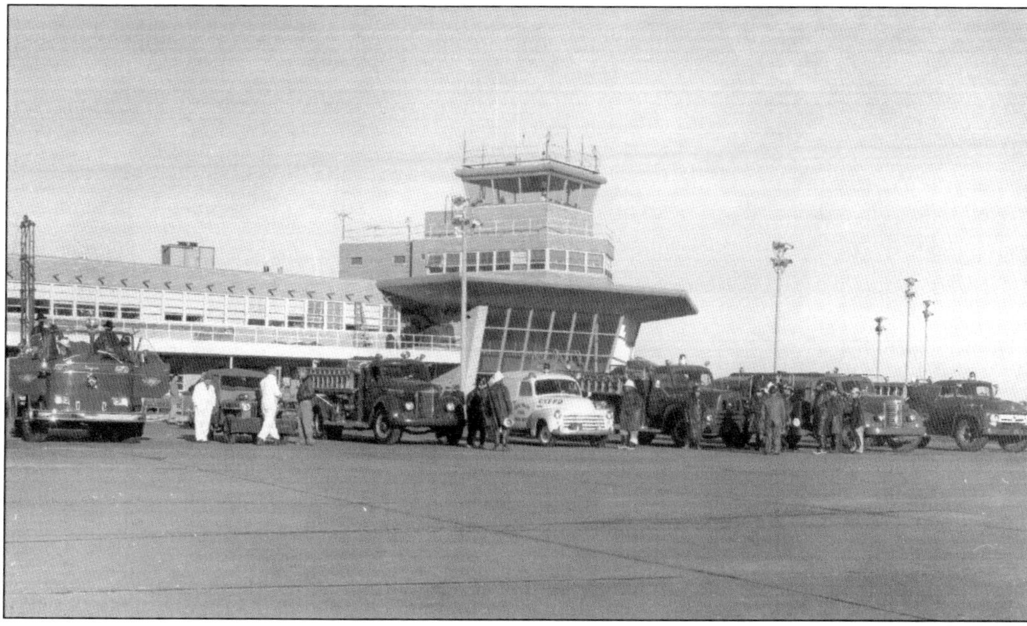

The airport's firefighting equipment is posed on the ramp for this 1961 photograph. Well within Federal Aviation Administration regulations but not as elaborate as today's requirements, the Coal Valley Fire Department provided manpower and equipment for any airfield incident. Moline and Rock Island Arsenal departments would also be called to respond. The equipment included pumper trucks, water tankers, and a foam supply vehicle. (Courtesy of QCIA.)

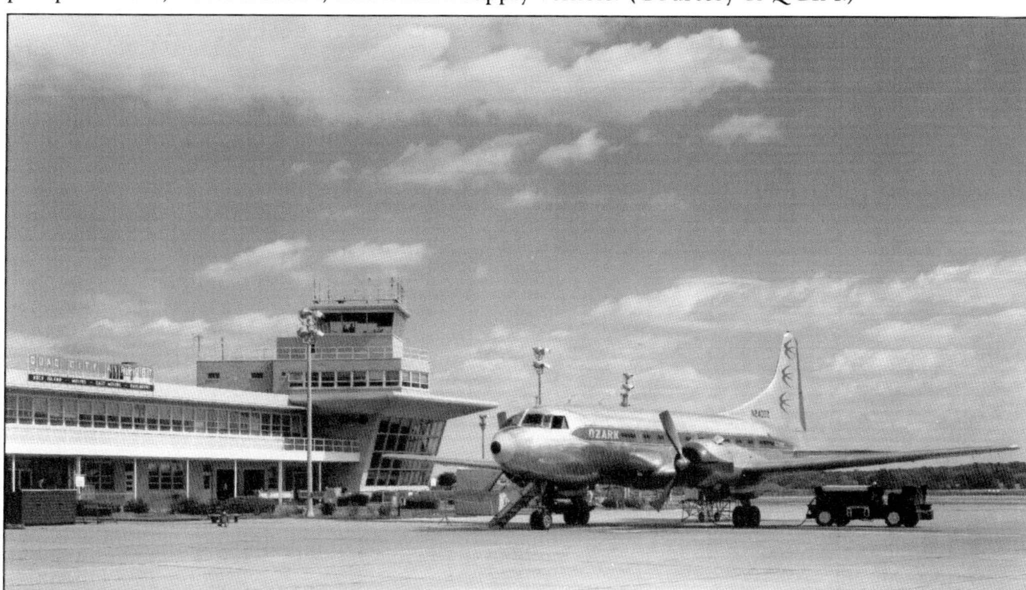

This 1962 photograph captures a Convair 240 in Ozark colors that would occasionally fly into Moline. Ozark used seven of this type of aircraft between 1962 and 1966. It was a slightly smaller version of the Convair flown by United. Self-contained boarding stairs can be seen on the right side of the aircraft. This may have been a former American Airlines plane, as American specified this model with passenger loading on the right. (Courtesy of QCIA.)

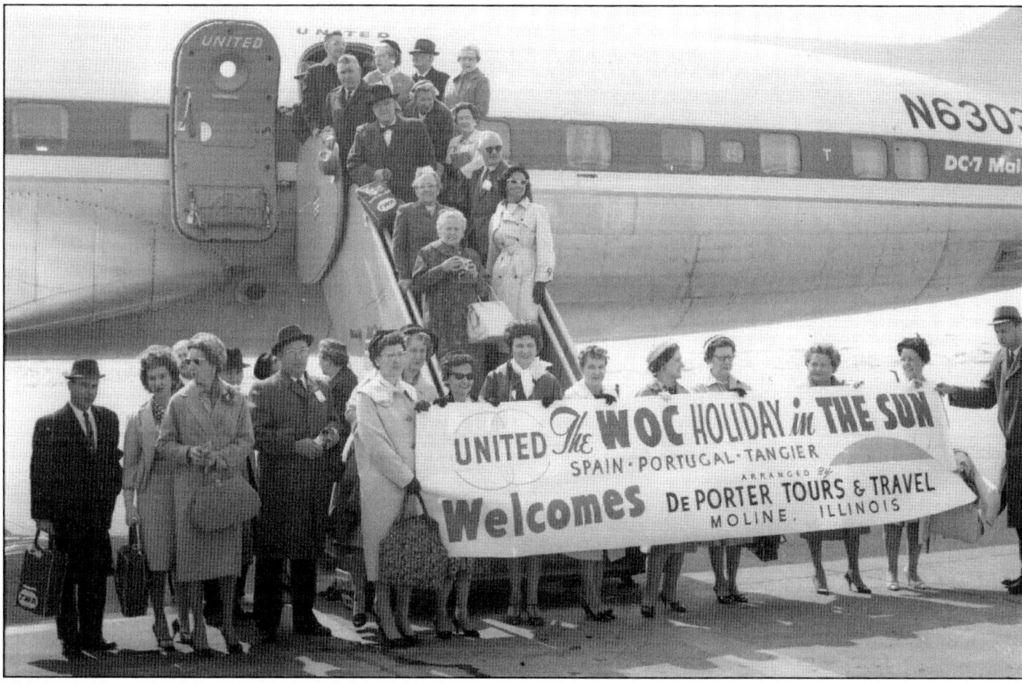

It was not uncommon for charters to originate from the Quad City Airport. Davenport's WOC Radio booked this tour of Spain, Portugal, and Tangier in 1961. Interestingly, the tour departed on a DC-7, an aircraft not normally seen in Moline at this time. Tour operator DePorter Travel and Tours originated many charters from Moline, including tours of Belgium that were popular with Moline's Belgian community. (Courtesy of Anita Sundin.)

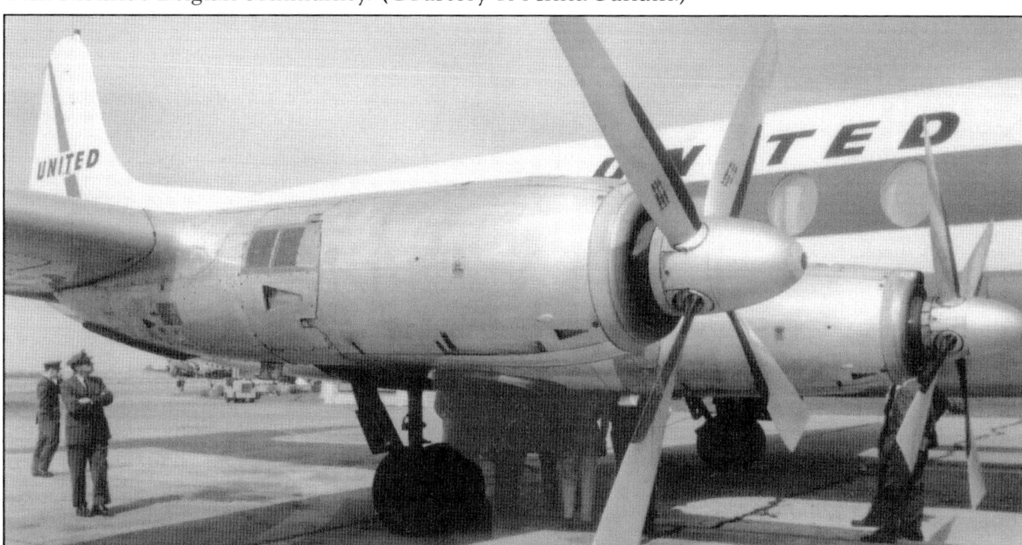

The Civil Aeronautics Board approved a merger between United Air Lines and Capital Airlines in April 1961. Capital had a number of British-built Vickers Viscount four-engined propjet airliners that United assumed. During the early 1960s, Viscounts would occasionally be used on routes through Moline. In this photograph, two Ozark DC-3 pilots wandered over to examine a Viscount that made its first trip into Quad City Airport. (Courtesy of Richard Shrader family.)

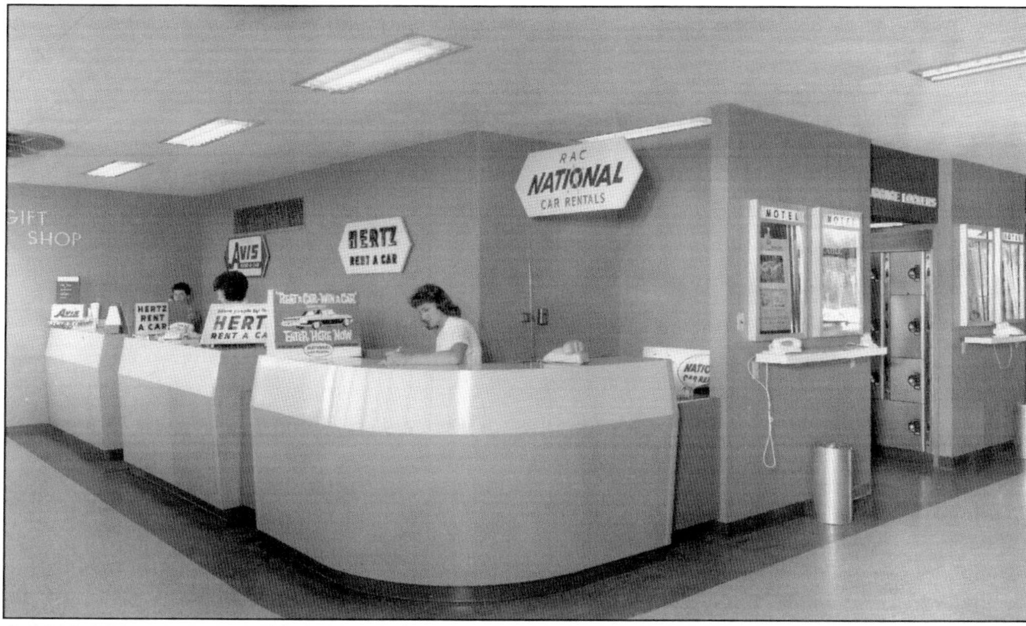

A $900,000 expansion added a second story to each wing of the terminal and a 120-foot extension to the east end of the main floor in 1961. The restaurant was moved farther east and enlarged, another passenger gate was created, lockers and more restrooms were added, and new rental car counters were enlarged and moved close to a new baggage claim conveyor system. (Courtesy of QCIA.)

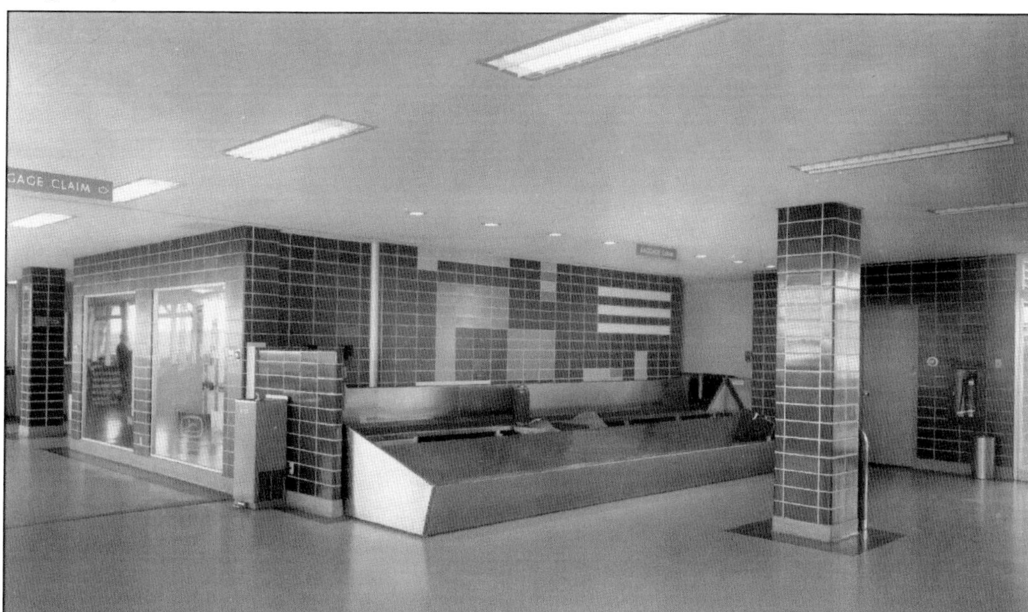

No longer did passengers have to crowd around a rather small window to retrieve their bags; they could now retrieve their luggage from a more advanced conveyor delivery system. Bags were placed on a horizontal conveyor. A vertical conveyor that traveled back and forth kicked the bags off onto the slanted collection table for ease of pickup. Unfortunately, a building column and an exit still caused congestion. (Courtesy of QCIA.)

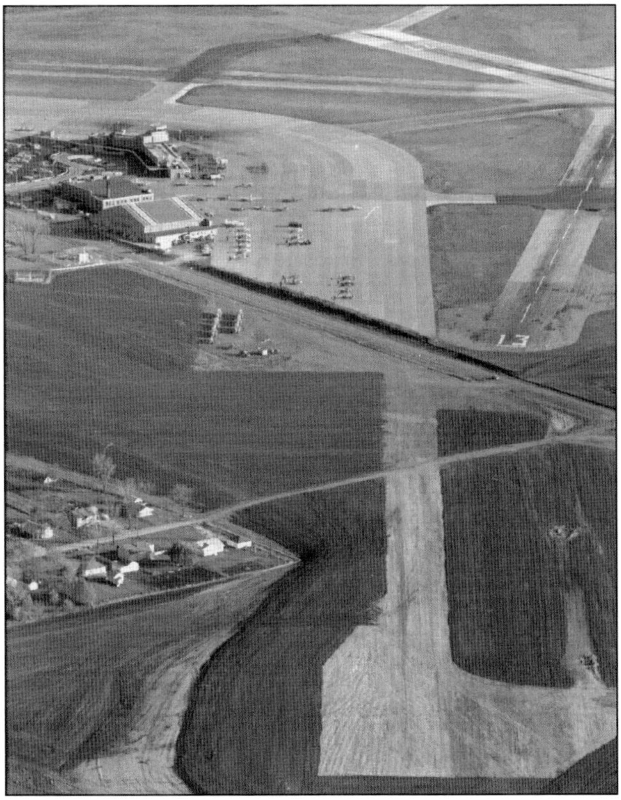

In 1963, the public parking lot in front of the terminal was doubled in size. Contractors moved over 800,000 cubic yards of earth to the northwest corner of the airport prior to building a new entrance road and relocating Route 92 (Airport Road) off airport property. The relocated road would pass through the property shown in the foreground. (Courtesy of QCIA.)

Following a nearby speaking engagement in April 1965, former US president Eisenhower visited Deere and Company headquarters in Moline. After his stop, he returned to his home at Gettysburg via the Deere corporate plane seen in the background. In this photograph are, from left to right, Dwight Eisenhower; his aide, Brig. Gen. Robert Schultz; radio newsman Harry King; and Iowa senator Jack Miller. (Courtesy of Harry Kirchman.)

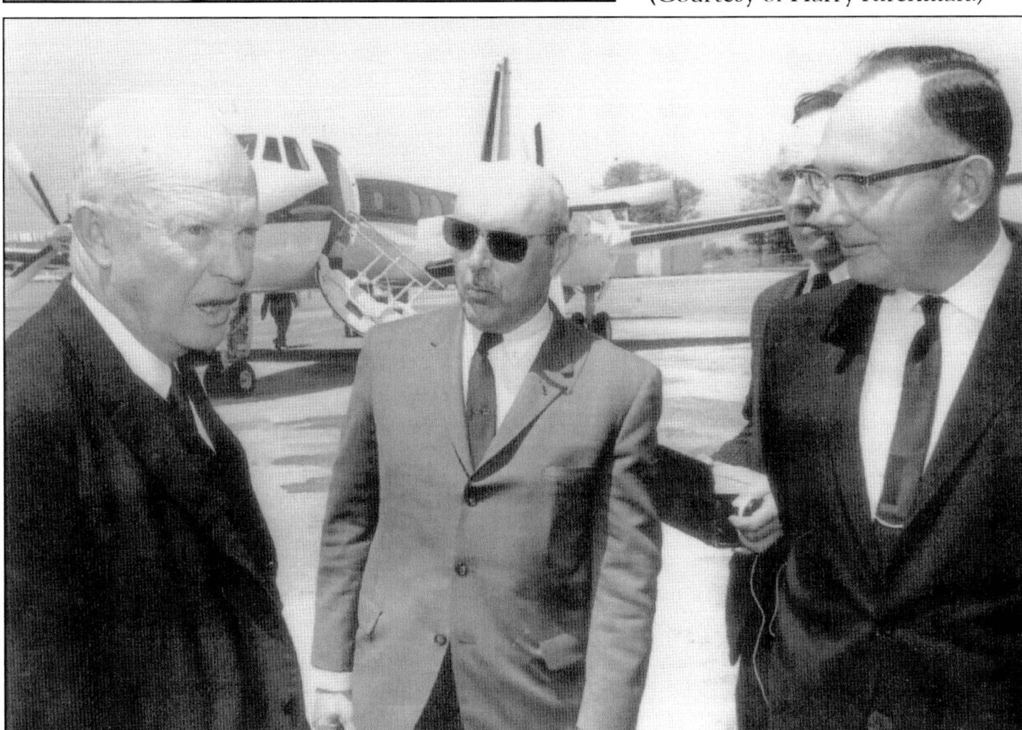

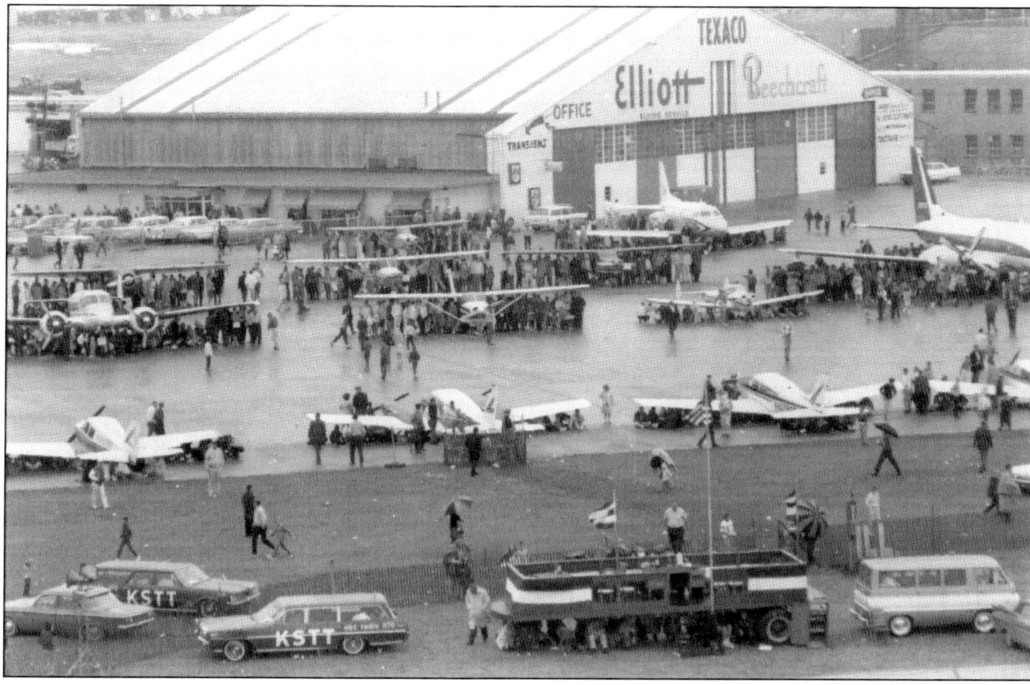

The Quad City Airmen's Association staged an air show that brought a number of civilian and military airplanes and the US Air Force Thunderbirds demonstration flight team to Moline in 1965. Although it rained during part of the show, the weather did not dampen the crowd's interest in the planes or the Thunderbirds' performance. Gathering under airplane wings assisted some of the spectators in their efforts to stay dry. (Courtesy of QCIA.)

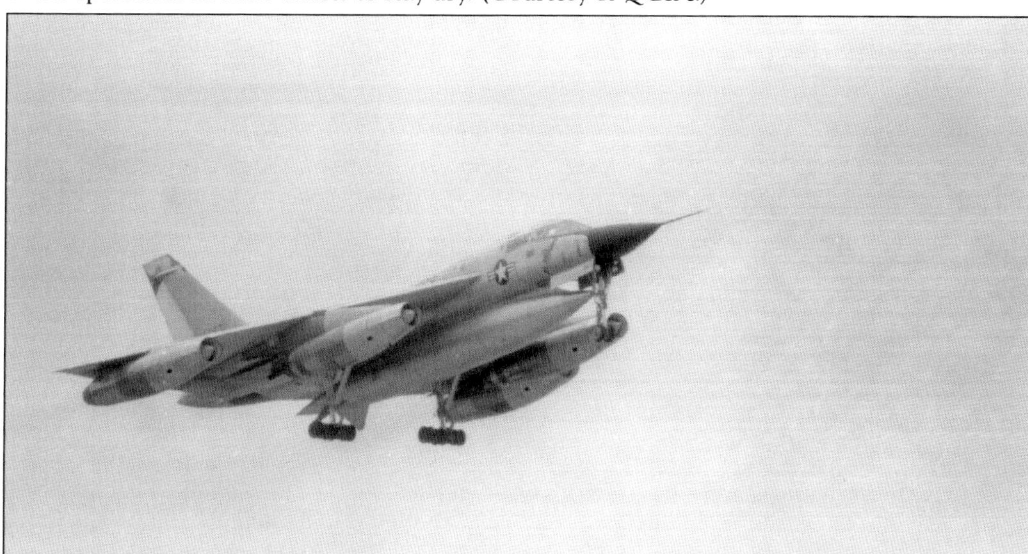

The Quad City Airmen also arranged for the Strategic Air Command's Convair B-58 "Hustler" supersonic bomber to make several low-level and high-speed flybys. Although the jet could fly at twice the speed of sound, it did not demonstrate that window-breaking ability at Moline. However, when the jet used its afterburners, the vibration caused bricks in Airport Road to pop from their resting places in the roadbed. (Courtesy of QCIA.)

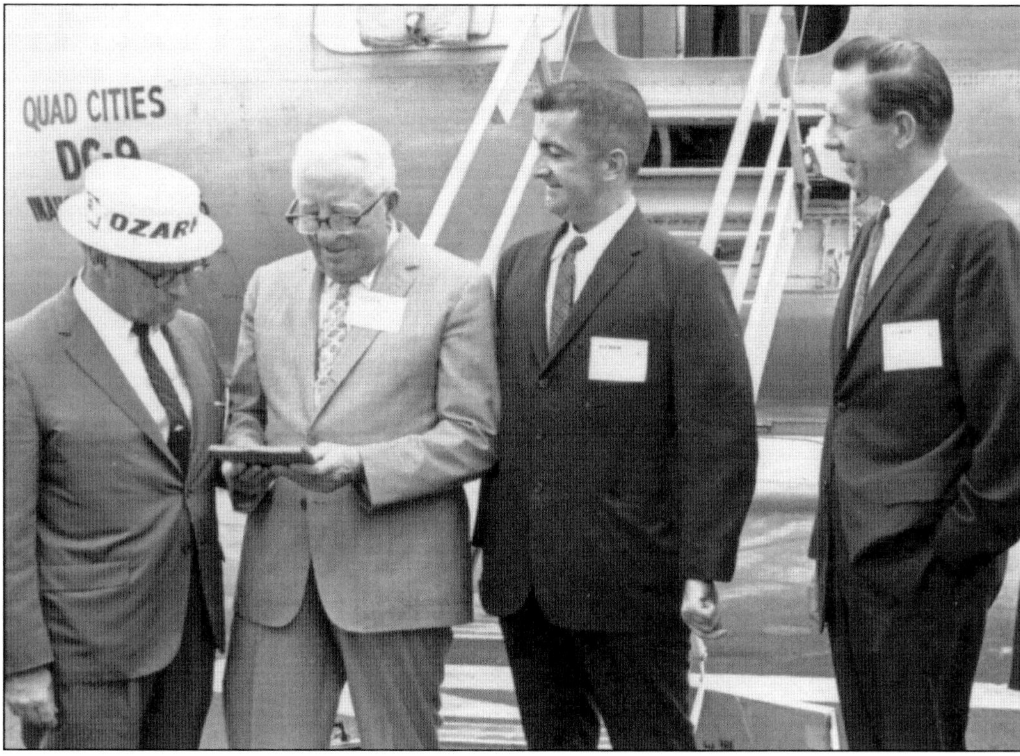

In August 1966, the first pure jet service at Quad City Airport was offered by Ozark Airlines, with a flight from Chicago. Taking part in the inaugural ceremonies are, from left to right, Ozark vice president Paul Rogers, Metropolitan Airport Authority chairman Judge Francis Coyle, airport commissioner Ben Potter Jr., and airport commissioner John Sundine. By 1969, Ozark was flying direct routes from Moline to New York and Washington, DC. (Courtesy of QCIA.)

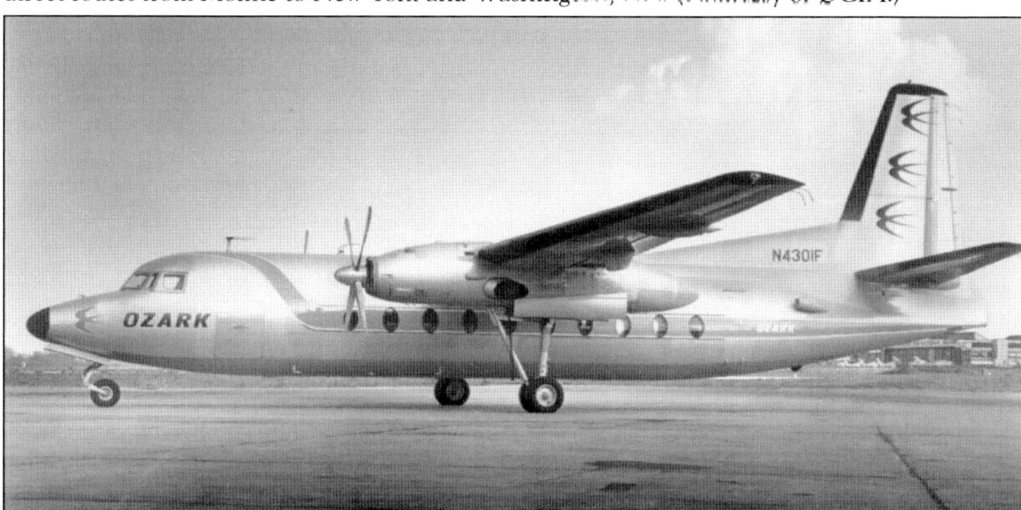

Ozark DC-3 flights to the Quad Cities were discontinued in August 1966 with the introduction of DC-9 jets. As Ozark added jet routes from St. Louis and Chicago, the Fokker F-27 was added to the airline's flight schedules in early 1967. In 1969, the FH-227, a stretched version of the F-27, entered service. This type was phased out in 1978 in favor of an all DC-9 fleet. (Courtesy of QCIA.)

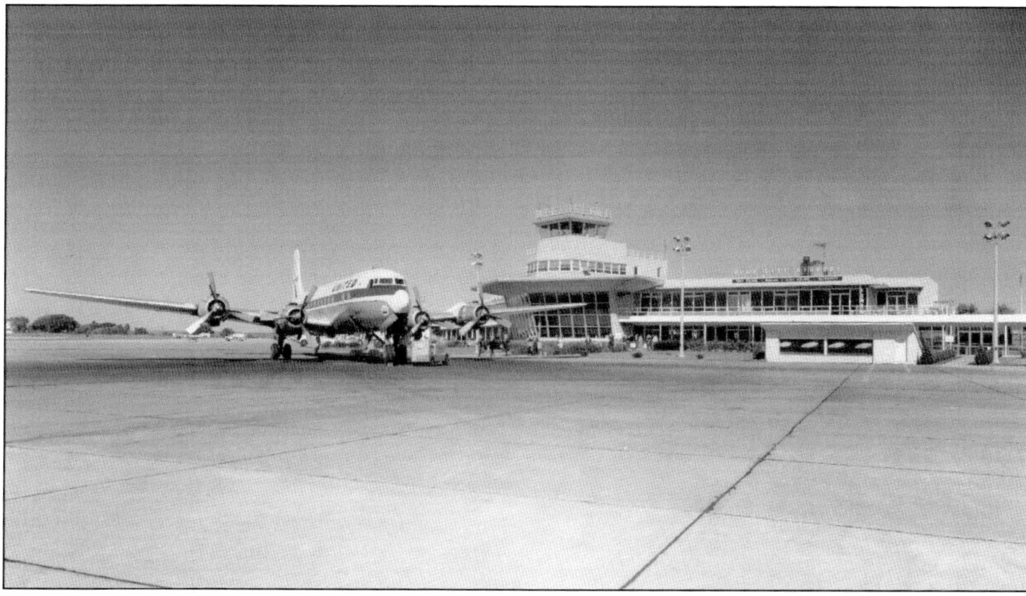

This United Air Lines Mainliner, photographed in September 1968 and sporting the livery adopted around 1960, may have been the last DC-6B flown into Quad City Airport. Its final destination was Chicago, where it was retired. United began replacing the smaller Convairs with DC-6Bs in the late 1950s. Until jets became the norm at Moline, the DC-6B was the workhorse aircraft used on routes through the airport. (Courtesy of QCIA.)

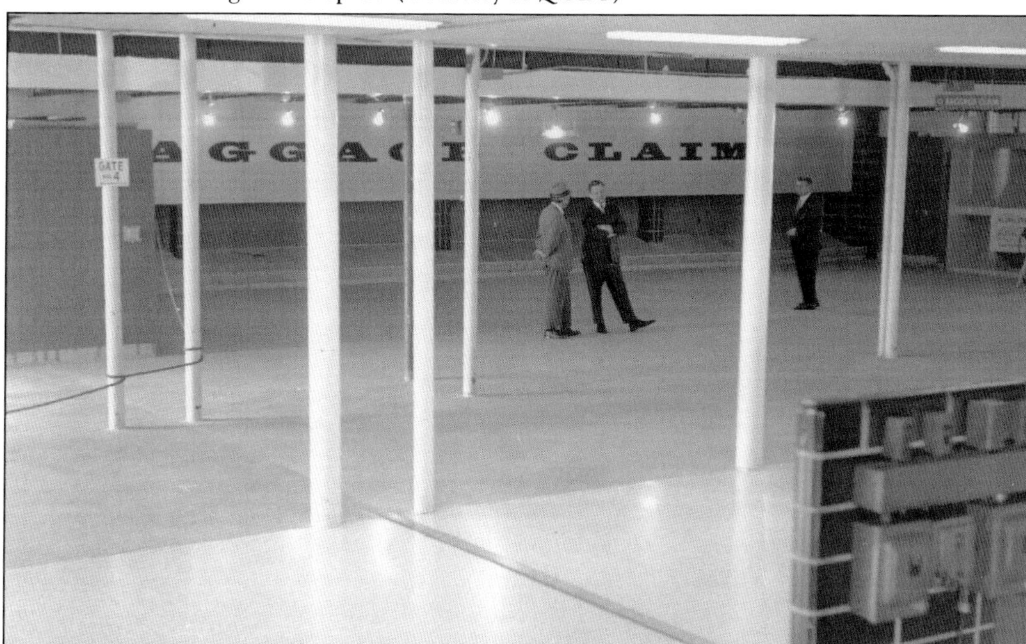

Improvements at the terminal in 1969 included enlarged passenger waiting areas and this much larger baggage claim area. The loop conveyor system was twice as long as that used previously, and remodeling eliminated most of the crowding at the former claim area. Baggage tugs pulled into a garage-like area behind the far wall, and bags were loaded onto the conveyor, where they circled until retrieved by their owners. (Courtesy of QCIA.)

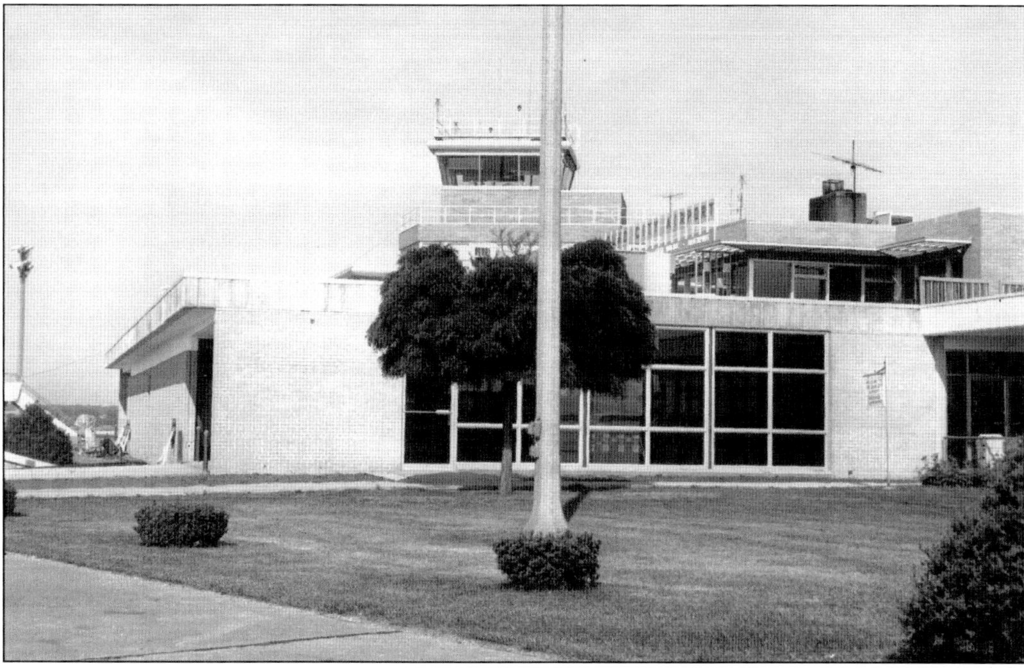

This photograph offers an exterior view of the new baggage claim and passenger waiting area addition on the east wing of the terminal. Baggage tugs entered at one end, off-loaded the luggage onto the circling conveyor, and then exited at the opposite end. Passengers knew by the sound of the baggage tug pulling up that their luggage would soon be available. (Courtesy of QCIA.)

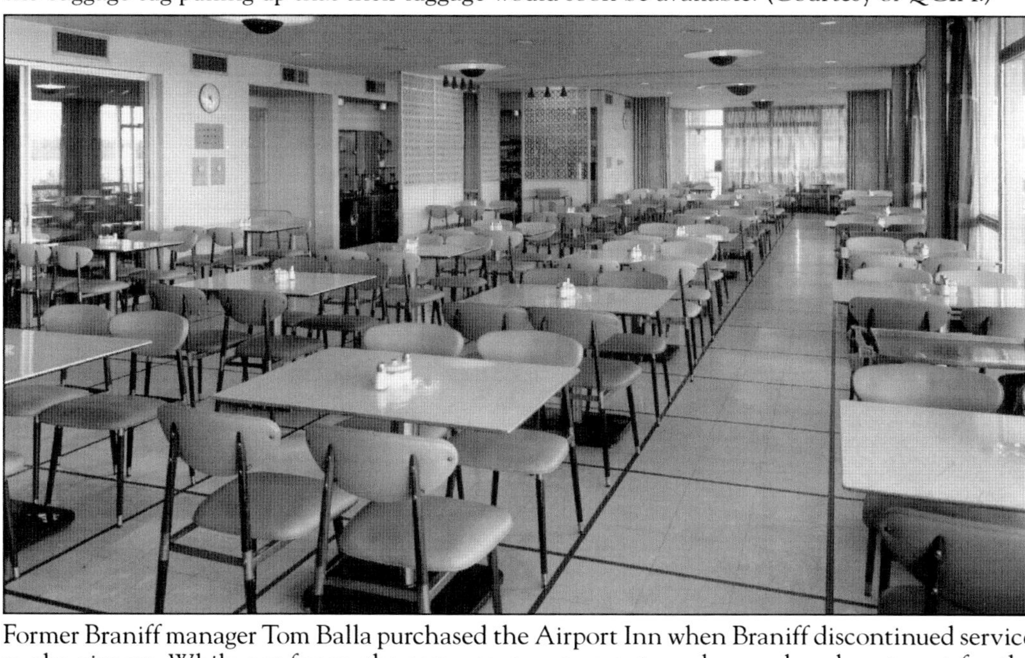

Former Braniff manager Tom Balla purchased the Airport Inn when Braniff discontinued service to the airport. While not fancy, the restaurant was an extremely popular place to eat for the general public. On Sundays, a wait of one hour for a table was not uncommon. Young and old alike were entertained while waiting by the action on the airfield. This 1961 photograph shows the restaurant's new addition. (Courtesy of QCIA.)

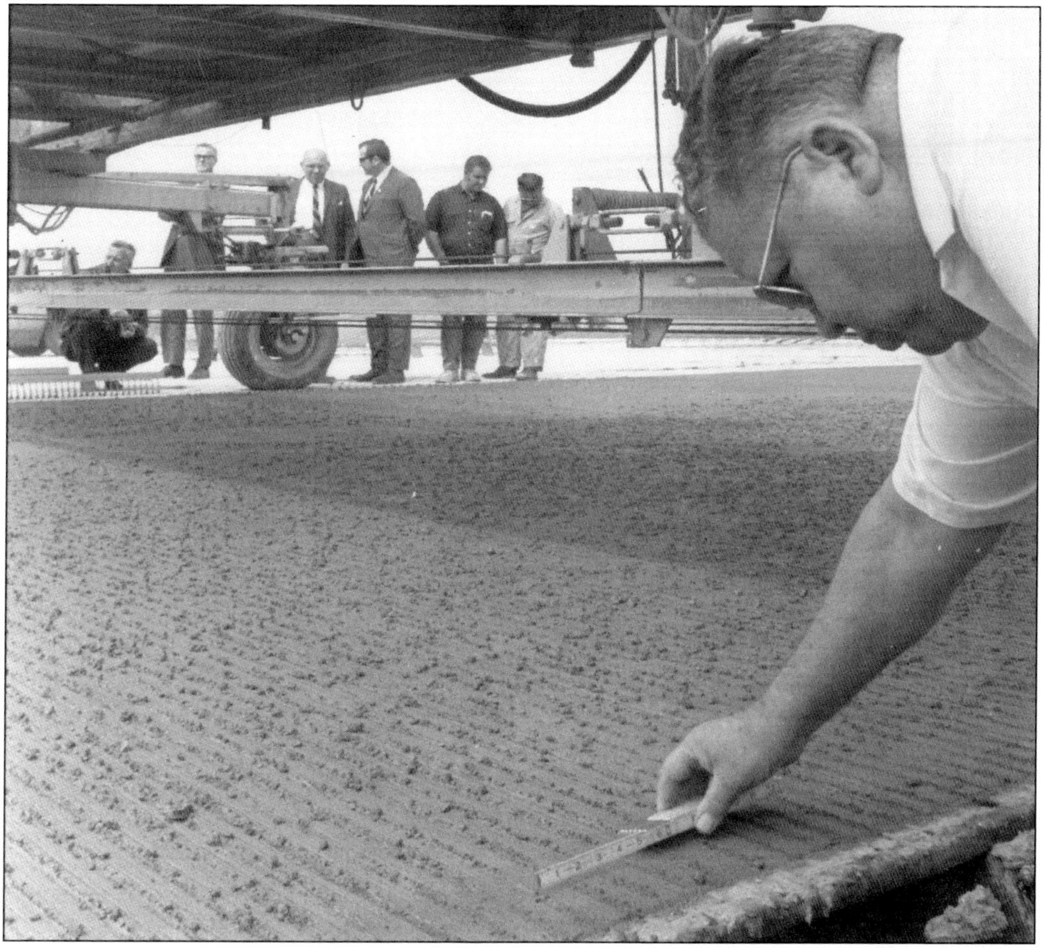

The northwest-southeast runway was totally rebuilt and extended 2,000 feet in June 1970. Financed by the Air Transport Association, experimental grooving to improve stopping capability on a wet surface was employed. Officials of the Federal Aviation Administration (FAA), airlines, airport, and Illinois Department of Aeronautics were on hand as FAA design engineer Curt Greve measured groove spacing. (Courtesy of Moline Dispatch Publishing Company.)

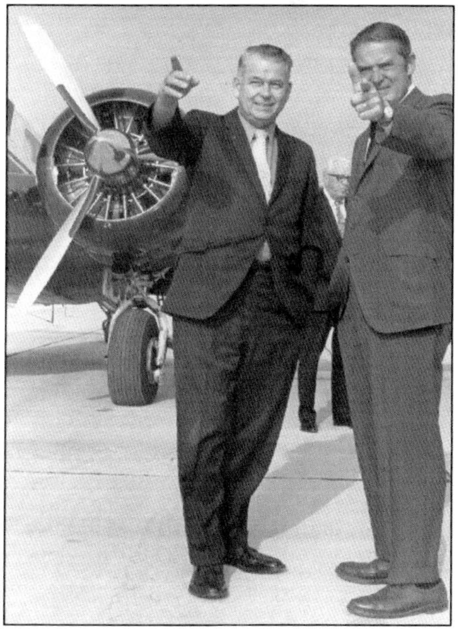

Metropolitan Airport Authority commissioner William Dowsett (left) and airport manager George Kirk pose with a Deere and Company Beech 18 during ceremonies for the completion of the new northwest-southeast runway. Seen behind and between the two is Judge Francis Coyle, commissioner. The runway was the last item in a $5 million airport improvement program, including additions to the main terminal. (Courtesy of QCIA.)

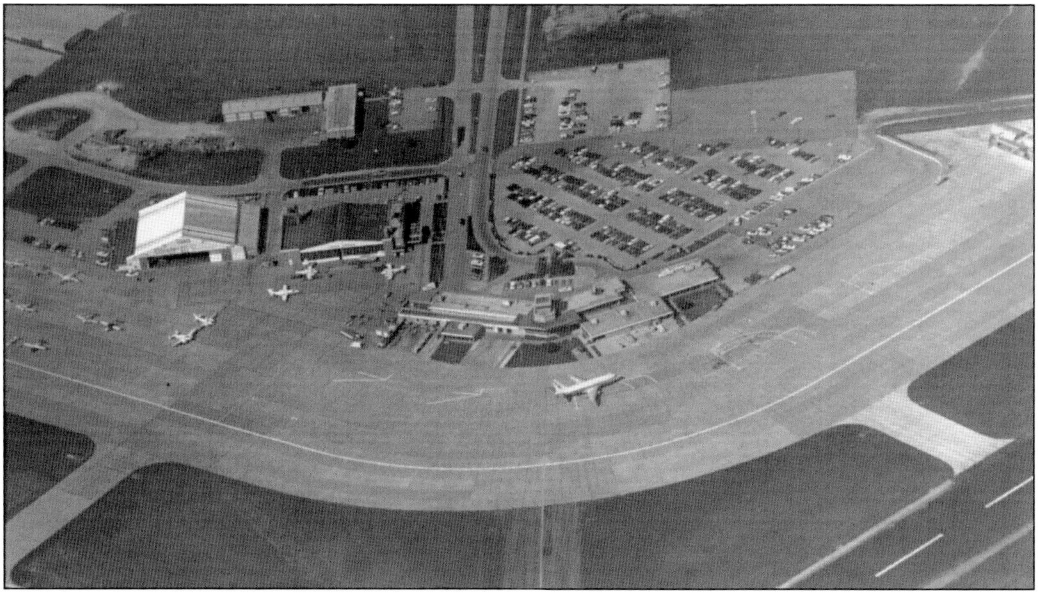

A mid-1970s aerial image provides this excellent northerly view of the Quad City Airport terminal area. Route 92 had been relocated farther north and new entrance and exit roads into the airport constructed. General aviation hangars are at the extreme upper left and right in this view. The field maintenance office and equipment garage can be seen north of the old hangar-terminal building. (Courtesy of QCIA.)

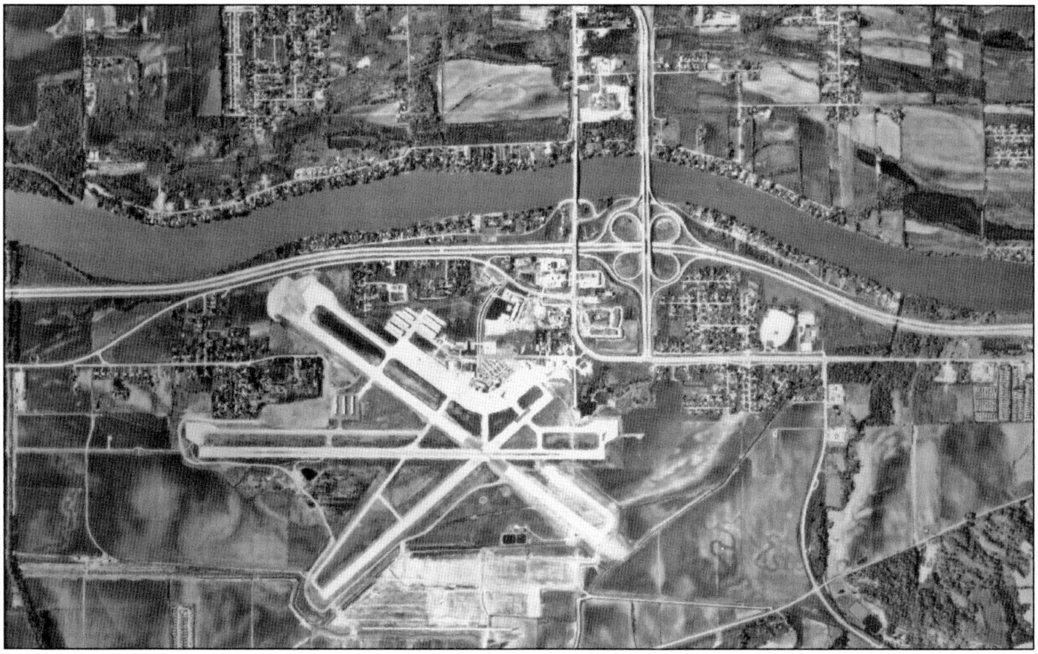

This aerial photograph taken in 1971 illustrates the surrounding growth of the city and changes to topography in relationship to the airport. North is at the top of the image. T-hangars are still northwest of the main terminal and Runway 9-27 has yet to be lengthened to the east, but the rebuild and lengthening of Runway 13-31, seen in the lower center of the image, is complete. (Courtesy of QCIA.)

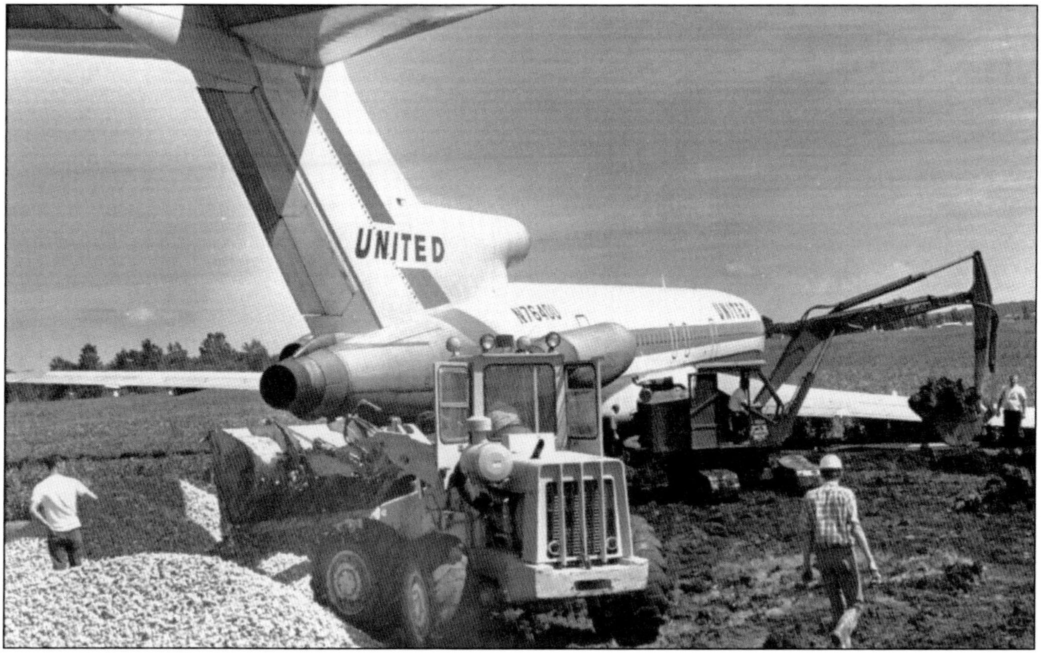

Labor Day weekend 1971 was not much of a holiday for these workers. Landing in a rainstorm, this United B-727 could not stop and ran approximately 100 yards off of the runway and into a soybean field at the east end of the airport. Cause of the incident was attributed to a layer of water on the runway that caused hydroplaning. None of the passengers or crew was hurt. (Courtesy of QCIA.)

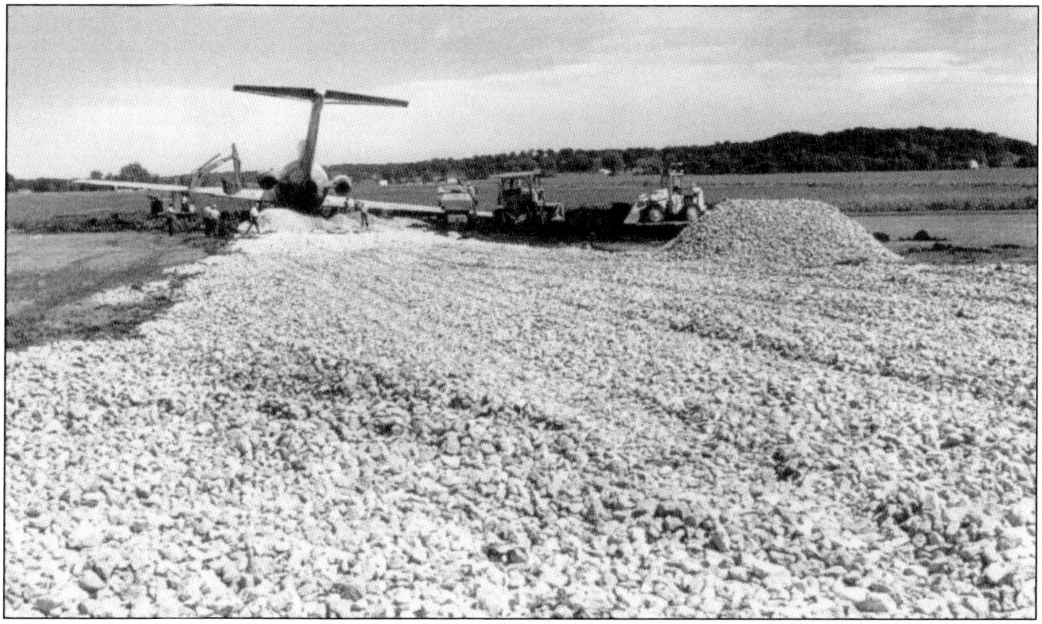

A backhoe and bulldozers work to remove soil from around the mired jet. A crane lifted each section of the airplane so railroad ties and plywood could be placed under the landing gear to keep the plane from sinking further. Over 100 tons of gravel was brought in to form a path for equipment to tow the jet back onto the runway apron. (Courtesy of Moline Dispatch Publishing Company.)

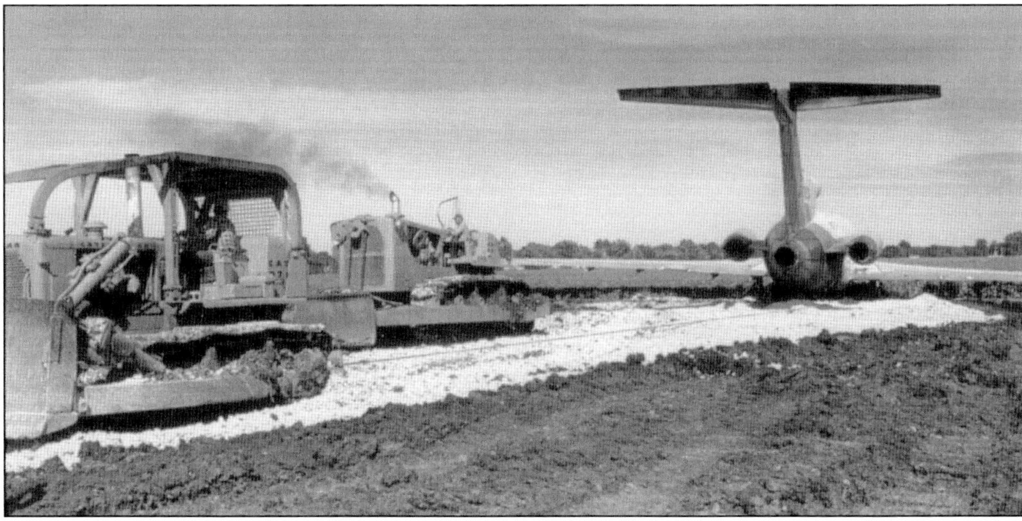

With steel cables hooked to the landing gear, bulldozers slowly and cautiously pull on the B-727, but the jet's weight kept pushing the landing gear through the gravel. Cranes again lifted the aircraft so steel mats could be placed under the wheels and along the gravel path to support the plane's weight. (Courtesy of Moline Dispatch Publishing Company.)

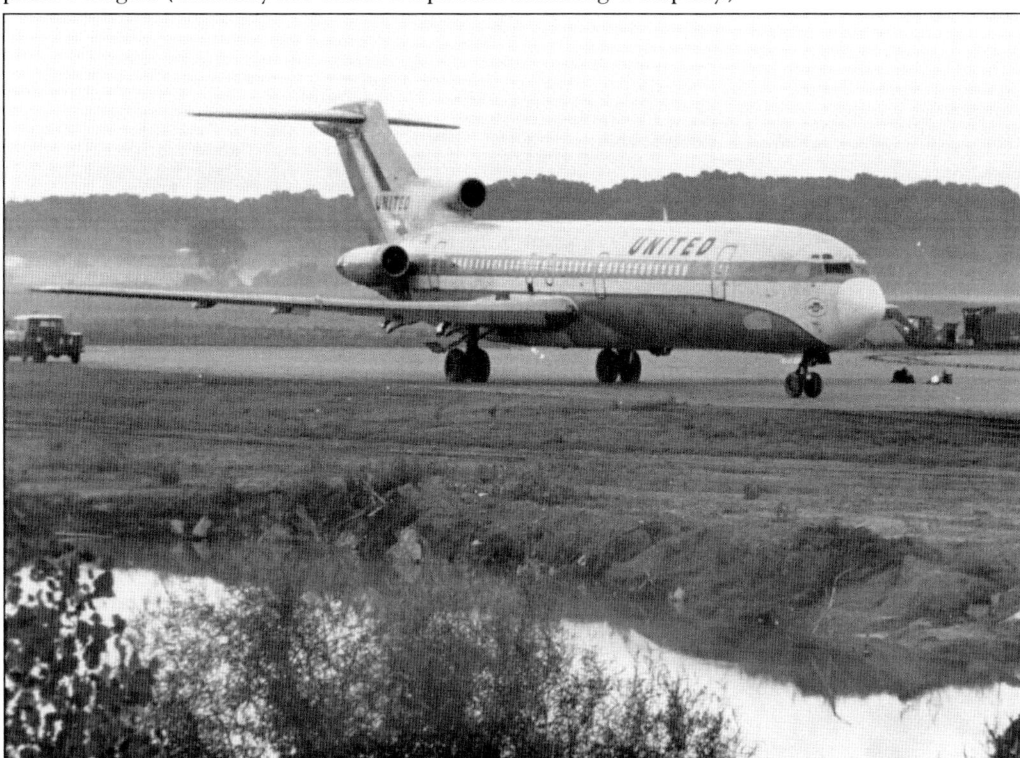

After more than two days stuck in the mud, the jet is back on solid ground. United Air Lines spokesmen stated that the plane appeared none the worse for wear. Its engines were started, and it taxied to the terminal ramp. The plane was washed down, given new tires, and inspected once again before it was flown back to Chicago to be put back into service. (Courtesy of QCIA.)

Aerorama '72 celebrated the 50th anniversary of the Quad City Airport. This program cover artwork captures the history of flight at Moline. The show featured a number of static displays of vintage and newer military aircraft, vintage and jet aircraft flybys, aerobatics, and a program presented by the US Navy's Blue Angels precision flight team. Today's annual air shows are held at the Davenport Municipal Airport.

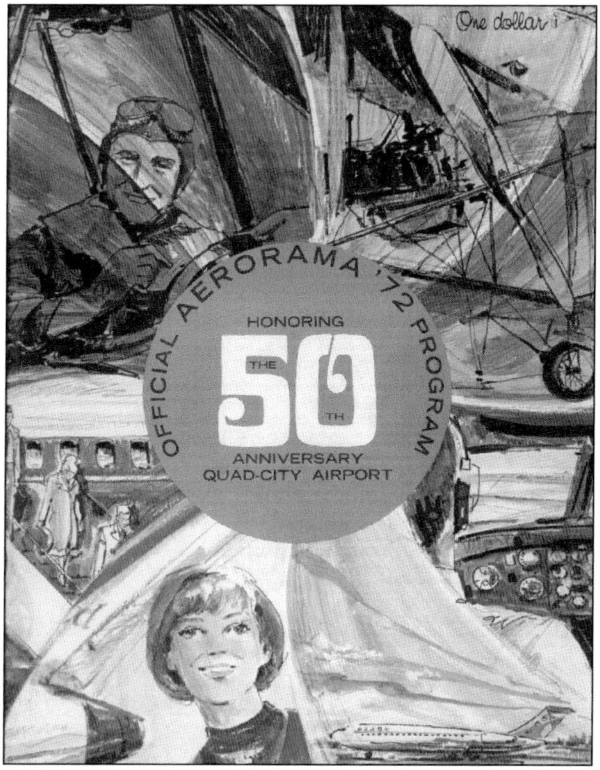

Geneseo, Illinois, native Harold Neuman learned to fly at Franing Field in 1926 and was a prominent barnstormer in the late 1920s. He went on to become a stunt flyer and national racer and won the Thompson Trophy at the National Air Races in 1935. A TWA pilot until retirement in 1966, Neuman is shown in this photograph at the 1972 Aerorama at the Quad City Airport. (Courtesy of QCIA.)

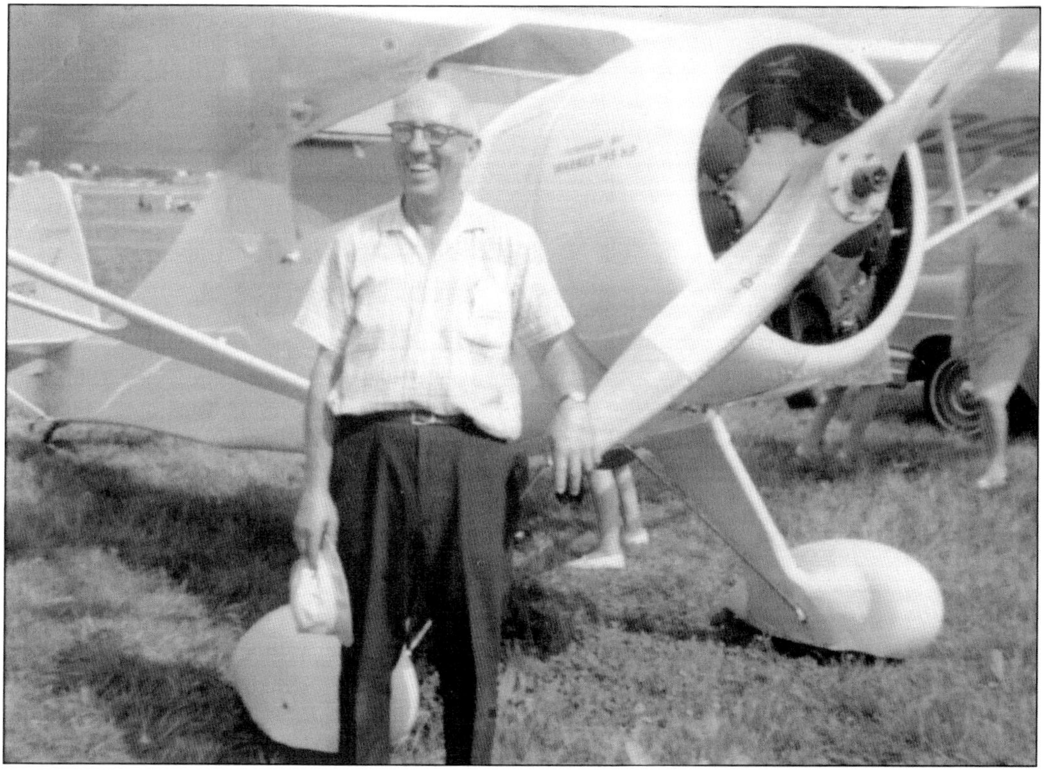

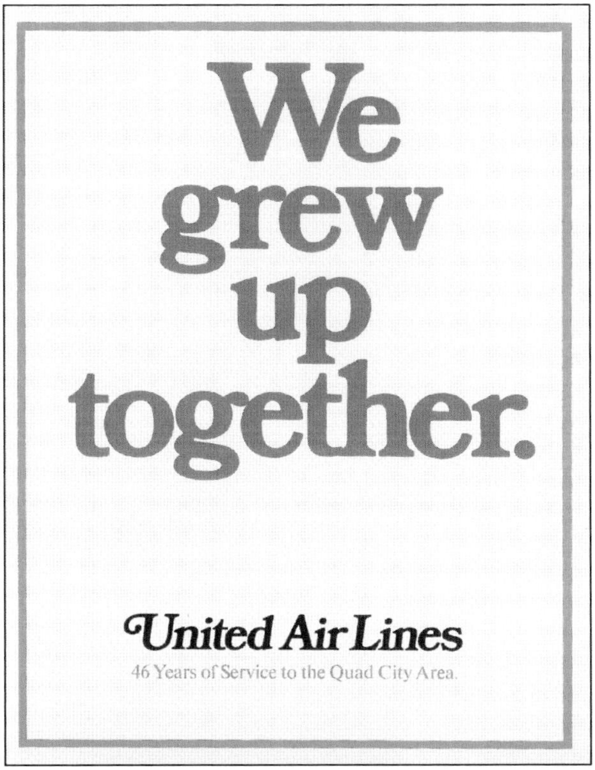

Still referring to itself as United Air Lines, the company placed this advertisement in the commemorative program for the Quad City Airport's 50th anniversary in 1972. United would introduce a new logo and begin using the shorter, more contemporary name United Airlines in 1974. United was created from former airmail carriers Boeing Air Transport, Stout Air Services, Pacific Air Transport, National Air Transport, and Varney Air Lines.

Normally, DC-10s did not fly into Quad City Airport in 1972. This one, a flight from Los Angeles to Chicago, made an emergency landing when a cockpit light signaled an engine fire. It was determined that no fire had occurred and the light was faulty. Passengers were flown on to Chicago on two United jets that were overnighting at Moline. (Courtesy of Moline Dispatch Publishing Company.)

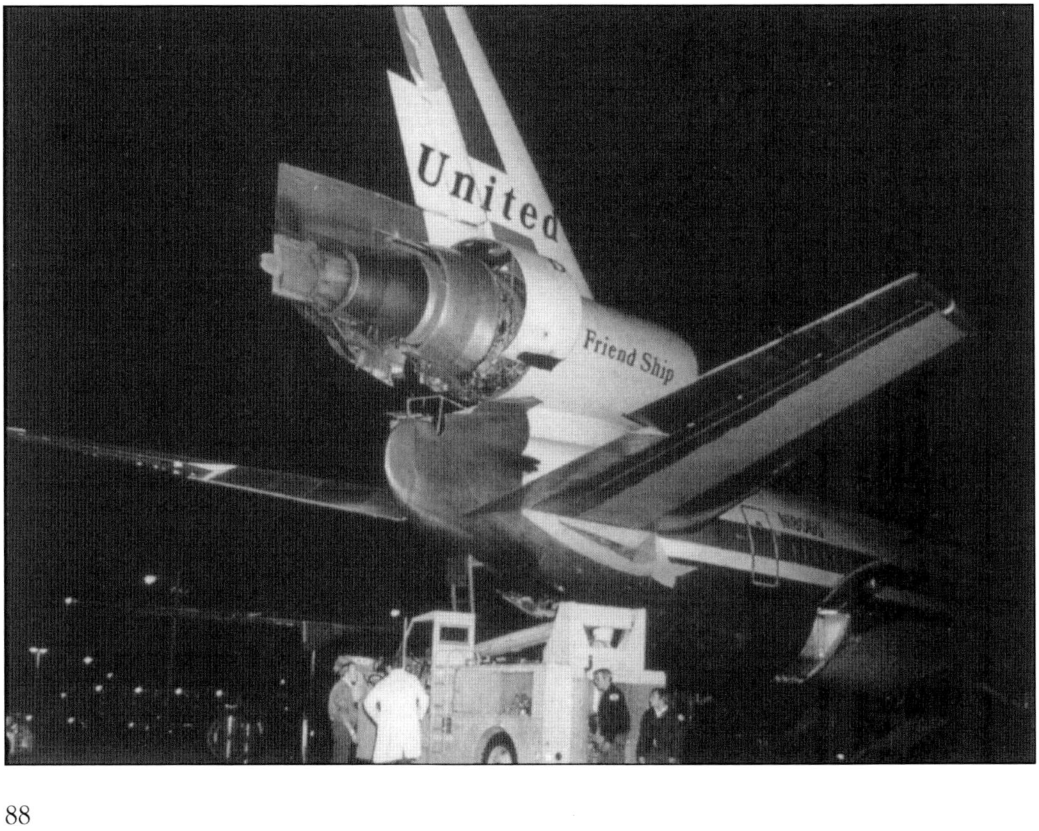

The DC-10's emergency landing was not its only problem. As the crew taxied to the runway, the plane turned wide and dropped the nose wheels off the ramp and onto rain-softened turf. Special jacks were flown in from Chicago on the next flight. While waiting, an airport crew with shovels, chain, and end-loader pulled the plane free. (Courtesy of Moline Dispatch Publishing Company.)

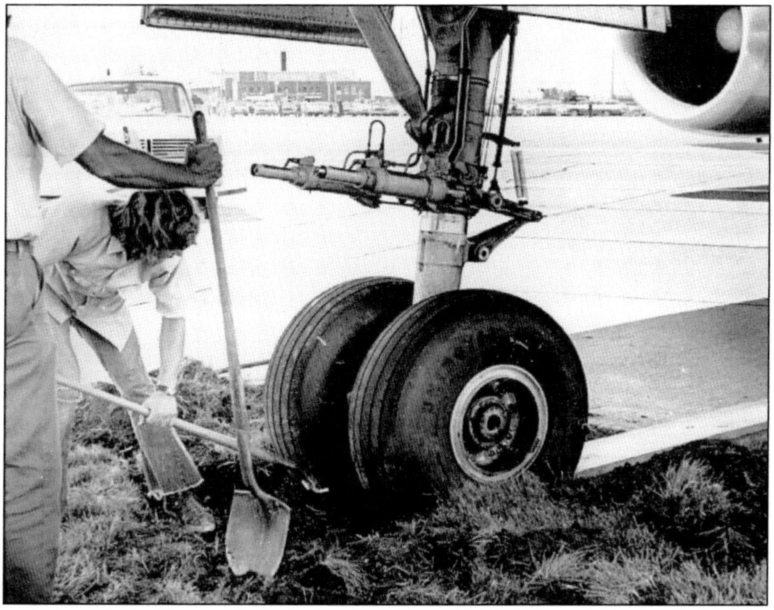

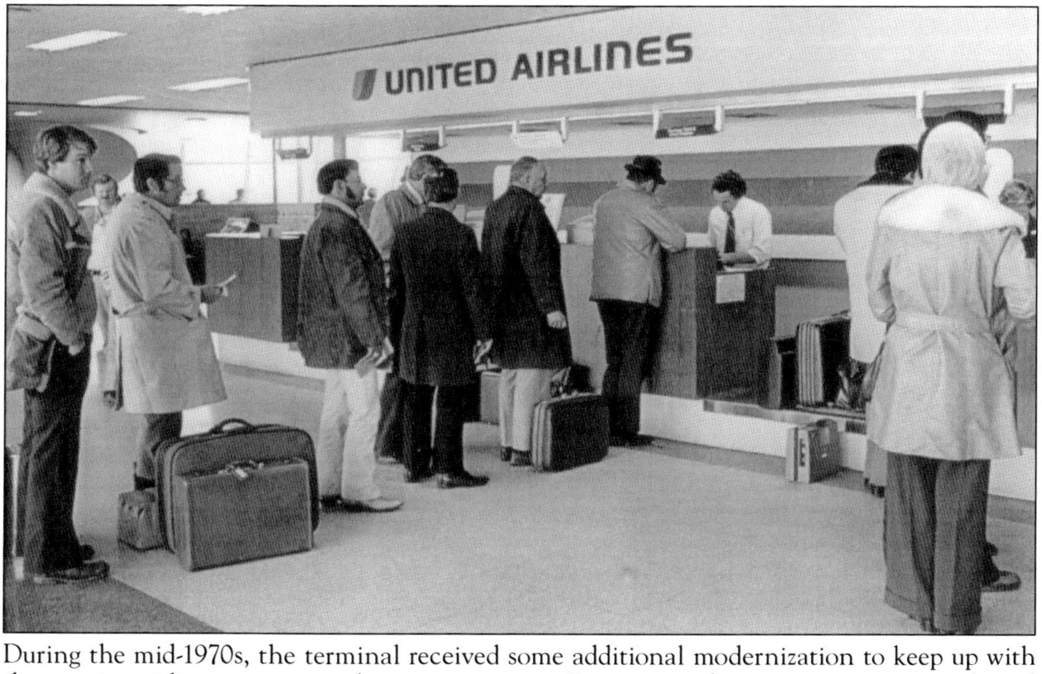

During the mid-1970s, the terminal received some additional modernization to keep up with the growing airline presence and passenger counts. Passenger ticketing counters were enlarged to quickly service the departing passengers, and boarding lounges were created to handle the crowds. In United's case, the remodeling also reflected the airline's updated corporate name, logo, and color changes. The change is apparent in a comparison to the image of United's ticketing position on page 67. (Courtesy of QCIA.)

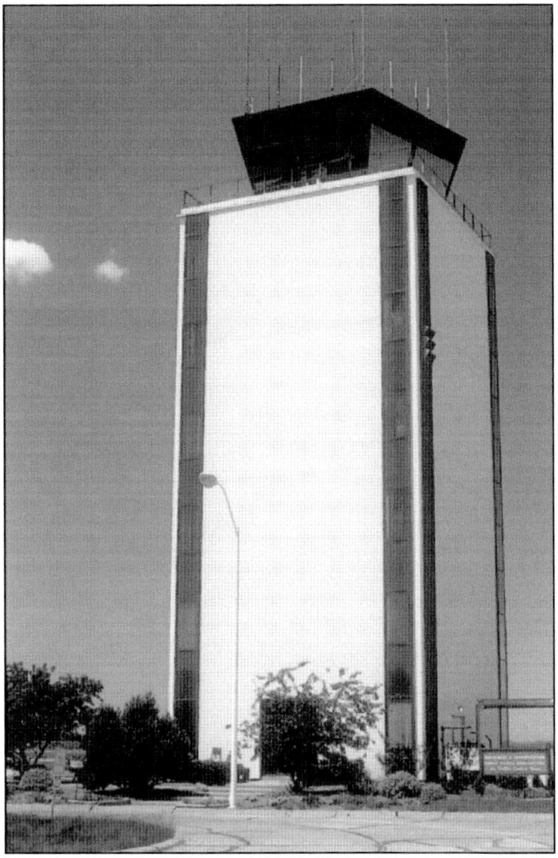

This seven-story Federal Aviation Administration (FAA) control tower was the first structure completed in 1975 on the south side of the airfield. The tower's move from atop the terminal building was the first step in separating general from commercial aviation. It also brought the airport's first installation of local surveillance radar. Prior radar coverage at Moline was provided by the FAA radar center in Aurora, Illinois. (Courtesy of QCIA.)

While the FAA control tower was being built, the airport's radar station was installed on a hill south of the field. The radar gave controllers the ability to watch traffic in a 40-mile radius. The Quad City tower also directs traffic at Davenport, Galesburg, Monmouth, Kewanee, Clinton, and Muscatine airports. Air traffic controllers Terry Hartley (left), Doug Jordan (center), and Molly Beserra keep watch from the tower cab. (Courtesy of QCIA.)

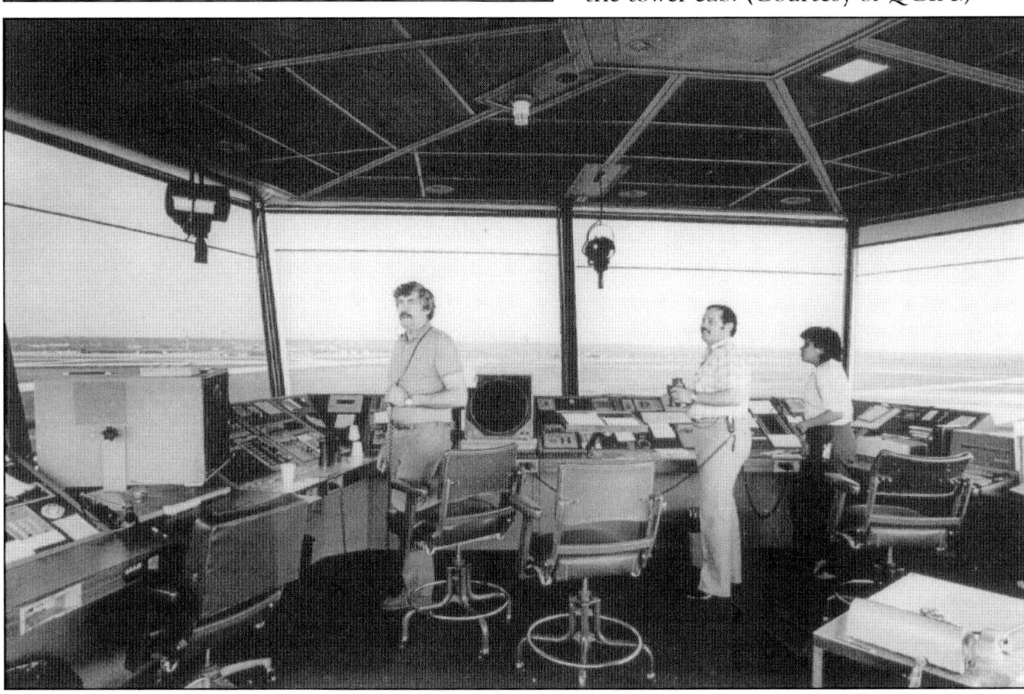

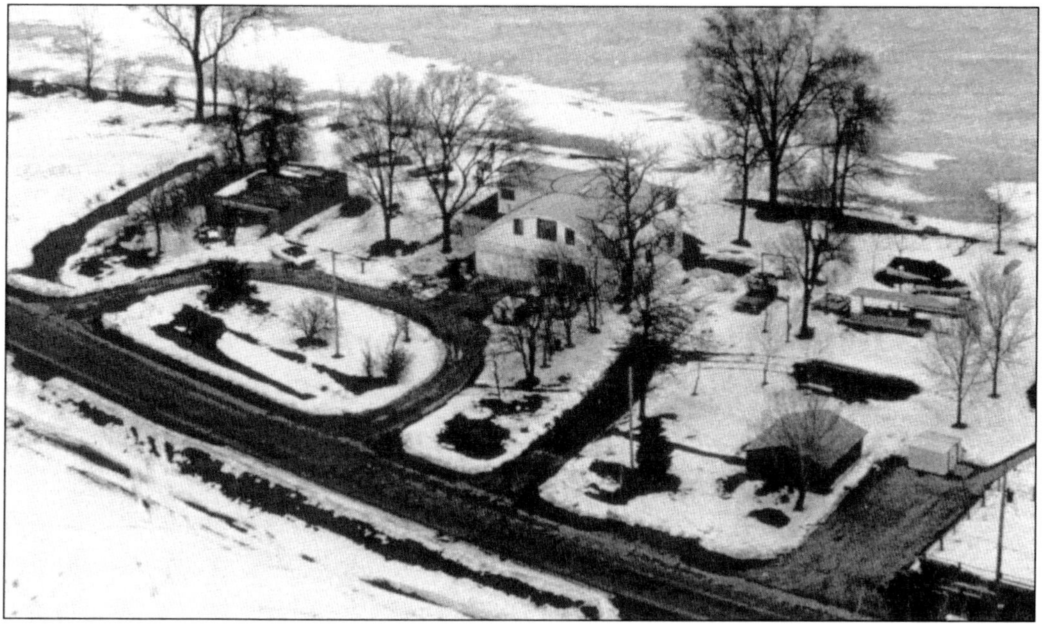

Quad City Airport is not the only landing field in Moline. The Quad City Seaplane Base is located within one mile of the airport, and it uses the Rock River as its runway. The base offers fuel, minor repairs, and tie-downs for any transient float planes. This photograph from the winter of 1978 shows the hangar located on South Shore Drive, just upstream from the bridge on Route 150. (Courtesy of QCIA.)

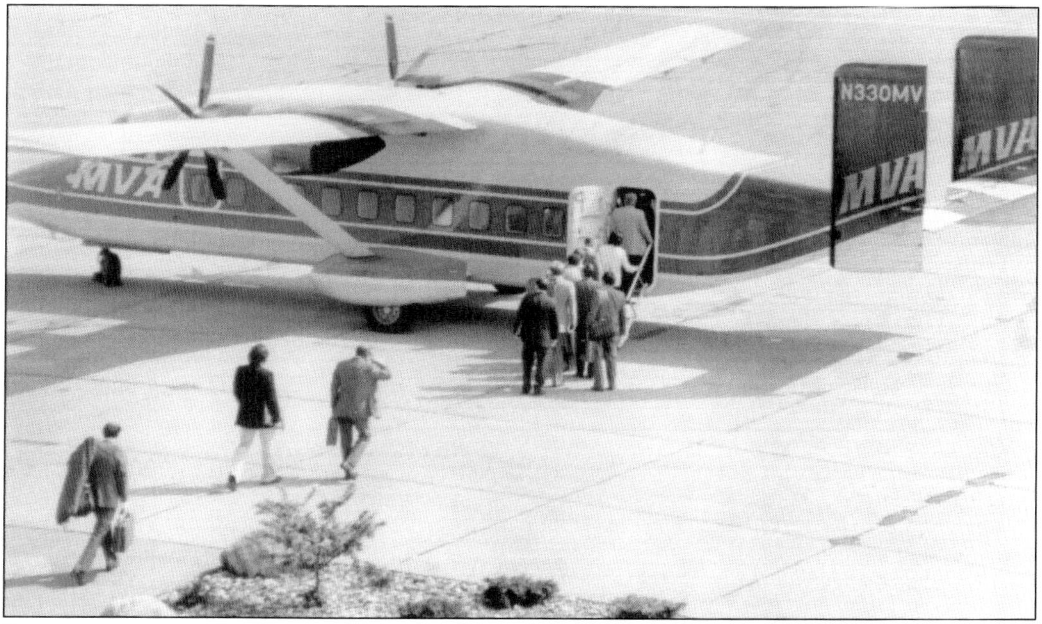

Passengers are seen boarding a Mississippi Valley Airlines (MVA) Short 330 at Moline. The regional airline was originally based in LaCrosse, Wisconsin. It began serving Quad City Airport in spring 1980 and moved its headquarters, maintenance base, and reservations center to Moline in 1982. MVA connected many smaller cities to several larger airline hubs. Chicago and Minneapolis were the two main destinations out of Moline. (Courtesy of QCIA.)

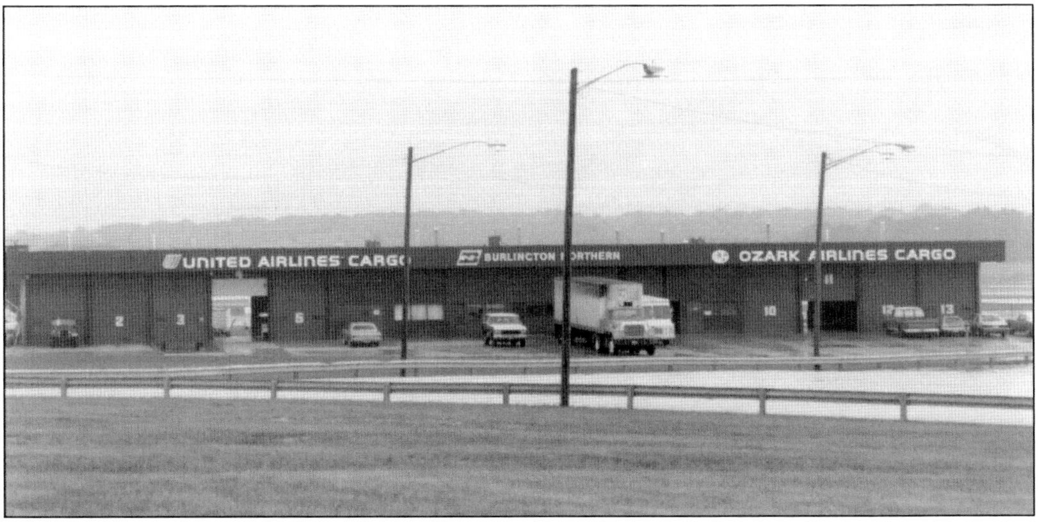

By the mid-1980s, cargo had become big business for airlines, and space in the small cargo facility at the west end of the terminal was no longer sufficient. This new cargo facility was built in 1991 to accommodate the needs of airlines and airfreight operators. The burgeoning freight business into and out of the Quad Cities would attract additional freight carriers in the early 1990s. (Courtesy of QCIA.)

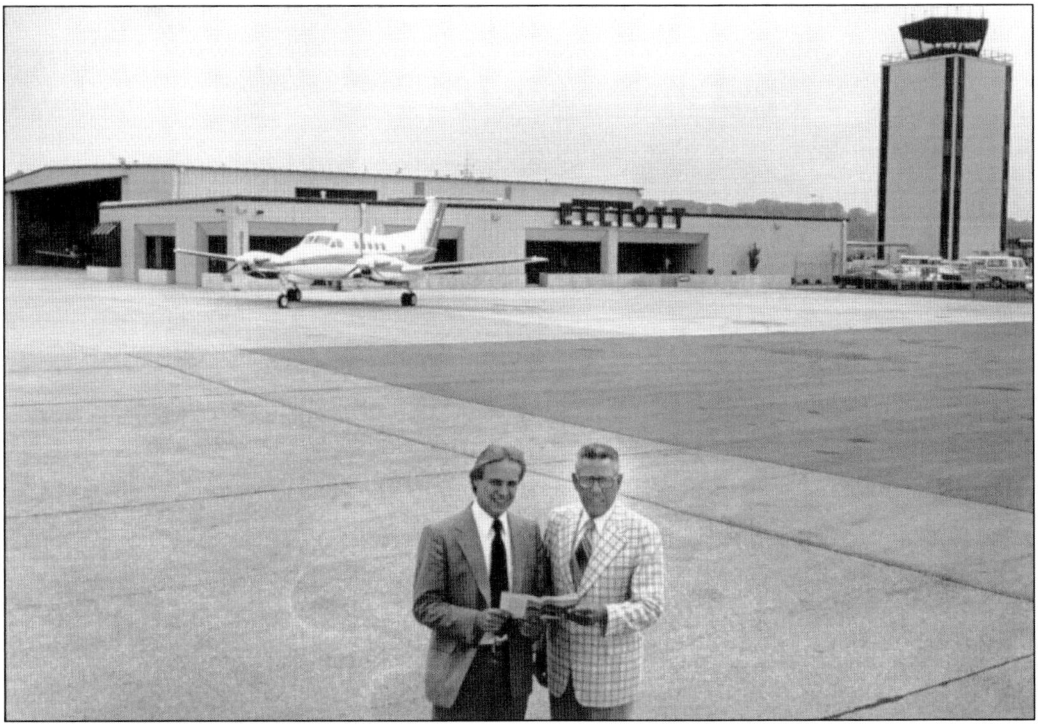

Founder Herb Elliott (right) and son Wynn pose in front of Elliott Aviation's new corporate headquarters and service center, completed in 1982. In business since 1936 and based at Quad City Airport since 1961, Elliott Aviation markets Beech aircraft and services all makes of private and business planes. The firm also provides custom interior design, avionics installations and modifications, noise reduction installations, and aircraft painting. (Courtesy of QCIA.)

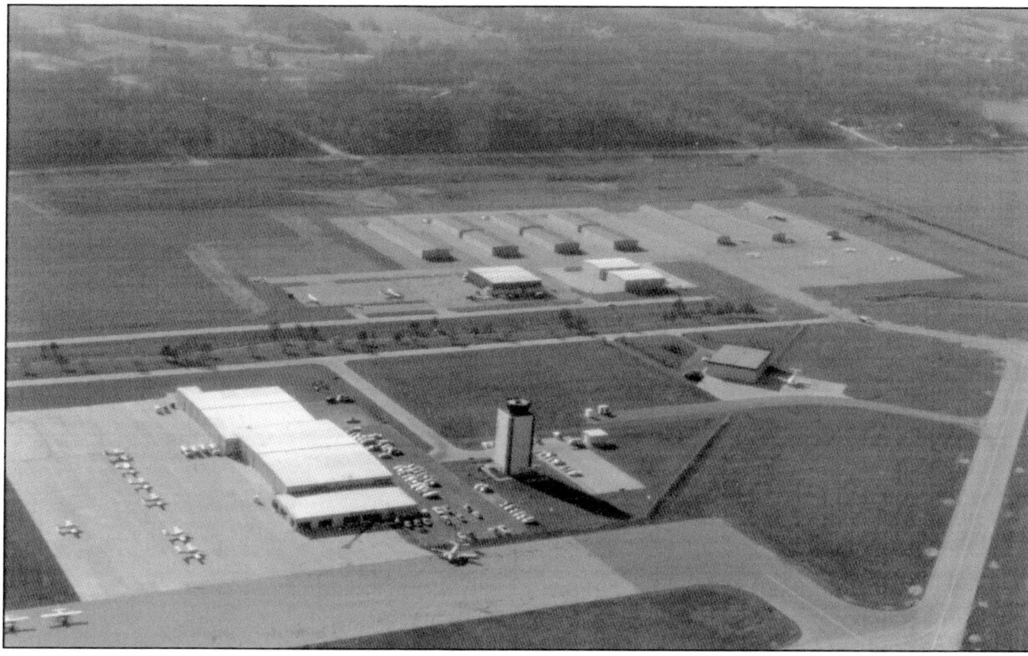

This 1982 photograph shows the growing development of the general aviation facilities on the southwest side of the field. Corporate hangars and US Army aviation facilities are seen in the center, and private T-hangars are in the upper center and right of this photograph. The newly completed Elliott Aviation is seen to the left of the tower. (Courtesy of QCIA.)

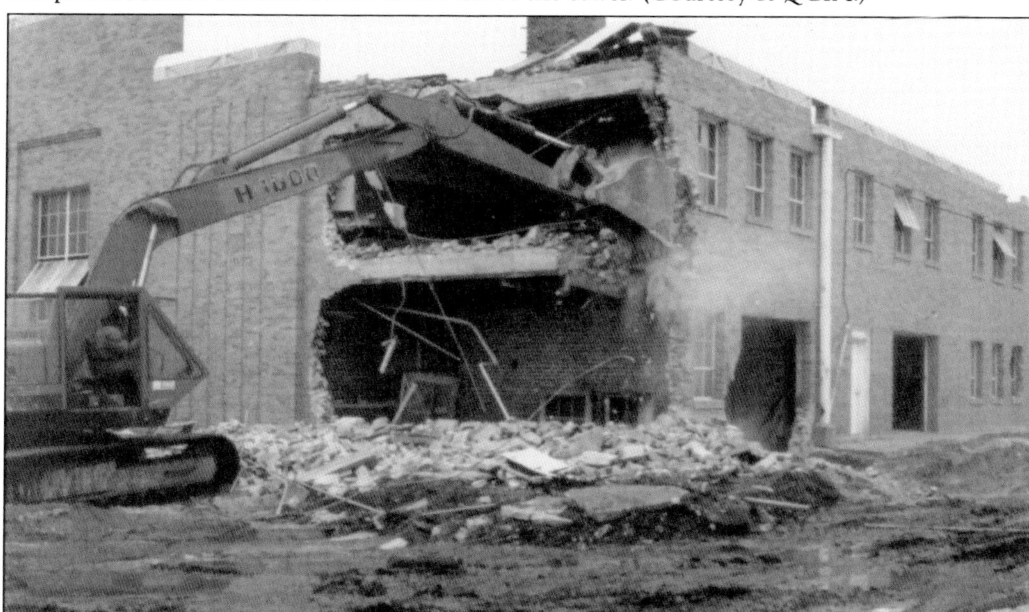

In March 1982, with the move of all general aviation facilities to the south side of the field having been completed, the old 1939 hangar-terminal building was demolished. Aeroline Flight Service and Deere and Company had used that building for many years after the 1954 terminal was built. However, it now stood in the way of the proposed new terminal building, ramp space, and access road. (Courtesy of QCIA.)

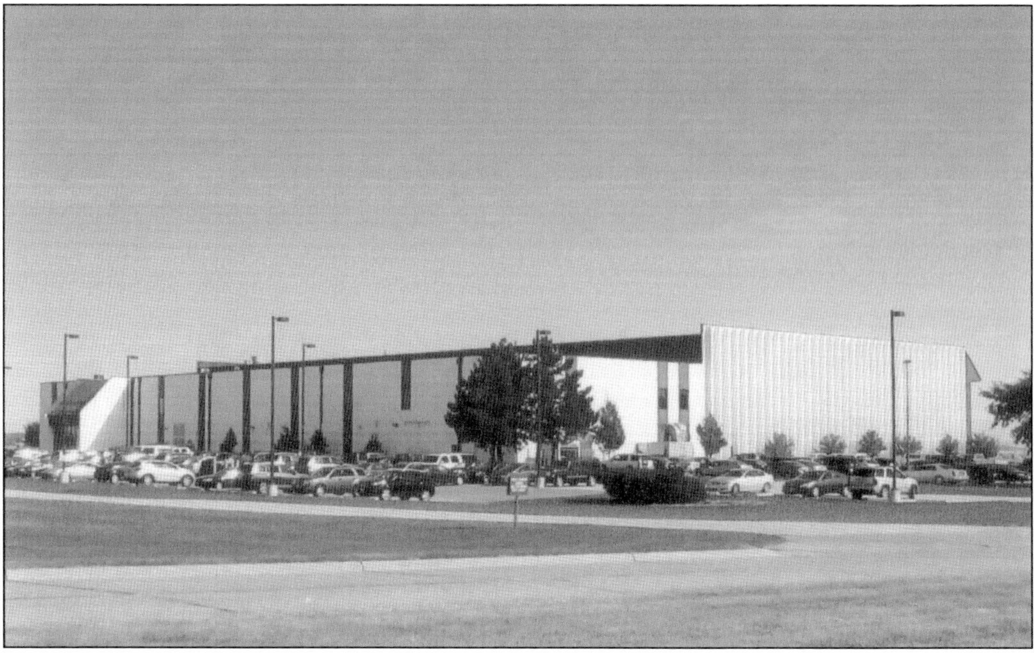

Formerly headquartered in LaCrosse, Wisconsin, Mississippi Valley Airlines (MVA) moved its corporate offices, reservations center, and maintenance base into this building at Quad City Airport. With the merger of MVA into Air Wisconsin Airlines, corporate operations moved to Appleton, Wisconsin. This facility became the maintenance base for all of Air Wisconsin's Fokker turboprop aircraft until the airline phased them out. Today, Deere and Company uses the building as a testing laboratory.

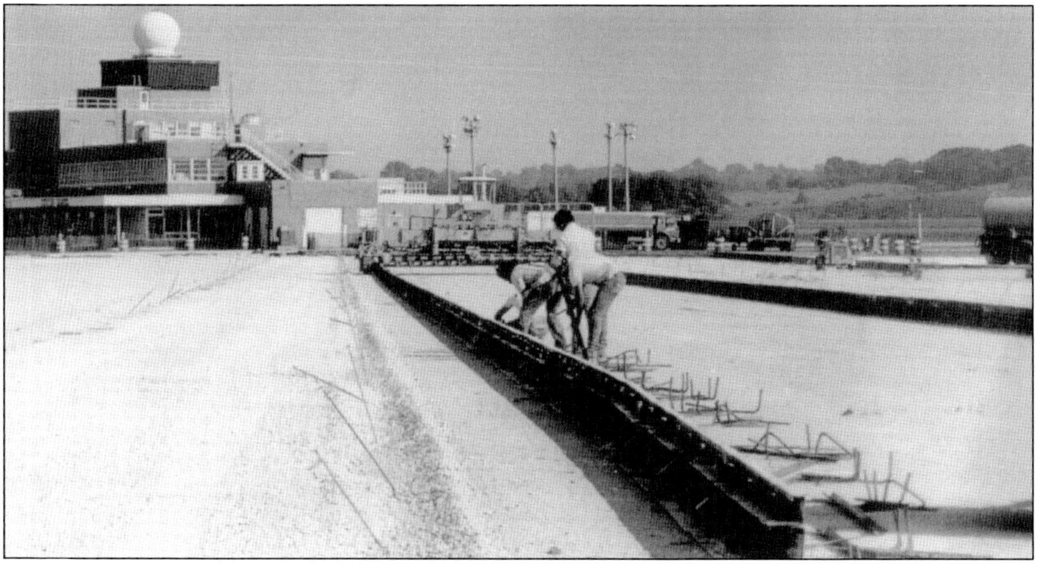

As part of the new terminal construction in 1983, a considerable amount of new concrete for aircraft parking ramps was needed. This photograph provides a good look at the compacted gravel subgrade that will support the thick concrete slabs. Workers are placing steel bars along the paving forms. These bars will tie each section of concrete together with the adjacent sections. (Courtesy of QCIA.)

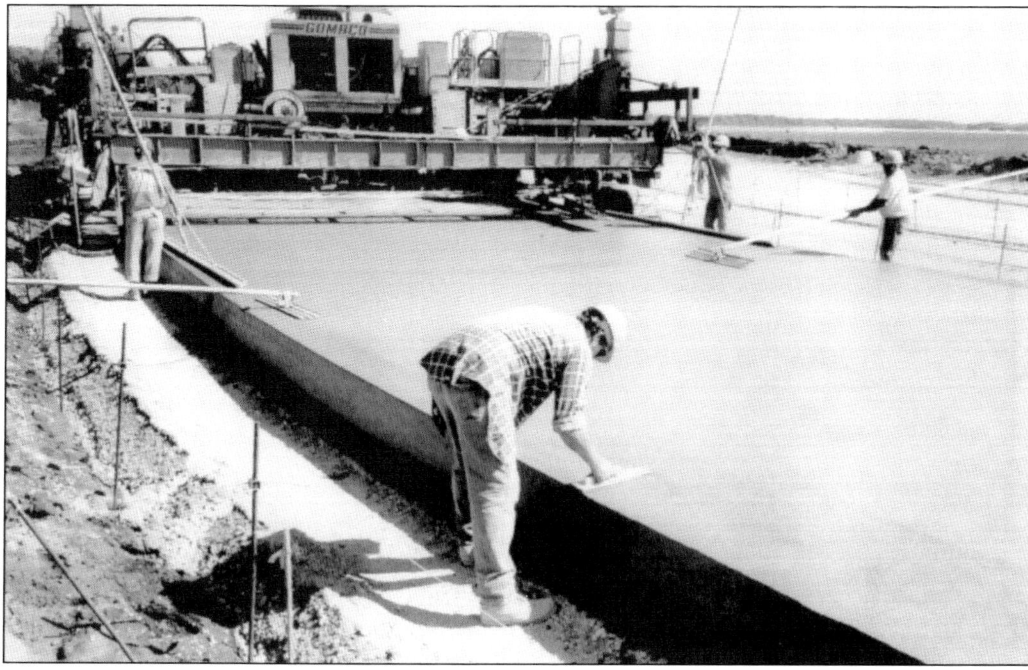

This photograph from a 1980s construction project shows just how thick runways must be to withstand the weight and punishment of landing and departing jet airliners. Working behind a slip-form paving machine, crews are finishing the 18-inch thick concrete surface of the new runway addition. Depending on the soil underneath the runway, there may be another 12 to 15 inches of crushed rock base beneath the concrete. (Courtesy of QCIA.)

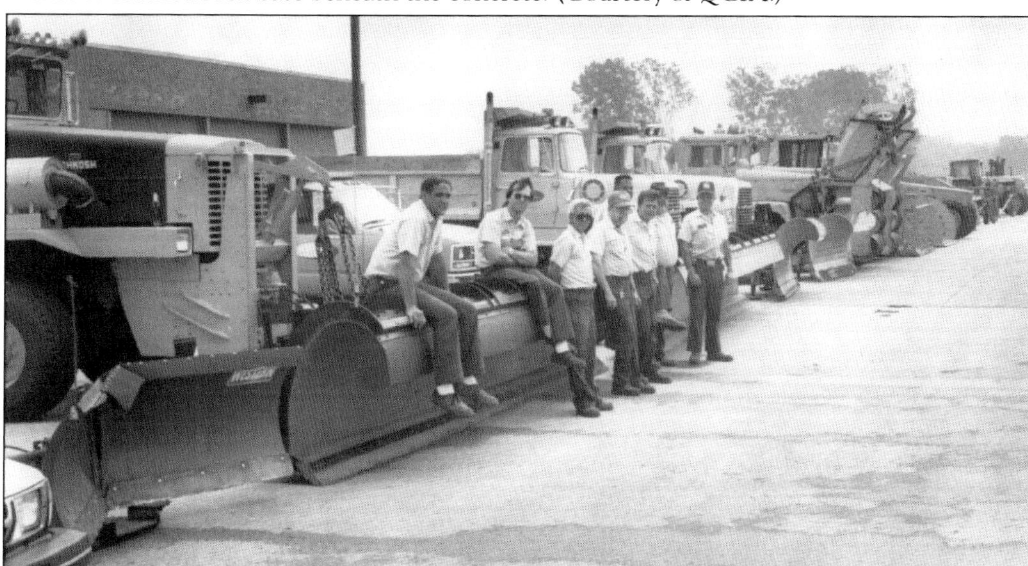

It takes a lot of equipment, large and small, to take care of the airport's 2,200 acres of real estate. In addition to snow removal equipment, the airport authority airfield maintenance department has a roster of trucks, tractors, and mowers to keep the grounds of the airport well groomed. These men, many of them longtime employees, pose for a group picture with the machines of their trade. (Courtesy of QCIA.)

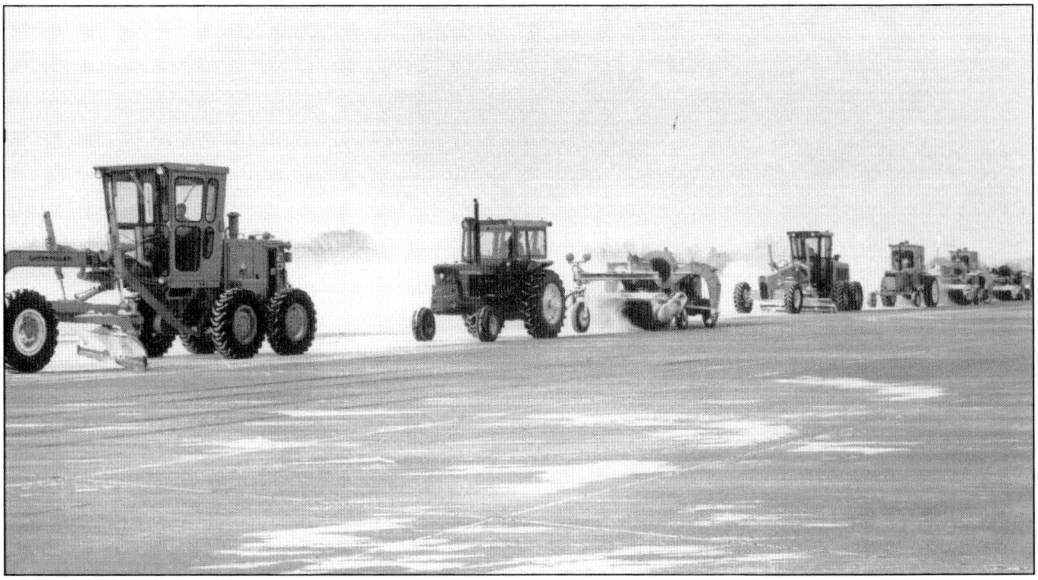

Snow removal is a big operation at Quad City Airport. Runways alone are equivalent to nearly 26 miles of city streets. And there are also taxiways, ramps, service roads, parking lots, and sidewalks. Graders, brooms, and self-propelled snowblowers form a line to clear snow. For deicing, special melting solutions are applied instead of salt, as salt is corrosive and cannot be used anywhere aircraft may travel. (Courtesy of QCIA.)

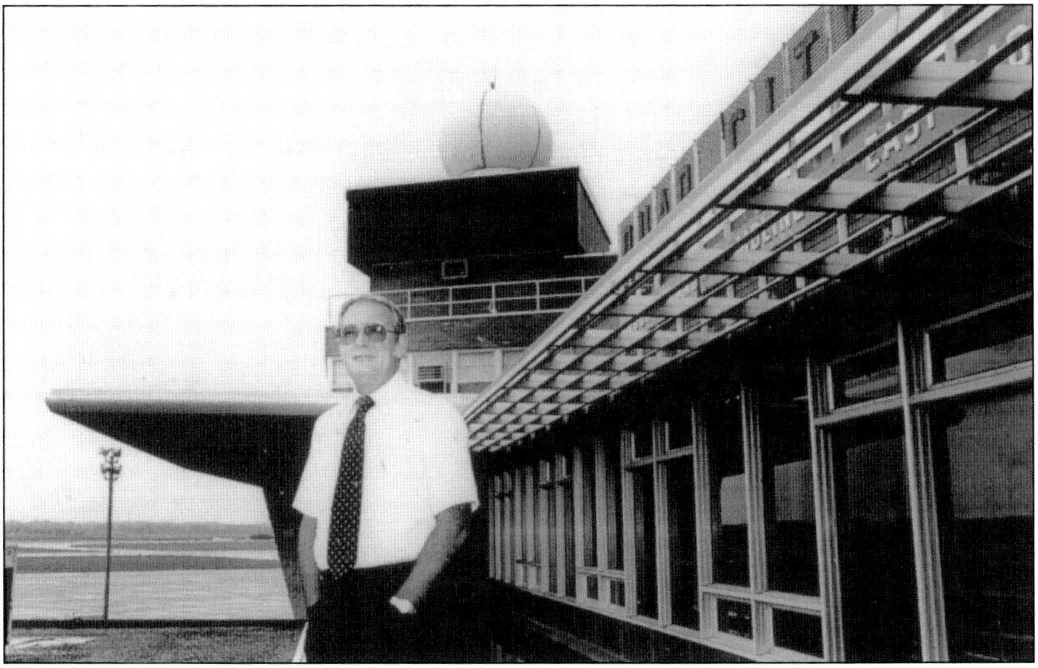

Moline native George Kirk was manager of the Quad City Airport from 1954 until 1983. He was a Navy fighter pilot and the recipient of two Distinguished Flying Crosses during World War II. Over his years as manager, he received national recognition for his management achievements in aviation. Much of the initial growth and improvement at the Quad City Airport were during Kirk's tenure. (Courtesy of QCIA.)

Four

Quad City International Airport 1985–Present

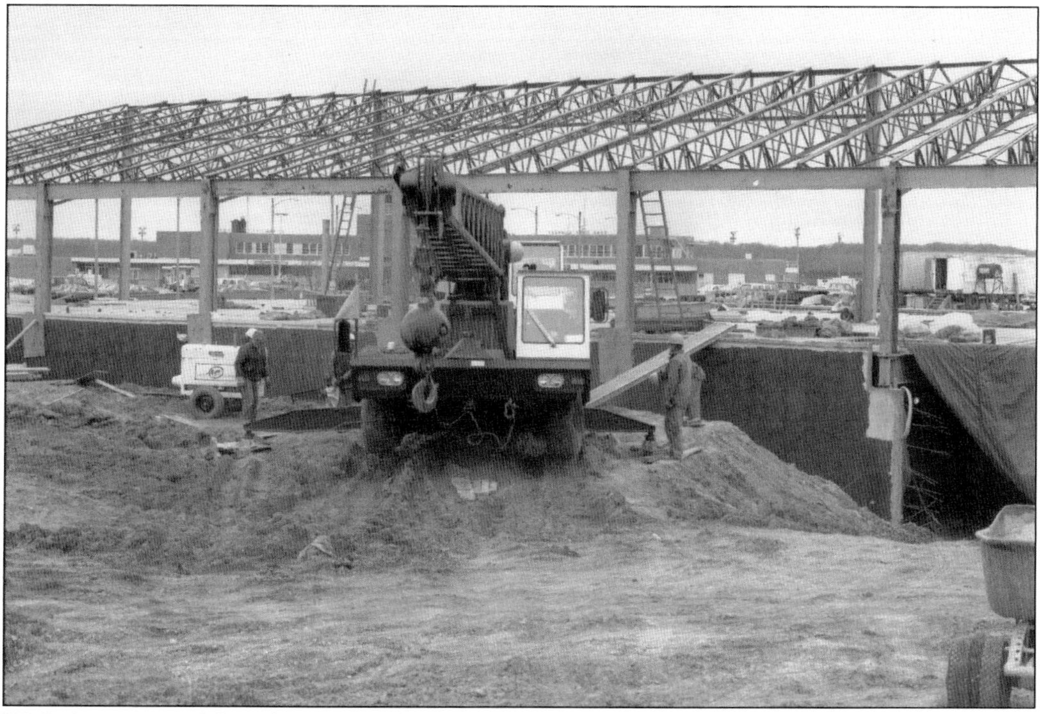

With footings and foundations in place, steelwork was being erected for the new $5.3 million terminal. Plans for the terminal were completed in 1983, and its construction was the last major project of a modernization plan that was begun in 1972. The plan's mission was to keep Quad City Airport as one of the best assets to attract business and bring vitality to the community. (Courtesy of QCIA.)

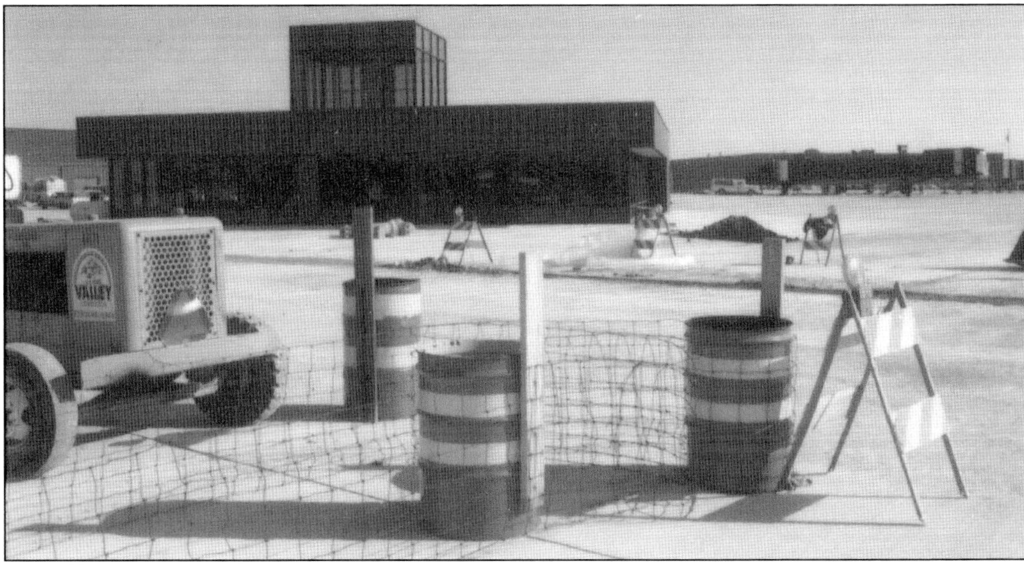

Construction on the 1985 terminal building is nearing completion. Pictured is the passenger lounge for the commuter concourse. The small tower seen atop the lounge will be used by Air Wisconsin for load-planning operations. With several flights departing for the same destination within a short time of one another, planners could decide how to distribute cargo and baggage based on weight-and-balance and passenger-load factors. (Courtesy of QCIA.)

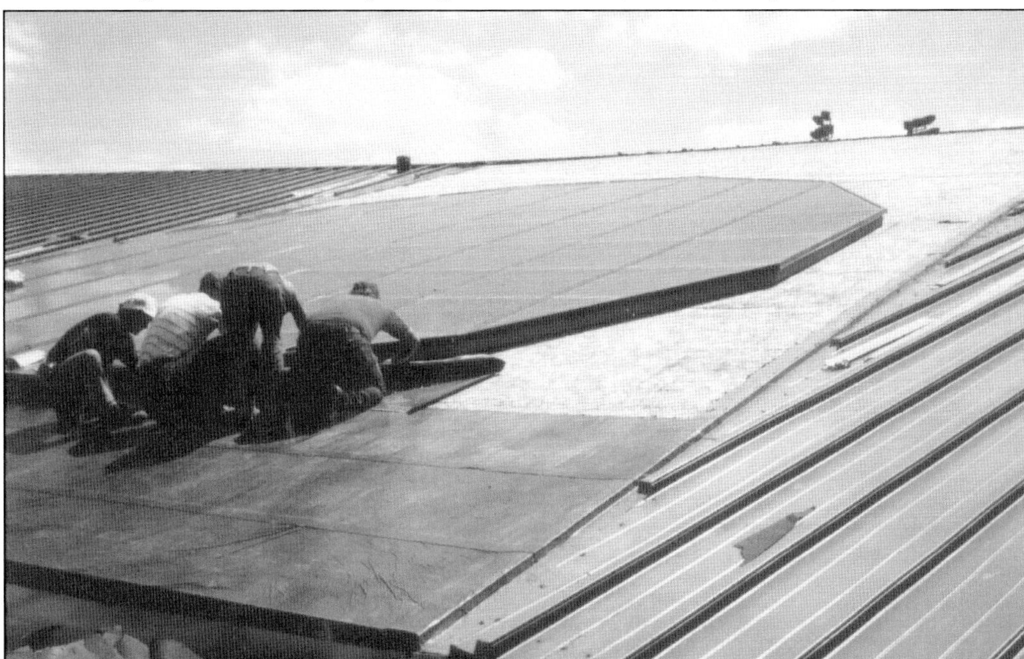

Workers apply roofing materials and flashing around the skylight above the central axis point of the new terminal. From this center point, airline ticketing counters stretched to the west; baggage claim, restaurant, and rental car counters extended to the east; and a public waiting lounge and passenger gates spread out to the south. Designers felt the design's openness, enhanced by the skylight, would be a fitting symbol for air travel. (Courtesy of QCIA.)

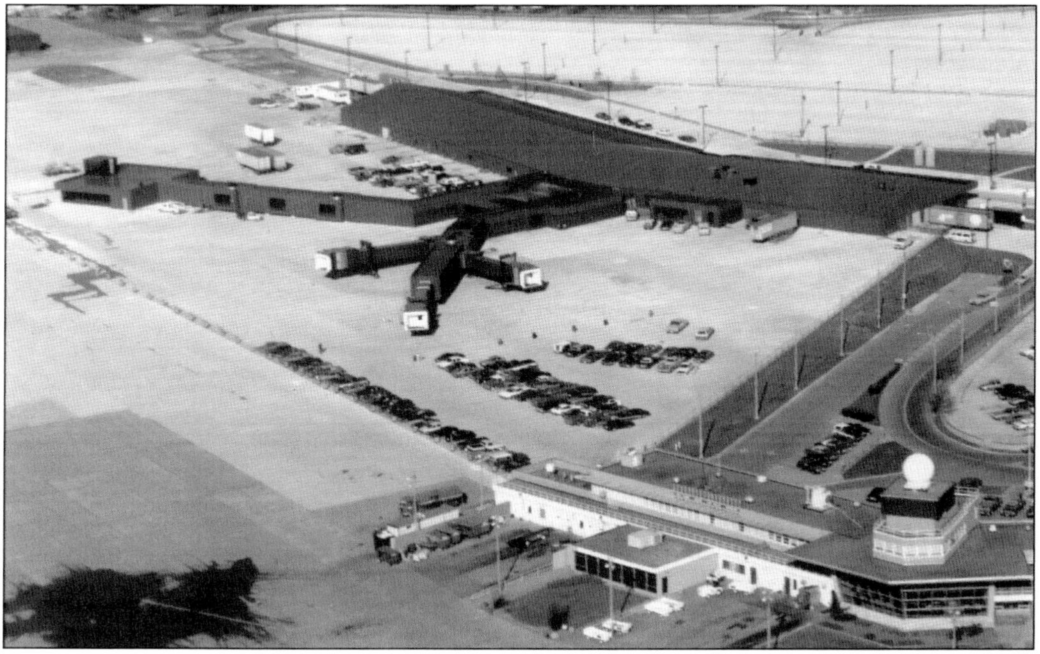

An aerial photograph shows the new terminal just prior to completion and nearly ready for use. The new entrance road and parking lot can also be seen. In the lower portion of this view, the passenger lounge at the 1954 terminal can clearly be seen. At the top right of the photograph, just beyond the parking lot, is the rental car fueling and make-ready building. (Courtesy of QCIA.)

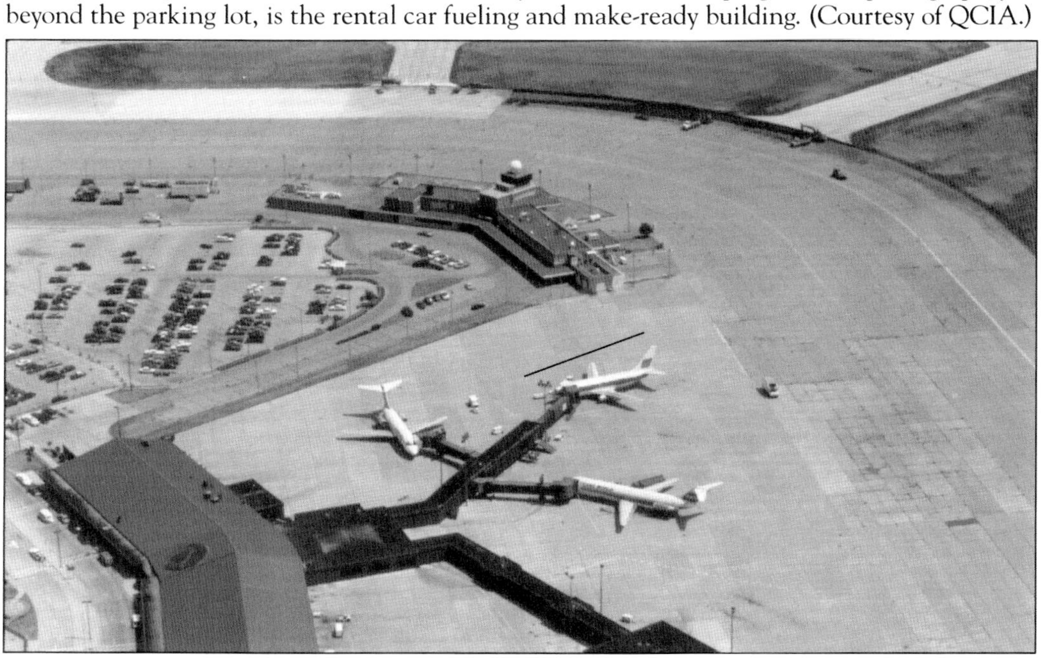

This 1985 photograph illustrates the newly opened terminal in relation to the 1954 terminal. It also happened to capture Republic (left), United (center), and TWA jets at their respective gates. There was still parking along the old terminal drive, and this was a great spot to shoot ground action photographs or watch the Republic jet perform a 270-degree turn to enable it to begin its taxi to the runway. (Courtesy of QCIA.)

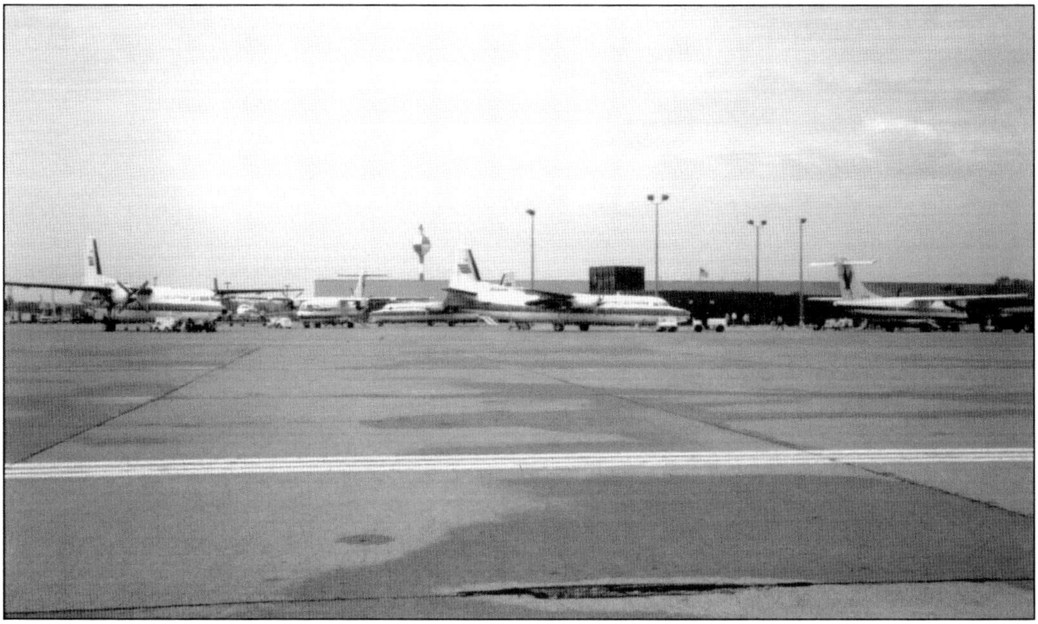

The commuter airline ramp at the west end of the terminal was a busy place in the late 1980s. Three Air Wisconsin Fokkers, two American Eagle ATRs, and an unidentified commuter can be seen parked at their gate positions. Most of the commuters, now referred to as regional carriers, had code-sharing agreements with the major airlines and offered additional flights to their airline partners' major hub cities. (Courtesy of QCIA.)

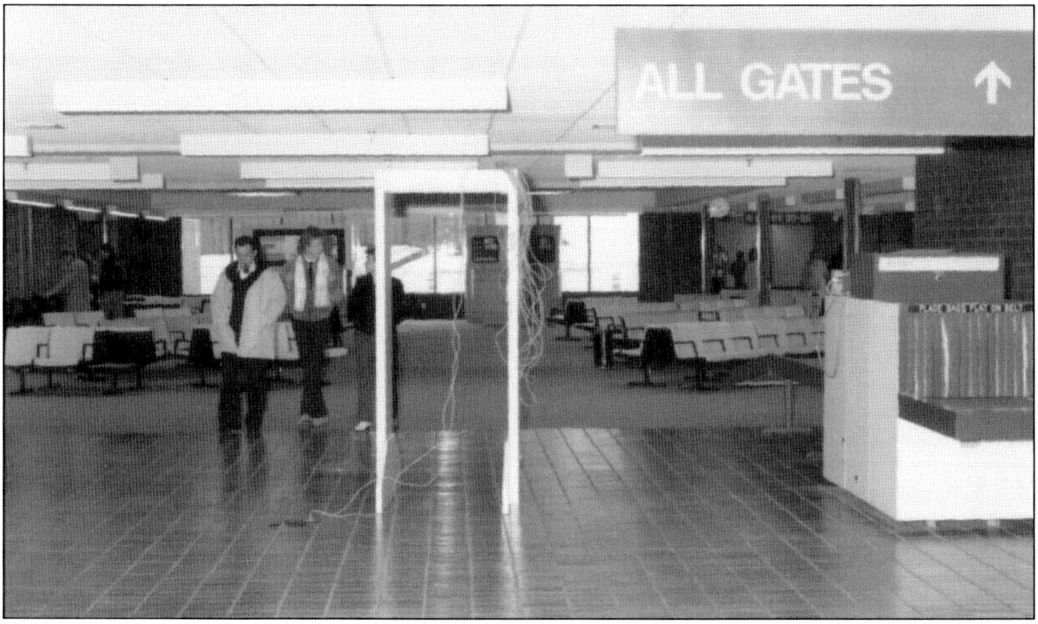

This undated photograph shows the main waiting area for passenger arrivals in the new terminal. Entrance to the boarding lounge for jet aircraft was at the back left corner, and the commuter concourse entrance can be seen at the back right. The photograph must have been taken in the later 1990s, as x-ray and magnetometer security equipment was beginning to be put into service. (Courtesy of QCIA.)

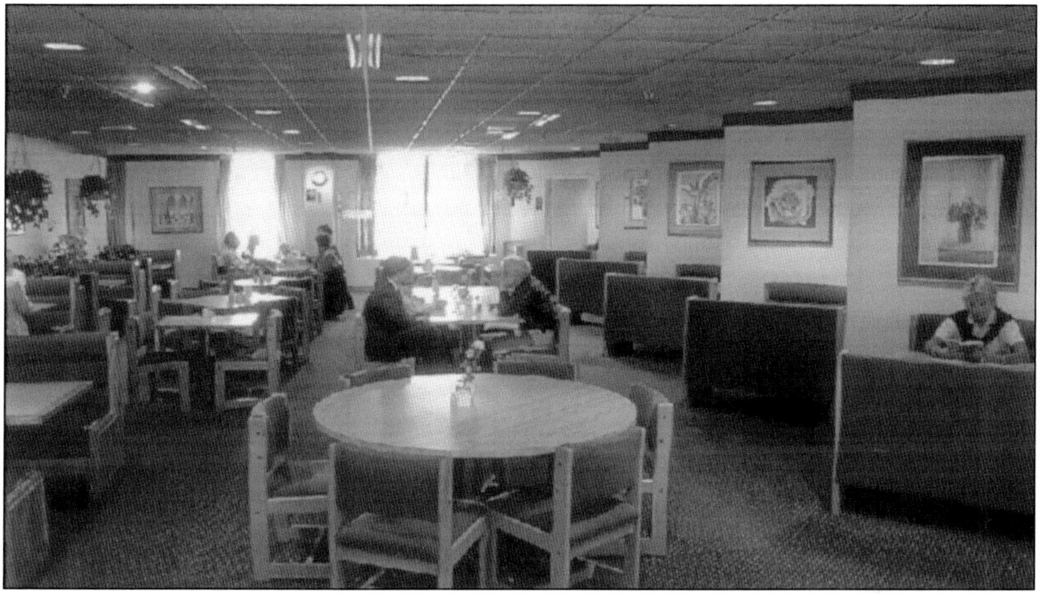

The Airport Inn restaurant in the old terminal was a popular spot to eat, especially on a Sunday. Patrons had no trouble waiting for a table, as they could always watch the airplanes come and go. But over time, the Airport Inn's decor could best be described as "coffee shop." The restaurant in the 1985 terminal offered a modern look and good food for hungry patrons before their flights. (Courtesy of QCIA.)

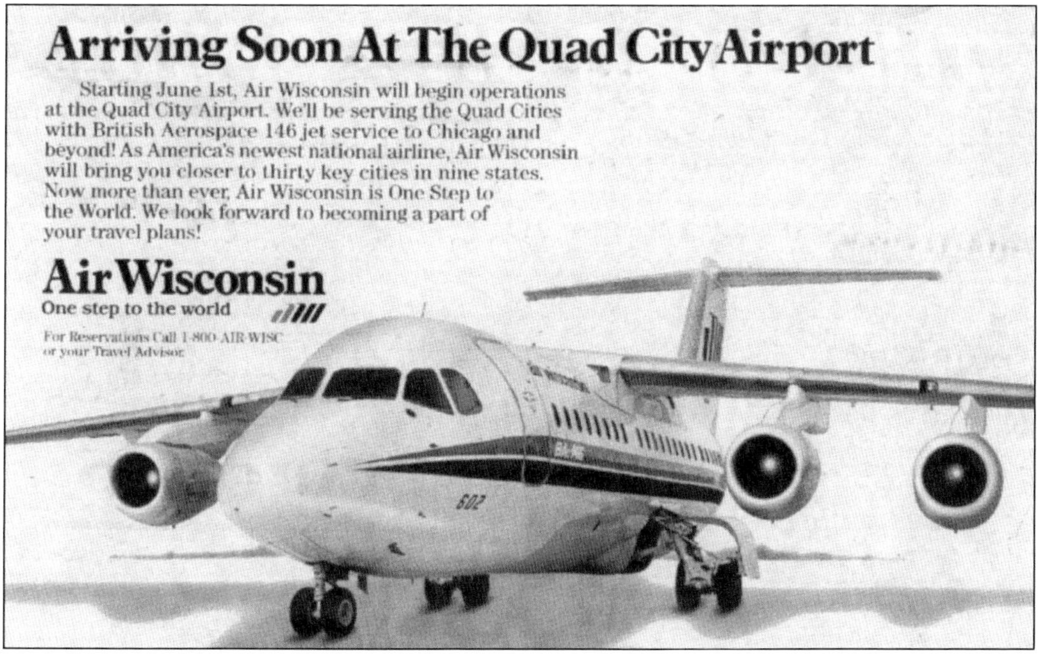

Mississippi Valley Airlines merged with Air Wisconsin in early 1985. This advertisement noted the new airline, new logo, and new aircraft type that would be serving Quad City Airport. The British Aerospace 146-100 jet carried 82 passengers and was noted for its quiet operation. Air Wisconsin also used Fokker F-27 turboprop aircraft at Moline. United Airlines partnered with them to create United Express and even owned Air Wisconsin for several years.

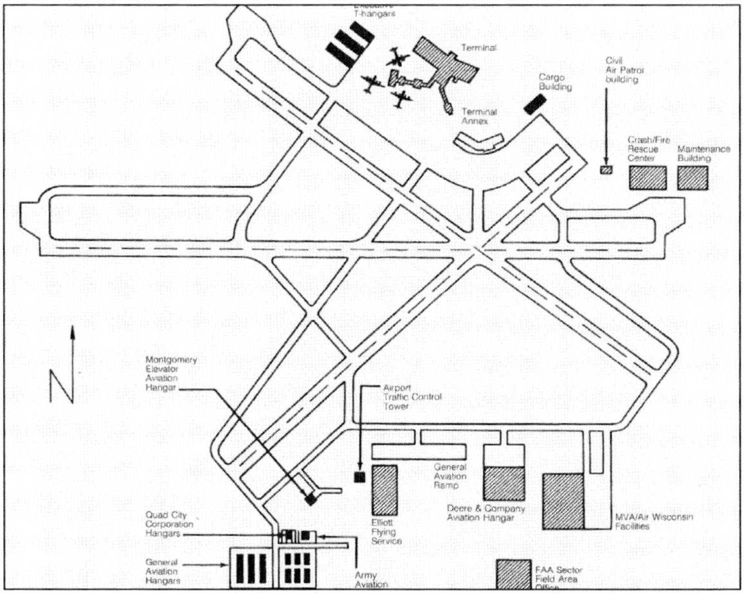

This diagram, from about 1990, illustrates the Quad City Airport layout. The graphic was used in a handout to showcase the businesses that were part of the expanded airport complex. Later, the executive hangars west of the terminal were moved to the south side of the field, the east-west runway was extended to the east, and new air cargo facilities were built farther to the east. (Courtesy of QCIA.)

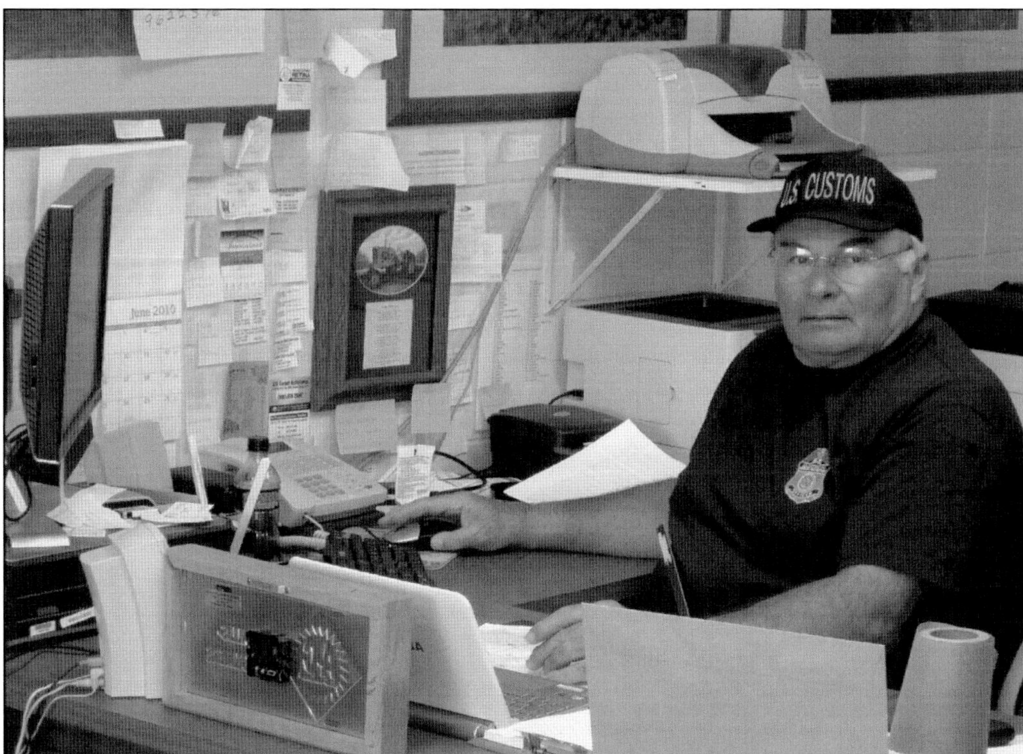

The Quad Cities was granted US Customs port-of-entry status in 1986. It allowed companies to save money on imported goods, as duties were levied when the goods arrived in the Quad Cities and not when they entered at a US border. Corporate aircraft arriving from outside US boundaries could also have passengers cleared through customs here. Anthony Howe has been customs officer at the airport since the office was opened.

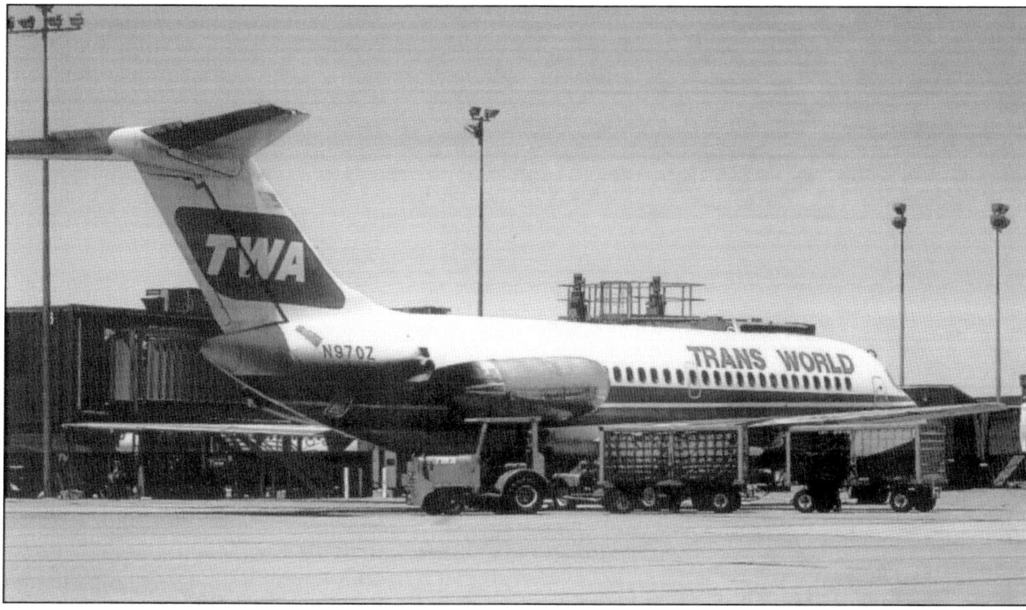

Trans World Airlines (TWA) aircraft began serving Quad City Airport in late 1986, when the airline purchased Ozark. Ozark had flown to Moline since 1950, except for a two-year hiatus to Davenport Municipal Airport. This particular aircraft was a former Ozark jet, as identified by its registration number. When American Airlines took over TWA in 2001, American logos and colors replaced those of TWA at Moline. (Courtesy of QCIA.)

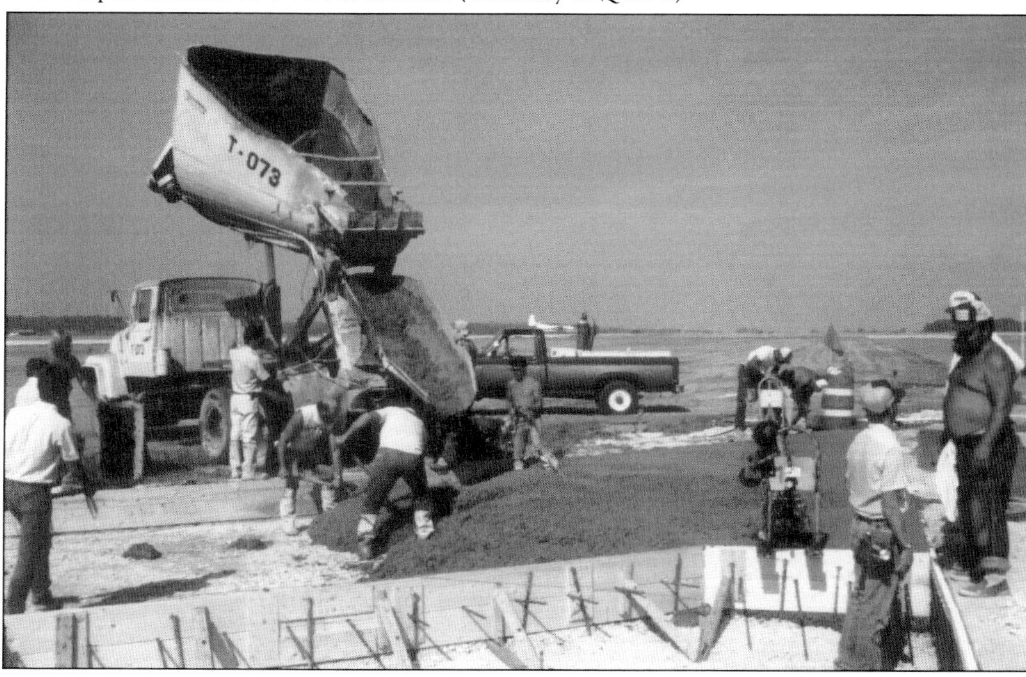

This 1987 photograph shows work on the east end of an east-west runway extension project. Normally a slip-form paving machine would be used, but with all the handwork being done by the crew, it appears they are working on a tie-in to a taxiway. The thickness of the concrete section reflects that it must hold up to the weight of a fully loaded jetliner. (Courtesy of QCIA.)

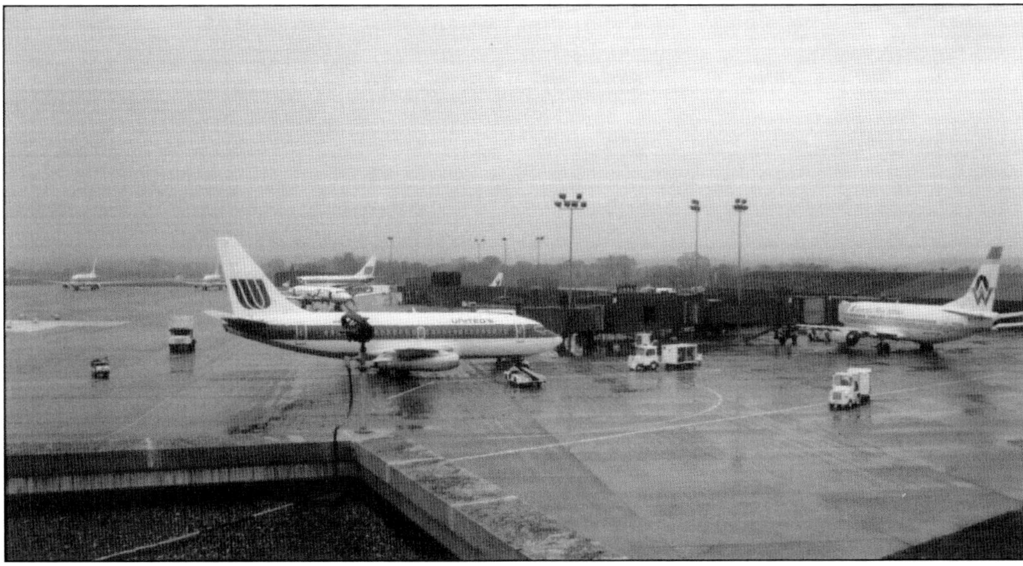

Seven airplanes can be seen on the ramp in this 1988 photograph. Quad City Airport normally did not see this many airliners on the ground at once. The three United jets in the far distance may have used Moline as an alternate airport due to weather. American West Airlines served Moline for several years, beginning in 1983. By 1987, the financially troubled airline had cancelled many of its routes. (Courtesy of QCIA.)

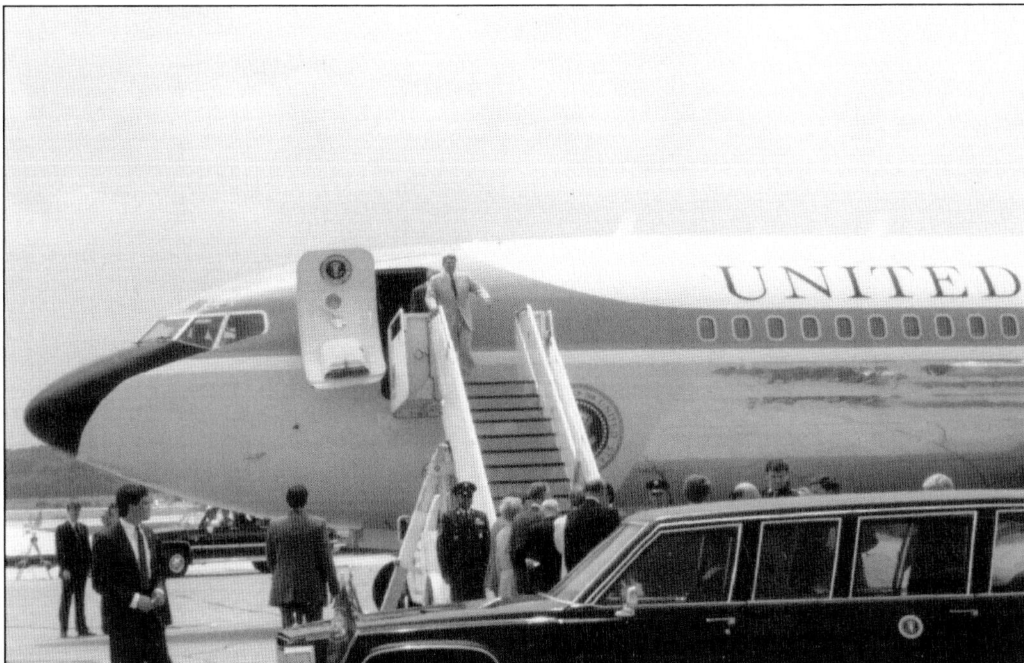

Pres. Ronald Reagan emerges from this version of *Air Force One*, a modified Boeing 707, after landing at Moline in July 1988. Born in Tampico, Illinois, and raised in nearby Dixon, Reagan arrived to celebrate the anniversary and dedicate the new facilities of WOC Radio in Davenport, Iowa. The station gave Reagan his start in broadcasting as an announcer and sportscaster. (Copyright Moline Dispatch Publishing Company, used with permission.)

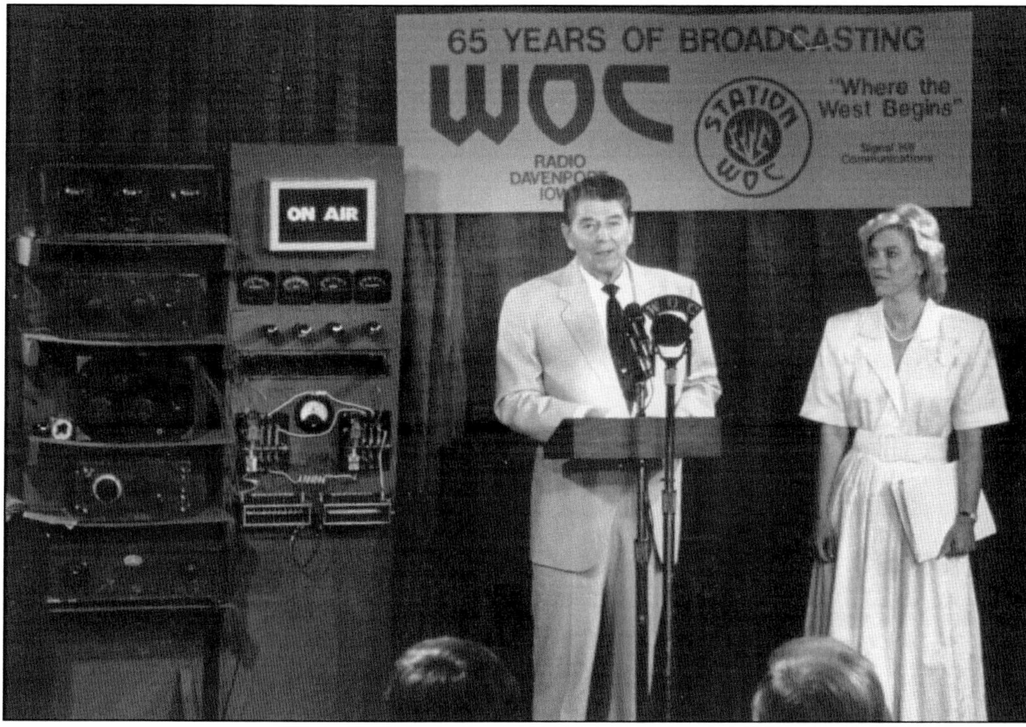

Behind a WOC microphone amid some 1930s-era broadcasting equipment, Pres. Ronald Reagan greets attendees at the dedication of WOC Radio's new studios, as station owner Vickie Palmer looks on. Reagan reminisced about how his broadcasting career was launched in Davenport and recalled, with great detail, his coworkers, where he lived, his on-air bloopers, and even the girls he dated. (Copyright Moline Dispatch Publishing Company, used with permission.)

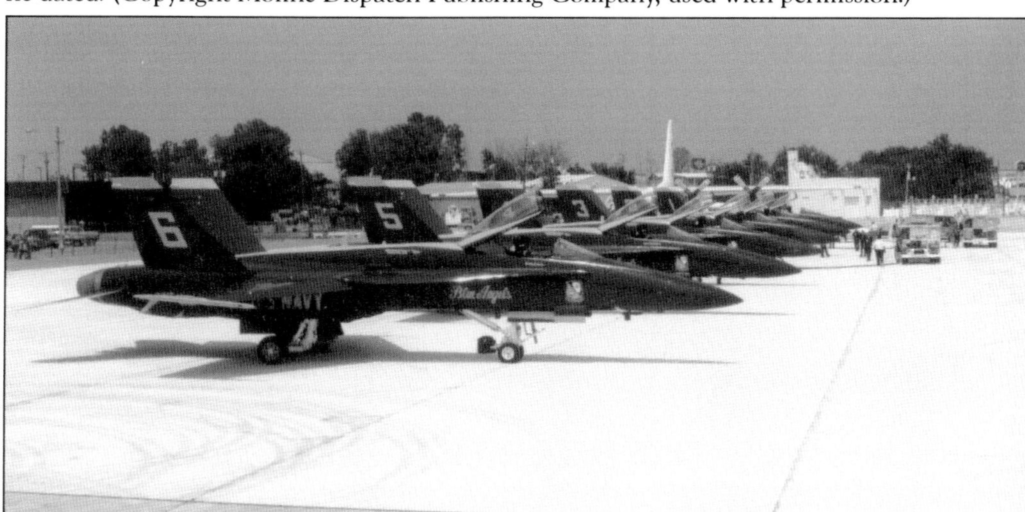

Since 1987, Davenport Airport has been the home to the Quad City Air Show. Airline schedules have made the logistics of a complete air show at Moline impossible. However, due to all the activities on the Davenport field, military demonstration teams like the Navy's Blue Angels operate from Moline. The precision preparation for takeoff by the Blue Angels' ground crew is quite a show in itself. (Courtesy of QCIA.)

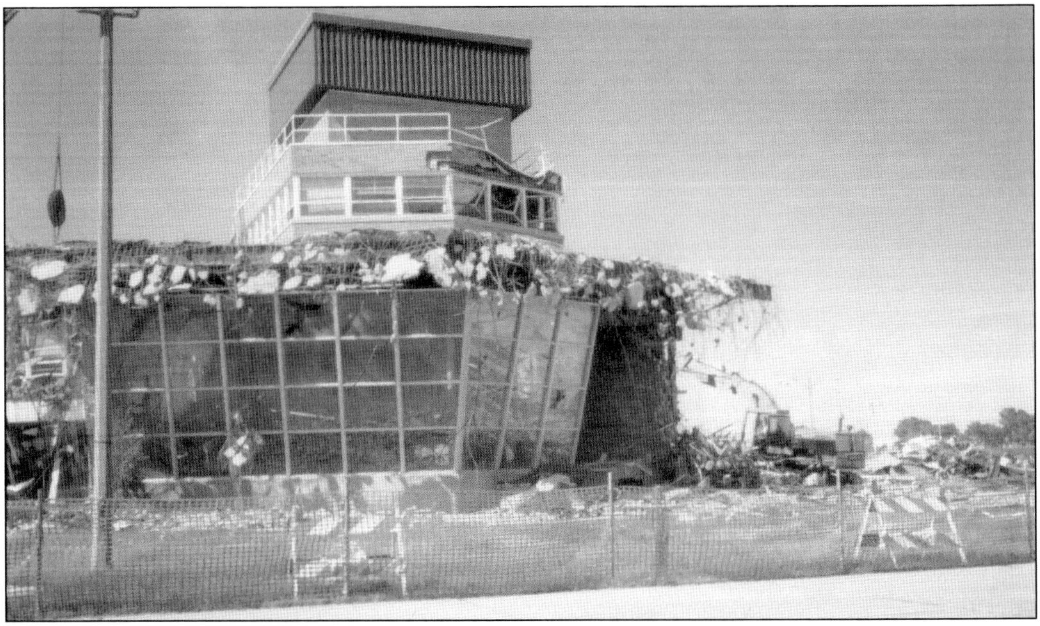

In the early 1990s, funds were obtained to build a new airfreight facility and to demolish the old 1954 terminal building. While the airport had a beautiful, modern terminal to serve the airlines and passengers, no doubt the demolition of the old terminal proved nostalgic to many. This photograph shows the central observation section coming down. One has to wonder how many thousands viewed airport action from that vantage point. (Courtesy of QCIA.)

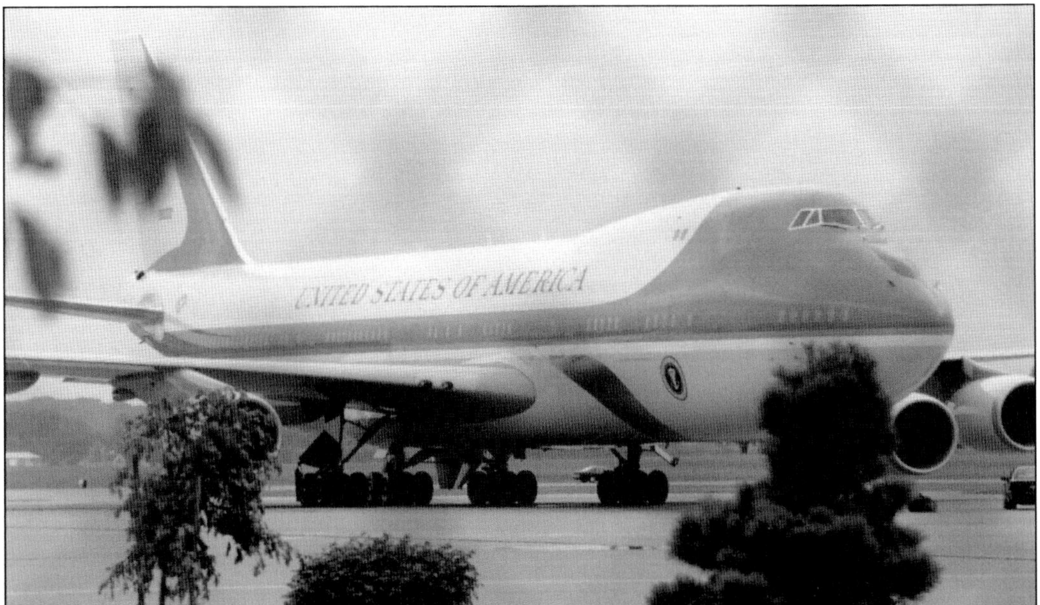

Air Force One taxis to its parking position and brings Pres. Bill Clinton to the Quad Cities to view the Mississippi River flooding of 1993. Pres. Ronald Reagan commissioned two identical versions of the Boeing B-747 in 1985. Delivered while Pres. George H.W. Bush was in office, the presidential transport has made several visits to Moline. Large crowds usually turn out to catch a glimpse of the president and the airplane.

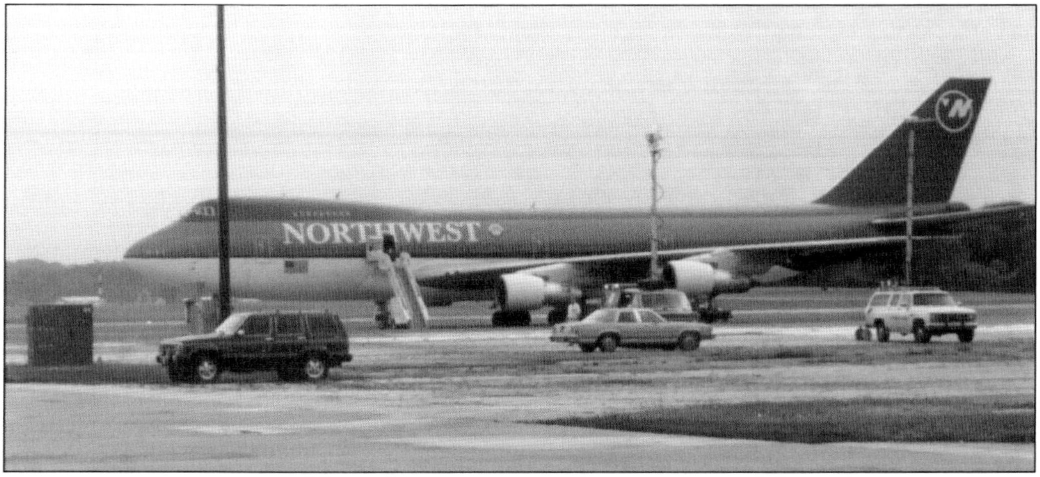

Where the president goes, so goes the press. Some of the major print, broadcast, and wire service reporters travel in *Air Force One*. Yet there were many more reporters and technicians who need to cover a presidential event. Those people travel in a chartered press plane. This Northwest Airlines 747 followed President Clinton into the Quad City Airport on his trip to view the Mississippi River flood damage in 1993.

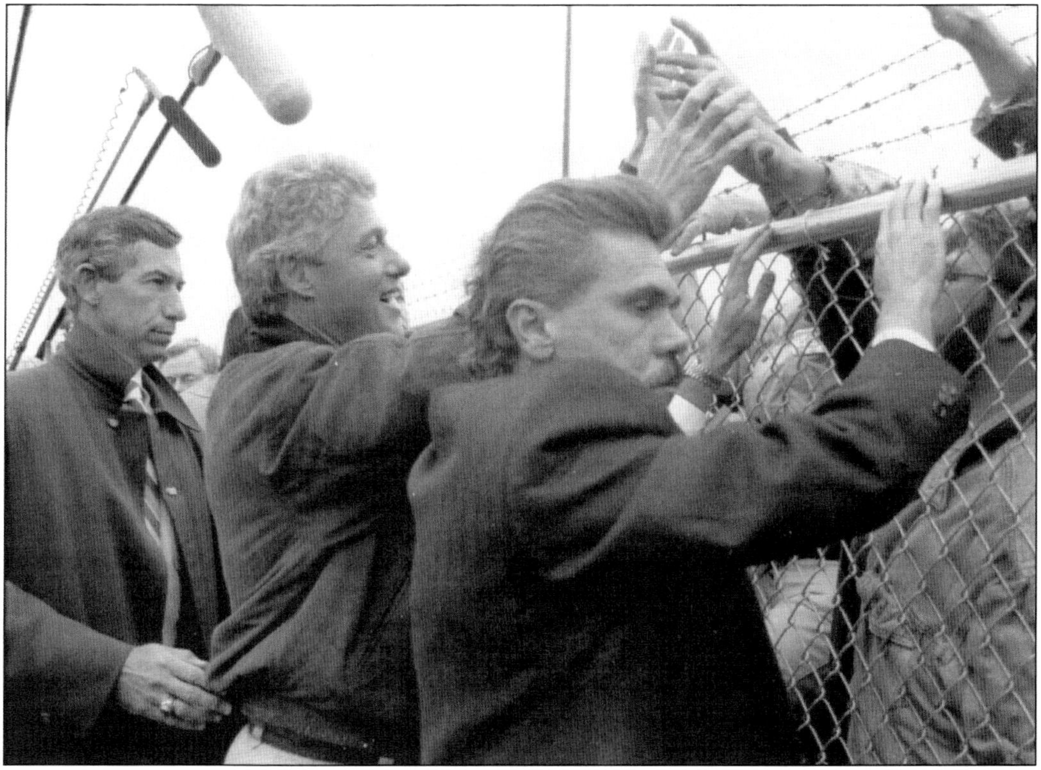

Pres. Bill Clinton (center), flanked by unidentified Secret Service guards, greets spectators to press the flesh while visiting the Quad Cities. Before landing, *Air Force One* and the following press plane made a low, slow flight along the river's path from Clinton to Muscatine, Iowa, enabling the president and the national reporters to see all the inundation and damage firsthand. (Courtesy of Moline Dispatch Publishing Company.)

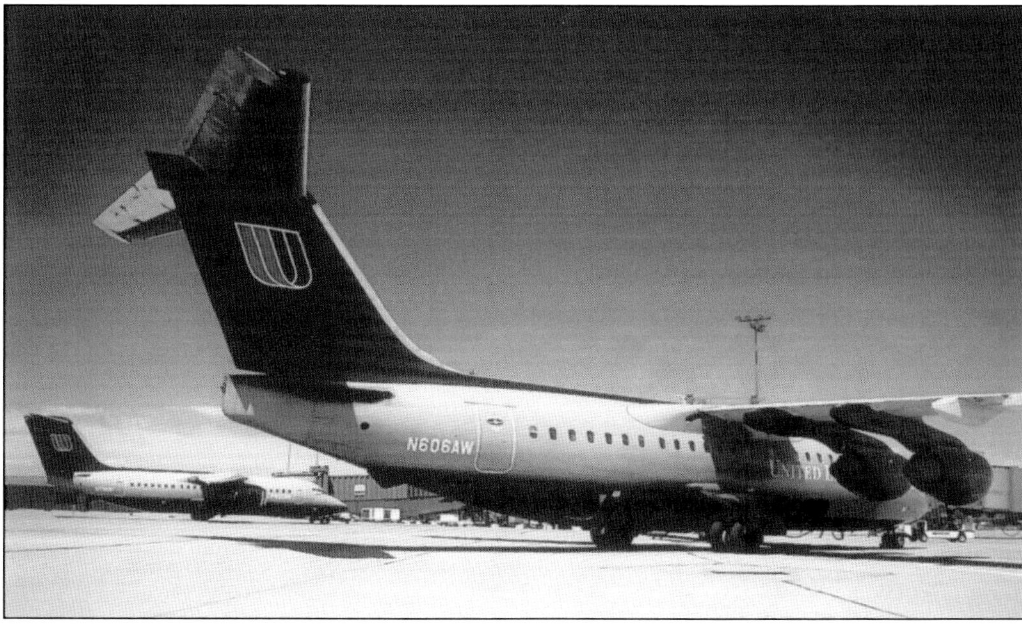

United Airlines partnered with regional carrier Air Wisconsin and rebranded it as United Express. This allowed United the ability to drop some of its flights in smaller markets, but through its partner, still feed passengers to the airline's hub. Planes were painted to match the look of United's mainline aircraft. Two of Air Wisconsin's BA-146 jets were photographed at their gates while they awaited passenger boarding. (Courtesy of QCIA.)

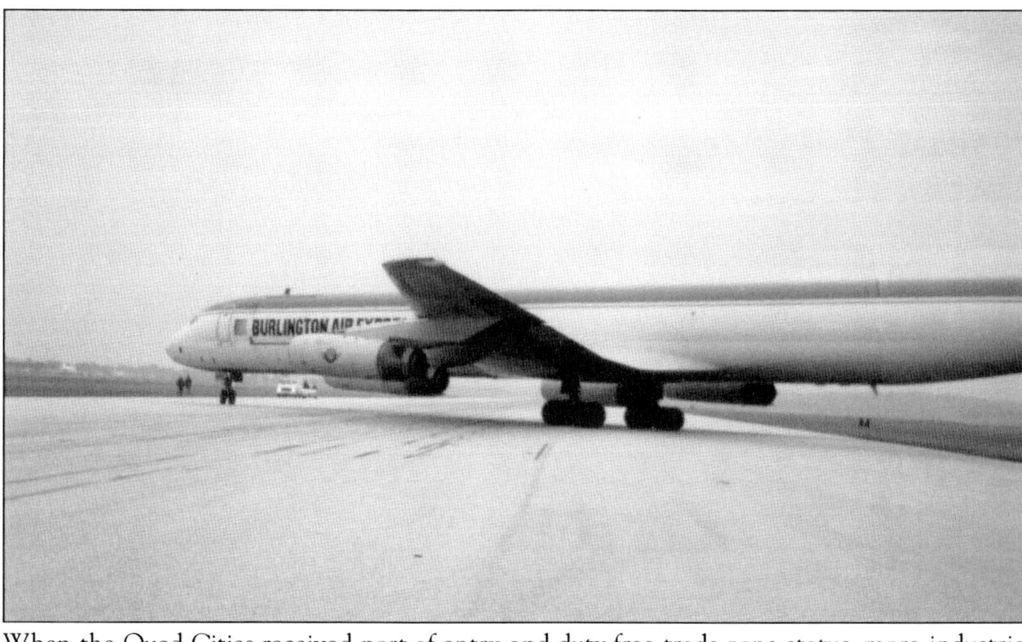

When the Quad Cities received port-of-entry and duty-free trade zone status, more industrial components began arriving and departing through the Quad City Airport. Several all-cargo airlines, including Burlington Air Express, launched service to the area. It was because of this customs status that the airport added the word *international* to its name. In this photograph from 1995, one of Burlington's stretch DC-8s is seen turning onto the runway. (Courtesy of QCIA.)

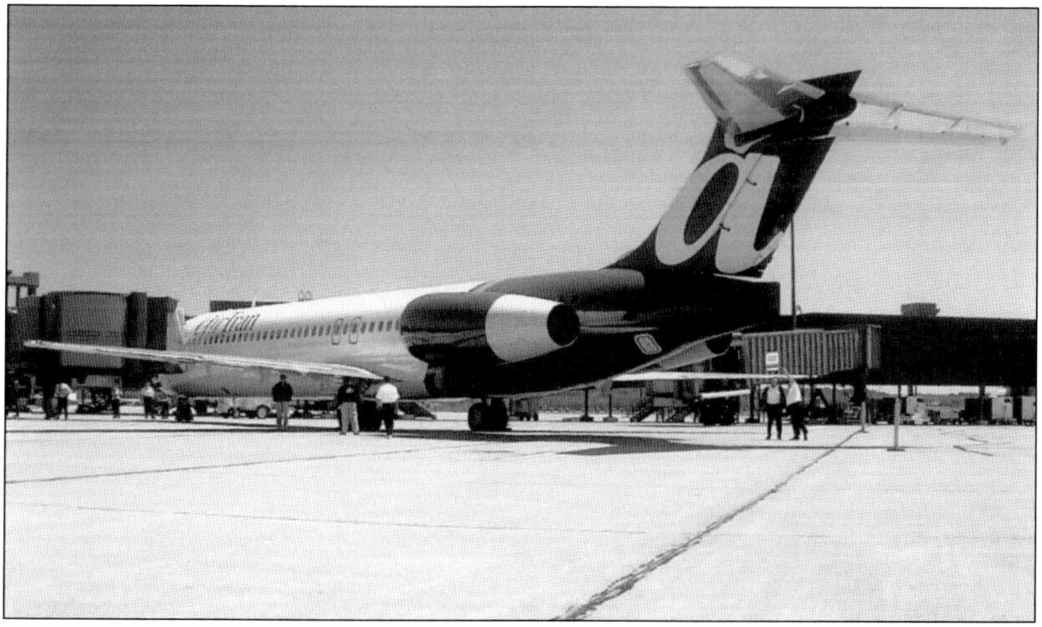

Low-fare airline AirTran Airways entered the Quad City market in 1997, with three flights per day to its Atlanta hub. It soon added flights to Orlando and Las Vegas, although the Las Vegas route was later dropped when fuel prices soared. In this photograph, airport personnel examine the AirTran DC-9 that made a promotional flight to Moline to announce the airline's new service. (Courtesy of QCIA.)

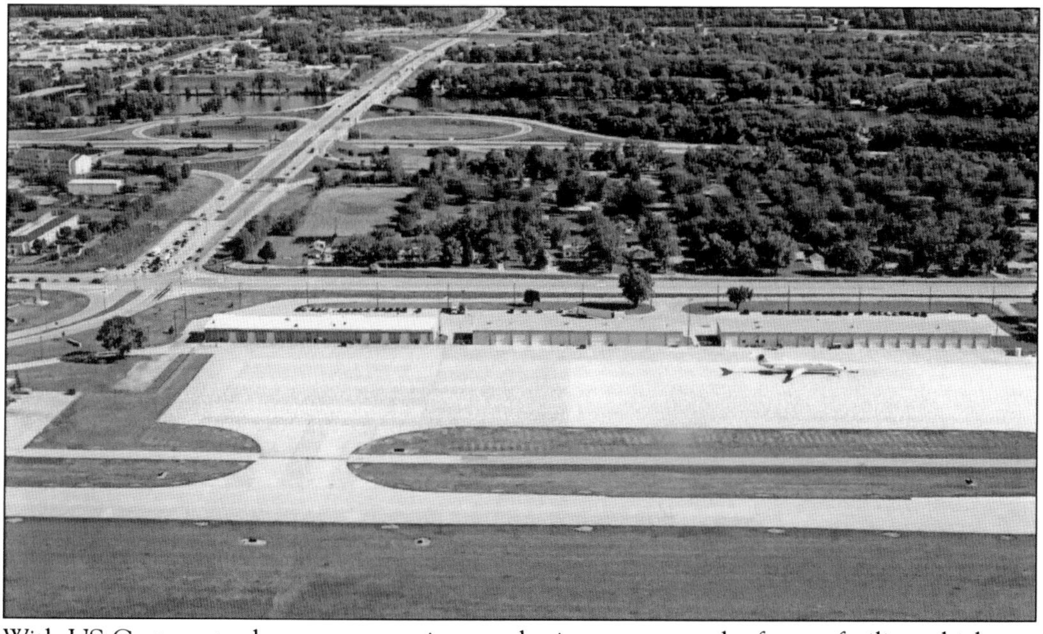

With US Customs trade zone status, air cargo business outgrew the former facility, which was built in 1981. The building on the left in this photograph was erected in 1991, and the structures in the center and on the right were added in 1998, as was the enlarged aircraft apron. The cargo ramp was a busy place until rising fuel prices and consolidations in the cargo airline industry cut operations. (Courtesy of QCIA.)

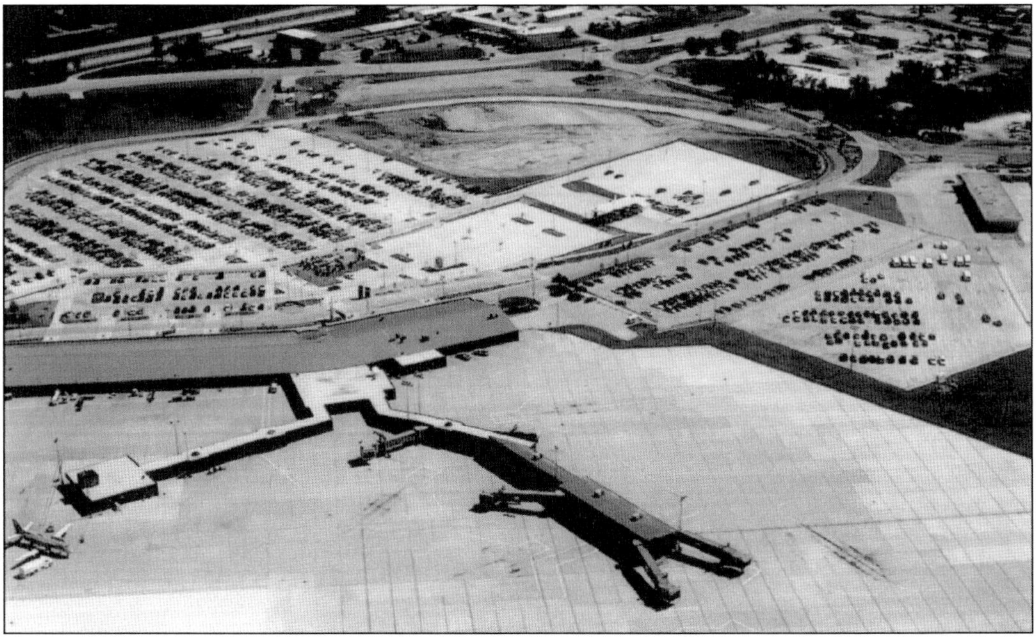

The early 1990s brought another expansion. Concourse A was extended and two additional jetways were installed to handle the increase in airlines and jet service. Additional short- and long-term parking was created as well as new entrance and service roads. Interestingly, the last vestige of Airport Road (Route 92) would disappear with roadway construction just north of the cargo building, seen in the upper right of this photograph. (Courtesy of QCIA.)

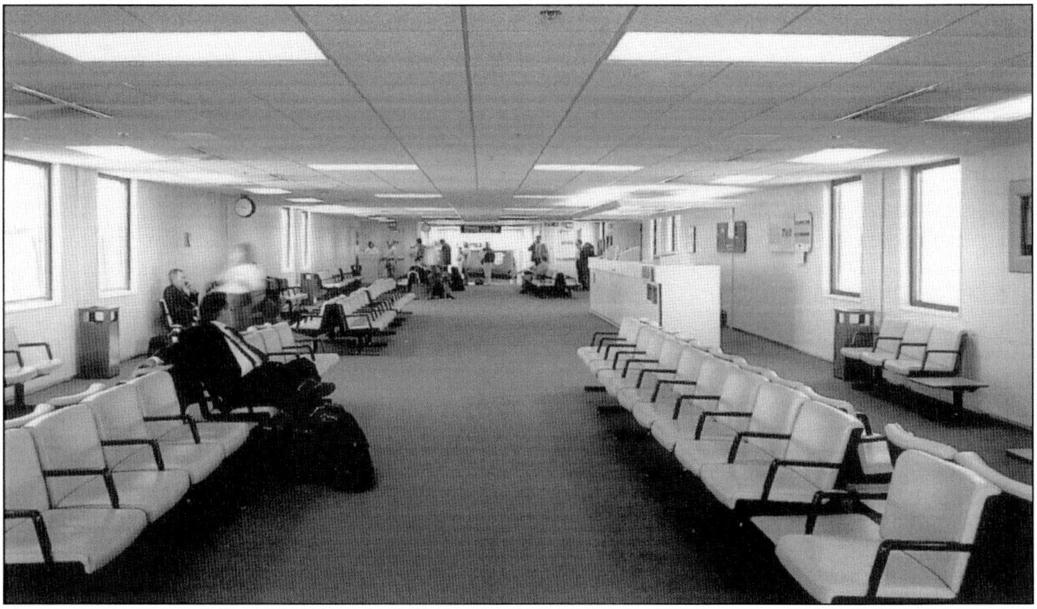

In the late 1990s, Concourse A had been lengthened and had two additional gate positions added prior to this photograph. While adequate when built in 1985, planners did not foresee the rapid growth in both the number of passengers or the airlines that were now using the airport. When several flights were departing about the same time, these gate areas would become quite congested. (Courtesy of QCIA.)

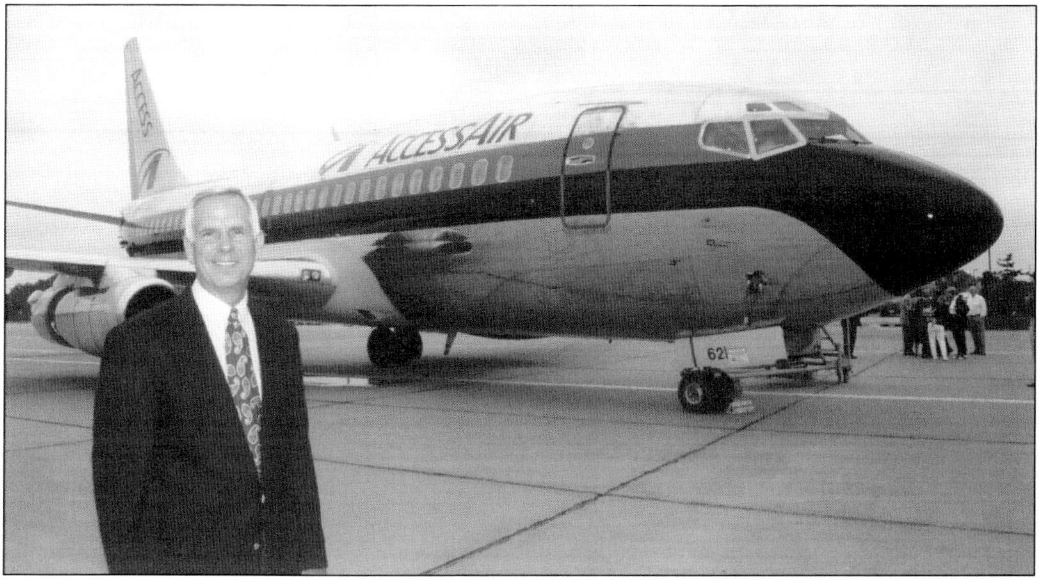

Airport manager Kent George was photographed in 1998 during a press preview visit for start-up airline Access Air. Headquartered in Des Moines, the airline offered point-to-point service to Los Angeles and New York through Colorado Springs, Moline, Peoria, and Des Moines. Access Air operated four B-737s and only flew for 10 months before it declared bankruptcy due to low ridership and lack of funding. (Courtesy of QCIA.)

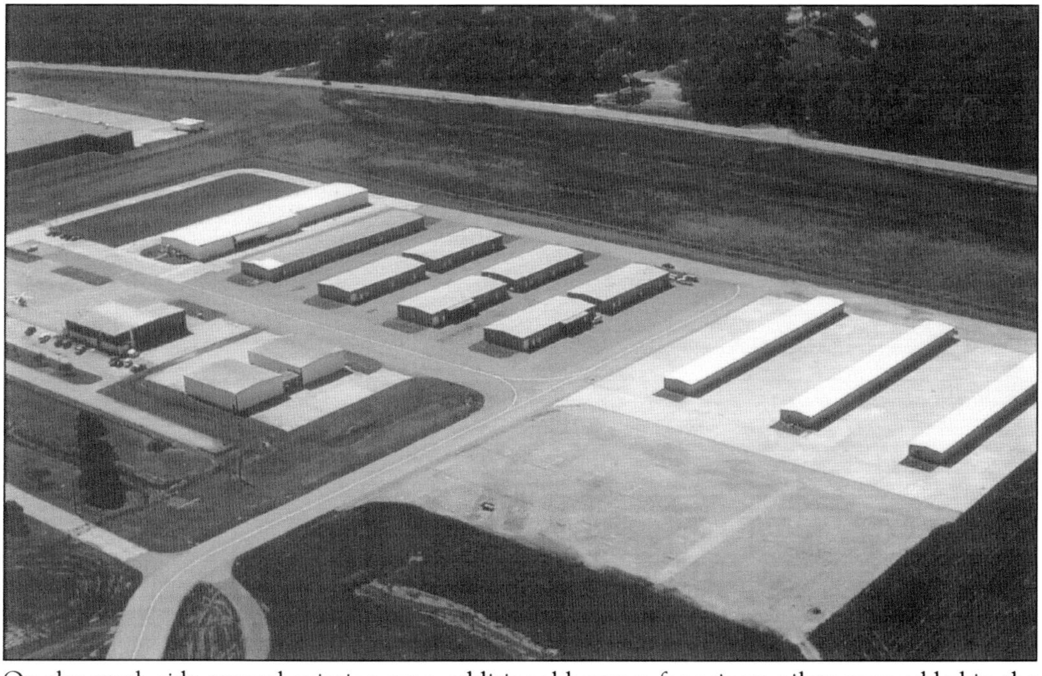
On the south side general aviation area, additional hangars for private pilots were added in the late 1990s. The building partially seen in the left corner of this photograph is the US Postal Service's regional sorting center. The airport has made good use of land it owns that is not directly involved with aircraft operations. Some lands were acquired to serve as sound buffer zones. (Courtesy of QCIA.)

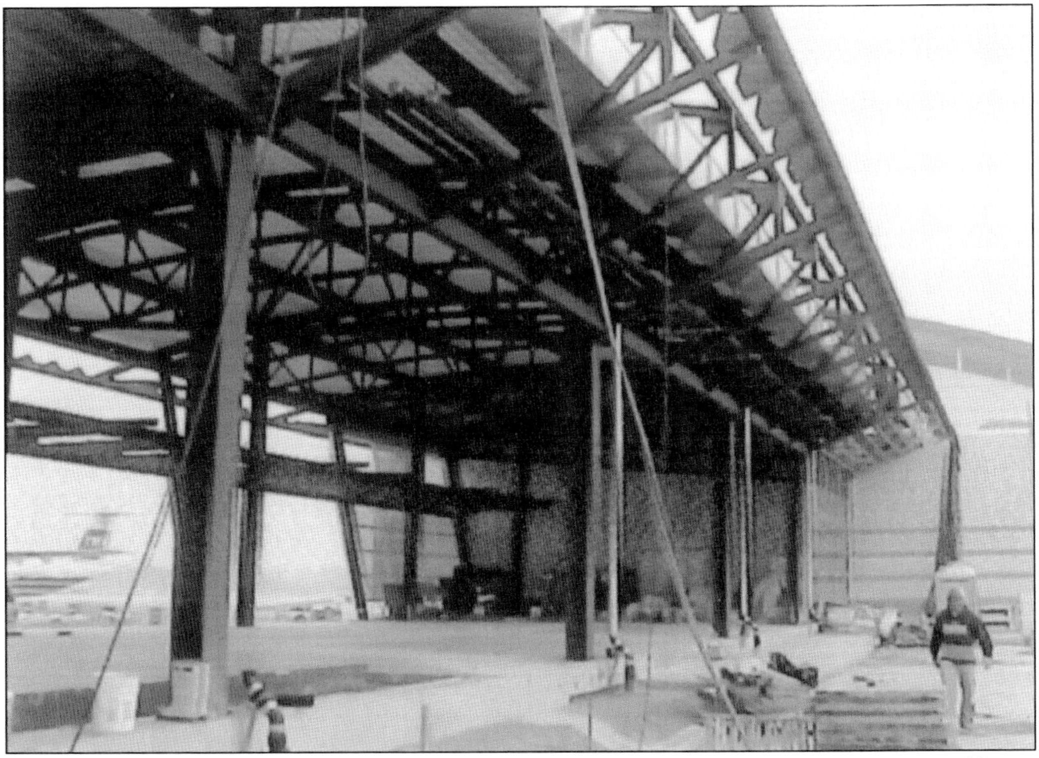

With yearly passenger counts growing to nearly 760,000 by 1999, it was evident that an addition was needed to Quad City International Airport. Ground was broken in November of that year for an $18 million project that would enlarge and modernize the passenger gates and waiting areas, enlarge the baggage claim area, and remodel some of the public portions of the main terminal. (Courtesy of QCIA.)

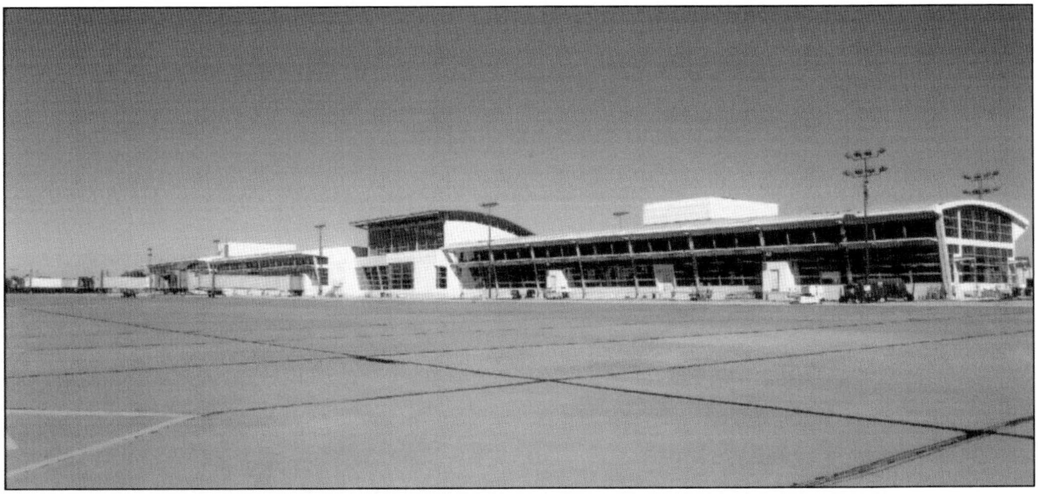

This 2001 photograph shows the terminal addition at completion. The large-jet concourse is to the left of the raised center section, and the regional jet concourse is to the right. Architectural firm Gere/Dismer used a "spirit of flight" theme in the addition's overall look, with an arched roof modeled after an airplane wing. Some old-time flyers say the atrium-like center section reminds them of an early airplane hangar. (Courtesy of QCIA.)

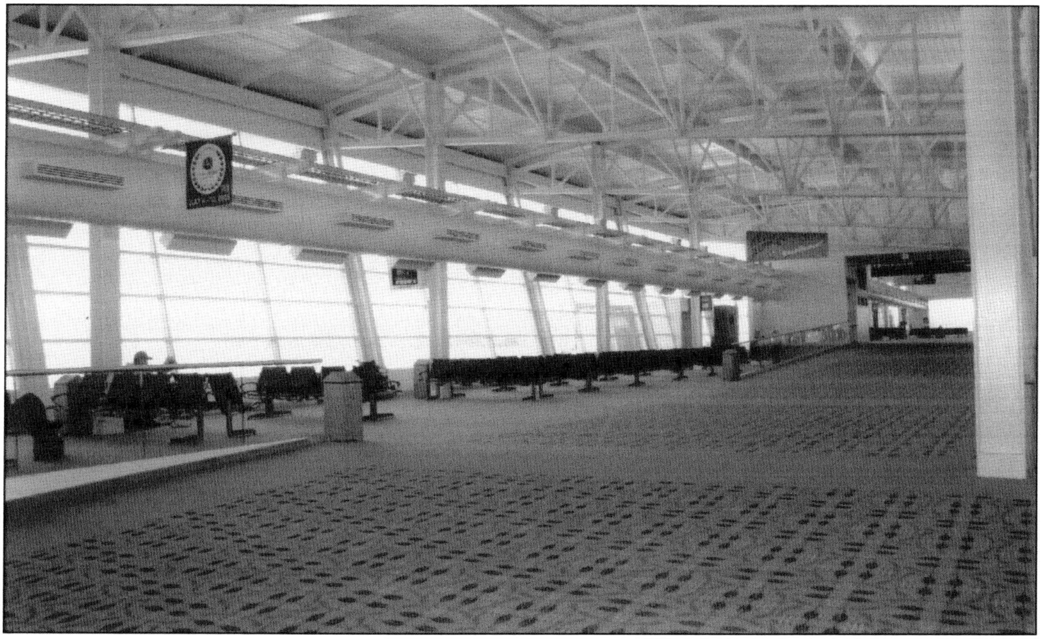

This view of Concourse B looks to the south and west. There are eight gate positions along this corridor, a business center, and an abundance of passenger seating areas. AirTran, Delta, and United Express aircraft primarily use this concourse. Floor-to-ceiling windows provide an open view of the field and aircraft ramp. (Courtesy of QCIA.)

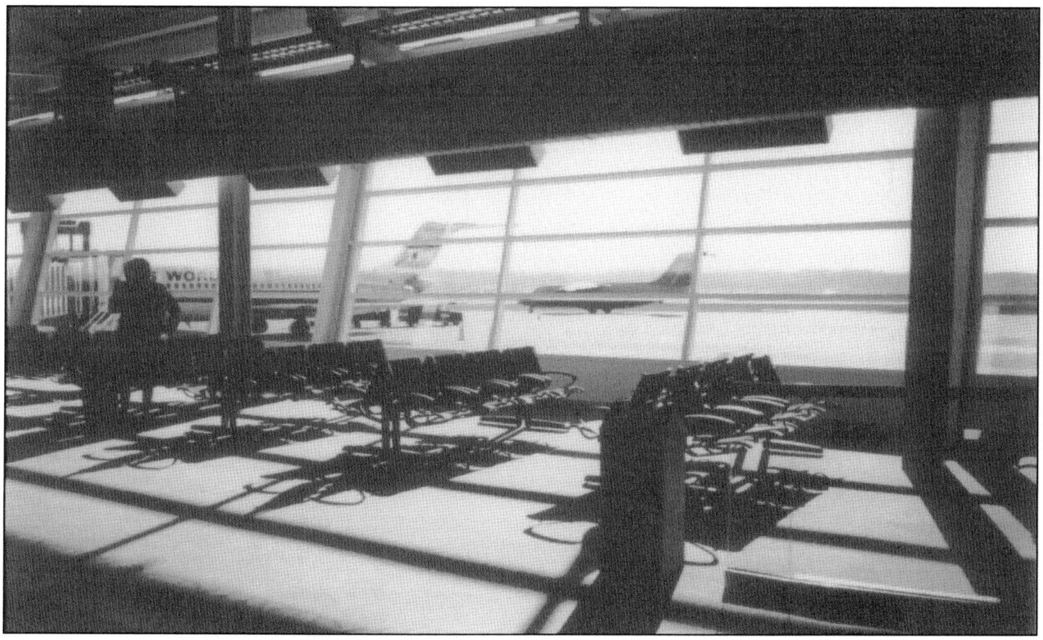

As originally planned, the terminal addition would offer views of the airfield, reminiscent of the observation area of the 1954 terminal, to both passengers and the general public. But security changes after September 2001 now limit the air-side concourses to ticketed passengers only. This rather artsy photograph provides a good example of the airy, open feel the architects desired. (Courtesy of QCIA.)

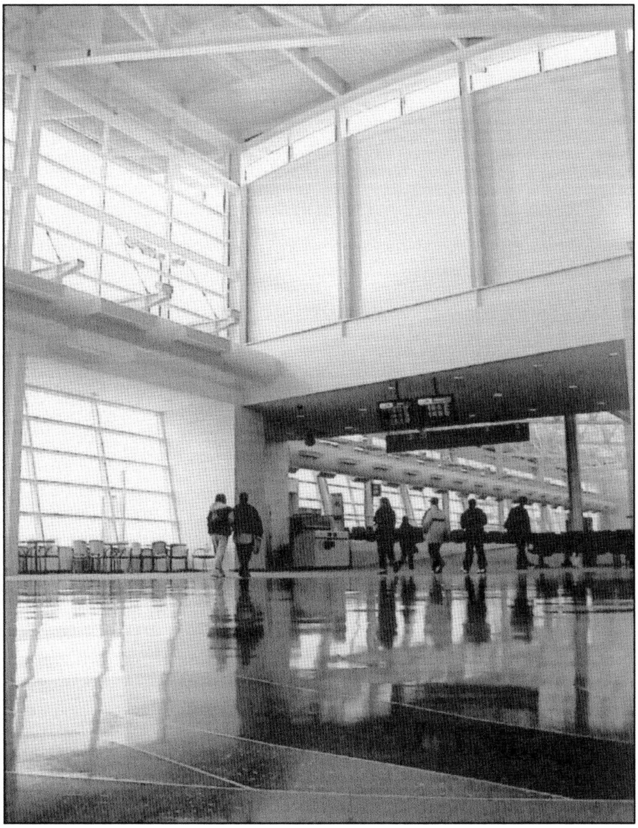

Passengers clearing security enter this central atrium area before heading towards their gate assignments. Again, this side of the terminal was originally designed to give a feeling of open space and to offer vast observation opportunities for passengers and those who might see them off or meet them. But shortly after the terminal opened, changes in security rules meant access was only available to passengers. (Courtesy of QCIA.)

Looking east from the central atrium, this photograph looks into Concourse A. On the right are the airport deli and its seating area. On the left is the corridor to the public portion of the terminal. Both concourses contain ample signage for airport amenities and monitors for up-to-date flight information. (Courtesy of QCIA.)

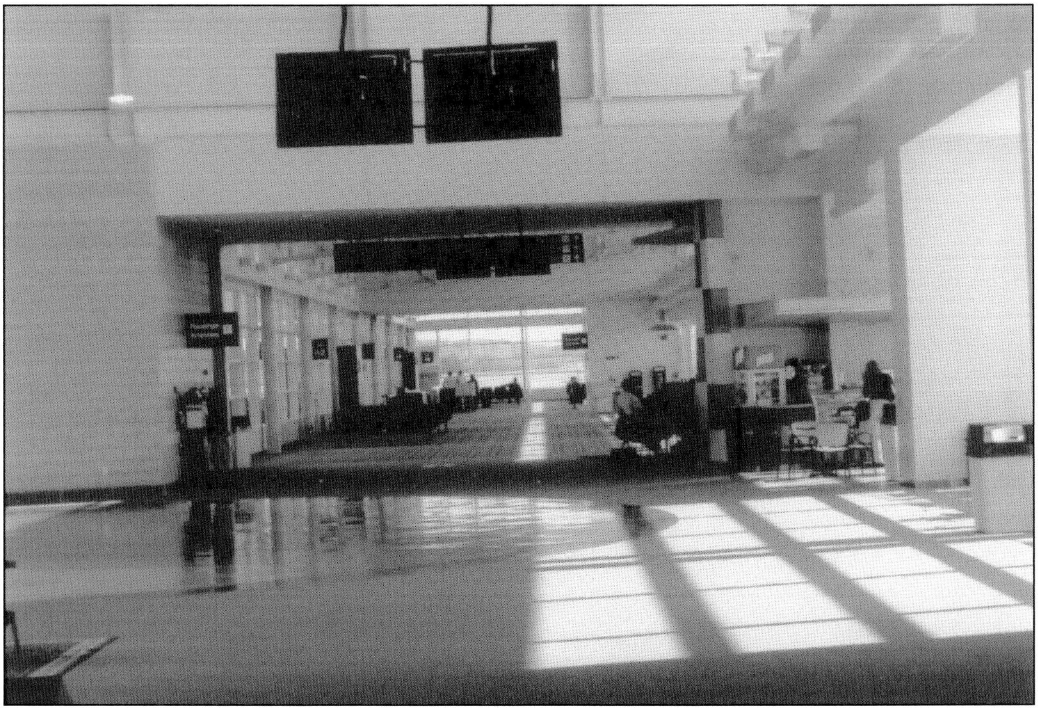

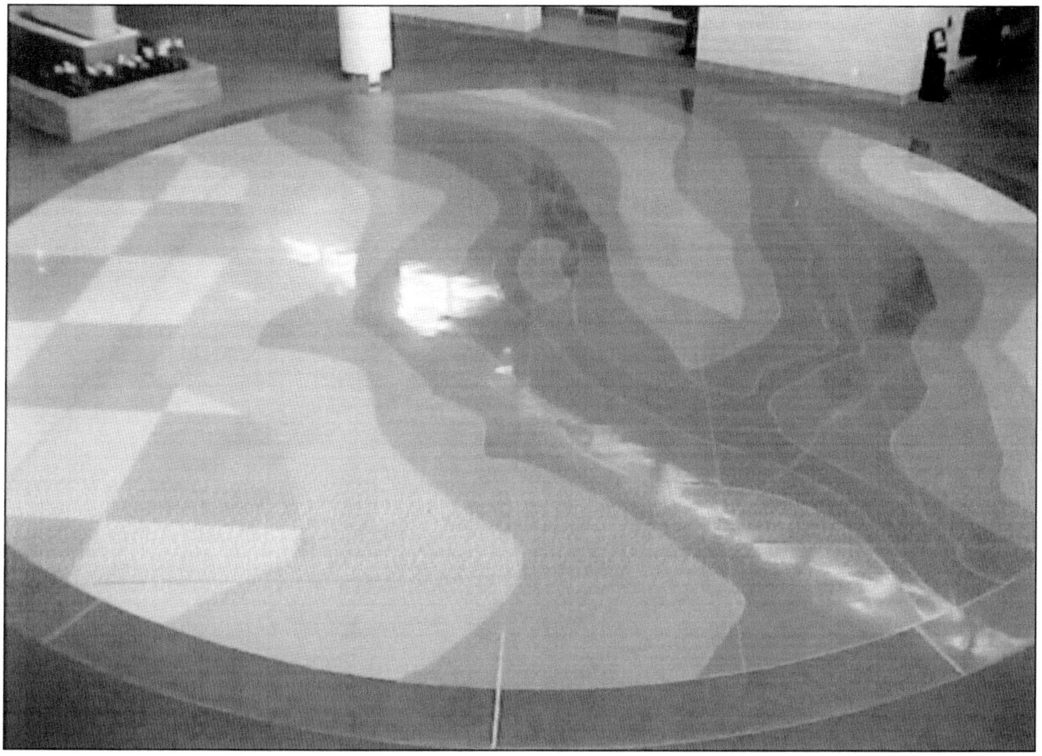

The Quad Cities is a geographical area consisting of four counties and nearly 400,000 people. It is the home of Deere and Company, several fraternal life insurance companies, and the Rock Island Arsenal. It is also the location of both large and small industrial and service firms, colleges and universities, medical centers, museums, and a great number of attractions and festivals, surrounded by the farms of its agricultural heritage. To illustrate the Quad Cities to arriving passengers, designers of the 2001 terminal addition installed this artistic rendering in the terrazzo flooring. The design greets arriving passengers at the atrium area as they exit the A and B Concourses, headed for the public portion of the terminal. The image below provides the "key" to the designer's vision. (Both, courtesy of QCIA.)

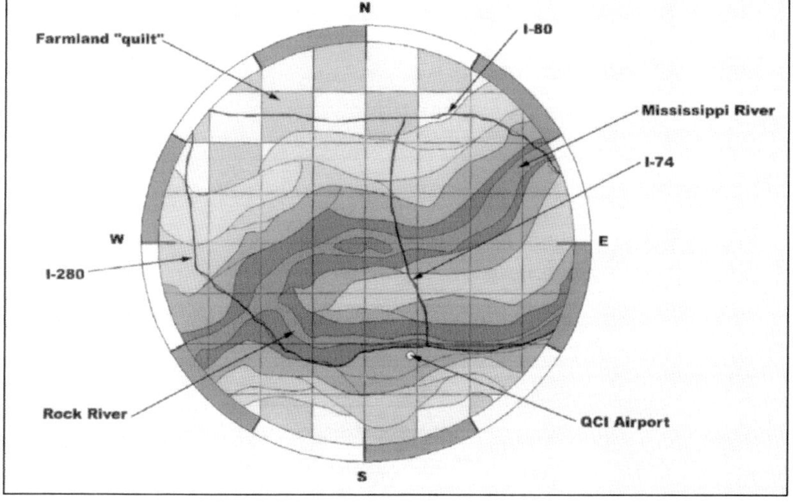

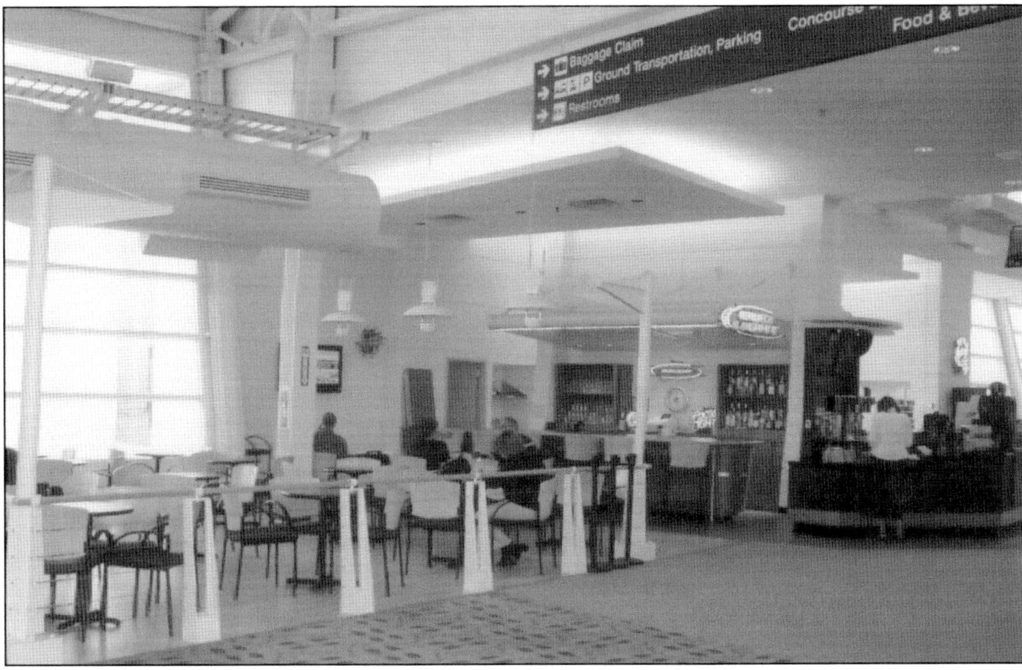

Specialty coffee shops are a growing trend everywhere. In addition to an airside deli, the airport has established a premium-brand coffee bar for passengers to enjoy a latte, espresso, or cup of Joe while waiting for their flights. Since liquids purchased elsewhere are not allowed through security, this is a welcome attraction. It shares handsome seating space with the cocktail lounge just inside Concourse B. (Courtesy of QCIA.)

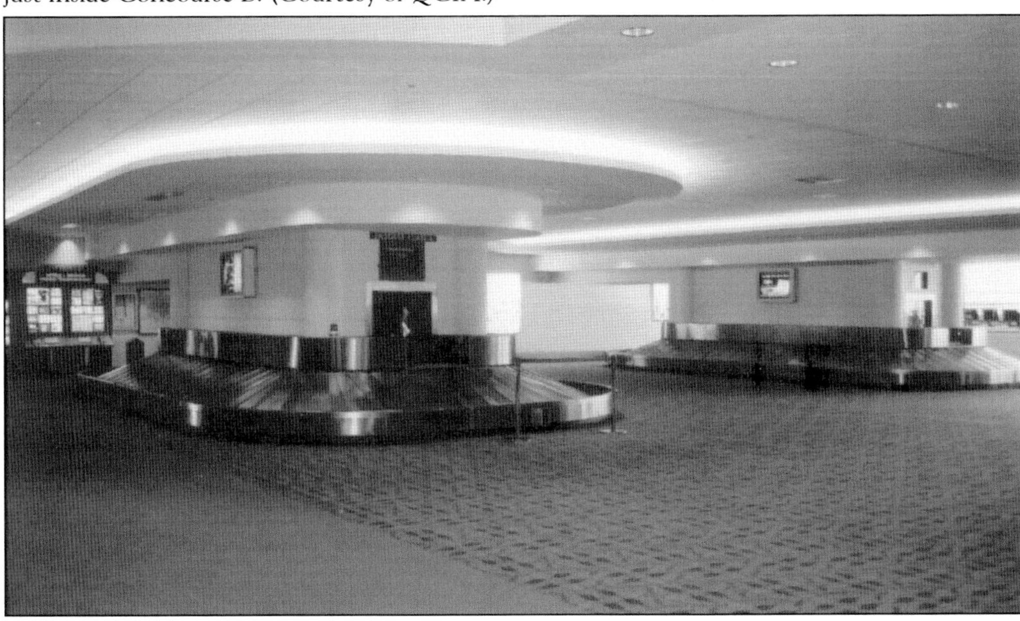

Compared with the earlier baggage claim locations at the airport, this claiming area is completely user-friendly. There is ample space for passengers and greeting family members to pick a place around the carousel to await the arrival of the luggage. When several flights arrive at the same time, alternating carousels are used to avoid confusion and crowding. (Courtesy of QCIA.)

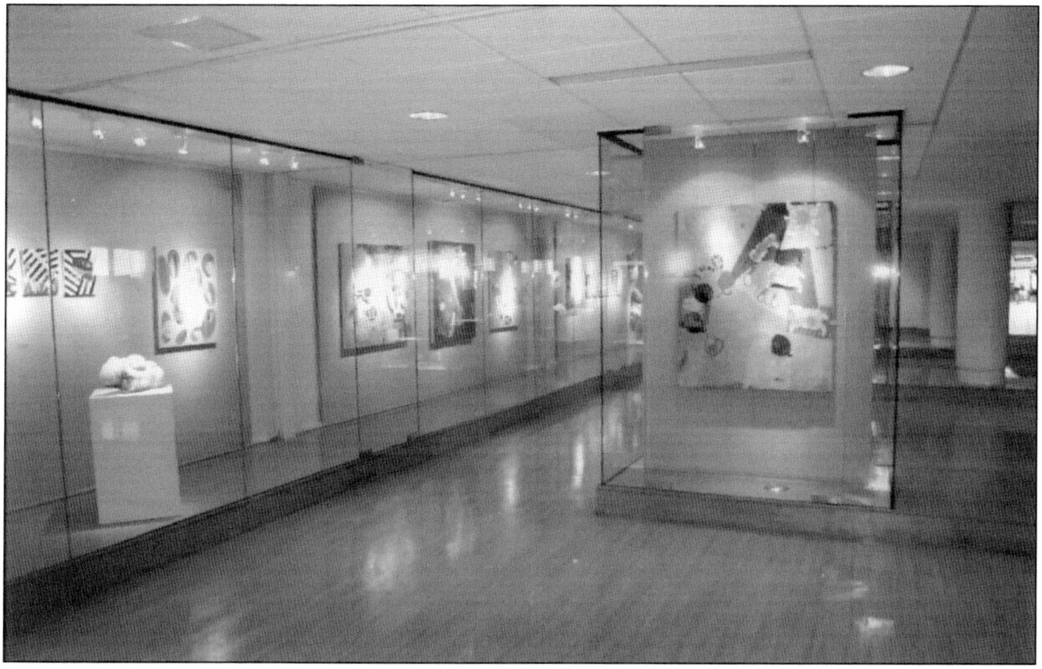

As part of the 2001 terminal improvement program, airport officials partnered with Quad City Arts to create Art at the Airport. The program showcases local artists' sculptures, paintings, and other forms of artwork and offers exposure for the artist and the artistic medium. The arts group provided an initial grant to pay for display lighting and assisted in picking appropriate places around the terminal building to display the works. Taking the program one step further, an art gallery was created in the connector between the ticketing and passenger gate concourses. Quad City Arts manages the gallery program, and any artist within a 250-mile radius can apply for placement. Displays are rotated every two months. Ironically, Gere/Dismer Architects and Quad City Arts are located in the same building that once housed the clothing store of early airport advocate Gabe Mosenfelder. (Both, courtesy of QCIA.)

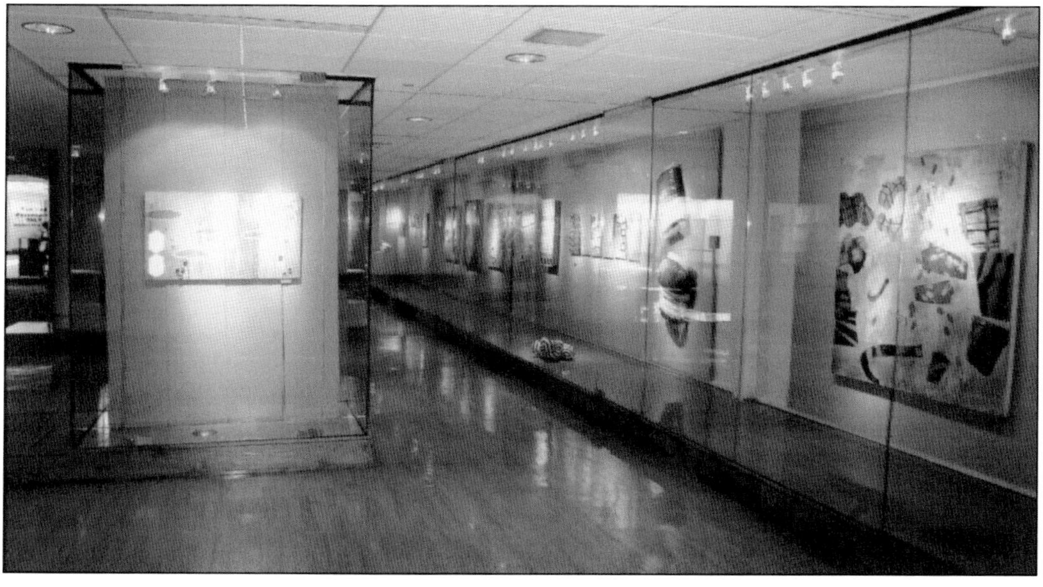

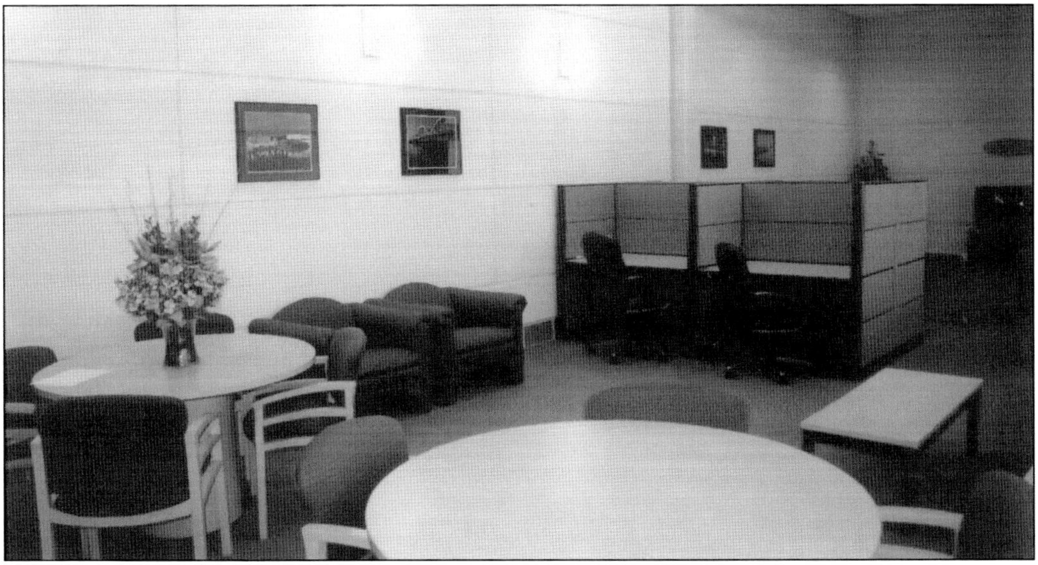

While QCIA does not have an airline club room, it does have a business center that offers a quiet place for the airport's most frequent business travelers to relax and work while waiting for their flights. There is no membership charge, but users are required to fly at least once per month. Airport officials stated that it is a perk to make the business traveler's airport experience more comfortable. (Courtesy of QCIA.)

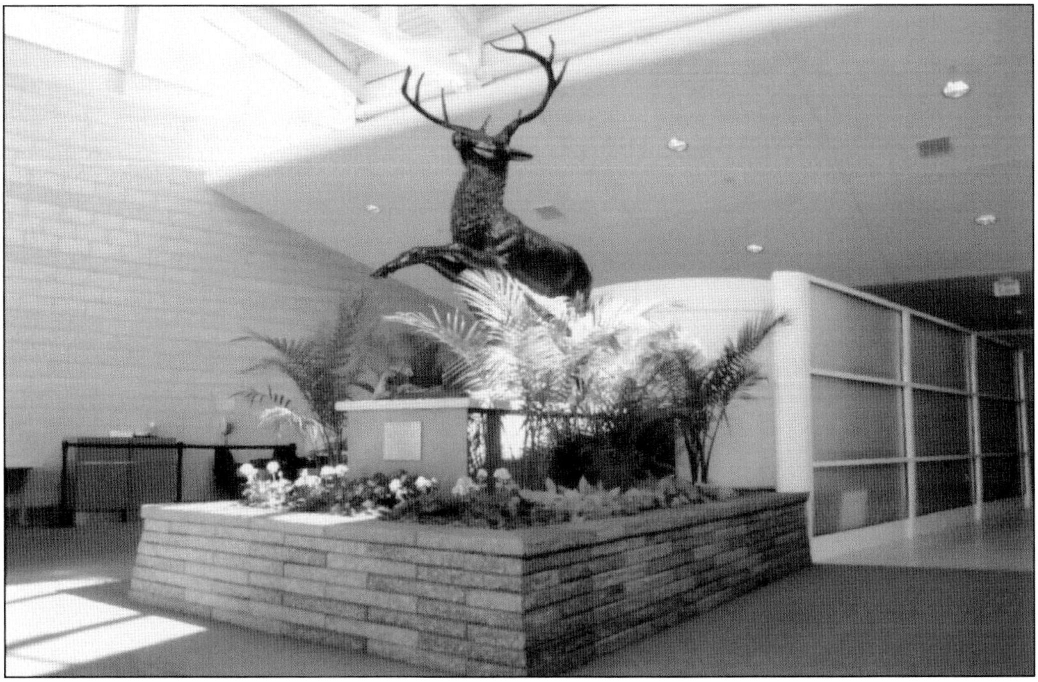

This 300-pound copper deer greets arriving passengers as they head toward the main terminal. Donated by Deere and Company, the statue once adorned one of its facilities. Produced in 1896, the deer is a reminder of Deere's trademark and that Moline is the firm's world headquarters. The statue is on permanent loan to the airport as part of Deere's corporate support of Art at the Airport. (Courtesy of QCIA.)

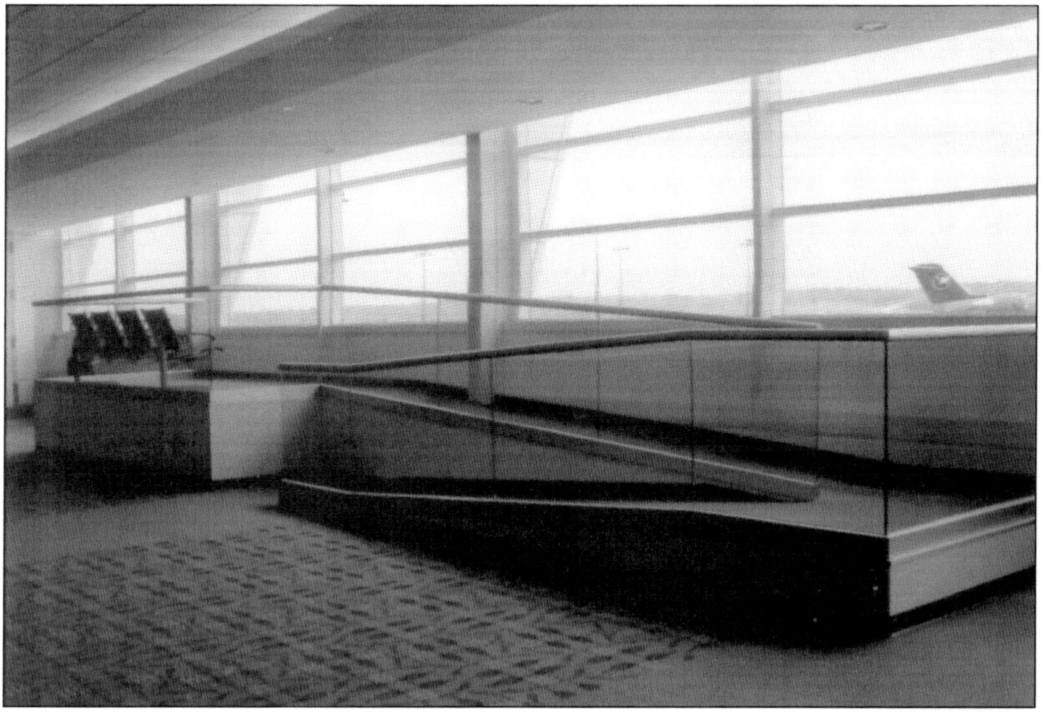

The new terminal was originally designed to give the public wide views of the airfield and its activity. Now, security rules allow only ticketed passengers access to the airfield side. To bring a little of the airfield view that was lost after September 2001, this platform was added to provide an opportunity to see some of the on-field activity. (Courtesy of QCIA.)

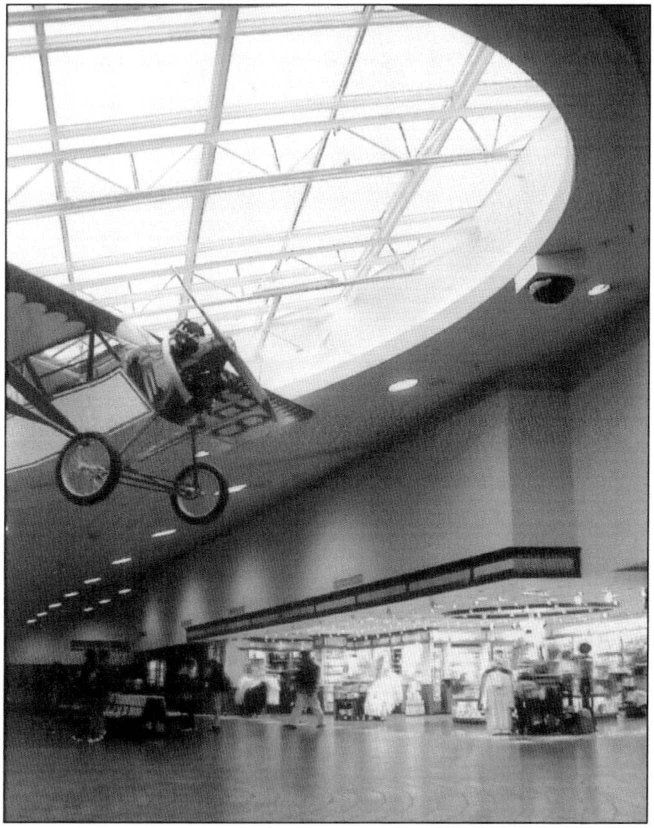

The focal point of the terminal's intersection with the ticketing and security concourses is the skylight. "Flying under the clouds" is a restored Velie Monocoupe, on permanent loan to the airport. With the 2001 addition and remodeling of the terminal, the airport's gift shop, seen in the background, was greatly enlarged and enhanced with lighting. Products promoting the airport and Quad City attractions are featured there. (Courtesy of QCIA.)

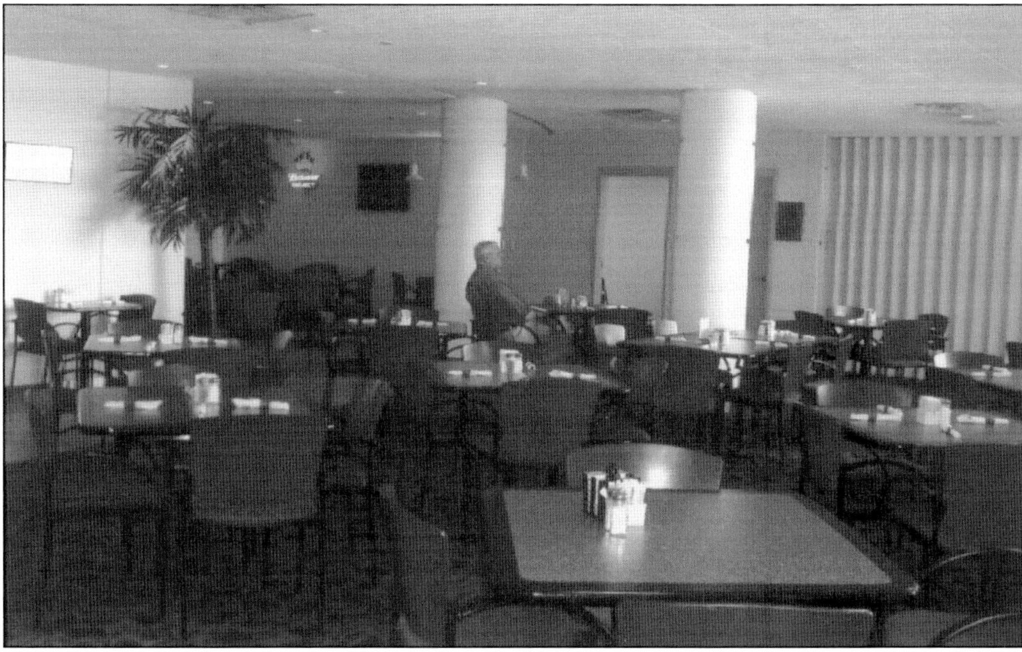

The terminal expansion and remodeling moved the restaurant around the corner and into the connector between the ticket and airline gate concourses. The facility was enlarged and utilizes two half-walls, giving it an open, airy feeling. The restaurant also includes a full-service bar and a banquet room. (Courtesy of QCIA.)

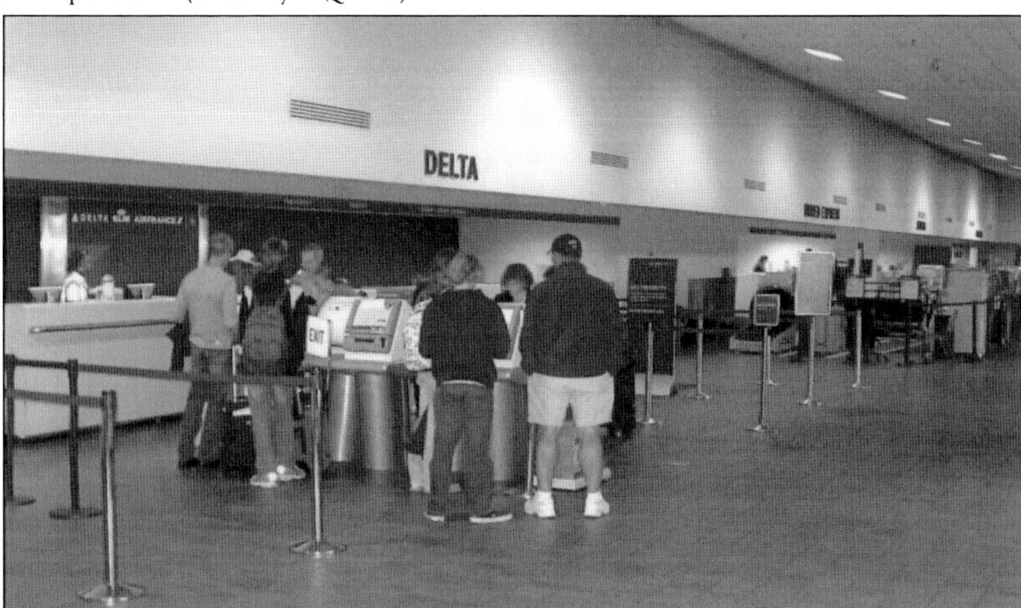

While the airline-ticketing concourse has not changed much since its construction in 1985, some of the equipment and activity has. In the foreground, passengers can now make or change seat assignments and print their boarding passes at these self-service kiosks. In the background, one of the two Transportation Security Administration (TSA) baggage x-ray centers for checked luggage can be seen. Airport executive offices are located at the far end of this concourse.

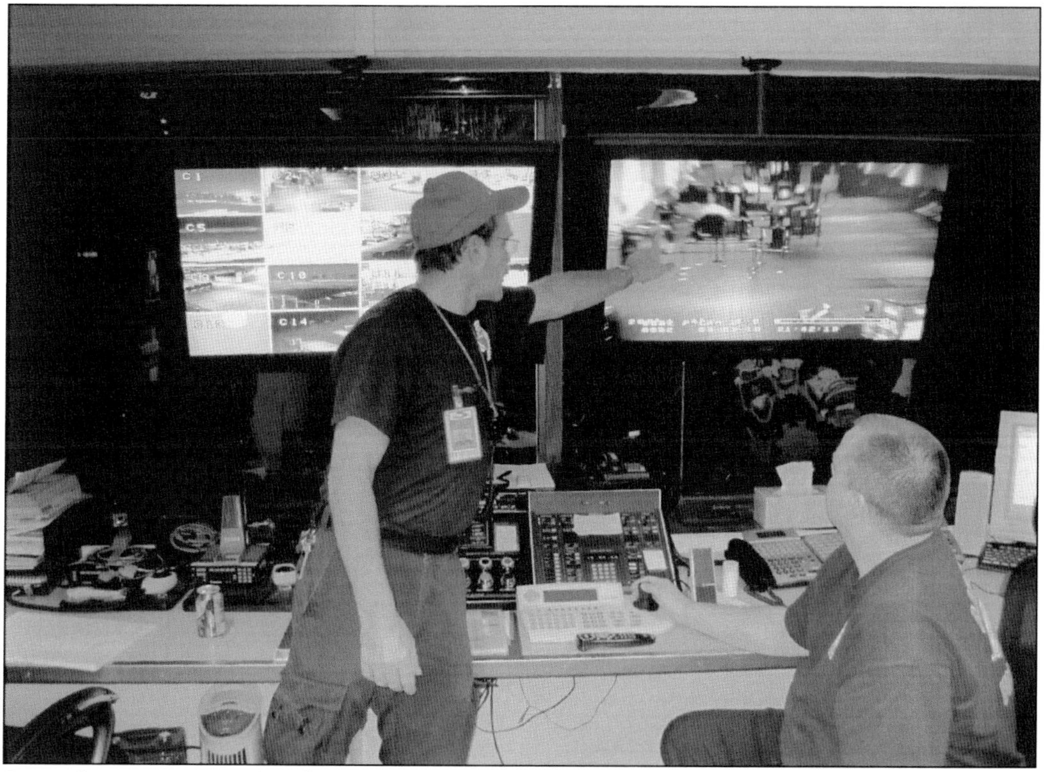

Since the terrorist attacks of 2001, airport security has become more prevalent and sophisticated. A large number of cameras pay close attention to the terminal and the airfield perimeter, watching for anything suspicious. Public safety officer Steve McGuire (left) has officer Mark Schipper zoom in on something suspicious in the main terminal. The cameras are of such quality that the officers can read a passenger's book over his or her shoulder.

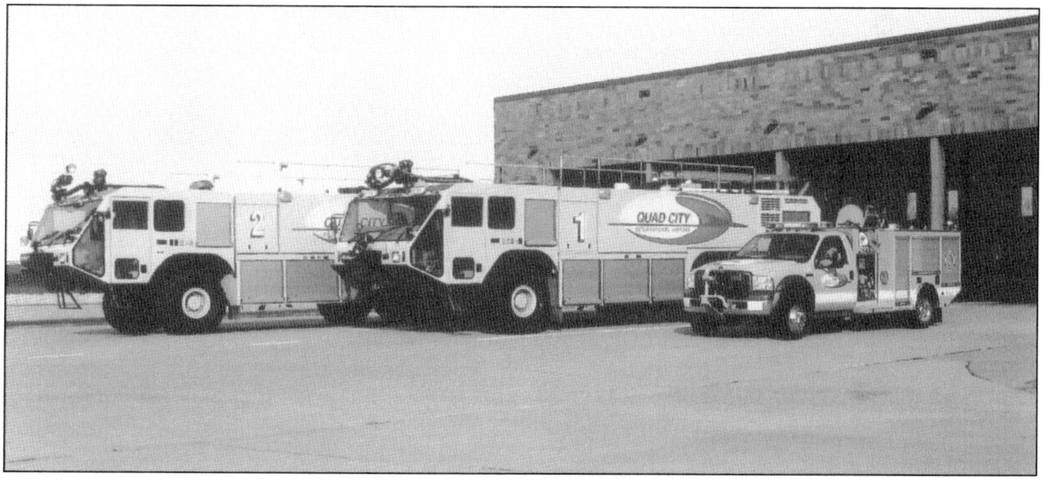

The latest airport rescue and firefighting vehicles sit on the ramp at QCIA. All three vehicles carry water and dry chemical, which is used to extinguish aircraft fires. The large units carry 3,000 gallons of water, and the smaller unit carries 300 gallons. Members of the Metropolitan Airport Authority Public Safety Department man the station around the clock and also provide security in the terminal and around the grounds of the airport.

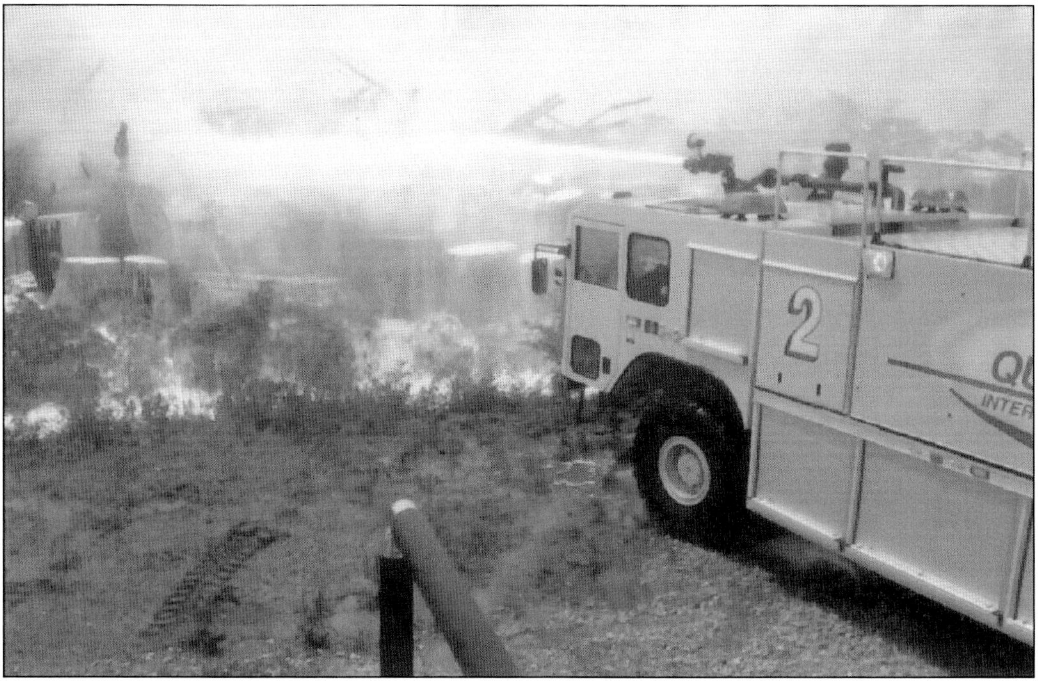

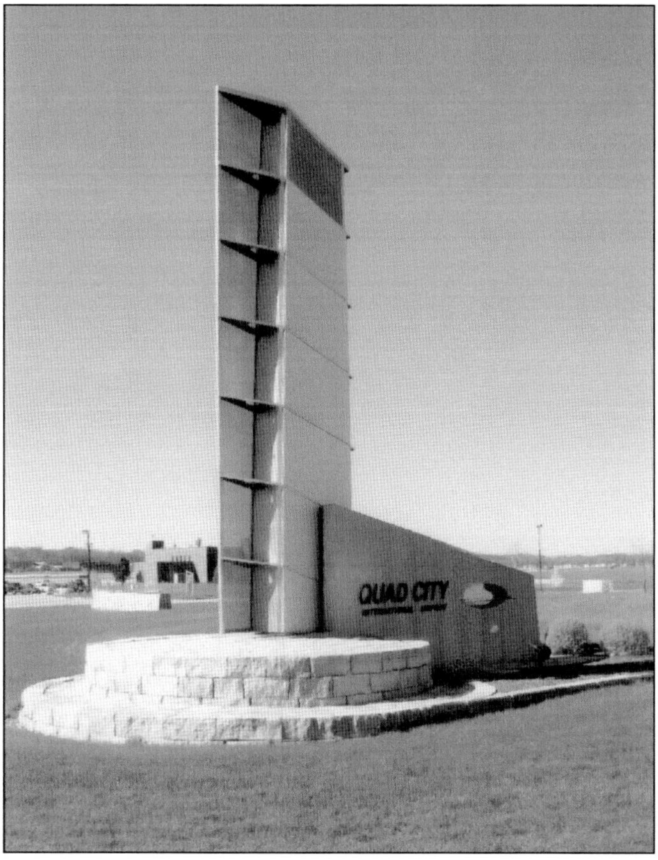

Occasionally the airport firefighters are called to neighboring cities. Here, the Moline Fire Department has been fighting a fire in a large pile of logs. Because the logs were piled high, water was not reaching the base of the fire. One of the airport's large trucks was brought in to lay down a blanket of foam, cutting off the fire's oxygen source. (Courtesy of John Lartz.)

With the 2001 terminal expansion complete, a new main entrance was created just off Interstate 74-280. Initial signage was adequate, but officials felt something unique and eye-catching was needed. In keeping with the modern design of the airport, this structure was erected. Resembling the vertical stabilizer of an airplane, it was made possible by a donation from the Alcoa Foundation. (Courtesy of QCIA.)

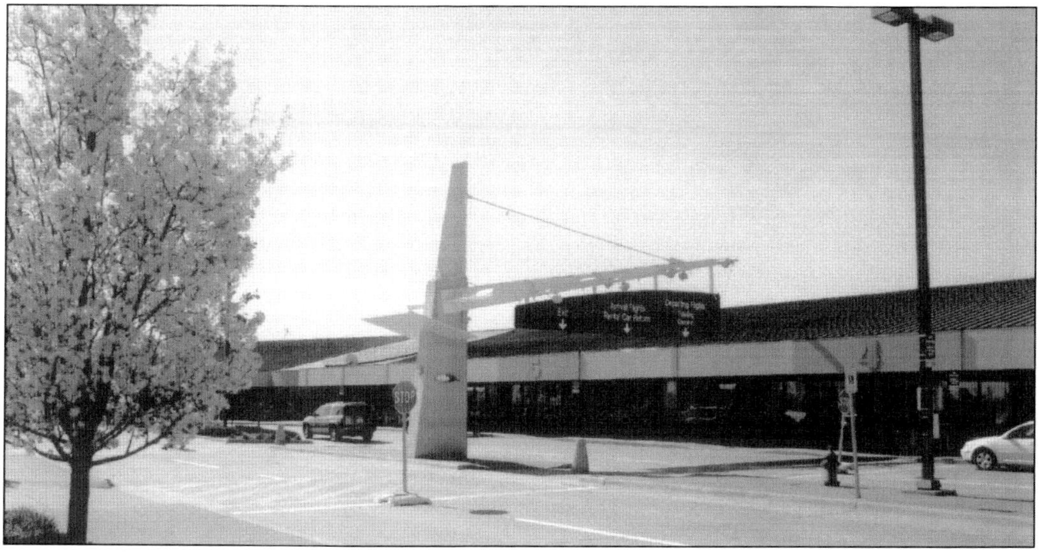

Directional signage throughout the airport gives clear guidance as to location of parking, rental car returns, airline gates, and local highways. In keeping with the modern motif of the main entrance sign, the directional signs are cantilevered from a support, looking very much like a stylized airplane vertical stabilizer and wing. This photograph shows one such sign at the terminal's front entrance. (Courtesy of QCIA.)

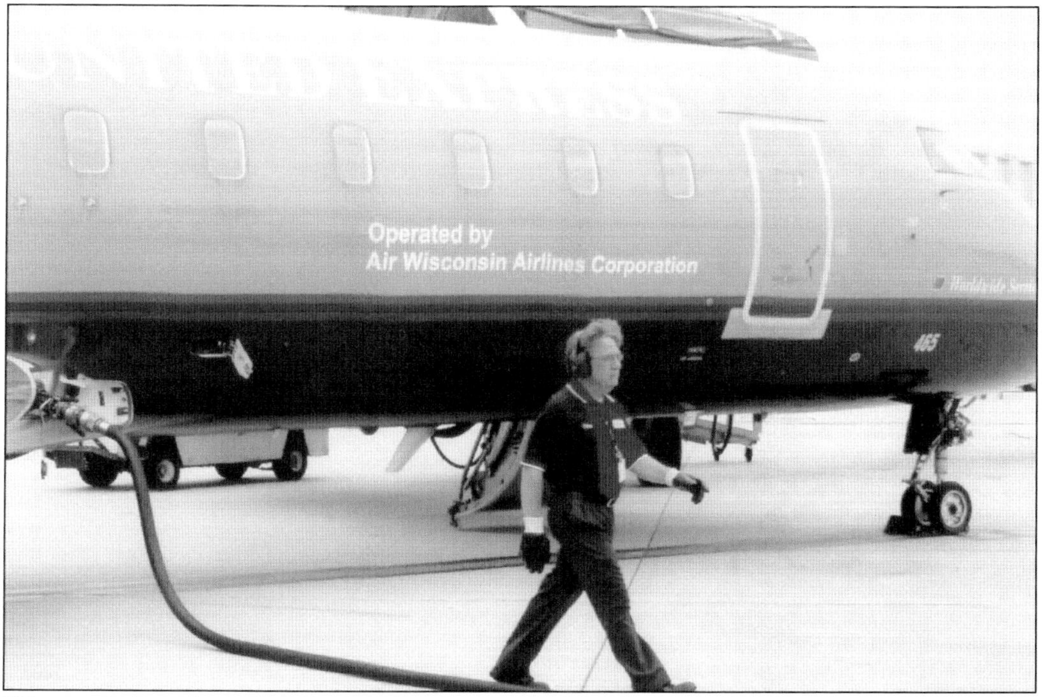

When a fuel vendor ceased operations at Moline in 2003, the Metropolitan Airport Authority saw an opportunity for revenue and created a subsidiary called QCIA Airport Services to provide fuel to the airlines and charters. Airport Services purchased the fuel tenders from the previous vendor and currently supplies the refueling needs for all commercial aircraft. Part of a 2010–2011 airport improvement plan includes building a new fuel tank farm. (Courtesy of QCIA.)

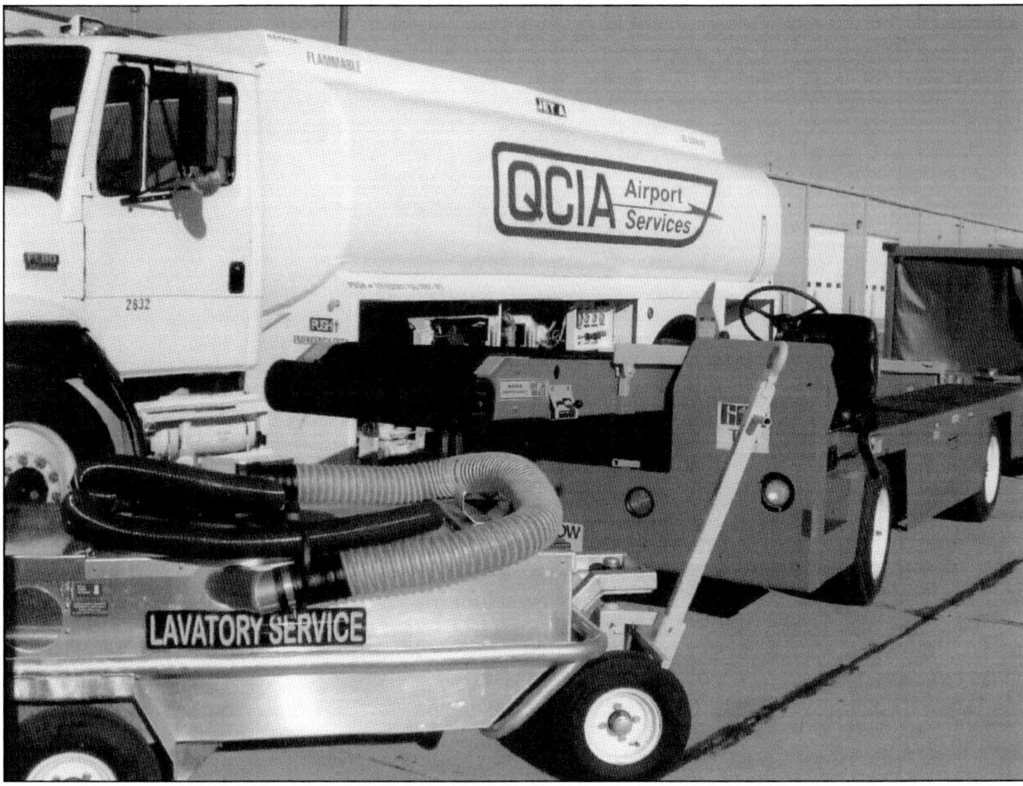

In 2005, QCIA Airport Services began providing ground-handling services to the airlines as a method of saving operational costs for the airlines and added revenue for the airport. It maintains a fleet of equipment for aircraft servicing, baggage loading and unloading, and aircraft cleaning. It can also provide ticket counter, baggage check-in, and boarding personnel. Airport Services currently provides all ground handling for AirTran and Allegiant Air. (Courtesy of QCIA.)

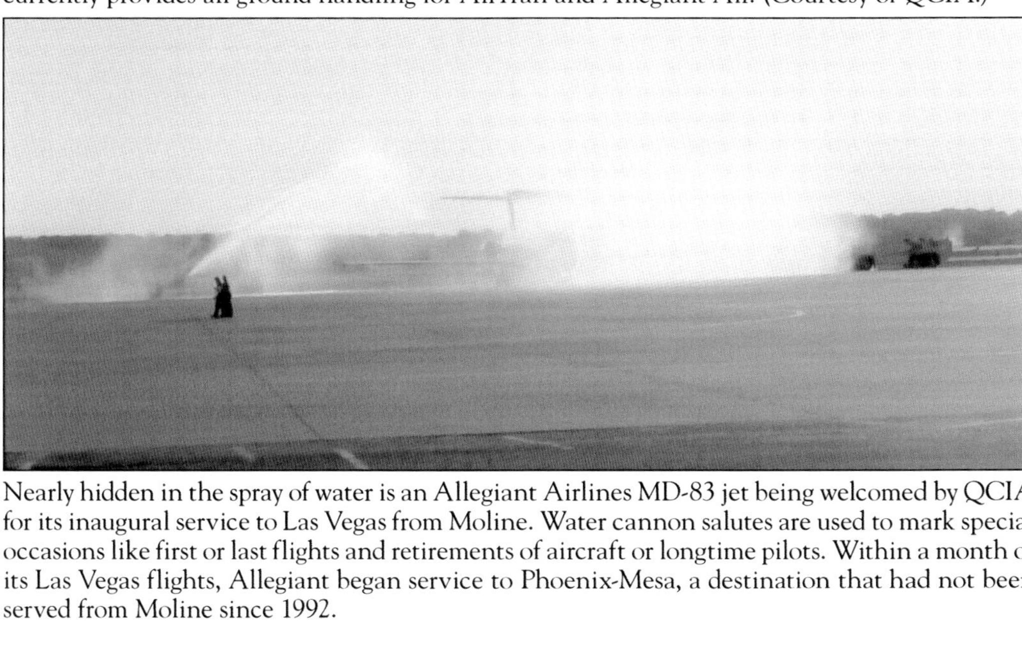
Nearly hidden in the spray of water is an Allegiant Airlines MD-83 jet being welcomed by QCIA for its inaugural service to Las Vegas from Moline. Water cannon salutes are used to mark special occasions like first or last flights and retirements of aircraft or longtime pilots. Within a month of its Las Vegas flights, Allegiant began service to Phoenix-Mesa, a destination that had not been served from Moline since 1992.

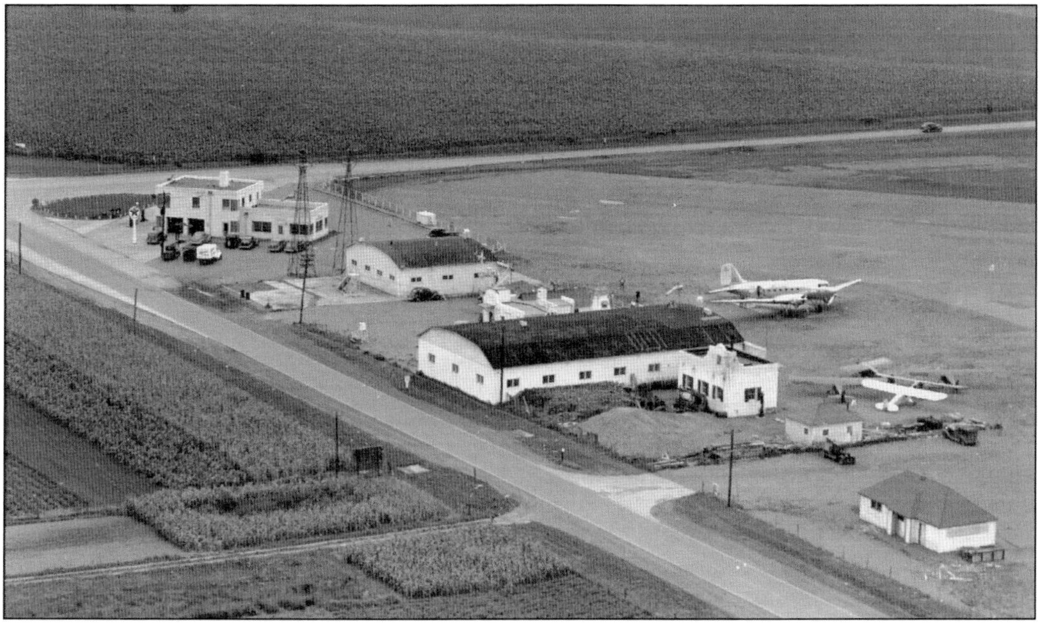

It is doubtful that founders Gus DeSchepper, Floyd Ketner, or Dr. C.C. Sloan ever envisioned their "little" airfield turning into the facility it has become today. Or maybe they hoped it would but did not realize the effort that it would take. The Moline Airport has weathered many a storm: financial insecurity, ownership, location, deregulation, the fortunes and misfortunes of the airlines, competition from other airports for flights and passengers, the instability of fuel prices, and changes since September 11, 2001. Yet with each adversity, the airport has prevailed through vigilant management by the airport authority, strong marketing efforts for airline destinations and passengers, the dedication of airport employees, and community pride in a great resource. This salutes those who have made Quad City International Airport what it is today and what it will continue to be tomorrow. (Both, courtesy of QCIA.)

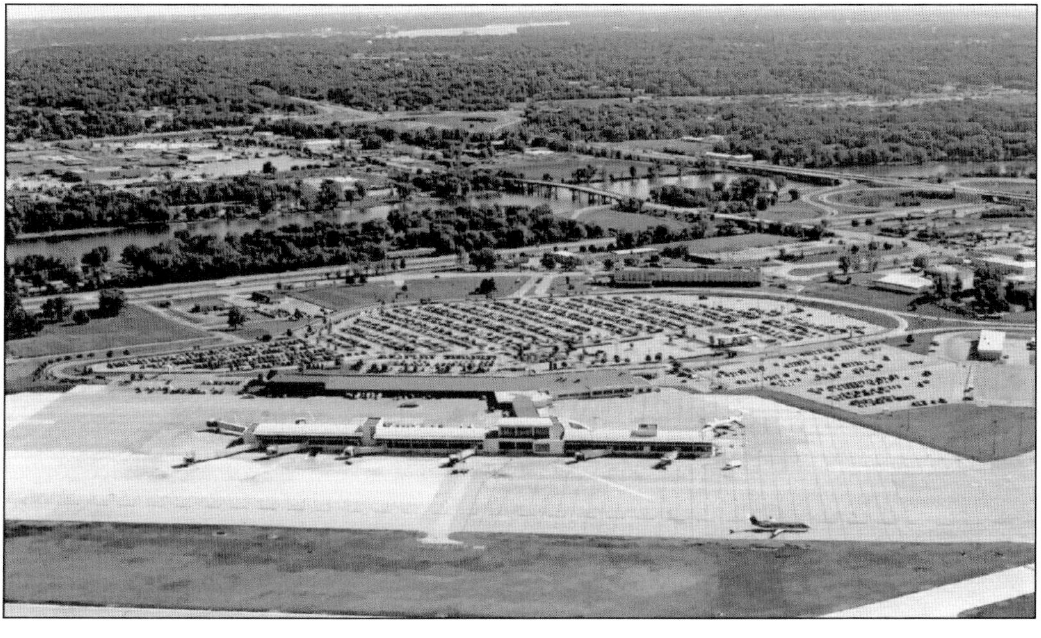

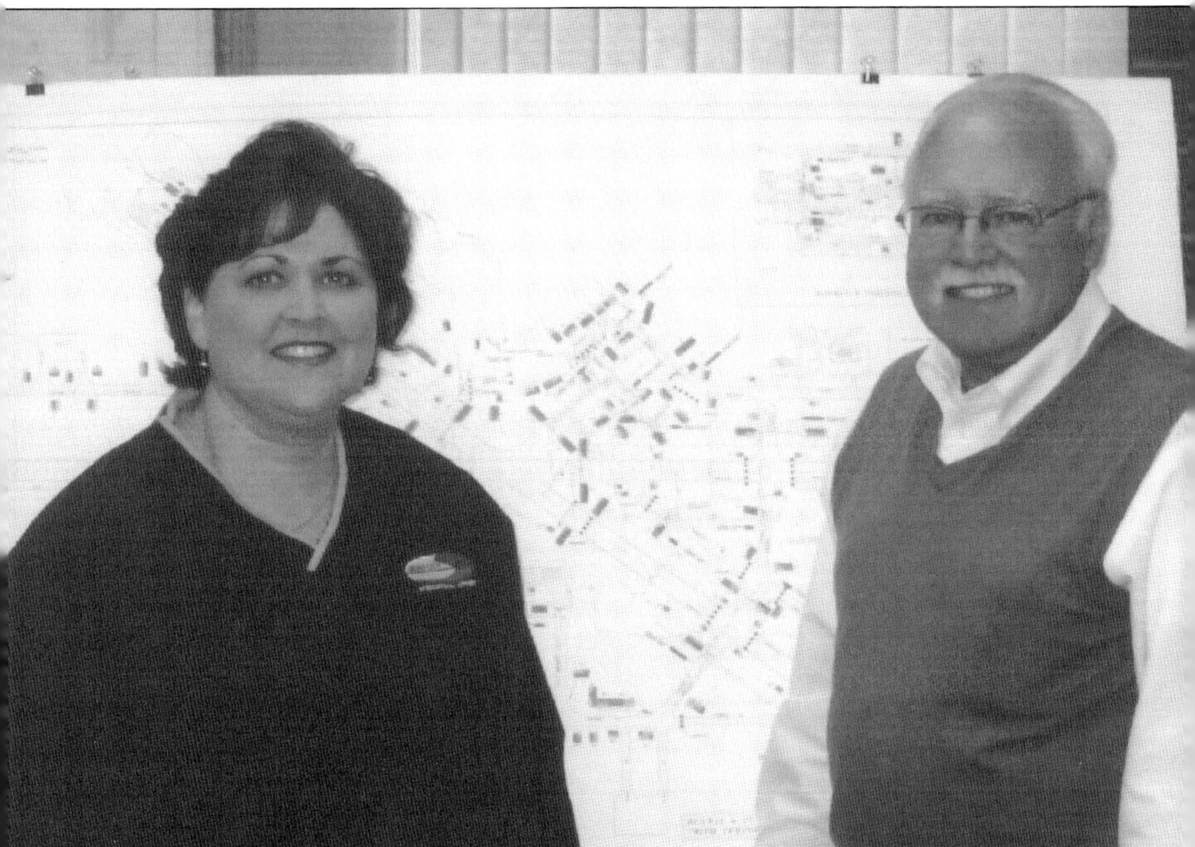

Marketing representative Cathie Rochau and director of aviation Bruce Carter, AAE, posed for this photograph during a planning session. Rochau handles Quad City International Airport's advertising and media programs and public relations and is the liaison for travel agents. Carter is a licensed pilot, former air traffic controller, and former manager of airports at Waterloo, Iowa, and Springfield and Peoria, Illinois. He joined QCIA in January 1999, just in time to oversee the airport's $18-million terminal improvement project. His celebration over the successful completion of the project was short-lived, as he and the rest of the airport staff had to deal with changes for the airlines and the airport brought about by the September 2001 terrorist attacks. Yet despite a chaotic beginning, Carter has led QCIA to constant increases in passenger usage, convinced new airlines to enter the Quad City market with new destinations, and found ways to partner with the airlines to save operational costs while developing additional revenue streams for the airport.

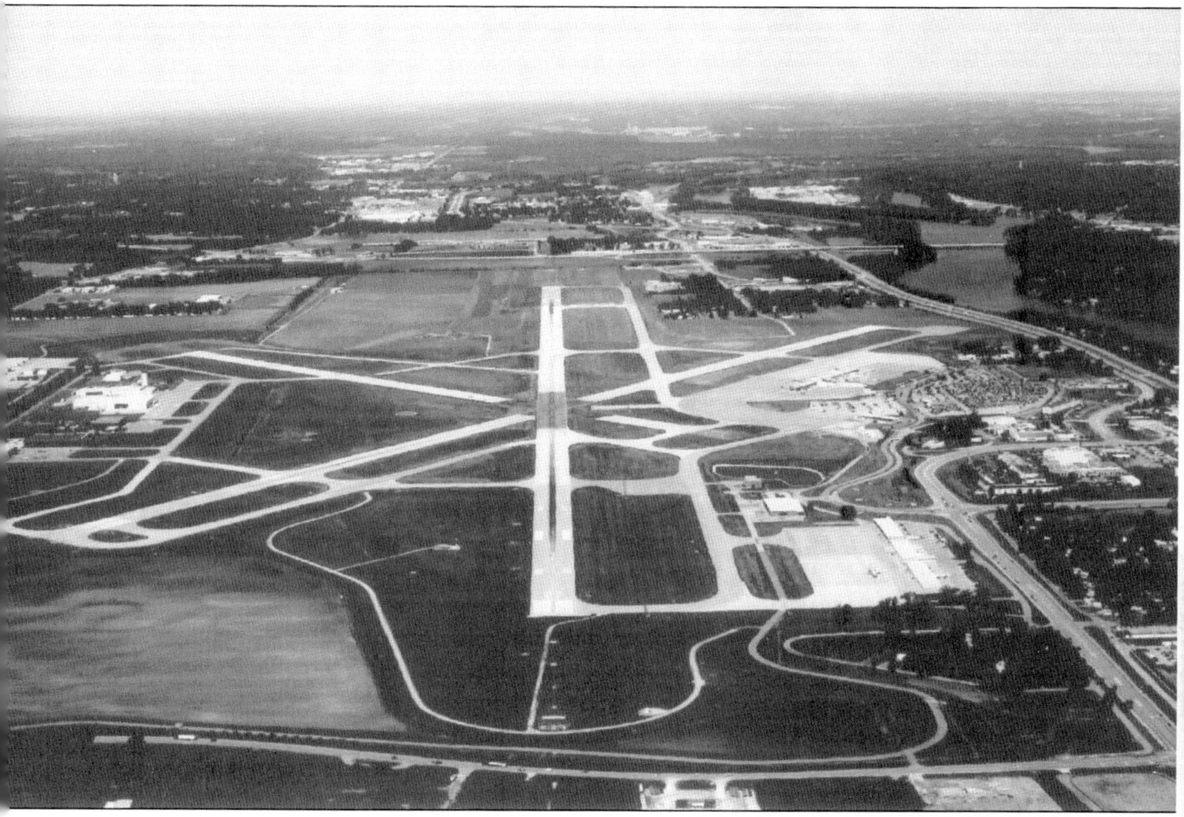

This photograph offers a pilot's-eye view of a landing approach to the west on Runway 27. To the right of the approach end of the runway are the cargo hangars and ramp, maintenance garage, and fire station. Opposite the midfield intersection are the terminal and ramp on the right and general aviation facilities on the left. But as this history is being written, major projects on the airfield are taking place. The main Runway 9-27 will have its center section replaced during 2011. Because this runway will have to be closed, a temporary 6,500-foot runway is being constructed between Runway 9-27 and the general aviation facilities. Electronic equipment, called a localizer, will be installed to aid pilots in aligning their aircraft with the temporary runway. When reconstruction of the main runway is complete, the temporary runway will be converted to a taxiway. Also included in the $39.3 million improvement package are a new fuel tank farm and rental car ready lot. All work is being done for the safety of the aviation community and convenience for the airport's customers. (Courtesy of QCIA.)